POLITICAL ACTION
HANDBOOK FOR NURSES

POLITICAL ACTION HANDBOOK FOR NURSES

CHANGING THE WORKPLACE, GOVERNMENT, ORGANIZATIONS, AND COMMUNITY

Diana J. Mason, RN, MSN

Susan W. Talbott, RN, MA, MBA

with Contributors

Foreword by Senator Edward M. Kennedy

Introduction by Eunice R. Cole, RN

Addison-Wesley Publishing Company
Health Sciences Division
Menlo Park, California
Reading, Massachusetts • Don Mills, Ontario
Wokingham, UK • Amsterdam • Sydney • Singapore • Tokyo
Mexico City • Bogota • Santiago • San Juan

Sponsoring Editor: Nancy Evans

Production: Newcomer/Muncil Associates, San Francisco

Book Designer: Gary Head

Cover Designer: Colleen McEvoy

Copy Editor: Elinor Schrader

Illustrator: Irene Imfeld

Library of Congress Cataloging-in-Publication Data

Main entry under title:

Political action handbook for nurses.

    Includes bibliographies and index.
    1. Nurses—Political activity.   2. Nursing—Political
aspects.   I. Mason, Diana J., 1948–   .   II. Talbott,
Susan W., 1939–   .   [DNLM: 1. Delivery of Health Care—
United States.   2. Nursing.   3. Politics—United States.
4. Public Policy—United States.   WY 16 P7685]
RT86.5.P6   1985   362.1'73   85-16804
ISBN 0-201-16368-3

   CDEFGHIJK-MA-898

Addison-Wesley Publishing Company
Health Sciences Division
2725 Sand Hill Road
Menlo Park, California 94025

DEDICATED TO

Wilma Scott Heide
(1921–1985),

The Contributors to This Book,

and

All Nurses Who Make a Difference

Wilma Scott Heide, RN, PhD, was a feminist leader and human rights activist. The only nurse president of the National Organization for Women (NOW), she led the organization from 1971 to 1974 with courage and vision. During her tenure, the U.S. Congress passed the Equal Rights Amendment and thirty-four states ratified it. Wilma was noted for her outspoken commitment to human rights, as well as her compassion and humor. While many people viewed her ideas and actions as "radical," the struggle for human rights would not have advanced so far without her activism.

Wilma supported the concept of this book. In particular, the editors consulted her on Chapter 3, "Coming of Age: Nursing and the Women's Movement," and regret that they could not receive her thoughtful critique of the final manuscript.

Truly, Wilma Scott Heide was a nurse who made a difference—for her patients, her nursing colleagues, her students, her sisters in feminism, indeed, for all human beings.

ABOUT THE EDITORS

Diana J. Mason

Mason is a lecturer at the New York City campus of the Lienhard School of Nursing, Pace University; an independent nurse clinician and consultant; and a doctoral student in nursing research and theory development at New York University where she is also a research fellow in nursing. She received a baccalaureate in nursing from West Virginia University and a master of science degree in nursing from St Louis University.

Mason is a member of the Board of Directors of the New York Counties Registered Nurses Association (District 13 of the New York State Nurses' Association) of New York City and is a member and former chairperson of its Committee on Legislation. A member of the New York State Nurses' Association (NYSNA), she was the recipient of the 1983 NYSNA Legislative Award. She has served as a delegate from New York State at annual conventions of the American Nurses' Association (ANA). In addition, she is a Congressional District Coordinator for the ANA and has worked with the New York State Nurses for Political Action in a variety of capacities: secretary, editor, and currently a senatorial district coordinator. Mason is a member of a number of other professional organizations, including the National League for Nursing, Nurses' Environmental Health Watch, Nurses' Alliance for the Prevention of Nuclear War, and the American Public Health Association.

Mason has authored publications on political action and issues and spoken on these topics to local, state, and national nursing groups. As a consultant, she has provided workshops on accountability, the nursing process, change process, workplace politics, and other topics to staff nurses and middle managers.

Susan W. Talbott

Talbott, a principal of Nurse Management Institute, has practiced public health and psychiatric nursing and taught both to baccalaureate nursing students. She received a BSN from Skidmore College, an MA in psychiatric nursing and nursing education from New York University, and an MBA from Adelphi University in health and hospital management.

She has been involved in legislative, political, and organizational activities for many years. She is currently president of District 13 of the New York State Nurses' Association and serves on the Governor's Commission on Domestic Violence, the National Coalition for Women's Mental Health, and the New York City Coalition Against Child Sexual Abuse. She was a founding member and former endorsement chair of the New York State Nurses for Political Action.

Talbott's publications include contributions on pay equity, legislative and political action, and management development and training for registered nurses. As a guest lecturer and seminar leader, she speaks on issues affecting the practice of nursing, legislative and political action, and organizational development.

Helen Margaret Archer-Dusté, RN, MSN
Head Nurse, Intensive Care Nursery
University of California Hospitals
San Francisco, California

Sarah Ellen Archer, RN, DrPH, FAAN, FAPHA
Consultant in Public Health and
Community Health Nursing
W. K. Kellogg National Public Health
Nursing Policy Center, School of Public
Health, Public Health Nursing Program,
University of Minnesota
Minneapolis, Minnesota

Pearl Skeete Bailey, RN, EdD
Director
Department of Nursing, York College, City·
University of New York
Jamaica, New York
Former Associate Director, Mid-Atlantic
Regional Nursing Association

Anne M. Barker, RN, MSN, CNAA
Chief, Nursing Service
Veterans Administration Medical Center
West Haven, Connecticut

Nettie Birnbach, RN, EdD
Associate Director
Mid-Atlantic Regional Nursing Association
New York, New York
Director, District 14, New York State
Nurses' Association; Director-at-large,
American Association for the History of
Nursing

Rachel Z. Booth, RN, PhD
Assistant Vice-President for Health Affairs
Professor and Dean of Nursing
Duke University
Durham, North Carolina
Vice-Chair, National Academy of Practice
in Nursing

Rosemary A. Bowman, RN, MBA
President
Health Care Partners, Inc.
Nashville, Tennessee

Janet Braunstein, RN, MPH, CPNP
Pediatric Nurse Practitioner
Minneapolis Children's Medical Center
Minneapolis, Minnesota

Gaye F. Bruce, RN
Coordinator of Marketing and Recruitment
Department of Nursing, Stanford
University Hospital
Stanford, California

Sheila P. Burke, RN, MPA, FAAN
Deputy Chief of Staff
Office of the Majority Leader
United States Senate
Washington, District of Columbia
Adjunct Lecturer, University of
Pennsylvania School of Nursing,
Philadelphia

Elizabeth Calderon, RN
Nurse Recruiter
District of Columbia General Hospital
Washington, District of Columbia
Chair, District of Columbia Nurses'
Association Political Action Committee

Caroline Camuñas, RN, EdM
Doctoral Candidate
Teachers College, Columbia University
New York, New York
Chair, Committee on Public Relations,
New York Counties Registered Nurses'
Association, District 13, NYSNA

Elaine McEwan Carty, RN, MSN, CNM
Assistant Professor
School of Nursing, University of British
Columbia
Vancouver, British Columbia

W. Carole Chenitz, RN, EdD
Associate Chief, Nursing Service for
Research
Veterans Administration Medical Center;
Assistant Clinical Professor
University of California at San Francisco
San Francisco, California

Joyce C. Clifford, RN, MSN, FAAN
Vice-President, Nursing, and
  Nurse-in-Chief
Beth Israel Hospital
Boston, Massachusetts

Donna Costello-Nickitas, RNC, MA
Grant Assistant Professor, Nursing
  Administration
Hunter College-Bellevue School of Nursing
New York, New York
Former Chair, New York State Nurses for
  Political Action

Dody Cotter, RN, MA
Gilbert, Arizona

Barbara Thoman Curtis, RN
Task Force on Health and Human Services,
  Consultant for Medicare and Medicaid,
  and Chairperson of Committee on
  Legislation, Illinois Nurses' Association;
  Former Chairperson (1975–1981) and
  Treasurer (1981–1982), Nurses Coalition
  for Action in Politics (N-CAP);
  Member, DuPage County Health
  Planning Council and Welfare Services
  Committee; Member, Board of Directors,
  ANA

Carolyne K. Davis, RN, PhD
Former Administrator
Health Care Financing Administration
U.S. Department of Health and Human
  Services
Washington, District of Columbia

Pamela McNutt Devereux, RN, MSN
Department of Nursing, Tampa General
  Hospital
Tampa, Florida

Barbara DiCicco-Bloom, RN, MA
Instructor
School of Nursing, Columbia University
New York, New York

Donna Diers, RN, MSN, FAAN
Professor
School of Nursing, Yale University
New Haven, Connecticut

Kathleen M. Dirschel, RN, PhD
Dean and Vice-Chancellor
University of Massachusetts Medical Center
Worchester, Massachusetts

Chairperson, Council of Baccalaureate
  and Higher Degree Programs, NLN;
  President, New Jersey State Board of
  Nursing; President, Mid-Atlantic
  Regional Nursing Association

Sr Rosemary Donley, RN, PhD, FAAN
Vice-President
The Catholic University of America
Washington, District of Columbia
Former Robert Wood Johnson Health Policy
  Fellow (1977–1978)

Karen Duffy-Durnin, RNC, MS
Nursing Education Specialist
Clifton Springs Hospital and Clinic
Clifton Springs, New York
Chair-Elect New York State Nurses for
  Political Action; Member, Democratic
  Committee, Ontario County

Rhetaugh G. Dumas, RN, PhD, FAAN
Dean
School of Nursing, University of Michigan
Ann Arbor, Michigan

Patricia A. Eberle, RN, PhD
Telecommunications Consultant
Denver, Colorado

Jo Eleanor Elliott, RN, MA, FAAN
Director
Division of Nursing, Bureau of Health
  Professions
U.S. Department of Health and Human
  Services
Washington, District of Columbia

**Vernice D. Ferguson, RN, MA, FAAN,
FRCN**
Deputy Assistant Chief Medical Director
  for Nursing Programs and Director of
  Nursing Service
The Veterans Administration
Washington, District of Columbia
President, Sigma Theta Tau (November
  1985–1987)

Sr Mary Jean Flaherty, RN, PhD
Chairman of the Graduate Program,
  Nursing of the Developing Family
The Catholic University of America
Washington, District of Columbia

Mary E. Foley, RN, BSN
Staff Nurse
St. Francis Memorial Hospital
San Francisco, California
Elected Nurse Representative from St.
Francis (1981-present); Nurse
Negotiator, affiliated contract (1981,
1983, and 1985); Treasurer, Region 12,
California Nurses' Association (CNA)
(1983–1987); Region 12 Commissioner,
Commission on Economic and General
Welfare, CNA (1983-present)
Member, Council on Economic and
General Welfare, ANA (1985–1987)

Patricia Ford-Roegner, RN, MSW
Field Director
Office of Political Education
American Nurses' Association
Washington, District of Columbia

Martha Fortune, RN, MS
Member, Council on Legislation
New York State Nurses' Association
(1981–1985)
Rochester, New York

Anne DuVal Frost, RN, MA
Assistant Professor
Graduate Program, School of Nursing,
College of New Rochelle
New Rochelle, New York
Consultant and Co-Founder, Health
Choices SNC

Sara T. Fry, RN, PhD
Assistant Professor
School of Nursing, University of Virginia
Charlottesville, Virginia

Shirley A. Girouard, RN, MSN
Doctoral Candidate
Florence Heller Graduate School, Brandeis
University
West Lebanon, New Hampshire
State Representative, New Hampshire
Legislature (1982–1984); Chairperson,
Government Affairs Committee, New
Hampshire Nurses' Association

Marilyn Goldwater, RN
Elected Member
Maryland General Assembly
Bethesda, Maryland
Member, Board of Directors, American
Nurses' Association

Ilene Tanz Gordon, RN, DrPH
Associate Professor
School of Nursing, Arizona State
University
Tempe, Arizona

Sandra A. Haff, RN, MPA
Latham, New York
Graduate Senate Legislative Fellow
(1983–1984), New York State Senate

Barbara E. Hanley, RN, PhD
Assistant Professor, Coordinator; Nursing-
Health Policy Program and
Governmental Affairs
School of Nursing, University of Maryland
Baltimore, Maryland
Member, Board of Nurses United for
Responsible State Elections (Maryland)

**Anne G. Montgomery Hargreaves, RN,
MS, CNAA, FAAN**
Executive Director
Massachusetts Nurses' Association
Boston, Massachusetts
Lecturer, School of Nursing, University
of Massachusetts, Boston; Lecturer,
School of Nursing, Columbia University,
New York

Susan Harris, RN, BSN
Staff Nurse, Pediatrics
Kaiser Hospital
Sacramento, California
Former Second Vice-President, American
Nurses' Association; Former President,
California Nurses' Association

Jacqueline Rose Hott, RN, PhD, FAAN
Chair, ANA Council of Nurse Researchers,
1985–1987
Acting Dean, Marion A. Buckley School of
Nursing, Adelphi University

Cathy Chapman Hughes, RN
Utilization Coordinator, the CARE olina
Health Plan, Inc.
Charlotte, North Carolina
Former Chair, North Carolina Nurses'
Association Political Action Committee;
First Vice-Chairperson, Mecklenburg
County Democratic Party
North Carolina Democratic Party State
Executive Committee

Clair B. Jordan, RN, MSN
Executive Director
Texas Nurses' Association
Administrator
TexN-CAP
Austin, Texas

Jacquelyn S. Kinder, RN, EdD
Senior Vice-President
Mennonite Hospital
Bloomington, Illinois
President, National League for Nursing

Karren Mundell Kowalski, RN, PhD, FAAN
Director
Women's Hospital at St. Luke
Denver, Colorado

Sydney D. Krampitz, RN, PhD
Associate Dean and Director of Graduate
Programs
School of Nursing, The University of
Kansas
Lenexa, Kansas

Lucille P. Leone, RN, MA
Coordinator, International Students
School of Nursing, University of California
San Francisco, California
Former Chief Nurse Officer, U.S. Public
Health Service; Charter Member,
Executive Committee, Institute of
Medicine; President, National League for
Nursing (1959–1963)

Bridget C. Loetterle, RN, PhD
Assistant Professor
School of Nursing, City College of New York
New York, New York

Mary N. Long, RN, BSN
Director of Public Affairs
American Arthritis Foundation
Atlanta, Georgia
President, Georgia Nurses' Association
Member, Board of Directors, ANA

Walter A. Lumley, RNC, BSN
Staff Nurse and President, Staff Nurse Forum
Veterans Administration Medical Center
Philadelphia, Pennsylvania

Diane J. Mancino, RNC, MA
Director of Program
National Student Nurses' Association

New York, New York
Former President, Nurses' Environmental
Health Watch

Pamela Maraldo, RN, PhD
Executive Director
National League for Nursing
New York, New York

Diana J. Mason, RN, MSN
New York, New York

Veneta Masson, RN, MA
Director and Nurse
Community Medical Care
Washington, District of Columbia
Former Director of Nursing, Project HOPE;
Past-President, District of Columbia
League for Nursing

Angela Barron McBride, RN, PhD, FAAN
Professor and Acting Associate Dean for
Research, Development and Resources
School of Nursing, Indiana University
Indianapolis, Indiana
First Vice-President, Sigma Theta Tau

Ann Marie McCarthy, RN, MA
Administrative Nursing Supervisor
Mt. Sinai Hospital and Medical Center
New York, New York
Former Democratic District Leader, 64th
Assembly District, Part B, New York
County (1979–1983); Delegate to
Judicial Convention, First Judicial
District of New York State (1976–1983);
Member, Board of Directors, New York
Counties' Registered Nurses' Association

Norma L. McKay, RNC
Staff Nurse and Past-President, Staff Nurse
Forum
Veterans Administration Medical Center
Philadelphia, Pennsylvania

Margaret A. Kessenich Meagher, RN, MS, CS
Private Practice: Clinical Specialist in
Psychiatric Nursing
Denver, Colorado

Patricia Moccia, RN, PhD
Associate Professor and Chair
Department of Nursing Education, Teachers
College, Columbia University

New York, New York
President, Health Policy Advisory Center;
Vice-President, New York Counties
Registered Nurses Association, District
13, New York State Nurses' Association

Janet N. Natapoff, RN, EdD
Associate Dean
Hunter College-Bellevue School of Nursing
New York, New York

Ann M. Newman, RN, MSN
Assistant Professor
College of Nursing, University of North
Carolina
Charlotte, North Carolina
Member, Legislative Committee and Nurse-
PAC, North Carolina Nurses' Association
(NCNA); Board of Directors, District 5,
NCNA; Precinct Delegate, 1984 County
and District Democratic Conventions

Barbara Nichols, RN, MS
Former President
American Nurses' Association
Madison, Wisconsin

Deborah Oakley, PhD
Associate Professor
Center for Nursing Research, University of
Michigan
Ann Arbor, Michigan
Executive Committee Liaison to
Congressman Pursell, Nurses Political
Action Committee; Former Chair,
Population Planning Section, American
Public Health Association

Joan O'Leary, RN, EdD
Associate Professor and Key Advisor
Graduate Program in Nursing Service
Administration, Villanova University
Villanova, Pennsylvania
President, O'Leary and Associates, Inc

Gretchen A. Osgood, RN, MA
Deputy Director
Division of Nursing, Bureau of Health
Professions
U.S. Department of Health and Human
Services
Rockville, Maryland

Patricia Anne Payne, RN, PhD
Nurse-Midwife
North Central Bronx Hospital

Bronx, New York
Former Co-chair, Government Affairs
Committee, District 5, Texas Nurses'
Association

Timothy Porter-O'Grady, RN, EdD
Nursing Administrator
Saint Joseph's Hospital
Atlanta, Georgia
President, Affiliated Dynamics, Inc;
Chairperson, Governmental Affairs
Commission, Georgia Nurses'
Association

Belinda E. Puetz, RN, PhD
Consultant
Continuing Education Unlimited
Indianapolis, Indiana
Adjunct Associate Professor, Graduate
Department of Psychiatric Mental
Health Nursing, Indiana University
School of Nursing; Former Member,
Executive Committee ANA Council on
Continuing Education; Member ANA
Cabinet on Nursing Education; Author,
Networking for Nurses

Thelma M. Schorr, RN
President and Publisher
American Journal of Nursing Company
New York, New York

Sandra Simmons, RN, MS
Doctoral Candidate
Michigan State University
Nursing Consultant
Big Rapids, Michigan
Former Director of Lifelong Education,
College of Nursing, Michigan State
University; Coordinator, Nursing Center
Ferris State College

Betty J. Skaggs, RN, PhD
Director, Learning Center
School of Nursing, The University of Texas
Austin, Texas
President, Texas Nurses' Association; Vice-
Chair, Constituent Forum, American
Nurses' Association; Chairman, Board of
Directors, Texas Nursing Coalition for
Action in Politics

Elizabeth Dorsey Smith, RN, EdD, FAAN
Assistant Director of Nursing
Mount Sinai Medical Center
New York, New York

Julie A. Sochalski, RN, MS
Doctoral Student
School of Nursing, University of Michigan
Ann Arbor, Michigan
Member, Michigan Nurses' Association
    Committees on State Legislation,
    Finance, and Third Party Reimbursement;
    Congressional District Coordinator,
    Michigan 2nd Congressional District,
    ANA

Sally B. Solomon, RN, MSN, CPNP
Director of Public Policy and Research
National League for Nursing
New York, New York
Cocoordinator of Senatorial Districts, New
    York State Nurses for Political Action

Susan W. Talbott, RN, MA, MBA
New York, New York

Sally Austen Tom, RN, CNM, MS, MPA
Annandale, Virginia
Former Government Liaison, American
    College of Nurse-Midwives

Connie N. Vance, RN, EdD
Associate Professor
Division of Nursing, New York University
New York, New York
Former Vice-President, Board Member and
    Chair of the Legislative Committee, New
    York Counties Registered Nurses
    Association, District 13 of New York
    State Nurses' Association; Former Chair,
    Public Relations Committee, New York
    State Nurses for Political Action

Diane Welch Vines, RN, PhD
Director of Special Programs

California State University
Long Beach, California
Former White House Policy Fellow
    (1982–1983)

Duane D. Walker, RN, MS, FAAN
Associate Hospital Director and Director of
    Nursing
Stanford University Hospital
Stanford, California

Richard S. Webster, PhD
Principal
Webster Systems International
Columbus, Ohio

M. Elizabeth West, RN, EdD
Nashville, Tennessee

Nancy West, RN, MSN
Faculty Member and Doctoral Student
School of Nursing, Adelphi University
Garden City, New York
Chair, New York State Nurses for Political
    Action; Former Public Policy Fellow,
    Center for Women in Government,
    Albany, New York; Cofounder, Nassau
    County Democratic Women's Committee;
    Democratic Committeewoman, Garden
    City, New York; Isabel Hampton Robb
    Scholar (1985–1986), Nurses'
    Educational Fund

Karen Zander, RN, MS, CS
Organizational Development Specialist
New England Medical Center Hospitals
Boston, Massachusetts
Private Practice in Psychotherapy, Newton
    Highlands, Massachusetts

Contents

Foreword

Nurses are America's largest group of health professionals, but they have never played their proportionate role in helping to shape health policy, even though that policy profoundly affects them as both health providers and consumers. The potential influence of the nation's 1.7 million nurses is enormous and virtually untapped. With the publication of this handbook, nurses now have a clear blueprint for wielding their power and transforming their profession into a major force for improving our health care system.

With this guide, nurses will be in a better position to influence the health and well-being of all Americans, particularly the young and the old, the poor and minorities, and others most likely to be affected by limited resources. Nurses have long understood that preventing illness and promoting good health in the home and in the community are more effective and economical than treating sickness in hospitals and other institutional settings. It is appropriate, therefore, that nurses should become more vigorous leaders in shaping current policy as the focus of health care in our society shifts back from hospitals and other institutions to the home and community.

As modern experience proves, many federal programs for those in need have been successful because of the involvement of nurses in identifying people at risk and helping them to help themselves. Adequate care of hospitalized patients, especially those who are most frail and vulnerable, is possible because of knowledgeable, watchful, continuing nursing care. And the same is true for millions of patients in the home, for whom decent care is available only because nurses are there to give it. Often, however, these vital services are provided behind the scenes, and are therefore undervalued.

But times are changing. As a profession composed primarily of women, nursing has been advancing in concert with the women's movement. Access of women to health care has improved. Nurses have catalyzed needed action on issues such as rape, spouse and child abuse, and reproductive freedom. Nurse researchers have spearheaded studies of prenatal care, aging, and treatment of the dying and their families. Nursing's daily involvement with the human aspects of care and caring has thrust nurses into the midst of the complex ethical questions facing modern medicine, and it is essential for their perspective to be heard in the current debate.

The monumental contribution that nursing makes to health care in America is probably the profession's best kept secret. As citizens more fully exercise their right to competent and affordable health care, nurses will play an ever greater role in achieving that goal. Nurses already understand their far-reaching capabilities. One of their most important missions now is to assume their rightful role in the public debate on the future of our health care system. By setting out the possibilities for contemporary political action, this important handbook brings that mission closer to fulfillment.

EDWARD M. KENNEDY
U.S. Senator from Massachusetts

Preface

A strong and effective nursing profession is needed by both nurses and consumers. A strong profession is dependent upon nurses who are able to individually and collectively influence public policy, institutional practices, professional organizations, and community action. Because the editors believe that nursing is essential to the public's health, this book was written to help nurses further develop this individual and collective influence.

The women's movement has been a mixed blessing for nursing. While providing support for nursing's desire for and efforts to achieve professional autonomy, the women's movement has provided women with opportunities to enter male-dominated professions. Many women, who in an earlier day would have chosen nursing, now select careers that offer more money and better working conditions. Also, the women's movement has contributed to a devaluation of traditional "women's professions." Today, many nurses feel a need to justify their selection of a career that society views largely as a nonprofession, one that attracts dependent individuals who want to be no more than handmaidens (Fagin & Diers, 1983).

Improving nursing's image depends upon nurses' ability to influence events in our society, including the ability to develop and foster competence, autonomy, and interdependence with other health professionals. While nurses talk of being the patient's advocate, hospitals hire non-nurse ombudsmen to fulfill this role. While nurses talk about primary prevention, health educators are hired by agencies to do just that. Many nurses do not see current threats to professional practice or the need to participate in determining health policy. Those who do perceive problems are often at a loss as to what to do because they have not been taught the principles of effective political action. Indeed, the editors believe that the chronic complaining of many staff nurses about conditions of employment and the problems they face in practicing their profession is a symptom of their feelings of powerlessness. Those who see nothing to do but complain are wasting precious time and energy, scarce resources that could be used to solve many problems encountered by nurses and consumers. A constructive way to channel this energy and reduce the sense of powerlessness is for nurses to take action on their own and their patients' behalf. This book was written to help nurses solve professional and health care delivery problems. It provides nurses with a framework, principles, and strategies for successful political action.

In a review of the Kalisch and Kalisch (1982) book, *The Politics of Nursing*, Diers (1982) discussed the importance of their landmark contribution, but identified the need for a book that dealt with the "how-to's" of political action. This book was written to fill this need. It outlines strategies for effective political action and illustrates them with examples contributed by a variety of authors who agreed to share their successes and failures so that other nurses might learn from them.

Contributions from a large number of authors were deliberately solicited. We believe our collective voices can send an important message to nurses who are not yet involved in the legislative and political process:

> Nurses have been and are continuing to use their political skills to bring about change in health care policies and programs. More needs to be done, and you can help. We offer our suggestions and examples of our work; won't you hone your political skills and join us?

Some of the contributors are renowned nurse leaders. Many say that their political skills have been essential to their becoming effective leaders. Other contributors are new staff nurses who are learning about political action by watching others and then doing it. Each person is committed to helping her nursing colleagues improve and expand their political acumen and effectiveness.

USING THE BOOK

This book is designed for nurses with little political savvy as well as those who are already quite skilled. It is a handbook that can be read from cover to cover or used as a reference. It will serve nurses throughout their careers—from novice to expert. While serving as an undergraduate text for leadership, issues, and policy/politics courses, it will also provide graduate students with a resource for health policy and politics courses. The book's focus on four key spheres of influence—the workplace, government, professional organization, and community—makes it a valuable reference for any nurse who wants to exert influence in these areas. Established and proposed political action committees, organizational and institutional committees on legislation, community activists, leaders, and members of professional nursing organizations—all can use this book as a source of ideas on how to "do politics" and influence the allocation of scarce resources in any arena.

ORGANIZATION OF THE BOOK

Although parts of the book have been organized to provide specific attention to each sphere, the reader is often referred to other parts of the book that discuss similar topics.

Such overlap is unavoidable in a book of this scope. It serves to reinforce important content by demonstrating how principles of political action are applied in each sphere.

The first part of the book, "Politics—A Nursing Perspective," provides the reader with the historical and feminist perspectives that we believe are invaluable to future political successes, as well as discussion of the challenging issues that require nursing to become a poltically astute profession. Chapter 4, "The Politics of Patient Care," and other chapters on the politics of each of the four spheres of influence discuss *why* nurses must be politically active.

The second unit of the book, "Analysis of Key Concepts," provides discussion of selected concepts that are integral to political action: politics, power, change, conflict, and conflict management. A final chapter in this section examines some of the ethical issues surrounding nursing practice and political action. We believe this area will grow increasingly important as health care resources shrink and nurses become more involved with politics and confront ethical dilemmas that arise when one tries to exert influence.

The third unit of the book presents chapters on "Generic Strategies for Political Action": analyzing formal and informal political structures and processes; developing one's interpersonal skills; using collective strategies; developing an issue; and using marketing skills to promote nursing. The strategies discussed in these chapters can be applied to each sphere of influence.

The remaining four units focus on political action in each of the four spheres. Considerable detail is presented in Unit 5, "Political Action in Government," reflecting the fact that this is the sphere where political action is not only accepted but expected. The book ends with a case study that demonstrates the overlap of political action among the four spheres as politically astute nurses worked successfully to save their school of nursing from the university budget cutter's ax.

The appendices include reprinted and original material that the editors believe will be valuable resources to many readers. Careful attention has also been given to the index, as the editors believe a thorough index facilitates the reader's use of a book of this scope.

Every effort has been made to avoid use of sexist language in this book. In the interest of simplicity and clarity, however, where singular pronouns were necessary, we have referred to the nurse as female. This is in no way intended to diminish the contributions that men continue to make to the profession.

ACKNOWLEDGMENTS

The development and writing of this book was a truly collective venture. The editors would like to acknowledge the people who contributed their time, effort, and support to this project.

First and foremost we thank the contributing authors for generously sharing their knowledge and experiences. All of the contributors are very busy people. Some hesitated to commit to writing for the book because of other life demands, but believed in the project so strongly that they agreed to make it a priority. The contributors not only enabled us to produce this book in a timely fashion, they apologized when deadlines became unrealistic. We particularly appreciate the encouragement they gave to us.

Several contributors deserve special acknowledgment because of their help with the development of the entire project. Connie Vance and Janet Natapoff assured us we could tackle the project and encouraged us when, halfway into it, we asked them, "Why are we doing this?" They shared their thoughts with us about the shape of the book, the framework, and targeted audience.

Another contributor, Pamela Maraldo, shared with us her national network of colleagues whom we contacted to ask for contributions. On several occasions she made personal requests to very busy colleagues, asking them to join the project. She did this for us while acknowledging that one day she hopes to write her own book on politics in nursing. We look forward to her book, as we have been fortunate to work with her in various capacities and have seen that her political wisdom makes her one of nursing's finest leaders with a political acumen that we admire and respect.

One of nursing's most eloquent leaders, Vernice Ferguson, gave us a great deal of support and encouragement in the early stages of our endeavor. We met with her in Philadelphia just after her return from an international journey. Despite jet lag, she invited us to her room, ordered coffee, and helped us think through our ideas. We admire her style and are indebted to her for helping us.

Other people who helped us to identify potential contributors include two committed and visionary members of the ANA Washington office staff, Joanne Symons and Pat Ford-Roegner, and ANA President Eunice Cole. We are also indebted to these individuals for their efforts in leading a revolutionary movement to develop a politically astute cadre of nurses. The American Nurses' Association's Political Education Department and Office of Governmental Affairs are helping to make nursing a visible and powerful force in Washington and in state houses across the country. Additionally, the staff in this office have been consistently accessible and helpful to us and other nurses across the country. We also thank Pat Jones, formerly an ANA staff member, who helped us identify potential contributors.

When we first approached publishers with the idea of a book that would include numerous original works on political action in nursing, the editors advised us not to include more than a handful of contributors. The Addison-Wesley Publishing Company, new to the nursing field, was the only firm that fully embraced our idea. Our selection of Addison-Wesley as our publisher reflects our respect for their efforts to undertake bold, new projects. The company has supported this project with competence and enthusiasm.

We have been particularly fortunate to work with Nancy Evans, the Senior Editor, Nursing Division, at Addison-Wesley. Known to many of our book's contributors from her years of experience in publishing, Nancy is the consummate editor. When we told her that we were committed to including a variety of contributors, Nancy not only agreed with us, she recruited several key contributors. She also pointed out the compromises we would have to make to involve many contributors, such as accepting a book that is not necessarily consistent in style and one that is complex to manage because of the number of authors. When we needed expert advice, she provided it. When we needed encouragement to keep going, she told us what we needed to hear. When problems arose that we were having difficulty handling, she knew when to take over and did so with competence and compassion.

We also thank Ellie Schrader for her work as copy editor of the book. Her editing smoothed many rough edges in the book.

Knowing the importance of the packaging of any product, we wanted a cover to the book that would make an impact at first glance. Colleen McEvoy used her expertise in design and project management to develop the striking cover of the book. We thank her for doing a superb job and for her interest in the book.

We would never have completed this project without the expert typing and editorial contributions of Susan Mannheimer. She often worked long hours to help us meet important deadlines. Additionally, Elaine Shen was a great asset in helping us prepare the final manuscript.

One of the important themes of this book is that nurses need to have and be mentors. Each of us has been fortunate to have mentors who have helped us in learning political lessons. Since the term was not in vogue twenty years ago, not all of these mentors realize that they were mentors to us. For Diana, her first faculty advisor, Patricia Diehl of West Virginia University School of Nursing, demonstrated how listening, compassion, and active support of people could encourage them to maintain commitments to difficult endeavors. Anita Golden Pepper and Edna Dell Weinel introduced her to the role of politics in everyday nursing when Diana was a graduate student at St. Louis University. They shared their knowledge, networks, families, and friendship with her. They are valued mentors and friends. Other special people include Candice Knight and Colleen McEvoy, whose friendship and "women's night out" provided welcome alternatives to working on the book.

For Sue, early lessons about the politics of interpersonal relations were learned from Jane Schmall Cattell, a dynamic psychiatric nursing instructor at Skidmore College. A fortuitous meeting with Claire Fagin, one of nursing's outstanding leaders, led Sue to enter the psychiatric nursing masters program at NYU. That educational experience, plus the role model provided by Sue's community service–oriented mother, set the stage for involvement in legislative and political activities in a wide variety of spheres: block association, antiwar movement, women's rights, and nursing/consumer advocacy.

The idea of mentors as peers has been described by Connie Vance, and Sue has been fortunate to have colleagues who are true peer-pals. Lois Mantel was a mainstay through the demanding program at NYU, Rosalyn Gershell was a key support during business school, and Connie Vance is a valued friend and colleague. Sharing struggles and successes with these special women has been a particular joy.

For both editors, putting together a book of this sort was often exceedingly demanding of our time and energies. Having each other as co-editor, friend, and colleague made it a mutually satisfying and rewarding endeavor. It reinforced our belief that working with others can be vastly more satisfying and productive than working alone.

We also want to thank our husbands, James Ware and John Talbott, and Sue's daughters, Alexandra and Sieglinde, for their support and understanding during the time it took to complete this book, for tolerating piles of copy that covered dining room tables, for birthdays missed, and for other times when the book took precedence over important family activities.

To all of our colleagues who supported us in this endeavor and were tolerant of receiving less than full attention to other projects and work commitments, we thank you. Our colleagues from New York State Nurses for Political Action and from the New York Counties Registered Nurses Association were particularly supportive of our efforts. We thank you for some of the political lessons we have learned with you and cherish having you as colleagues.

We are grateful to the following reviewers who shared valuable insights at various stages of the book's development:

Mickey Beil, Associate Administrator, Government Relations, Illinois Nurses' Assn, Springfield, IL

Rosemary A. Bowman, RN, MBA, Health Care Partners, Nashville, TN

Donna Diers, RN, MSN, FAAN, Yale University

Catherine J. Dodd, RN, MS, President, San Francisco NOW

Laurie Ferris, RN, MA, University of North Carolina at Chapel Hill

Phyllis M. Gallagher, JD, RN, Attorney at Law

Debra M. Hardy, RN, BS, FNP, Vice-President, Capitol Associates, Inc., Washington, DC

Edith P. Lewis, MN, RN, FAAN, Consultant, Southbury, Connecticut

Shirley Martin, PhD, University of Missouri, St. Louis

Nancy Rothman, BSN, MEd, MSN, Villanova University

Marilyn T. Spikes, RN, MS, Elmhurst College, Diecke Center for Nursing, Elmhurst, IL

Margretta M. Styles, EdD, RN, FAAN, University of California at San Francisco

Pamela Swearingen, Special Projects Editor, St. Louis

Lillian Waring, RN, EdD, Baylor University

Nancy West, RN, MSN, Adelphi University, Garden City, New York

Edith Wright, RN, MS, Texas Woman's University, Houston, Texas

Their comments helped us to both refine and enrich this work.

And finally, we want to acknowledge our foremothers in nursing, for they have provided us with a rich heritage of effective social activism. They were women who used their political skills to better the lives of the less fortunate and to promote the delivery of health care and the growth of the nursing profession. We hope our readers will reflect upon the past while learning from today's activists how to use effective political action to translate their vision of a better world into a shining legacy for tomorrow's nurses.

D.J.M.
S.W.T.

References

Diers D: Book Review. *Nursing Outlook* 1982; 31: 20–22.

Fagin C, Diers D: Nursing as metaphor. *Am J Nurs* 1983 (Sept); 83(9): 1362.

Kalisch BJ, Kalisch PA: *Politics of Nursing.* Lippincott, 1982.

Introduction

As a profession inherently responsive to people, nursing cannot separate itself from politics and public policy. We understand in human terms what, to policy makers, appears as flat abstractions on paper. Only by being willing to enter into the political arena can we ensure that our elected representatives legislate in the interests of the health needs of their constituents.

Nursing's abilities to influence the legislative process have not gone unnoticed. U.S. Senator Daniel Inouye of Hawaii has publicly recognized the unique legislative contributions of nurses. He credits nurse interns on his staff for many of the insights that have helped him formulate bills for federal policy. As information givers, nurses perceive health care as including the promotion of wellness, both psychosocial and physiological well-being. As advocates, we support the rights of children, families, and the elderly. Nurses have the ability to personalize issues in powerful ways that have made important differences in legislative decisions.

The 1980s mark a decade of revolutionary change in the health care industry. Everywhere we look, issues demand nursing's attention. Growing numbers of older Americans, rapidly increasing health care costs, and technological advances that can dehumanize the care given to individuals—all are problems that nursing must help to solve.

Consumers, government, and business and industry are forced to consider a new focus in the health care delivery system on wellness and the prevention of disease and on a system that can save money and yet improve the quality of care. A new system of Medicare payment for inpatient services has sought to give incentives for shorter lengths of stay at hospitals based on diagnosis and a prospective pricing system. It has helped to preserve the endangered Medicare Trust Fund by controlling escalating costs. This increased emphasis on cost savings in health care has encouraged competition, creativity, and innovation among facilities and providers.

The nursing profession has always supported cost containment in health care—in the total range of health care delivery in hospitals, in long-term care facilities, and in the community. Nursing must be ready to assume the added responsibilities inherent in the changes occurring throughout the health care system. We will have added responsibilities in care of the acutely ill, during and after their shorter hospital stay. We will continue to be a critical link from hospital to community and increasingly involved in delivery of a full range of health care services.

These unprecedented public needs mean that our voices must be heard in the political arena. Nurses have sought recognition as cost-effective providers of high quality care in many new legislative programs. We must be represented in all forums in which health care policy is developed and implemented—from the institutions in which we practice to the highest level of federal government.

Political Action Handbook for Nurses encourages nurses to exercise their political prerogative and speak out on health care issues. This handbook is a complete resource on the political process and how nurses can work within it. Experts in all areas of nursing and politics discuss politics within the profession, in the workplace, in the community, and with public officials. This book will be a useful reference for each step of your involvement in health care issues—from your initial understanding of political action, into areas where you are directly involved in decision making, and through the broader concepts of political power, change, conflict, and ethics. Practical chapters help increase your personal skills in communicating and in planning strategy. Other chapters will help you work more effectively with groups you may encounter in your networking. Entire sections are devoted to explaining the political process as it operates in the workplace, the government, organizations, and the community.

Because our culture has generally not socialized women to use power, many nurses find the concepts of power and politics remote from their daily lives. Political influence, however, includes the concept of power. The power we possess is as strong as our ability to do or our capacity to act. We must be able to accomplish our objectives, whether in the workplace or in government. Nursing has power, and we must continue to develop and use it effectively.

The American Nurses' Association (ANA), the professional organization for the nation's nurses, is working to increase political power for nursing. Through its Department of Political Education, ANA recruits volunteers to work on local, state, and federal election campaigns and to educate public officials to nursing's concerns. These volunteers serve as congressional district coordinators, active in every state in the nation. With funds raised by the political action committee N-CAP (Nurses' Coalition for Action in Politics), ANA offers campaign and financial support to candidates nursing endorses.

During the 1984 election, N-CAP distributed more than $300,000 in campaign contributions—money contributed voluntarily from state nurses' association members. These efforts helped elect 88 percent of our endorsed candidates for the U.S. House and Senate. Monetary contributions played a large part in the success of these efforts and assured us of access to the decision makers for discussion of issues with them. Political access is vital to sharing the information that is unique to our profession.

Nursing must join together as a profession to address the vital issues in health care. We cannot work in isolation from the society that gives us our mandate to practice. As citizens and as spokespersons for the profession, we must be involved in our communities on a political level, educating the policy makers and speaking out for our patients as well as for our profession.

This handbook gives us the tools we need to strengthen our political efforts. We will be challenged by the issues, by the process, by the possibilities of our individual and collective power to change our health care system. Together we can meet these challenges; together we and our society will share the benefits.

EUNICE R. COLE, RN
President, American Nurses' Association

POLITICAL ACTION
HANDBOOK FOR NURSES

UNIT I

POLITICS—
A NURSING PERSPECTIVE

Unit I explores politics as it relates to nursing and demonstrates why political action is relevant to every nurse in a variety of contexts. In Chapter 1, a framework for political action is presented in which politics is defined as influencing the allocation of scarce resources in four spheres: the workplace, professional organizations, government, and the community.

Chapter 2 describes the development of the nursing profession in the political arena and identifies some of the important contributions of the profession's leaders. Two vignettes illustrate nurses' efforts to secure registration legislation and make nursing research a priority for the profession and the country.

The women's movement continues to influence the personal and professional lives of nurses and encourages them to gain and exert power. Chapter 3 explores the women's movement and nursing's impact on women's health and feminist ideology.

The final four chapters examine political issues relevant to the nurse in the four spheres of influence. Chapter 4 discusses the politics of direct patient care, an important sphere for staff nurses as well as nurse managers. A differentiation between politics and health policy is explored in Chapter 5, while Chapter 6 examines the role of the professional organizations in nursing and some of the political issues confronting them. Finally, Chapter 7 illustrates how the community encompasses the other spheres through discussion of political issues in communities from one's hometown to the international community.

Chapter 1

Introduction: A Framework for Political Action

Diana J. Mason, RN, MSN
Susan W. Talbott, RN, MA, MBA

Politics.

What images does this word conjure up?

Smoke–filled rooms where deals are being made by male power brokers . . . Watergate . . . bribes . . . unethical compromises . . . money trading hands under tables . . . pork barreling. . . .

Or perhaps less negative images come to mind: legislation . . . negotiating . . . elections . . . campaigns . . . power . . . public officials. . . .

The word "politic" evokes a variety of images related to government activities. Some of these images have negative connotations. The dictionary includes several definitions of the term. The words "crafty" and "unscrupulous" are included in *Webster's New World Dictionary of the American Language*. However, Webster's first definition is more positive: "having practical wisdom."

Politics can also be defined as "influencing the allocation of scarce resources" (Talbott & Vance, 1981, p 592). It is a word, then, that is not only related to government. Rather, it is applicable to every aspect of life where resources are limited and more than one person or group competes for them (Ehrat, 1983).

Even this broader definition of politics conjures up negative images among nurses. For example, how often have you heard this: "I like her. She doesn't play politics." Some may think this a compliment, but if this person is the head of a nursing department, school of nursing, or home care agency, he or she needs to be politically astute and skillful to influence who gets what share of the available resources. While nurses expect nursing leaders to be politically astute—to "wheel and deal" with other power brokers—some have reservations about whether political and professional behavior should coexist in trusted colleagues.

Nurses must beware of complacency regarding their political power. As the nursing profession struggles for educational standards recommended in the early 1900s; for economic accountability and reimbursement for its services; for ensuring that nursing services are provided by qualified professional nurses rather than nonnurses; it must take stock of its political skills and savvy. Nurses' discomfort with "politics" may have made these struggles more difficult.

NURSES' DISCOMFORT WITH POLITICS

Until recently, little was written on the politics of nursing. Politics was considered a dirty game that was not an openly acknowledged and accepted part of the professional nurse's role, eg, "nice girls don't do it." Why?

First, the majority of nurses (97 percent) are women. Before the women's movement, politics was seen as an aggressive, men-only endeavor. The men-only barrier is still not completely broken. Although in 1984 Geraldine Ferraro became the first woman to be nominated for the vice-presidency by a major political party, speculation continues over when the United States will elect a woman as president. News reports show interviews with the "person on the street" expressing doubt about a woman's ability to lead the nation. Women, however, are participating in political campaigns in unprecedented numbers. The Nurses' Coalition for Action in Politics (N-CAP), the political action committee of the American Nurses' Association, has reported annual increases in nurses' participation in political campaigns and in monetary contributions to the PAC. In 1980, nurses contributed $99,000 to N-CAP; in 1984, they contributed $300,000. State nurses' PACs are growing in number, size, and influence, and an increasing number of nurses are running for political office.

In spite of these optimistic trends, nurses still have difficulty expanding their acceptance of and involvement in politics to other than government arenas. Although being politically astute in government and political campaigns is acceptable, many nurses are still not sure that politically astute behavior in the workplace is professional. A nursing leader, for example, told a group of nurses: "You cannot be both political and professional at the same time." One wonders how this nurse was able to maneuver successfully as the chief of a division of nursing in a major teaching hospital without using political skills. Perhaps she did not see herself as involved in politics because of an aversion to the word. As a leader in her workplace and professional association, however, she unquestionably demonstrated political prowess.

The male-dominated institutional hierarchy rarely encourages or rewards nurses who influence resource allocation if it results in a loss of resources for a male-dominated group in the institution. Nurses who take a "get tough" position are often labeled brassy, bitchy, belligerent, aggressive, or unfeminine.

Because women have been socialized differently than men, women are often unable to influence the male-dominated professional and business worlds. Women have not been encouraged to engage in team sports. Men are, and they learn valuable lessons in the process. Although this idea was first discussed in relationship to business women (Hennig & Jardin, 1977; Harragan, 1977), the findings are applicable to nursing, where team play is crucial to the patient's welfare.

What lessons are learned by playing team sports? One learns that the object of the game is scoring the most points, and this can only be done if team members work together. Whether two team members like each other becomes irrelevant. While the game is being played, personal relationships are subordinated, and all energy is focused on winning.

In team sports, the coach's word is law. Disagreement is not tolerated, and no one undermines the coach. The coach is the acknowledged expert and commands the attention and devotion of the team players. The coach sets the game plan for the team members to follow. If one member deviates from this plan because he disagrees with it, the team cannot function effectively.

One also learns that although winning is the object of the game, competition is as important. Men relish competition in personal and business affairs, but most women are uncomfortable with competitive situations. The message has been clear: women should not compete—not with each other and certainly not with men.

A key role of a team player is to make sure the team star gets the ball. Although the star receives the glory, the other players try to make this player shine, since the team benefits whenever the ball crosses the goal line. The star player's own ambitions, however, should not outshine the team's success. Personal ambition has its place only as it contributes to the team effort and winning.

A good politician is a team player. The denizens of Wall Street play the game so that their corporations succeed in business. How do nurses score on team effectiveness? Most nursing leaders shake their heads when someone talks about the infighting among nurses. Nursing rarely speaks with one strong voice. The arguments over entry into practice are a case in point. One legislator told his nurse constituents:

> When you folks decide among yourselves what the entry level should be, you let me know, and we will write and enact a bill into law that says what you want. Until you can publicly agree, I do not want to hear any more about it. You would do yourselves a favor if you kept your intraprofessional arguments to yourselves. Airing disagreements before your legislators does not help your image or your cause.

This does not imply that nurses must adopt male behaviors to be successful change agents. A growing body of literature suggests that women bring a unique perspective to the business, professional, and political worlds (Rosener & Schwartz, 1977). For example, Miller (1982) points out that while men strive singularly to achieve power, women demonstrate the ability to develop the concept of "power-sharing."

A second block for nurses is insufficient appreciation of nursing history. Many nurses have made significant contributions to the profession and to health care because they were consummate politicians. Florence Nightingale is a good example. Reflecting on her first administrative position in nursing, Nightingale wrote:

> When I entered into service here, I determined that, happened what would, I *never* would intrigue among the Committee. Now I perceive that I do all my business by intrigue. I propose in private to A, B, or C the resolution I think A, B, or C most capable of carrying in Committee, and then leave it to them, and I always win (Huxley, 1975, p 53).

Indeed, Nightingale oversaw the development of British health policy from her bed. She sent flowers to her new student graduates, invited them to tea, and then sent them on difficult assignments that they rarely protested. She was a leader who knew how to garner the support of her followers and colleagues.

Nurse historians are paying greater attention to the political savvy and strategies of nurses in earlier times. Such knowledge can help nurses appreciate the importance of political action to the development of the profession and health policies. Knowledge of the political efforts of nurses such as Florence Nightingale, Lavinia Dock, Margaret Sanger, Harriet Tubman, Lillian Wald, and others may encourage nurses to emulate them.

A third reason why nurses are uncomfortable with political action is that they are not educated to be politically astute. In a study of 1,086 nurse administrators from various settings, Archer and Goehner (1981) found that:

> Respondents attribute nurses' lack of political involvement mainly to inadequate preparation, failure to realize the importance of participation, socialization of nurses into passive roles, ignorance of issues, and failure to realize our potential clout. All of these factors are related to the inability of both formal and continuing nursing education to provide opportunities for nurses to learn the importance of political participation and how to be prepared for political effectiveness (p 52).

Although many nursing curricula include the concepts of change agent, teamwork, and leadership, the rules of team play and effective politics are seldom discussed. A few schools of nursing include an elective or required course in health policy and politics. These, however, are the exception. Most programs include little content on influencing governmental politics and none on workplace politics.

The factors underlying nurses' political naiveté and ineptitude are beginning to be addressed. This book addresses these factors to encourage nurses to develop and use their political skills, individually and collectively.

SPHERES OF INFLUENCE

Because the word "politics" is primarily associated with government, nurses have often confined their political activities to this area. While there have been numerous articles in the nursing literature on the politics of health policy and legislation, there is little on politics in other arenas.

Three other spheres of influence are the workplace, professional organization, and community. Although we will discuss the four spheres separately here and elsewhere in the book, the reader is encouraged to keep in mind that activities associated with each of these spheres overlap and affect what happens in other arenas or spheres (see Figure 1-1). Ignoring one can lead to defeat in another. In fact, one of the reasons why nursing, the largest health profession in this country (1.7 million registered nurses), does not have the influence its numbers warrant is that nurses have not always been politically active in each of these spheres. Recognition of the importance of and interrelationships among these four spheres is part of the evolutionary or developmental process that the nursing profession is experiencing.

The most obvious sphere for nursing involvement is government. The government

Figure 1-1 The four spheres of political influence where nurses can effect change: workplace, government, organizations, and community (the encompassing sphere).

provides society with a legal definition of nursing. It influences reimbursement systems for nursing services, and it determines who will get what kind of health care. It often influences which health problems will be researched and targeted for government-coordinated treatment programs. It is also an important part of any community, although local government has not received the attention it deserves from nurses. With the societal trend towards decentralization (Naisbitt, 1982), local governments will become increasingly important. Furthermore, persons elected or appointed to government offices are frequently influential in the community. They may be members of the boards of hospitals, nursing homes, or home care agencies. They and their families are also potential consumers of health care.

The second sphere of influence is the workplace—hospitals, nursing homes, home care agencies, public health departments, schools, mental institutions, and schools of nursing. Over 66 percent of nurses work in hospitals, and like other workers, spend the majority of their waking hours at their place of employment. Yet these bureaucratic organizations are rarely described as satisfying places to work. Few nurses speak glowingly of their ability to practice professional nursing the way they would like it to be practiced. Will the day come when we have more than a handful of "magnet hospitals" (McClure, Poulin, Sovie & Wandelt, 1983)? The magnet hospital study examined hospitals across the country that were successful at attracting and retaining professional nurses. The rate of turnover among nurses and the periodic nursing shortages our country experiences indicate that all is not well in nurses' place of work.

Nurses' dissatisfaction with their work is too often a reflection of their inability to establish and maintain standards of care. Hospitals are becoming more concerned with reducing operational costs as the government and private insurors attempt to cap escalating health care costs. As a result, the maintenance of minimal standards of patient care is in jeopardy. Politically effective nurses in the workplace can have a positive effect on patients' well-being by working to influence how the institution allocates its resources.

The third sphere is professional organizations. Many nurses complain that their professional organization does nothing for them, or that they do not like what their professional organization does. Fewer than 25 percent of all nurses are affiliated with the American Nurses' Association through membership in constituent state associations. Although specialty organizations are growing in number and size, the same complaints are heard about these professional organizations. Just as chronic complaining in the workplace indicates nurses' sense of powerlessness, nurses complain about these groups, don't join them, or drop out because they do not feel they are influential.

While some leaders in these organizations may say this is nonsense—that because they were able to influence their organization means that anyone can—one must question how or where nurses are supposed to learn how to exert influence. Few organizations are so secure as to want to give classes on "Influencing Your Professional Organization." Those in power would often prefer to keep the general membership ignorant of how to exert influence. Yet, an active, knowledgeable, involved membership is essential to the growth and influence of the organization itself.

A strong professional organization should be a visible force within its community. A national organization should have a national presence. A local organization should be known in the local community. These organizations should identify issues of concern to nursing and health care and bring them to the attention of the public.

The fourth sphere of influence is the community. In years past, nurses such as Lillian Wald viewed the community as more than a practice site. It is a social unit with a variety of special interest groups, community activities, health and social problems, and numerous resources for solving those problems. The other three spheres of influence are an integral part of the community. As members of a community, we have a responsibility to promote the welfare of the community and its members. In turn, the community's resources can be invaluable assets to health promotion and health care delivery. Government officials, hospital administrators, patients, corporate managers, presidents of private and public organizations—all players who can effect change in health policy—are affiliated with at least one community, the one in which they live. When nurses become visible in the affairs of their communities, they represent an entire profession. Community networks can be called upon to support nursing agendas. Nursing should be called upon to support the agendas of communities that are trying to develop a better place in which to live.

The interrelationship among these four spheres becomes more obvious as the nurse develops and uses political skills. Ignoring one sphere can endanger one's effectiveness as a change agent. Developing one's influence in all four spheres, however, takes time and effort. While striving to develop such influence, collaboration with colleagues who have already achieved significant influence in any one arena, should be sought.

THEMES

There are pervasive themes throughout this book. This book illustrates a shared belief of the authors in our responsibility to effect change. Authors have contributed their work without fee, and a portion of the book's proceeds will be contributed to N-CAP. A number of authors told us that they do not ordinarily write for contributed books, but in this case felt they had a responsibility to contribute to the political education of nurses.

Indeed, nurses are known for their altruism. While altruism is laudable and should be cherished, nurses must find better ways to achieve altruistic aims. Political action becomes a positive concept when it is used to ensure a humanistic health policy.

The vignettes and case studies illustrate another idea: that politics is a humanistic endeavor. Nurses are educated in the art of interpersonal communication. We must learn to transfer techniques for effective patient communication to other spheres of influence, including relationships with one another. Colleagiality, team work, and collective action require that we respect each other and our differences.

The reader will undoubtedly identify other themes, but the main message remains: savvy nurses—including students, staff nurses, public health nurses, clinical specialists, researchers, lobbyists, educators, and administrators—all kinds of nurses across the country are using political knowledge and skills to bring about change in the spheres of government, workplace, community, and professional organizations. Many have shared their knowledge and skills in this handbook. We hope you will reap the benefits of their collective wisdom. Use this handbook in good health, to promote the health and welfare of your colleagues, neighbors, patients, and yourself.

References

Archer S, Goehner PA: Acquiring political clout: Guidelines for nurse administrators. *J Nurs Admin* (Nov–Dec) 1981; 11:49–55.

Ehrat KS: A model for politically astute planning and decision making. *J Nurs Admin* (Sept) 1983; 13:29–35.

Harragan BL: *Games Mother Never Taught You: Corporate Gamesmanship for Women*. Warner, 1977.

Hennig M, Jardin AJ: *The Managerial Woman*. Anchor Press/Doubleday, 1977.

Huxley E: *Florence Nightingale*. Putnam's Sons, 1975.

McClure ML, Poulin MA, Sovie MD, Wandelt MA: *Magnet Hospitals: Attraction and Retention of Professional Nurses*. American Nurses' Assoc, 1983.

Miller JB: Colloquium: Women and power. Stone Center for Developmental Services and Studies. Wellesley College, 1982.

Naisbitt J: *Megatrends: Ten New Directions Transforming Our Lives*. Warner, 1982.

Rosener L, Schwartz P: *Women, Leadership and the 1980s: What Kind of Leaders Do We Need?* (Background paper, NOW legal defense and education fund) Dec 1977.

Talbott SW, Vance C: Involving nursing in a feminist group—NOW. *Nurs Outlook* 1981; 29:592–95.

Chapter 2

Historical Overview of Nursing and Politics

Sydney D. Krampitz, RN, PhD

The actions of nurses as political activists are well recorded in the profession's proud history. This chapter will give an overview of the milestones in the political evolution of nursing in the U.S., beginning with the movement to enact registration laws. Acknowledgment of Florence Nightingale, a consummate politician, must precede discussion of recent nursing history.

Nightingale's political activity extended far beyond her years in the Crimea. As a reformer and political activist, she helped to establish a new attitude toward the contributions of nurses in a military environment and the education of women (Dock, Vol. 2, 1935). Nightingale's influence culminated in extensive reform of the British Army, resulting from public awareness of statistics she obtained and analyzed related to the sanitary condition and material welfare of the population and military establishment of India (Agnew, 1958).

Although Nightingale is one of the most recognized nurse reformers, other prominent nurses have gained public recognition for contributions to improving the quality of patient care and for advances in nursing service and education. The structuring of hospitals by the pioneer nurse graduates of the first American training schools, as well as early attempts to establish a nursing organization and publication, influenced later developments in nursing and initiated organizational developments with political and social impact on the fledgling nursing profession.

The problems attendant upon urbanization, industrialization, and immigration had special significance for the nursing profession. It became increasingly important for nurses to focus not only on the treatment of acute and chronic illness but also on the prevention of disease and disability. This forced nurses into the political arena. Early campaigns for public health originated in the late nineteenth century as drives against poor housing, rat infestation, and filth. Later reforms broadened into attacks upon particular diseases and eventually resulted in integrated, city-wide health care programs.

As early as 1877, the New York City Mission sent trained nurses into the homes of the sick poor. The New York Ethical Society later (1881) placed nurses in dispensaries to instruct in the prevention and control of illness and disability. The first visiting nurse association was established in Buffalo, in 1885. These visiting nurses were affiliated with settlement houses in major industrial cities and, consequently, they became acutely aware of the living conditions that plagued the poor city dweller. It would be difficult to overestimate the impact of these visiting nurses on later innovations in the field of health, hygiene, and medical care in America.

ORGANIZATION OF AMERICAN NURSING

A unique opportunity presented itself to the nurse leaders of the 1890s. Mrs Bedford Fenwick, a nurse leader in the English nurse registration movement, came to Chicago in 1893 to arrange the English nursing exhibit to be displayed in the Women's Building at the World's Fair. As part of the Congress on Hospitals and Dispensaries, a nursing section included papers on establishing standards in hospital training schools, the establishment of a nurses' association, and nurse registration (Dock, Vol. 3, 1935). These papers and discussion by nursing leaders led to: (1) the establishment of the American Society for Superintendents of Training Schools for Nurses; (2) the initiation of preparatory courses for nurses preparing for positions as heads of training schools for nurses at Teachers College, Columbia University; and (3) the move for state licensure for nurses. The development of the hospital economics course at Teachers College, Columbia University, ushered in a new era in preparation of nurse leaders in America. This one-year certificate course was extended to a two-year postbasic training program in 1905 (Christy, 1969). The commitment of key nursing leaders to advancing educational preparation for nurse faculty fostered the subsequent development of baccalaureate education in nursing during the first quarter of the 20th century.

By the turn of the century, nurse leaders were expressing a need to establish a state nurses' organization, principally to influence legislation. " . . . we go before the legislature, not as graduates of any one school but as citizens of the state. . ." (Dock, Vol. 3, 1935, p 147).

Nurses participated in political activities to gain support for passage of registration acts. These activities included involvement in preparation of legislation as well as gaining support from various legislators and other organized groups. Birnbach (1982, p 2) held that these activities " . . . constituted efficient political pressure groups." Often, in attempts to establish standards for education and practice, nurse leaders met with resistance not only from other professional groups but also from within the nursing profession. Graduates of training schools offering a ten- to twelve-week training program criticized proposed educational standards and protested attempts to initiate state licensure. Individuals operating short courses or correspondence schools also protested against the proposed licensure of nurses (Kinney, 1905).

Despite this opposition, the movement for legislation to protect the public from the untrained nurse spread across the country. Although New York nurses began to organize for passage of legislation in 1901, the first state to pass a nurse practice bill was North

Carolina in 1903. By 1914, forty other states had passed similar legislation for nurse registration. (See vignette, p 17, by Nettie Birnbach.)

Dock states, "It was a new thing to see women coming forward, nurses at that, demanding the same guarantees which had been granted to the medical, dental, and other professions, and to skilled callings, such as that of a plumber, engineer, and horseshoer" (Dock, Vol. 3, 1935, p 149). Unfortunately, many nurses failed to see the relationship between their struggles for professional licensure, educational standards, and greater autonomy as related to broader women's issues of the period.

ISSUES IN THE EARLY 1900s
Women's Issues

Although nurses engaged in political activities related to nursing practice, they did not support the movement to gain the vote for women. In 1908, the membership of the Nurses' Association Alumnae of the United States (renamed the American Nurses' Association [ANA] in 1912) failed to endorse the following resolution:

> Whereas the thinking women of America are striving more earnestly than ever before to be a helpful part of the people, in the firm belief that men and women together compose a democracy, and that until men and women have equal political rights they cannot do their best work, therefore be it. . .
>
> Resolved, that the Nurses' Association Alumnae of the United States, numbering fourteen thousand members, as a company of workers, heartily endorse every well directed movement which tends to emancipate the women of our land and give them their rightful place in government (Dixon, 1908, p 442).

Dock, nurse leader and political activist, responded:

> It is so shortsighted not to perceive that full political equality for women would make it immediately possible for them to express themselves actively in reformative movements such as moral prophylaxis, and in administrative work such as better housing and homemaking of public institutions, that it is distressing to see nurses, who ardently desire the reforms, refusing to acknowledge the virtue of democracy's most potent instrument, the ballot, for attaining reforms of this character. I am sure that only a little study is needed to place our American nurses in the army of intelligent modern thinkers on this the most pressing of all present social reform (Dixon, 1908, p 446).

The delegates at the convention in San Francisco indicated that they felt that nurses ". . . had affairs enough of their own to attend to without getting mixed up in politics." Others disagreed, stating that ". . . we were mixed up in politics before we were born, and that it is impossible to attend to the smallest part of our own affairs without taking politics into consideration." (Dixon, 1908, p 442). Although nursing leaders often faced opposition within their own ranks, the turn of the century witnessed the increasing involvement of professional nursing at a national level.

Social Reform

Nurses today, although the majority of professional workers in the health field, often continue to focus on narrow interests rather than the broader concerns of such nursing leaders as Florence Nightingale, Lavinia Dock, and Lillian Wald. At the turn of the century, nursing was a visible force for social reform— influencing hospital reform, child labor legislation, and the establishment of minimum wage standards for working women. Dock (1907) repeatedly denounced the idea of nurses limiting their political activity to professional issues.

Military Service

The entry of the U.S. into World War I in 1917 brought opportunities for nurses to serve their country. Nurses in military hospitals soon realized their efforts were restricted by the lack of military status. Problems in maintaining discipline and morale compounded the struggle to maintain professional standards. The military nurses ". . . advanced that the reason for their demanding rank was to promote the efficiency of the nursing service for the Army" (Petersen, 1942). The Lewis-Jones-Raker bill for military rank for nurses was controversial. The Secretary of War was actively opposed to it. However, with support of the Federation of Women's Clubs, the American Nurses' Association, and thousands of telegrams from nurses to their congressmen, the bill passed in 1920. This accomplishment, among others, showed that nurses were gaining an awareness of power inherent in organized political action.

University-based Education

After the war, increasing numbers of women entered colleges and universities, and nurses were again caught up in the social change affecting women's roles. In response to the demand for increased nursing services in new settings, such as school and industry, university programs expanded educational opportunities for nurses. Teachers College, Columbia University, offered the first postbasic college courses to prepare educators.

Social Change

Growing awareness of the need for political and economic reform brought pressure for change in the existing social order. Initiated by the middle class, the Progressive movement had an urban, national perspective with emphasis on social reform. Led by professionals rather than rural, farming groups, the Progressive movement spawned "muckraker" articles about conditions in mills and the poverty of immigrants. Legislation during this period expanded nursing practice. The passage of the Sheppard-Towner Act, actively supported by nurses, expanded services to mothers and children in underserved areas. This act provided for a rapid expansion of health conferences, centers for prenatal care, and visiting nurse services. During this period, other demonstration projects had far-reaching implications for public health nursing. Smillie (1952, p 10) states that the period of 1919–1929 ushered in ". . . the nationalization of the public health." Legislation to improve health care for women and children

". . . provided for the employment of public health nurses in a variety of capacities" (Roberts, 1954, p 199).

ANA COMMITTEE ON LEGISLATION

In October 1923, the ANA Board of Directors established a Special Committee on Legislation. Activities were confined to legislative action related to health, nurses, and nursing. When this original resolution was reviewed in 1934, child labor legislation was added.

In the mid-1920s, Burgess (1928) and the Committee on the Grading of Nursing Schools recognized the problem of nurse "overproduction." The vulnerability of the private duty nurse to changes in the community socioeconomic status and to continued expansion in the number of nursing schools and student enrollment was well documented. The problem was compounded by decreased numbers of patients admitted to the not-for-profit hospitals and thus fewer opportunities for private duty in the hospital setting.

The depression years of the 1930s brought special health problems as a huge army of drifters searched across the country for employment. Many families were dispossessed from their homes during the depression following the Hoover Administration. These individuals lived "in empty lots on the edge of industrial cities . . . in crude shelters of packing crates and old pieces of metal. In large cities, whole colonies of these Hoovervilles were established" (Leuchtenburg, 1958, p 253). As numbers of homeless Americans increased, the need to provide health care to these populations was clearly evident. Roberts (1954) states, ". . . clinics became overcrowded and public-supported hospitals overflowed with patients" (p 223). Public health nursing agencies had an ever increasing patient workload amidst wide unemployment of private duty nurses.

The rise in the number of unemployed or severely underemployed nurses brought an organized response from the professional organization. ANA established the Committee on Distribution of Nursing Services with representation from the National League of Nursing Education (NLNE) and National Organization of Public Health Nurses (NOPHN), resulting in a joint effort to encourage the use of graduate nurses in staffing hospitals with a plea for the reduction of admissions of students to hospital schools of nursing. Although the response was less than anticipated, it became evident during this period in American nursing that professional nursing had to move forward in an organized effort to ". . . elevate, advance, and sustain the profession" (Christy, 1971, p 1783).

The 1930s ushered in a period of rapid expansion of social legislation—the passage of the National Labor Relations Act, the Social Security Act, the Wealth-Tax Act, and unemployment legislation. The Wealth Tax Act stimulated philanthropy, resulting in nursing scholarships and later funds for research. Opportunities for nurse employment resulted from the passage of the National Recovery Act (NRA), the Federal Emergency Relief Act (FERA), and Works Project Administration (WPA). The WPA, for example, funded direct patient care activities through community health agencies, which hired public health nurses. Nursing organizations supported federal intervention to alleviate the unemployment of nurses.

POLITICAL ACTION AT MID-CENTURY

A phenomenal increase in the use of hospital facilities occurred during the 1940s. "Between 1935 and 1943, the number of births in hospitals increased by 96% . . . and approximately four and one-half million persons were enrolled in plans approved by the Blue Cross Commission of the American Hospital Association" (Roberts, 1954, pp 259–60). The early 1940s brought a significant increase in employment of private duty nurses, the rapid expansion of public health nursing, and the establishment of standards for industrial health nursing. The impact of the Social Security Act and amendments in the 1940s on nursing and other federal programs indicated the role federal government would play in determining manpower needs and the allocating of support for nursing.

The first federal nursing education legislation was enacted in 1943. The Bolton Bill established the Cadet Nurse Corps, initiating a series of nursing training legislation that significantly affected nursing education and the development of nursing practice.

After World War II, nurses, together with other veterans, flocked to the universities under the GI bill. This stimulated the movement of nursing into the halls of higher education.

During the war, there had been a high rejection rate of military recruits because of mental illness or disability. As a result, programs to fund the training of nurses as key mental health professionals were initiated. The focus was on prevention, with the desire that if we were to go to war again, the nation would not be faced with the high incidence of mental illness in the population. The realization that nurses with special preparation could be in the forefront of prevention and health promotion was a significant step.

World War II also brought expansion of the number, size, and quality of hospitals in rural as well as urban communities. The Hill-Burton Act of 1946 funded the building of hundreds of new hospitals as well as nursing education facilities.

In 1946, ANA's Special Committee on Legislation outlined a program on federal and state legislation and expanded its membership to include representatives of the NLNE, NOPHN, and the American Association of Industrial Nurses. The committee maintained this structure until 1952 when ANA and NLN were reorganized as separate organizations.

When the Cadet Corps program expired in 1948, ANA sought new ways to gain federal support for nursing education. It supported a bill proposed by Senator Frances Payne Bolton (Ohio) to provide financial assistance to nursing education programs on a federal-state matching formula. The bill, however, failed to get adequate support from other legislators. This documented the need for the professional organization to act directly on behalf of nurses to influence federal legislation related to nursing education and health care programs. A more active presence in Washington was needed if the nursing profession was to gain federal support for nursing education programs.

Political Influence

ANA established a Washington office in 1951 to provide increased support and visibility for its legislative efforts. In 1954, the ANA Standing Committee on Legislation held a conference on legislation in Chicago to address issues relating to federal legislation. This conference was followed by the publication of *Legislative News* in 1955 and a series of conferences on legislation held in Washington.

The Health Amendments Act (1956) provided traineeships for nurse educators, consultants, and supervisors, and funds for training public health nurses and public health personnel. Legislation to support nursing education continued to be an issue addressed by the professional nursing organizations. Thompson (1972, p 43) states that, ". . . despite the apparent lack of progress, the word was being spread in the legislative halls of the need for federal aid to nursing." The need for federal support of nursing was formally recognized by President John Kennedy in 1961, when appointment of a consultant group to the Surgeon General of the Public Health Service was announced.

The Surgeon General's Report (1963) introduced legislation for nurse training. The report recommended expansion of federal support to nursing education, nursing service, and nursing research, and resulted in the passage of the Nursing Training Act of 1964. This action ". . . represented the efforts of many years' work with the Congress and Department of Health, Education and Welfare. It accomplished much of what the Association had set out to do in 1951" (Thompson, p 45).

Other legislation passed during this period supported selected nursing groups. The Mental Hygiene Bill (1946), the Health Amendments Act (1956), and Partnership in Health Act (1967) provided expanded training and research opportunities. The U.S. Public Health Service established an intramural research program in 1950 and initially allocated nursing research funds to the Division of Nursing (1954) for training of predoctoral fellows. (See "The Beginnings of Nursing Research," a vignette by Lucille P. Leone, p 20.) The establishment of the nurse-scientist programs marked a new era in federal support for nursing.

Nurses in the Political Arena

During the late 1960s and early 1970s, federal support for nursing education decreased markedly. Political action efforts appeared essential. Members of the American Association of Colleges of Nursing initiated political action to maintain support for baccalaureate and higher education.

Other nursing groups were also organizing to become more effective in the political arena. The California Nurses' Association (1971) and, later, the Colorado and Washington Nurses' Associations developed legally separate political action units. These nurses, ". . . concerned about trends in health care and the impact or lack of impact on these trends, organized so that they might exert greater influence. . ." (Stanton, n.d.). In New York State, nurses from New York City and Long Island incorporated to form "Nurses for Political Action."

In 1972, the Nurses for Political Action established a formal liaison with ANA. In September 1973, the ad hoc committee of ANA recommended "the establishment of a carefully structured nonpartisan political action unit (PAU)." These purposes were identified by the ad hoc committee: (1) to educate nurses and others on the relevant political issues; (2) to assist nurses and others in organizing for effective action in the political arena and in carrying out their civic responsibilities; (3) to raise funds and make contributions to candidates for public office who have demonstrated or indicated supportive positions on the issues of importance to nurses and health care. The ANA Board of Directors approved the establishment of a ". . . nonpartisan political action unit to be a voluntary, unincorporated nonprofit association of nurses and others."

Professional nursing organizations have educated nurses to their rights and responsibilities for political action. Increasing numbers of nurses are participating in political campaigns and helping to draft health care legislation. Early nurse leaders recognized action in the political arena as a necessity of life—a skill to be learned, developed, and taught to the new professional.

The professional nurse has greater responsibility today for political involvement as the struggle for resources becomes more complex and increasingly competitive. Individually and collectively, nurses must expand their legislative and political action, because the future of nursing as a profession will be determined by legislators and health policy makers at all levels of government.

References

Agnew LRC: Florence Nightingale—statistician. *Am J Nurs* 1958; 58:665.

Birnbach NS: The genesis of the nurse registration movement in the United States, 1893–1903 (dissertation). Teachers College, Columbia University, 1982.

Burgess MA: Nurses, Patients, and Pocketbooks. Committee on the Grading of Nursing Schools, 1928.

Christy TE: *Cornerstone for Nursing Education: A History of the Division of Nursing Education of Teachers College, Columbia University: 1899–1947.* Teachers College Press, 1969.

Christy TE: First fifty years. *Am J Nurs* 1971; 71:1783.

Dixon MB: Votes for women. *Nurs J Pacific Coast* 1908; 4:442–447.

Dock L: *A History of Nursing.* Vol 2. GP Putnam's Sons, 1935.

Dock L: *A History of Nursing.* Vol 3. GP Putnam's Sons, 1935.

Dock L: Some urgent social claims. *Am J Nurs* 1907; 7:895–901.

Kinney DH: Some questionable nursing schools and what they are doing. *Am J Nurs* 1905; 5:224–29.

Krampitz S: Historical Development of Baccalaureate Nursing Education in the American University: 1895–1935 (dissertation). University of Chicago, 1978.

Leuchtenburg WE: *The Perils of Prosperity: 1914–32.* University of Chicago Press, 1958.

Petersen A: The nurse's fight for military rank. *Trained Nurse Hosp Rev* 1942; 109:98–100.

Roberts M: *American Nursing: History and Interpretation.* Macmillan, 1954.

Smillie WG: *Preventive Medicine and Public Health,* 2nd ed. Macmillan, 1952.

Stanton M to Jacobi E: Folder 77, Nurses for Political Action, Central File. American Nurses' Association, n.d.

Thompson J: *ANA in Washington.* American Nurses' Association, 1972.

Vignette: Political Activism and the Registration Movement

Nettie Birnbach, RN, EdD

Political activism, a recurring theme in American nursing, can be traced to the early 1900s, when trained nurses were struggling to achieve legal recognition of educational standards through the enactment of nurse registration laws. The registration movement had begun earlier in response to the rapid growth of irresponsible nurse training schemes. Recognizing that the absence of legal restraints would permit those abuses to continue, nurse leaders embarked on a crusade to institute legal requirements for the education and registration of trained nurses. Legal regulation was a priority for nursing organizations. But, the opposition to registration included, besides physicians, owners of short courses or correspondence courses in nursing.

It was soon apparent that the new associations needed assistance in implementing effective campaign techniques. Sophia F. Palmer and Lavinia L. Dock provided the necessary leadership on a national scale. The publicity they generated and strategies they recommended reflected a degree of political sophistication and assertiveness uncommon to most women of that era. Palmer, as first editor-in-chief of the *American Journal of Nursing*, wrote editorials advocating immediate planning for the achievement of nurse registration. Dock, because of her knowledge of the law and prior experience with the British registration movement, aided the registrationists in both New York and New Jersey.

Strategies used to effect the initial laws centered on: (a) obtaining expert legal advice in the preparation of bills; (b) increasing pro-registration publicity in professional journals and popular periodicals; (c) eliciting support from various women's groups, organized medicine, legislators, and prominent citizens; (d) delivering addresses at public hearings held in the legislatures; and (e) responding to the obstructive attempts of the opposition. In the various states, nurses constituted efficient political pressure groups. Despite hostile criticism from powerful adversaries, the involved nurses conducted themselves in a manner befitting an aspiring profession. In 1903, their labors resulted in the enactment of legislation in North Carolina, New Jersey, New York, and Virginia, respectively.

Although North Carolina was the first state to pass registration legislation, nurses there were forced to compromise their goals because of the intransigence of the opposition. Consequently, a weaker law than the one originally drafted was enacted. Similar setbacks were encountered in the other three states, but each subsequent experience served to increase nurses' power, influence, and political savvy.

In New Jersey, Irene T. Fallon, president of the New Jersey State Nurses' Association (NJSNA) from 1902 to 1903, is credited with being the driving force behind the successful enactment of that state's nurse registration act. Fallon, who was associated with the Cooper Hospital in Camden, made a number of trips to the State House at Trenton during March 1903 to promote the nurses' bill and convince undecided legislators to vote in favor of its passage. In a series of letters and telegrams to Sophie A. Bruckner of Newark, former member of the Ways and Means Committee of the NJSNA, Fallon described her activities in behalf of the bill.

In the pursuit of registration, Bruckner also assumed a pivotal role—in fact, she was identified by Fallon as "the champion politician of the bunch." By virtue of her political expertise and personal association with several influential persons, she was frequently called upon to generate support for the bill. On more than one occasion, she was requested to bring a delegation of nurses to the capitol to demonstrate strength and unity. In the struggle to defeat the opposition, Bruckner was responsible for motivating the patronage of Chief Justice William Stryker Gummere of the New Jersey Supreme Court. Strongly supporting the nurses' cause, Chief Justice Gummere used his influence to promote the bill and persuade assemblymen and senators to vote favorably. When the opposition failed to halt the bill in the legislature, attempts were made to obtain a veto from the governor. Once again, the NJSNA, with the assistance of Chief Justice Gummere, was successful in thwarting the opponents' plan.

In New York, the campaign for registration began in April 1902 with the formation by the New York State Nurses Association (NYSNA) of a Committee on Legislation. Eva Allerton, superintendent of the Homeopathic Hospital in Rochester, NY, was appointed chairman of the Committee on Legislation and empowered with the selection of other members who would serve with her.

In conjunction with Sophia F. Palmer, Allerton is acknowledged as instrumental in New York's enactment of a registration law. During the summer of 1902, Allerton conferred with The Rev Thomas A. Hendricks, regent of the University of the State of New York, and State Senator William W. Armstrong of Rochester to obtain guidance in preparing the legislative proposal. Father Hendricks's suggestions were particularly relevant because of the unique supervisory role of the Board of Regents in safeguarding educational requirements, including "admission to professional schools and professional practice," in New York State. Consultation with Senator Armstrong was helpful in determining the actual provisions to be incorporated in the bill. With the able assistance of both men, NYSNA entrusted Allerton's committee with the task of drafting a bill.

The publicity campaign initiated by the NYSNA Committee on Publication and Press was designed to increase public awareness of the bill's provisions and stimulate support throughout the state prior to the bills' introduction in the legislature. Letters were sent to various women's groups, the New York State Medical Society, and other organizations, reinforcing NYSNA's position that legalized standards for nurses would offer greater protection to the public. Articles and editorials supporting registration appeared with increasing frequency in the *American Journal of Nursing*. Individual nurses were urged to communicate with physicians, legislators, and private citizens, requesting their cooperation.

Every effort was made to secure the cooperation of prominent persons to promote the bill. Allerton recommended that the NYSNA contact the eighteen members of the Public Health Committee, urging their endorsement. Anna C. Maxwell, superintendent of the Presbyterian Hospital in New York City, solicited the assistance of Elbridge T. Gerry, chairman of the Law Committee of the Board of Governors of New York Hospital.

Sara Cocke of Brooklyn was owed a debt of gratitude for generating Governor Odell's rapid endorsement of the nurses' bill. Cocke was employed as a nurse in Albany and promoted the bill via her cousin, Calvin McKnight, the governor's secretary.

In Virginia, Sadie Heath Cabaniss and Agnes Dillon Randolph led the registration movement. As the first elected president of the Virginia State Nurses' Association (VSNA), Cabaniss helped frame Virginia's registration law. Randolph, a charter member of the VSNA, was considered an outstanding "lobbyist" and is credited with having a primary role in the achievement of registration in Virginia.

To convince the Virginia legislature that the registration movement was not confined to a select few, members of the VSNA traveled throughout the state to solicit support from other nurses and promote letter-writing campaigns. Furthermore, endorsement of the goals of the VSNA was obtained from a number of Virginia's physicians and attorneys. These strategies proved effective in overcoming resistance to the proposed legislation. In the General Assembly, despite limited opposition from several legislators, and "a doctor, a druggist, and president of a hospital board," the major provisions of the bill were approved by the General Assembly on May 1 and signed into law on May 14, 1903.

Conditions affecting the political freedom of women impinged on nursing's goals. Stereotyped notions about gender differences were obstacles facing the nurses' campaign for legalized reform. The absence of universal suffrage was an additional barrier. Despite those limitations, organized nursing was able to promote and obtain official endorsement of its proposals. Many of the nurses involved in the registration movement identified their achievement as a step forward for women in general.

Over the years, nursing's connection with the advancement of women became more tenuous. Organized nursing adopted a conservative stance and, until recently, remained conspicuously silent on the subject. Although women's suffrage has been a fact since 1920, many women choose not to exercise their rights. In nursing's case, this lack of political involvement is particularly significant. Nurses, by virtue of their number, have the potential for exerting considerably greater political influence. Their failure to do so is probably one of nursing's most serious handicaps.

This vignette is based upon the author's doctoral dissertation, *The Genesis of the Nurse Registration Movement in the United States, 1893–1903*, Teachers College, Columbia University, 1982. Portions of this vignette have been previously published in: "The Origin of Political Activism in American Nursing," *Nursing News* September–October 1982, 40(4). They are reprinted with the permission of the Nurses' Association of the Counties of Long Island, Inc, the publisher of *Nursing News*. Due to space limitations, the original citations are not included. Interested readers should refer to the author's original research.

Vignette: The Beginnings of Nursing Research

Lucille P. Leone, RN, MA

Research puts nursing into the mainstream of health care. It moves nursing as a profession into new levels of maturity, beyond the search for autonomy and independence and on to partnership and collaboration. It develops nursing as a designer and giver of creative patient care and an instigator of wellness. And it places nursing, with its unique sensitivities, among scientists.

When did nursing research start? In the 1920s and 1930s, landmark surveys were done, but few would now characterize them as research. In some baccalaureate programs, courses called "experimental nursing techniques" included "development of scientific method." Some of the students' studies were published. Some nurse teachers and students enrolled in advanced courses in statistics in preparation for research. A few pioneer nurses acquired doctoral degrees in education, a social science, or some other field. In addition to the knowledge they brought to nursing, their degrees were useful when the school initiated doctoral programs.

The word "research" appeared more and more frequently in the literature of nursing. The need for research, its values and potentials were discussed by an increasing number of nurses, particularly by those teaching in universities.

World War II opened the door for federal funding of nursing education and nursing research. A small number of applications for research funds by nurses were received by the National Institutes of Health (NIH) in the early 1950s.

Nurse leaders both outside and inside the U.S. Public Health Service were convinced that research in nursing must be encouraged and that it merited federal support. The staff of the Division of Nursing and I, the chief nurse officer, were in close contact with nurses and other leaders in schools and colleges of nursing in universities throughout the country. Professional organizations and journals were urging action. Many members of the staff of NIH, though not all, and some key members of NIH committees supported a proposal for a nursing research program. The Division of Nursing could serve as an institute, and its staff members were prepared to develop a national program of research, including consultation services to universities and schools of nursing.

Although the top leadership at NIH encouraged nurses to seek action, some other staff members and some members of the Council and Study Sections opposed this idea. These are some of the dissenting comments:

- Nursing is not researchable.
- Nursing has no scientific base except that of medicine, and medical scientists have conducted and will conduct that research and share with nursing whatever it needs.
- Nurses are not qualified to do research.
- Nurses cannot learn to do research.
- Nursing has no mechanism for operation of a national research program.

Nurses heard these dissenting comments, sometimes in their own universities, and tried to show dissenters evidence of the need for nursing research, of investigations ongoing or planned in their institutions, and of current or prospective nurse researchers and their advisors.

The next step in the move toward organized, federally financed research in nursing was securing from the National Advisory Council the approval of the idea and its action to finance and locate the administration of the program, including its own Study Section.

Bringing the Issue to the Table

This episode occurred in the early 1950s when public attitudes toward science were favorable. Nurses and their advocates were fully convinced of the need for research in nursing and were ready to apply findings to practice. They were confident that nurse researchers and prospective researchers were available in large enough numbers to implement a growing movement. Nurses with vision of the health needs of the future knew that the creative results of nursing research could supply needs that would not otherwise be met.

An arrangement was made to have the subject of nursing research brought up at the next meeting of the NIH Advisory Council. I attended many of the Council's meetings. At this one, the chairman introduced the subject of nursing research and asked for my comments. Dissenting views, enumerated above, were then expressed. I suggested it was time we all found out whether nursing was researchable, and whether nurses could conduct research. I recommended a small committee be appointed to visit two or three universities where I knew nursing research was being carried on. I suggested that the committee report to the Council, and that it include representatives from biological sciences, social sciences, and nursing. The committee was appointed, and its members included a biological scientist from the NIH staff, a social scientist from a prestigious midwestern university, and me, as the nurse.

I made arrangements to visit two universities in the west where research was already in progress and visible. At one, we met the dean of the School of Nursing and those she had invited to demonstrate that nursing research was underway and to discuss plans for immediate action should federal financial aid become available.

The group included diverse disciplines. The head of the Anthropology Department advised master's students in nursing on their theses. He had encouraged one to embark on a doctoral program in anthropology. Also present was a professor of physiology in the medical school. One of his students, a nurse, was about to receive her PhD in physiology. He believed that nurses could do good research. A sociologist who had had several nurses in his graduate courses agreed that nurses could handle doctoral level study. A professor of pharmacology who had taught a special course for graduate students in medical nursing said nurses were capable of carrying out doctoral level study in pharmacology or in nursing, with a pharmacology segment.

A nurse, head of the Department of Community Health Nursing, spoke to us about the projects she and her students had in mind as dissertation subjects related to community organization, the economics of health care, and problems of health in the workplace. An administrator of nursing in one of the university hospitals spoke of problems she hoped graduate students in nursing would explore and of her dream of having a nurse researcher on her staff. Interspersed with these informal presentations were comments by the dean of the nursing school. She referred to interdepartmental collaboration and the plans for a doctoral degree in nursing.

There seemed to be little doubt that nursing was researchable and that there were nurses who wanted to conduct research and could do so effectively. A spirited luncheon with this group of academics who, nurses and others alike, knew first-hand the challenges of nursing, made a pleasant ending for the observation visit. The report was written in the hotel room that evening.

At the next meeting of the Council, the report of the committee was presented, and its recommendations were accepted. Annual funds from a general research appropriation were earmarked for nursing research. The Division of Nursing was instructed to prepare a staff and create a study section. Soon there was a line item for nursing in the budget.

If we were to drop in on these trained investigators today, many would be outstanding professors and researchers working on exciting projects. We could trace back improvements in patient care to these investigators. We could find new understandings of ethical dilemmas related to health technology. We would find policymakers and planners of health services whose goals are more courageous because of nursing research. We would find new vision in our participation in international health actions.

Chapter 3

Coming of Age: The Women's Movement and Nursing

Connie Vance, RN, EdD

Susan W. Talbott, RN, MA, MBA

Angela Barron McBride, RN, PhD, FAAN

Diana J. Mason, RN, MSN

The advent and growth of the women's movement in the twentieth century have changed dramatically and irrevocably the role of women, including behaviors, attitudes, standards, and beliefs. The consciousness-raising encouraged by the feminist movement has led to major changes for *all* women as well as for men. A feminist is one who advocates for women the same rights which society accords men, particularly in economic and political spheres. Since most nurses are women, feminist ideology has affected the professional and personal lives of nurses. It influences how nurses see themselves, their patients, and the health care system. Indeed, feminist ideology has legitimatized nurses' interest in developing and using power and politics to reshape society's definitions of health and roles for nurses in developing programs for health and illness.

This chapter will explore the interaction of feminist ideology, the women's movement, and nursing. It will become apparent that nursing, in turn, has influenced the women's movement, particularly in terms of women's health and changing feminists' attitudes, ideology, and responsiveness towards female-dominated professions.

AN UNEASY RELATIONSHIP

Feminist women and nurses have frequently experienced an uneasy relationship. Much of the energy in the women's movement has been directed toward moving into nontraditional fields of study and work. Nursing has been seen, therefore, as one of the ultimate female ghettos from which women should be encouraged to escape. Indeed, as Muff (1982) points out, for some women, becoming "conscious" has involved identification with masculine characteristics and a denial of females who espouse traditionally feminine ones. The profession of nursing has not been valued for its autonomous social contributions, independent decision-making, scholarly productivity, or for its collective striving for recognition, power, and legitimization in professional, political, policy-making, and community circles. Feminists have sometimes failed to look beyond the inaccurate, sexist stereotypes of nurses and to even acknowledge the multiple dimensions of professional nursing. For example, in the late 1970s, Judy Chicago's feminist art project *The Dinner Party* paid tribute to women who have made significant contributions to society since the beginning of recorded history. Among the hundreds of women acknowledged was Florence Nightingale. She was identified as a social reformer, medical reformer, statistician, policy maker, and several other labels—but not as a nurse. Margaret Sanger was also part of *The Dinner Party* but not identified as a nurse.

The organized women's movement has often ignored nursing as a career choice or as an authentic voice for women's rights. For example, a major leadership conference for women, sponsored by the Legal Defense and Education Fund (LDEF) of the National Organization of Women (NOW) in 1980 did not initially include a single nurse on its program or invitation list (Talbott & Vance, 1981).

A leading feminist scholar, Florence Howe (1975), urges women to consider another viewpoint:

> . . . rather than bemoaning the fact that women numerically dominate the teaching, nursing, and social work professions, why not consider that fact important strategically? . . . Women should focus on building their potential for strong and effective leadership in those areas where they are currently numerically dominant—education, social work, nursing, for example—rather than diluting their possible power base by urging that those most energetic and talented serve as additional tokens in nontraditional fields of study. . . . To focus feminist energies on them now would be to develop 'womanpower' to change three of the most important service institutions in the society (pp 14, 166, 169).

The nursing profession has not always embraced feminist ideology. However, more and more nurses are identifying with the goals of the women's movement. They are viewing their profession as an important career, rather than seeing it as preparation for marriage and motherhood. They are changing their self- and public-images. Nurses are joining with other women to work for women's rights, including:

- equal pay for work of comparable worth
- an end to sexual discrimination in education and in the workplace
- election of women to political office
- provision of adequate child care and women's health programs
- reproductive rights
- a safe work environment

THE EVOLUTION OF NURSES AS WOMEN

Nursing's tenuous connections with the women's movement points to the contradictions inherent in women's search for their "proper place" in society (Rothman, 1978). What is valued in our patriarchal society has created conflict for women between their own desires, needs, and values and those prescribed for them by men. A "proper woman" and a "proper nurse" are relegated to defined roles that even other women will endorse and perpetuate. Social and personal sanctions are imposed on those who do not carry out these "proper" roles. Women can pay heavy emotional, career, and economic prices for noncompliance with tradition.

Yet how different women and nurses really are from many of the traditional labels and images that plague and impede us. Virginia Woolf (1929) pointed out that "it is obvious that the values of women differ very often from the values which have been made by the other sex" (pp 76–77). A contemporary nurse writer writes, "Because ours is a patriarchal society, these differences, which could have been merely considered as differences without any value judgments, have been judged as negative toward women" (Meleis, 1985, p 41).

Only recently, through the efforts of feminist scholars, researchers, and writers, have we begun to learn about the different developmental paths women follow. Their work will help women and nurses to understand and reject the burdens of sexism, sex-role discrimination, destructive images, and devaluing of women's work in our society. Miller (1976) points to women's critical need to develop in a context of attachment and affiliation with others, leading to valuing a more cooperative mode of life. Research by Gilligan (1982) points to the centrality of the concepts of responsibility (connection with others) and care in women's moral development. For women, this ethic of care—the tie between relationship and responsibility—creates tensions between responsibilities and rights—to others and to oneself. "It is precisely this dilemma—the conflict between compassion and autonomy, between virtue and power—which the feminine voice struggles to resolve" (p 71). It is the feminist struggle to both reclaim the self and to solve moral problems in such a way that no one is hurt. Gilligan points out that changes in women's rights have finally enabled women to consider it all right not only to care for others but also for themselves.

The development of nursing embodies this dichotomy of tensions experienced by the developing woman. Nursing, defined by the ethic of care, has been rightly valued for its virtues of empathy, compassion, and nurturing. At the same time, this view of nursing has been negated by images of nurses, such as "housekeepers of the sick," domestic servants, doing mere woman's work. A second-career nursing student and anthropologist applied Gilligan's view of male and female morality to medicine and nursing and noted that society places a higher value on the male version:

> Unfortunately there is more social and economic value placed on the male version of morality. Nurses are awarded only a fraction of the status and financial remuneration of physicians despite their comparable "life-and-death" responsibilities. Yet female morality has so much to offer (London, 1985, p 114).

Nurses must not only reject the negative aspects of society's determination of their worth, they must also change society's sexist perceptions of nursing. This requires nurses to change their own perception that it is immoral to care for oneself or further one's own interests. Indeed, nurses must place such high value on what they have to contribute to society and health care that they recognize that advocating for their own interests will serve society as well.

As more nurses become career oriented and remain in the workforce, the pressures to create more equitable conditions will increase. Greater availability of female role models and mentors, increasing opportunities for advanced education and training, role-restructuring in the family, and continuing gains by women in the workplace, government, the classroom, and at home will ensure an acknowledgment and respect for "women's work" and "women's place" in society. "As institutions—and thus roles—change, the value system and normative structure change; transition periods cause ambivalence but also mean that new values are formed and many outmoded values and beliefs are discarded" (Epstein, 1970, p 49). This transition of changing value systems will continue to be a struggle in the 1980s and beyond. Continuing discrimination will fan the fires of the feminist movement. As Jeane Kirkpatrick, former chief U.S. delegate to the United Nations, told a meeting of the Women's Forum: "Sexism is alive. It's alive in the U.N., it's alive in the U.S. government—and it's bipartisan" (*New York Times*, Dec. 31, 1984).

ISSUES AND OPPORTUNITIES

"Nursing . . . is struggling with a history of submission and male domination. It is learning to reach for and obtain power, authority, and control over its own destiny—it is a profession that is coming of age" (Sovie, 1978, p 368). For nurses who have been practicing for many years, it is sometimes difficult to accept the fact that nursing is still evolving as a profession, that it has yet to "arrive." On the other hand, it is an exciting time of growth and opportunity as nurses contribute to the women's movement by confronting issues that include sexism, equal pay for work of comparable worth, power, and women's health.

Sexism

Sexism is discrimination based on sex, especially against women. Most nurses can identify incidents in which they or their colleagues have been victims of blatant or thinly disguised sexism. One still hears male administrators and physicians refer to nurses as "the girls." Unfortunately, we also hear our nursing colleagues refer to themselves and associates as girls. This type of sexist language is demeaning to educated, professional women. Although some believe that concern over words is a semantic game, Wilma Scott Heide, a nurse and the first president of NOW, argues that sexism is perpetuated by language, and that until language changes, sexism will continue. Unfortunately, many words referring to women have acquired negative connotations of the female experience. Spender (1980) discusses the fundamental semantic rule in society as being male-as-norm; and, along with Schulz (1975), documents the working of this semantic rule. The double standard in language can be seen in the different connotations attached to the same condition in men and in women. Consider the following:

Male	Female
mister	mistress (a kept woman)
governor	governess (a servant class woman)
sir	madame (a fallen woman who promotes prostitution)
bachelor	spinster (old maid nobody wants)

Sexism is also related to the public's image of nurses. Beatrice and Phillip Kalisch (1983a) believe that the present image—nurse as sex object—is the most negative media image since Charles Dickens's pre-Nightingale character, "Sairy Gamp." Too often, "female physicians and other professionals are now accorded all the glamour and heroic proportions that once were accorded media nurses" (p 19), while nurses are portrayed as sexual mascots for the medical team. Nurses may have been ignored and undervalued when women were only supposed to look pretty, and they may be ignored and undervalued, now that women are supposed to have careers, on the grounds that nursing is not a profession.

The stereotype of the nurse as handmaiden to the physician persists. It implies that the nurse possesses neither scientific knowledge nor the capacity to be an independent thinker. The disparity between the availability of state and federal funds for medical versus nursing education suggests that our society does not see a need to spend money in this area. The perception that nurses leave nursing for marriage and motherhood causes legislators to question the logic of investing in nursing education. Also, why spend tax dollars on nursing education when we "know" that it's the doctor who does the "important" work, ie, "cures," while the nurse does the "unskilled, emotional" work, ie, "cares." The stereotype of the intellectual physician (male) and the nurturing (nonintellectual) nurse (female) persists (Muff, 1982). It is a powerful thread in the web of sexism. The frequently asked question, "Why does she need a college degree?" validates the image of nursing as a nonscientific, nonintellectual occupation.

Recently, however, there has been recognition of the need for nurses to be image-makers (McBride, 1983). When you perceive yourself to be helpless to change the situation, you feel enervated; when you perceive yourself as able to effect some change, you feel energized. Specific strategies for improving nursing's image include seeking news coverage for real-life events, distributing press packets, and making talk show appearances (Kalisch & Kalisch, 1983b). Sigma Theta Tau's writers' seminars help nurses build the communication skills necessary to influence the media. Duane Walker, director of nursing at Stanford University Hospital, has been particularly effective in developing a magazine, *Stanford Nurse*, which communicates a positive image of nursing service and research. This publication dispels, through its many photographs and stories about nurses, stereotypes about nursing.

Some nursing faculty members feel the sting of sexism when male professors in other departments are paid on a higher scale than female nursing professors. Staff nurses feel its sting when male nurses are treated with greater deference than females by physicians, hospital administrators, or female nurses. Both male and female nurses recognize that deeply rooted sexism underlies the fact that nurses are paid less than those in male-dominated professions that require the same or less skill.

EQUAL PAY FOR WORK OF COMPARABLE VALUE

Comparable worth has been called the women's issue of the 1980s—and perhaps the 1990s. It is an important issue for nurses, whose salaries are depressed because they are in a female-dominated profession.

The concept of comparable worth, which goes beyond equal pay for the same job, calls for employers to evaluate different jobs based on educational requirements, required skills, responsibilities, and work environment. Job-evaluation studies weigh these factors in different jobs. Thus a secretary's job can be compared to a truck driver's, or a nurse's to a pharmacist's.

Comparable worth got a boost from a landmark decision in the state of Washington in 1983. The state was ordered to pay back wages and raise salaries of women paid less than male workers in comparable jobs. The job evaluation revealed the wage disparity in the marketplace. While registered nurses received the highest number of points (573) of any job, the lower-rated computer systems analysts (426 points) earned about 56 percent more than the registered nurses.

Because nurses are directly affected by comparable worth, the American Nurses' Association and state nurses' associations have strongly supported the concept. But there have not been successes in the courtroom. In 1984, ANA and the Illinois Nurses' Association filed suit against the state of Illinois, charging that the state's job classification and pay structure illegally discriminated against nurses and other employees in traditionally female occupations. The state had failed to take action on the results of a state-commissioned study that showed a large sex-based differential in pay between male and female job classifications. The case was dismissed before coming to trial. In another case, six nurse practitioners filed suit against the Student Health Service of the University of Georgia because they earned substantially less than male physician's assistants who did essentially the same work. They lost the suit.

In the spring of 1985, the U.S. Civil Rights Commission rejected the comparable worth concept, further recommending that the Justice Department resist the doctrine and that Congress not adopt legislation that would establish comparable worth in the federal or private sector.

There are several reasons why nurses face a difficult pay equity problem. Women's work is not valued as highly by society as men's. The federal government, for example, carefully records the contribution of each major industry to the gross national product (GNP). The output of those who labor in the home, as homemakers and mothers, however, is not tabulated as part of the GNP. Similarly, the cost of nursing service is rarely identified as a separate entity on hospital bills. Nursing care is perceived as supportive of the physician and as work that is attributable to the physician's skill (Ashley, 1977). This is ironic because patients often are not admitted to hospitals unless they need nursing care. One could conclude that the work of nurses is without recognition and without monetary value because it is perceived to be nonrevenue producing (Lowery-Palmer, 1982).

Another sign of the undervaluing of nurses' work is revealed by a comparison of nurses' incomes with that of physicians. In 1981, Aiken, Blendon, and Rogers reported that nurses were being paid less than one-fifth of what physicians earned; whereas in 1945, nurses earned one-third of physicians' incomes. Of course, few people know about this disparity because traditionally nursing care has been lumped with room charges, laundry, housekeeping, and supplies on hospital bills. Nurses are beginning, however, to insist that the economic value of their work be identified ("Maine legislature," 1983).

Secondly, most nurses are employees. Few nurses own their own business, and there has been the expectation that nurses ("good girls") will willingly accept the salaries and benefits offered in the marketplace. This is definitely changing (Witzel, 1984).

Another factor that contributes to the pay equity problem for nurses relates to the fact that nursing is a female-dominated profession. Studies show that ". . . the more women dominate a profession, the less it pays" (Bellamy, 1984). The "free" market forces continue to undervalue nurses' work. Even in the federal government, women employees earn less than men working in the same job categories (Hunter, 1985). In addition, Hunter reports a survey done by the Capitol Hill Women's Political Caucus showing that few women (15 percent) hold policy-making positions.

Considering the extent of wage discrimination in female-dominated professions uncovered by states that have used job-evaluation studies (approximately 18 by 1984), the resolution of pay inequity will take decades. Many argue against "tampering" with the marketplace, but at least two states—Minnesota and Connecticut—have set up pay equity funds. There are indications that other states will do the same, or face suits from labor unions. Nurses have much to gain from the combined efforts of women's and professional organizations and labor unions as they press the issue of pay equity.

POWER

Nursing and feminist literature abounds with books and articles on power and influence, but many nurses still do not like to discuss such "loaded" topics. Why are nurses and other women uncomfortable with their actual or potential individual and collective power? Howe (1975) suggests that because women are socialized to please others and have a particular need for affiliation, they avoid the pursuit of achievement and power that men are encouraged to attain. Furthermore, this socialization contributes to women's feelings of powerlessness because they measure themselves against others' standards, not their own. Friedan (1977) noted that "we are so unused to success, recognition, even a taste of power, that we hardly know how to handle it when it is offered to us. . ." (p 209).

What can nurses do to overcome the aversion to seeking and using power on behalf of themselves, their patients, and their community? Some feminist writers like Miller (1982) have described ways in which women traditionally use power. Miller defines power (p 3) as "the capacity to produce a change." This definition, which is not complex or intimidating, describes the way women use power. For example, women, and particularly nurses, are adept at fostering the growth and development of others to effect change. A nurse who works with a young girl who has diabetes knows that she needs to use herself and her knowledge and skills to empower the patient to cope with the disease. The nurse does not exert power over the child; rather, she searches for ways to interact with the child and to enhance learning and coping skills.

While women may be comfortable using their power to foster the development of others, there is reluctance to use their power on their own behalf. Miller (1982) refers to this as "self-determined power" and explains why women fear the use of power. For example, a nurse may avoid using her access to influential nurse leaders to promote her career because she perceives such behavior as selfish. On the other hand, she may find it more comfortable to support and promote a colleague, for this involves enhancing the power of others.

Nurses avoid using their power to advocate themselves because they fear they may be abandoned. Women's affiliative needs influence their efforts to work on behalf of others, while they avoid self-promotion for fear of severing their intricate framework of relationships.

Janeway's (1980) dynamic view of power should encourage nurses who fear the destructive nature of self-determined power. She suggests that power can be a positive force to rearrange social relationships.

Miller (1982) suggests that women may bring a unique perspective to power as a force for rearranging society. Women are demonstrating, by their affiliative and caring priorities, that they may be more comfortable with power-sharing. While some powerful women have been criticized by men and women for playing the men's power games, women may have to play by men's rules until a sufficient cadre of powerful women is developed who can change the rules of the game so that power sharing is valued. Women who want and have power should evaluate what it means to be a powerful woman, and whether women, by bringing a unique perspective to power, can play a better game.

The infighting in the nursing profession on issues such as educational preparation might cause nurses to question whether women prefer power-sharing. On the other hand, such infighting could be interpreted as a manifestation of powerlessness. Grissum and Spengler (1976) note that while the women's movement has helped women learn to "love, value, trust and respect other women" (p 95), many of us are still very isolated from one another because we mistrust and are uncomfortable with other women. The self-hatred demonstrated by oppressed groups, like nurses, is another factor that promotes isolation and precludes group cohesiveness (Roberts, 1983). Nurses' internal power struggles may not diminish until our sisterhood ceases to perceive nursing as an oppressed group (Heide, 1973) and, instead, takes organized action in support of the profession. As the women's movement has demonstrated greater concern for female-dominated professions and as the profession's political power is growing, coalition-building and unity among the professional organizations have become more common.

A number of nurses have written about the nursing profession and its relationship to power and influence, and some have outlined guides for acquiring and using power (Brooten, Hayman, & Naylor, 1978; McCurdy, 1982). In addition, this book includes a chapter that analyzes the concept of power (see Chapter 9). Nurses must thoroughly understand and integrate the concept of power into their self-concept if they are to be effective political activists. The book also contains practical "how to's," which nurses can use to overcome their individual and collective powerlessness. Nurses no longer have to accept the premise that those who *say* they have all the power do indeed have it all. Or that "nice girls" should not seek and use power. If the nursing profession is to prosper and grow (some would say survive), and if nurses are to help shape health care policy, then they must use their individual and collective power, influence, and authority.

WOMEN IN HEALTH AND ILLNESS

The women's movement has influenced nursing in terms of practitioners' concepts of women, both as patients and as caregivers, and definitions of health. Since Friedan

(1963) wrote about "The Problem That Has No Name"—the terrible tiredness that took so many women to physicians in the 1950s—there has been an awareness of the health consequences of sexist stereotypes. Women's health encompasses more than prenatal care or the need for an annual gynecologic exam. It means redefining the nature of health care so that "physical and psychological well-being are always presumed to be intertwined, as well as determined by the context (interpersonal, socioeconomic, political, and environmental) in which the individual operates" (McBride & McBride, 1981, p 41). This means being concerned about the overall experience of women and their diseases, not just their diseases or childbearing functions (Stevenson, 1979).

Nurses realize they may be the health care providers best suited to meet consumer demands for self-determination, because their professional mandate has long been expressed in terms of helping the patient "to gain independence as rapidly as possible" (Henderson, 1961, p 42). Indeed, the public demand for nurse midwifery services in freestanding childbearing centers and hospitals attests to the value families place on the care of nurse midwives. Ruth Watson Lubic, a leader of the nurse midwifery movement, acknowledged in a 1982 speech to the American College of Nurse-Midwives the demand for nurse midwifery services while advocating strong ties between midwives and their nursing sisters. While warning nurses that separation into disconnected specialty groups is folly, she reminded nurses that together they can exert the political clout needed to alter the system to provide consumers with the care they desire.

An expanded view of what should be considered under women's health has led nurses to become concerned about matters previously not deemed worthy of serious consideration. For example, dysmenorrhea (Jordan & Meckler, 1982), perimenstrual distress (Woods, Most & Dery, 1982), and menopause (MacPherson, 1981; Muhlenkamp, Waller & Bourne, 1983) are now viewed as complicated phenomena still not well understood. Menstrual cycle fluctuations are being tracked after nongynecological surgery (McKeever & Galloway, 1984) and in working women (O'Rourke, 1983). The effects of nurse counseling on sexual adjustment after hysterectomy are being scrutinized (Krueger, Hassell, & Goggins, 1979). Beliefs about breast cancer and breast self-examination (Schlueter, 1982; Stillman, 1977), and the relationship of women's overall preventive practices to their practice of breast self-examination (Turnbull, 1978), are being studied in the hope of being able to improve survival statistics for the cancer affecting American women the most. At the same time, the life experience of women cured of breast cancer is being described (Woods & Earp, 1978). Nurses are exploring facets of the maternal role, including what happens to mothers when their children have chronic health problems (Butani, 1974; Gordeuk, 1976; Holaday, 1981).

Obesity in women is being reexamined as a health problem that is one consequence of encouraging women to compete in the kitchen at the same time that they are denied access to the athletic arena. The experience of female joggers is being scrutinized (Rudy & Estok, 1983) as well as the overall effects of sports training on the menstrual cycle (Macvicar, Harlan & Ouellette, 1982). The psychological and physiological factors affecting obesity in women during the childbearing years are being explored (McBride, 1982) as well as the adverse effects of weight control in teenage girls (Mallick, 1981).

Prior to the women's movement, rape was not of much concern to health care professionals; it was thought to be primarily a legal problem. But nurses have taken the lead in being concerned about recovery from rape (Burgess & Holmstrom, 1978). Nurse researchers have found that rape victims are not only traumatized physically but emotionally and need support and guidance (Ipema, 1979). They want clarification, advice, and the opportunity to talk through their feelings (Burgess & Holmstrom, 1974).

The women's movement is influencing nurses in their perceptions of women's health care needs even more than is obvious from a quick perusal of the nursing literature. Nurses are generally more concerned that females be included as subjects in health care research. For example, studies of alcoholism, coronary disease, and job-related stress have often ignored the experience of women. Nurses are more concerned that women not be excluded from decision-making as to treatment choices. For example, the mastectomy patient should be informed of treatment options and the availability of reconstructive surgery.

Nurses are concerned about searching for sex-related health differences and calling attention to women's health problems (eg, osteoporosis, depression, agoraphobia [fear of being in public places]). They are also offering services hitherto unavailable. In 1972 Turner, a Boston psychiatric nurse, founded Coping with the Overall Pregnancy/Parenting Experience (COPE) to draw pregnant women and new mothers together in small groups to share their experiences. By 1978, more than 600 women had participated in these support groups, and COPE groups were operating in over 20 communities (Turner & Izzi, 1978). Lipson (1980) points out that nurses have been particularly active in different self-help groups, possibly as an outlet for ideas not always sanctioned by professional colleagues or employing agencies. Nurses' involvement in mutual-aid groups (eg, La Leche and caesarean support groups) may also reflect the affiliative orientation of women as described by Gilligan (1982).

Nursing's commitment to women's health is also politically important. When the needs of women are met by the health care profession dominated by women, then the competence of nurses can be demonstrated at the same time that sisterhood is affirmed. Consumers are asking for what nurses are best able to deliver. All considerations of etiology, diagnosis, treatment, and prognosis should begin with the consumer's view of her own situation. The feminist clinician asks: "What do you think is your problem?" "How do you think that you came to have this problem?" "What do you think needs to be done to help you with this problem?" "What do you think your own chances for getting better are?" Nurses have been schooled to build assessments on the patient's perception of his or her experience and to promote self-help.

The workplace has not only been altered by new views of women as patients, but also by new views of women as caregivers. Nurses are less defensive about being therapeutic and are promoting their effectiveness in health care delivery. Nurses are taking action against health hazards on the job (Selby, 1984b). Nurse-managed centers (eg, Loeb Center for Nursing and Rehabilitation in New York, Erie Family Health Center in Chicago, and the Pennsylvania State Consultation Nursing Center) are regarded as fine alternatives to traditional health care and are effective in meeting the needs of unserved and underserved populations (Selby, 1984a). Many services provided are geared to the needs of women; for example, the University of Wisconsin-Milwaukee Nursing Center has sponsored group sessions for divorced women.

In the last decade, nurses have worked to get state nurse practice acts that define clear areas of independent practice. They want to promote the notion that the authority for nursing is based on a social contract, not doctor's orders. A social contract between the profession and society means that the latter grants the former self-regulation to assure quality in performance (American Nurses' Association, 1980). Nursing's struggle for the right to practice as an autonomous professional is a longstanding feminist issue. For example, Rothman (1978) has pointed out that after enactment of the Sheppard-Towner Act in 1921, authorizing and funding maternal and well-baby centers that were staffed largely by nurses, physicians decided pregnancy was a disease and, therefore, inappropriate for nurses to manage. In the 1920s, "woman's proper place" did not include challenging male bastions of power and authority. Today, the women's movement has helped nurses to realize that their proper place includes not only protecting their right to practice but reclaiming lost rights to work with consumers in the role of an independent professional. But there is still work to be done. The nurse practice acts in most states do not reflect the real scope of nurses' work. Nurses are still expected to play wife-like, deferential roles toward physicians (Roberts & Group, 1973) rather than to exert their own authority in a collegial relationship.

SUMMARY

This chapter has considered the profound influence of the women's movement on nursing. Nurses are contributing to the women's movement, particularly in the field of women's health, and influencing feminists' responsiveness to female-dominated professions.

One major outcome of the women's movement is that politics is no longer considered inappropriate for women. Nurses have responded to this change in definition of "women's proper place" by developing their political skills. They are becoming more knowledgeable about publicizing their effectiveness in health care delivery and are establishing independent nursing practices. In addition, lobbying for the needs of women consumers, such as for maternity benefits, has had a positive effect on the lives of nurses themselves.

The women's movement is still necessary. Indeed, the problems that the nursing profession faces in gaining its right to autonomy and ensuring reimbursement of its services speak to the need for nurses to build even stronger alliances with feminists. Change invites risk, and we need to heed Gloria Steinem's (1983) warning that "the armies of the status quo will treat (us) as something of a dirty joke. That's their natural and first weapon. (We) will need sisterhood" (p 117).

Both the women's movement and the nursing profession represent the embodiment of a great diversity of ideas, styles, and strategies. Significant change in women, health care, and society can be brought about if nurses actualize their potential power—if they move beyond their "proper place." What would happen if:

• Nurses proudly identified themselves as such, including writing "RN" after names and almost arrogantly identifying themselves as nurses in social situations. (For a discussion of the latter, see Fagin & Diers [1983].)

- Nurses became knowledgeable about the issue of equal pay for work of comparable worth and in their workplace questioned and challenged unfair pay structures.
- Nurses who are continually confronted with practicing under unsafe staffing conditions did so only "under protest" written, copied, collected, and shared with the director of nursing, board of trustees, and press.
- Every practicing nurse refused to perform nonnursing tasks, such as housekeeping and secretarial chores.
- Every director of nursing demanded the establishment of formal collaborative practice arrangements between nursing and medicine, as well as other disciplines.
- Every nurse acted as a mentor to at least one other nurse—helping, teaching, supporting, and sharing opportunities with protégées.
- Nurses valued one another as colleagues and worked to develop a system of mutually supportive relationships.
- Nurses used their connections or demanded as part of contract negotiations that nurses be included as members of the boards of trustees of hospitals, nursing homes, and home care agencies in at least equal numbers as any other health care provider.
- Every nurse who watches television or movies protested, in writing to the producers, the sexist and archaic portrayal of nurses and, by the same token, wrote to praise positive portrayals.
- Every nurse joined the relevant professional organizations including the American Nurses' Association, the National League for Nursing, and nursing specialty organizations and made a commitment to contribute something more than just dues to one of them every year.
- Every nurse supported at least one women's organization, such as the League of Women Voters (LWV), the National Organization for Women (NOW), and the National Women's Political Caucus (NWPC).
- The leadership and membership of the various professional nursing organizations agreed to disagree in private and to develop a means for resolving interassociation disputes that would demonstrate power-sharing and women's morality at its best.
- The leaders of local, state, and national nursing associations made coalition-building with women's groups (such as NOW and NWPC) a top priority.
- Every nurse gave at least $1 to the national and state political action committees (PAC) for nurses, such as N-CAP (Nurses Coalition for Action in Politics; to become "ANA-PAC" in 1986), the PAC for the ANA.
- Nursing organizations ensured that nurses sat on every health-related task force or commission in local, state, and national government.
- Every nurse who has a connection with a public official (elected or appointed) invited that official to spend a day with a practicing nurse.
- Every nurse knew her legislators' names and participated in a letter-writing or lobbying campaign on at least one health care issue each year.
- Every nurse worked at least half a day a year on behalf of a legislator's election campaign.

- There was at least one nurse in Congress and in every statehouse in the nation.
- A nurse were president of the United States of America.
- Every nursing school and department of nursing valued and encouraged the activities outlined above.

We must act in different ways to accomplish our goals. We each have a responsibility to contribute our special abilities to transform the workplace, community, government, and professional organizations. As Gloria Steinem (1983, p 355) says, ". . . a movement depends on people moving. What *are* we going to do differently when we get up tomorrow?"

References

Aiken L: The nurse labor market. *Health Aff* 1982; 1:30–40.

Aiken L, Blendon RJ, Rogers DE: The shortage of hospital nurses: A new perspective. *Amer J Nurs* 1981; 81:1612–1618.

American Nurses' Association: *Nursing: A Social Policy Statement.* ANA, 1980.

Archer S, Goehner P: *Nurses: A Political Force.* Wadsworth, 1982.

Ashley J: *Hospitals, Paternalism, and the Role of the Nurse.* Teachers College Press, 1976.

Bellamy C: Pay ruling sends "loud message" to New York. *NY Law J* (Apr 9) 1984; 191:1.

Brooten D, Hayman L, Naylor M: *Leadership for Change: A Guide for the Frustrated Nurse.* Lippincott, 1978.

Burgess AW, Holmstrom LL: Crises and counseling requests of rape victims. *Nurs Res* 1974; 23:196–202.

Burgess AW, Holmstrom LL: Recovery from rape and prior life stress. *Res Nurs Health* 1978; 1:165–174.

Butani P: Reactions of mothers to the birth of an anomalous infant: A review of the literature. *Matern Child Nurs J* 1974; 3:59–76.

Epstein CF: *Women's Place: Options and Limits in Professional Careers.* University of California Press, 1970.

Fagin C, Diers D: Nursing as Metaphor. *Amer J Nurs* 1983; 83:1362.

Friedan B: *Feminine Mystique.* Dell, 1963.

Friedan B: *It Changed My Life.* Dell, 1977.

Gilligan C: *In a Different Voice: Psychological Theory and Women's Development.* Harvard University Press, 1982.

Gordeuk A: Motherhood and a less than perfect child: A literary review. *Matern Child Nurs J* 1976; 5:57–68.

Grissum M, Spengler C: *Womenpower and Health Care.* Little, Brown, 1976.

Heide W: Nursing and women's liberation—a parallel. *Amer J Nurs* 1973; 73:824.

Henderson V: *Basic Principles of Nursing Care.* International Council of Nurses, 1961.

Holaday B: Maternal responses to their chronically ill infants' attachment behavior of crying. *Nurs Res* 1981; 30:343–348.

Howe F: *Women and the Power to Change.* McGraw-Hill, 1975.

Hunter M: Hypocrisy of in-house job bias. (Jan 23) *New York Times* 1985; A20.

Ipema DK: Rape: the process of recovery. *Nurs Res* 1979; 28:272–275.

Janeway E: *Powers of the Weak.* Knopf, 1980.

Jordan J, Meckler JR: The relationship between life change events, social support, and dysmenorrhea. *Res Nurs Health* 1982; 5:73–79.

Kalisch B, Kalisch P: *Politics of Nursing.* Lippincott, 1982.

Kalisch B, Kalisch P: Anatomy of the image of the nurse: Dissonant and ideal models. Pages 3–23 in: *Image-making in Nursing*. Williams CA (editor). American Academy of Nursing, 1983a.

Kalisch B, Kalisch P: Improving the image of nursing. *Amer J Nurs* 1983b; 83:48–52.

Krueger J, Hassell J, Goggins D: Relationship between nurse counseling and sexual adjustment after hysterectomy. *Nurs Res* 1979; 28:145–150.

Lipson JG: Consumer activism in two women's self-help groups. *West J Nurs Res* 1980; 2: 393–405.

London F: Why choose nursing? *Amer J Nurs* 1985; 85:114.

Lowery-Palmer A: The cultural basis of political behavior in two groups: Nurses and political activists. In: *Socialization, Sexism, and Stereotyping: Women's Issues in Nursing*. Muff J (editor). Mosby, 1982.

MacPherson KI: Menopause as disease: The social construction of metaphor. *Adv Nurs Sci* 1981; 3:95–113.

Macvicar MG, Harlan JD, Ouellette M: What do we know about the effects of sports training on the menstrual cycle? *MCN* 1982; 7:55–58.

Maine legislature orders hospitals to break out nursing costs. *Amer J Nurs* 1983; 83:1251.

Mallick MJ: The adverse effects of weight control in teenage girls. *Adv Nurs Sci* 1981; 3: 121–123.

McBride AB: From being concerned about our image to becoming image makers. Keynote address at the biennial convention, Sigma Theta Tau, Boston, 1983.

McBride AB: Leadership: Problems and possibilities in nursing. *Amer J Nurs* 1972; 72: 1045–1049.

McBride AB: Nursing: Let's turn around the image. *New Woman* (Nov)1978:95, 100.

McBride AB: Obesity of women during the childbearing years: Psychosocial and physiological aspects. *Nurs Clin North Am* 1982; 17:29–38.

McBride AB, McBride WL: Theoretical underpinnings for women's health. *Women Health* 1981; 6:37–55.

McCurdy JF: Power is a nursing issue. In: *Socialization, Sexism, and Stereotyping: Women's Issues in Nursing*. Muff J (editor). Mosby, 1982.

McKeever P, Galloway SC: Effects of nongynecologic surgery on the menstrual cycle. *Nurs Res* 1984; 33:42–46.

Meleis A: *Theoretical Nursing: Development and Progress*. Lippincott, 1985.

Miller JB: *Toward a New Psychology of Women*. Beacon, 1976.

Miller JB: Colloquium: women and power. Stone Center for Developmental Services and Studies. Wellesley College, 1982.

Muff J: Handmaiden, battle-ax, whore: An exploration into the fantasies, myths, and stereotypes about nurses. In: *Socialization, Sexism, Stereotyping: Women's Issues in Nursing*. Muff J (editor). Mosby, 1982.

Muhlenkamp AF, Waller MM, Bourne AE: Attitudes toward women in menopause: A vignette approach. *Nur Res* 1983; 32:20–23.

O'Rourke MW: Subjective appraisal of psychological well-being and self-reports of menstrual and nonmenstrual symptomatology in employed women. *Nur Res* 1983; 32:288–292.

Riley WJ, Schaefer V: Nursing operations as a profit center. *Nurs Man* 1984; 15(4):43–46.

Roberts JT, Group TM: The women's movement and nursing. *Nurs Forum* 1973; 12:303–322.

Roberts SJ: Oppressed group behavior: Implications for nursing. *Advances Nurs Science* 1983; 5:21–30.

Rothman S: *Women's Proper Place: A History of Changing Ideals and Practices, 1870 to the Present*. Basic Books, 1978.

Rudy EB, Estok PJ: Intensity of jogging: its relations to selected physical and psychological variables in women. *West J Nurs Res* 1983; 5:325–334.

Schlueter LA: Knowledge about beliefs about breast cancer and breast self-examination among athletic and nonathletic women. *Nurs Res* 1982; 31:348–353.

Schulz M: The semantic derogation of women. In: *Language and Sex: Difference and Dominance.* Thorne B, Henly N (editors). Newbury House, 1975.

Selby TL: Nurse-managed centers show their potential. *Amer Nurs* (May) 1984a; 16:1+.

Selby TL: RNs take action against job hazards. *Amer Nurs* (Apr) 1984b; 16:24.

Sovie M: Nursing: a future to shape. In: *The Nursing Profession: View Through the Mist.* Chaska NL (editor). McGraw-Hill, 1978.

Spender D: *Man-made Language.* Routledge and Kegan Paul, 1980.

Steinem G: *Outrageous Acts and Everyday Rebellions.* Holt, Rinehart and Winston, 1983.

Stevenson JS: Women's health research: why, what, and so what? *CNR Voice,* Ohio State University School of Nursing (Fall) 1979:2–3.

Stillman MJ: Women's health beliefs about breast cancer and breast self-examination. *Nurs Res* 1977; 26:121–127.

Talbott SW: Issue for the '80s: Equal pay for comparable worth. *NYSNA J* (Mar) 1981; 134–135.

Talbott SW, Vance C: Involving nursing in a feminist group—NOW. *Nurs Outlook* 1981; 29:592–595.

Turnbull EM: Effect of basic preventive health practices and mass media on the practice of breast self-examination. *Nurs Res* 1978; 27:98–102.

Turner MF, Izzi MH: The COPE story. A service to pregnant and postpartum women. Pages 107–122 in: *The Woman Patient. Sexual and Reproductive Aspects of Women's Health Care.* Notman MT, Nadelson CC (editors). Plenum, 1978.

Witzel L: From the bedside to independent practice at the bedside. *Nurs Econ* 1984; 2:294–295.

Woolf V: *A Room with a View.* Harcourt and Brace, 1929.

Woods NF, Earp JAL: Women with cured breast cancer. *Nurs Res* 1978; 27:279–285.

Woods NF, Most A, Dery GK: Toward a construct of perimenstrual distress. *Res Nurs Health* 1982; 5:123–136.

Chapter 4

The Politics of Patient Care

Diana J. Mason, RN, MSN
with an episode by Ann M. McCarthy, RN, MA

The ultimate reason for enhancing the nurse's political power, be it in the workplace, community, government, or professional organization, is to improve the health care that patients receive. Politics plays a role in every aspect of health care, ranging from what kind of care gets funded to whether a patient gets adequate teaching before being discharged from the hospital. Whereas the politics of health policy are acknowledged and accepted, the politics of bedside patient care are not so obvious, but hardly less important.

The powerlessness experienced by many staff nurses may arise from the failure of nurses to recognize the existence of the politics of patient care, let alone be politically effective. This is true of nurses working in hospitals, where the presence of multiple special interest groups precludes apolitical decision-making (Ehrat, 1983). Although 92% of all newly licensed nurses are employed in hospitals six to eight months after graduation (National League for Nursing, 1984), only 66% of all employed nurses choose to continue to practice there (American Nurses' Association, 1983).

The end result of powerless, politically naive, frustrated nurses is inadequate nursing care.

DEFINING POLITICS

Politics can be defined broadly as "influencing." More specifically, it means influencing the allocation of scarce resources. Those who claim that professional nurses should not be political are really saying that nurses should not try to influence their own practice and the care that patients receive.

In the following episode, Ann Marie McCarthy, RN, MA, describes her realization that politics are a fact of life in the nurse's delivery of quality patient care:

From 1972 to 1973, I worked as a staff nurse with the Visiting Nurse Service (VNA) of New York. I joined my local political club primarily because it was supporting George McGovern for President, and I was concerned about our nation's involvement in the Vietnam War. I did not see the importance of the role of local politics in patient advocacy.

One patient's situation changed that. My patient, a man in his 60s, had suffered for many years from severe chronic hypertension and peripheral vascular disease. He was being treated as an outpatient at a local hospital. I received a call from his physician in the clinic. The physician was convinced that the patient was not getting better because he was not following the regimen of diet, medication, and exercise the physician had prescribed.

It was clear to me the physician didn't realize his patient lived in a run-down, rat- and roach-infested SRO (single room occupancy hotel). SROs are aptly named: the tenant's rooms are so tiny that one person can barely fit in with a few belongings. The only place for my patient's bed was right underneath a part of the ceiling where the plaster was falling. After assessing the patient's concern about the ceiling, I realized that to help him control his blood pressure, his ceiling would have to be fixed.

My initial effort was to pursue what I thought were "appropriate channels." From my VNS desk, I contacted the SRO landlord, thinking that if he were aware of the falling plaster, he would surely want to get it fixed immediately. How naive I was. I couldn't understand why my calls to the landlord were not returned.

In my frustration, I mentioned this to one of my fellow political club members. She suggested that I contact a local tenants' association that fought for tenants' rights in the area. I did this. The tenants' association was able to get my patient's ceiling fixed within two weeks. With the removal of this environmental stress, the patient's blood pressure soon came within a normal range.

Why did the tenants' association succeed and I fail? Very simply, it had *political clout*, and I did not. It was in touch with the local legislators and actively participated in the campaigns of politicians who supported tenants' rights. When the tenants' association called the local politician's office, it responded immediately.

This episode illustrates how a nurse successfully mobilized a community's resources to reduce the stressors in the life of a hypertensive patient. She did so indirectly through a group that had more political clout than she had. Developing such connections in the community may seem imperative for the community health nurse; however, it should be no less so for the hospital nurse, who may find that the head of that tenants' association is also a member of the hospital's board of directors.

Patient care consumes resources of time, manpower, money, and equipment/supplies—all of which can be influenced or manipulated by the nurse who chooses to do so. If only one special interest group were involved in making a decision, that decision could be based on the facts rather than politics. Most health care institutions, however, include multiple interest groups, making it almost impossible to allocate resources based solely on the facts (Ehrat, 1983). Nurses are known for their altruistic motives. Unfortunately, this altruism has not always been accompanied by the political savvy needed to achieve their altruistic goals.

Indeed, Stevens (1984) suggests that nursing must shift from a goal-driven to a resource-driven model of practice that acknowledges the reality of a society that is becoming increasingly aware of its limited resources:

When a patient refuses to confront an obvious reality, we worry. When we do it as a profession, we congratulate ourselves on maintaining principles. Instead of blaming health care institutions for failing to supply the necessary resources for delivery of excellent nursing care, we must recognize that they are responding to a clear national mandate: no more growth in the cost of health care. . . . In a resource-driven model, the planner asks what goals can be achieved with the available resources (p 184).

Such a model demands that nurses evaluate available resources and determine which can be strengthened or added and which require too much energy and time to change.

IN THE HOSPITAL

One would like to think that the hospital nurse does not have to contend with falling ceilings. In one old hospital, however, the nurses in the neonatal intensive care unit warned the administrators that the unit's cracked ceiling posed a threat to their patients and asked that it be repaired. But, the nurses did not have the political clout to get administration to heed their warnings. The ceiling finally collapsed when a water pipe burst, flooding the unit and endangering the lives of both the patients and the staff. The nurses were outraged. They related this story with altruistic indignation ("We were right, after all."), anger ("No one would listen to us."), and frustration and powerlessness ("They're still not listening to us."). That the nurses did not know who sat on the hospital's board of directors or who their city council representative was seemed irrelevant to them.

Less dramatic examples of the politics of patient care abound. This episode illustrates the more subtle aspects of the politics of patient care in everyday hospital nursing practice through the experience of a nurse who was a member of the patient's family:

Several years ago, my 31-year-old brother, John, was found to have a benign intracranial tumor pressing on the facial and acoustic nerves, resulting in symptoms of hemiparesis of the face and a unilateral hearing deficit. Although his surgeon had prepared him for the risk of permanent damage to these nerves, John was not prepared for the dysphagia and high-pitched voice postoperatively as temporary results of trauma to other cranial nerves manipulated during surgery. After 24 hours, he was transferred from the ICU to a general neurosurgical floor in stable condition.

Two days after the surgery, I arrived at the hospital to be greeted by his distraught wife, crying, "He can't eat—every time he tries to swallow something, it comes out his nose. So they're talking about putting a tube in him to feed him and he'll have to stay in the hospital longer. Will his voice always be that way?"

I found John lying in his bed, looking depressed and helpless. He confirmed in an embarrassed, high-pitched voice that he was unable to swallow the liquids brought to him for lunch. Furthermore, I assessed that although his bed had been made in the early morning, he had not shaved, washed, brushed his teeth, nor been out of bed. I am not compulsive about patients having their beds made and baths by 10 am; however, I do believe that the nurse must assess when such rituals would physically or emotionally benefit the patient. In John's case, his self-concept needed all of the support it could get since the voice change and loss of swallowing control were unexpected assaults to his own image, particularly if he realized how these changes had upset his wife.

After setting John up in the bathroom to do his personal care, I discussed with his primary nurse the inappropriateness of a liquid diet for a patient with a hemiparesis of the esophageal muscles and was able to find a dish of Jell-O to teach him how to learn to swallow in spite of the paresis. I took about five to ten minutes to teach him basic self-care, such as tilting his head slightly forward and to the unaffected side when eating, and to give him a few words of encouragement when he tried to put these suggestions to use. I also showed him how he could lower the pitch of his voice.

He was no longer helpless. He practiced the swallowing, had an uncomplicated recovery, and was discharged within the week.

When and what kind of contact did John have with his primary nurse? She made his bed each and every morning. She gave him intravenous steroids for three days and then oral steroids every morning. She took his vital signs periodically and several times spent at least five minutes looking for one of the floor's two electronic thermometers or one of the two sphygmomanometers. She collected urine specimens as ordered, removed the intravenous line, and recorded his intake and output. I also assume that she wrote daily progress notes. In general, her time with him was confined to carrying out medical orders. She had 8 to 10 other patients, most of whom were sicker than John.

I gave much thought to this situation and concluded that: (1) nurses have not mastered the politics of patient care, but (2) nurses must do so to provide quality health care to patients.

The politics of patient care in this episode are not as obvious as those in the first episode. This shows a patient who was not getting the nursing care he needed. If his sister had not been a nurse, it is likely that he would have had a nasogastric tube inserted for feeding, a prolonged hospitalization, further assaults to his self-esteem, and been at greater risk for other complications.

Why were politics a determinant in the care John received— or didn't receive? Recall that politics means influencing the allocation of scarce resources. In John's case, several political questions can be raised. Why did the institution have the latest expensive medical technology (such as a CT scan) but inadequate bedside equipment for basic nursing care (two electronic thermometers and sphygmomanometers for a floor of 34 patients)? Why did the nurse spend time pouring and handing John his oral medication (which he was going to have to take on his own once he was discharged) and making his bed (which he could have done himself after the first day) but not find time to teach him information that he needed for self-care and to prevent an unnecessarily complicated and prolonged hospitalization? Why has the nurse-patient ratio outside of the intensive care unit remained the same over the years even though patients are sicker and require much more care? Why did the nurse place a higher priority on executing medical orders than on developing and implementing a nursing care plan?

If patient care decisions were based upon "the facts," John would have made his own bed, been responsible for his own medications to the fullest extent possible, and been guided to use the nurse's time and expertise (resources) to help him respond as favorably as possible to his health problems. But the kind and quality of health care a patient receives, and from whom he receives it, are political issues that involve the resources of money, time, equipment/supplies, and personnel.

MONEY

Money is probably the most important resource to be considered when discussing the politics of health care. The other resources of time, equipment, and personnel usually can be translated into dollars.

Money determines who gets what kind of health care. Physicians have controlled the health care dollar, not because consumers need medical care more than nursing care, but because physicians have garnered the power to shape health care resources to their liking. A review of the politics of the development of the U.S. health care system, although beyond the scope of this chapter, demonstrates this point. The nurse who is not familiar with this history is urged to read such works as *The American Health Empire: Power, Profits, and Politics* (Ehrenreich & Ehrenreich, 1970); *American Medicine and the Public Interest* (Stevens, 1971); *The Social Transformation of American Medicine* (Starr, 1982); and *Hospitals, Paternalism, and the Role of the Nurse* (Ashley, 1976).

Physician control of access to health care and the health care dollar has been accompanied by skyrocketing costs. As society tries to control this escalation through legislated programs such as prospective payment plans (Shaffer, 1984a; Shaffer, 1984b; Hamilton, 1984; Toth, 1984), one might be fooled into thinking that discussions of cost effectiveness preclude politics. Certainly, economic efficiency, in principle, operates from the premise that ". . . resources should be allocated to those projects or activities for which the benefits are greater than the cost. . . . The necessary assumption for this premise is that society is rational and that decisions are made in a rational fashion" (Hicks & Boles, 1984, p 177). Unfortunately, society does not operate this way.

A rational society, responding to factual information, would value nursing care as much as medical care. Leslie (1981) examined the extent to which institutionalized patients with incurable medical conditions, such as emphysema and cerebral vascular accidents, had nursing problems that were irreversible. She found that all patients had nursing diagnoses that were amenable to improvement or resolution through good nursing care. Indeed, the patients were there because they needed nursing care.

Furthermore, reluctance by federal and state governments and insurance companies to approve direct reimbursement of nursing services continues, despite the fact that numerous studies document the cost effectiveness of nursing services (Fagin, 1982; Maraldo, 1982; Mason, 1982). Reimbursement for nursing care is a political issue. Those with power (the American Medical Association and insurance companies) and those influenced by those with power (legislators) do not wish to share scarce resources (money) with nurses, despite the logic (cost effectiveness) of the argument in favor of reimbursement for nurses. Had John's brain tumor been malignant and incurable, he would not necessarily have been entitled to reimbursement of supportive nursing care that would have allowed him to die with comfort and dignity. One of the most important advances in care of the terminally ill patient has been the hospice movement, which grew out of a need for humanistic terminal care that institutions were not providing. The facts suggest that hospice care, which is predominantly nursing care, should be embraced by the health insurance industry since it is at least as cost effective as regular hospital care and is certainly more humanistic (Vladeck, 1984; Birnbaum & Kidder, 1984). Instead, the movement faces an uncertain future since hospice care is not reimbursed to the same extent as regular hospital care.

Even though Naisbitt (1982) has identified a trend toward a greater need for "high touch" care as "high tech" care increases, our society continues to value "high tech" more than "high touch" care through its reimbursement policies. Kimble (1980) pointed out that "insurance reimbursements for technology are increasing far more rapidly than reimbursements for 'physician-patient interaction,' and doctors can double or triple their income merely by adopting a high-technology 'style'" (p 62).

Since nursing is a "high touch" service, the struggle for reimbursement of nursing services is likely to continue to be difficult—but not impossible. Maine has already passed legislation mandating that nursing services be costed out and listed separately on a patient's hospital bill. Such economic accountability is critical to nursing's survival and the patient's assurance of receiving quality health care. As hospitals contend with the realities of prospective payment mechanisms, the pressure is on all nurses to demonstrate that improvement in nurse-patient ratios outside of intensive care units and efforts to have nurses spend their time on nursing rather than nonnursing activities will result in shorter hospital stays and long-term cost savings. Sovie (1984) has proposed that magnet hospitals—hospitals identified in a national study as not having difficulties recruiting and retaining nurses—will have a distinct advantage in maintaining economic viability in this changing competitive market: ". . . a hospital's investment in selected components of magnetism can result in economic efficiencies, that is, a less costly approach to meeting the health care needs of patients coupled with the same or increased benefits to patient care" (p 89).

At the very least, nurses and consumers need to be concerned about the attempts by some hospitals to "save money" by undercutting nursing services. The largest nurses' strike to date in the nation's history lasted for five weeks in 1984, as 6,000 Minnesota nurses protested layoffs, involuntary reduction of hours of senior nurses, and hiring of junior nurses and part-time nurses without benefits to replace the senior nurses. Interestingly, these hospitals did not propose to lay off senior medical staff and replace them with junior physicians to save money.

How the hospital allocates its monetary resources is influenced by nursing to a greater extent when nursing has control over its own budget. This allows nursing to have more power over the allocation of other resources that influence patient care. Greater control and influence by nurses in institutions are occurring. Nurses have the professional right to be economically accountable to the consumer; and, the consumer has the right to know what his health care dollar is buying.

Even if nurses do not have control over their own budget, we must be able to document that nursing is an income-generating activity. As hospitals adjust to prospective payment plans, such as DRGs (diagnosis-related groups), nurses have the opportunity to demonstrate that it is good nursing care that will make a difference in the patient's length of stay, and thus, the hospital's revenues. For example, nurses might design a pilot project in which financial outcomes on a pulmonary unit with an improved nurse-patient ratio and primary nursing are compared with a pulmonary unit with usual staffing patterns.

There are numerous other economic issues relevant to this discussion of the allocation of money in health care. The ones mentioned here illustrate that nurses must be concerned about this important political resource and be alert to other economic issues that determine who gets what kind of health care.

TIME AS A SCARCE RESOURCE

One of the most precious resources in a nurse's practice is time. How it is spent can influence whether an administrator metes out rewards or punishments—whether a patient has an uncomplicated recovery or pays heavy emotional, physical, and monetary tolls to beat preventable, often iatrogenic, complications of hospitalization—or whether the nurse walks away from a hard day of work feeling that it has been a worthwhile, meaningful effort or feeling as if she has been bloodied and defeated in battle. How the administrator, patient, physician, nurse, and others think the nurse should spend his or her time is likely to vary tremendously, depending upon their priorities, values, motives, and knowledge about nurses' roles and responsibilities.

State nurse practice acts updated in the past thirteen years usually define nursing as "diagnosing and treating human responses to actual or potential health problems . . . and executing medical regimens." The Nurse Practice Act of New York (the first state to pass a progressive practice act and one which has served as the model for other states) does not specify that execution of the medical regimen must take precedence over other aspects of nursing care. And yet, as illustrated in the second vignette below, many nurses make executing medical orders the priority, even if it is not in the patient's best interests.

This point was illustrated to me in a disturbing fashion two years ago, when I witnessed the care of a 90-year-old woman who had been admitted to the hospital from a nursing home for congestive heart failure:

> Mrs. Smith's medical condition and the change in the environment exacerbated a problem with confusion accompanied by a loss of interest in eating. She was on a 40-bed medical unit that had a nurse-patient ratio of 1:8 to 12. The nurses were "too busy" to spend much time trying to feed her, particularly since she ate only small, frequent meals. They had sicker patients who demanded their time and attention, including a comatose patient on a respirator.
>
> As the patient continued to lose weight, she became obviously malnourished and more confused. The physicians ordered that she be fed by nasogastric tube. When she tried to pull out the NG tube, wrist restraints were ordered. The bolus tube feedings, for which the nurses now made time, gave the patient diarrhea, which quickly led to decubiti, since the restraints prevented her from turning her buttocks away from the incontinent stool. As the diarrhea continued, she became more malnourished and finally died after suffering great humiliation and classic iatrogenic "unhealth" care.

The nurses, who did not find the time to offer a few bites of food to the woman whenever they came into the room, found time to give both the tube feedings, which took longer than oral feedings, and the decubitus care because they were "ordered" by the physician. Their time was allocated not because of "the facts," but because they were in a hospital in which medical care is more highly valued than "patient care." This is another hospital where the latest in medical diagnostic equipment—CT (computed tomography), PET (positron-emission tomography), and MRI (magnetic resonance imaging) scanners—can be found, but basic equipment for bedside patient care is inadequate. It is a hospital where medical student "rounds" are mandated, but no interdisciplinary rounds exist because, as one of the staff nurses told me, "the doctors don't have time." It is a hospital where nurses frequently run from room to room looking for clean towels, because linen is in short supply. It is a hospital that supplies housing for interns and residents, but not for nurses, even though affordable housing is in great demand and would assist with recruitment of nurses in an area of the country that still had a shortage of nurses in 1984.

How nurses spend their time is influenced by the mission and priorities of the institution. In the hospitals in the two previous vignettes, the institutions were first and foremost sites for medical education and research. In one large metropolitan medical center, visitors were greeted in the lobby with a large display celebrating the hospital's anniversary and recounting its accomplishments and mission. The first mission listed on the colorful display was medical education. The second was medical research. The third was patient care. The sign gave a clear message as to the priorities of the hospital and the political power of its physicians. It was, thus, not surprising to find a sign in the cafeteria designating one part of the room, "For Doctors Only."

Historically, physicians have been the power-brokers in health care. Although this traditional position is being challenged by other players in the health care arena, the air of paternalism continues to pervade hospitals (Ashley, 1976). Although it is rare for a nurse to sit on a hospital board, physicians often dominate them. Some visiting nurse services still have medical rather than interdisciplinary advisory boards.

Although how the nurse spends her time is theoretically a professional decision that should be based upon the patient's needs and the availability of other resources, decisions regarding time allocation are usually influenced by a system that may overvalue medical care to the point that patient care is jeopardized. Certainly, nurses continue to assert their professional right to be accountable to the patient, as opposed to being accountable to physicians. Changes in nurse practice acts are putting an end to legislated dependency; but it will take knowledgeable, politically astute nurses to develop truly autonomous, professional practice in systems where nursing care is not highly valued or perceived to be an important aspect of the patient's care.

MATERIAL RESOURCES

The power and influence of physicians are demonstrated by the way the hospital allocates its material resources such as supplies and equipment. In the two vignettes, nurses wasted precious time looking for one of the two electronic thermometers designated for units of thirty or more patients. In discussions with nurses across the country, I have found this is a common situation. Electronic thermometers replaced mercury ones for reasons of speed and accuracy, which has been substantiated by nursing research (Baker et al., 1984). The number of electronic thermometers allocated per unit, however, is not always predicated on need. At one hospital, each unit had two because that is how many thermometers manufacturers gave—yes, gave—to the hospital.

Why are hospitals given free thermometers? So the manufacturers can make money on the disposable sheaths used for each temperature reading. The nurses at this hospital were told the cost of the thermometer sheaths came out of the nursing budget for their unit. They were disturbed by this fact, because they did not recognize the influence they could have over their own unit budget. Certainly, such situations warrant further attention, including studies of the cost of the nurses' time wasted trying to locate thermometers. Such studies might reveal that, unless there is a significantly larger ratio of thermometers to patients, electronic thermometers are not time-efficient.

One hospital medical unit of forty patients had one unit-dose medication cart for two wings. The carts were old. Drawers would stick and have to be yanked open, pulling out completely if jerked too hard. A mid-level drawer of ampules and vials of common parenteral medications would regularly stick, be yanked too hard, and then spill on the floor. Thousands of dollars were undoubtedly wasted every year in broken vials of medications and wasted nursing and janitorial time. Although the nurses complained to each other, they did not see themselves as able to change the situation.

The same unit usually had at least ten diabetic patients at any one time who had frequent fingerstick blood sugar readings, using the unit's one Dextrostick machine. Nurses would run from a patient's room at one end of the hall to the treatment room, balancing a drop of blood on a Dextrostick that had to be rinsed off within sixty seconds from the time it touched the stick. Precious time was wasted and patients restuck when sticks were dropped during the rushed transit to the treatment room, or the nurse arrived to find someone else doing a reading or the machine malfunctioning.

Nurses, however, are beginning to recognize the influence they can have over the allocation of material resources. With the trend toward decentralization of nursing departments and unit budgets under the control of the nurse administrator of the unit, staff nurses have the opportunity to control more of the unit's supplies and equipment. Some nurses are also recognizing the influence they have with the supply manufacturers. For example, if a nursing unit with budget control determined that two electronic thermometers were insufficient and costing money in terms of nursing time, it could inform the manufacturer that more electronic thermometers were needed or the unit would return to mercurial ones the patient would pay for and take home upon discharge—or seek out a competing manufacturer for a better arrangement on the electronic thermometers.

Although one may prefer to believe that hospitals and other health care agencies purchase equipment and supplies on a competitive, cost-containing basis, Strelnick (1983) has pointed out that both medical supply manufacturers and hospitals have been indicted for illegal, anticompetitive practices that have resulted in higher costs for the patient. One supply company moved from sixth place in the medical supply industry to first over an eleven-year period. Although the company claimed to have reached that position because of good "salesmanship" and competitive prices, the fact was that the company ". . . could not boast of low prices because on many standard items its prices were not only uncompetitive, they were outrageous. A Becton-Dickinson surgical clip that some distributors sell for a penny was sold by [this medical supply manufacturer] for as much as $6.55" (p 9). Strelnick concludes: "Consumers and patients ultimately pay for such practices—in higher prices and defective products" (p 14).

At times, the "big business" of the health care industry has taken heavy tolls on the consumers in terms of the care they receive and the care they do not receive (Harding, Bodenheimer & Cummings, 1972). Certainly, nurses need to be aware of these realities and examine how to influence the process in a "healthier" way. One large city hospital never had sufficient linens or important basic medications, such as anti-biotics, yet had the latest in medical diagnostic equipment. In such situations, nurses must usually grapple with the city's politics, questionable purchasing practices, and an institutional mission that does not value nursing care, in spite of the fact that patients are admitted to a hospital for nursing care or else they would be treated on an out-patient basis (Maraldo, 1982).

With hospitals becoming increasingly concerned about their ability to remain finan-cially solvent under prospective payments, nurses have an opportunity to demonstrate that they can benefit the institution by having input into not only their unit's supplies and equipment, but also the hospital's overall plan for allocation of monies to material resources. This includes how hospitals are designed. Any nurse who works in a hospi-tal or nursing home or who lives in a community whose hospital is being renovated or newly constructed should make sure that nurses are involved in the design process. Otherwise, the result may be a lovely unit with sprawling corridors, a nursing station the size of a closet, no office for the head nurse, and a spacious "room-with-a-view" for the chief of medicine. One major West Coast teaching hospital found that the archi-tects had not made the doorways to patient rooms large enough for wheelchairs to pass through. All doorways had to be rebuilt at an enormous cost.

At one rehabilitation unit in a hospital where patients often stay for several months, the nurses recognized that the patients needed a room on the unit where they could go for quiet and solitude. Most of the patient rooms had four to eight beds, and the so-larium, or "TV room," was usually noisy. The nurses identified two rooms that were not being effectively used. One was the relatively large office of the service's previous chief physician; the other was a smaller room used to store supplies. Since the new chief physician had not yet arrived, the nurses decided to experiment. They moved the sup-plies into another supply closet and the physician's office furniture into the former sup-ply room. They asked the local veterans' organization to donate an aquarium, found some comfortable furniture in a storeroom, and had the patients make pictures and hangings for the walls. The patients loved the room. The nurses were quick to elicit patients' written comments and present them to their chief nurse, with copies to the chief-of-staff and the hospital administrator. When the new physician arrived and in-quired about the office in which he had been interviewed by the former chief-of-service, the nurses talked about the positive effects of the new "quiet room" and showed him the substantiating evidence obtained from patients. When the chief-of-service went to the chief-of-staff to ask for the old office back, the chief-of-staff reiter-ated the nurses' statements about concern for the patients' emotional well-being on a long-term rehab unit. The "quiet room" stayed.

As a nursing consultant, I have worked with head nurses who are making the transi-tion to the role of nursing care coordinator in nursing departments that have changed to a decentralized structure. The coordinators frequently identified a problem with role conflict that arose when they tried to find time to take care of their management tasks when others were expecting them to do patient care. When I suggested they retreat to their offices and shut the door, they often reported they had no office or their office was the nurses' lounge. Of course, the chief-of-service would usually have a spacious office that was seldom used.

Although this may seem a trivial concern, its impact goes beyond the coordinator having an adequate working environment. It is an indicator of how the coordinator is seen by self and others. One new vice-president for nursing recognized the importance of what one's surroundings communicate to people. Her predecessor had a small, shabby office and little clout within the institution. The new vice-president told the hospital administrator that she would need larger quarters and wanted to talk with the hospital's decorator about its design. She refused to list her name on her temporary quarters because she wanted to make sure that people with whom she was meeting knew it was temporary. She knew that first impressions can be lasting, and that one's surroundings can influence how one is perceived.

Although not all nurses need to be concerned with decorating their offices, it behooves all nurses, regardless of where they are working, to take stock of the environment, supplies, and equipment available to meet the needs of patients and nurses. Where these material resources are insufficient or costly in terms of time, money, and patient well-being, nurses should collaborate on strategies for changing them.

PERSONNEL: WHO PROVIDES NURSING CARE?

"Who provides nursing care?" appears to be a rhetorical question. However, it is a relevant and political one that will grow in significance as health care resources become scarcer. And if nursing care is essential to the patient's health, the question of who delivers it must be promoted as an issue of critical concern to the consumer.

Two other groups competing with nurses to provide professional nursing care are: (1) technicians, who do some tasks that nurses perform, without having the preparation and skill to make the necessary professional judgments; and (2) physicians, whose numbers are growing, resulting in increasing competition among themselves and moves toward claiming aspects of nursing care as their turf.

Presently in New York, the Nurse Practice Act exempts state mental institutions and juvenile facilities from having to use professional nurses to provide nursing care. If the facts were the only basis for this "exempt clause," it would be repealed via a bill promoted by the nursing community for a number of years. Evidence that the use of "mental health technicians" instead of professional nurses in these facilities is detrimental to patient care is accumulating. For example, two young adult patients died while in isolation at a New York psychiatric center because of inadequate professional evaluation of patients and supervision of their care. Mental health technicians staffed the units. The unions for the technicians have fought the repeal, arguing that it will cost the state significantly more money to hire nurses, when in fact a beginning staff nurse earns what a senior mental health technician makes.

The nursing profession's struggle to guarantee that qualified professionals will practice nursing continues across the country. Denver tried to replace nurses in its city hospital with "health aides" who were "trained" by the hospital and paid less than nurses. Operating room technicians, skin graft technicians, dialysis technicians, IV technicians, and school health technicians are prevalent. The argument for the use of "substitutes" is primarily an economic one, since technicians are paid less than professional nurses. The same idea, however, of substituting "physician technicians" for physicians has not been promoted vigorously. At the same time that substitution of technicians for nurses has gained favor, the ratio of physicians' incomes to nurses' incomes has increased dramatically (Aiken, Blendon, & Rogers, 1981).

Nurses are increasingly fighting for their right to practice nursing. In Missouri, two nurse practitioners who were providing family planning and gynecological services for women in a rural clinic were taken to court for practicing medicine without a license. Although the Missouri Supreme Court finally ruled in favor of the nurses, the primary care turf promises to be a battleground for nurses and physicians competing for limited health care dollars (Andrews, 1983).

In workshops that I have led on accountability for staff nurses, less than 1% of the participants have been able to define nursing in accordance with the nurse practice act of their state. And yet, the practice act is a powerful legal tool for assuring the public and the profession that professional nursing care will be provided by professional nurses. The staff nurse, however, has seldom used it to justify a refusal to spend time on nonnursing functions or to challenge the use of nonnurses to provide nursing care. While medicine seeks to restrict nursing's turf, nurses often stand by while nonnurses practice nursing.

Another example demonstrates the extent to which nursing undervalues the expertise required for professional nursing care. In 1982, the news media and several professional publications reported on a physician who, sympathetic to the difficult job of the hospital nurse, decided to practice nursing in an intensive care unit for a week to find out what it was like. At the end of this week, he commented on how physically exhausting it was to be a nurse—what with having to lift patients on and off bedpans, turn them, get them out of bed, and generally be running all day. Furthermore, he asserted that all physicians should have to do as he did to gain a greater appreciation of nurses. The news reports did not indicate that he had expressed any understanding of the cognitive aspects of the nurse's job.

Perhaps the most surprising aspect of this example is that the newsletter of a national nursing association reported the story without commenting that what he was doing was illegal (Week as ICU nurse, 1982). Should a nurse reverse the situation to find out what it is like to be a physician, he or she probably would not get through a full day without being hauled into court for practicing medicine without a license.

Some hospitals in areas of physician surpluses have contemplated using new medical interns who needed a job to replace nurses in intensive care units. As one hospital saw it, why not pay a little more to get someone who can do what a nurse does plus what a physician does? Another hospital hired a physician's assistant to teach cancer patients about self-care at home. And, some hospitals have been trying to replace emergency room nurses with emergency medical technicians (SNAs seek laws, 1984).

The question of who will provide nursing care may be answered with "no one." While the hospital has acknowledged the need for higher nurse-patient ratios in ICUs, it continues to expect the "floor nurse" to take care of the same number of patients as she did twenty years ago. Because these "floor" patients are sicker now and because there is more technical care available, most patients are not getting the professional nursing care they need. Any nurse who continues to play secretary, janitor, physician's handmaiden, transporter (in situations not requiring a professional nurse), or stock-boy/girl, needs to examine whether patients need a nurse to do these things, or whether they are suffering because he or she is not providing the professional nursing care that nonprofessionals cannot provide. At best, the nurse will have to admit that he or she is an expensive janitor or secretary, and the hospital, whether it realizes it or not, is not getting its money's worth. This situation is often made worse by the ways in which nurses allocate their time, energy, and other resources.

THE PATIENT AS A RESOURCE

In the U.S., the health care consumer has been socialized to regard the hospital as a hotel and the nurse as a maid. Once patients walk through the hospital doors, they are regarded as unable to be responsible for their own care, even if they are physically and mentally competent. They cannot take their own medications. They cannot make their own beds. The family is not encouraged or instructed how to participate in caring for the patient. In some institutions, diabetic patients do not test their own urine or blood sugar, even though they will be expected to do so after discharge.

Although there are exceptions to this generalization—most notably in the armed forces and on psychiatric and rehabilitation wards—they are too few in this age of limited resources and escalating health care costs. In the vignette describing John's experience after surgery, the nurse did not regard John as a valuable resource. The nurse wasted her time doing for him what he could have done for himself, while things that only she could do went undone. Had his sister not intervened, he could have had complications and a prolonged hospitalization.

While nursing students are often taught to maximize the patient's assets, they usually depart from this principle when they are confronted as staff nurses with abiding by hospital policies—written and unwritten—that keep the patient in the helpless role. When I have suggested to staff nurses and nursing care coordinators that they change their practices to ones that encourage self-care as much as possible, a frequent response has been: "But the patient will never stand for it. They're paying all this money for a hospital room so they expect certain things from the nurses. They'll never make their own bed. If we try to make them do it, they'll complain to the hospital administrator."

Certainly, the patients might react this way if the change in expectations of patients is not presented appropriately. Hospitalized patients, however, are all too aware of the inadequate nursing time patients receive these days when nurse-patient ratios are not improving. Most would welcome the opportunity to be more responsible for their care if they were informed about the benefits. This is particularly true if the change in expectations of patients is marketed to the community as a new philosophy that will improve health care.

Even without the community marketing, it is the nurse's professional right and responsibility to develop a care plan for newly diagnosed diabetics that encourages maximum activity during the hospital stay, so that the patients will not experience hypoglycemia when they return home and increase their activity, which reduces their insulin requirements. Would patients refuse self-care if they were told that making their own beds, testing their own urine and blood after proper instruction, returning their own food trays to the racks, and taking their own meds when possible would result in a prescription of insulin more in keeping with what they will need after discharge? Wouldn't they understand that it would permit nurses to use their time in more valuable ways, such as assuring adequate teaching before discharge and providing proper skin care for debilitated patients? Many routine surgical patients would welcome the opportunity to do more self-care if they knew it would facilitate recovery, shorten hospitalization, and lower the risk for complications.

The same questions can be asked about the patient's family and significant others. Too often the family's reluctance to touch the hospitalized patient is interpreted as a lack of desire or interest in participating in the patient's care, when it may be due to the family's fear of pulling out a tube or otherwise doing harm because of their lack of knowledge. Although some patients and families do not want to participate in patient care, nurses should never assume this is so. Patients and their families are valuable resources nurses can use.

CONCLUSION

The question of who receives what kind of care from whom is a political issue. Since nursing care is vital to the restoration and promotion of the consumer's health, the nurse *must* recognize the political nature of patient care and develop political skills for influencing the allocation of resources that affect patient care. These resources include money, time, material resources, personnel, and the patient.

Certainly, being politically effective in institutions such as hospitals and nursing homes is difficult because of their complexity. Where nurses are not politically effective, one often finds a powerless, frustrated staff, a high rate of attrition, and a paucity of competent senior clinicians. Such a scenario is not conducive to quality nursing care. The study of magnet hospitals (McClure et al., 1982) demonstrates, however, that when an institution is organized to facilitate nurses' collaboration on the institution's decision-making, recruitment and retention of nurses are not a problem.

Health care consumers frequently do not recognize how important quality nursing care is until they are patients and cannot find a nurse when they need one. Consumers need nurses to be politically effective. They need nurses to document that good nursing care is an income-generating activity. They need nurses to lobby for legislation that improves access to cost-effective health care. They need nurses to assure that only properly prepared professionals provide nursing care. They need nurses to act as advocates for safe and adequate care. They need nurses to lead a revolution in the roles the patient and family are expected to play or not play. They need nurses to assure that they are not wasting precious health care dollars on overpriced equipment and inappropriate technology at the expense of humanistic care. And, they need nurses to educate them that they need politically effective nurses.

References

Aiken LH, Blendon RJ, Rogers DE: The shortage of hospital nurses: a new perspective. *Am J Nurs* 1981; 81 : 1612–18.

American Nurses' Association: *Facts About Nursing.* ANA, 1983.

Andrews LB: *Deregulating Doctoring.* People's Medical Society, 1983.

Ashley JA: *Hospitals, Paternalism, and the Role of the Nurse.* Teachers College Press, 1976.

Baker NC et al: The effect of type of thermometer and length of time inserted on oral temperature measurements of afebrile subjects. *Nurs Res* 1984; 33:109–11.

Birnbaum HG, Kidder D: What does hospice cost? *Am J Public Health* 1984; 74:689–97.

Ehrat KS: A model for politically astute planning and decision making. *J Nurs Adm* (Sept) 1983; 13:29–35.

Ehrenreich B, Ehrenreich J: *The American Health Empire: Power, Profits, and Politics.* Vintage, 1970.

Fagin CM: Nursing as an alternative to high-cost care. *Am J Nurs* 1982; 82:56–60.

Hamilton JM: Nursing and DRGs: proactive responses to prospective reimbursement. *Nurs Health Care* 1984; 5:155–9.

Harding E, Bodenheimer T, Cummings S: Billions for Bandaids. Medical Committee for Human Rights, 1972.

Hicks LL, Boles KE: Why health economics? *Nurs Econ* 1984; 2:175–80.

Kimble C: In pursuit of well-being. *Wilson Q* 1980; 4:61–74.

Leslie FM: Nursing diagnosis: use in long-term care. *Am J Nurs* 1981; 81:1012–14.

Maraldo P: Reimbursement for nurses in the primary care arena. *NLN Public Policy Bull* 1982; 1:1–4.

Mason DJ: Reimbursement for RNs. *Cost Containment* (Nov 23) 1982; 4:3–6.

McClure ML et al: *Magnet Hospitals: Attraction and Retention of Professional Nurses.* American Nurses' Association, 1983.

Naisbitt J: *Megatrends: Ten New Directions Transforming Our Lives.* Warner, 1982.

National League for Nursing: *Nursing Data Book.* NLN, 1984.

Rose M: Laying siege to hospital privileges. *Am J Nurs* 1984; 84:612–15.

Shaffer FA: Nursing: gearing up for DRGs. Part II: Management strategies. *Nurs Health Care* 1984a; 5:93–99.

Shaffer FA: A nursing perspective of the DRG world, part 1. *Nurs Health Care* 1984b; 5:48–51.

SNAs seek law to bar EMTs, paramedics from assuming nursing roles. *Am J Nurs* 1984; 84:255+.

Sovie MD: The economics of magnetism. *Nurs Econ* 1984; 2:85–92.

Starr P: *The Social Transformation of American Medicine.* Basic Books, 1982.

Stevens BJ: But it shouldn't be that way. *Nurs Outlook* 1984; 32:184.

Stevens R: *American Medicine and the Public Interest.* Yale University Press, 1971.

Strelnick H: Look out for number one. Illegal practices in the "ethical" medical supply industry. *Health PAC Bull* (Mar–Apr) 1983; 14:7–14.

Toth RM: DRGs: imperative strategies for nursing service administration. *Nurs Health Care* 1984; 5:197–203.

Vladeck BC: The limits of cost-effectiveness. *Am J Public Health* 1984; 74:652–3.

Wandelt MA, Pierce PM, Widdowson RR: Why nurses leave nursing and what can be done about it. *Am J Nurs* 1981; 81:72–77.

Week as ICU nurse opens eyes of physician, says AMA News. *Am Nurse* 1982; 14:30.

Chapter 5

Policy and Politics

Donna Diers, RN, MSN, FAAN

Once upon a time, a real time, political leadership in Europe, then the organized church, needed to establish authority. One way to do that was to interpret any thought or behavior not prescribed as the devil's work. It was thought then that the cat, especially black cats, led unsuspecting human beings directly to hell. It was also thought that cats were the companions of witches, their "familiars" who spoke the devil's words into the witch's ear. So, the policy was made that cats were evil and had to be destroyed, and eventually there were weekly ceremonies in which cats were collected and put in bags and burned to the cheers of the crowd.

Any woman with a cat was suspected of being a witch, and there was wholesale slaughter of such women, especially midwives who knew the secrets of the human body, because cats had told them.

About the same time, and for many of the same policy reasons, the church organized and sent crusades to remote places to bring the heathen into the fold. When the crusaders returned triumphant to Europe, their ships carried some stowaways—rats. Since the cat population had been depleted, the plague-bearing rats took over (for some reason the plague bacillus does not survive in cats, even when they eat the rats). And so, in some areas, up to seventy percent of the population succumbed to disease, and the course of civilization was profoundly altered. Policy changed, and cats were restored to their domestic role, but it was too late for Europe. England, which had not executed cats, rose to power.

All of the facts in this anecdote are true, even if I have taken liberty in relating them (Voight, 1976; Ehrenreich & English, 1973). There are several points to be drawn from this story. First, policy determines politics. Second, policy may not be right, but it is always powerful. Third, policy can change but much more slowly than politics.

POLICY

Policy is not politics. Policy deals with the "shoulds" and "oughts"; politics implements (and sometimes impedes) policy. Politics is the use of power for change. Policy sets directions and determines goals or other principles.

One of the problems nurses might have in understanding and dealing with policy and politics is that there has never been coherent policy for nursing. Nursing has had to learn and use political tactics and strategies to accomplish political goals, leaving the policy considerations unstated.

For example, the most hotly debated issue in nursing—entry into practice—has lost its policy goal. In its present form, entry into practice deals only with educational credentials. Were it conceived as a policy thrust, the "rightness" of the position would be explicit. A policy statement might say that nursing is complicated work and the American people deserve the most intellectually able and best-educated practitioners to deliver care and humanize institutions. To produce such nurses, education should include not only carefully supervised clinical experience, but also change theory, theories of health and disease, and all the rest, so that nurses would be properly equipped to meet the policy goal. One way to guarantee the policy to the public would be to require evidence of such preparation for licensure. (Actually, the original Position Paper said much the same thing.)

Stating the policy issue in this way makes clear the limited agenda that has occupied nursing since 1965 and caused us to fight each other in public forums. The concern over the "1985 proposal" to require a minimum of the bachelor's degree in nursing for entry (meaning professional licensure) has been converted into a political concern. And politics shift with pressure, as we have seen in the twenty years since the Position Paper.

Because policy deals with large issues, it moves slowly, in tiny increments (Lindblom, 1980). Change, especially change in values, which is what policy is, is resisted even more than changes in power, which is what politics is.

The first step in policy-making is simply "getting on the agenda" (Lindblom, 1980). When potential new policy runs counter to entrenched ideas or outdated values (as is often the case in nursing's issues), getting noticed will be difficult and resisted. Thus, one strategy for policy-making in nursing is to figure out what the existing agendas are and how nursing might fit into them.

For example, there was no coherent national health policy until the passage of the National Health Planning and Resources Development Act in 1974. That act created a whole grid of health planning structures, including Certificate of Need bodies and Health Systems Agencies. The policy was to increase access to care, especially for the medically underserved; to decrease costs of care; and increase quality. It is not surprising, then, to see in the years immediately following the great growth of primary care nurse practitioner programs and clinical practices and change in legislation to permit reimbursement to them. Nursing was in a position to help meet a policy challenge and was "on the agenda."

Another example. The most important policy issue in health care now is controlling costs. With the change in Medicare reimbursement from retrospective to prospective payment, and to a case-mix methodology using diagnosis-related groups, a concern about nursing costs arose. Nursing is now in a position to help meet a policy agenda item.

The State of Maine has passed legislation mandating that the costs of nursing services in institutions be broken out of the hospital bill. There have been some nurses who have worried about the wisdom of this move. Historically, nurses have had trouble justifying what we do and why we have the right or intelligence to do it. Now, nursing is being asked to justify that as well as why it costs what it does.

Yet nursing's policy point here might be what we have said for years: that nursing is an independent profession that has a set of activities, theories, and practices requiring intellectual and clinical autonomy; and that its authority in institutions does not match its responsibility and accountability. One way in which this mismatch occurs is in nursing's economic invisibility. We cannot have it both ways. We can never claim the role of authority to determine our own practice unless we can see what the work is. The only way to see it is to figure out how much there is and what it costs.

Early studies that break nursing costs out of the hospital bill (Walker, 1982) have shown that nursing costs are a much smaller fraction of the bill than even laboratory costs for selected diagnoses. Nursing earns income for the institution. Such information gives nursing a policy tool. It is possible to argue that nursing ought then to have a larger chunk of the revenue produced by its services.

WHERE POLICY IS MADE

Politics occurs in smoke-filled rooms and by organized bodies, dealing and trading or marching and writing. Policy is made in any setting in which values are at issue. "Public" policy is simply the acts of government or governmental agencies.

Policy in health is often the result of national commissions, either mandated by Congress or by presidential order. For example, the President's Commission on Mental Health was created by executive order of President Jimmy Carter. Its massive report (President's Commission, 1978) revealed the failure of the community mental health movement and the shattered promises of deinstitutionalization. It advocated new legislation and other political action to concentrate services for certain underserved groups: women, the elderly, adolescents, the deaf, and others physically handicapped. Among the recommendations were direct reimbursement for psychiatric nursing services in organized settings and changes in the present reimbursement practice, which makes it difficult for the mentally ill to be served. The report was careful to make its recommendations as *policy*, leaving it to the appropriate political bodies (such as Congress and professional associations) to implement them. Legislation was written—the Mental Health Systems Act—but did not pass. It was opposed by political forces who saw their entrenched authority being eroded, as well as by others who may have believed that the mentally ill have no "right" to treatment in the least restrictive setting.

A more recent example of the policy-making role of a commission is the 1983 report of the Institute of Medicine's Committee on Nursing (Institute of Medicine, 1983; Aiken, 1983). The Institute of Medicine of the National Academy of Sciences was charged by Congress to study the federal role in nursing and determine what it should be. The study was prescribed because there was a growing sense in Congress that the nursing shortage, to which federal funds had been devoted, was over, and it was time for the federal role to change.

The report recommends, among other things, that the federal role in nursing should concentrate on advanced nursing practice, providing funds for training clinical nurse specialists and nurse practitioners. Further, it recommends that states should change their laws to allow direct reimbursement for nursing services when lack of such funding can be shown to be a barrier to care. A relatively minor recommendation has caused considerable debate: that an organizational entity be established within the federal structure to place nursing research in the mainstream of scientific inquiry and accountability.

That policy recommendation was taken up in the political arena, with a bill introduced to create an Institute for Nursing within the National Institutes of Health. The bill passed both houses of Congress but was vetoed by the president. Plans are to resubmit the bill to Congress in 1985. However, the split in the nursing community over the proper policy (Dumas and Felton, 1984; Commentary, 1984) may complicate things. Congress likes clear signals.

Here is a clear instance of policy-making and its relationship to politics. That is not to say that political action strategy has no place in policy conferences. Indeed, the Institute of Medicine Committee was riddled with politics from its composition (a minority of nurses) (Jacox, 1983) to its interim report. That document essentially advocated a return to diploma schools. Exposed to the nursing community by the nurse members of the group, it brought national outrage. The final report reflects reconsideration.

Policy is also made officially by Congress. One example of that is the Community Mental Health Centers Act of 1963 which revolutionized treatment for the mentally ill and created a public policy that said psychiatric illness was in part a result of social problems, and thus treatment should also be aimed at eliminating poverty, discrimination, and other injustices. This example is one of the few in which the policy change was truly revolutionary. Most policy change is much more modest.

Policy is made by the judicial system as well. Here, the recently settled case in Missouri in which two family planning nurse practitioners were sued for practicing medicine without a license is instructive (Sermchief v. Gonzales, 1983). The Missouri Supreme Court stated firmly and clearly that the nurses were practicing within the authority of the nurse practice act of Missouri, which contemplated not only this expansion of the nursing role but others as well (Doyle & Meurer, 1983; Wolff, 1984). This decision affirmed if not actually set policy for expanded roles in nursing and will be a precedent for other cases.

States, of course, create policy, and when the state is large and powerful, policy can transcend state boundaries. An excellent example is the change in the nurse practice act in New York State (1972), which defined nursing as "diagnosing human responses." For the first time, nursing had the right to claim diagnostic functions and use the word out loud. For the first time, the core function of nursing in dealing with human responses to illness or treatment was stated and debated (Diers & Molde, 1983).

That policy-making act led to the ANA Social Policy Statement (ANA, 1980), which uses the New York State language to define nursing. The ANA statement itself is a policy statement for nursing, if not actually public policy.

Policy made in the private sector sometimes becomes public policy. For example, the Robert Wood Johnson Foundation, with massive amounts of money to distribute, has tilted the direction of medical service and education toward primary care. The Foundation adopted primary care as an early agenda. The Foundation's present support of twenty projects to consolidate services for high-risk adolescents provides a base for policy for health services to this underserved group. The W. K. Kellogg Foundation's support to the National Council of State Boards of Nursing effectively took the control of the licensure examination out of the hands of the ANA (under whose umbrella the Council had once stood) and the NLN (which used to write and validate the licensure examination). The policy impact of this move is yet to be felt entirely. Since the operational work of licensure is in the hands of the states, there may be random attempts by states (as there have been in Connecticut) to write their own exam rather than require the State Board Test Pool Examination for licensure. The California legislature believes the present examination discriminates against certain groups and is not a bona fide test of occupational qualification. Because the national group in charge of the content of the examination is no longer a part of an organized nursing body, it is easier to challenge. It has no constituency.

Policy-making also occurs at local levels. Moves to institute primary nursing, for example, are policy moves that balance authority, responsibility, and accountability (Manthey, 1980). Proposals for governance structures for nurses in institutions that would make nursing report directly to the trustees, as medicine does, are another example of policy-making at the local level (Kimbro & Gifford, 1980).

Regulatory agencies also participate in policy-making. The Federal Trade Commission (FTC), for instance, is interested in the extent to which organized medicine restricts the practice of nurse-midwives, a case in Tennessee (McCarty, 1981). Two privately practicing nurse-midwives were denied hospital privileges, and the malpractice coverage of their backup physician was terminated. With the FTC's help, a physician-controlled malpractice carrier has signed a consent order to end its practice of cancelling coverage for physicians who provide backup to nurse-midwives. (Lerner, 1983).

HOW POLICY IS MADE

It is not difficult to describe where policy is made. *How* it is made is something else. Political scientists and others have difficulty understanding it (Lindblom & Cohen, 1979; Doty, 1980).

Some groups have the defined mission of policy-making—certain commissions, Congress, the executive branch, the judicial system. Professional organizations also make policy for the issues that concern them. What is confusing and controversial is that policy is often made because it is politically expedient, not because it is right.

The notion that it might be sensible to figure out what should or ought to be done, what is "right," and then derive the political strategies to make it happen is hardly revolutionary. Yet in the midst of the activity of frenetic political work, it is difficult to step back to see the big picture. In nursing, we have all too often compromised ourselves with such maneuvering, and we have also been pushed into this strategy by others. It is in the interest of those with historical or entrenched power to keep it, and one way to do that is to divide those who would seek it. There would be less division in nursing if we were to try first to say out loud what ought to happen and why, before we start strategizing to make something happen that might turn on us. (Remember the cats?)

Saying why something should happen requires some data or theory from which to argue. The case of nurse-midwifery is instructive here (Diers & Burst, 1983). When the policy issue was access to care, nurse-midwives had the data that said they could increase access. When the issue was "safety," the data were there as well. Now the issue is cost, and nurse-midwives have been accumulating data on that for years.

Nurse-midwifery has been successful in using data because it was already there. Every nurse-midwifery service in the country is required by the American College of Nurse-Midwives to collect information on every patient. When a policy question comes up, the nurse-midwives add up the numbers to answer whatever the question is—access, safety, cost.

In every hospital in the country, data are being accumulated on every shift, every day, and then stuffed in some administrator's file to be shredded when the pile gets too high. Such reports routinely list critically ill patients, new admissions, VIPs, or other patients who deserve extra attention. They list absences of the staff, needed repairs, or accidents. They are an absolute goldmine of information, but rarely used.

Any service that has nurses functioning in independent roles (clinics in which nurses have caseloads, for example) can pull out data on numbers served, time, and cost. When those data are linked with the medical record, one can monitor quality of care. Schools of nursing have data on alumnae (or should). Personnel records contain masses of information on the relationship between, for example, educational preparation and length of service, specialty choice, and even some rough measures of quality such as merit increments.

When the issue of breaking nursing costs out of the hospital bill comes up, some are worried that if we collect that data, it will be used against us. Surely data can be dangerous, but not if it is valid, reliable, presented carefully, and collected by people who know what is in it. Data are almost always more valuable than no data when policy considerations come up. Thus, it is in our interest to accumulate information regularly, even if it is not immediately apparent how important it is, for it will be, somewhere, someday. With computer technology, such accumulation is easy, but nurses must seize the opportunity before some clerk somewhere erases the files.

CONCLUSION

Nursing is just beginning to realize the strength of its numbers and its issues. The remarkable success of nursing in the political sphere is but the tip of the iceberg. When nurses begin to get on the policy agenda, we will finally be where we should be. When we are, the frustration we may now feel with limited gains on small issues will be over, and we will be in a position to act to make policy, rather than react to policy proposals of others.

References

Aiken LH: Nursing's future: Public policies, private actions. *Am J Nurs* 1983; 83:1440–44.

American Nurses' Association: *Nursing: A Social Policy Statement*. ANA, 1980.

Commentary: Should there be a National Institute for Nursing? *Nurs Outlook* 1984; 32:74+.

Diers D, Burst, HV: Effectiveness of policy related research: Nurse-midwifery as case study. *Image* 1983; 15:68–74.

Diers D, Molde S: Nurses in primary care: The new gatekeepers? *Am J Nurs* 1983; 83:742–45.

Doty P: *Guided Change of the American Health System: Where the Levers Are*. Human Sciences Press, 1980.

Doyle, E, Meurer J: Missouri legislation and litigation. Practicing medicine without a license. *Nurse Pract* (June) 1983; 8:41+.

Dumas RG, Felton G: Should there be a National Institute for Nursing? *Nurs Outlook* 1984; 32:16–22.

Ehrenreich B, English D: *Witches, Midwives and Nurses—A History of Women Healers*. Feminist Press, 1973.

Institute of Medicine: *Nursing and Nursing Education: Public Policies and Private Actions*. National Academy Press, 1983.

Jacox A: Significant questions about IOM's study of nursing. *Nurs Outlook* 1983; 31:28–33.

Kimbro CD, Gifford AJ: The nursing staff organization: A needed development. *Nurs Outlook* 1980; 28:610–16.

Lerner, AN: Impact of antitrust on the health professions. Unpublished paper. American Association of Nurse Anesthetists, 50th Annual Meeting, New Orleans, 1983.

Lindblom C: *The Policy Making Process*, 2nd ed. Prentice-Hall, 1980.

Lindbolm C, Cohen D: *Usable Knowledge*. Yale Press, 1979.

Manthey M: *Primary Nursing*. Blackwell Scientific, 1980.

McCarty P: Nurse-midwives forced out of practice. *Am Nurse* (Feb) 1981; 13:1+.

President's Commission on Mental Health: *Report*. U.S. Government Printing Office, 1978.

Sermchief v. Gonzales. Missouri Supreme Court #64692: 1983.

Voight J: The black death plague and the cat. Pages 17–19 in: *Cat Catalog*. Fireman J (editor). 1976.

Walker D: The cost of nursing care in hospitals. Pages 131–44 in: *Nursing in the 80's: Crises, Opportunities, Challenges*. Aiken L (editor). Lippincott, 1982.

Wolff MA: Court upholds expanded practice roles for nurses. *Law Med Health Care* 1984; 12:26–29.

Chapter 6

Politics and the
Professional Organization

Pamela Maraldo, RN, PhD
Jacquelyn Kinder, RN, EdD

In the early 19th century, Tocqueville, a Frenchman studying American democracy, remarked on the American propensity for forming organizations. In American society, membership organizations, like all private associations, have been symbols of liberty. They have historically been the public's vehicle in taking stands for or against the state and served as a pluralist attack on the state's power. Associations and membership organizations are one of the cornerstones of democracy in America.

THE NATURE OF ORGANIZATION

In the 20th century, associations have proliferated. Yet, they still have common characteristics:

- They are private, not controlled by the state.
- They are autonomous and assert the right to be self-determining and self-governing.
- They are limited in their purpose. They do not purport to concern themselves with all aspects of their members' lives. Rather, they have a specific mission.
- They are homogeneous. Within the scope of the association, there will be only people of similar interests, since the autonomous association selects its membership and has limited purposes.
- They are voluntary. Members belong to the association by choice (Lipset, 1960).

Some membership associations meet these criteria to a greater extent than others. Some membership associations have trivial aims; others serve an important mission in the larger community. Some organizations are clearly more homogeneous than others.

The most important principle of organization is that it is politically necessary in a democracy because through its numerical strength and coordination, it is the only way to overcome adversarial forces.

This aspect is evident in the case of nursing organizations such as the American Nurses' Association (ANA), the National League for Nursing (NLN), the National Federation for Specialty Nursing Organizations, and the National Student Nurses' Association. Nursing's strength in the political arena lies in its numbers. That is why it is essential for nurses to be organized into a cohesive "body politic." For regardless of the expertise and care-giving nurses have to offer to humanity, their view of how health care is delivered will be unheard without the leverage of numbers—without a collective strength. Such is the purpose of organization. Ultimately the mission of every membership association must be to be heard in a large public policy arena, regardless of its more narrowly focused mission and goals. Because we are a society of special interests in a representative democracy, it is the charge of membership associations to speak for their constituents in the arenas that will affect them or their interests.

Such is the raison d'être of national nursing organizations. The ANA speaks for the profession in public policy discussions, establishes the standards of practice for registered nurses, and certifies nurses for excellence in areas of practice. These are activities geared toward the individual professional nurse. The NLN, on the other hand, advocates nursing as an enterprise to consumers, to the higher education community, and to other health professions as well as nurses. The NLN, then, is in the business of ensuring the quality of the enterprise—the quality of nursing education and community-based nursing services.

It is important that nurses support their national nursing organizations, rather than forming new organizations, so that the national nursing organizations can effectively represent these missions. New organizations are diversionary and futile because they fail to advance nursing's cause in public policy. Yet movement to other organizations or to new allegiances has characterized nursing in this country for some time.

The governance and politics of membership organizations determine their effectiveness. Whether they meet their stated goals and whether their members remain involved and loyal to the organization are the keys to making a mark in the larger societal arena.

Even though associations are a symbol of liberty, the questions remain: How are they governed and what is the political process employed in their governance (Dahl, 1961)? In national nursing organizations, many believe that governance lies in the hands of the membership. But is it the membership that is accountable for the successes and failures of national nursing organizations?

THE IRON LAW OF OLIGARCHY

Oligarchy is control by a few. Political analyst Robert Michels (1962) presented a bold and disturbing thesis that is still troublesome to many political leaders. He said, "Who says organization, says oligarchy." Referred to as the iron law of oligarchy, this provocative thesis implies that democracy, whether in government, trade unions, political parties, or membership organizations, must result in domination by a few individuals—the elected leaders. Michels concluded this based on a study of the pre-World War II German Social Democratic Party. He examined socialists' behaviors and views because of their devotion to democratic ideals. They fought for adult suffrage, free speech, and for popular participation in the operation of governmental and economic institutions at every level. He reasoned that, if democracy existed in associations, then surely it could be found among those organizations which were most engaged in the preservation of a democracy. Yet Michels did not find it there. In a comparison of members' and leaders' opinions and values, he found the leaders always prevailed.

Oligarchic tendencies have probably lessened over the past twenty years in keeping with general societal trends toward decentralization, increased educational levels, and diversification. But some still believe that a handful of opinion leaders dominate and control membership organizations. Justifications given for oligarchic rule or control by a select few in voluntary organizations have been:

- It better enables organizations to fulfill their roles in general social conflicts in the political arena.
- There is no structural basis for conflict from within since they are homogeneous.

The major political argument in opposition to Michels' theory is the concept of direct popular democracy, which is the basis for much of traditional democratic theory. The concept of popular democracy was originally the ideal behind organizations and continues to be today.

IS THERE DEMOCRACY IN NATIONAL NURSING ORGANIZATIONS?

To some extent, tendencies toward both oligarchy and "popular" democracy can be seen in modern nursing organizations. First, according to the characteristics of organization, the major national nursing organizations—ANA and NLN—violate the homogeneity that sometimes encourages oligarchy. The more homogeneous an organization is, the more the leadership of the organization will tend to feel free to speak for the members without their input. A pluralistic constituency serves as its own check-and-balance system on the administration as well as the elected leadership. These organizations have a structural basis for conflicts that must be resolved over and over again. The structural makeups of ANA and NLN must necessarily contend with nursing's age-old struggle over educational credentials to enter the profession. The variety of entry levels through which an individual can enter the profession creates a fragmentation of the nursing body politic into several special interest groups—practical nurses, diploma nurses, associate degree nurses, baccalaureate and higher degree nurses. In the case of NLN, each of these groups constitutes its own separate membership unit. The members feel strongly about associating with their peers, who hold similar sets of values, especially as concerns accreditation, which is a peer process.

The major determinant of how democratically an organization is run rests in the degree of participation of its members. The greater the participation, the more democratic the organization. For most Americans, participation in voluntary associations is a peripheral aspect of their lives (Milbrath & Goel, 1977). The family and occupational roles are the centers of activity. Participation in organizations is marginal.

Participation in any organization appears to be related to the number and importance of the functions it performs for its members and the degree of the members' personal involvement (Milbrath & Goel, 1977). In some cases, participation in organizational affairs provides rewards in the form of higher status, improved professional opportunities, or valued social relations. Such incentives and opportunities exist in national nursing organizations.

To the extent that members view their jobs as an important aspect of their lives, participation will be higher. The organization that serves as a status reference group will increase members' participation. If the profession or occupation has a high status, participation in the national organization will be greater (Lipset, 1960).

Membership in nursing and other health professional organizations at the national level has been decreasing. Even though the American Dental Association still has about three quarters of the dentists in the country in its ranks, it used to have 90%. The American Medical Association currently has less than 50%; just a few years ago over half of the physicians in the country were members. Prior to a change in its structure in 1982, the ANA was concerned with loss of membership. NLN's numbers have also shrunk: In 1970, NLN had 25,000 individual members; it currently has 16,000.

Some in nursing have made a strong case that membership needs in national nursing organizations have not been met, and members participation has been stifled. Therefore, some groups have broken away to form their own organization. In fact, many of the 60 national nursing organizations are the result of ANA or NLN members seeking greater autonomy, different purposes, and/or greater response to the demands of their members.

Does this separating from the parent organization occur because of the lack of adherence to a democratic process in organizations? It's difficult to say. Maybe if these organizations had provided greater autonomy and decision-making authority to these groups of members they would have remained within their original matriarchal structures. The inevitable dissension and power struggles among opinion leaders are undoubtedly responsible for separations of this nature.

Another reason for the universal decline in membership in organizations is the many changes in society that affect the nature of participation in organizations. The backbone of America has been its patriarchal institutions. The government, the medical establishment, the corporation, and the educational system were paragons of authority and control. Shielding Americans against many responsibilities, institutions have been America's decision makers, caretakers, and unchallenged authorities. Slowly we are weaning ourselves from our institutional dependence; the lack of authority was too high a price to pay (Lipset, 1960).

Despite the decrease of nurses' involvement in national nursing organizations, there is a political process in organizations that must respond to its members to be viable—not unlike the political process in the govermental arena.

THE POLITICAL PROCESS WITHIN NATIONAL NURSING ORGANIZATIONS

Just like the legislative arena in Washington or on the state level, national organizations have pressure points. Like a congressman or state legislator, the elected leadership serves a constituency. And just like a legislative representative, if an elected official of a membership organization receives ten letters or phone calls of concern from members on a particular matter, he or she will be more responsive. Even though elected heads of membership organizations aren't in a position to run for election every two years indefinitely, the possibility of membership attrition is a strong incentive to be conscientiously responsive.

In the same way, it is possible to effect change in national nursing organizations. How the process can work was illustrated at the NLN convention in June 1983 in Philadelphia. A position statement specifying that the baccalaureate degree should be required for professional nursing was proposed to the membership. At the time, major nursing organizations—including the American Society for Nursing Service Administrators (now the American Organization of Nurse Executives), an affiliated group of the American Hospital Association—had taken the position that professional nursing practice should be at the baccalaureate level. NLN was one of the few national nursing organizations that had not taken such a stand. The Council of Baccalaureate and Higher Degree Programs leadership in the League, in conjunction with the associate degree council leadership, guided the two groups to join forces. Even though Pennsylvania, where the convention was held, has one of the highest percentages of diploma schools in the country, the position was carried.

The frenzy and politicking in the conference rooms at the Mayflower Hotel brought to mind the lobbying and networking typically seen at the Republican and Democratic national conventions or in congressional corridors in Washington. In these circumstances, the principles governing the activity of the body politic were similar: coalition-building to achieve cohesion and consensus is the key to success. A successful vote taken in Congress would be orchestrated in much the same way as the successful vote establishing the NLN's position on the baccalaureate degree. That is, there is a crossfire of lobbying through letters, phone calls, and person-to-person meetings before the vote is to be taken.

While the leadership and the personalities at the top are always key to the outcome, the practical efforts of the group must be geared toward increasing the numbers of votes. Numbers are the measurement of success in membership organizations just as they are in the legislative process. In the NLN scenario, the baccalaureate council knew it was essential to link up with the large numbers of associate degree (AD) council members to accomplish its mission. Even though the baccalaureate council and many members of the associate degree council believed that establishing the baccalaureate as the professional level of practice would benefit the entire profession, many in the associate degree council perceived their support as a trade-off for a political favor. To maintain a good political rapport with that group, the baccalaureate council will have to address this perception in dealing with future issues and potential alliances with that group.

Strength in numbers is essential to be effective in the public policy arena. From a public policy perspective, there is no right or wrong in a democracy on many issues that concern the general public. There is only difference of opinion and divergent, conflicting interests and views that must be reconciled to the satisfaction of the majority. Staunch, unbending ideological postures are inevitably destined for failure. Compromise to reach consensus should always be nursing's political goal.

ISSUES FOR PROFESSIONAL ORGANIZATIONS

If nurses are to be consistent with their raison d'etre, which is first and foremost to meet the health needs of people, then it is nursing's responsibility to gain strength in the public policy arena so that nurses have a voice in how health care is delivered. Without that voice, efforts to improve health care will be impotent and futile.

The most effective way to influencing federal policy decisions in health care is through membership in national nursing organizations, which have nursing's greatest numbers. These organizations, to have any impact, must be in concert on issues of major import to the profession. In the past, there have been too many instances when the ranks of nursing have been divided, allowing politicians to dismiss the issue and the nursing profession. Unwilling to enter into nursing's internal conflicts, they can easily plead neutrality and dismiss the issues and the nurses.

During the past decade, there have been occasions when the ANA and the NLN have been at odds. More recently, there has been a growing awareness of the need to enter into joint ventures, to support each other, and to come to consensus on important matters. There are external threats to the profession as a result of the severe economic constraints on health care. If nursing does not join forces, it may jeopardize the progress we have made. Under prospective payment, nursing is vulnerable.

Whenever resources shrink, the system becomes more political and nurses often bear the brunt of the retrenchment. Some institutions may use the budget ax to chop the biggest chunk out of the nursing department. Some key hospital officials have made public statements regarding the potential cost savings that would accrue from using cheaper labor instead of registered nurses. To cite an example, when Medicare cutbacks began, National Medical Enterprises dispatched a team of corporate consultants to its 90 hospitals. The team reported that a number of hospitals can improve their "effective level of operation by altering the mix of staffing" in the nursing department, largely through increased use of licensed practical nurses (LPNs) and aides instead of registered nurses. Robert Rubin, president of Superior Care, Inc. (a proprietary nursing agency), stated in an interview with *AMA News* that to keep expenses down, Superior Care would use an increasing number of unskilled aides rather than LPNs and RNs. Eventually, he believes that insurance contracts will probably even stipulate the use of skilled aides instead of costly nurses.

Nurses may have to fight for their professional lives. Nursing service directors need to make their budgets defensible. Accounting methods that identify nursing costs separately will be needed to allocate nursing resources in the most rational, efficient manner. As resources shrink, conflict is inevitable. When conflict occurs between nurses and other providers, whether in hospitals or in other political arenas, nurses will be on much firmer ground if they have the support of the body politic behind them.

Nurses have made progress. In terms of having many nurses in policy-making positions in government and the private sector, there has been progress. There has also been progress in nursing's autonomy. The growing number of nurses who are receiving third party payment for services is a major step forward in control over nursing practice. In fact, many nurses have established their own practices; and nurse-run enterprises in home health, chronic illness, and illness prevention are appearing.

There has also been progress in nursing's ability to approach policy issues in a unified manner. The Tri-Council on Nursing, consisting of the presidents and executive directors of the ANA, the NLN, and the American Association of Colleges of Nursing, has consistently been in accord on funding priorities. In 1984, the three organizations supported establishment of a National Institute of Nursing in the National Institutes of Health. In addition, these three organizations and the American Society for Nursing Service Administrators (now American Organization of Nurse Executives) received funding from the W. K. Kellog Foundation to reach consensus throughout the nursing community on credentialing. This undertaking promises to be far-reaching in its impact on the state of the art of nursing.

There is still much to be done before nurses are credited with the professional status and authority they need to be effective. There is still a counterproductive power struggle for center stage among national nursing organizations. Nonetheless, considering the importance of unity among the national nursing organizations and all that is at stake, the members of the respective organizations have every right to demand cohesion. No matter how noble nursing's aims or how legitimate its goals, without the strength of nurses' numbers as a cohesive group, nursing is destined to rehash its conflicts and replay its old themes.

References

Anderson VF, Van Winkle RA: *In the Arena: The Care and Feeding of American Politics*. Harper & Row, 1976.

Dahl RA: *Who Governs? Democracy and Power in an American City*. Yale University Press, 1961.

Kalisch BJ, Kalisch PA: *Politics of Nursing*. Lippincott, 1982.

Lane RE: *Political Life: Why People Get Involved in Politics*. Free Press, 1959.

Lipset SM: *Political Man: The Social Bases of Politics*. Doubleday, 1960.

Maraldo P: *Open-Closed Mindedness*. Dissertation, New York University, 1984.

Michels R: *Political Parties*. Collier Books, 1962.

Milbrath LW, Goel ML: *Political Participation*, 2nd ed. Rand-McNally, 1977.

Chapter 7

Politics and the Community

Sarah Ellen Archer, RN, DrPH, FAPHA, FAAN

Politics affects virtually all levels of individual and community life in every country. Let us look at some examples.

- The place we call home is subject to building codes. These standards have been set up to ensure homeowners and renters that the structure they live in is safe. Builders and contractors, however, often resist these standards as unnecessarily increasing construction costs.

- To ensure the food we consume is safe, standards for food production, packaging, labeling, and distribution have been developed. However, each year new pesticides, food additives, and preservatives are among the more than 1,000 new chemical substances introduced into our environment. Often little is known about their long-term effects on humans.

- Water supply purification and protection are taken for granted in the United States. Yet we read about cities in this country where the water is contaminated by toxic industrial wastes, many known to be hazardous to health. Laws are on the books to prevent this from happening, but it continues. The polluters, if they can be found, are often not held responsible for their actions or the consequences, although the courts are intervening on behalf of the public in some instances.

- There is increasing concern by some that even the United States, one of the world's richest nations, does not have sufficient resources to provide for the needs of its population. Others argue that the United States has resources to meet its own peoples' needs and to increase its role in assisting other nations to do the same. What prevents this from happening is not so much a scarcity of resources, as it is political decisions about how those resources are to be allocated. We must realize that neither we nor the rest of the world with whom we are interdependent can have both "guns and butter." The political and military elites, most of whom are men, make decisions that increase weapons arsenals. The world's people, a majority women and children, plead for food and many continue to go hungry.

Two objectives are addressed in this chapter. One is to increase nurses' awareness of the effects that political decisions have on health care, women's concerns, and the environment. These three key arenas are chosen because of their importance to all levels of communities, from the village to the planet. The second objective is to emphasize why nurses, in concert with others, must participate in political decisions that affect us, our patients, and the communities where we live and work.

HEALTH CARE

The availability and quality of health care to which we, our families, and our patients have access is increasingly a political subject if not a political football. As consumption of health care approaches 11 percent of the gross national product (GNP), the increasing politicization of issues related to health care is not surprising. The increasing costs of health care make even clearer that political priorities need to shift to implementing ways to prevent illness and disability.

Health promotion and disease prevention, although considered by the Department of Health and Human Services Secretary Margaret M. Heckler to be a top priority, received only $8 million in the administration's fiscal year 1985 budget proposal. Heckler says that prevention activities are "a question of emphasis," rather than of funding.

There are a few bright spots, however, in the political arena for health. Congress is moving to create a network of Centers for Research and Demonstration on Health Promotion and Disease Prevention as part of the National Institutes of Health. Also, the Prevention '84 meeting in Atlanta brought together leaders from all of the major public health and preventive medicine organizations to discuss the state of the art of prevention. The cost benefits of preventive efforts are of increasing interest to members of the business, labor, and insurance communities, as well as to government third-party payers. Opportunities for broad coalition formation to advocate for health across these communities are evolving; nurses must be involved.

The production and use of tobacco is an example of a complex constellation of political, economic, and health issues (Milio, 1981). On the one hand, the federal government, for political and economic reasons, continues to subsidize tobacco production. These same resources could be used to help the farmers to produce other crops less hazardous to people's health.

Despite reports over a 20-year period by the surgeon generals about the hazards of smoking, 53 million people in the United States still smoke. Estimates are that 300,000 people die of smoking-related causes each year or 15 percent of all deaths in the United States (Smoking . . . after 20 years, 1984). How much smoking-induced illness and disability cost taxpayers is difficult to estimate, but the amount is substantial. The hazards for nonsmokers of inhaling second-hand smoke are being documented. Surgeon General Everett Koop has warned, "A parent interested in the welfare of his (or her) child should stop (smoking)." (Where there's smoke, 1984).

In 1984, the Department of Health and Human Services launched a cancer prevention campaign that emphasizes eight recommendations, one of which is not to smoke or to use tobacco in any form. The American Public Health Association is seeking endorsement and cooperation from the Department and other organizations toward a "nonsmoking society" by the year 2000. Stronger warnings have been approved to appear on cigarette packets stressing the linkage between smoking and cancer, heart disease, and complications of pregnancy. All of these government-sponsored efforts are aimed at reducing the consumption of a product that is clearly hazardous to both smokers' and nonsmokers' health. At the same time, the government pays out millions of dollars to subsidize tobacco production.

After several unsuccessful attempts to pass an antismoking initiative in San Francisco, a coalition of citizens organizations succeeded in 1983. Obtaining the needed number of registered voters' signatures to qualify the initiative for the ballot was relatively easy. Our problems began in earnest during the campaign. As is often the case with citizen-generated initiatives, there was much enthusiasm, expertise, and volunteer time but little money. The opposition, much of it from the tobacco industry, poured thousands of dollars into the campaign. Radio and TV advertisements asserted that the antismoking initiative was the first of what could be many infringements on people's personal freedom. One of the factors we believe influenced the antismoking initiative's passage was that the sponsoring coalition made it known that the opposing position was supported by money from outside of the community. This appeal to preserve community autonomy, as well as the merits of the proposed legislation itself, led to its successful passage. This is another step toward raising people's level of consciousness about smoking and its hazards.

Many people view cost containment as the major health care issue facing the United States. Health care spending has increased from $27 billion in 1960 to $356 billion in 1983 and now consumes 11 percent of the GNP. A 1985 Census Bureau Survey of Income and Program estimates that 35 million, or 15 percent, of all Americans have no health insurance coverage. In 1983, health care costs rose by 12 percent, more than triple the rise in the overall consumer price index (Davis, 1984). A number of political decisions have been made to contain costs. Medicare and Medicaid are major targets for cuts in appropriations as Congress and the states try to find ways to reduce the federal budget deficit. Some of the proposed changes include increased deductibles and co-payments for Medicare recipients, thus increasing their out-of-pocket costs for care. More stringent eligibility requirements for Medicaid are also proposed. These changes fall disproportionately on the elderly and the poor, many of whom are members of minority groups. Many of these groups need help and advocacy to promote and to protect their interests.

The passage of the 1983 Social Security Amendments that introduced prospective payments for hospital services for Medicare recipients is another approach to cost containment. Of particular interest to community health nurses is the impact this legislation is having on community-based nursing and home care services. Clients are discharged earlier with greater nursing care needs. As the demand grows for increased nursing services in clients' homes, involving higher levels of expertise and technology, policy changes to provide adequate reimbursement for these services will also be needed. Visiting Nurses' Associations and other home nursing service agencies must carefully document the effects of these changes in their clientele and services so they can use these data to show the need for appropriate reimbursement. This need for different and expanded reimbursement for home nursing services is one of many opportunities for nurses to form coalitions with patients and their families, community groups, and other health care providers. Nurses need to take a leadership role in these coalitions to lobby state and federal legislators to assure that members of the community have access to the kinds of home care and other community-based services they need.

WOMEN'S CONCERNS

Women's concerns have become increasingly prominent in the political arena, particularly because of the effects of the gender gap on election outcomes since 1980. As Theodore White notes, "Any politician who ignores the ancient resentments and new ambitions behind the thrust of the women is blind to what probably is the most formidable new force in American politics" (Kucherov, 1984, p 47). Most of our patients are women and their children. Most nurses are also women, so we share many of these same "ancient resentments and new ambitions." Together with patients and women from our communities, nurses can be an increasing part of that "most formidable new force in American politics." Here are some reasons, particularly since the failure of the Equal Rights Amendment, why we must mobilize our own and others' resources at all levels of community on behalf of women.

The feminization of poverty is an increasingly recognized phenomenon. As Dion Aroner (1984), staff person for the California Lt. Governor's Task Force on the Feminization of Poverty, points out: 150,000 women per year are becoming poor. After divorce, women experience a 73 percent decrease in their standard of living, while men experience a 42 percent increase in theirs. Even with court-ordered payment of child support, only one-half of the parents in California with custody of children receive what they are entitled to, and one-fourth receive nothing. As of 1984, one out of seven families in the United States was headed by a woman; approximately 40 percent of these families had incomes below the poverty line. Starfield (1982) notes that "poor children are 75 percent more likely to be admitted to a hospital in a given year. They have 30 percent more days when their activity is restricted and 40 percent more days lost from school" (p 245). That was in 1980. The situation now, with inflation and reductions in Social Security, Medicare, and Supplemental Security Income benefits, is even worse for many elderly, particularly for elderly women.

Unemployment is also a women's issue. Unemployed persons and their families are deprived of health insurance and other fringe benefits tied to employment. The result is increased morbidity, mortality, and domestic violence among the unemployed (Brenner, 1973; Brenner & Mooney, 1983; Spruit, 1982). For example, the infant mortality rate in Detroit between 1980–1982, when unemployment was at a peak, increased

Table 7-1 Comparison of Men's and Women's Average Salaries 1980

Vocational Area	Men's Salary	Women's Salary	Women's Salary as a percent of Men's
White collar	$20,705	$9,235	44.6%
Blue collar	13,419	7,361	54.9%
Service	6,213	3,258	52.4%

Source: U.S. Census, 1980.

4 percent, while the infant mortality rate for the state of Michigan decreased by 5 percent.

Pay equity continues to be a major concern for women. As of 1983, according to the U.S. Department of Labor, women made up 43 percent of the workforce. Table 7-1, based on 1980 U.S. Census data, compares the average salaries of men and women in the major vocational areas and shows the percentage of men's salaries that women are paid. The greatest discrepancy is in the white-collar vocational area where women are paid 44.6 percent of men's salaries or 44.6 cents for every $1 a man is paid. This wage gap increases in some white-collar positions over time. For example, female Stanford Business School graduates start with an average salary that is 94 percent of what male graduates are paid. Five years later, females are paid only an average of 79 cents for every dollar their male classmates receive (The first fully comparable city, 1984). Across all three vocational areas, women are paid an average 50.6 cents for every dollar paid to a male worker. More recent reports indicate that women are now being paid 62 percent of what males make. This continuing wage gap is ". . . fostered by the clustering of women in such 'pink-collar' fields as nursing, elementary-school teaching, and secretarial work" (Kucherov, 1984, p 47). A concentration of women workers in a field has traditionally depressed salaries. Ramsey, professor at Golden Gate University and chairperson of the San Francisco Commission on the Status of Women, said:

> Wage discrimination based on sex aims at the bottom of the pay pyramid and [correcting it] potentially is of much greater value to minority women than affirmative action. It also offers a potential benefit to minority men, especially in the South, where the highest paid black job rates are below the lowest paid white job rates. Comparable worth is not about pulling down men's jobs but about pulling up women's (The first fully comparable city, 1984).

The goals for pay equity are to evaluate jobs in a sex-neutral way and then to enforce the 1963 Equal Pay Act requiring equal salaries for men and women doing comparable work. Nurses have a considerable stake in the pay equity issue, as do many of our patients. There are many local and national organizations such as NOW and the ANA that support comparable worth. They need nurses' participation, and we need them.

Women are repeatedly told that the United States cannot afford pay equity. Indeed, in 1985 the U.S. Civil Rights Commission recommended that the federal government, including Congress, agencies, and the Justice Department, reject the concept of comparable worth and rely only on the principle of equal pay for equal work. Yet at the same time, the government finds funds, through deficit spending if necessary, to finance the billions of dollars needed for the MX missiles and other expensive military hardware. The United States has emerged as the world's leading arms merchant, exceeding the USSR by almost $2 billion. Many of these arms have been sold to Third World nations. Indeed, arms sales in the early 1980s have become "a major instrument of this country's diplomacy." This is contrasted with previous United States policy of limiting arms sales, especially to Latin American countries. To discourage poor countries from wasting resources on arms, the late President Dwight D. Eisenhower said in 1953, "Every gun that is made, every warship launched, every rocket fired, signifies in the final sense a theft from those who hunger and are not fed, those who are cold and are not clothed."

Political decisions to shift spending priorities from domestic services to defense are affecting women. One way is as a result of opportunity costs, since money spent for defense cannot be spent for other purposes, such as social services. Sidel (1984) gives an indication of what some of these opportunity costs actually are. "Scrapping of the MX missile and the B-1 bomber programs would save $51 billion over the next five years in the U.S. alone. A nuclear freeze would save the U.S. $84 billion over the next five years and $200 billion over the next 10 years" (p 9). Those funds could be put to more humanitarian purposes.

Cuts in social programs are having a marked effect. Children's Defense Fund data show that:

• Over 35 percent of all preschool children in the U.S. are not immunized against diphtheria-tetanus-pertussis.

• Almost 40 percent are not immunized against polio, nor 50 percent against mumps.

• Four million children living in poverty are not covered by Medicaid, which reaches fewer than half of all poor Americans.

• Poor women pregnant with a first child are now precluded from Medicaid in six states. Thirty-two states do not provide Medicaid to poor pregnant women who are married.

• Seven migrant health centers have lost federal funding, affecting 70,000 people (Edelman, 1984).

Smeal (1984) states that defense spending means job loss for both women and men. She cites a 1982 Michigan study that showed for every $1 billion of defense spending, women lose 9,500 jobs and men lose 500 jobs. Much of this loss in female jobs can be attributed to the fact that social programs are those most heavily cut in order to fund defense spending. Female workers, as noted, predominate in the "pink-collar" jobs such as nursing, elementary school teaching, and social services. Also, the majority of clients of these programs are women and children. Thus, women are hit twice by defense spending increases. Smeal also notes that reductions in federal spending are aimed ". . . to cut 'overlapping' benefits. The value of food stamps is counted in determining housing-assistance eligibility. What this means is that the poorest of the poor can choose between eating and shelter" (p 48).

Staggering and frustrating as these inequities are for women in the United States, women's status in much of the rest of the global community is worse. This is eloquently summed up in a statement from the Programme for Action developed at the 1980 Mid-United Nations Decade for Women: "Women suffer dual oppression of sex and class within and outside the family. The effects are strikingly apparent in the present world profile of women. While women represent 50 percent of the world population, they perform nearly two-thirds of all working hours, receive only one-tenth of the world income and own less than one percent of world property" (Fraser, 1984).

Hard as the opportunity costs of the arms race and military spending are on women in the United States, they are more devastating for women in less developed countries. In 1980, world military budgets were estimated to be 450 billion U.S. dollars, just over half of what they are estimated to be in 1984. Less developed countries are estimated to "spend as much on the military as they do on agriculture, while food production per person declines and people starve" (Terris, 1982). The following estimates were made as part of the Brandt Report (1980):

- The world was spending less than 5 percent of the total military budget on official development aid to less developed countries.
- One-half of one percent of one year's world military expenditures would pay for all of the farm equipment needed to increase food production and to help food-deficit, low-income countries to approach food self-sufficiency by 1990.
- One-half of one day's military expenditures would have financed the World Health Organization's entire successful malaria eradication program and would more than cover the costs of eradicating river blindness, which is still a scourge of millions of people (p 14).

Harrison (1981) provides additional information on what other uses military spending might have:

- For the price of one jet fighter plane, 40,000 village pharmacies could be set up.
- For the same amount of money, approximately 30 million U.S. dollars, classrooms could be provided for 600,000 children.
- 15 billion U.S. dollars per year could provide clean water and sanitation for all people by the year 1990.
- Less than 200 million U.S. dollars could provide immunizations for all children against six major childhood diseases—pertussis, tetanus, diphtheria, measles, tuberculosis, and polio (p 457).

Estimates are that in 1984 only 10 percent of the children born in less developed countries were immunized against these six childhood diseases. Infant mortality rates in some of these countries exceed 250 deaths per 1,000 live births—one-fourth of all infants born die before reaching their first birthday (April 7 is World Health Day, 1984).

Because the women of the world are the mothers and caretakers of its people, women are the ones upon whom the burdens of poverty, disease, and war fall disproportionately. In many countries of the world, including the United States, women do not enjoy equal rights. This is yet another example of inequities that political decisions per-petuate. Women rarely participate in these decisions.

ENVIRONMENTAL ISSUES

Political decisions about the environment affect people in all kinds of communities all over the world. We are increasingly aware of the interdependence of environment and life on this planet. Concern is also growing about the effects we have on the environ-ment, particularly with toxic, chemical, nuclear, and other kinds of pollution. The effects that environmental contamination have on human health are becoming more frightening with every day's news. In 1984, the fears became reality when an American-owned chemical company in Bhopal, India, accidentally released a cyanide compound into the air, resulting in the death and injury of thousands of Bhopal's citizens.

The National Academy of Sciences reports that little is known about the effects on humans of 80 percent of the approximately 50,000 chemicals currently in use. For ex-ample, data are inadequate on 38 percent of more than 3,300 pesticides, 25 percent of 1,800 drugs, and 46 percent of food additives (Work & Taylor, 1984). Approximately 1,000 new chemicals and compounds are introduced into the environment every year.

The Environmental Protection Agency (EPA) was created by federal law to protect the environment. To do that requires a great deal of money in increasing amounts. The administration's fiscal year 1985 budget request for the EPA is estimated to be 27 percent below its 1981 budget after inflation (EPA: Increased, 1984).

Inadequate funding is not the only difficulty EPA faces in trying to do its Herculean tasks. The Supreme Court agreed to hear an appeal in a suit by Monsanto against the EPA. Monsanto charges that EPA's regulation requiring review of manufacturers' data on health and safety testing of new pesticides to determine whether they are safe to be approved for marketing constitutes the unlawful taking of private property. Monsanto believes that health and safety testing data are part of its "trade secrets" that it does not want to be available to its competitors. EPA does not believe that health and safety testing data are "trade secrets."

The American Public Health Association, the American Association for the Ad-vancement of Science, and the Society for Clinical Ecology have filed *amicus curiae* briefs with the Supreme Court, arguing that in a number of instances EPA's ". . . closed regulatory scheme has failed to reveal fraudulent and inaccurate pesticide data, resulting in serious risk to public health and the environment. . . ." These organiza-tions want open scientific peer review and critique as ". . . the most basic and effec-tive means of ensuring accuracy in science" (Case on pesticide, 1984). Much of the testing for risk determination of chemicals and other substances, particularly those thought to be carcinogens, is done on laboratory animals. Even these results are sus-pect. Walker and Wade (1982) point out: ". . . it should be recognized that no data may provide absolutely definitive evidence—one way or another—as to whether can-cer is caused in humans by a substance that has been demonstrated to be an animal carcinogen" (p 412).

The public is entitled to as much information about adverse effects of chemicals and other substances in our environment as is known. Suspicions are growing that we are not being told the whole story. A group of over 100 labor, environmental, and consumer groups have formed a National Campaign Against Toxic Hazards, whose objective is passage of stronger laws against chemical contamination. The campaign needs to add law enforcement to its agenda as well as law enactment. Nurses should be involved in this coalition.

Disposal of chemical and radioactive toxic wastes is an increasing problem. Toxic waste disposal sites are turning up in communities from New York to Missouri to California. The effects of the materials dumped in these toxic waste sites on human health is unknown, although present evidence is increasingly frightening. Voices are being raised by and on behalf of victims of exposure to toxic wastes to compensate them for ". . . medical, rehabilitation, and relocation expenses and for lost wages" (APHA testifies, 1984, p 6). Congress is reviewing testimony on this problem. How, one asks, can innocent people be adequately compensated in money for loss of health, home, and community?

Many of these waste sites were created as a result of a convenient business practice of externalizing as many manufacturing costs as possible. Thus, unwanted and hazardous byproducts (such as dioxin in the manufacture of pesticides), rather than being stored, recycled, or properly destroyed, are dumped at waste disposal sites. This enables the manufacturers to reduce production costs and maximize profits. The costs of cleaning up these toxic waste disposal sites, when they are discovered, are then borne largely by the public. The "superfund" created for waste site cleanup received $210 million in fiscal 1983, $410 million in fiscal 1984, and the administration asked for $640 million in fiscal 1985. EPA increased its removal activities from 51 sites in 1982 to 94 sites in 1983 (EPA: Increased, 1984). There may be more than 16,000 uncontrolled toxic waste dumps (APHA testifies, 1984). No one really knows how many or in what communities they are.

The magnitude of the threat of nuclear wastes to the public's health remains largely unknown, although it, too, stalks communities throughout the country. Communities such as those around Three Mile Island have already experienced the fear of meltdown or other nuclear reactor catastrophes. The actual effects on these people are yet to be measured. As Peterson points out, "In the case of nuclear power, the build-up of radioactivity in reactors and in waste storage sites represents a potential for serious environmental contamination and poses a health threat to future generations for thousands of years to come" (1982, p 135).

While environmental contamination by toxic chemical and nuclear wastes is hazardous, we face the possibility of the ultimate environmental horror—nuclear war. Nuclear war is the greatest threat to the survival of every creature in every community on this planet that we have ever faced. Most people seem content to deny the increasing probability of nuclear war; it is simply too awful to contemplate. Others believe that nuclear war, waged on a limited scale, would not have devastating planet-wide effects. Still others have faith that civil defense and evacuation measures will save much of the population, who then can return to life as usual. These are myths (Lown 1982). "Prevention, not preparation, is a policy approach that strives for health and well-being and sets us on a positive course toward a peaceful future. Through public awareness and citizen involvement, prevention can supplant preparation as the dominant approach to nuclear war" (Myers, 1982, p 121).

NURSES' POLITICAL RESPONSIBILITIES

As nurses, 96 percent of whom are women, we must be aware of the effects of these and other political issues on our patients and ourselves as professionals, citizens, and human beings. We are in a unique position to serve as advocates for patients who are victims of political decisions in which they rarely participate and in which they are relatively powerless, but which directly and drastically affect them and their communities. Caring for and about people is not enough. We must act politically. We must not permit the victims to be blamed for their own conditions or merely to help them adapt to the present socio-politico-economic system. Second order changes—those that change the system and how it functions—are needed (Archer, Kelley & Bisch, 1984; Watzlawick, Weakland & Fisch, 1974), and we must participate in them.

As the largest group of health care providers in the United States, we must use our expertise and power as nurses and citizens to expand and alter the bases on which political decisions are made and implemented at all levels of community. We must become increasingly concerned with issues of equity and redistribution. We must look beyond nursing and nurses for political support and coalition formation. We must become involved in all kinds of communities and work with people from all walks of life to bring about needed changes to improve health and well-being for all. This book provides examples of strategies we can use in concert with others. We must learn to use them consistently and effectively. To do less is to abdicate our humanitarian and professional responsibilities.

References

APHA testifies: Plan needed to compensate toxic victims. *Nation's Health* 1984 (Mar); 1+.

April 7 is World Health Day. *Int Health News* 1984 (Mar–Apr); 4.

Archer SE, Kelly CD, Bisch SA: *Implementing Change in Communities. A Collaborative Process.* Mosby, 1984.

Aroner D: Feminization of poverty. (Paper, meeting of the California Public Health Association, Northern Division), 1984.

Brandt W: *North-South: A Programme for Survival.* MIT Press, 1980.

Brenner MH: Fetal, infant, and maternal mortality during periods of economic instability. *Int J Health Serv* 1973; 3:145–59.

Brenner MH, Mooney A: Unemployment and health in the context of economic change. *Soc Sci Med* 1983; 16:1125–38.

Case on pesticide safety. Data comes before Supreme Court. *Nation's Health* 1984 (Jan); 1, 6.

Davis CK: The time is right for the NLN initiative. *Nurs Health Care* 1984; 5:227.

EPA: Increased, but still below fiscal 1981. *Nation's Health* 1984 (Mar); 11.

Edelman MW: What's happening to people? *Child Church Society* (Mar) 1984; 75:7–9.

The first fully comparable city. *San Fran Exam* (April 24) 1984; B-10.

Fraser AS: Looking to the future: Equal partnership between women and men in the 21st century. University of Minnesota, H. H. Humphrey Institute of Public Affairs, Women, Public Policy, and Development Project, 1984.

Harrison P: *Inside the Third World.* Penguin Books, 1981.

Kucherov A: Ten forces reshaping America. *US News & World Rep* (Mar 19) 1984; 40–52.

Lown B: Nuclear war and public health. *Public Health Policy* 1982; 3(1):12–21.

Milio N: *Promoting Health through Public Policy.* F. A. Davis, 1981.

Myers BA: To plan for a hoax is a disservice to the people. *J Public Health Policy* 1982; 3(2): 119–21.

Peterson RW: Health, energy, and the environment. *J Public Health Policy* 1982; 3(2):130–39.

Sidel VW: APHA tells democrats: US security is aided by domestic stability. *Nation's Health* (May) 1984; 9.

Smeal E: *Why and how women will elect the next president.* Harper & Row, 1984.

Smoking . . . after 20 years still the public health challenge. *Nation's Health* 1984 (Feb); 1, 6.

Spruit IP: Unemployment and health in macro-social analysis. *Soc Science in Medicine* 1982; 16:1903–17.

Starfield B: Family income, ill health, and medical care of U.S. children. *J Public Health Policy* 1982; 3(3):244–59.

Terris M: The 1% fund (editorial). *J Public Health Policy* 1982; 3(3):239–40.

Walker B Jr, Wade DR: Issues in the regulation of environmental carcinogens. *J Public Health Policy* 1982; 3(4):408–18.

Watzlawick P, Weakland JA, Fisch R: *Change: Principles of Problem Formation and Problem Resolution.* W. W. Norton, 1974.

Where there's smoke. *New York Times* (May 27) 1984; D-1.

Work CP, Taylor RA: Toxic chemicals: Just how real a danger. *U.S. News and World Report* (May 21) 1984; 90:64–67.

UNIT II

ANALYSIS OF KEY CONCEPTS

Unit II analyzes several concepts basic to an understanding of political action: politics, power, change, and conflict. Chapter 8 examines politics as an interpersonal endeavor. Although power is discussed in Chapter 3, two nursing leaders present additional perspectives in Chapter 9. For nurses to be political activists, they must come to terms with this important concept with which many nurses are not yet comfortable.

The goal of political activism usually is to change something. Chapter 10 examines theories of change and illustrates these with examples from the four spheres of influence—the workplace, professional organizations, government, and the community. Influencing is also associated with conflict. Chapter 11 explores several perspectives on conflict and presents strategies for conflict management. One strategy that deserves particular attention in any discussion of political action is negotiation. An overview of Principled Negotiating and Steps to Informal and Formal Negotiating is presented.

As nurses become politically active in the four spheres of influence, they will face ethical dilemmas regarding how, when, and to what extent they should develop and use their influence. Chapter 12 explores some of these ethical issues. Analyses of ethical issues surrounding political action should not end here. Nurses must continue to explore such issues and in doing so, perhaps from a women's perspective, bring a more noble ethic to the male-dominated game of politics. Chapters 3 and 12 may stimulate the reader to develop a personal ethic of political action that may differ from what is now accepted political behavior.

Chapter 8

Politics Is People

Pamela Maraldo, RN, PhD

We speak of politics as though we all know what politics is. We identify "becoming political" as getting more involved with Washington, DC, and state legislatures. But to confine politics to Capitol Hill or state legislatures is to miss the point. Politics is ubiquitous, occurring wherever two or more people are gathered.

Most people still confuse the art of politics with under-the-table deals and morally reprehensible wheelings and dealings. People censure the political life. As Henry Fairlie, a British political journalist, chides—even politicians try not to be politicians.

Others who are not hung up about the immorality of politics see it as an abstraction. They hold reified notions of the political arena, considering it to consist of those societal institutions established to govern members of the state. These theorists hold lofty ideas of politics' purpose, such as: to maintain and foster an environment in which our national life and individual freedom can survive and prosper. Traditionally, political scientists and philosophers have considered politics to be a complex and necessary social institution and process, which includes such aspects as stability or change in governments and the pursuit and attainment of normative goals (justice, order).

The truth of the matter, however, is that everybody who functions in society must be, to some extent, a political animal. There's no escaping politics in any arena.

Politics is little more than human behavior in the raw, or, as one political writer put it, the art of who gets what, when, and how. The study of politics and the study of human behavior are one and the same. Aristotle believed that man is a political animal. Wilhoite (1973) also held that politics and human behavior are inextricable phenomena. He claimed that a propensity for power, authority, and influence may be part of man's biological nature.

Plato was the first of several political thinkers to describe the importance of understanding the relationship between human nature and politics. In the *Republic*, when he talked about developing in young people those human qualities necessary to become political leaders, he was actually talking about the traits of leadership in general.

Aristotle's and Plato's views of politics as intrinsic to human behavior have not been heeded over the years. Despite the growing evidence, for example, that psychological dynamics are the key to any political process, political scholars have paid little attention to the psychological aspects of political behavior. In the 19th century, political science was shaped by works espousing an abstract notion of politics that ignored people. It was similar to sociologist Max Weber's (1968) theoretical concept of bureaucracy, which assumed that to function effectively, organizations have to be as passionless and dehumanized as possible. Thus, political scientists have often considered politics from a sterile standpoint, leaving out the analysis of human behavior. Even in the 1960s and 1970s in the midst of student riots and sit-ins, the study of stable, safely observable, easily quantifiable phenomena continued to be the trend.

POLITICS IS GOOD
INTERPERSONAL RELATIONS

Adapting noted interpersonal theorist Harry Stack Sullivan's adage, it would be fitting to say: Politics is more simply human than otherwise. Stated simply, politics is interpersonal relations. That is, the pattern or dynamics of relations among persons in a given setting reflect its politics. When we hear people talk of politics of the family, partisan politics, the politics of nations, or of nursing, they are simply referring to the relations and behaviors of the persons typically found in these settings. Too often people are mystified or intimidated by situations and scenarios of state legislatures or Washington, DC, that are considered to be "political." In fact, they are no more political or no different than if they had occurred at the local grocery store, university, or hospital. If we speak of university politics, hospital politics, or Capitol Hill politics, what are we talking about and what do the three have in common? They are all characterized by interests and personalities amongst which one must maneuver to have a say in the situation, and at the very least, to protect one's own territory lest it be gobbled up by a more aggressive professor, physician, or Congressman. A politician's tools in any setting—the university, the hospital or Washington, DC—are people and events. Paramount to understanding the politics of a situation is understanding the persons in the setting and the interrelationships and psychodynamics of the interactions among them. Politicians call it "knowing the players."

To "know the players" in a political situation, a model for understanding interpersonal behavior will be appropriate.

Bales (1970) provides a model well suited to analyzing the political process in any setting. Taking one person in a group (someone who figures prominently in the setting) as the beginning focus, Bales provides a set of questions that one may ask about that person, such as:

- Does he or she seem to receive a lot of interaction from others?
- Does he seem personally involved in the group?

- Does he assume responsibility for leadership?
- Does he seem dominating?
- Does he seem warm and personal?
- Does he seem to stand for the most conservative ideas and beliefs of the group?
- Does he seem introverted, serious, shy, introspective?
- Does he seem resentful?
- Does he seem to identify with some group of underprivileged persons?

Bales suggests his method of analysis be used when a group is task-oriented, and there is pressure to allocate the group's resources constructively (time, money, members' abilities, and efforts). This is by definition a political situation, because politics is often defined as the allocation of scarce resources.

After the focal figure in the group has been analyzed, Bales makes a distinction between behaviors related to the individual's personality versus his or her group role and the need to distinguish between the two. The group role of any given person is determined in part by other group members—the way they behave and evaluate the acting person. In most cases, their evaluation, expectations, and behavior profoundly affect the individual. This is an important facet of understanding the political factors of a situation, given that one's aim in politics is to influence the behavior of others.

To influence a person's group role, one may have to influence others in the group. On the other hand, group members may be reacting mainly to special features of the major player's personality. In this case, it may be easier to modify the behavior of the individual than to change the attitudes and behaviors of all the group members.

For example, suppose the Congressional staffer of a major Senate committee, in a period of stringent cost constraint, is asked by nursing lobbyists to include nurses as providers under Medicare. He does not favor the idea. He claims that an action of this nature will be an add-on cost and not a cost-savings measure as the nurses argue it would.

Obviously, from the nurses' perspective, this person's thinking must be influenced to support their position. But first, it would be essential to know whether the response represented "party line" thinking (reflecting loyalty and responsibility to his or her reference group, eg, political party, department, committee, or other group) or whether the position was a reflection of his or her personality and values. This preliminary analysis would be fundamental to pursuing the issue further.

Bales' model examines each person in a given group. It advises us to pick out strategic pairs, trios, and larger coalitions within the group. Bales also suggests it is important to examine the way the values and beliefs of individuals conflict with those of others in the group.

Most importantly, Bales' model tells how power is being transferred back and forth in the group. Power is defined as the ability to control or dominate the actions of others. For instance, speaking in a small group is exercising power over the other members during that time. Observing who speaks how much and to whom can clarify the major power holders. In interactions, persons tend to maintain continuity with regard to who communicates with whom. Thus, the power holders tend to remain constant.

Political situations, then, represent the psychosocial systems that need to be analyzed in psychologically meaningful terms such as motivations, values, and ideologies, psychodynamics, and the personalities of the actors.

Political scientists have concentrated too heavily on the social backgrounds and other social characteristics of the political player (ie, age, sex, race, and geographic region) in search of the causal link between the individual and political behavior. Social characteristics provide descriptions of phenomena; but explanations of political situations that rely upon sociological analysis fail to explain why an individual behaves the way he does, which is the most critical information to a politician.

WHAT MAKES A GOOD POLITICIAN?

Persons who enjoy interacting with others are most effective in political situations. They participate more in political activities. Not much empirical research has been conducted in the area of personality as it relates to political activity, but the work that has been done examining electoral politics clearly demonstrates that individuals who relate well to others are the ones that make the best politicians. Studies have demonstrated that individuals who score highest in sociability also score highest in political efficacy and political participation. Persons with self-confidence are more likely to be politically active. Individuals who rank high in ego strength participate in politics to a greater extent than those who rank low in this area; and political participation was found to be most highly correlated with striving to fulfill self-actualization needs (Maraldo, 1984; Milbrath & Goel, 1977).

Thus, a profile of a politically active person is someone who is gregarious, self-confident, and psychologically stable enough in basic areas to pursue higher level needs. Several political researchers have asserted that persons with neurotic problems will probably not be attracted to political action in a democracy (Milbrath & Goel, 1977).

But there is more to politics than enjoying daily social exchanges with others. Politicians are not simply managers or administrators, or actors, or nurses. At their best, politicians are a different breed. Often politicians are thought to be drawn to political situations because of needs for power and ambition. Not true. Take a peanut farmer from Georgia who serves one term as governor and decides that he wants to be president. In less than four years he makes it. Ambitious? Yes, but it is not ambition alone. He could have moved into a corporate setting, bought more farmland, or started a new business empire. Power? In Jimmy Carter's last days in the White House, the mayor of Dayton, Ohio is said to have had more power than the president.

President Reagan provides another example of the nature of politics. "Dutch" Reagan started off as a sports announcer with an ambition for acting. At twenty-six, he took off for Hollywood to satisfy his deepest ambition. After his first screen test, he signed on with Warner Brothers. As an actor, his principle outlet for leadership was union work. In his second year in Hollywood, the Screen Actors Guild put Reagan on its board as representative of the young contract actors. He served the Guild for twenty-two years, six as president. Reagan's move into partisan politics was not driven by ambition as was his acting career. His political career moved at a much slower pace.

He became "hooked" on politics as a Democrat for Nixon, delivering over 200 speeches for the Republican presidential nominee. Neither was power the drive behind Reagan's entry into politics. At the time, friends and colleagues report, he was more interested in developing his acting career.

Any politician worth his salt is aware that making it to the top does not ensure power. Although ambition is necessary, it is not the same ambition that leads one to the heights of a career in law or nursing or economics. Remember that Woodrow Wilson said, "The profession I chose was politics; the profession I entered was law. I entered one because I thought it would lead to the other."

The point is that the politician—no matter what his or her profession—wants to act in the political arena. What interests him or her most is not running a large organization, be it a corporation, or a membership association, or a hospital. His or her major drive has its roots in the rough-and-tumble and day-to-day conflict. It's the cause, the battle, the confrontation, the crisis that makes the blood surge through a politician's veins. The daily combat does not tire or frighten him or her; he thrives on it.

Since power is transient and elusive, a good politician knows he or she must make his or her own. Assumptions about what will happen in political situations bloom and fade so rapidly that a skilled politician must form new coalitions by the moment and for the moment. Alliances change from occasion to occasion and issue to issue based on the personalities in the situation and what they want from the exchange.

Besides the sheer delight he or she takes in it, what distinguishes a good politician from the rest of the world is the ability to know what "makes people tick." In Bales' model, this translates into acquiring a grasp of others' personalities and value systems. This demands some understanding of human behavior, but nurses are good at that. It is said, for example, that President Carter could never remember how to pronounce Congressman Jim Santini's (Nevada) last name. Santini's was the one vote by which hospital cost-containment failed in the House of Representatives during the Carter administration. Politics begins at this basic human level.

Knowing how to read human behavior leads to the capacity to see the heart of things, detecting the point on which the controversy depends. Reagan won the 1980 presidential election because he, not Carter or Anderson, articulated an approach to governance and provided a vision about America's future direction. Political leaders reduce uncertainty about the future, not because they have ready-made answers, but because they express essential tenets that strike a responsive chord among constituents because of the values they embody.

One may fault President Reagan for his policies, but not his political instincts. In early 1984, a member of the American Association of Retired Persons (AARP) was bemoaning the fate of Medicare and the recent cutbacks. When asked how the 16 million AARP members would voice their concerns in the upcoming election, the individual responded, "Oh, they'll support the president. They're angry about the cutbacks, but they don't blame President Reagan. They fault the administration and don't associate the cutbacks with the president." That is political genius at its best.

Perhaps most important in making a good politician is flexibility. The maneuverability that comes from following political instincts (or interpersonal sensitivities) allows for priorities that shift from one minute to the next. The rapid-fire sequence of trade-offs, compromises, smoke screens, and power plays that constitute the political world demand skillful posturing and gearshifting. The ability to move quickly to another set of agendas should not be construed as "selling out" or immoral behavior. To the contrary, this is politics at its best. The political actor is simply moving in synchrony to the nuances, emotions, undertones, and overtones.

NURSING'S POLITICAL SCORECARD

Considering its beginnings, nursing fares well in politics. Nurses hold high political positions (governmental as well as nongovernmental) throughout the nation. Indeed, nursing has come a long way from the days when its only political concern was the Nurse Training Act.

There is now a much keener awareness of the potential power that resides in the number of nurses as the largest group of providers in every hospital in the country. Numbers are the lifeblood of politics. Representatives are attentive around election time when they hear about the numbers of nurses in their district. This was the likely political impetus for legislation to establish a National Institute of Nursing (NIN).

In the summer of 1983, a Republican Congressman, who was a prominent member of a health committee in the House of Representatives, suggested to a group of nurses that a proposal to establish NIN be developed. He would introduce it if the major nursing groups could agree on it. Even though the Congressman's initiative may have arisen from a deep, longstanding commitment to nursing, it is equally important to realize that the representative knew Republicans had not received high marks on women's issues. Seeing nursing, a profession that is 97% women, he seized the opportunity to gain their support by introducing the NIN measure as part of a bill to reorganize NIH. In fact, Edward Madigan (R-Ill) and his colleagues deserve much credit and support for introducing and nurturing the legislation in the Congress. The bill passed in the House of Representatives, ultimately in the Senate, only to be vetoed by President Reagan in the fall of 1984.

This passage, despite opposition of the leadership of NIH and the administration, is testimony to the strength nursing can have if unified. The achievement of unity, however, was precarious. Indeed, at several junctures, support for the NIN was in jeopardy for several reasons.

First, it is simple for any lawmaker to dismiss nurses and nursing issues when nursing groups don't agree. In the case of the NIN, although the Tri-Council for Nursing (the American Nurses' Association, the National League for Nursing, and the American Association of Colleges of Nursing) were in agreement in supporting the proposal, others in nursing's vocal ranks were not (Commentary, 1984).

The second problem encountered by nursing in legislative matters is that everybody wants to be directly involved. Yet the complex communication networks that exist in any given political situation involve an equally complicated set of exchanges, negotiations, affections, and disaffections that distant political actors are not privy to and do not understand. Nursing should have faith in its lobbyists and permit them flexibility and decision-making power on legislative matters. If the lobbyist's judgment is poor, he or she should not hold the position.

The NIN scenario gathered many distant actors along the way that complicated the picture. Partially, the legislative process itself was to blame. Gathering the complete undivided support from the nursing community was impossible—given the short turnaround time from the introduction of the bill. Yet, there was room for improvement with regard to the human approach to the situation. The proposal was developed in a hostile environment. The National Institutes of Health, the medical community, and the administration opposed it. It was developed as a complete package, just waiting to be picked apart. In the political arena, when substantial opposition is anticipated, the first move is to win over key players, encouraging them to see the merits of your proposal (players within the nursing community as well as the Congress). It is during *this* process that the proposal takes shape. The final product is a combination or amalgamation of the brainstorms and leanings of nursing's key opinion leaders. Flexibility in developing proposals little by little, player by player, in an unfriendly environment is the only way a self-respecting politician would proceed.

In defense of politics, this flexibility (perhaps considered a piecemeal approach to its opponents) is its beauty. Staunch ideologues may refer to behavior of this sort as selling out or as prostituting one's values. But in a pluralistic society, a rigid adherence to an ideology is considered to be myopic, self-serving, and narrow-minded.

In the end, politics saves us from having one disagreeable notion imposed on us. Politics deals with a balance of special interests, to protect us from harsh government or subjection to an unpalatable ideology. Politics is what freedom and democracy are all about.

References

Bales RF: *Personality and Interpersonal Behavior.* Holt, Rinehart and Winston, 1970.
Commentary: Should there be a National Institute for Nursing? *Nurs Outlook* 1984; 32:74+.
Maraldo P: *Open-Closed Mindedness.* (Dissertation.) New York University, New York, NY, 1984.
Milbrath LW, Goel ML: *Political Participation,* 2nd ed. Rand McNally, 1977.
Wilhoite FM: *The Politics of Massive Resistance.* Braziller, 1973.
Weber M: *Economy and Society.* Bedminster Press, 1968.

Chapter 9

Two Perspectives on Power

Power in Nursing

Vernice D. Ferguson, RN, MA, FAAN, FRCN

Power is generally not associated with nursing. The media and many organizations refer to the power of corporations, trade unions, and medical associations, for example, but seldom to the power of nursing. On the contrary, nursing and nurses are often perceived as powerless, particularly by physicians, the acknowledged power group in the health care system. Kennedy (1984) found that physicians are reluctant to build trust relationships within the hospital except with nurses—whom they feel they control. They do not perceive nurses as part of the hospital hierarchy, but rather as personal possessions.

Many nurses are uncomfortable with the idea of power, particularly personal power. Nursing as a profession, however, is acknowledging its right to and need for collective or collaborative power. Those at the heart of this change, though sometimes the target of criticism, are leading the way toward a new era in American nursing.

> Confronting those in the health care system who react with anger toward nurses who are breaking stereotypes and demanding nurses' rights can be an exhilarating experience, particularly to those who are skilled in the art of confrontation. Role-breakers must be knowledgeable regarding the issues, articulate in expressing them, and skilled in using confrontation and negotiation to gain their ends—a leadership role in the health care of this country, power to control our own profession and autonomy for our individual practitioners (Grissum & Spengler, 1976, p 248).

DEFINITION AND SOURCES OF POWER

Power is the ability to do or act. It is the possession of control or command over others. Power is access. It is the ability to deliver goods and services on your terms. Power is achievement of the desired result.

Power is multidimensional. In planning strategies, one must understand the dimensions of power relevant to the prevailing environment, circumstances, and the goals to be achieved. In a period of stability, when the majority is comfortable with the prevailing mood and circumstance, the individual has little leverage. When restlessness is pervasive, and the status quo is unacceptable, the individual's power and leverage are enormous. Individuals and groups who can assess the environment and understand the dimension of power are positioned to become more powerful.

Power is derived from specific sources or bases. Five bases were identified by French and Raven (1959) and expanded on by Hersey, Blanchard, and Natemeyer (1979), yielding a typology of seven power bases—coercive, reward, legitimate, expert, referent, information, and connection power. Understanding these derivatives makes possible analysis and prediction of individual and organizational behavior.

Coercive power is rooted in real or perceived fear of one person by another. *Reward power* affects behavior as one person perceives the potential for rewards or favors by honoring the wishes of a powerful person. *Legitimate power* derives from an organizational position or title rather than from a personal quality. *Expert power* comes from knowledge, special talents, and skills; it is person power as contrasted with position power. *Referent power* is apparent when a subordinate identifies with and follows the direction of a leader based on admiration and belief. *Information power* results when one individual has (or is perceived to have) special information that another individual desires. Persons are accorded *connection power* when they are thought to have a privileged connection with powerful individuals or organizations.

How one uses the power bases is determined by one's power "orientation," or how one perceives and values power (Heineken & McCloskey, 1985). Cavanaugh (1979) identified six possible power orientations:

Power as good: A belief that power is natural and desirable. This orientation fosters a positive attitude and probable use of reward, legitimate, and expert power bases.

Power as resource dependency: A belief that power depends on possession of resources, such as knowledge and information. An individual with this orientation will likely use information power, withholding rather than sharing valuable information.

Power as instinctive drive: A belief that the desire for power is inherent rather than learned. This orientation often implies use of referent power, the influence of a "power" person.

Power as charisma: The belief that certain individuals exude a special magnetism giving them power over others. Such an orientation can lead to election of leaders on the basis of personality and charm rather than actual qualifications for a particular position.

Power as political: The belief that links power with an ability to successfully negotiate "the system." This orientation draws on referent and connection power.

Power as control and autonomy: The belief that power depends on controlling others. An individual with this orientation may combine the use of coercion, information, and connection power.

Understanding the sources or bases of power and the types of power orientation can help nurses analyze the dynamics of power in specific situations. Fortunately, the study of power and politics is beginning to find its way into nursing education even as nurses in practice are beginning to apply these concepts toward positive change.

Washington, DC, is a city of the powerful and the would-be powerful. The following examples offer insight into power and its sources. During a major thunderstorm in the Cleveland Park section of Washington, home of many powerful people, a junior senator's wife telephone a senior senator's wife and asked: "Do you have power?" The senior senator's wife replied, "Power over whom?" Status symbols and trappings of power once included long chauffeur-driven limousines, elegant offices, and a hierarchy of secretaries making the powerful boss almost inaccessible. Today new power symbols have emerged, one of which is the entourage that surrounds powerful leaders in public, responding to orders, offering information, and just being available. Members of this entourage can also act as gatekeepers, granting or denying access to the powerful.

THE NEED FOR POWER

Nursing comprises a predominantly female work force. Two-thirds of all nurses work in hospitals, which are male-dominated power structures. Furthermore, the majority of these nurses spend most of their time in direct patient care as staff nurses (DHHS National Sample Survey, 1980). The functions of governance and management are not usually identified with nurses at this level in the organization. In recent years, nurse administrators have made gains, achieving increasing recognition at the top management level and in some instances, in the governance arena. The ease with which these leaders are removed from their positions, however, reminds us that longevity and role acceptance by others have not been assured (American Hospital Association, 1980).

Nurses need power to ensure their ability to provide competent, humanistic, affordable care to people. Nurses need power to help shape health policy, power commensurate with their knowledge and experience as the care givers closest to patients. Nurses need power proportionate to their number and their right to be heard. They need power to alter the disproportionate leverage of physicians who represent only 7.3 percent of the total health care labor force, yet exert enormous decision-making power within the health care system. Nurses need power to ensure that nursing is an attractive career option for "the best and the brightest" women and men who expect to influence nursing, health care, and health policy.

Some questions for nurses who seek power include:
• What expertise do I own from which I can gain power?

- How can I be perceived as powerful when that is important?
- What can I do to encourage collaboration so that collectively nursing can increase its participation and influence in decision making?
- How can we as nurses gain and maintain power commensurate with our responsibility and contribution to health care?
- In a particular situation, was it important that I simply carry out policy or should I have been involved in shaping it?

POWER THROUGH INTERDEPENDENCE

Nursing is only beginning to learn the benefits of collective action, mutual support, and interdependence. By acknowledging their own expertise and that of their peers, nurses increase the power of all nurses (Boyle, 1984). Sharing expertise gives nursing a "positive sum" power base in which the whole is greater than the sum of its parts. This approach differs greatly from a "zero sum" power base, in which a system has a fixed amount of power, and one person's gain means another's loss of power (Beck, 1982).

In addition to interdependence within nursing, nurses need to discover, according to Styles (1982), that "there is power where our claims overlap those of other claimants and form a basis for forging coalitions in the negotiation. Where do our goals merge with those of consumers or other professional groups with respect to needed reimbursement or management reform?"

POWER THROUGH EXPERTISE

Power is gained, maintained, and expanded as nurses give sustained attention to perfection of practice, education for practice, research to improve practice, and administrative activity to enable practice. The emergence and performance of competent and confident clinical nurse specialists, nurse practitioners, nurse researchers, and nurse administrators offer the surest way of establishing and sustaining nursing's power base in health care (Fagin, 1982).

The nation's labor force increasingly comprises college graduates. Professionals and managers now hold one out of four of the nation's jobs (Ginzberg, 1979). This is significant as nurses compete for increased participation in management, governance, planning, and policy development in the health care system. Nurses must value scholarship and continually translate it to practice. Knowledge is power. Those who possess it and use it well can influence and often control events, money, and people.

POWER IN CARING

Nurses need to acknowledge to themselves and to each other the power inherent in caring. As Benner (1984) writes:

I am concerned when I hear nurses say that the very qualities essential to their caring role are the source of their powerlessness in the male-dominated hospital hierarchy. Such a statement disparages feminine qualities and elevates a masculine view of power, one that emphasizes competitiveness, domination, and control. But to define power or nursing exclusively in traditional masculine or feminine terms is a mistake. The disparagement of feminine perspectives on power is based on the misguided assumption that feminine values have kept women and nursing subservient, rather than recognizing that society's devaluing of and discrimination against women are the source of the problem (p 207).

Benner identifies six different qualities of power associated with the caring provided by expert nurses: transformative, integrative, advocacy, healing, participative/affirmative, and problem solving.

Caring nurses can help their patients in such a way that the patients' lives can be permanently *transformed*. One young man entered a long and complicated illness feeling helpless, unattractive, and socially deficient. The nursing care he received made a profound impression. Formerly believing that life is a contract that gives you only what you earn, the young man emerged from the illness with the view that sometimes you get what you are unable to ask for.

Through caring, nurses *reintegrate* individuals into their meaningful life activities despite prolonged illness or permanent disability. Nursing's ability to interpret patient to doctor and doctor to patient is what Benner terms *advocacy power*—helping the patient retain some control over his or her life.

Caring has the power to *heal*. By establishing a healing relationship and creating a healing climate, the nurse evokes the patient's internal and external resources, sometimes described as "the placebo effect."

Benner describes the *participative/affirmative* power of caring as an engagement and involvement in a demanding situation and gaining strength from that involvement. A caring involvement is essential to expert, creative problem solving because it makes the nurse sensitive to subtle cues that aid in the search for solutions. "To abandon the power inherent in caring relationships is to . . . become alienated from our own identity and to thwart our own excellence. Ultimately, our power in terms of mastery, status, and control over our own practice depends on excellence" (Benner, p 216).

GOVERNANCE AND INFLUENCE

Recently, attention has been focused on the formulation of bylaws in organized nursing service. These bylaws become the organizational mandate for self-governance of the nursing department and professional nurses (see Chapter 21). Through bylaws, professional nurses in an organized clinical department ensure commitment and accountability for the decisions affecting nursing. The nursing department's bylaws are a powerful instrument for the recognition of nursing as a professional discipline in control of nursing within the health care institution.

Bylaws also become a tool to enhance the socialization and professionalism of nurses. Reaching consensus on the organization, administration, and practice of a department of nursing fosters accountability. Involving nurses in the decision-making process enhances group cohesiveness, a requirement for a profession that would be powerful in the larger social order.

ACQUISITION OF SKILLS

"Power is assumed, not bestowed. Acknowledging that nurses, as individuals and as a profession, need and want power is the first step in gaining it" (Persons & Wieck, 1985). Nurses have taken that first step. The next steps include acquiring and developing a deeper understanding of the dynamics of power and the skills related to it:

- communication
- persuasion
- negotiation
- leadership
- parliamentary procedure
- group dynamics
- networking

Citing the number of nurses as a potential powerful force is not enough. A group's wealth, its organizational cohesiveness, and the importance of the organization to the social system are critical to its effectiveness as a powerful and influential force. Nursing must plan its strategic agenda, giving full consideration to each of these factors and their dynamic interface. Achieving nursing's goals of autonomy in patient care, economic security, and professional status requires full participation and commitment from all members.

Frederick Douglass, the abolitionist, orator, and journalist, said:

> If there is no struggle, there is no progress. Those who profess to favor freedom, and yet deprecate agitation, are men who want crops without plowing up ground. They want rain without thunder and lightning. They want the ocean without the awful roar of its many waters. Power concedes nothing without a demand. It never did and it never will.

These words are instructive to nursing as it seeks to understand and use power on behalf of the public it is privileged to serve.

References

American Hospital Association: Profile of the nursing service administrator revisited. In: The 1977 Survey of Nursing Service Administrators in Hospitals. AHA, 1980.

Beck CT: The conceptualization of power. *Adv Nurs Science* 1982; 4:1–2.

Benner P: *From Novice to Expert: Excellence and Power in Clinical Nursing Practice.* Addison-Wesley, 1984.

Boyle K: Power in nursing. *Nurs Outlook* 1984; 32:164–167.

Cavanaugh MS: A formulative investigation of power orientations and preliminary validation of relationships between power orientations and communications. Dissertation, University of Denver, 1979.

Department of Health and Human Services: National Sample Survey of Registered Nurses. DHHS, 1980.

Fagin C: Nursing's pivotal role in American health care. In: *Nursing in the 1980's: Crises, Opportunities, Challenges.* Aiken L, Gortner S (editors). Lippincott, 1982.

French JRP, Raven B: The bases of social power. In: *Studies in Social Power.* Cartwright D (editor). University of Michigan, 1959.

Ginzberg E: The professionalization of the U.S. labor force. *Scientific Amer* 1979; 240: 48–53.

Grissum M, Spengler C: *Womanpower and Health Care.* Little, Brown, 1976.

Heineken J, McCloskey J: Teaching power concepts. *J Nurs Educ* 1985; 24:40–41.

Hersey P, Blanchard K, Natemeyer W: Situational leadership: Perception and impact of power. *Group Org Studies* 1979; 4:418–28.

Janik A: Power base of nursing in bargaining relationships. *Image* 1984; 16:93–96.

Kennedy MM: *Power base: How to build it: How to keep it.* Macmillan, 1984.

Persons C, Wieck L: Networking: A power strategy. *Nurs Econ* 1985; 3:53–57.

Styles, M: *On Nursing: Toward a New Endowment.* Mosby, 1982.

Women and Power*

Rhetaugh G. Dumas, RN, PhD, FAAN

Inherent in the notions about women and power are some complex dilemmas posed, on the one hand, by the traditional gender stereotypes and the desire to transcend them, and, on the other hand, by the fear of powerful women that lies hidden just beneath rationality not only among men but among women as well.

At the Yale School of Nursing, we faced such a dilemma during the sixties. We were charting new directions for the school. We were pioneering clinical nursing research and therefore operating on the cutting edge in the scientific development of nursing. We were negotiating new relationships within the school and between the school and other units of the university. Before these were settled, we were being challenged by the civil rights movement, the black power movement, and the contemporary women's rights movement to expand our perspective beyond traditional psychological, social, and cultural boundaries of mission and goals. We were being pressured by groups and organizations within the New Haven communities to pay greater attention to their respective prerogatives and needs. Some of our colleagues in nursing education were challenging our strong emphasis on research at the master's level, which they believed was more appropriate to doctoral preparation. Within the profession, nursing roles were expanding and nurses were having to deal with the resistance of colleagues in other disciplines. The demand for "community control" signaled the rise of a stronger consumerism that raised critical issues concerning the balance of power between consumers and health care providers. It was during those times of turmoil and exciting advances that Donna Diers and I worked to better understand the dynamics that were

*Adapted by permission from address delivered at Yale and reprinted in *The Yale Nurse*, September 1984.

occurring within the faculty as a whole and among the various subgroups. All were women struggling to gain greater power within the School of Nursing and on a number of fronts outside. None was willing to admit to their fierce competitive strivings nor to their power tactics. They also lacked the awareness that often we were probably as frightened by the prospects of success as by the fear of failure. The struggle continues and is more intense today in the groups and organizations in which we live and work. Without that struggle there is no progress. Power is an important consideration in all social relationships, often unacknowledged among women. Whether or not they acknowledge it, people (and women are not exempt) are concerned about their ability to influence the events that have important implications for their lives, and this ability may not exist without some degree of power.

FEAR OF POWERFUL WOMEN AND FEAR OF BEING POWERFUL

The myth of the weaker sex appears overtly to have been attenuated, but covertly it is lurking in the crevices of the minds of women as well as men. I propose that this myth functions to conceal the fear of powerful women and the fear of being powerful. There is implicit support for this proposition in the works of Freud, more explicit in Melanie Klein. Wolfgang Lederer (1968) has perhaps the most explicit treatment of this issue in his book entitled, *The Fear of Women*. He speaks only of man's fear of women. Of all the things that occupy the thoughts of men, he says, relationships with women are perhaps the most basic. These relationships have been variously described in other literature and in conversations as intricate, perplexing, elusive, and so on. Lederer presents cases in which strong men fret about their experiences in relation to women. Their fantasies contradict the notion that women are shy, timid, or weak. Rather, women are seen as powerful and inescapable beings who arouse in men feelings of inadequacy, anger, bewilderment, fear, horror, awe, and at the same time, love, devotion, and dependence. The myth of the weaker sex masks these feelings and stereotypes of masculine and feminine roles and forces society to consider the recognition and expression of such fears unmanly and hence unacceptable behavior. While overt expression can be suppressed, its impact is nonetheless powerful. The fear is manifested covertly and has far-reaching ramifications in the lives of men and women. Fantasies about the power of women and what will happen if this power is unleashed prompt men and women to hold potentially powerful women in check. Even today, many women are threatened by reference to their aggressive and competitive strivings or their power potential. Their strivings and struggles for power find expression in subtle, passive-aggressive behavior.

THE NEGATIVE IMAGE OF POWER

When I began to speak publicly about women and power ten years ago, many of my colleagues in nursing became anxious. They denied having any interest in power, and they were concerned that I would convey the "wrong impression" to our colleagues in other disciplines and to the public. In their thinking, the concept of power and the concept of nursing as a helping profession were incompatible. They stressed the importance of concepts such as leadership, teamwork, cooperation, and collaboration without realizing that success in achieving these relationships involves the exercise of power.

They stressed the role of nurse as change agent, apparently unaware that the concept of change and the concept of power are inextricably tied together. They were unwilling to examine how nurses use power, because they were preoccupied with the negative connotations of the concept. The saying that power corrupts, and absolute power corrupts absolutely held special meaning for them. They believed that power exists in some fixed quantity, and that the exercise of power by one person or group renders another or others powerless. They associated power only with conflict, ignoring the fact that power can also foster cooperation. The desire to avoid conflict reinforced their resistance to deal openly with power issues. While some resistance still remains, larger numbers of nurses are realizing the need to give greater attention to this concept. Furthermore, issues regarding women and power, although still somewhat elusive in the minds of many, are being viewed as relevant to the status and progress of the nursing profession. That is progress.

SOCIALIZATION AND STEREOTYPING

There is still much work to be done to overcome the pitfalls of the early socialization of males and females, pitfalls that perpetuate gender stereotypes and retard progress towards ensuring equal rights for women in this society. This is not to discount our progress toward this goal. We have come a long way since the early days in New England when Anne Hutchinson challenged church and state on behalf of new ideas of tolerance and religious freedom and questioned for the first time the validity of the place assigned her because of her sex. Or when Lucretia Mott, Elizabeth Cady Stanton, and Susan B. Anthony championed the cause for women's suffrage, and since the time that Sojourner Truth, a former slave, turned the full force of her eloquent elocution against those who ridiculed women as too weak and helpless to be entrusted with the vote. That was in 1851 at a women's rights convention in Akron, Ohio. One of the women present seemed unable to answer an outbreak of heckling, and it looked as if their cause would be worsened at their own gathering. Truth gained the podium over the objections of many of the women who feared that she might do greater harm to the cause. Nevertheless, the chairperson gave her permission to speak—and she saved the day.

With a gesture that electrified the audience, Sojourner Truth raised her black arm (in defense of women's causes and in demand for the respect and rights they deserve).

Look at my arm, I have ploughed and planted and gathered into barns, and no man could head me—and ain't I a woman? I could work as much and eat as much as a man—when I could get it—and bear the lash as well—and ain't I a woman? I have born thirteen children, and seen most of them sold into slavery, and when I cried out with my mother's grief, none but Jesus heard me—and ain't I a woman?

Lucretia Mott, Elizabeth Cady Stanton, Susan B. Anthony, and their followers paved the way for the work for equal rights for women under the Constitution of the United States. That work continues to this very day.

Attitudes towards women have been changing. We have witnessed increasing efforts to eliminate sex-role stereotypes and discrimination. Educational opportunities have continued to expand and women have now reached parity with males in the median number of years of schooling completed. Career opportunities are expanding, and there have been progressive increases in the number of women in the labor force. Small numbers of women now head business enterprises. The number of women in high governmental positions has increased considerably. None could have occurred without some degree of power; yet we still have far to go before true equality is achieved.

In 1984 women comprised 53 percent of the voting population in this country but held only 12 percent of all public offices. There was only one woman serving as governor of her state, and seven women serving as lieutenant governors. Two women were members of the president's cabinet; one woman was on the Supreme Court; one on the Federal Reserve Board; one woman was named general counsel for the National Labor Relations Board; and a woman was confirmed as deputy attorney general.

Our power is increasing, but this is still a man's world. Law, architecture, natural sciences, and engineering, for example, are still male professions. Men hold the high academic posts. With only a few exceptions, men are the presidents of the major institutions of higher learning. They head the major economic institutions. They dominate the political arena and the military establishment. The proportion of women to men on boards of trustees of academic institutions is too low to be significant. The privately endowed institutions depend in large part upon the corporate sector for survival. Only a small number of women serve on the boards of directors of large banks and corporations. Although a considerable proportion of the nation's wealth is owned by women, it is controlled by trust officers and executives who are men.

These and other glaring inequities are not likely to change significantly unless women are able to develop and mobilize stronger power bases. Otherwise, we may never fully realize equal rights under the law for all Americans.

POWER IN SOCIAL AND POLITICAL RELATIONSHIPS

In my conceptual schema, power is defined as that force that enables persons or groups to realize their will even against opposition. This definition refers to power in social and political relationships. Thus, a clearer understanding of power demands a clearer understanding of the nature of social and political relationships, the context in which power exists.

By definition, the social relationship refers to the behavior of a plurality of parties in which each party takes into account and is oriented to the behavior of the others (a party might be an individual or a group). According to the Weberian definition: "The social relationship consists entirely and exclusively in the existence of the probability that there will be in some meaningful understandable sense, a course of social action."

For a social relationship to exist, there must be at least a minimum of mutual orientation of each party to the action of the other or others. In general, social relationships can be dynamic, flexible, variable, and they may provide unlimited possibilities for influencing the course of events. It is important to realize that the meaning attached to a social relationship need not be reciprocal. In fact, those in which there is total correspondence between attitudes are often limiting cases. The consistent desire among women for consensus is a signal of the tendency to define social relationships too narrowly.

A social relationship can be temporary or of varying degrees of permanence. The subjective meaning of the relationship may not always remain the same. However, when the subjective meaning remains relatively constant, it is possible to formulate that meaning in terms of maxims that the parties involved expect their partners to adhere to. The more rational the action is in relation to values or to given ends, the more possible this becomes. Rational formulations of the subjective meaning of business relationships are, of course, much easier than those of intimate relationships. Business contracts are easier to formulate, negotiate, and keep than are contracts dealing with emotional relationships and personal loyalty.

SOURCES OF POWER

No one can be truly powerful unless he or she has access to the command of major institutions (Mills, 1956). Not all power is anchored in and exercised by such institutions, but only within and through them can power be more or less continuous and important. Mills continues:

> If we took the one hundred most powerful men in America, the one hundred wealthiest, and the one hundred most celebrated away from the institutional positions they now occupy, away from their resources of men and women and money, away from the media or mass communication that are now focused upon them, then they would be powerless and poor and uncelebrated. For power is not of a man, wealth does not center in the person of the wealthy, celebrity is not inherent in any personality. To be celebrated, to be wealthy, to have power requires access to major institutions, for the institutional positions men occupy determine in large part their chances to have and to hold these valued experiences (pp 10–11).

Mills refers to the power elite—men in positions to make decisions having major consequences. They are in command of the major hierarchies and organizations of modern society. They rule the big corporations. They run the machinery of the state and claim its prerogatives. They direct the military establishment. They occupy the strategic command posts of the social structure. Below the elite, there are those at the middle levels of power—members of Congress, pressure groups, members of the upper class. Although such individuals or groups may not hold top posts in any dominating hierarchy, they are able to gain the ear of those who do hold such positions and who can exercise direct power on their behalf, if they choose to do so.

Zaleznik (1976) describes the initial "capitalization" that makes up an individual's power base. Three elements provide the capital for an individual's power base: (1) the amount of formal authority vested in his or her position, (2) the amount of authority vested in his or her expertise and reputation for competence, and (3) the attractiveness of his or her personality to others—how much he or she is respected or liked. He suggests that the capitalization of power requires one to internalize all the sources of power capital in a manner similar to that in which she or he develops a sense of self-esteem. The individual knows that he or she has power, assesses it realistically, and is willing to risk personal esteem to influence others. To retain this power base, he says, the individual must perform and get results. Attrition in the power base may erode confidence, which often leads to self-doubt and undermines the psychologic work that enabled the individual to achieve power in the first place.

Mills cites society's major economic, social, and political institutions as the primary sources of power, and Zaleznik cites personal characteristics and formal authority as power capital.

Starr (1983) gives a brilliant historical account of how American physicians, who were bitterly divided and financially insecure in the nineteenth century, have united to form one of the most powerful and authoritative professions in the twentieth century. How they have achieved an especially persuasive claim to authority in health affairs, and how they have converted their clinical authority into social and economic privilege and power is instructive.

Medicine was transformed into an authoritative and powerful profession by the interaction of factors related to its internal development and those related to the social, economic, and political context of the times. Social and scientific advances in the late nineteenth century promoted more internal cohesiveness as physicians became more dependent upon each other for referrals and use of facilities. Greater cohesiveness strengthened their authority. Better diagnostic technology strengthened their authority.

Before the profession consolidated its position, some physicians had great personal authority. They offered opinions on all kinds of problems not limited to physical illness. Until the authority of the physician was institutionalized, it remained limited and dependent upon individual character and lay attitudes. Once this authority was institutionalized, standards for education and licensing conferred authority upon all who passed through them. It also regulates the relationships among physicians. People have become increasingly dependent upon medical authority for a variety of gatekeeping functions, and physicians have become dependent upon each other's referrals and sanctions. Both of these developments have contributed to the ability of the profession to confirm and strengthen its authority. The conversion of that authority into power and privilege involved gaining control over the markets for health services and over the various social, economic, and political hierarchies in health-related arenas. That control was gained by shaping the structure of hospitals, insurance, and other private institutions that impinged upon medical practice. Organizational and political arrangements have been important to the rise of the medical profession and to its defeating national health plans that incorporate physicians as employees. Their gatekeeping authority has given physicians a strategic position in relation to health-related organizations. Their authority to decide whether and where to admit patients, to prescribe drugs, and to select expensive equipment gives them greater leverage over hospital policy and wins them good will and financial and political support from drug companies and other businesses that profit from the practice of medicine.

LESSONS FOR TOMORROW

There are lessons here that might be useful to women.

1. Authority is a significant source for generating power—but its greatest value is derived when that authority transcends the mere command of actions—or social authority. We must be able to influence thoughts, ideas, information, and experience. We must have cultural authority. This would mean that we are able to have our definitions of reality, our judgments of meaning and value prevail, and to have them sanctioned as valid.
2. Professionalism and social unity are sources of power.
3. Command or control of markets is a source of power.

Finally, the importance of sound organizational and political strategies can never be overemphasized in any consideration related to women and power. None of this will be effective until we have found ways to diminish the fear of powerful women—by men and women.

Throughout the history of this nation, women have struggled to transcend gender stereotypes of their "place" in society as subordinate to men. They have continued in the quest for the respect and status that they deserve and for more significant numbers in high positions of authority and power in major institutions.

Women are extending the boundaries of "woman's place," and a new woman has been emerging, insisting that neither providence nor anatomy blueprints her for all times. The status and role of women are socially determined and thus subject to social amendment. The broad social policy sanctioning a wider scope of functions and prerogatives and higher positions of authority and power for women will be better not only for women but for society (Reeves, pp 16–17).

References

Lederer W: *Fear of Women.* Grune & Stratton, 1968.
Mills CW: *Power Elite.* Oxford University Press, 1956.
Reeves N: *Womankind: Beyond the Stereotype.* Aldine, 1971.
Starr P: *The Social Transformation of American Medicine.* Basic, 1983.
Zaleznik A: In: *Management for Nurses.* Stone et al. (editors), Mosby, 1976.

Chapter 10

Making a Difference: The Courage to Change

Janet N. Natapoff, RN, EdD

Bridget C. Loetterle, RN, PhD

There is nothing permanent but change.
HERACLITUS, 513 BC

Life shrinks or expands in proportion to one's courage.
THE DIARY OF ANAÏS NIN, 1941

Change is constant and universal. It is an enduring and powerful force—a force we can control. Why a chapter on change in a book on political action, you ask? Political action is change. It occurs because someone wanted to change something and took control of the process.

Creating change takes courage, and nurses who want change must be aware of the difficult but satisfying road ahead. There are powerful groups to confront, such as the American Medical Association and even the legislators. These groups are powerful, but so are we. Some of the techniques for mobilizing our power to create change as well as guidance and inspiration from proven innovators will be found on the following pages. But, why change? Why make the effort? That brings us back to politics again.

The desire for change gives impetus to political action. Almost everything about nursing is determined through the political process. Educational standards, entry into practice, practice definitions, and even payment for services are legislated. Legislative changes, often imposed on nursing from outside, profoundly influence our profession. Instead of being forced to react to these changes, we can use our power to control them.

In the workplace (also political but less obvious), nurses can rally together to bring about desired goals. Sometimes change happens without obvious or deliberate effort on anyone's part. Policies, rules, and regulations, however, are frequently imposed on nurses by others. We want control of our own practice in the workplace, yet this control often eludes us. Many attribute our lack of autonomy to the powerful male-dominated medical profession and hospital administrators. Controlled, planned change can be used to bring power to nursing as well as alter the way hospitals are ruled and health services delivered.

Brooten and her colleagues (1978) define change as "the process which leads to alterations in individual or institutional patterns of behavior." Planned, or controlled change, is defined as a "deliberate and collaborative process involving a change agent and a client system." This kind of productive change occurs when an individual or group intervenes according to a comprehensive strategy.

There are many theories of planned change, and while these are useful, it is often the academician who thrives on them, while the practicing nurse who should make change "bumbles" along. Nurses are more often the recipients rather than the initiators of change. Some understanding of change theory is necessary if ideas are to be implemented. Most of us are familiar with the nursing process, basically a problem-solving approach to organizing and planning care. Change theory is similar. Kurt Lewin (1947, 1951) is the most frequently cited change theorist. Table 10-1 shows how this theory and another by Lippitt (1958) relate to the nursing process.

Stevens (1977) discusses management of continuity and change. Continuity is represented in traditions, patterns of behavior, and policies. At times, these traditions should be preserved. However, continuity for its own sake is meaningless, just as change is when not used to accomplish some well-defined end. Lewin has studied how change is accomplished and how it can be controlled. Change often occurs by coercion, or does not occur at all. Somewhere between coercion and maintenance of the status quo is change that is designed to meet a desired end.

Table 10-1 The Nursing Process and Change Theory

Change Theorist	Nursing Process and Steps in the Change Process			
	Assessment	Planning	Implementation	Evaluation
Lewin	Unfreezing	Unfreezing Moving	Moving Refreezing	Refreezing
Lippitt	1. Identification of need for change 2. Establishment of a change relationship 3. Clarification and diagnosis of system's problem*	3. Clarification and diagnosis of system's problem* 4. Examination of alternative routes and establishing goals	5. Transformation of intentions into actual change efforts	6. Generalization and stabilization of change 7. Termination of the relationship

*This step in Lippitt's theory takes place during the last part of the assessment phase and the first part of the planning phase.

THEORIES OF PLANNED CHANGE

Lewin believes that change is a push-pull situation. There are forces desiring change and sometimes equal or greater forces resisting it. *Driving forces*, desiring change, are in dynamic equilibrium with those opposing it, *restraining forces*. For planned change to occur, driving forces must increase or restraining forces decrease. The first step in Lewin's theory is called *unfreezing*. The balance between forces must be upset. People must become uncomfortable enough with the old system to want to change it.

This first step in Lewin's theory is similar to the first step in the nursing process. Suppose Ms Greene, a 60-year-old woman, has been in bed for several days and now must get up despite her great reluctance. The nurse must determine what might motivate Ms Greene to walk—her driving and restraining forces. This assessment process is completed when the nurse gathers data and plans how to proceed. She determines what will motivate Ms Greene and makes her uncomfortable enough with the status quo that she wants to get up more than she wants to stay in bed. She is "unfrozen." This approach that worked so well with Ms Greene can be used to change complex organizations.

Lewin's second stage is called *moving*. At this point, driving forces have overcome restraining forces, people want change, and positive action is planned. Participants must look at the problem from a different perspective (cognitive redefinition) before they can come up with a novel and workable solution. Then they move in the desired direction. This is similar to the planning and implementation phases of the nursing process. The nurses decide the goal for Ms Greene is not to force her out of bed but to help her want to walk. As a group, facilitated by a leader who helps them to see things differently, they plan a novel approach for Ms Greene. The plan is implemented and she is walking, but how long will she remain walking? Is her desire to return to bed stronger than her desire to remain upright?

Lewin's last stage is called *refreezing*. The idea, now implemented, must be integrated within the larger system and made a part of familiar routines. With repeated practice sessions and sufficient rewards, the new approach becomes automatic. Change has occurred. Ms. Greene is mobile and leaves the hospital. This is the evaluation phase of the nursing process. If something works, keep it. If it does not work, change it. This statement, even if it sounds trite, has important implications.

Planned change does not just happen. It is based on a carefully developed plan using evidence to document the need for change and the actual approach. It relies on research findings to support the correct alternative. If the change should work theoretically but recipients are dissatisfied with it, it can be altered during the moving phase. That is why trials are used to evaluate the idea before it becomes institutionalized. The new idea is harder to alter once it has become frozen into the system. When that occurs, the system must be unfrozen again.

By dividing Lewin's stages into several subphases, Lippitt (1958) developed the theory further (see Table 10-1). These subphases, also similar to the nursing process, are useful to nurses interested in making change. Lippitt emphasized the individual more than Lewin and paid particular attention to the change agent.

In phase 1, the change agent identifies a *need for change* and translates this need into a desire. While the entire system may not become aware of this need, at least some must feel that a more desirable state of affairs is possible. Some will actively resist the idea. The change agent offers help to those who want change and works to increase awareness of the others. The second phase is, therefore, the *establishment of a change relationship*. Here the system to be changed, the target, evaluates the change agent's ability to give help, an important point. The change agent must be prepared to cope with constant evaluation and possible criticism. A mutual assessment takes place between the agent and the target, both evaluating the other's capabilities. Lippitt feels this might be the most significant part of the process. Nurses know this from interactions with patients on a day-to-day basis.

In phase 3, the system's problem is *clarified* or *diagnosed*. The change agent needs information about the system and the change itself. A few days of reading and contemplating are important before the nurse fully understands the problem. In the next phase, the nurse, with the target system, *examines alternative routes and establishes goals*—the planning stage of the nursing process. If the change agent's ideas are supported with results as well as intimate knowledge of the system, success is more likely. In phase 5, the agent *transforms intentions into actual change efforts*. This phase corresponds to Lewin's moving stage and the implementation of the nursing process. At this point, the change agent may begin to step back from the process just as when teaching a patient self-care. If the nurse offers supportive assistance, the patient or political system is likely to continue on the desired path. Without such support, the system may give up.

The next phase involves the *generalization and stabilization of change*. Here the goal is to make the change a permanent characteristic of the system—the refreezing. Positive evaluations and rewards are needed. If the change spreads to other systems, this helps to stabilize it. A nurse who initiates change might want to publicize it and take credit. In doing so, credit is given to the system, bringing further rewards to both system and nurse. This writing about change, or "spreading the word," is new to nursing but long overdue.

The last phase is *terminating the relationship*, a process familiar to nurses. If the change is to become institutionalized, the agent must withdraw or terminate the role as change facilitator. The nurse then moves back into the system, at least temporarily.

With this understanding of the process, the nurse can begin to develop appropriate strategies for implementing change. Chin and Benne (1976) have grouped strategies for change into three categories: empirical-rational, normative-reeducative, and power-coercive.

The *empirical-rational* strategy builds on the idea that individuals are guided by reason, and that they will use self-interest to determine the need for change in behavior. Knowledge is the power that motivates change. Educational campaigns to increase the target system's information will lead to rational decision making.

Another strategy, the *normative-reeducative*, is based on the assumption that humans seek impulse and need satisfaction. They are guided in their actions by social beliefs and norms—a normative culture. Change occurs when people are persuaded that they should abandon their old habits and adopt new needs. People are reeducated to accept a new normative culture. Lewin's and Lippitt's theories draw primarily on normative strategies.

The third strategy, described by Chin and Benne as the *power-coercive*, relies on the use of power by one group or individual to change another. The target system is coerced to change by a more powerful force. Power may be legitimate or illegitimate and may rely on laws and policies, or on bribery, threats, and even extortion. Laws promulgated without consent of the governed are an example of a power-coercive strategy.

These are strategies helpful to nurses who want to make changes. To assist the potential change agent, there are numerous references, many listed at the end of this chapter. After nurses have prepared themselves to make change and fully assess the situation, they select an appropriate strategy and proceed with the plan. This discussion of change theories and strategies, however, is a bit academic. What happens in real life? The following examples illustrate how change has been made by nurses in four spheres.

GOVERNMENT

"Oregon RNs push for, and win, state maternity-care program," declared the headline (Oregon RNs, 1984). This project began in 1982 when two nurses, Mary Ann Curry and Carol Howe, became concerned because they were seeing more women coming to maternity care centers with little or no prenatal care. The unemployment rate in Oregon was high, and there were no funds for medically indigent women not on welfare. At the same time, there was less money available through the new maternal-child block grant because of federal budget cuts and transfer of funds. The two nurses decided to convince the state legislature to provide more money for maternal-child services. They wanted to change things. How did they do it?

First they needed to "unfreeze" the legislators, but they could not just appear at the state house asking for money. They had to gather evidence to convince not only legislators but also voters that a serious problem existed. They conducted a study using volunteer nurses as data collectors to document the need for more money for prenatal services. Timing was crucial. The study had to be completed before the legislative year ended and funding decisions made. The study, admittedly, had weaknesses but timing was more important than design (Curry, 1983). The two are now repeating the study using a different methodology to gather data for future change efforts.

Meanwhile, they had to convince people that a problem existed. They identified concerned segments of the population and enlisted the help of nurses in key spots, including Donna Zajonc, a state legislator, Kristine Gebbie, a director of Oregon's state health division, and Marianne Remey, a state maternal-child health coordinator. The five nurses outlined a plan for action and proceeded to convince legislators of its importance and usefulness through public appearances, speaking at open hearings, and meeting with legislators. Thus, while they were planning the moving phase of the change, they were unfreezing those who could help. They identified allies and used individuals and groups powerful enough to speak for their cause. In Lewin's terms, they had identified driving and restraining forces.

They developed a statewide constituency for improved maternal-child care, outlined a plan for action, implemented that plan, and refroze the system through legislative action. Although they did not identify their change strategy by name, they apparently used the normative-reeducation strategy outlined by Chin and Benne (1976). They changed the political culture and won. Maternal-child services received a higher priority on the legislative agenda. They did this by reeducating the target to a new way of thinking.

The nurses' statements (Oregon RNs, 1984) outline the entire change process. Table 10-2 relates these quotes in the context of Lewin's theory of planned change. The table reduces the contributions of each participant to a few boxes, although each worked throughout the process and made many contributions that do not show in the table. What it *does* show is that nurses can make change. These five nurses were able to influence the state budget to a significant extent.

Making governmental changes means that lawmakers must be convinced that the desired change is more important than changes desired by others. They must also be convinced that the change agents can and will influence significant numbers of voters. Lobbying efforts, described elsewhere in this book, ultimately involve large numbers of people, but the idea for change often comes from a small group of concerned individuals.

WORKPLACE

While making change in the workplace may not involve as many people and resources as legislative efforts do, the process is similar. Resistance may be greater because change affects persons more directly. Their day-to-day routines, job security, or status may be threatened. The change agent, too, is often well known in the organization. The relationship between the change agent and the target system is a vital part of the process, as Lippitt (1958) points out. Many times hospital or agency administrators and physicians act as change agents, and nurses react rather than initiate. Lack of control over practice is commonly expressed by nurses as one reason for dissatisfaction. Yet, nurses have made changes. Some of the most important ones include:

- change from team nursing to primary nursing
- increase in nurse-patient ratios in critical care areas
- humanizing hospital routines to include more rooming-in facilities, flexible visiting hours, and less rigid policies
- elimination of many nonnursing tasks, freeing nurses to provide professional care
- more orientation, staff development, and on-the-job training for nurses
- more nurses in private practice and nurse-owned and -managed health care businesses
- participation on interdisciplinary committees
- experimentation with staffing patterns.

The last change, experimentation with staffing patterns, began in response to two trends in hospitals during the late 1970s. A shortage of nurses forced hospitals to rely on outside agencies to meet staffing needs. Nurses were attracted to these agencies, the

Table 10-2   How Oregon Nurses Changed Funding Mechanism for Maternal-Child Care

	Lewin's Stages of Planned Change		
Change Agent	Unfreezing	Moving	Refreezing
Curry: "The consequences are incalculable."	Collected data on prenatal care Presented testimony using data	Convinced legislators that idea should receive priority	Continued to gather data for future efforts
Howe: "We all pay the costs."	Collected data on prenatal outcomes Organized nurse volunteers	Helped convince legislators that idea should receive priority	Continued to gather data for future efforts
Zajonc: "We did our homework. . . . We had a plan."	Identified key people	Helped organize statewide constituency Worked with legislators	
Remey: "Access is critical."		Developed document for legislators outlining plan for expansion of services	
Gebbie: "We had to set priorities."	Identified key people	Helped develop statewide plan	Implemented plan after funding
Legislators			Increased funds for maternal-child services

Quotations from: Oregon RNs win battle to upgrade maternity services. *Am J Nurs* 1984; 84:111.

second trend, because they could set their hours and felt more in control of their practice.

Directors of nursing, together with staff nurses, began experimenting with staffing patterns based on hospital needs and nurses desires. The result is flextime, a change initiated in a few hospitals by small groups of nurses. The nurses started by collecting data about why colleagues quit, patient care needs during different hours of the day, and the cost of traditional staffing (including overtime). Patient care needs and the cost-effectiveness of flexible staffing patterns were emphasized (Price, 1981; Dison, 1981).

When nurses want to make changes, they must be prepared to support their ideas with facts and figures. This means they must anticipate possible questions and use research findings to substantiate strategies. It is also helpful to determine trends. A program is more likely to be accepted if it is in harmony with current ideas, policies, and

Figure 10-1   Flow Sheet for Change from Standard to Flextime Staffing

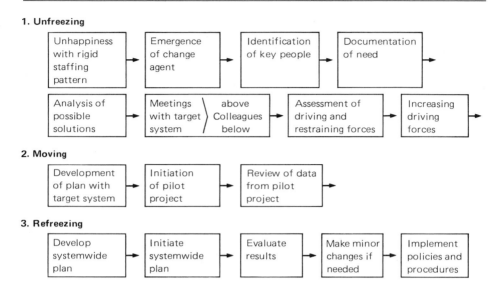

even language. In this case, cost-effectiveness was emphasized. All this helps in the unfreezing process.

To decrease resistance, pilot projects were started on individual units. Data about effectiveness were collected. Instead of changing an entire hospital, nurses initiated change on one unit. Because the nurses in one area were involved in the change, they were the pushers—the ones who wanted change. Superiors had to be persuaded, perhaps using one of the models suggested by Rappsiller (1982). Results of the pilot projects were analyzed, and changes made throughout the hospitals. This process of introducing flex time is diagrammed in flow sheet format (see Figure 10-1). Developing such a flowchart is a helpful technique for a change agent during the assessment and planning phases. Details of how the goal in each box is to be met would be included with the actual proposal for change.

Articles written by nurses involved in the change appeared in the nursing journals. Flextime spread to many institutions. Analysis indicates that there is less need to hire agency nurses, and the various plans are cost-effective. The effect on patient care and well-being, however, has yet to be documented. This missing piece should be considered before the change becomes "frozen" into the system. An important part of the change process is to evaluate results of the change before it becomes institutionalized. It is easier to try another idea during the moving phase of change than during the last phase of refreezing.

PROFESSIONAL ORGANIZATIONS

Professional organizations are composed of "rank and file" members and what many consider an elite corps of leaders. This may be more image than reality. Through our professional organizations, we can gain power to increase the effectiveness of political participation through collective action. Nurses tend to believe, however, that their professional organizations do little for them.

A group of nurses wanted to form a political action committee formally affiliated with the state nurse's association. The board of directors did not support the idea and voted against formal endorsement and affiliation. The nurses interested in making the change brought the proposal to the floor of the annual convention for debate. Members voted to form an official political action arm, but again the board of directors turned down the proposal. What to do now? Give up? Change the board?

The involved nurses analyzed forces for and against the proposal and decided the impediment to change was the board leadership. What could be done to remove this obstacle? They decided to get someone on the nominating committee who could influence the committee enough to propose a candidate in favor of their idea. The person selected to run for the nominating committee had to be someone who could win but also someone valued by the organization's leaders. A known "loyalist" who could garner votes (an analysis of forces was done first to see who could win) was selected and agreed to run.

After winning election to the nominating committee, the nurse used her influence within the committee and the result was a presidential candidate in favor of the change who later won and supported the development of a political action arm of the association. It was not an easy process, however, and it took time, as planned change often does. The nurses interested in making the change spent considerable effort analyzing forces for and against the idea as well as the electoral process itself. Figure 10-2 illustrates some of the driving and restraining forces considered by the change agents. To bring about the desired results, they had to increase the weight of driving forces and decrease the restraining—a necessary part of planned change.

There are numerous examples of change brought about by professional organizations. Many nurses have participated in collective bargaining, one of the most effective ways an organization can bring about change. Because nurses have the backing of their professional colleagues and organizational resources, they are able to bring about more equitable contractual agreements. This has improved the economic status of nursing and working conditions in many hospitals and home health agencies.

Using *power-coercive* techniques (Chin & Benne, 1976), nurses have bargained effectively. They have, for example, learned to use the media. The public is made aware that nurses will strike if contract disputes are not settled. Power-coercive techniques can be used appropriately when change is necessary and other techniques have not been successful.

COMMUNITY

A community is defined as a social system with semipermeable boundaries determined by individuals, interest groups, societies, and even cultural groups. Nurses can participate in or initiate community change as members of community groups such as women's organizations or as nurses in a variety of capacities. Nurses have been involved in community change for generations. Public health nurses have profoundly influenced com-

Figure 10-2   Getting a Political Action Arm: Force-Field Analysis for Making Change (Lewin)

Driving Forces	Change Target	Restraining Forces

A. Forces within society

- Increasing participation in political process → | ←
- Rise of special interest PACs in American politics → | ←

- Belief that politics and political committees are "dirty"
- Vote buying
- Apathy

B. Forces within the organization

- Large portion of membership in favor of change → | ←
- Small committed group with knowledge of how to institute planned change →
- Established electoral process known to all members →

- Feeling by some members, particularly the older established leaders, that participation in politics is unprofessional
- Board of directors opposed to proposal ←

C. Forces within the profession

- Increasing recognition of political action as important for nursing → | ←
- Political action committees (PAC) formed by ANA and many states →

- Ambivalence about political participation
- Apathy ←

D. Forces within the individual (Person selected for nominating committee)

- Loyal member of organization → | ←
- Member of district with largest number of votes →
- Known to many members of district →
- Committed to desired change →
- Respected by other candidates running for nominating committee →

- Unknown to members living in other districts
- Believed to be a "troublemaker" by some members ←
- Only one member of nominating committee ←

Adapted from a diagram by C. Vance, 1984.

munity health and life. Some, notably Lillian Wald and Margaret Sanger, have made important changes that ultimately affected all of us. Nurses have also operated as liaisons between the community and the hospital, as a later example will illustrate.

The first step in making community change is to define the community of interest. Let's see how one nurse did it.

The nurse, together with a hospital chaplain and a community college instructor, decided to plan a hospice facility in a medium-sized town with the backing of a local hospital. This small group found itself in competition with a community-based group, which also wanted a hospice. Boundary battles were the inevitable result. Before any hospice service could be established, the two groups had to define each other's community and find ways to join together across what is often a rigid boundary—the hospital and the community around it. The nurse involved in the change stated that the major factor opposing their goal was the "community atmosphere of noncollaboration, competition, and turf sensitivity" (Theado & Scarry, 1983, p 569). The community members may have said something similar about the hospital-affiliated group.

How did the hospital nurse work with a community that seemed so hostile? She and her colleagues identified their strengths and weaknesses as well as the community's and made compromises where necessary. They included community members in the planning process. Because the nurse was able to articulate concerns of both groups, she emerged as a group leader. The original plan identified the nurse as a bridge between groups, and she worked to implement this part of the plan. As leader, she was also able to act as an advocate for her group's interests. The final product was different from what either group had envisioned at the beginning but acceptable to both.

This change involved cooperation between hospital staff and community residents. In another example, Ida Martensen and Marjorie Jamieson started a block health care program for the elderly in their own neighborhood. Unlike the nurse interested in starting a hospice, they did not have a large, powerful hospital backing them. They worked closely with block residents and community health agencies. As part of the change, the two nurses were able to secure third party reimbursement for their home health service.

The professionals involved in the Martensen project lived in the same community as the recipients and could provide care within a few minutes if called. This exciting project might be duplicated in other communities. "There are nurses living in every community. You just have to locate those nurses and get them working together" (Selby, 1983 p 15).

When working together, nurses must follow a carefully developed plan, or they will drift apart before the change is made. They also have to include influential community people such as those who can arrange for reimbursement, community residents who will be using the service, and community leaders who influence the users. They also will find that the service they provide (or the change they make) will not last unless they gather data about its effectiveness and use this data to "institutionalize" the change, something the block health program leaders did. Institutionalizing a change involves identifying local sources of power who can support that change. These sources may not be the expected political leaders or elected officials. In Harlem, for example, community influentials are the clergy. Without their cooperation, change might not occur.

PROFITING FROM EXAMPLE

The nurses described in the last few pages have been successful change agents. Why? In the unfreezing or assessment stage, each nurse carefully analyzed the situation. They assessed the interest in change, the motivation of involved parties, and the environment within which the change will occur. The nurses then developed strategies. The first step in each plan included mechanisms for increasing the target's readiness for change.

To increase this readiness, the nurses had to arouse discomfort and create tension. They also had to create enough psychological safety to make it possible for the target to pay attention to the discomfort while developing motivation for change rather than resistance.

Brooten recommends developing a power base early in the process. Such a support group has advantages, including numbers (vital for political change), skills to accomplish tasks, credibility, financial support when needed, and contacts. Each of the successful change agents developed a support group as part of the unfreezing or planning phase of making change. This is particularly evident in the Oregon situation where five nurses built a large support group.

Based on assessment data, analysis of target system readiness, and support group input, each change agent developed specific change strategies. These strategies were based on logic and hard facts as well as clear identification of issues. All paid attention to potential and actual resistors. Each change agent also developed a working relationship with the target system before attempting change, thereby gaining respect and acceptance. As stressed by Lippitt (1958), this may be the most important part of the change process.

A relationship of respect is developed between the target and the change agent. The agents must have enough internal leverage (carefully developed by each) to influence the system, but this power leverage alone is not enough. Even power-coercive strategies are built upon a predeveloped relationship between target and agent. Note that the nurses who wanted a political action arm chose a person respected by the target group.

After selecting strategies, each nurse implemented the plan. They did not proceed to the implementation phase (moving) without a plan, and they did not act spontaneously or without thought. The changes they made were planned changes. They controlled the process and the results.

CONCLUSION

This chapter has discussed major theories of planned change, notably by Lewin and Lippitt, and compared these theories with the nursing process. Strategies for implementing change were summarized from Chin and Benne (1976). These ideas of change may be viewed as a continuum from the low key rational model to the midpoint normative model (and most commonly used model) to the high-pressure power-coercive model.

The ultimate goal of planned change is to improve the quality of care and the environment in which we live for our patients, neighbors, and communities. Frances Storlie (1970) helps us to realize that change is always possible if we have the courage of our convictions and are willing to believe that things can be different. She said:

> There is always the dream, deep down, that things can be changed; that those elements of society that chafe can be softened, those laws that bind us excessively need not be—that ordinary man can make himself heard.
>
> I will do nothing to undermine another's dreams, or shed my light on his illusions. For where there are no illusions there can be no dreams; where no dream exists, the spirit dies.
>
> As a nurse, I cherish the dream that quality health care, with dignity, will become a reality for all people. As a member of my organization, I hold the illusion that the status quo can change—will change to welcome challenge and accommodate dissent so that our efforts will be better channeled to the benefit of mankind. . .(p ii).

References

Archer SE, Goehner PA: *Nurses: A Political Force.* Wadsworth Health Sciences, 1982.

Bennis WG, Benne KD, Chin R, Corey KE: *The Planning of Change.* Holt, Rinehart and Winston, 1976.

Brooten DA, Hayman L, Naylor M: *Leadership for Change: A Guide for the Frustrated Nurse.* Lippincott, 1978.

Chin R, Benne KD: General strategies for effecting changes in human systems. Pages 22–45 in: *The Planning of Change,* 3rd ed, Bennis et al. (editors), 1976.

Curry MA: Personal communication, 1983.

Dison CC, Carter N, Bromley P: Making the change to flextime. *Am J Nurs* 1981; 81:2162–64.

Gillies DA: *Nursing Management: A Systems Approach.* Saunders, 1982.

Kalisch BJ, Kalisch PA: *Politics of Nursing.* Lippincott, 1982.

Lancaster J, Lancaster W: *Concepts for Advanced Nursing Practice: The Nurse as a Change Agent.* Mosby, 1982.

Lewin K: Group decision and social change. In: *Readings in Social Psychology.* Newcomb T, Hartley E (editors), Holt, Rinehart & Winston, 1947.

Lewin K: *Field Theory in Social Science.* Harper & Row, 1951.

Lippitt R, Watson J, Westley B: *The Dynamics of Planned Change.* Harcourt, Brace, 1958.

Olson EM: Strategies and techniques for the nurse change agent. *Nurs Clinics of North America* (June) 1979; 14:323–36.

Oregon RNs win battle to upgrade maternity services. *Am J Nurs* 1984; 84:111.

Price EM: Seven days on and seven days off. *Am J Nurs* 1981; 81:1142–43.

Rappsiller C: Persuasion as a mechanism for change. In: *Concepts for Advanced Nursing Practice: The Nurse as a Change Agent.* Lancaster J, Lancaster W (editors). Mosby, 1982.

Selby TL: Block nurse program provides home care for older residents. *Amer Nurs* (Dec) 1983; 15:1, 15.

Stevens BJ: Management of continuity and change in nursing. *J Nurs Adm* (April) 1977; 26–31.

Stevens KR: *Power and Influence: A Source Book for Nurses.* Wiley, 1983.

Storlie F: *Nursing and the Social Conscience.* Appleton-Century-Crofts, 1970.

Theado GC, Scarry KD: Networking community services: Politics of hospice development. *Nurs and Health Care* 1983; 4:568–72.

Welch LB: Planned change in nursing: The theory. *Nurs Clinics of North America* (June) 1979; 14:307–21.

Chapter 11

Conflict and Conflict Management

Rachel Z. Booth, RN, PhD

Walk into a staff meeting and inform the group that two staff nurses are involved in a conflict. In most instances, the group reacts with anger, hostility, fright, disagreement, and other negative behaviors. This response indicates the indoctrination most individuals have to conflict. The socialization process in playing, learning, and maturing has trained individuals, particularly women, to maintain harmony and to minimize conflict at all cost. The goal is peace and cooperation.

Synonyms for conflict include fight, battle, contend . . . to be antagonistic or incompatible. If there is no effort to resolve the incompatibilities, the consequences are usually detrimental, leaving individuals in adversarial and destructive positions. Historically, the tendency has been to minimize and suppress conflict rather than stimulate and resolve it. Conflict management, however, includes both the stimulation and resolution phases.

Nurses are at high risk for conflict due to their service functions, relationships with many different groups, and overlap of roles with other health professionals. In attaining both individual and organizational goals, it is important to recognize and manage conflict.

PHILOSOPHIES OF CONFLICT

The traditionalist philosophy of conflict considered it to be negative and destructive and that it should be dissipated at all costs. Conflictual behaviors were not acceptable for either children or adults. Children were taught to cooperate, obey, and not to question adult judgment. The negative and destructive view of conflict persisted until the 1940s.

The traditionalist philosophy was replaced by the behavioralist philosophy, which continued until the 1960s. This approach considered conflict inevitable and proposed that it be minimized. There was acknowledgment that conflict might have some positive aspects. An attempt was made to rationalize its existence, but emphasis was placed on finding ways to suppress it.

The current philosophy of the interactionists suggests that conflict is both functional and dysfunctional. It must be present in an organization to maintain a dynamic state; and it must be both stimulated and resolved. Supporters of this view provide examples of businesses that failed because conflict was not encouraged. Likewise, the absence of conflict in an organization will result in stagnation and complacency, leading to gradual deterioration.

These three different philosophies (Robbins, 1974) provide a meaningful perspective for nurses in examining their beliefs about conflict and deciding how functional or dysfunctional those beliefs are to their achievements in an organization. The different philosophies also provide a framework for understanding how conflict may be used to attain the goals of the individual and the organization.

RELEVANCE TO NURSES

Nurses are at a high risk for experiencing conflict because of the differentiation and integration that occurs in health-care settings (Lawrence & Lorsch, 1967). Differentiation refers to the differences among individuals in relation to their education, socioeconomic status, values, attitudes, and responsibilities. In an organization, differentiation is ". . . the state of segmentation of the organizational system into subsystems, each of which tends to develop particular attributes in relation to the requirements posed by its relevant external environment" (Lawrence & Lorsch, 1967, pp 3–4). Integration is the bringing together of individuals, tasks, units, and subsystems into a workable, coordinated activity.

Although nurses comprise the largest practicing group of health professionals, they have the lowest level of academic credentials. No other profession allows less than a baccalaureate for entry into practice, yet only about 20 percent of all practicing nurses have this degree. To compensate for this gap between the educational level of nurses and other professionals, nurses must strive harder to establish a power base built on expertise through experience and continuing education.

The medical profession dominates the health system, while nurses struggle with an image of subservience. Because of this historical pattern and the positive changes occurring in the women's movement, human rights, and the nursing profession itself, conflicts will occur.

Another factor that places nurses at risk for conflict is the stereotypical roles ascribed to males and females. Although these images are diminishing, there is a long history to overcome. The dominance and aggressiveness ascribed to males have overshadowed the deference and nonassertiveness ascribed to females. Societal changes are merging these stereotypes. In the 1980 presidential election, as many women as men voted, a first in the history of our country. A 1983 study (Booth, Bausell-Vinogard & Harper) compared men's and women's desire for social power. Social power was defined as a facilitating factor used by an individual when striving to influence others in the achievement of organization goals. The results showed no significant difference in that desire, whereas in 1972 Good and Good found that men had a significantly higher desire for social power than did women. This is one example indicating fewer differences between the behavioral characteristics of men and women in contemporary society.

The complexity and interrelatedness of health care causes overlapping of authority and responsibility among nurses, physicians, and administrators. Nurses are assuming managerial positions that frequently expand beyond the nursing department. The position of vice-president for nursing has become common. Nurse managers are also assuming responsibility for other departments such as pharmacy, environmental services, and unit management. Titles are changing to reflect the expanded responsibilities.

With increasing acuity of illness and expansion of knowledge and technology, nursing is becoming more specialized. As professions become more specialized, they become more interdependent. Nurses working in intensive care units, tertiary care units, and primary care centers have roles interdependent with other professions, increasing the potential for conflict.

Another risk factor is involvement in multiple tasks. In many settings, nurses are involved in practice, research, administration, and professional and community service. Each task requires a different orientation, knowledge base, and time commitment, creating areas of potential conflict. Weisbord and others (1978) found a positive relationship between the number of tasks one is performing and the degree of conflict. If staff nurses are involved in research projects and professional organizations in addition to practice responsibilities, they are likely candidates for conflict.

Role conflict, including both overload and ambiguity, is a major problem for nurses. Role overload is common when nurses are required to assume the tasks of other disciplines and professions as well as provide nursing care for patients. During the nursing shortage of the late 1970s and early 1980s, nurses experienced burnout due to the stresses from overload. Role ambiguity is another aspect of the same problem. Roles are changing so rapidly that practice changes often precede organizational policies and legislation. Therefore, risks are taken in expanding responsibilities or engaging in activities commensurate with increased need and demand. In some settings, the nurse's role has not been clarified and legitimized, creating the potential for conflict. One way to minimize this is to develop a position description with approval by the supervising staff of the health care organization. Periodic conferences and discussions maintain clarity and understanding among all parties.

In the current economy, resources are diminishing, while pressures mount for increased accountability. Ethical issues and cost-containment measures create stresses that place nurses at the center of conflict. The decline in hospital occupancy rates is necessitating shorter workweeks, layoffs, or other cost-reduction measures. The result is a potential for conflict among physicians, nurses, patients, and other workers in the health care system.

STAGES OF CONFLICT

For conflict to occur, there must be antecedent conditions such as unclear roles; scarce resources; differences in values, interests, goals, and work characteristics. All of these may exist in a health care setting (Pondy, 1967). Conflict then evolves through a process of five stages identified by Kast and Rosenzweig (1970). Identifying the stage of the conflict is important to anticipate the events of the next stage.

The first stage, *latent conflict*, is always present in an organization where workers are highly differentiated, ie, have different cognitive and emotional orientations. Another frequently occurring latent situation is when important differences that are valued exist between two or more parties. For example, in patient unit A, the schedule of working hours and weekends off is better than for nurses on unit B. Unit A is also better staffed than unit B. The conditions have been set for conflict; but until it occurs, the situation is latent.

The next stage is *perceived conflict*. This happens when the nurses on unit B realize that they are not as well staffed and do not have the same working schedule as unit A. Nurses on unit B do not perceive themselves as having the options that have been given to unit A. The conditions for the next stage are created.

The process moves into the third stage, *felt conflict*, where hostilities, anxieties, and stress erupt. The nurses on unit B experience the conflict but it is not recognized by others. Such feelings may exist for a limited period of time before the fourth stage is reached.

In the fourth stage of *overt conflict*, the nurses on unit B interact with supervisors and the nurses on unit A. Their hostilities, anxieties, and stresses are manifested through overt behaviors, which may be so laden with emotion that no meaningful discussions can be held. If conflict reaches the stage of open dispute with no attempts at resolution, it is difficult to resolve without outside intervention. Conflict should be identified early so the affected parties may be able to resolve it among themselves.

The final and fifth stage, *conflict aftermath*, follows the resolution phase when the outcome is known to all the participants. The outcome may or may not be optimal for either unit. If the outcome is not acceptable to the participants, a range of behaviors could occur from full cooperation to passive-aggressive resistance.

Deviations from these five stages can occur, and the progression may not be recognized as discrete stages. Nurses should pay particular attention to the latent and conflict aftermath stages because extensive damage to relationships can occur at these times if conflict is not recognized and managed appropriately. If possible, intervention should occur in the latent stage to minimize the dispute, otherwise serious disruptions to unit functioning may result. All five stages may be applied to both individual and organizational conflict.

TYPES OF CONFLICT

Individual Conflict

Intrapersonal.   Intrapersonal conflict exists in the cognitive and affective domains of an individual. There is no overt behavioral display that indicates to others that the individual has a problem, yet the problem may eventually cause physiological or emotional stress. If intrapersonal conflict persists, it will manifest itself in some type of behavior that will precipitate interpersonal conflict.

This type of conflict could occur when a nurse is having difficulty fulfilling the role of a mother while fulfilling the role of a staff nurse in an intensive care unit. Or a nurse may believe a certain act she is required to do is not consistent with professional ethics, yet it achieves organizational goals. The question arises as to whether the individual should act according to a professional value or the organization's goal.

Interpersonal. When an inner experience becomes disturbing enough to cause problems in relationships among individuals, the conflict is interpersonal. It may manifest itself in verbal or nonverbal behavior or, in some cases, physical behaviors. The individual with the conflict may display angry, hostile, punitive, or passive-aggressive behaviors. While the conflict exists, it may be destructive in damaging attitudes, morale, work efficiency, and goal achievement. Avoiding resolution perpetuates the destruction. The longer one waits to initiate resolution, the more difficult it becomes. In general, good interpersonal relationships are essential for preventing dysfunctional interpersonal conflict. Seven guidelines for fostering healthy interpersonal relationships are:

1. Be descriptive rather than judgmental.
2. Be specific rather than general.
3. Deal with things that can be changed.
4. Give feedback when it is desired.
5. Consider the motives for giving and receiving feedback.
6. Give feedback at the time the behavior takes place.
7. Give feedback when its accuracy can be checked with others (Luthans, 1981, p 378).

There are many areas where interpersonal conflict occurs in a health care setting, but one of the most fertile areas is role conflict. Role overload indicates responsibilities and expectations beyond the capabilities of the nurse. Usually the more capable one is, the more responsibilities one is given. The capable nurse is singled out as one who can continue to be stretched. The problem arises when a saturation point has been reached, and the nurse cannot accept more responsibility.

Two techniques available to reduce overload are delegation and negotiation. Delegation is assigning selected responsibilities with commensurate authority to another individual. Then, the nurse's role is to hold the person accountable for executing those responsibilities. When overload occurs, the nurse should explore the feasibility of delegation by ascertaining the capabilities of other workers carrying out tasks not solely in the nurse's realm. Fear of responsibility for delegated acts sometimes dissuades nurses from delegating. If the nurse consistently finds that other workers are not functioning at the appropriate level for that particular unit, it may be necessary to reassess the type of workers needed to minimize supervision time.

Another strategy for role overload is negotiation—two or more individuals reach an agreement with stated conditions and expectations. The interests of all individuals are served, but usually each makes compromises. This strategy for resolving conflict will be discussed in greater depth later.

Table 11-1   Responsibility Charting

Activities		Individuals			
	Supervisor	Head nurse	Staff nurse A	Staff nurse B	Physician

Role ambiguity is another area of potential conflict. When the boundaries between a nurse's role and that of another health professional are unclear, tension is created at the point of overlap. As health care increases in technology and specialization, this area becomes ripe for conflict. Clinical specialists and nurse practitioners are groups that have a high potential for conflict because of role ambiguity.

A technique that can be used to resolve conflicts from role ambiguity is *responsibility charting*, which allocates responsibilities among several individuals (Beckhard & Harris, 1977). A grid is drawn with vertical and horizontal axes; activities to be performed are listed on one axis, and the individuals involved in these activities are listed on the other axis (see Table 11-1).

The role for each individual designated on the horizontal axis is identified as either: (1) Responsible (R); (2) Approve/veto (A/V); (3) Support (S); or (4) Inform (I). In the matrixed square for the supervisor, any of these four roles would appear for the activity listed on the vertical axis. The same process would occur for all individuals on the horizontal axis and for all activities listed on the vertical axis.

Only one person may be responsible (R) for any one activity. That person may delegate the task to someone else but is still responsible. If there is a disagreement over who should have the (R), this indicates the activity should be broken down into several activities or moved up one level higher in the organization.

The person in the support role supports the individual who has the (R) with resources and encouragement. More than one person may be assigned the (S). If resources are not available to support the activity, then a request for them must be taken to the next higher level. If the resources are unavailable from the higher level, then the responsible person must decide to continue or discontinue the activity.

The individual in the inform role on the horizontal axis needs to be informed prior to the implementation of the activity and be kept informed of its progress. More than one person may be assigned the (I); however, they do not have authority to alter the activity.

Development of a responsibility chart requires careful thought and discussion among those involved. A full understanding of the process and an appreciation of the need to allocate responsibilities are critical. To ensure a greater chance for success and acceptance, a simple activity can be used to orient the group to the process. Decisions about the assignment of roles and responsibilities may be made individually and brought to the group to discuss any differences before making the group decision, or the group may convene to work through the total process together.

Although used in business and industry, responsibility charting is a new technique for use in the health field. It brings all concerned parties together and forces a decision, reducing the ambiguity and uncertainty in any individual's role. Since all concerned parties are involved in the decision, greater commitment to implementation can be expected.

Organizational Conflict

Increasing complexity and specialization within organizations have made conflict more prevalent. If conflict is not managed, the organization experiences inefficiency and ineffectiveness. One of the most important functions of a successful manager is the ability to manage conflict.

The hierarchy of relationships in organizations creates tension. When one individual controls another by having the authority to reward, hire, fire, or discipline, it may breed suspicion, competition, and other strained relations between the supervisor and worker or among workers. The supervisor must be explicit, fair, and candid about the rules, policies, and guidelines used in making decisions. Expectations must be communicated so workers will know what is expected of them.

The size of an organization affects relationships among workers. Robbins maintains that ". . . as a structure increases in size, goals will become less clear, relationships will by necessity become more formal, specialization will increase pressure to protect one's bailiwick, and more opportunities for distortion will occur. . . ." (1974, p 42). Organizations establish levels of management, rules, policies, and procedures to standardize operations and relationships. Standardization and formalization can become so inflexible that the organization's work is impeded. It then becomes even more crucial for the nurse to possess expert skills in managing human relations and conflicts.

Allocation of resources may cause competition among units, especially if resources are scarce or if the allocation is unfair. The scarcer the resources, the greater the potential for conflict. For example, if the nursing supervisor has funds to support two head nurses to attend a workshop and selects two favorites, he or she is sure to precipitate dissatisfaction. The supervisor should have specific guidelines and criteria for making the decision, and these should be known to all affected. A preferable method might be to ask the head nurse group or a representative group of head nurses to make the decision.

Health professionals may also experience a professional-bureaucratic conflict. The professional ideology for self-governance and autonomy may supersede the bureaucratic ideology. New nurse graduates are often caught in the conflict between the professional ideology learned in the educational program and supported by the profession and bureaucratic practices. Unfortunately, experienced nurses and nurse administrators often criticize the new graduate's ideals. How often have you heard a nurse administrator say, "I just cannot assign more than two of those bright, young graduates to a unit. They think they can change the world, and are they ever surprised when they face reality"? The experienced nurse can assist the new graduate in establishing an equitable exchange between the beliefs of the profession and those of the organization.

Another built-in conflict is the staff-line relationship. In nursing service, the clinical specialist is often placed in a staff position that has no formal authority over the workers on the unit. This creates a strain between the clinical specialist and the staff. Some nurse administrators have resolved this conflict by delegating line authority to the clinical specialist for standards of care in the unit. Others have appointed the clinical specialist to an administrative position such as head nurse or supervisor. Responsibility charting could be used in this particular situation.

Intragroup. Conflict within groups depends on the personality and behaviors of group members as well as the organizational climate. Different motives among group members may disrupt the group's work. When groups are established, the purpose should be made explicit, and every member should know why he or she is a member.

Once the group is functioning, process may be a problem. Process is the means a group uses to achieve the outcome. If this occurs, an outside consultant with process skills should be used to observe and identify problematic areas. The consultant may have to work with group members until they have the skills necessary to complete the task or achieve the outcomes. Aldag and Brief (1981) propose the following guidelines for a group:

1. Focus on defeating the mutual problem rather than each other. Try not to personalize the conflict; instead, view the *problem* as a *depersonalized objective* to be mutually achieved through joint problem solving.
2. Avoid voting, averaging, or trading to reach a solution. Talk things out.
3. Seek facts to resolve points of disagreement. Don't make decisions based on pure speculation.
4. Recognize that conflict can be helpful. Avoid making conflict a threatening or defense-invoking process.
5. Recognize others' needs and positions. Avoid acting solely on behalf of your own interest (p 400).

Intergroup. Conflict between groups is related to the environment. Multipurpose organizations, which have more than one mission, have a higher potential for conflict because of different individuals, groups, and missions. A common disagreement among groups is the allocation of resources, such as budget, space, and people. When organizational groups have varied values, goals, and tasks to mesh with the multimissions of the organization, a high level of integration is necessary to attain goals and allocate resources in a fair manner. The integrative function, assumed either by an individual or a group, is to coordinate and establish unity among the elements of the organization.

An effective integrator has a balanced orientation, influence based on competence, and expert skills in communication and conflict management (Charns, 1976). Lawrence and Lorsch (1967) maintain that the greater the need for interdepartmental collaboration, ". . . the more need there is for integrative roles to be formally identified so that such activities are seen as legitimate" (p 144).

The intensity of conflict is greatest at the point of coordination or integration. Thus, the integrator must possess a unique set of communication and interpersonal skills to maintain a high quality of relationships among the groups (Weisbord, 1978b).

RESOLUTION STRATEGIES
Individual

In any attempt to win a disagreement or discussion, it is necessary to develop a strategy that yields the greatest benefit for the parties involved. The benefit is not always equal for both parties, but an acceptable resolution is paramount or lasting negative attitudes and behaviors may develop. Nurses need to be able to understand conflict and prepare in advance for its resolution. There is rarely a conflict that demands immediate resolution. It is advisable to take time and carefully think through the situation and options.

The mode of resolution most beneficial in a majority of situations is *problem solving* or confronting. These two terms are used interchangeably and convey that there is open discussion of the problem, a thorough investigation of its dimensions, and an outcome that provides a win-win situation for both parties. Confronting requires a high level of interpersonal skill and if problem solving occurs, the outcome lasts. Weisbord (1978a) offers the following steps for problem resolution:

1. Acknowledge the other person's position as legitimate for him.
2. Differentiate the other person's position from yours.
3. Check to see whether you hear the other person clearly and vice versa.
4. Accept angry and/or hostile feelings in yourself and others as real. Be responsible for your own feelings. Leave the other person free to feel differently.
5. Don't problem solve until differences are fully analyzed.
6. Ask the other person to state his or her preferred solution. Be prepared to state (and differentiate) yours.

It is important to identify the issue rather than a symptom or a sign. Also, be sure both parties are interested in resolving the conflict prior to the discussion. Otherwise, the expected problem solving may turn into another form of resolution. If the power bases are grossly unequal, the result could be forcing, withdrawing, or some other less desirable mode of resolution. Another requisite is to have adequate information and data concerning the problem prior to the discussion. It may even be necessary to postpone the discussion while more information is collected. If too much time elapses, however, other problems may be generated.

For example, a clinical specialist and a supervisor who disagree over the responsibilities of a nursing assistant enter the discussion with near equal power bases. The clinical specialist possesses expert power because of her knowledge base. The supervisor possesses legitimate power because of her position. They are both motivated to resolve the issue because it is affecting patient care and other personnel. They schedule a meeting date. When they attempt to identify the issue, they discover the incident is a manifestation of a longstanding disagreement between them about the patient classification-employee assignment system. Once this is acknowledged by both sides, the classification-assignment issue is assigned to a task force for investigation and decision making. The task force recommends an acceptable system, and both parties are pleased with the outcome. The resolution is long term.

Another form of resolution is *negotiation* or bargaining. This means that usually neither party gains an optimal solution. Instead, each loses something but also gains something in return. Negotiation or bargaining is a favorable technique to use in resource allocation. The technique can be used on an informal or formal basis. (See "Steps to Informal and Formal Negotiating" at the end of this chapter.)

Positional negotiating, the most common form, is the usual method for collective bargaining. It entails identifying one's bottom line and optimal positions, and making trade-offs to get a final agreement as close as possible to one's optimal position. In recent years, others—most notably Fisher and Ury (1981)—have proposed another model called *principled negotiating*. This involves developing options that satisfy both parties and selecting one or more according to mutually agreed upon criteria. Dirschel discusses this method in more detail in the vignette following this chapter. The positional method will be used here to explain negotiating in greater depth.

For bargaining to be successful, both parties must be sincere in their desires to negotiate. The issue to be negotiated must be clearly identified, and all relevant information collected to respond to questioning or probing by either party. Issues amenable to compromise should be differentiated from those which are not. It is also wise to decide in advance the lowest concession one will accept, the most ideal position one would desire, and the middle or less than ideal position for which one would strive. A mental rehearsal of anticipated positions and responses will be beneficial in responding to the other party. With such preparation, the nurse enters the process with a feeling of self-confidence built on knowledge and is less likely to lose ground to the opposing party.

Common pitfalls are negotiating on an emotional level and allowing oneself to be placed in a defensive position. Also, it is easy to talk *at* a person instead of talking *with* a person. If the nurse has prepared thoroughly and rehearsed mentally or with a peer, there is less likelihood that these pitfalls will occur. In a successful negotiation, the issues, goals, and outcomes must be clear to both parties. When there is a need for concession, Laser (1981) suggests:

1. Avoid making the first concession, and *never* make the first major concession. Doing either raises the expectations of the other party unnecessarily and dangerously.

2. Use a trade-off in making concessions. By saying "If I do that for you, what can you do for me?" there is always the possibility of getting something in return.

3. If forced to give concessions to the other party, be sure that the concessions are progressively *decreasing* in value.

4. Keep a scorecard of the concessions that have been exchanged during the course of the negotiation. You can then explain that the other party has received considerably more than you have from them (pp 27–28).

Concessions are made by both parties. If at a certain point neither one is willing to go any further, the decision that is reached is temporary, and the parties will need to return to the issue later. During the interim, the issue may disappear or accelerate. Negotiation should be on a factual basis, not on an emotional, personal, or judgmental one. It is often acceptable to concede on a particular issue in exchange for gaining support for a pending or future issue. Such an approach serves as a bank account, and both parties gain an attractive solution. If a prolonged discussion occurs with little or no progress, it may be best to cease deliberations and engage a neutral third party or arbitrator. Both parties must agree to abide by the decision of the arbitrator.

Smoothing is a form of short-term resolution. It usually does not resolve the problem and may displace the conflict to another situation or person. Smoothing frequently occurs when there is a power differentiation and may result in intimidating behavior. The more powerful person de-emphasizes differences but emphasizes points of agreement. There are times, however, when smoothing is appropriate to reach a short-term solution. If emotional behaviors defeat attempts at resolution, it may be more productive to smooth the current discussion and attempt to resolve at a later time.

Avoidance, another mode of resolution, occurs when one party withdraws from the resolution process and ceases discussions. Since the problem was not resolved, it will resurface. In certain situations, avoidance may be preferred, especially if there is a need to "cool off" or gather additional data.

Forcing is a means of conflict resolution that uses power, influence, or some other method to impose one's preference on another. This method is used in power differentiation, where one has the authority to make the decision, and the other person feels powerless to challenge or pursue it. This situation may occur between the director of nursing and the supervisor, or between the supervisor and the staff nurse. One party feels he or she has more to lose than gain by pursuing the matter so accepts the decision imposed by the other. A variation of forcing may occur when someone at a lower level in the organization bypasses normal levels and goes to a higher level for a favorable decision or resource. This is usually considered unacceptable and places all concerned in vulnerable positions.

The best mode of resolution to use depends upon the situation. No one mode fits all situations. It may be necessary to use one type of resolution for a temporary solution while stalling to gain strength through information, resources, or simply maturity.

Practicing confronting or negotiating skills instills confidence. Starting out with a situation that is not too complex increases chances of success. It may help to role play different resolution strategies with a peer, and have others critique the interaction. Whatever strategy one chooses, self-confidence, direct eye contact, effective communication skills, and knowledge are crucial ingredients to a successful resolution. Observing others in role-playing or in real situations is an excellent learning experience. For any meeting to resolve conflict, one should prepare ahead of time by gathering the facts, identifying one's options, and rehearsing the approach.

Although most conflict studies have been done in industry, there is a beginning interest in conducting similar studies among health workers. Weisbord, Lawrence, and Charns (1978) studied conflict resolution among physicians in five academic medical centers. Bargaining was most often used, and forcing was used least among this group. In contrast, Lawrence and Lorsch (1967) showed that confrontation was most often used, and smoothing was least used in industrial organizations. In a study (Booth, 1978) with five different health professions as subjects, the most frequently used mode was bargaining, and the least used was forcing.

Organizational

Three approaches have been identified by Pondy (1967) in resolving organizational conflict. Although similar to the strategies for resolving individual conflict, these approaches are more conceptual in nature. Realizing that individuals and groups make up the organization, both sets of strategies could be applied.

Bargaining. The bargaining approach is useful when there is competition for resources such as personnel, space, or monies. As these resources become scarcer, more conflict occurs as each group is intent on establishing its need as greatest. Representatives of the groups engage in negotiations, starting with the most attractive solution to each. Realizing that the optimal solution is not possible, further discussions will most likely be needed. If the groups are unable to reach an acceptable settlement, then a third party may need to be brought in as an arbitrator. The groups must agree to the arbitrator's decision and accept it as final.

Bureaucratic Approach. Rules, policies, and procedures are used to establish authority. The nurse supervisor can say, "This is the policy, so we must do it this way." This shifts the responsibility for control and decision making from the individual to the organization. This approach can result in rigidity and inflexibility, stifling creativity and innovation. Frequently, professionals become dissatisfied if it is used too often and leave the organization. Costs are then incurred in the turnover of personnel. A balance of supervisory control and policies and procedures is preferable.

Altering human or structural variables may be beneficial in organizational conflicts (Robbins, 1974). If an individual is a consistent source of dysfunctional conflict, efforts should be made to change that person's behavior through education or counseling. It is the next level manager's responsibility to identify the problem, counsel the individual, and alter the dysfunctional behavior. Altering the structural variable would involve changing the organizational structure creating a grievance process, developing an employee resource program, or giving decision-making responsibilities to committees.

Systems Approach. A systems approach to organizational conflict requires an integrator who can coordinate both vertical and horizontal lines of communication and activities. This person must recognize, appreciate, and manage the differences in attitudes, behaviors, expectations, and goals that exist within the system and facilitate conflict resolution when necessary.

Defining a superordinate goal (Robbins, 1974) is a strategy that could be used in the systems approach. This involves setting a goal that needs the cooperation and support of all contending parties. Each party recognizes that it cannot achieve the goal without the assistance of the other party. For example, a new member of the state legislature wishes to become visible and influential in her efforts to become chairperson of the political party. Nurses in the health department would like legislation granting more autonomy to their practice. The superordinate goal agreed upon by these two parties is for the legislator to be successful in introducing a bill granting third-party reimbursement for professional nurses. Nurses in the health department assist the legislator in writing the bill, lobbying other legislators and influential groups to support the bill, and mobilizing nurses throughout the state to lobby their legislators and other influential groups. The bill is enacted, and both parties benefit. The delegate has gained visibility and success, while the nursing profession has gained autonomy in practice.

CONCLUSION

Nurses will be exposed to greater levels of potential conflict and must be able to identify causes, anticipate effects, and choose the most appropriate mode of resolution. It is crucial to acquire highly developed skills in confronting and negotiating—the two most effective resolution modes. Nothing is inherently wrong in using any one of the five modes; some are more effective in certain situations than others.

All nurses should possess a repertoire of skills to manage organizational behaviors. The clinical specialist, staff nurse, and manager deal with other individuals and groups within and external to the organization, making conflict management a necessary tool.

References

Aldag RJ, Brief AP: *Managing Organizational Behavior.* West, 1981.

Beckhard R, Harris RT: *Organizational Transitions: Managing Complex Change.* Addison-Wesley, 1977.

Booth RZ: The management of an interprofessional program in an academic health science center: A case study. Dissertation, University of Maryland, 1978.

Booth RZ, Bausell-Vinogard C, Harper D: Social power need and gender among college students. *Psych Rep* 1984; 55:243–46.

Charns MP: Breaking the tradition barrier: Managing integration in health care facilities. *Health Care Manage Rev* 1976; 1:55–67.

Fisher R, Ury W: *Getting to Yes: Negotiating Agreement Without Giving In.* Houghton Mifflin, 1981.

Good L, Good EK: An objective measure of the motive to attain social power. *Psych Rep* 1972; 30:247–51.

Kast FE, Rosenzweig JE: *Organization and Management: A Systems Approach.* McGraw-Hill, 1970.

Laser RJ: I win-you win negotiating. *J Nurs Adm* (Nov-Dec) 1981; 11:24–29.

Lawrence PR, Lorsch JW: Differentiation and integration in complex organizations. *Adm Sci Q* 1967; 12:144–47.

Luthans F: *Organizational Behavior.* McGraw-Hill, 1981.

Pondy LR: Organizational conflict: Concepts and models. *Adm Sci Q* 1967; 12:296–320.

Robbins SP: *Managing Organizational Conflict.* Prentice-Hall, 1974.

Weisbord MR: Anatomy of Confrontation. Management seminar, University of Maryland School of Medicine, Baltimore, 1978a.

Weisbord MR: *Organizational Diagnosis: A Workbook of Theory and Practice.* Addison-Wesley, 1978b.

Weisbord MR, Lawrence PR, Charns MP: Three dilemmas of academic medical centers. *J Appl Behav Sci* 1978; 14:284–304.

Vignette: Principled Negotiation
Kathleen M. Dirschel, RN, PhD

Everyone negotiates something every day. Negotiation is a basic means of getting what you want from others through an agreement considered fair to both parties. It is back-and-forth communication designed to reach an agreement between individuals or groups. The process involves "give and get" on matters of value to those negotiating.

Effective nurses are effective negotiators. They negotiate for better care for patients with other members of the health care team, including social workers, secretaries, dieticians, housekeepers, physicians, and colleagues. Nurses negotiate for themselves with supervisors about issues such as work schedules, raises, changes in responsibilities, or other working conditions. Sometimes they negotiate with physicians, lawyers, and other nurses about issues such as the scope of nursing practice. They may also negotiate with other health care workers whom they believe are encroaching on nursing practice. They may help negotiate with nursing supervisors and others to avert a strike or to reduce the required amount of "floating" to other units.

The format for a negotiation may be one-to-one or a small group representing a particular interest. A negotiation session may be a formal meeting or an informal discussion. The issues may be contractual, work-related, or personal.

Regardless of these circumstances, the process of negotiating can take on two different forms: positional or principled negotiating. Booth (preceding this discussion) has outlined the former method. While there are similarities between the two methods, principled negotiating is based upon a different philosophy—namely, that negotiating positions can interfere with a successful negotiation. This approach has been developed by Fisher & Ury (1981). The reader is encouraged to refer to their work for a more indepth discussion of principled negotiating.

While successful negotiation is important to professional survival and growth, few nurses are expert negotiators. The ideas about negotiation presented here just scratch the surface of a skill important to professional growth and success.

Tips for Successful Negotiation

A successful negotiation should produce a fair agreement. It should be an efficient process and improve (at least not damage) the relationship between the parties. The following tips should help you improve your negotiating skills (Fisher & Ury, 1981).

1. Separate the people from the problem. Persons who hold views different from yours are also human beings. They are emotional, have values, and are unpredictable—just like you. They may get angry, frustrated, or offended. While you are dealing with issues, you are also dealing with a relationship. It is important to maintain a good relationship while dealing with another who may hold a substantially different point of view on an issue. If there is a lot of emotion, find ways to let off steam. If there is misunderstanding, attempt to clarify the issues. It is helpful to take an extra step and "put yourself in their shoes" so that you can see the issue from another's point of view. As a result, you may be able to align your views more closely with the other person's. This may help you change their opinion. Don't blame others for the problem under discussion. While it is easy to think that the hospital administration is responsible for low nursing salaries, stating this belief, and placing blame, is usually counterproductive. See the other side not as the cause, but rather as a resource to use for solving the problem in a mutually agreeable way.

The solution agreed upon should prevent either side from "losing face." Often in a negotiation, persons will hold out, not because the proposed solution is unfair, but because they don't want to appear to be backing down. If a solution can be presented as "fair" to all parties then a "win-win" outcome has been achieved. Chances are good that the proposal will be accepted.

By separating the people from the problem, you can think of dealing with the persons as human beings and with the problem on its merits. Direct your thinking away from the idea of adversaries in a confrontation and toward the vision of side-by-side partners searching for a fair agreement advantageous to each. Stating one's wish to work jointly to satisfy collective interests (in many circumstances the needs of the patient) is usually appropriate and facilitates the negotiating process.

2. Analyze the problem, focusing on each side's interests, rather than positions. Identify the facts and feelings behind each side's desires and concerns. Behind opposing positions often lie shared and compatible interests. If the focus is on positions rather than interests, the parties will have difficulty brainstorming other options, because they will be intent on keeping their "bottom line" positions.

For example, Jane has been told by the dean that she will be teaching the clinical portion of pediatric nursing next semester because the pediatric nursing coordinator needs time to write a grant. Not having worked in pediatrics for many years, Jane does not want to accept the assignment because, in her view, she is not qualified to teach pediatric nursing. She is also concerned about her liability. The dean indicates that if Jane will not fulfill this assignment, she can look for another job. At this point, Jane takes it upon herself to initiate a negotiating meeting that includes the dean, the pediatric course coordinator, and herself. Before the meeting, she identifies the interests of all parties. The dean wants to have someone assigned to teach pediatric nursing before it's too late to hire someone else. The course coordinator wants sufficient time to write her grant. Jane wants to have a teaching assignment that does not compromise her professional integrity and accountability. During the meeting, Jane articulates these interests and obtains validation from the other parties that these interests are correct. All three now explore other options for addressing these interests.

3. Brainstorm about possible options and discuss these so that both parties can envision more than one outcome. A single answer to any disputed situation is counterproductive. Resolution becomes a joint effort as both sides identify and discuss a variety of solutions and the benefits to each party.

In the above example, Jane had done her homework by brainstorming the night before the meeting. She presents five options acceptable to her and asks the dean and pediatric coordinator for other options she has not identified. The dean identifies another that would be acceptable to Jane. Jane then invites the pediatric coordinator to select the option she prefers, since all of the options on the table are acceptable to her. The coordinator accepts the option that calls for her to teach the clinical portion of the pediatric course, while Jane assists her in teaching the didactic portion of the course and in coordinating related activities, such as exams, handouts, and meetings.

Many people have ethical difficulties with *positional* negotiating because they believe it entails a certain amount of withholding of information and perhaps even dishonesty. Principled negotiating may appear to be more ethical. Both parties, however, must be willing to engage in principled negotiating for it to work effectively. Otherwise, positional bargaining will be used. Thus, it is helpful for the nurse to be versed in both methods.

References

Fisher R, Ury W: *Getting to Yes: Negotiating Agreement Without Giving In.* Houghton Mifflin, 1981.

Vignette: **Steps to Informal and Formal Negotiating**
Richard S. Webster, PhD

Formal and informal negotiations have similarities as well as differences. Formal negotiating builds on the strategies used in informal situations. This chart outlines the steps in any negotiating process and compares formal and informal methods.

Steps in Negotiating	For Informal/Colleague Negotiations	For Formal/Contract/Team Negotiations, ALSO CONSIDER:
1. Preparation	Gather information: learn the facts; consult experts; seek advice.	
	Understand how the other person(s) sees the situation.	Understand the position of the other side.
	Decide what you want and your priorities; identify your "bottom line."	
	Plan your strategies.	Plan strategies for each team member.
2. Entrance		Learn the scope of authority of the person with whom you will be negotiating.
	Start on a positive note.	
	Establish goodwill; seek common interests.	
	Propose (or take) control, eg, by hosting the meeting.	. . . or by writing the agenda.
		Agree on ground rules and procedures for the overall negotiations; eg, size of team, frequency of meetings, scope and duration of the negotiations, environmental factors.
3. Work with people	Be courteous.	
	Present your position with confidence.	
4. Explore	Inform the other persons.	Inform the other team.
	Identify issues and related interests.	

Steps in Negotiating	For Informal/Colleague Negotiations	For Formal/Contract/Team Negotiations, ALSO CONSIDER:
	Ask questions: why, how, what, where . . . ?	
	Seek agreement ("yes" responses) on minor issues.	Seek agreement first on exploration ground rules; eg, alternate presentation of points, exchange draft statements, mutually brainstorm options.
	Look for common interests, shared objectives, and opportunities for mutual benefit.	
5. Invent	Review steps 1–4.	
	Brainstorm, evaluate, and select actions to improve situations and solve problems. Consider both sides' beliefs, facts, forecasts, interests, objectives and priorities, costs and benefits.	Invent mutually shared benefits. Write alternative solutions.
	Structure choices into informal terms of agreement.	. . . more formal, written terms of agreement.
6. Bargain	Exchange for mutual benefit. Use reason, be reasonable. Make your requests legitimate, rational, routine, and rewarding for all concerned.	
		Use tactics: start with large demands; be precise in demands and responses; have your negotiator's authority limited to be able to recess, ostensibly for consultation, when you need time to reassess your position and develop other strategies; consider "good guy-bad guy" roles for team members; expose others' abusive tactics.
	Listen for hints of offers, opportunities to make or change your offers.	
7. Agree and Close	Delay if pressure to settle is inappropriate.	Adjourn if pressure is inappropriate.
	Assure that terms are operational; ie, who is to do how much of what by when?	

Steps in Negotiating	For Informal/Colleague Negotiations	For Formal/Contract/Team Negotiations, ALSO CONSIDER:
	Include incentives for following the agreement.	Include contractual incentives.
	Consider arrangements for settlement of disputes; eg, outside consultant.	*Include* formal arrangements, eg, arbitration, fact finding, mediation.
	Celebrate the achievement.	Publicize the agreement.
8. Implement	Follow through and support the agreement.	Encourage your team to do the same.
	Use dispute settlement arrangements whenever necessary.	

Adapted from program materials developed by Roy J. Lewicki, PhD, College of Administrative Science, The Ohio State University, Columbus, Ohio. Professor Lewicki's contribution is gratefully acknowledged.

Chapter 12

Ethical Issues: Politics, Power, and Change

Sara T. Fry, RN, PhD

Nurses in politics are receiving more attention in the news media. Nurses are running for public office in many states; others have been elected or appointed to state and federal offices. One reason is that nursing responsibilities are not confined to employment settings. Nurses are citizens and therefore may voice their opinions, give their support, and participate in activities affecting the health of citizens. Another reason is that each nurse has a responsibility to support the goals of the nursing profession in political issues related to the distribution of health care to consumers. Since the nursing profession is the largest provider of health care services in this country, it is appropriate that the nursing profession, as a collective voice of all nurses, takes a stand on political issues affecting health care services. The individual nurse has a responsibility to support and participate in the profession's efforts whenever possible.

To understand the roles and responsibilities of nurses and the nursing profession concerning political issues, it seems prudent to examine the sources of nursing responsibilities in social and political activities. My thesis is that there is an interesting ethical tension between the responsibilities of the individual nurse and the responsibilities of the nursing profession concerning involvement in political issues. There is also an ethical tension between the traditional role of the nurse and political involvement considered appropriate and inappropriate to that role.

In examining the sources of nursing responsibilities in social and political activities, it is clear that nurses have individual responsibilities to participate in political issues as citizens. It is also clear that the nursing profession has responsibilities as a collective entity to participate in political issues. Yet there are indications that involvement in some political issues is not appropriate to the professional role. Apparently the kind of political issues nurses or the nursing profession are involved in is directly related to the correlation between political issues and health matters. This chapter discusses: (1) political responsibilities of the individual nurse; (2) political responsibilities of the nursing profession; and (3) the dimensions of the professional role in political issues.

INDIVIDUAL RESPONSIBILITIES OF THE NURSE

The profession's code of ethics, *Code for Nurses* (American Nurses' Association, 1976), describes individual responsibilities of the nurse. The introduction to the code states that "upon entering the profession of nursing, each person inherits a measure of the responsibility and trust that has accrued to nursing over the years and the corresponding obligation to adhere to the profession's code of conduct and relationships for ethical practice" (p 1). Each point in the code specifies what is expected of the individual nurse.

In relation to political activity, the code specifically states: "The nurse collaborates with members of the health professions and other citizens in promoting community and national efforts to meet the health needs of the public." Since all citizens have a right to quality health care, the interpretive statements state that nurses have a responsibility to become involved with political issues to enhance consumer health, further asserting: "An effective way of ensuring that nurses' views regarding health care and nursing service are properly represented is by involvement of nurses in political decision making" (p 19).

Yet a nurse's views concerning quality health care may conflict with views of other health professionals, especially with those of the medical profession. The ANA *Code for Nurses* mandate to be involved in political issues is qualified by the pronouncement that nurses should collaborate with other health professionals in political involvement. It states: "The complexity of the delivery of health care service demands an interdisciplinary approach to delivery of health services as well as strong support from the allied health occupations" (p 19).

This general professional mandate to be involved in concert with other health disciplines is echoed in the *Definition and Role of Public Health Nursing in the Delivery of Health Care*, a statement of the Public Health Nursing Section of the APHA (APHA, 1980). This document notes, "Because so much of health care has become a political issue, leaders in the field, including nurses, must be able to function in the political arena to effect decisions supportive of public health. Part of this leadership role includes working with consumers in planning and evaluating health care. . . . This will involve working with . . . other health disciplines" (p 3).

Direct involvement in political issues affecting consumer health often creates ethical conflict for many nurses. The nurse may have to decide whether to support cost-effective efforts that might decrease the quality of health care services. Nurses may also have to decide whether their position on professional issues is too costly in terms of potential loss of collaborative support from other health colleagues, especially the medical profession. Consider the dilemma of the nurse in the following case study:

> Rose McGovern, director of nursing of an 80-bed nursing home in a small, urban community, has been involved in a joint effort among physicians, nursing home and long-term care administrators, and county health officers to provide cost-effective quality health care services for the elderly or chronically ill in their region. She has just learned that a bill has been introduced in the state legislature to allow medications to be administered by unlicensed technicians in nursing homes throughout the state. McGovern is concerned. As a longstanding advocate of skilled nursing care in nursing home settings, she

knows that the administering of medications to elderly or chronically ill patients is much more than merely giving ordered dosages of chemical substances. The administering of medications is an important but adjunct part of nursing home care. Its effectiveness in the total care plan for the elderly or chronically ill patient requires optimal surveillance from licensed personnel: practical or registered nurses.

Although medication technicians have been allowed, by law, to give medication in state-owned and psychiatric hospitals within her state for many years, the practice has never been legislated for general hospitals or for nursing homes. In fact, the state nurses' association and the state association of nursing homes have always agreed that the administering of medicines in nursing homes is a nursing function and must be performed by licensed nurses. Now, that position is being challenged in the legislature.

After a few hurried phone calls, McGovern and her colleagues in the state nursing home association learn that the bill has been referred to committee. They also learn that the bill was introduced by a representative in support of a group of businessmen and physicians who are building a nursing home facility in his rural district. The businessmen have argued that medication technicians in nursing homes are more cost-effective than licensed personnel and, if properly trained and supervised, present no additional risk to nursing home residents. Since the number of elderly residents needing this kind of care and the cost of employing licensed nursing personnel have risen dramatically in the last few years, the bill is viewed as a means to help provide low-cost nursing home care for the state's residents. The bill has the support of the state medical association and the state pharmaceutical association.

When the bill comes out of committee, McGovern and many of her colleagues testify against the bill. To her dismay, many of her physician colleagues on the joint effort group testify in favor of the bill. To make matters worse, many registered and practical nurses employed by nursing homes attend the hearing and testify through their representatives that the use of medication technicians will "free us of the time-consuming task of medication administration to devote more time to the delivery of needed nursing care to patients." A number of the nurses have received the day off with pay to testify for the bill.

The bill is passed and sent to the governor for signature. McGovern, other directors of nursing homes, and officials of the state nursing home association send an urgent message to the governor opposing the potential legislation. They also request time for a governor-appointed task force to study the use of medication technicians in nursing homes. There is nothing more they can do but hope that someone close to the governor will speak on their behalf.

The need for individual participation in the political process is evident in this case situation. Three issues create ethical conflicts on different levels. The first issue is the quality of patient care in nursing home settings and the risk to nursing home residents if medications are not administered by licensed personnel. For McGovern and her nursing home colleagues, this is a critical situation. If the bill is passed, they will be responsible for the expertise of those administering medication in their institutions. Since they are personally opposed to the giving of medications by unlicensed personnel, they might be put in the uncomfortable position of being responsible for a practice they are opposed to.

The second issue involves the trade-offs necessary to achieve cost-effective nursing home care. McGovern and her colleagues take the position that high quality nursing home care translates into the giving of medications by licensed nursing personnel.

Physicians and others, including many nurses, argue that cost-effective nursing home care means that high-cost nursing care be replaced, in part, by unlicensed personnel giving medications. The crucial question is whether the quality of nursing home care ought to be sacrificed for cost-effective care. The ethical tension between the two choices is a classic example of one of the most common ethical dilemmas in health care: between what is right according to universal moral norms and what is right according to outcomes or consequences.

A third issue concerns the mandate for collaboration between members of the nursing profession and members of other health professions. The fact that many physicians support the bill, including the state medical association, creates tension between nurses and physicians. At what point should members of one profession feel obligated to negotiate their differences with other professionals? Is compromise on important issues ever ethically acceptable? If so, under what conditions? If not, how can tensions between professionals be resolved to preserve joint effectiveness on larger political issues concerning health? These are important concerns in political involvement. While professional documents mandate individual involvement on political issues, the complexity of the issues may require a considerable amount of professional compromise to create change or wield power in political arenas affecting health care.

COLLECTIVE RESPONSIBILITIES OF NURSING

The responsibilities of nursing as a collective body are presented in *Nursing: A Social Policy Statement* (American Nurses' Association, 1980). This document states that the nursing profession has leadership responsibilities in five areas frequently addressed as political issues: (1) the organization, delivery, and financing of health care; (2) the development of health resources; (3) preventive and environmental measures to provide for public health; (4) the development of new knowledge and technology through research; and (5) health care planning.

The political process is often used to shape public perceptions of needs and create public demands. Thus it can be used to advance vested interests where the public good may be of lesser or no concern. The nursing profession's overriding concern, however, must always be the public good. Thus, the nursing profession is expected to work through political channels to help protect the public good, not vested interests of any particular group. Since political priorities for action are often based on society's values and its needs, the nursing profession should focus its attentions on the health orientations of the public.

Two means by which the nursing profession carries out its responsibilities for political involvement are the American Nurses' Association (ANA) and its political action affiliate, the Nurses' Coalition for Action in Politics (N-CAP). The ANA has a government relations office in Washington and is registered as an official lobby. The functions of the ANA are: (1) to evaluate and promote legislation; (2) to advance the goals of the association; (3) to publish a legislative newsletter; (4) to monitor federal and state legislation; and (5) to study trends in government in terms of their implications for nursing practice, services, education, economics, and goals of the ANA. The positions on political issues are developed by representatives on various cabinets and councils, members of its house of delegates, and officials of the organization. The Political Education Department of the ANA also works to: (1) encourage nurses to take a more active part in governmental affairs; (2) increase the political consciousness of nurses; and (3) assist nurses in organizing themselves for political action.

As the political action committee of the ANA, N-CAP endorses and makes contributions to political candidates regardless of party affiliation who by their voting record and statements have demonstrated their interest in the health of the nation (Humphrey, 1979). Since ANA is a lobbying group, it is not allowed to use membership funds for contributions to political candidates. N-CAP solicits funds for campaign contributions from members of its constituent state nurses' associations.

The responsibilities of the nursing profession are more clearly stated and supported than the responsibilities of the individual nurse in professional documents and statements. Although the individual nurse is urged and expected to be politically active, this involvement is viewed as supporting the professional or collective responsibility, often in cooperation with other health disciplines. The nursing profession and individual nurses have fundamental responsibilities to protect and advance citizens' interests in matters of health. The role of the individual nurse in political issues supported by the collective voice of nursing, however, may prove difficult when the nurse's individual values and goals conflict with professional values and goals. The following case illustrates the conflict of individual values with values held by the profession. It also questions the moral authority of the profession where the health status of the individual patient is at issue.

As Marge Tomlinson, the evening nurse on A-Wing, a primary care unit for patients with chronic diseases, completed her charting, she wondered who would be taking her place during the remainder of the week. She and most of Memorial Hospital's nurses would be on strike starting at 7 a.m. the next morning. The decision to strike had been reached several days ago by the urban hospital's nurses after many hours of meetings, conferences with hospital administration, and heated discussion among the nursing staff.

Tomlinson strongly supported her colleagues' efforts to increase salaries, fringe benefits, and general working conditions for all nurses employed by Memorial Hospital. She had personally experienced many frustrating evenings in recent months due to loss of nursing staff dissatisfied with the low morale, poor salary, and short staffing. She had also experienced decreased support services for the consistently high number of chronic disease patients on her 35-bed unit. Yet now that the strike was imminent, Tomlinson wondered whether further reducing the available nursing services to the patients in A-Wing by striking was in their immediate best interest.

During the previous two days, some patients had been sent home early in preparation for the strike. Several elderly patients whose care was too involved for families to manage had been placed in nursing homes, much to the distress of the patients and their families. But other patients, like Ralph Osborn, a 63-year-old recent amputee with diabetes mellitus and congestive heart failure, could not be moved. Osborn and other patients without families or other resources were dependent on the nursing staff of A-Wing to meet their daily physiological and nursing care needs. Tomlinson had been Osborn's primary care nurse for five weeks. During that time, he had progressed from a dependent, irresponsible individual with chronic disease to an individual willing to begin assuming his physical care. She hoped that within another month, Osborn could be discharged to a nearby rehabilitation center to complete his adjustment to chronic disease and life as an amputee. Without good nursing care during the coming weeks and careful monitoring of his medication, blood sugar levels, and self-care efforts, he would be at risk for reoccurrence of the multiple problems that had necessitated this hospital stay and his recent surgery. Yet there was no way Tomlinson could guarantee the availability of the kind and level of care and supervision he needed during the next few days or weeks. Like the other nurses at Memorial Hospital, she could only hope that the collective efforts of the nursing staff would quickly bring about improved working conditions for the benefit of future patients.

Many of her nursing colleagues considered the decision to strike as a professional responsibility. They also claimed that it was ethical to strike because the ANA *Code for Nurses* stated that "the nurse participates in the profession's efforts to establish and maintain conditions of employment conducive to high quality nursing care." Yet Tomlinson questioned whether these efforts should be carried out when nursing services were already operating at a minimal level of care and safety for the patient. She also wondered whether the profession should direct the actions of individual nurses through its code of ethics. The expectations of patients like Osborn and the obligation to provide the best possible care under any conditions made her wonder whether the *Code for Nurses* should be interpreted as encouraging nurses to "collective action . . . to achieve employment conditions to which the professional standards of practice can be implemented. . . ." Following professional expectations and directives might result in nurses walking a picket line while patients received minimal standards of nursing care.

The nurse in this case situation is torn between two courses of action; both can be considered morally correct. Choosing one course of action acknowledges that working conditions at Memorial Hospital directly affect patient care. Not only are nurses already working in less than optimal conditions, but as more nurses find the situation intolerable, they leave, making conditions worse. Thus, by striking, nurses can use the loss of their nursing care as a tool to create change in the working conditions of the hospital and eventually improve patient care (Muyskens, 1982).

Choosing a second course of action acknowledges that certain patients may be placed at risk or denied beneficial care while the nurses are striking. Since the nurse has an obligation to provide patient care and safety, she should not strike unless optimal nursing care can be provided for each patient. Unfortunately, optimal nursing care is not always possible during strikes. Thus the nurse must decide which "good" is of higher importance—improved nursing care for all future patients or beneficial care for an identified patient. Not to participate in the strike is to acknowledge that the provision of beneficial care to the identified patient is more important (Veatch & Bleich, 1975).

In deciding between these possible courses of action, the nurse may appeal to several authorities. If Tomlinson appeals to the ANA *Code for Nurses* as her authority, she will be considering the ethical code the source of rules for ethically appropriate conduct for nurses. While codes of ethics often provide broad guidelines for ethical conduct among members of a profession, we usually do not agree that ethical conduct is actually created by the professional group. Ethics are not a matter of what some social group decides. Ethics encompass what is morally right for the whole of life and not just what is right for the professional role. Thus Tomlinson should consider whether the social group—the nursing profession—knows what is right in that situation or whether there are other authorities to which she might appeal—for example, her religious group, her peers, the broader values of society, or even the patient's value system. Regardless of which authority she selects, she will have to consider the justifications for her particular moral judgments in that situation and their universality for all relevantly similar situations (Muyskens, 1982).

Tomlinson should also consider the dimensions of her professional role in each of the possible courses of action (Bowie, 1982). She should ask the following questions: Does the individual who is also a nurse always primarily represent that role? Is it permissible for nurses just to represent their role as citizens? Do nurses have a responsibility to voice their individual opinions or support the profession's positions in matters not directly related to health?

In professional documents, the mandate to be involved in political issues as a nurse and as a supporter of the nursing profession seems clear. The individual nurse and the nursing profession are presumed to have fundamental responsibilities to protect and advance citizens' interests in health matters. The role of the individual nurse and the nursing profession is less clear in political issues not related to health. Thus it is necessary to understand the dynamics of the professional role and the moral adequacy of involvement in political issues not related to health care.

POLITICAL ACTIVITIES AND THE PROFESSIONAL ROLE

Downie (1982) states that there are two dimensions of the health professional's role relevant to political involvement. The first dimension is concerned with the role of the individual as a professional representative expressing the collective values of the profession. Individual action necessarily expresses collective responsibility since it is "through the individual that the profession is represented." The health professional involved in political issues actually represents his or her profession as: (1) the ascriptive representative (meaning that his actions are authorized by the profession by virtue of professional education), and (2) the values of the profession insofar as the professional acts in terms of its ethics.

The interesting question to ask is: Who bears primary moral responsibility for ascribed actions? Are nurses, in representing the profession, morally responsible for their actions? In a sense, yes. When one acts in terms of a social role, not merely in a private capacity, the individual bears moral responsibility for the actions done in the name of a particular profession. There is a certain "morality of role acceptance," which means that when individuals accept a given role, they act in capacities defined by the nature of the profession, *as a collective* (Downie, 1982). Downie states, "We can say that individuals are authorized by their collectives to act in certain ways, depending on the function of the collective" (p 49). Thus, even though one may act as an individual, he or she also acts as a representative of a profession with responsibility to uphold the rights, duties, and values of the profession.

There is, however, a richer dimension of the professional role relevant to political involvement. This dimension provides a strong directive for collective responsibility in matters of health and involves sharing concerns for health and welfare with other professions. It means that nurses must act as representatives of society and must act in concert with the other health professions mandated by society.

This view of involvement in political issues by the nursing profession is consistent with the ANA document, *Nursing: A Social Policy Statement* (1980), and the profession's code of ethics. From the assumption that "nursing is owned by society . . . and must be perceived as serving the interests of the large whole of which it is a part" (ANA, 1980, p 3), to the ethical obligation to "enhance citizens' health through political involvement" (ANA, 1976, p 19), nursing is expected to serve society's interests in the area of health. Thus, involvement in political issues is an appropriate activity for individual nurses when such involvement ultimately serves society's interests in matters relating to health care. It is also an appropriate activity for the nursing profession when done in collaboration with other health professions mandated by society.

References

American Nurses' Association: *Code for Nurses with Interpretive Statements*. ANA, 1976.

American Nurses' Association: *Nursing: A Social Policy Statement*. ANA, 1980.

American Public Health Association, Public Health Nursing Section: *The Definition and Role of Public Health Nursing in the Delivery of Health Care*. APHA, 1980.

Bowie NE: 'Role' as a moral concept in health care. *J Med Philos* 1982; 7:57–63.

Downie RS: Collective responsibility in health care. *J Med Philos* 1982; 7:43–56.

Humphrey C: Introduction: Mandate for nurses: involvement in health policy. Pages 1–10 in: *The Emergence of Nursing as a Political Force*. National League for Nursing, 1979.

Muyskens JL: Nurses' collective responsibility and the strike weapon. *J Med Philos* 1982; 7:101–12.

Veatch RM, Bleich D: Interns and residents on strike. *Hastings Cent Rep* (Dec) 1975; 5:7–8.

GENERIC STRATEGIES FOR POLITICAL ACTION

Effective political action requires skillful application of strategies that can be applied to one's sphere of influence. Some of these strategies related to politics, power, change, and conflict were introduced in Unit II. The reader is encouraged to review this preceding unit, particularly the discussions of conflict management and negotiation. Unit III presents additional strategies basic to effective political action and elaborates on some of the strategies introduced in Unit II.

Just as a nurse must assess a patient before developing a nursing care plan, so must the politically astute nurse analyze the structures and processes of the sphere she wants to influence. Chapter 13 describes how to analyze these structures and processes and offers ideas and strategies for action by nurses.

Using data from the political analysis, nurses can begin to develop appropriate political strategies. In Unit II, politics was defined as an interpersonal, humanistic endeavor—a description that fits nursing as well. Most nurses already possess interpersonal skills, although application of these skills has too often been confined to nurse-patient interactions. In Chapter 14, development of these interpersonal skills and their application to the four spheres of influence are discussed. The author focuses on politics as the exercise of influence and describes three components: communication, collectivity, and collegiality.

The importance of collective action is stressed throughout this book. In Chapter 15, collective strategies receive in-depth attention. This chapter stimulates the nurse to think about possible sources for collective support. Coalition building and networking are important means for developing a support base. Chapter 15 also includes an important example of coalition building—the Nurses in Washington Roundtable—an ongoing collaboration of nurses in Washington, DC.

Chapter 16 turns the reader's attention to the principles for pursuing an issue by analyzing the case of the Tennessee nurse-midwives forced out of private practice by competing physicians. The midwives' and consumers' response to this challenge is told in an exciting way by the author, a colleague of the midwives.

As competition for scarce resources increases among multiple special interest groups, nurses are becoming more aware of marketing. Chapter 17 introduces nurses to the concept and principles of marketing. These principles are illustrated by two vignettes that describe the successful marketing efforts of the Stanford University Medical Center Nursing Department.

Unit III concludes with a case study of a court case involving comparable worth. The case against the City and County of Denver was brought by seven nurses who believed that it was not equitable for the city to pay nurses less than city tree trimmers. The case extended over five years. The story, written by one of the plaintiffs, describes the efforts of a group of committed nurses and a national network of nurse supporters, who used the courts to pursue an issue of great importance to nursing and the women's movement.

Chapter 13

Political Analysis: Structures and Processes

Susan W. Talbott, RN, MA, MBA

With a Section on Parliamentary Procedure by Barbara Nichols, RN, MS

Nurses who understand the systems in which they work can function better and provide better patient care. Nurses can expand their influence by learning how to use the formal and informal structures and processes in the workplace, professional organization, government, and their own communities.

FORMAL STRUCTURE AND PROCESSES

Nurses who work in hospitals (about 67 percent) can learn a great deal about institutions by examining key documents, including the table of organization; statement of mission, goals, and objectives; and policy and procedure manuals. Nurses who want to learn about a professional association, a community organization, or a government structure can examine similar documents plus the organization's constitution and by-laws, annual report, or long-range planning document. The following review of these documents, as well as a brief discussion of important structural processes (budget, committees, and policies and procedures) will help nurses understand the formal structure and processes of organizations.

Table of Organization

A table of organization presents the "big picture" of the organization with its divisions, departments, and units. The solid lines on such tables show the chain of command or "who reports to whom" and indicate, to some degree, who holds formal power in different parts of the organization. For example, the director of nursing who is responsible for a staff of 500 RNs, the management of all patient units plus the OR, OPD and unit management, and a budget in the millions has an important role in the

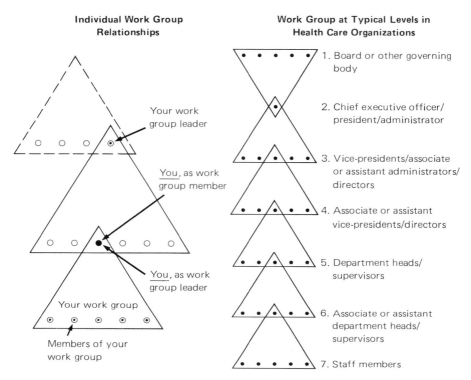

Figure 13-1 Work Groups and the Organization (Adapted from Likert R: *New Patterns of Management*. McGraw-Hill, 1961.)

overall goals of the organization. The span of the nursing director's control will be illustrated by the organization chart.

Examining an organizational chart of the workplace will enable the nurse to:

1. Understand her place within the organization
2. Understand the chain of command, eg, who reports to whom
3. Visualize the relationship of the nursing department to the larger organization.

This vignette illustrates the importance of knowing and following the rules dictated by a formal table of organization:

A staff nurse on a medical unit wants to transfer to the surgical ICU. If she is unaware of the need to follow the department policy for transfers (which takes into consideration the chain of command), the nurse might go directly to the chief nurse in the surgical ICU. The chief nurse will probably ask if she has discussed the transfer with her head nurse and, finding she has not, instruct her on the appropriate manner in which to make a transfer request, following the chain of command.

1. Inform your boss; never "jump over" his or her head. No boss likes surprises, and hearing that an employee is applying for a position in another division other than from the employee will not go over well.

2. Demonstrate your awareness of how to negotiate the chain of command in formal situations like a transfer. Review the nursing department policies to get an idea of how other policies reflect the need to follow the formal chain of command.

3. Remember that the table of organization serves as a map for an organization. Use it as a guide in your formal relationships with others.

Tables of organization are changing in many hospitals because of decentralization. This process entails the "flattening of the organization." For example, in many hospitals there are no longer supervisory nursing positions. Instead, all head nurses in a particular division report directly to an assistant director of nursing. Modern management theory advocates this trend because it reduces layers of administration and enhances the nurse's accountability for her professional practice. Involving employees in decision making that affects them results in their having a vested interest in "doing a good job"—in working for, not against, the organization (Porter-O'Grady & Finnigan, 1984).

Mission Statement, Goals and Objectives

Many nursing departments and nursing organizations have written their philosophy with a statement of mission, goals, and objectives. A statement of philosophy consists of fundamental beliefs underlying the activities of an organization.

A mission statement describes the business with which a group of individuals, such as a nursing department, is charged. It is an enduring statement, frequently discussed, and changed only after careful consideration. It should be communicated to all who work in the organization and discussed by work groups, because it provides general guidelines for individual and work group behavior. An example of a hospital's mission statement might be: Evans Memorial Hospital seeks to provide the highest quality nursing and medical care for consumers in Addison County.

Goal statements outline how the mission statement will be implemented. They provide a framework for defining objectives. Goal statements are usually written in terms of expected results (outcomes) to be achieved over a period of time, often a year or more. Review of goal statements by each work group concerned should occur during budget planning each year. A goal statement written by school health nurses in a city health department might say: "Teenagers attending schools with a high rate of adolescent pregnancy will be identified and included in a reproductive health education program."

Objectives focusing on high priority concerns are written to support the mission and goal statements. They are guides to action, measurable, and defined by results. They provide a basis for performance evaluation and for formulating revised and new objectives. They should be prepared by those who will be doing the work, such as the nursing staff who work together on one unit. They should be feasible, recognizing the limits of key resources (people, money, time) and double within a year. An objective set by nurses in an extended care facility, for example, might be to set up a rehabilitation program for poststroke patients, including a plan for evaluation of the program.

A careful study of the mission statement, goals, and objectives assists in understanding the essence of the organization. When you apply for a nursing position, ask for a copy of the mission statement for the organization as well as the nursing department. The mission statement of the nursing department should mesh with the institution's. If you work in an organization that has not developed a statement of mission, goals, and objectives, you and several of your colleagues might offer to develop a draft for consideration by the leadership group (Penberth-Valentine, 1984). Defining the mission, goals, and objectives can help improve the quality and cost-effectiveness of nursing practice. Nurses who work on the same unit or team are more inclined to work toward a goal if they have defined it and made a public commitment to it. On a personal level, involvement in the development of formal statements can help nurses learn how to effect change. Participation in the process of organizational change often stimulates personal growth and development.

Policy and Procedures

All nurses are familiar with policy and procedure books, but how many take the time to review nonclinical policies and procedures? Because knowledge is power, a review of policies and procedures that govern most organizations is worthwhile. This is especially true if you have an idea for a new approach you want to introduce. For example, you believe the transfer policy, which makes it difficult for nurses to transfer from one position to another, causes staff nurses to resign and take positions in other hospitals. You might suggest to a receptive and responsible administrator that the transfer policy be evaluated and changed to reduce nursing turnover. You could offer to help carry out the evaluation and make recommendations. Many hospitals invite nurses to serve on recruitment/retention committees that look for ways to encourage qualified nurses to join and remain on the staff.

Despite the fact that policy and procedure manuals appear formidable, they often need revision. Does your organization have a committee that systematically reviews them? If not, maybe you should help organize one.

The Budget Process

In this period of scarce resources, nurses are looking at how funding is allocated. The nursing association committee chairperson wants a fair piece of the financial pie just as the head nurse does. Nurses are also looking at how funding can be generated to support special projects. Nurse entrepreneurs, many of whom own their own businesses, know the importance of the budget process.

How can you find out about the financial picture of your organization or employer? Ask the chief administrator for a copy of the annual report, which should include a report of the financial status of the organization. After you have studied this document and the mission, goal, and objective statements, ask for details about how the budget is drawn up. In a hospital, you might ask your head nurse if she is responsible for drafting the budget for your unit. With the trend toward decentralization, many head nurses have assumed this responsibility. In the workplace, nursing association, community organization, or legislative body, there will be a formal system of tracking income and expenses and correlating them with allocation of monies to various cost centers or budget categories.

If you work for a privately held corporation, you might not be able to review its financial statements. For public institutions, you should be able to obtain reports and budget information. In some organizations and institutions, it will take time and effort to obtain the information you want. You may have to be persistent, and a group approach with a clearly defined purpose is recommended.

What might you want to learn about the budget process?

- How much money is allocated to a particular cost center, for example, to a 28-bed medical unit or to a legislative committee of your district nursing association?
- Who decides how the funds will be used? Is this determined by a board of directors, a budget committee, or does one person, a head nurse for example, make the decisions? Can members of the work group submit requests for funds for specific projects or question decisions on allocation of resources?
- How is the use of funds evaluated? Does the head nurse write an annual report describing the work of the unit and analyzing the expenditures?
- If you have an idea for a project that will require funding, how and where can you submit your request?

Nurses and nursing administrators must take charge and be accountable for costs associated with patient care. Some see prospective reimbursement, such as the DRG system (diagnosis-related groups), as an opportunity to end the lumping of nursing care costs with other costs. Nurses in Maine have taken a strong stand on accountability by convincing the state legislature to pass a law that requires hospitals to break out nursing care costs as a separate item on patients' bills (Hospitals must, 1983).

Committee Structure

Much of the work of an organization is carried out by committees. Take time to find out about the various standing committees in your nursing department. Some committees include only RNs, eg, a committee on continuing education or peer review. Others are multidisciplinary, such as those on equipment selection, space allocation, pharmacy, or nurse-physician relations. The functions of committees vary; some have policy-making responsibilities and others advisory functions. Most organizations have standing committees, such as the membership committee of a nurses' association, while ad hoc committees are created to carry out specific projects in a limited time period.

Service on a committee enables nurses to influence the decision-making process. For example, nurses use a variety of equipment in caring for patients and should have a say in determining what will be purchased. Participation in decision making fosters a sense of accountability and a spirit of loyalty.

Committee work affords nurses an educational opportunity to learn about the process as well as content areas. It also provides an opportunity to meet other people,

---

Checklist of Documents to Review

1. Table of organization
2. Statement of mission, goals, and objectives
3. Constitution and bylaws
4. Annual reports, including budget
5. Long-range planning documents
6. Nursing department statement of philosophy
7. Listing of organization's or department's standing committees
8. Listing of organization's board of directors and committee chairs. (Check to see how many nurses are on the hospital board.)
9. Policy and procedure manuals

---

developing personal and professional networks. (See Puetz, Chapter 15.) Active involvement with committees is an antidote to burnout and reduces feelings of isolation and impotence. Committee work also fosters collegial relationships, a lively exchange of ideas, and opportunities for shared problem solving. Tips on committee involvement (Tropman, 1980):

- The person who chairs a committee and sets the meeting agenda has a major influence on the direction of the committee's work.
- The person who takes minutes influences the manner in which the committee activities are recorded.
- The committee secretary can also keep the participants focused on the agenda by alerting the chair when the groups' attention strays. She might also offer to summarize discussion to help the committee determine a plan of action.
- Prepare to influence action on an item of concern to you by lobbying committee members before the meeting.
- If your effort to influence action fails, you might succeed the second time.
- If you want to work on a particular committee, seek out the chair to find out details of the committee's work. Then ask to be appointed.

Parliamentary Procedure

This section is contributed by Barbara Nichols, an expert on parliamentary procedure and past-president of the American Nurses' Association. She summarizes how to manage a meeting.

Parliamentary procedure provides a democratic process that carefully balances the rights of individuals, subgroups within an organization, and the membership of an as-

Basic Principles of Parliamentary Procedure

1. All business is brought before the meeting by a motion, resolution, a report of a committee, or a communication. The terms "motion" and "question" are synonymous; when first stated it is referred to as a "motion"; when it is repeated by the presiding officer (the chair), it is referred to as a "question." The motion should be worded in the affirmative whenever possible.

2. To make a motion, the individual must be recognized by the presiding officer (chair).

3. Every motion must be seconded, or it dies. Seconding a motion does not commit the person to support it in any way. A person seconds a motion to indicate that he or she believes that the motion should come before the meeting.

4. Only the presiding officer can place a motion before the group or assembly. She does this by restating the motion (reads it) and asking, "Is there discussion?"

5. Once the presiding officer has restated the motion, the motion is said to be "pending." It is then open to debate. The maker of the motion is entitled to speak first on the motion.

6. Only one main motion may be considered at one time. Until it is disposed of, either by a vote on the motion itself or by a vote on a secondary motion affecting it, no new main motion may be made.

7. Secondary or subsidiary motions most commonly used include those that amend, table, refer to a committee, postpone to a later date, or close debate. These are called subsidiary motions because they can only be made when a main motion to which they apply is "pending" or before the group. Each of these motions requires a second before it can be considered. Each is open for discussion before a vote is taken, except the motion to close debate, which is nondebatable.

8. Motions must not be in violation of local, state, or federal laws; the organization's constitution, bylaws, or standing rules.

9. The maker of a motion can vote against but cannot speak against his or her own motion, despite the fact he might have changed his opinion since introducing the motion.

10. The presiding officer may require that main motions, amendments, or instructions to committees be presented to her in writing before discussion is permitted. This is common practice at the ANA House of Delegates (annual business meeting of the American Nurses' Association) and business meetings of many state and student nursing associations.

sembly. Fundamental to the understanding and use of parliamentary procedure is respect for fairness and order in assemblies, organizations, or groups. Respect is demonstrated by a participant's willingness to adhere to an orderly method of procedure guided by the will of the majority, while protecting the rights of the minority and safeguarding the interests of absent members.

The basic rules of parliamentary procedure are clearly delineated in *Roberts' Rules of Order Newly Revised* (1981). This has been accepted throughout the United States as

Motions and Procedures

Motions are classified as follows:

1. A *main* motion brings before the group or assembly some new subject upon which action is desired.

2. *Privileged* motions do not pertain to the question or main motion but are of such urgency and importance that they take precedence over other business and are not debatable. There are five privileged motions:
   - call for the orders of the day (force consideration of a postponed motion)
   - questions of privilege (make a personal request during debate)
   - to take a recess
   - to adjourn
   - to fix the time at which to adjourn

3. *Incidental* motions arise from debate of a main motion and must be decided before any other business is taken up. They have no special rank, but they yield to privileged questions and take precedence over subsidiary motions. There are seven incidental motions:
   - to appeal the decision of the chair (reverse the chair's ruling)
   - to suspend the rules (change convention rules)
   - to call for point of order (to ask a question or correct parliamentary error)
   - to object to consideration of a question (to suppress action)
   - to withdraw or modify a motion
   - to divide the question (consider its parts separately)

4. *Subsidiary* or secondary motions may be applied to a main motion and to certain other motions for modifying, delaying action, or otherwise disposing of them. Subsidiary motions are the most frequently used motions in parliamentary procedure and yield to privileged and incidental motions. Anyone can make amendments to the main motion or an amendment to an amendment. If a motion becomes too cluttered with amendments, it may be wise to offer a substitute motion that corrects the situation by restating the proposal in a clear fashion.

   There are seven subsidiary motions. They are made while a main motion is pending for the purpose of delaying action or otherwise disposing of the main motion:
   - to table (to defer action)
   - previous question (force immediate vote)
   - modify debate (extend or limit time for debate)
   - postpone to a certain time
   - refer to committee (for further study)
   - amend (modify a motion)
   - postpone indefinitely (to suppress action)

5. Miscellaneous and unclassified motions are used to take up a question again or to change or undo an action previously taken. These motions are to: reconsider, rescind, and take from the table. They provide an opportunity for members of an assembly to reconsider a subject. The group may or may not reverse its decision.

the standard authority on parliamentary law and procedure and is the reference for this section.

Parliamentary law, evolved from the customs and rules for conducting business in the English Parliament, forms the basis for the conduct of our Congress, state legislatures, and local assemblies. Parliamentary rules and procedures are based upon the principles of law and have been adapted for use by groups other than legislative bodies. Parliamentary procedure assists a group in determining what it wants to do and how it will carry out its decisions.

The outline of key points and procedure (shown in the box at left) is offered as a basic guide.

Conducting a Meeting. The presiding officer or chair leads the activities of a formal meeting. The chair must keep order, expedite the business of the meeting, and ensure that the rules of the group or assembly are enforced. The presiding officer must know basic parliamentary principles and how to apply them. The chair should:

1. Call the meeting to order on time
2. Refer to himself or herself as "the chair," not "I"
3. Follow the agenda and keep the members informed about the status of the business under consideration
4. Deal firmly with disturbances, frivolous motions, or debate-delaying tactics
5. See that debate is confined to the merits of the motion
6. Remain calm and deal fairly with all sides, regardless of personal opinion.

Group Member Participation. As a group member, you want to:

1. Prepare carefully for meetings
2. Assist in clarifying problems and tasks
3. Promote efficient, orderly, and fair deliberations
4. Contribute to objective review of all pertinent information
5. Support decisions consistent with the organization's mission, goals, and objectives.

Voting. The vote needed to pass a motion or elect an official is based upon the votes actually cast, unless otherwise specified by the bylaws or rules:

- By consent of an assembly, a formal vote can be avoided on routine matters when there is no opposition.
- A voice vote or a show of hands is a common way to take a vote when the group is small.
- When the presiding officer is unsure of the result of a vote, he or she can request a standing vote or a roll call (division).
- A motion for a ballot (written vote) can be made if the bylaws do not already require one. This motion is not debatable and requires a majority vote.

The rules and principles of parliamentary procedure are intended to help, not hinder, democratic decision making by groups. Applied with common sense, they ensure efficient and effective meetings.

If you take time to study the formal structure and processes of your workplace, your professional association, governmental bodies, or a community organization, you will have a broader understanding of how and why they work and be in a stronger position to influence the organization. Who knows, one day you may be the CEO or president of the organization where you now participate as a staff nurse, volunteer, committee member, or elected/appointed official.

INFORMAL STRUCTURE AND PROCESSES

All organizations have an "informal life" not bound by a formal chain of command, board of directors, or committee structure. Anyone who wants to influence an organization should take stock of the informal structure and processes. This is not easy to do because there are no formal documents to study. Nobody writes an annual report about the activities of informal networks of staff or members who influence decision making in the nursing department, professional organization, or local political club. To learn about informal connections or networks, it is important to be an insider.

Informal Communication

There are ways to identify and influence the informal structure and process. One nursing director, for example, wanted to expand interactions with nursing staff. She initiated walking rounds on a different nursing unit each week. Although a nurse was asked to make a formal presentation on a patient, there was time for informal exchanges as the nursing director moved through the halls or sat in the nurses' station. The nursing director learned that nursing care was impeded because there were too few medication carts. While information about this problem would have ultimately made its way through channels to the appropriate committee on hospital equipment, direct access to the nursing director brought the problem-solving process into action more quickly.

In another hospital, a group of head nurses set up an informal luncheon meeting. Despite the hours they spent each month in formal meetings, they realized they needed time to talk together about common problems and achievements. Self-help (support) groups of this sort are frequently developed by nurses for their patients, eg, ostomy groups, postmastectomy groups, but nurses fail to see how such groups can help them personally and professionally (Kirschenbaum & Glaser, 1978). Even an informal gathering over coffee before or after a formal meeting provides time for colleagues to share ideas and offer counsel to one another.

There are other informal processes that can be used to advantage. The evaluation process is usually formal, but effective managers keep staff members up to date on their performance in informal ways. Has your boss ever taken you aside and paid you a compliment, telling you what a good job you've done on a particular project or patient care assignment? Everyone appreciates receiving praise from peers, subordinates, and superiors without waiting for a formal meeting to be arranged.

Sending a quick note or memo is an informal communication process. It is always advisable to keep a copy "for the record" so you will know exactly what you said. For example, you want your supervisor to cover for you so that you can attend a conference. You asked her during an informal meeting over lunch, and she agreed to help you, but you confirm it in writing by sending her a brief memo, keeping a copy for your files. It could happen that on the appointed day your supervisor tells you she does not recall your request, but you have the memo to show her:

May 3, 1985

Memo TO: Sally Jenkins, RN
From: Mary K. Herman, RN

Thank you for agreeing to cover for me on June 1, 2, 3, 1985 while I attend the ICU conference at Evans Memorial Hospital.

Copy: Nursing office scheduling secretary

If you confirm in writing what you agree to in informal conversations with others, misunderstandings can be averted.

Power and Influence

Those with formal titles usually have power and authority. But others who do not have important titles also wield power and influence. It is important to analyze where the power lies, because you may need to involve "power people" in your efforts to make change.

On many units, nurse's aides wield informal power despite their status. An aide on one unit was a close friend of the man who delivered linen to the floor. The aide's floor always had an adequate supply of linen. Another example is a nurse who, as a new member of her political club, was nominated to run for a key committee position based on her friendship with the club president. Because of connections in city politics, a nursing director in a large city hospital always seemed able to obtain the necessary funds for nursing department projects.

When assessing the sources of power and influence in your organization, keep in mind both the formal and informal channels. The board of directors of a hospital or community organization has the authority to direct the work of the organization. But, members of this group are often influenced by their friends and colleagues. For example, a group of nurses in one legislator's district worked with her to draft a bill relating to the restoration of prenatal care funds. The legislator in turn discussed the importance of this bill with her uncle, who was a prominent member of the city hospital board of directors. He in turn mobilized his colleagues to pressure their city council representatives to vote for passage of this important health care bill.

Old Boy-New Girl Networks

Many important decisions are made outside of formal board or committee meetings. The idea of the "old boy" networks conjures up visions of men on golf courses or at private clubs. Hennig and Jardin (1977) discuss how men use networks. The "old boys" club in your hospital may include prominent physicians, often chiefs of service. In some hospitals, there are still dining rooms reserved for physicians. Hospital administrators, also a powerful group, have extensive networks beyond the institutions they manage.

Nurses are beginning to use "new girl" networks. For example, a group of nursing directors in a large city has begun to meet informally to discuss common concerns. They share ideas, ask for help in solving problems, compare notes on reimbursement and cost-cutting initiatives. Another group of nurses with a variety of professional interests, such as teaching, administration, independent practice, direct service, and consultation, get together for dinner every month or two to socialize and exchange ideas and information. An informal gathering of nurses centers around the management of a district nurses' association. A newly elected president, realizing the vast scope of opportunities to exert leadership, invites a group of district members to meet over brunch every month or two. The purpose is to keep in close touch with different areas of nursing practice as well as generate ideas for action by the association. National leaders have "kitchen cabinets," informal groups of individuals who can be counted on for honest opinions on issues. Nursing leaders also can benefit from such informal advisory bodies. Ideas can be generated at such gatherings, and individuals or small groups take them back to their workplace, professional association, community, or governmental spheres.

Nurses also need networks with other professionals who share common interests. One group of female mental health professionals organized informally around their common concern with women's issues such as equal pay, the equal rights amendment, and access to health care. This group included nurses, psychologists, and social workers. A different group of mental health professionals (nurses, psychiatrists, social workers, psychologists, and administrators) met regularly to discuss concerns about state support for psychiatric care in the large city where they worked. They conveyed their recommendations to the state's commissioner of mental health.

A nurse member of the New York State Governor's Commission on Domestic Violence uses her interdisciplinary networks whenever legislation needs support or opposition from health professionals. In 1984, the Commission supported a bill to remove the corroboration requirement in cases of child sexual abuse. Because of opposition from a few key legislators, the nurse knew that expert testimony in support of the bill from health professionals would be essential for passage. She alerted the New York State Nurses' Association, which arranged for a nurse who is an expert in the treatment of victims of sexual abuse to testify. She also urged the lobbyist of the State Psychiatric Association to lobby for the bill and asked the chair of the Child Psychiatry Committee to testify on behalf of the bill. Additionally, the nurse contacted colleagues on nursing faculties and asked them to review the bill with their students and to encourage them to write their state legislators on behalf of the bill. Members of the commission contacted other groups, such as the Women's Bar Association, to generate support for the bill. All Commission members used their professional networks and the result was a victory—the bill was passed and signed by the governor. Professional networks and informal coalitions can be powerful forces in any arena.

Social Circles

Social contacts are also an opportunity for networking. One nurse, a neighbor and friend of a powerful state legislator, has spent hours talking with him about nursing and health care issues, and he calls upon her when he has questions in these areas. He keeps her informed when key nursing or health bills are moving through the legislature and uses his influence to get them passed or defeated. This mutually beneficial arrangement illustrates the concept of quid pro quo—something for something—you help me and I'll help you.

In another social setting, a nursing home board member attends the same church as a young staff nurse. They often talk about the nursing home. During a period of high nursing turnover, the board member asked the nurse for her opinion on why the turnover was so high and solicited her suggestions for reducing it. After their informal discussion, the board member convinced the board to fund the task force on recruitment and retention that the new nursing director had requested. He also told the nursing director he was impressed by the young nurse's ideas for solving the recruitment/retention problem and suggested that the director consider appointing her to the task force.

Access to Resources

Whom do you know who has power and influence and access to resources? Resources include money, time, positional connections, and intangibles, such as creative ideas. One nursing director has used her personal relationship with the hospital auxiliary chairwoman to lobby for funds to bring prominent nurses to speak at nursing grand rounds four times each year. Often drug companies will provide funding for projects or programs initiated by nurses who work with officials or representatives of a particular company. Nursing history acquaints us with nursing leaders who were effective fund raisers. Lillian Wald's work at Henry Street was supported almost single-handedly by Jacob Schiff. Wald worked so closely with him that he always knew what services were in need of funds. Our foremothers found access to resources and so can we.

GUIDING PRINCIPLES UNDERLYING POLITICAL ACTION

The previous section discussed principles that support political action. This section discusses ten additional principles essential to effective political action (see box on p 157).

Look at the Big Picture

It is human nature to view the world from a personal standpoint, focusing on the people and events that influence everyday life. Sometimes this results in a narrow view of life. We fail to step back and take stock of the larger environment. For example, a staff nurse who works in a hospital that is "over-bedded" may be oblivious to the fact that he or she could lose her job. Job security has become a major concern for nurses across the country. It was the major factor in the five-week strike by nurses in Minnesota in 1984 (Minnesota strike, 1984). If nurses are not aware of the conditions in their hospital, community, or state, they could find their professional future in jeopardy.

Nurses also need to take a broader perspective in the legislative sphere. Many legislators believe that nurses are single-issue oriented. They tend to focus on nursing legislation or a single issue that affects them rather than building coalitions to influence a wider spectrum of health issues (Lake, 1984). This problem may be remedied as more nurses participate in their local legislative committees and state political action committees and engage in coalition building with other groups.

Each of us must take stock of the realities of our professional life, including the economic and governmental spheres that determine our employment opportunities. For example, since the ANA issued its 1965 statement on entry into practice, many nurses have either obtained basic education in an associate degree (AD) or bachelor of science in nursing (BSN) program or gone back to school to obtain a BSN. While no law dictates that nurses must have a BSN, the future is apparent. Staff nurses who want to move into nursing management or education know chances for promotion will be greater if they have a BSN. In urban medical centers, management positions may require a master's degree.

Awareness of the "big picture" should extend to the working environment. The staff nurse is usually a member of a work group in a hospital or agency, and this work group in turn is part of a larger department of nursing (see Figure 13-1).

Political decisions affecting nursing practice are made every day. The head nurse may be confronted with a hiring freeze, dictated by the director of the city hospital in response to an economic crisis. Word of the freeze comes down through the chain of command: hospital administrator to department heads (director of nursing, chief of medicine) to unit chiefs. The head nurse's response may be to plan staffing so that each day-shift nurse must accept a rotation to a night shift. Staff nurses' personal lives will be affected and their ability to care for patients will be altered by the reduced staffing pattern. Nurses may think decisions are unfair, especially if nursing staff and supplies are cut, but the hospital's executive director keeps his full administrative staff.

Looking at the "big picture" can help you and your colleagues understand your professional environment and enable you to function most effectively given existing constraints. It can give you a more objective perspective and increase your credibility as one who is broad minded, has vision, or can see beyond personal needs.

This does not mean you must accept or agree with a particular trend or the majority opinion. You may be confronted by "conflicting rights." Consider a situation in which one group wants the town's limited funds (scarce resources) used to clean up a polluted stream, while a group of public health nurses advocates services to reduce child abuse. When the decision is to deal initially with only one of the "conflicting rights," the individuals whose project was put aside are advised to work to achieve the chosen priority. Learning how to be a team player should be a priority of every nurse. A broad understanding of the health care scene will benefit your patients, staff, and the public.

Principles for Political Action

- Look at the big picture
- Do your homework
- Nothing ventured, nothing gained
- Get a toe in the door
- Quid pro quo
- Walk a mile in another's moccasins
- Strike while the iron is hot
- Read between the lines
- Half a loaf is better than none
- Rome was not built in a day

Do Your Homework

In the nursing process, nurses evaluate the patient's status in terms of history, health habits, family, and community circumstances. The same principle can guide nurses in their evaluation of the formal and informal aspects of their professional life. What does "doing homework" entail? It means, for example, clarifying your position on an issue you are concerned about so you can explain it to others. This process includes gathering data to support your position as well as lining up individuals who will support you. Development of a strategy to carry out a plan should be a key aspect of doing one's homework. Use of a model will facilitate political planning and decision making and avoid mistakes. A basic undertaking such as career planning requires much thought, yet how many nurses set aside time to work on this aspect of their life? (Nowak & Grindel, 1984).

Assessing one's ability to maneuver in the political environment is important. On a nursing unit, for example, how might you get support for your idea to implement primary nursing? First, read the literature on primary nursing, including articles that describe how to initiate it. You can test your ideas on peers. Once you have outlined a plan and lined up supporters, you can arrange to present your proposal at a unit conference.

In another instance, a public health nurse wants to have her district nursing association cosponsor a health fair. She alerts the district president that she plans to present her request to the membership at the next meeting. Having secured the president's support, she prepares for the meeting by recruiting supporters who will speak in favor of the proposal. She also writes down her ideas and practices delivering her statement in front of the mirror. She wants to be sure she can present her proposal clearly and concisely. She also tries to anticipate questions so she can give thought-out replies.

A wise staff nurse will do her homework prior to receiving an evaluation from her head nurse. She will review the notes she has kept since to document her efforts to respond to suggestions for improvement at the last formal evaluation. She will review goals and objectives for personal/professional development and write out questions or ideas she wants to raise. She might also think about the way the unit is managed, the strengths and weaknesses of the nursing staff, the relationships among the staff nurses, and her role and responsibilities as a member of the work group.

Building networks among colleagues through participation in professional associations is another important aspect of doing one's homework. Many nurses join a committee or special interest group of their professional association to work collectively on behalf of shared professional goals and consumer advocacy issues.

The influence of an organized group (network) of nurse administrators, working through their district nursing association, will have more impact on the delivery of nursing care in a community than the efforts of one nursing director working alone. For example, in one community, a group of nurse administrators realized that each hospital had a shortage of operating room (OR) nurses, and each was spending scarce resources on recruitment. They formed a task force to determine the regional supply of OR nurses. After reviewing data (homework) submitted by each nursing director about recruitment efforts, the task force reported that few OR nurses were available to fill numerous openings. Another way to solve the problem had to be devised. Using their networks, the nursing directors found that many RNs wanted OR training, but it was not available. They pooled a portion of each of their inservice education budgets to set up one OR training program for nurses. This could increase the supply of OR staff nurses in a shared, cost-effective manner, while diverting scarce recruitment dollars to targets that were more likely to pay off.

A thorough approach to doing your homework should include development of an historical "6th sense." Most nurses know a little about major figures in nursing: Florence Nightingale, Margaret Sanger, and Clara Barton. But other important nursing leaders, such as Lavinia Dock, a political activist and colleague of Lillian Wald at Henry Street, are not well-known to contemporary nurses because their biographies have yet to be written.

Few of us will do classical historical research, but we can undertake practical ministudies of nursing history in our professional communities. For example, before a nurse begins a campaign to change some aspect of nursing policy, it would be important to find out the origin of the policy—who wrote it and why. The following example illustrates this point.

A nursing administrator was appointed to direct the inpatient units of a psychiatric hospital. She had previously directed a day hospital and she, along with the professional staff, had worn street clothes. The nurse noted that nurses on the psychiatric units wore white uniforms. She made a mental note to investigate this practice, thinking it was more appropriate for nurses to wear street clothes. Fortunately, the new chief nurse met with each member of the nursing staff to ask questions about current nursing practice and the underlying rationale. She found out from one of the nurses who had worked on one unit for five years that in prior years, nurses had worn street clothes on the inpatient units on orders of the medical director. Subsequently the nursing staff, believing that the patient response to the change in nurses' attire was counterproductive, designed a study to assess the effect of the change on patients. Following the study, the medical director concurred that patients were better served when nurses wore uniforms.

The new chief nurse polled the head nurses, asking their opinion. Finding that they believed nurses should wear uniforms, the new leader did not pursue a change in policy, realizing it was not politically wise to do so.

Doing your homework, individually and collectively, centers upon the development of a sound plan, based on a thorough assessment of the pertinent history and the current situation. The following check list can serve as a guide to assessing your skills:

- clarify your position
- gather data, search literature
- plan strategy
- develop a model
- assess strengths and weaknesses
- evaluate ability to maneuver in political arena
- expand and use networks
- line up support

Nothing Ventured, Nothing Gained

Nurses have always been risk takers. Margaret Sanger fled to England after she was sentenced to jail for providing women with information about birth control. Clara Maas lost her life while participating in research on malaria. What about the courage of the Denver nurses who took their case for equal pay to the U.S. Supreme Court? (See Unit III Case Study.) Or Susie Sizemore and Vicki Henderson, two nurses who are fighting for the right to practice midwifery? (See Chapter 16.)

Thoughtful risk takers weigh the costs and benefits of their actions. They consider possible outcomes in relationship to the expenditure of available resources. For example, a nurse may decide to run for city council, even though she has little chance of winning. She risks losing because running for office will give her the opportunity to bring important health issues to the public's attention.

In another situation, a head nurse decides she has nothing to gain from continuing her opposition to her boss's plan to decentralize the nursing education department. In fact, if she fails to support the decision, her management career may be in jeopardy. She has more to gain from being a team player.

Get a Toe in the Door

Incremental changes or actions may have a better chance of success than a project of major proportions. Resistance to change can often be overcome if a pilot project or task force is set up to test an idea on a small scale. For example, if you were a nursing director, and a group of nurses proposed changing all units in the hospital from team nursing to primary nursing, you would not be likely to allocate the necessary resources.

If a group of nurses on one unit, however, wrote a proposal to institute primary nursing on a 32-bed unit, you might support such a project, viewing it as a worthy pilot test.

The need for change can be evaluated by a task force appointed to explore an issue and report back to the director, board, or head nurse. In one hospital the nursing director responded to staff nurse concerns about administration of experimental medications by appointing a task force, chaired by the nurse director of quality assurance. As a result of the task force report, new policies and procedures were developed for review by the hospital's chiefs of service, including the directors of nursing, medicine, pediatrics, and surgery.

An effective way to call attention to an issue or to gather data is to conduct a survey. To raise the consciousness of legislators concerning health and nursing issues, the New York State Nurses for Political Action (NYS-NPA) distributed a survey to all 211 state legislators. In addition to asking them how they would vote on upcoming nursing legislation, the survey raised questions about larger health practices and social issues, including disposal of radioactive waste, costing out of nursing care on hospital bills, and equal pay for work of comparable worth. The survey provided the PAC and the nursing community with a wealth of information. It also stimulated legislators to think about major public health and economic issues. One legislator said, "The nurses' PAC survey really made me think about some pretty big issues; I am glad they sent it to me."

Quid Pro Quo

"Something for something." "You scratch my back, I'll scratch yours." "Everything and everybody has a price." Some say these phrases represent a cynical view of human/organizational relationships, but others acknowledge that they represent a realistic approach to life. Consider your informal relationships at work. The director of the hospital laundry asks your advice about selecting a pediatrician. She knows you have young children, and she trusts your advice. After she consults one of the physicians you have recommended, she comes to your unit to thank you. As she leaves, she tells you, "If you have any linen problems here, you just give me a call and I'll fix you up." Interchanges like this occur every day in business, in hospitals, and in families.

When assessing your position within nursing and the health care arena, review your friendships, connections, and pragmatic relationships. Frequently men say, "He owes me one," implying the person has been the recipient of a favor and will be asked to reciprocate. Women or nurses rarely talk this way. Perhaps we are uncomfortable with the idea of "owing," being "in debt," or being in a position to "call in a favor," despite the fact we participate in "give and take" situations every day. For example, your willingness to interview a staff member's relative for a potential position on the nursing staff will probably be remembered by the staff member when you ask her to work overtime at a later date. We can agree that what you know is important, but who you know can be just as important. The qualified job applicant who has connections and knows somebody important is most likely to be selected. While some find "using pull" distasteful, the politically astute nurse will seek help from influential people who are available to her. She will also use her clout to promote those in whom she has particular confidence (Vance, 1982).

Sometimes a person is asked to repay a favor, but feels it would compromise her principles. For example, a nursing leader was asked to serve on a state legislator's re-election committee. While the legislator had worked hard to pass a key nursing bill, he had a poor record on environmental issues—an area of particular concern to the nurse. She declined to support the legislator saying, "I would like to help, but I cannot, due to your position on toxic waste disposal programs. However, you might contact Nurse A, she may be able to work with you." While a favor is not always returned by the person who has been helped, someone else may be found to assist.

Walk a Mile in Another's Moccasins

Nurses are astute evaluators of patients, but do we employ the same skills in our dealings with others? How often do you try to ascertain how another colleague, your boss, or your friend is feeling about something? For instance, when you talk with your head nurse about the next year's goals for the unit, do you consider whether your goals are in harmony with those of the head nurse and her vision of the unit's direction? Perhaps you want to expand your cardiac nursing expertise. You know your unit is slated to receive a greater number of very sick cardiac patients and that the head nurse wants the staff to upgrade its cardiac nursing skills. Considering your personal goal, the needs of the unit, and the head nurse's plans, you might offer to work with her to develop a course or self-study program that would meet your needs and the unit's. Nurses on the lookout for "win-win" situations—those which benefit the nurse, patients, and the organization—are often winners themselves. The ability to "tune in" to what others need or are interested in allows one to plan strategies that benefit all concerned.

A related idea is the concept of equity or fairness. When you seek something for yourself, a promotion or maybe a day off to attend a conference, do you consider the fairness as it relates to your colleagues and coworkers? Those who act in relationship to others, whether boss or colleague, with a sincere interest in achieving equity are likely to get more of what they want while contributing to a more pleasant and productive work environment.

Strike While the Iron Is Hot

You may have a well thought-out plan only to have it fail because your timing is off. Judging the right time to act is tricky, and you take a calculated risk when you decide to act or not act.

The importance of timely vote counting is illustrated by this example. A group of nurses submitted a resolution to the annual meeting of their nurses' association to ban smoking at association meetings. After lobbying key leaders, they determined that the outgoing president's opposition would lead to defeat. Realizing they did not have the necessary votes, they withdrew their resolution. Later they discovered the president-elect favored their position and had suggested the resolution be introduced at the next annual meeting when she would support it. In another situation, a staff nurse wanted to submit a proposal for job-sharing. She decided to approach the nursing director after the director had returned from maternity leave, thinking that the director would be more receptive once she too had experienced the delightful, but demanding aspects of motherhood herself.

Many timing decisions should be based upon common sense, a principle many of us forget in our eagerness to act. One nurse was so sure her proposed staffing plan would solve the shortage of night staff that she submitted it to the nursing director on the eve of a walkout of nonprofessional staff. The staffing proposal was relegated to the pile of low-priority projects, and the author was written off, at least temporarily, as politically unsophisticated.

Read Between the Lines

Some people tell you a lot by what they choose not to disclose. For example, after an interview for a head nurse position, you ask the assistant director of nursing if you are a strong candidate for the job. When she says she has not finished interviewing candidates, but then outlines your strengths, you can read between the lines. She is sending a strong signal that you are a contender for the position. At a large teaching hospital, top management has made drastic cuts in the next year's budget. The chief of nursing helped to determine where staff cuts would occur but was not at liberty to share this information prior to the hospital administrator's announcement of the total plan. Meanwhile, two assistant directors of nursing had to meet a grant application deadline but did not want to go ahead if their key staff person was to be fired. When they asked the nursing director for guidance, she replied that they should complete the grant application, indirectly telling them that the staff person needed to carry out the grant would not be laid off.

Half a Loaf Is Better than None

Some of us are more gracious than others when it comes to sharing. We have all had experience with people whose behavior reflects the "me" or "I" approach to life. There are the others who, if they do not get exactly what they want, go stomping off in a crabby mood. It is hard to work with these individuals.

How often have you had a goal for getting or doing something, only to find that you can achieve only part of it? You may want to attend a management development workshop but cannot because you must cover for your head nurse who is attending the workshop. Your head nurse, knowing of your disappointment, offers to share the reading materials and meet with you an hour each week to help you develop your own personal management development program. You would have preferred attending the workshop, but the alternative offered by your head nurse is likely to be worthwhile.

Another example involves the endorsement decisions made by political action committees. The board of one state nurses' PAC wanted to reward legislators who sponsored a nursing bill that passed the legislature by endorsing each sponsor's bid for reelection. But examination of the sponsors' full voting records showed that several had opposed passage of the ERA and Medicaid funding for abortion. Both these bills were listed among those supported by nurses. The board investigated each instance and realized that two factors—pressure from conservative leadership and personal opposition to abortions—led to the legislators' negative votes on the ERA and Medicaid funding for abortions. Despite this, the board believed it was in the best interest of nursing to endorse all legislators who sponsored the nursing bill.

This example also illustrates the concept of "quid pro quo"—something for something. The bill sponsors got something—endorsement—for something—their sponsorship of the bill.

Many times we are confronted with situations in which we may not get all that we want. It pays to figure out acceptable solutions or alternatives. Identification of alternatives represents a good way to test your convictions and to consider what you want in the long and short term. (See Chapter 11 vignettes on negotiation.)

Rome Was Not Built in a Day

When I was a student nurse on my first assignment as team leader, I was impatient with the system. I thought I was keeping my opinions to myself, but to my amazement the head nurse called me aside and said: "I realize you disapprove of the way this floor is managed, and I agree that many outmoded practices need to be altered, but my dear, I've been head nurse on this unit only two months and do not forget, Rome was not built in a day." I was flabbergasted. I could not figure out how this woman could read my mind, and I didn't understand why things could not be changed STAT. I later found out that I was no different from other impatient students with whom this capable head nurse had worked. During the past two years, she had specialized in "rescuing" floundering units—like this one—that needed strong, capable leadership.

Summary

Successful political action requires a thoughtful analysis of the formal and informal processes that will be part of the anticipated change. The reader is encouraged to discuss and perhaps outline such an analysis with her colleagues. Collectively, a group of nurses may be able to identify nuances in the informal structures and processes, clarify priorities within the formal structures, and uncover hidden agendas held by the institution, organization, community, or government.

The nurse must also develop a keen understanding of political principles and themes, such as the importance of timing and being sensitive to the "larger picture." Development of skill in political analysis will only come with practice. One's failures, thus, become one's successes. The novice, however, is encouraged to tackle problems or changes that are short term and likely to be successful. After all, "nothing succeeds like success."

References

Brown B (editor): Politics and power. *Nurs Adm Q* (Spring) 1978; 2 [entire issue].

Ehrat K: A model for politically astute planning and decision making. *J Nurs Adm* (Sept) 1983; 13:29–34.

Hennig M, Jardin A: *The Managerial Woman.* Anchor/Doubleday, 1977.

Hospitals must cost out nursing care under landmark Maine law. *Am J Nurs* 1983; 83:1251.

Kirschenbaum H, Glaser B: *Developing Support Groups.* University Associates, 1978.

Lake RD: Legislator's opinions about nursing: Results of a pilot study. *Nurs Health Care* 1984; 5:204–7.

Longest B: Institutional Politics. *J Nurs Adm* 1975; 5:3, 38–41.

Minnesota strike settlement termed victory for nurses. *Am Nurse* 1984; 16(7):1.

Nowak J, Grindel C: *Career Planning in Nursing.* Lippincott, 1984.

Patients pay for nursing services under hospital's new billing plan. *Am J Nurs* 1982; 82:1333.

Penberth-Valentine J: *Health Planning for Nurse Managers.* Aspen, 1984.

Porter-O'Grady T, Finnigan S: *Shared Governance for Nursing.* Aspen, 1984.

Talbott SW, Vance CN: Involving nursing in a feminist group—NOW. *Nurs Outlook* 1981; 29:592–95.

The Scott, Foresman Roberts' Rules of Order Newly Revised, 1981.

Tropman J: *Effective Meetings.* Sage, 1980.

Vance CN: The mentor connection. *J Nurs Adm* (Apr) 1982; 12:7–13.

Wieczorek RR (editor): *Power, Politics, and Policy in Nursing.* Springer, 1985.

Chapter 14

Political Influence: Building Effective Interpersonal Skills

Connie N. Vance, RN, EdD

Politics is an interactive phenomenon; it assumes relationships between people. It cannot be a solitary pursuit, or merely an intellectual exercise. The term "political" refers to the lively, interpersonal activity that each of us is involved in on a daily basis.

This chapter focuses on politics as the exercise of influence. The use of influence is the generic basis of all political activity. Influence is dynamic activity that springs from one's particular power. Influence implies a reciprocal relationship that affects all parties in some way. An important assumption about influence is the expectation that all parties will get something out of the exchange. Influence is exercised when:

- You convince a director of nursing to assign additional staff to your unit.
- You mobilize a group of nurses to go to the state capitol to lobby for an insurance reimbursement bill for noninstitutional nursing services.
- You teach a parenting skills class in your community.
- You work on a membership drive in your district nursing association.
- You pull the lever in a voting booth in your neighborhood.
- You persuade your colleagues to institute daily interdisciplinary rounds on all patients.
- You telephone your congressperson to protest against a presidential veto of a nurse training act.
- You testify before a city council hearing against the dumping of toxic wastes near a congested urban area.
- You write a memo to your supervisor, documenting the need for additional sphygmomanometers on your unit.
- You send a check to your state senator's re-election campaign.
- You attend a meeting to plan for the installation of additional stop signs in your community.

165

In each of these activities, you are influencing others to effect change. At the same time, you are achieving collective goals and competing for scarce resources—all part of politics.

As nurses, we must expand our conception of the political influence process to include all kinds of efforts to guide and change decisions. This is especially important for us, because nurses have remained a relatively weak, uninfluential group in the policy-making political arena, as well as in everyday professional, work-related matters. Decisions are made daily that affect every aspect of our lives and the public we serve. It is our choice whether we will be part of the process surrounding these decisions. If we actively participate in the influence process known as "politics," we will become strong in decision making and in directing change. If we do not participate in the influence process, others will make decisions for us, often not with our best interests at heart.

THE THREE "Cs" OF POLITICAL INFLUENCE

The exercise of influence involves three components, or the three "Cs" of political influence:

- communication
- collectivity
- collegiality

First, by putting the entire repertoire of communication activity—the verbal and the behavioral—to work for us, we become influential professionals. Through skillfully applied communication skills, we can more effectively influence others to achieve our goals. Some theorists view communication simply as influence (French, 1968). Political influence skills are communication skills.

Second, we can be more effective in the influence process by joining with others. Unfortunately, many nurses continue to act alone rather than in collaboration with other nurses, professionals, or consumer and community groups. They fail to recognize that professional and political matters are largely group affairs. A group approach assumes that individuals act in professions and in politics largely as members of groups with shared attitudes, beliefs, and values. People act together because they perceive that by doing so they will more likely achieve their goals and thus gain similar rewards (Schmidt et al., 1977).

Third, influence should involve collegiality—a spirit of cooperation and camaraderie with our associates. Collegiality is an attitude of mutual respect and shared convictions and values. Collegiality is the feeling for each other that eventually draws us into collaboration. Styles (1982, p 143) believes that "collegiality is the actual sharing of that innermost core identity with our colleagues, a spiritual brotherhood or sisterhood."

The remainder of the chapter discusses each of these three Cs to: (1) demonstrate their importance for those who want to become effective influentials in the political process; (2) provide examples illustrating their application to the four spheres of political influence—the workplace, community, government, and professional organizations; and (3) suggest some "how to's" for action. Although the three Cs are discussed separately, they overlap and are interwoven in the work that nurses do to influence and thereby create change and reach their goals.

COMMUNICATION AS POLITICAL INFLUENCE

"The ability to influence social action is primarily a communication process" (LeRoux, 1978). As nurses, we subscribe to the notion that communication is a basic element of nursing practice. In a national study, nursing leaders rated communication skills as the single most important source of influence in nursing (Vance, 1977). Still, it can be a bit more difficult for us to connect communication skills to politics, collective action, and influence. For instance, many nurses are still exclusively attuned to the one-to-one dimension of nursing practice, discounting its large social and political elements. The attitude that "all I want to do is be left alone at the bedside" is a head in the sand view of the multiple forces that have a great impact on both the practice of nursing and the recipients of nursing care. The nurse practice acts, legislation on prospective reimbursement, nurse training acts, federal research funding laws, and the insurance acts are all legislative-political matters that powerfully influence all aspects of professional nursing—its practice, education, research, and accessibility to the public. In spite of this reality, many nurses still view only patient-related communication as worthy of attention and virtuous, while viewing politically related communication (eg, lobbying) as beneath the dignity of the professional nurse. This naive viewpoint reveals a lack of knowledge of the inevitable commingling of the practice and political elements of all professions, including nursing.

There are, however, many signs that point to growing sophistication in making the connection between communication in nursing and the political influence process. Many of my nursing colleagues and I have received letters from the president, governors, congresspersons, and state and city officials responding to our communication activity (ie, letters, telephone calls, telegrams, and visits) on behalf of nursing and health care bills.

There are other examples of nurses' political communication activity: A nurse writes her state and local legislators, congratulating them on their recent elections and inviting them to a nurse-sponsored "meet your legislators" party. Busloads of nurses and nursing students go to their state capitol to discuss nursing education issues with their legislators. A university nursing department holds a series of voter registration drives on the campus. Nurses joined thousands of women during the summer of 1983 in Washington, DC, appealing to Congress for a positive vote on the Equal Rights Amendment. Nurses are testifying at public hearings on a variety of social, educational, and health-related topics. Across the country, nurses are participating in election campaigns for legislators who support nursing and health care bills. They are doing this as individuals and as members of groups such as Nurses Coalition for Action in Politics (N-CAP), state nursing political action committees (PACs), the Women's Political Caucus, the National Organization for Women, Women's Campaign Fund, Women's Vote Project, and local political clubs.

We are establishing the important connection between communication in nursing and political influence. A few examples follow to illustrate the application of communication to the four spheres of political influence—the workplace, community, government, and professional organizations.

In the Workplace. As nurses, we influence our patients and their families, our co-workers, and administrators daily. We do this through personal appearance, use of time, facial expressions, posture, gestures, vocal tone, touch, and listening. What are *you* communicating when you:

- Carefully explain every treatment for your patient and his family?
- Never speak up at the team meetings on your unit?
- Always wear neat, clean, and appropriate professional attire?
- Can't find the time to write nursing diagnoses and nursing orders?
- Go out of your way to assist new nursing personnel on your team?
- Rarely volunteer for special projects on your unit?
- Carefully inform your patients' physicians of your judgment of their needs, progress, and your nursing interventions?
- Don't go out of your way to help colleagues who are carrying a heavy assignment?
- Encourage your associates to problem solve rather than be chronic complainers?
- Are often late for work?
- Openly confront co-workers about conflicts rather than talking behind their backs?
- Budget your time for direct nursing care as well as executing medical orders?

In the Community. In the larger community, nurses must be the spokespersons for our profession. Information power is an important source of influence for us in our communities. Information power refers to a person's ability to use persuasion to influence others (French & Raven, 1959; Raven, 1965). If we broaden our communication networks in the community, we will be able to contribute important information and thereby gain influence.

Nurse educators at one school of nursing are offering free health education programs for the community on a variety of topics such as teenage suicide, infant mental health, substance abuse, breast self-examination, and sexually transmitted diseases. Two nurse representatives of a district nursing association have been holding a monthly radio show in their community for several years called "EverywomanSpace." This radio program educates women about health issues. Nurse experts are invited to speak on issues important to women. Topics have included childbirth alternatives, family planning, domestic violence, breast cancer update, women and alcohol, women's role in politics, and nurse practitioners.

Testifying at public hearings is another way for nurses to use informational power to influence others. Nurses in New York State, for example, have testified on many issues: comparable worth, home care legislation, environmental health hazards, access to health care in urban areas, domestic violence, child abuse, and entry level for professional nursing practice. Nursing students, with assistance, can also be effective. Two of my undergraduate students wrote and presented testimony at city hall against the dumping of toxic wastes in congested urban areas, with input from the president of Nurses' Environmental Health Watch.

I offer another example of how nurses can develop their influence in a community setting. A colleague and I, in attempting to influence our state senator to vote for a third-party reimbursement bill for noninstitutional nursing services, recognized the need to involve community constituents. We live in the same suburban community and have a broad community network of friends, professional colleagues, and organizational, school, service, and town officials (my colleague's husband is a former mayor of the town). We realized that, although we were adept at organizing voter constituents within nursing, we had paid little attention to other constituents. This is a serious error when one considers the influence and power that rest with such a large number of potential allies. Most of these people are past or future consumers of nursing care. This vested interest, if activated, could heighten political support for nursing.

We therefore set about to organize what we call a community constituent task force for nursing. This task force is still in its planning phase. The method for implementation will depend on our initiative to create an image of nurses' competency, involvement, and expertise in a wide variety of special interest needs for the constituent groups. For example, on-site consultation by nurses will be offered to each constituent group, including information on legislation. Potential networks for ongoing collaboration, support, and information related to mutual interests will be identified. Examples of constituent groups in our community include: nurse-police task force on rape; women's task force on domestic violence; nurses' and League of Women Voters' project on voter registration; teenagers and nurses for health; and the senior citizens and nurses coalition.

In the Government.   If you want to influence the decision of a government official, you must: (1) get the information to that person, and (2) present it so the decision maker will listen and be receptive. "The lobbying process, then, is essentially a communication process, and the task of the lobbyist is to figure out how he/she can handle communications most effectively in order to get through to decision-makers" (Milbrath, 1965, p 178).

There are two basic ways to get information to your legislators. First, you can directly communicate with them. You can telephone, write letters, send telegrams, visit them, and testify at public hearings—all are effective communication-lobbying strategies. I have found that sending a personal note, attending a fund-raising party, or working on an election campaign are effective ways to influence my legislators. I always identify myself as a nurse with definite nursing and health concerns. In addition, I always place RN after my name when I sign a contribution check.

The second, indirect way to communicate with legislators, involves voting. Even if one's candidate does not win, a strong show of votes indicates the desires and power potential of a large bloc of the candidate's constituents (Milbrath, 1965). This is proving to be true of the women's bloc and the growing power of nurses' votes. As the largest female-dominated professional group, we can use the "gender gap" to exert critical leverage in the election process. Unquestionably, voting is a powerful political influence tool.

One collective way to assist and inform potential voters is through conducting voter registration drives. The New York State Nurses' Association, at its fall 1983 convention, passed a unanimous resolution that it conduct, in conjunction with New York State Nurses' for Political Action, voter registration programs with the goal of registering every one of the 200,000 registered nurses in the state. The American Nurses' Association also collaborated on a national voter registration drive with a broad coalition of various women's groups (Abzug, 1984).

We also have the choice to vote for women and nursing legislators as more women and nurses run for office. The political reality is this: Those who produce votes, contribute money, and communicate directly with government officials will acquire political clout. Activating our political communication skills to influence health policy decisions is vital for us as advocates of the public's health and to control our profession (Archer & Goehner, 1982).

In the Professional Organizations.   You can become an important influence in professional organizations by first, sending in your membership check, then actively participating in meetings, becoming an officer, and working on committees. In addition to your state and district nursing associations, N-CAP, and state political action committees, there are literally hundreds of special interest organizations. (See Appendix E for a listing of national nursing organizations.)

One method that local nursing legislative committees use to activate their collective voice is the telephone tree or network. This network can be used to convey information to members or for political-legislative action. For example, one person calls six people, who each in turn call six others, until a large number of people have been contacted. If action on a bill is needed, the people contacted are either asked to send a letter, make telephone calls, or send public opinion telegrams or mailgrams if time is of the essence (Messer, 1980).

Activists in various nursing organizations are now being asked to consult with government agencies, such as the Food and Drug Administration. This is an exciting development in political influence by nurses. Since these agencies have the task of interpreting and implementing legislation, nurses can be involved in yet another method of influence.

THE HOW-TO'S OF COMMUNICATIONS

• **Build a professional image**

What images do you have of yourself? Tough, assertive, confident, competent, powerful? Some people view the political process as a mutual modification of images through communication and feedback (Boulding, 1969). To be politically influential means that we must be effective image-shapers (Grissum & Spengler, 1976). What images do you put to work in the workplace, the community, the government, and professional organizations? Our behavior conveys powerful messages about how we view ourselves and influences how others feel about us. The following checklist will help you identify some of your messages.

In your daily encounters with patients and their families, do your verbal and non-verbal behaviors convey that you take pride in your profession? That you are devoted to quality patient care?

Do you actively listen to the concerns of your patients and their families?

Do you document your nursing care in carefully written progress notes?

Do you spend time every day teaching your patients?

At staff and interdisciplinary meetings, do you set the tone for serious collaboration by asking questions and giving your opinions?

When you meet other professionals, public officials, and community people, do you offer a firm handshake, direct eye contact, and a confident greeting such as, "Hello, I'm . . . , RN"?

Do you regularly communicate your ideas, concerns, and suggestions to your supervisors? To community groups? To public officials? To organizational leaders?

What does your body language communicate? Do you stand tall or shrink invisibly out of sight?

Do you consistently write nursing diagnoses and orders on your patients' charts?

Do you vote at every local and national election?

Do your voice, posture, and gestures convey that you are confident—positive—bold (Chenevert, 1983), or disinterested—ill-at-ease—passive?

Do you call or write "thank yous" to supervisors, community people, public officials, and organizational leaders when they have helped you with a problem or issue?

Does your attire communicate that you are a serious, businesslike professional?

Do you practice good health habits as a health professional? Do you smoke? Are you overweight? Do you exercise? Do you eat properly?

Do you carry a business card to solidify contacts with persons you meet?

- **Refine your communication skills**

    Work on developing your writing and speaking skills. These skills are indispensable in sending messages that will be taken seriously.

    Register for workshops and continuing education courses on assertiveness training, public speaking, and writing.

    Volunteer to speak at programs in your workplace, at nursing association meetings, and in the community. Testify at public hearings. Write out your speech, no matter how small, as this will give you confidence. Practice in front of a mirror, using a tape recorder or videotape to evaluate and improve your spoken image (Linver, 1978).

    Develop your lobbying skills. For assistance, see Chapter 29, the NLN *Guidelines* (1976) for *Meeting with Your Legislator; Presenting Testimony on Legislation;* and *Writing Your Congressman;* the League of Women Voters' *Self-Advocacy* (1968) and *The Citizen Lobbyist* (1976); the National Student Nurses' Association's *Legislative Handbook* (1983); N-CAP's *Clout: Handbook for Political Action* (1977).

Practice communication skills with an experienced colleague.

Go in teams to visit legislators, to write an article, to testify, or to speak on a radio show or at a workshop. You will learn from the shared experience, bolster each other's confidence, and enjoy it more.

Learn invaluable political influence skills through committee work and involvement in nursing organizations, work-related committees, political action committees, multidisciplinary and consumer groups, and political clubs.

Vote and get others to vote.

COLLECTIVITY AS POLITICAL INFLUENCE

"The disposition to work through groups stems from the experience of ordinary men and women that an individual . . . is politically rather helpless, but a group unites the resources of individuals into an effective force" (Dahl, 1961, p 5). Nurses have group power to influence decisions that affect the public as well as professional practice. However, this potential group power must be transformed into influence through a collective voice. To make an impact, to be heard, to be taken seriously, nurses must act together—in pairs, in small groups, and in large organizations.

A legislator told me that even though the medical profession had great political power by virtue of its financial resources, nurses were in a better position to wield influence because of their numbers and because of their identification with broad social concerns. We represent a large number of concerned, educated, professional citizens who can be powerful lobbyists and an important voting bloc.

Collectivity is the attitude underlying "groupness"—those behaviors that result from joining together—the quality of wholeness, or being one body, and of augmenting one's power (Styles, 1982). Collectivity is the foundation for networking, coalition-building, and collaboration—all crucial in the struggle for influence.

Why have nurses found it difficult to act collectively? For one thing, we are a diverse group. Our collective body is composed of multiple subcultures, interest groups, and specialty organizations. Often, our interests are split in many directions. Others blame our female-role indoctrination, with its emphasis on domestic relationships and solitary achievements. It is believed that boys, more than girls, seek a group identity, manifested by their involvement in team sports (Hennig & Jardin, 1977). Women have not had the experience of being team players. A third reason for our collective indifference may lie in the professional socialization of nurses, which places great emphasis on individual, one-to-one care, and a personalized approach.

As a professional group, nurses are learning that strong, well-organized groups can bargain and enforce agreements (Swingle, 1976). Such group thinking can create a resonance that gives rise to new and different insights and activity. Group membership enables people to share power, to blend individual power centers, and to empower each other and their professional group. Such group awareness and collective action are increasingly evident in nursing today, as can be seen by the following examples.

In the Workplace. Enlightened hospitals in contemporary society have witnessed the growing collective involvement of nurses in the committee structure of the hospitals—for governance, for investigation and problem solving, for creating change, and for conflict resolution (American Academy of Nursing, 1983). Nurses who are collectively involved in their workplaces believe they have a powerful voice, use this collective voice in many situations, and make changes in their work environments. One of the best-kept secrets about group work is that it is a "turn-on" to be involved with others in significant, worthwhile activity—it is energizing, satisfying, and fun.

Collective bargaining is, of course, another form of collectivity. Autonomy (ie, both the authority and responsibility for one's practice) will be gained by nurses organizing on behalf of professional issues. Organizing collective bargaining units rests on the assumption that the authority for professional practice resides with professionals collectively and not with an individual administrator or with administrative units. Historically, nurses have been reluctant to engage in collective bargaining because of its questionable "professional" nature. They are receptive to it, however, as a form of professional collectivism (Flanagan, 1983). Those who regularly read the "News" section of the *American Journal of Nursing* know that nurses across the country are using collectivism to bring about improved working conditions and greater control of their practice in the workplace.

In the Community. A colleague and I demonstrated the power of a small pressure group by getting nurses invited to a national leadership conference held by the National Organization of Women in 1980. When the conference was announced, we were disappointed to note that not a single nurse had been included in this important women's convocation. We set out to correct this oversight with letters and phone calls to the organizers. We pooled our political know-how, gained at the state and local levels, and planned strategy to provide nursing input at a conference on women in leadership (Talbott & Vance, 1981). We achieved our goal: invitations were extended to representatives of our national and state nursing organizations. Eleven nurses attended the convocation. A nursing leader was a panelist, with her picture and interview in the convocation report; and the event was covered by the professional nursing press. Other important ripple effects included coalition building, lobbying, image-building, information sharing, and mutual benefit contracts. All of these are outcomes of successfully applying political skills.

In 1982 a fund-raiser for the Equal Rights Amendment campaign was held in the New York City apartment of author Elizabeth Janeway. Each contributor's ticket cost $400. Recognizing that few, if any, of us could afford to attend this important event, I spent a weekend calling my network of nurse colleagues and friends and raised $900. Using the telephone tree idea, I asked each person to contribute $25 and to call one or two others for a contribution. We sent two nurses to this fund-raiser. By pooling our resources, we achieved several important political objectives: (1) money was raised for a "cause" having critical ramifications for women; (2) nurses were present at a women's meeting where networking contacts were made for future work; (3) it was a learning experience in collective action and served as a model for our ongoing fund-raising activities for various causes.

In the Government. Examples of collective networking by nurses to influence governmental policies are numerous. N-CAP and the state political action committees permit nurses to pool their resources and make campaign contributions to candidates who support nursing and health care issues. These groups also sponsor workshops, forums, lobby days, voter registration drives, and publish newsletters with endorsement information. N-CAP and state political action committees have held auctions at nursing conventions to raise money. These events have produced thousands of dollars for political education and action on behalf of nursing. (Nurses in Tennessee, for example, charged $25 per person at a reception for Senator Albert Gore and raised $10,000 for his campaign.) These activities are fun and draw nurses together.

Nurses frequently travel in groups to attend lobby days in Washington, DC, and in their state capitals. As an educator, I have helped student nurses work together on legislative programs, letter-writing campaigns, voter registration drives, lobby days, and testimonies at public hearings. These are all excellent ways to learn firsthand the benefits of group influence.

In the Professional Organizations.   We cannot achieve our goals unless we support our professional organizations. Nurses who collaborate in committee work at the national, state, and local levels of these organizations are enhancing their individual power as well as the power of the group. Legislative committees and the political action committees of the professional organizations are putting their collective political influence to work and are experiencing many victories. At some district nursing associations, legislative committees are helping nurses in local hospitals and schools of nursing to start agency-based legislative committees. They help set up objectives and strategies and serve as ongoing consultants. Other state and local nursing associations are organizing task forces on impaired nurses and developing peer counseling programs. The message in this instance is that we take care of our own in cooperation with local, state, and federal regulations.

THE HOW-TO'S OF COLLECTIVITY

- **Use your networks**

  Networking is an essential strategy in influencing others. Networks can exist for a variety of purposes—support, advice, information, access, and action.

  Join established groups with professional and political purposes that match your own goals and interests. These include various women's groups with goals relevant to nurses' concerns.

  Start your own network if existing ones do not serve your purposes (Puetz, 1983; Archer & Goehner, 1982).

  Have business cards readily available to network with others.

  Collect other people's business cards and review these periodically for networking purposes.

- **Develop a collective voice**

  Join and be active in committees and coalitions in your workplace, community, government, and professional organizations.

Become a committee member or contributor in political action committees (N-CAP and state PACs). Join, work for, and contribute to organizations that support political causes related to nursing and health care. (For guidelines, see Archer and Goehner's "Nurses' Political Yellow Pages" pp 243–257).

Keep an up-to-date address book of your associates' telephone numbers. Such lists can be used for telephone networking and as an information resource.

Join the League of Women Voters, whose purpose is to promote informed, active participation of citizens in government, and other women's organizations active in political matters affecting women (Abzug, 1984).

Vote and encourage others to do likewise.

Conduct voter registration drives at your workplace and in the community. For assistance, see Appendix A and contact Women's Vote Project, Voter Education Project, Operation Big Vote, National Women's Political Caucus, or Human SERVE Fund (Abzug, 1984).

- **Cultivate a collective mentality**

  When there is something to be done, a change to be made, some money to be raised, or a decision to be reached, think how to involve at least one or two others to work with you to achieve your goals.

  When you are dissatisfied, think of ways to solve the problem, using your professional associates as resource people or as helpers.

  Practice working effectively in a group, either as a leader or as a member/follower. Both skills are necessary in collaboration and negotiation.

COLLEGIALITY AS POLITICAL INFLUENCE

"Collegiality is as sacred as a vow; it is a solemn promise whereby we bind ourselves to those who share our cause, our convictions, our identity, our destiny" (Styles, 1982, p 143). The third C of political influence—collegiality—is an ideology. It is an attitude that underlies why we do or do not behave as full-fledged professionals, why we act in isolation or in concert with others. Collegiality is about community, camaraderie, and sisterhood. Esteem for and trust in one's associates are its foundation. Support and nurturance of associates are manifestations of collegiality.

As women and as nurses, we are frequently accused by detractors and by ourselves of not being good colleagues, not supporting each other, being poor team players, and putting each other down. Many women, and nurses in particular, are redrawing this caricature. They are breaking the tradition of mistrust, jealousy, isolation, and low self-esteem by joining together in powerful ways for mutual benefits. To be a political activist and a risk-taker requires support from colleagues. It is simply impossible to "go it alone" and be successful in political endeavors.

But we are neophytes in this kind of work and must consciously train ourselves for it. Too many nurses (including deans, directors of nursing, and nurse educators) still do not know the names of their legislators or have never communicated with them. Our training can come in various ways—through friendships, formal courses of study, professional organizational work, and contacts with work associates. Often, a cause helps people join forces and mobilize for action. Pursuit of such causes can provide fertile training ground for the development of political influence skills. There is so much important work that needs to be done that it is never difficult for nurses to find causes. For example, any time the nursing community has been threatened with the loss of nurse training funds (a cause), it has banded together with so mighty a force that legislators, with their telephones ringing off the hook, have been known to ask, "Where have all these nurses come from?"

The importance of collegiality as a political influence skill is underscored by Kalisch and Kalisch (1982, p 445), who say: "In order for nurses to become fully mobilized, they must develop an identification with and allegiance to other nurses; they have to see their problems as similar to those of all nurses, and realize that improvements occur only as they work collectively." Nurse colleagues can do this by consciously developing strong alliances and networks, work teams, peer connections, and mentor-protégé relationships. "Our training in nurturing, as members of a helping profession, coupled with increasing awareness of the benefits of working together can help us to be highly effective mentors" and colleagues (Vance, 1982).

Nurses are turning to their nurse colleagues for:

- advice
- guidance
- assistance
- support
- encouragement
- inspiration
- information
- access
- advocacy

In the workplace

   In the community

      In the government

         In the professional organizations

This collegial activity is effective as a political influence skill. Why is this? Simply because collegiality builds self-confidence and expands the power of each person. Collegiality increases each one's power, effectiveness, and capabilities. A real plus my colleagues and I have also discovered is the enjoyment we get working together on our causes. It is a powerful feeling to be involved in something you and your associates believe is important and to know the satisfaction of achievement and a job well done. Once we learn to activate the real power of collegiality, we will never again act in our old isolationist ways. Instead of using influence techniques that stem from weakness (eg, manipulation, reaction, and ingratiation), we will use influence strategies that stem from power (eg, assertiveness, initiative, collaboration).

One form of collegiality occurs in mentor-protégé relationships and "peer-pal" relationships. These relationships are characterized by a conscious, nurturing involvement over a period of time, in which each person's resources are used to promote and help the other. This help can take many forms: advice, guidance, role-modeling, inspiration, support, and intellectual stimulation (Vance, 1982). Research indicates that these helping relationships assist in developing individuals who are happier, more competent, self-assured, and successful. In addition, such relationships increase the influence and effectiveness of a professional group by increasing the number of its committed, powerful leaders. Each of us can serve as mentor and protégé and peer-pal; there are always persons ahead of and behind us, professionally.

Another setting in which collegiality is promoted is the professional support group. Nursing educators and administrators in some hospitals have developed support groups to help their staff. Some groups assist new graduates (Leiske, 1984); others are for nurses who work in high stress units such as ICUs and burn units (Skinner, 1980; Webster et al., 1982). Team building is a key purpose of one support group (Scully, 1981), while leadership development is the focus of another (Turner, 1983). A variety of positive outcomes have been reported by nurses involved with support groups:

1. Nurses are better able to deal with stress, including work related conflicts.
2. Productivity seems to increase.
3. Team work improves.
4. Turnover decreases and morale is higher.

A colleague-friend and I have developed a personal version of the professional support group (Kirschenbaum & Glaser, 1978). The two of us had been meeting regularly for several years over lunch or dinner to discuss the role juggling we do as professional women with family responsibilities. Out of our get-togethers have come creative problem solving, support for risk-taking ventures, and many ideas for action. We wanted to share this experience by expanding our peer-pal relationship to include a few other nurses with similar needs and backgrounds. We meet in restaurants for dinner every three to four months for personal/professional sharing and support. Recently, for example, we realized that we were doing more public speaking and will hire a public speaking expert to work with us for a day or two. We are developing articles as a result of our meetings, although sometimes we just help each other get through another month filled with work and family pressures and deadlines.

The classic mentor-protégé relationship is often hard to establish, but peer mentoring relationships are possible for each of us. These relationships represent collegiality at its best and are essential to support the risk behaviors necessary for political activity. Good colleagues are one of the most important resources we professionals can have.

THE HOW-TO'S OF COLLEGIALITY

- **Identify with other nurses.**
    Feel pride in the accomplishments of nurses.

Respect and trust nurse colleagues and their work.

Form strong alliances with your nurse associates. Turn to them for help and consultation.

Show active interest in each other's work and projects.

Identify areas where you can work with your colleagues for mutual benefits.

- **Establish peer-collegial and mentor-protégé connections**

    Build strong support relationships with your peers. Promote and nurture each other.

    Consciously establish yourself as a mentor to your less experienced associates. Offer your guidance and support in various ways, depending on your own background and strengths and the needs of your protégés.

    Actively seek the assistance of a more experienced colleague who might serve as a mentor to you—to counsel, promote, open doors, and sponsor you in various ways.

- **Develop collegial strategies for mobilization**

    Consult and act with your colleagues when influence is needed in any situation.

    Collegial strategies include cooperation, collaboration, and compromise. It is not always possible to achieve a complete consensus with colleagues.

    Agree to disagree with your colleagues, and a healthy diversity of ideas will evolve.

    Form a professional support group with colleagues who share common interests and want to support and learn from one another. Kirschenbaum and Glaser (1978) provide guidelines for starting a professional support group.

SUMMARY

"The endeavors of small blocs of opinion-holders often energize . . . the machinery of state. Little bands of dedicated souls leave their imprint on public policy" (Key, 1964, p 6).

Nurses, as the largest group of health care professionals in this country, have great potential for exerting political influence. Influence lies at the core of all political activity. Nurses can build influence skills by applying the three Cs of political influence: (1) communication; (2) collectivity; and (3) collegiality. Through activities in the workplace, community, government, and professional organizations, nurses will directly influence professional and social issues and policy decisions. By converting their considerable power into political action, nurses will ensure the future strength of their profession and establish themselves as a strong force for improved health care and other social concerns.

References

Abzug B, Kelber M: *Gender Gap: Bella Abzug's Guide to Political Power for American Women.* Houghton Mifflin, 1984.

American Academy of Nursing: *Magnet Hospitals: The Attraction and Retention of Professional Nurses.* American Nurses' Association, 1983.

Archer S, Goehner P: *Nurses: A Political Force.* Wadsworth, 1982.

Boulding K: *The Image.* University of Michigan Press, 1969.

Chenevert M: *STAT: Special Techniques in Assertiveness Training for Women in the Health Professions,* 2nd ed. Mosby, 1983.

Dahl R: *Who Governs?* Yale University Press, 1961.

Flanagan L: *Collective Bargaining and the Nursing Profession.* Monograph: *Economic and Employment Issues for Registered Nurses.* American Nurses' Association, 1983.

Fleischhacker V: Writing your legislator: Some dos and don'ts. MCN 1977; 2:153–54.

French J: A formal theory of social power. Pages 557–68 in: *Group Dynamics: Research and Theory,* 3rd ed. Cartwright D, Zander A (editors). Harper & Row, 1968.

French J, Raven B: The bases of social power. Pages 150–67 in: *Studies in Social Power.* Cartwright D (editor). University of Michigan Press, 1959.

Grissum M, Spengler C: *Womanpower and Health Care.* Little, Brown, 1976.

Hennig M, Jardin A: *Managerial Woman.* Anchor/Doubleday, 1977.

Kalisch B, Kalisch P: *Politics of Nursing.* Lippincott, 1982.

Key V: *Politics, Parties, and Pressure Groups.* Crowell, 1964.

Kirschenbaum H, Glaser B: *Developing Support Groups.* University Associates, 1978.

League of Women Voters of New York State: *The Citizen Lobbyist.* League of Women Voters, 1976.

League of Women Voters of New York State: *Self-advocacy for New York's Citizens.* League of Women Voters, 1978.

Leiske M: Support groups: From student to employee. *Nurs Manag* (Sept) 1984; 15:14–22.

LeRoux RS: Communication and influence in nursing. *Nurs Adm Q* (Spring) 1978; 2:51–57.

Linver S: *Speak Easy: How to Talk Your Way to the Top.* Summit, 1978.

Lowery-Palmer A: The cultural basis of political behavior in two groups. Pages 189–202 in: *Socialization, Sexism, and Stereotyping.* Muff J (editor). Mosby, 1982.

Messer S: *Politics for Nursing: Threat or Opportunity?* National League for Nursing, 1980.

Milbrath L: Lobbying as a communication process. Pages 176–192 in: *Information, Influence, and Communication: A Reader in Public Relations.* Lersinger O, Sullivan A (editors). Basic Books, 1965.

National Coalition for Action in Politics: *Clout: Handbook for Political Action.* N-CAP, 1977.

National League for Nursing: *Guidelines for Meeting with Your Legislators; Guidelines for Presenting Testimony on Legislation; Guidelines for Writing to Your Congressmen.* NLN, 1976.

National Student Nurses' Association: *Legislative Handbook.* NSNA, 1983.

Puetz B: *Networking for Nurses.* Aspen, 1983.

Raven B: Social influence and power. Pages 371–82 in: *Current Studies in Social Psychology.* Steiner I, Fishbein M (editors). Holt, Rinehart, 1965.

Schmidt D et al. (editors): *Friends, Followers, and Factions: A Reader in Political Clientelism.* University of California Press, 1977.

Scully R: Staff support groups. *J Nurs Adm* 1981; 11:48–51.

Skinner K: Support group for ICU nurses. *Nurs Outlook* 1980; 28:296–99.

Styles M: *On Nursing: Toward a New Endowment.* Mosby, 1982.

Swingle P: *The Management of Power.* Wiley, 1976.

Talbott SW, Vance CN: Involving nursing in a feminist group—NOW. *Nurs Outlook* 1981; 29:592–95.

Turner SL: Building a nursing support group. *Nurs Health Care* 1983; 4:387.

Vance CN: *A Group Profile of Contemporary Influentials in American Nursing.* Dissertation, Teachers College, Columbia University, 1977.

Vance CN: The mentor connection. *J Nurs Adm* (April) 1982; 12:7–13.

Wagner R: The concept of power and the study of politics. Pages 3–12 in: *Power: A Reader in Theory and Research.* Bell R, Edwards D, Wagner R (editors). Free Press, 1969.

Watzlawick P, Beavin J, Jackson D: *Pragmatics of Human Communication.* Norton, 1967.

Webster S et al.: The support group: A method of stress management. *Nurs Manag* (Sept) 1982; 13:26–30.

Chapter 15

Collective Strategies

Developing a Support Base

Patricia Moccia, RN, PhD

Who:	Nurses
	Coworkers
	Consumers
When:	Ongoing
How:	Dialogue
	Identify themes
	Make the ordinary extraordinary
Why:	Because . . .
	"Health Care Is for People, Not for Profit"
	(Motto of the Health Policy Advisory Center)

In increasing numbers and in a variety of ways, nurses are discovering the power of collective action in their ongoing professional struggles for a humane health care system. Whether they are lobbying against federal budget cuts in health and human services, organizing in state nurses' associations and trade unions, or joining institutional committees, community coalitions, and nationwide networks, nurses are finding there is strength in unity.

Through collective actions, nurses are trying to control their practice and working conditions. In seeking such control, nurses are threatening existing power structures. The attempt itself, whether or not successful, is a radical one since it implies fundamental changes in the philosophies underlying policy and program development, research and planning agendas, funding and reimbursement, and professional and social responsibilities. Responsible collective action depends, therefore, on understanding its practical advantages and implications for the transformation of health care.

The powers that control health care in this country are long established, well entrenched, and not about to share their positions (Starr, 1982). The strong opposition to nurses' recent activities, therefore, is no surprise and may be expected to continue. As nurses become more successful, the opposition will likely become more vehement.

Some nurse activists like Maraldo (1982) see their ultimate goal as allying themselves with those in power. Others are seeking to develop new power networks among those out of power. There is an understandable tendency among many of these activists, who have lost difficult battles with the established powers of the health care system, to eschew collaboration. Whether this tactic is effective will have to be evaluated in each situation. Before doors are shut, however, there is a critical lesson to be learned from the way these special interest groups have become powers.

COMMON INTERESTS

Nurses can learn about extending their support base from the example of the existing power networks within the health care system. While the American Hospital Association (AHA) and the American Medical Association (AMA) come to mind, insurance and pharmaceutical companies exert a considerable, less obvious, influence on health care in this country (Kotelchuck, 1976). The power and influence of this medical-industrial complex is based on more than their financial resources. Their real strength, analysts like Navarro (1975) argue, is derived through the interrelationships they share with those groups that exert parallel influence and control throughout society—the predominantly white, male, corporate class. Physicians, hospital administrators, the heads of insurance and pharmaceutical companies sit on the same boards of directors, attend the same alumni meetings, play golf at the same country clubs, live in the same parts of the same towns, read the same newspapers and journals, and vacation in the same places. They have common interests.

To build the support base essential for any successful collective action, nurses must first recognize the people, groups, and organizations with whom they share a concern for a humane health care system. Finding common links is not the easiest task in a system such as ours characterized by fragmentation and alienation for both providers and consumers (Sidel & Sidel, 1981; Knowles, 1976). But finding areas of mutual concern is vital to immediate and long-term success. Once these areas are identified, subsequent activities will fall more easily into place. Furthermore, if the follow-up strategies are designed to acknowledge and capitalize on existing connections, the links will be strengthened, which will then establish a base for further extension of nurses' supporting networks.

WHERE IS NURSES' SUPPORT TO BE FOUND?

Since nurses' main interest is health promotion and restoration, we will find our support among groups similarly concerned such as other nurses, coworkers, and consumers.

Nurses. We are our own best allies. The profession continues to grow, change, and seek creative, fair, and just ways to promote health. Some of our recent gains have occurred when we have focused on what we had in common. Lobby Day 1981, for instance, was successful because the three major professional organizations, the American Nurses' Association (ANA), the National League for Nursing (NLN), and the American Association of Colleges of Nursing (AACN), put aside their differences and lobbied together to save advanced nurse training funds from drastic budget reductions.

Coworkers—Hospital and Health Care Employees. One of the easiest ways to identify potential support is simply to look around us at work. For at least eight hours a day we share experiences with coworkers across an occupational hierarchy that seems designed to promote conflict (Ehrenreich & Ehrenreich, 1973). If we refuse to accept the divisive stratification of the workplace, nurses will find support from other employees who work with identical environmental and occupational health hazards, who face the same institutional attitudes and policies and who share the responsibility for providing consumers with hospital and health care services.

Coworkers also see what nurses do; they know our work and can testify to its significance. For nurses who are continually fighting for recognition from groups such as medicine and administration, this can be invaluable. The benefits of such a relationship are discussed in relation to the cooperation between the California Nurses' Association (CNA) and Local 250 of the Service Employees International Union (SEIU) in the section, "When To Start."

Consumers. Nurses' largest support base and the one with the most potential to be the significant factor in changing the power relationships within the health care system is also the one most overlooked—the consumer population. Although this relationship was truncated by the rise to dominance of the medical-industrial complex and has been since hidden by its structures, it will not be denied. The leadership of two of our professional organizations recognize this critical connection. According to the ANA's *Social Policy Statement* (1983), "Nursing shares a partnership with the people it serves." According to past NLN President Virginia Jarratt (1984), "Nursing is the consumer's 'natural ally.'"

There is untapped support in the general population among those who need health services but can't get them, those who can get health services but can't afford them, and those who can get health services and can afford them but, nonetheless, do not feel healthy (Knowles, 1977). Given its current design, the health care system insures that just about everyone falls into one of these categories. Nurses have only to find the most effective ways of reaffirming the relationship we share with consumers.

Consumer groups are looking to nurses' organizations for assistance in a wide range of mobilization campaigns. One consumer group in California, DES Action, recently sought nurses' support in the casefinding of children of DES (diethylstilbestrol) mothers ("Nurses help," 1983). The Day Action Council of Illinois recognized the political influence of the Illinois Nurses' Association in their broad-based coalition that was successful in overriding a state-level veto of day care and human service funding ("Day Care Action," 1982).

Nurses are extending their support base by sharing their expertise and political influence with consumers at local, state, federal, and international levels. The School of Nursing at the College of New Rochelle (New York), for example, is one of the many schools where faculty and students play a major role in annual community health fairs. Another example is the Minnesota Nurses' Association joining the Minnesota Equal Rights Alliance. Together with the National Organization for Women, the League of Women Voters, the Women's Political Caucus, and several other groups, it conducted community education programs about issues relating to the Equal Rights Amendment ("Minnesota Equal Rights," 1983).

At the national level, the ANA joined sixty women's organizations to form the Coalition on Women and the Budget to investigate the impact of Reagan's budget cuts on women ("ANA joins," 1983). At the international level, the Michigan Nurses' Association was one of several state nurses' associations joining the worldwide Infant Formula Action Coalition (INFACT). Infant formula has been associated with high infant mortality rates in underdeveloped countries and poverty communities in the United States ("Infant Formula," 1981). The coalition supported the 118-1 vote by the World Health Organization to restrict the promotion of infant formula in these areas. The United States cast the lone dissenting vote, expressing concerns over free speech and freedom of information.

WHEN TO BEGIN COLLECTIVE ACTIONS

When collective actions have been successful, it has been because existing networks were mobilized. There is, however, a Catch-22 in when and how to build our support. While support systems should be in place before they are needed, the most effective way to establish a collective identity is to organize around a specific, immediate issue. We can only avoid the catch by (1) recognizing that each of our struggles is part of the larger, ongoing, developmental struggle for a humane health care system, and (2) jumping into the fray.

The recent settlement of the nine-week strike by SEIU's Local 250 against Peralta Medical Center in the San Francisco Bay area, for example, was attributed by an SEIU assistant director to the support of CNA, which had been supported by SEIU in a previously threatened strike against Associated Hospital in the East Bay ("250 Settles," 1983). The future impact of this collaboration was identified by SEIU, "Their (nurses') strong commitment to the cause of Local 250 will have far-reaching effects on their own contracts as well as the contracts of all other nurses throughout the Bay Area."

HOW TO BUILD OUR SUPPORT

As social beings, we are always engaged in a multitude of ongoing interactions, having more in common with other social beings than we realize. To demonstrate how much smaller the world is than it generally appears, I'd like you to try the following exercise. Given a maximum of ten interactions we are presumed to be connected to every one else in the world and can, in fact, share information, ideas, opinions, etc., with people who seem very far away. Telephone trees, networking, and "legislative alerts" are based on a similar premise.

Suppose you're in a continuing education course and have a teacher (that's one interaction), who went to school with the dean of a major university (that's two), who sits on a federal commission (three), the head of which reports to the president (five), who is on his way to meet with several world leaders at a summit conference (six, seven, . . .). Something you say in class might start a chain reaction that could conceivably influence a nuclear freeze agreement. Now abandon linear time and imagine what you might have said to Freud, Einstein, or Marx.

The game is great fun, goes a long way in the "temporary relief" of feelings of alienation, insignificance, and impotence and, I hope, makes the point of our existing, albeit obscured, interrelationships.

The unity of purpose necessary for the success of any collective action starts with the recognition of our interrelationships and common ties. Such a recognition depends on a three step process: (1) dialogue, (2) identifying themes, and (3) making the ordinary extraordinary (Friere, 1973; Shor, 1980).

Dialogue.   Because we need to compare our experiences with the experiences of others, we must begin an ongoing dialogue. We must start talking with and listening to everyone we see during the course of our workday—other nurses, our coworkers, patients, their families, and our families.

This is more important than it sounds. Our work is organized around tasks, and our interactions are structured around sharing specific information about which tasks have been done and which are yet to be done. Just think about your daily work routine, visualize your treatment plans or look at your nurses' notes. All record or disseminate discrete pieces of information. They are explicitly developed to increase the efficiency of our work.

Since efficiency depends on reducing the human or subjective element of any work process to a negligible level, any interpersonal relation or communication threatens that efficiency. In the context of such a social organization, talking with each other becomes a revolutionary act. Talking turns the social order on its head; this is the first step towards collective power.

Dialogue is itself a mobilizing activity. By voicing and naming our experiences, we begin to control them in the same way that in psychotherapy we name our fears and anxieties to control them. The significant difference is that dialogue requires two people interacting, and so the move toward control becomes a collective action rather than an individual one.

When and how we communicate depends on the organization of our institutions and our communication skills. In any institution where nurses already have some degree of delegated authority to make decisions affecting practice or working conditions, dialogue can become a part of established policy. In a structured bureaucracy, however, dialogue will first take place during routine activities. For instance, it might occur during change of shift reports or patient rounds. In either case, nurses hoping to extend support throughout their institutions must be sure to talk with all levels of personnel and with patients and families.

The nurse's role in dialogue changes relative to the extent of fragmentation and alienation within the institution, the number of people and groups already engaged in some form of dialogue, and the general level of communication skills. The leader's role

Guidelines for Forming and Working with Coalitions

"A coalition is an alliance of individuals and/or organizations working together to gain specified goals or mutual advantages" (AAUW, 1981, p 207). They are formed to prevent needless duplication of effort, pool and maximize resources, and engender greater publicity than might be possible if participants acted separately. Some coalitions are loosely organized, informal alliances of individuals whereas others are formal, official organizations.

Because the issues and goals for which a coalition is formed can vary tremendously (short-term vs long-term, legislative vs nonlegislative, public vs private, local vs national or international), the resources needed and how they are used will also vary. The following guidelines should help those who want to develop and work with a coalition:

1. Define your issue or goal and examine whether it is or could be of interest to other individuals or groups.

2. Identify these individuals or groups, being sure to include those with interests that differ from yours or with minimal interest in your issue. The American Association of University Women (1981) further recommends:

   • Be sure there is no organization that regards the territory defined by the coalition as its exclusive domain.

   • Develop arguments based on potential member organizations' interests to persuade them to join the coalition.

   • Allow time to recruit other organizations. Be available to meet with their boards or members to present the case for joining (p 208).

3. Examine the role you want to play in this coalition, roles others might want to play, potential resources each might be expected to contribute, and potential problems with competition among the individuals or groups.

4. Contact these individuals or organizations in writing or through formal and informal contacts. Invite them to designate a representative to come to a planning meeting; or, if the coalition is already underway, invite them to join in.

5. At the planning meeting, define the issue, objectives, and tentative plans. Ask individuals or the representatives of other organizations to identify the role they want to play and the resources they can contribute.

6. If necessary, decide upon a name for the coalition. This is particularly important for coalitions operating on a formal, official basis that may want to print stationery or other materials to publicize their cause.

7. Care must be taken that one individual or organization does not take over control of the coalition in a manner that would jeopardize the standing of others or the issue. For this reason, the coalition should establish a means for obtaining group approval of coalition activities.

8. For formal coalitions, obtain the written approval of organizations that want to be included.

9. Different individuals or representatives of participating organizations should be spokespersons for the coalition, depending upon the occasion and needs of the participants.

10. Keep members of the coalition informed of the group's activities and progress.

11. Since many individuals or organizations participate in coalitions to acknowledge their stand on an issue, make certain that the coalition's efforts are sufficiently publicized. This often requires that the coalition include strategies and resources for publicity in its plan of action.

12. In informal coalitions, individuals may want to support the coalition's issue or goal but may not want their support made public. This should be ascertained when an individual agrees to participate in the coalition.

13. Disband the coalition when the goal is achieved, but maintain contact with the participants for future networking and collaboration.

14. Evaluate the success of the coalition, including the value of the various participants for future coalitions.

Reference

American Association of University Women: *Community Action Tool Catalogue: Techniques and Strategies for Successful Action Programs.* AAUW, 1981.

(in our case, the nurse's) in dialogue might be as "convenor, facilitator, advocate, lecturer, recorder, mediator, clearinghouse of information" (Shor, 1980). The role is fluid, depending on the group's needs, is different at different times, and often multifaceted. Not only must nurses be prepared to assume these responsibilities, we must be ready, in the name of real dialogue, to relinquish roles to others.

Identifying Themes.   Themes are recurring patterns that identify, characterize, and define individuals, families, communities, and societies. The presidency of John F. Kennedy, for example, was portrayed as "Camelot." Themes serve as descriptions of the collective experience, indicators of the central issues for those concerned, and reference points for developing meaningful activities. To the extent that they are self rather than other defined, themes provide a basis and logical context for collective actions.

Some Contemporary Themes:

For the health care system	Impact of prospective reimbursement
For the nursing profession	Autonomy and control of practice
For nurses	Job dissatisfaction
For all hospital employees	Job security
For consumers	How to stay healthy, out of the hospital, and out of debt

Specific themes, particular to a group or institution, emerge through dialogue. The process of identifying themes bonds people in new ways and strengthens existing ties.

It provides those involved in dialogue with a consensual validation for their experiences. The process of identifying themes through dialogue further empowers nurses and their allies.

A group's theme may break through the general social consciousness and become a "new slant" for researchers, writers, and media slogan makers. "Nurses' burnout," for example, is the term analysts now use to tell us what nurses and their families have known for years: nursing is physically exhausting and emotionally draining.

The process of identifying themes, however, is more than a search for a term that accurately describes an experience. As Freire (1973) states, it is the realization of people's "aspirations, concerns, and values as well as the obstacles to their fulfillment" (p 5). He goes on to emphasize that to the degree that people recognize their themes and *act on them*, they move towards a fuller, more human existence.

The relationship between working conditions and the health of nurses and other hospital employees is an example of how themes emerge through dialogue. Recognition of occupation-related illness has been delayed. One of the reasons is the diseases are chronic rather than acute. The symptoms develop gradually, often have a long latency period, and seem either far removed or an expected part of the job (Stellman & Daum, 1973).

Nurses who talk with and listen to their coworkers know how many employees are straining and injuring their backs by lifting and turning patients alone because there isn't a second person available. Nurses in the operating room will notice the unusual number of personnel who are suffering spontaneous abortions (which research links to traces of waste anesthetic gases); or the number of times x-ray technicians tell about former coworkers developing cancer. Before research studies show it, nurses and their coworkers know their work is making them sick. Since occupational hazards are collectively encountered, they are a logical place for a collective response.

Make the Ordinary Extraordinary. The ordinary experience of nurses, employees, and consumers in the health care system has been one of little control, much dissatisfaction, and no hope for change. But organized nurses at the grass roots are reversing the expected social order through collective actions. Through dialogue and the identification of themes, nurses have developed innovative ways to make the ordinary extraordinary.

In the early 1970s, nurses in community mental health centers in Boston were seeing the withdrawal of financial support from programs that had held political favor only a few years before. Patients visiting drop-in clinics could not be seen because of short staffing and were given appointments as long as three weeks later. After several months of dealing with irate patients and their families, the nurses decided they would do something extraordinary.

Together, the nurses decided to channel their professional frustrations and their patients' anger into a letter-writing campaign directed toward the source of the problem—the state legislators on the budget committee. A list of legislators was prepared and kept at the front desk. Electoral districts were outlined on a map on the wall, and a series of sample complaint letters was drafted and made available at the desk. When patients who were expecting to be seen that day, were given appointments for the next or following week, they asked, "Why do I have to wait so long?" In response, the nurses surprised them (and probably themselves) with the real answers. Instead of asking the patients to accept the situation, the nurses helped them write letters.

The nurse-patient interactions at the center were transformed into a cooperative effort to change things. While the letter-writing campaign was not immediately effective, it led to the formation of a community task force that subsequently monitored and publicized state legislation for health services.

I have a favorite scenario for making the ordinary extraordinary that, to my knowledge, is as yet untested. The theme is a familiar one—patients in hospital beds at night, ringing the call lights "for hours" without a nurse responding. Taking into account any differences in time perception, we would still have to admit that this is a real and too frequent occurrence given our usual patient loads. Consider the possible effects on nurses' demands for increased staffing levels if we were to share with the patients a list of the home phone numbers of both hospital administrators and the members of the board of trustees. Then each time fifteen minutes passed with no response to the call bell, the patients could call those with the real power in the situation.

It's a safe bet that there would be some changes were this scenario played out. That is the message of this chapter—nurses changing the system until the slogan becomes a reality—"Health care is for people, not profit."

References

Alinsky S: *Reveille for Radicals*. Vintage Books, 1969.

American Nurses' Association: *Nursing: A Social Policy Statement*. ANA, 1980.

ANA joins coalition on gender gap. *Ohio Nurses Rev* (Nov) 1983; 58:14–15.

Day care action council of Illinois thanks INA. *CHART* (Mar) 1982; 79:3.

Ehrenreich J, Ehrenreich B: Hospital workers: A case study in the "new working class." *Month Rev* 1973; 24:12–29.

Freire P: *Pedagogy of the Oppressed*. Seabury Press, 1972.

Freire P: *Education for Critical Consciousness*. Seabury Press, 1973.

Infant Formula Action Coalition (INFACT). *Mich Nurse Newsl* (Mar) 1981; 54:1.

Jarret V: Editorial. *Nurs Health Care* (Feb) 1984; 5:59.

Knowles J (editor): Doing better and feeling worse: Health in the United States. *Daedalus* (Winter) 1977; 106: [Entire issue].

Kotelchuck D (editor): *Prognosis Negative: Crisis in the Health Care System*. Vintage Books, 1976.

Maraldo P: Politics: A very human matter. *Am J Nurs* 1982; 82:1104–5.

Minnesota equal rights alliance. *Minn Nurs Accent* 1983; NV:145, 155.

Navarro V: Health and the corporate society. *Soc Policy* (Jan/Feb) 1975; 5:41–49.

Nurses' help needed in DES casefinding. *Calif Nurse* (Dec) 1982; 76:11.

Rogers ME: *An Introduction to the Theoretical Basis of Nursing*. Davis, 1970.

Shor I: *Critical Teaching and Everyday Life*. South End Press, 1980.

Sidel V, Sidel R: *A Health State*. Pantheon, 1980.

Starr P: *The Social Transformation of American Medicine*. Basic Books, 1982.

Stellman J, Daum S: *Work Is Dangerous to Your Health*. Vintage Books, 1973.

Successful passage of Child Safety Seat Law. *Oreg Nurse* (June/July) 1983; 48:7.

250 settles with RN support. *Calif Nurse* (Oct) 1983; 79:3.

Networks

Belinda E. Puetz, RN, PhD

Networking has always existed. Men traditionally establish "old boys'" networks in business, a source of information that permits them to move ahead more rapidly.

On the other hand, women did not begin to network until they started to enter the business world in greater numbers and discovered they weren't moving up the corporate ladder as rapidly as male counterparts. These women soon realized there was no "old girls'" network, and they began to establish their own networks.

Women now are networking with each other (and with men) for personal as well as professional gain. A 1980 publication (Kleinman) listed over 1,400 women's networks, and more are formed each day.

Although nurses are becoming aware of networking, some are still not familiar with networking. They ask, "What is networking, and what does it mean for me?" Welch (1980, p 15) defines networking as ". . . the process of developing and using your contacts for information, advice, and moral support as you pursue your career."

Advocates of networking enthusiastically describe its benefits. These benefits—information, feedback, referrals, improved self-esteem, and a sense of "collegiality" with others—are available to nurses as well as to women in general who network.

Benefits of Networking

Information, the major benefit of networking, is necessary at all points in an individual's career path. Information is necessary for those seeking to get ahead in a field of practice as well as for those who wish to remain where they are. Information is useful to learn about job opportunities, changes in the employment setting that will have an impact on a nurse's practice, upcoming professional events, and more.

Many career counselors, for example, say that an indiscriminate job change can be "career suicide." In many instances, a nurse might receive information through networking that will help him or her avoid this costly professional mistake. Nurse Anne Jones, who is contemplating a job change, can take advantage of her professional networks to get the information she needs to make an appropriate decision. She might talk with the individual who held the job previously, or others who work there. She might find out, for example, that the job is perceived as a "dead-end" position, with little opportunity for promotion or advancement. Based on that information, Anne may choose not to pursue obtaining the position. Had she taken the job, she might end up in what the career counselors call a "nonrecovery position" with relationship to her career advancement.

Networkers give and get feedback on their ideas, approaches to situations, and their behavior. A nurse gets a great psychological lift when a colleague says, "I was impressed with the way you handled Mr. Sterling's request for a room transfer. You were so tactful and concerned about his viewpoint as well as his roommate's. I think you did a lot to help them understand their differences. It certainly could have turned out with hard feelings on both sides—and because of you, it didn't!"

Feedback helps the nurse decide whether what is being tried will accomplish the desired results. When a nursing service administrator is planning a budget presentation to the hospital's finance committee, her colleagues' feedback on the content and the delivery of the presentation may help her make it more informative and dynamic and, ultimately, assure that the committee members will listen.

Referrals are a significant benefit of networking. Nurses, and others, make referrals when opportunities arise that they are unable to take advantage of and when they know an appropriate person to accept the referral. Thus, individuals in a nurse's network may refer the nurse to professional opportunities that might not otherwise be known to her.

For example, one nurse might say, "I would like to teach that continuing education course for you, but I'll be at a conference during that time. My colleague, however, has had as much experience as I have and does an excellent job teaching inservice activities. I'm certain he would want to take advantage of this opportunity. May I have him contact you?"

Or, "I've noticed a great deal in the nursing literature lately about research findings applied to practice, and I think the study you conducted that changed our decubitus care could easily be written up. I have a friend who has published extensively. Maybe I could ask her to help you get started with an article. Are you interested?"

Referrals can provide opportunities such as presenting a paper, serving as faculty for a continuing education offering, or participating in an invitational conference. A referral may consist of being asked to consider taking another position, either a promotion in a current employment setting or for a new employer, or any one of numerous other professional activities.

In networking, referral, information, and feedback should be reciprocal benefits. It often happens that someone is not able to return a "favor" to the same person from whom a favor was received. The favor returned may not be to the same individual, of the magnitude of the favor received, or even in a timely manner. Reciprocity means that favor is passed along to someone else.

In exchange for information or assistance, the nurse helps others by providing information they can use. Nurses who network support their colleagues by giving them constructive feedback on their ideas and behaviors. In turn, these nurses accept similar feedback offered to them.

How to Network

Networking helps the nurse achieve his or her professional goals. Networking involves establishing and using "contacts" to help move in the direction of professional goals. Most nurses already have many personal and professional contacts: family members, relatives, neighbors, colleagues, supervisors, teachers, schoolmates, or other health care professionals. Patients, their family members, health care agency personnel, legislators, politicians, and others may be contacts.

Those individuals with whom the nurse interacts for giving or getting information, feedback, and referrals are contacts who comprise existing networks. Existing networks may either be personal or professional. They may include nurses only or may be composed of nonnursing contacts as well. The choice of contacts, networks in which to become involved, and the extent of involvement is entirely up to the nurse.

Once existing networks have been identified, a review of the individuals who comprise those networks is in order. If individuals needed to help the nurse achieve his or her career goals are not in existing networks, networks must be expanded.

In one situation, a nurse may want to enroll in a graduate degree program but cannot decide whether the degree should be in nursing or education. The nurse may use contacts in an existing network to obtain information about advantages and disadvantages of those degrees. Or the nurse may have to make new contacts with some individuals who have those degrees.

If the nurse wants to publish an article in a nursing journal, contacts can be nurses who have published. The nurse might attend a continuing education course on writing for publication and establish contact with other potential authors or with the editor of a nursing journal who may provide guidance and encouragement.

Contacts are particularly helpful in advancing a person's career, but they can be useful in any setting. For example, a nurse who has a "difficult patient" problem to solve will find encouragement and support from nurses in existing networks who have experienced a similar situation and have helpful advice to offer.

Networking happens wherever a nurse's contacts are gathered. Professional networking can occur during a nurse's participation in activities of local, state, or national nurses' associations. Networking for professional purposes can happen at work, at conferences, continuing education meetings, or any other places where nurses meet. Professional networking can occur any time the nurse is in the company of those individuals who are actual or potential contacts.

Meeting people probably is the best way to make contacts. While it may be uncomfortable at first, meeting people gets easier with practice. A good place to practice is a continuing education offering, where the nurse can meet both participants and faculty. Setting a goal, such as meeting three new contacts at each event, helps to focus efforts.

District nurses' association meetings or local meetings of specialty nursing organizations are another good place to meet contacts in similar areas of practice. Sharing common concerns often provides a key idea that results in solving a nurse's particular problem. For example, a nurse may be having trouble with a head nurse. Others may have worked with a similar individual in the past and can offer helpful advice about how to cope: "I found it worked best if I put everything we talked about in writing. That way, neither of us could 'forget' our discussion." "It helped in my case when I talked over our difficulties with the supervisor present. The supervisor helped us keep on-track with the conversation; she made us focus on our job-related problems, not our personality differences."

When the nurse meets new contacts, exchanging business cards helps individuals remember each other. The back of the business card can be used to enter notes about where the meeting occurred, other significant details of the conversation, or the contact's area of expertise. If the nurse promises to send the new contact some information, such as a copy of a recent journal article, a note on the back side of the business card will help the nurse remember the follow-up needed. Keeping business cards in a filing system helps organize networking efforts. Business cards can be filed in alphabetical order by name, by geographic location, or by area of expertise.

NETWORKING EFFECTIVELY

Networking effectively means that the nurse tries to take advantage of all opportunities to meet people. In the workplace, the nurse makes an effort to meet all those with whom he or she works, either directly or indirectly. The nurse networks by helping to orient new employees. Involvement in the agency's collective bargaining program is an example of nurses' networking efforts. Changes in the working environment of nurses can be effected more skillfully and encounter less resistance when networking is used. The individuals in a nurse's network can be used to help identify the need for change, diagnose the problem, design a plan for the change, try out the change, and evaluate it (Puetz, 1983).

In the community, the nurse networks by being actively involved in organizations, such as health care organizations and others. Positions on boards of directors and committees of these and other organizations can provide a nurse with many valuable contacts. The nurse uses these contacts for personal or professional reasons: "I am planning to run for president of the state nurses' association. I wonder if you would endorse my candidacy. The experience I have had as a board member of the Mental Health Association has contributed immeasurably to my understanding of associations that I can use in office if I'm elected. I would appreciate your writing a letter of support."

In government, the nurse networks to obtain passage of legislation that affects the nursing profession. Contacts can provide information that will allow the nurse to monitor legislative activity. Contacts can give feedback about a nurse's testimony to the legislature or provide a referral to a key legislator.

The nurse can network during a campaign for election. The nurse may even choose to run for political office. At this point, his or her contacts are a source of invaluable support: "I've worked with nurse Martin for a number of years. She is articulate, poised, and skilled at working with people. She is consistently fair and reasonable. I think she would make an excellent officeholder. Can we count on your vote?"

In professional associations, nurses network with each other and members of other professional associations to implement the work of the association. Nurses networking in professional associations deal with education and practice issues and, in general, seek to enhance the profession and the image of its practitioners.

In concert with each other, nurses develop standards of practice and strategies to implement them. They identify the scope of their professional practice and adhere to a professional code of ethics. They plan and implement programs of quality assurance, so that consumers can be certain about the quality of the nursing care they are receiving.

Networking effectively involves following the "rules." The rules require that relationships with contacts be maintained on an on-going basis, not just when needed. Keeping in touch means periodic contact with individuals in a nurse's network through a note or telephone call.

Keeping in touch with those from whom referrals for professional opportunities were received is called "reporting back." The report back consists of a "thank you" and a description of the event.

Contacts should not be asked to provide feedback, information, or a referral if they are not in a position to do so. Networking effectively means not putting contacts into awkward positions. Requests for information, feedback, or a referral should be addressed to those persons who are most likely to be able to meet them without placing themselves in a compromising situation.

Information that may be useful to someone in a nurse's networks should be shared. Information that is crucial to someone else must be given.

All relationships with individuals in a nurses' network should be honest. For example, in accepting a referral, the nurse first determines that he or she has the ability (and time) to do what is required. The nurse must represent his or her skills and abilities accurately when accepting a referral. The nurse does not accept a referral, regardless of how attractive the offer, when he or she is unable to meet the responsibility.

Above all, the effective nurse networker is careful not to burn bridges. Past contacts may be most useful in future situations. Former employers, supervisors, coworkers, and colleagues should remain part of the nurse's network.

References

Kleinman C: *Women's Networks*. Ballantine Books, 1980.
Puetz B: *Networking for Nurses*. Aspen, 1983.
Welch MS: *Networking*. Harcourt Brace Jovanovich, 1980.

Vignette: Washington Nurses' Roundtable
Thelma M. Schorr, RN

Sheila Burke and I had been friends and colleagues for many years when, in 1978, she went to Washington to work as a health adviser to Senator Robert Dole (R., Kan.), who was then a minority member of the Senate Finance Committee.

Sheila had been program director of the National Student Nurses' Association, and often the programs she planned involved people in Washington who could speak at student meetings, teaching such things as the art of politics or the implications for nursing in a bill before Congress. So Sheila knew Washington—to a degree.

But when she actually got to the "Hill" as a staffer, she found it was a lonely place for a young nurse. Most of the LA's (legislative assistants) for health were physicians with a medical orientation. So she looked for support from other nurses. And, sure enough, she found some—about six nurses were LA's on the staffs of various congresspersons. But they didn't know one another as nurses, they didn't know other nurses in Washington who could keep them abreast of the nursing scene, and they weren't involved with the nursing organizations.

At that time I was editor of the *American Journal of Nursing* and so not only did I have personal and professional interest in Sheila's tale, but it whetted my journalistic interest.

Couldn't we have a story about the opportunities for nurses on Capitol Hill, about the fact that there were jobs in which nurses could have influence on health policy, and that in fact there was a cadre of nurses already in them?

Of course we could, and we could get the nurses on the Hill together with nurses in

Washington's other power structures. We decided to set up a roundtable session. Doing this would mean that people could get to know one another, exchange phone numbers, discuss similarities and differences in their positions, find ways to find out more about what they needed to know—in other words, establish a network of nurses who could help one another when a need arose.

So that's how the Nurses in Washington Roundtable got started—with 13 nurses invited, first for luncheon in the Senate Office Building and then on to the roundtable discussion that eventually turned into an article in the January 1981 *AJN.*

Each of the nurses at that first meeting described her background and how she had found her place on the Washington scene. All were enthusiastic about the idea of a nursing support system. Just trading telephone numbers was seen as useful.

As the afternoon wore on, occasional, and perhaps even regular, meetings of the emerging network were suggested. Volunteers offered to plan upcoming sessions— and this has indeed continued. At first, subjects for discussion were announced by the volunteering host who would arrange an inexpensive dinner meeting. But as the word spread around Washington, the group grew steadily and now a typical network dinner will have 50 to 60 nurses attending. This growth brought with it the establishment of more formal programming with speakers on subjects announced well in advance.

This growth has also brought pluses and minuses to the Roundtable's original mission. The group is no longer small enough to allow for the vigorous interchange enjoyed early on. Yet it still affords the opportunity to meet other nurses and get telephone numbers, which are so often the backbone of a successful networking function.

An interesting thing happened at that first meeting in 1980. Two nurses came who had not been invited but had heard about the meeting. Both were in Washington on that day, testifying before a Congressional committee, and both should be role models for other nurses who seek to be politically involved. One was Carolyne Davis, who would eventually become head of the Health Care Financing Administration in the Reagan administration. The other was Barbara Nichols, then president of the American Nurses' Association, who was later to become a member of the governor's cabinet in Wisconsin as the secretary in charge of all the state's licensing activities.

Both these women, destined for high political office, recognized the importance of networking with other nurses, had the fortitude to come uninvited, and the confidence to know they had something to offer to the discussion. Their contributions were welcomed, and their actions perhaps set the pattern for the network's growth.

The Roundtable is known throughout the country, and new recruits to the Washington scene often call and ask how they can get into the group. Conceived as a place for nurses in power positions to meet one another and renew their nursing interests, the network has enlarged to the point where some feel it is too large. However, in a city like Washington, with frequent and sometimes surprising power shifts, perhaps the larger the better, so long as the original purpose is not abrogated. For the Washington Nurses' Roundtable, that purpose is to provide a way for nurses to network with other nurses so they are all knowledgeable about current issues and not working at cross purposes with each other on issues that can often be resolved with some professional sophistication and unity.

Initial members of the Washington Nurses' Roundtable: Faye G. Abdellah, Cheryl Beversdorf, Sheila Burke, Carolyne K. Davis, Mary Jo Dennis, Sister Rosemary Donley, Vernice Ferguson, Debbie Hardy, Patricia Jones, Beverly Malone, Pamela J. Maraldo, Marion Murphy, Barbara Nichols, Thelma Schorr, Mary Ann Tuft.

Chapter 16

Recognizing, Developing, and Pursuing An Issue

Rosemary A. Bowman, RN, MBA

Months of preparation preceded the opening of Nurse-Midwivery Associates in May 1980. Vickie Henderson and Susie Sizemore, both certified nurse-midwives, opened a practice to give families in Nashville a new type of maternity care. They contracted with a physician group to provide medical backup for their patients, and they applied for practice privileges at hospitals in the community where their backup physicians practiced.

The hospitals with birthing rooms at which they sought privileges did not offer nurse-midwifery practice privileges. The other hospitals, which had approved nurse-midwifery privileges, did not have birthing rooms. Henderson and Sizemore considered birthing rooms essential to their practice. They submitted applications for practice privileges and protocols to those hospitals that had birthing rooms. Henderson and Sizemore had excellent clinical credentials, and as they began their practice, community support for nurse-midwifery practice in hospitals seemed strong.

In spite of these positive factors, problems became apparent soon after they opened their practice. In June, the Hendersonville Community Hospital revoked tentatively approved privileges because staff pediatricians refused to examine babies delivered by the nurse-midwives. In August and October, Vanderbilt University Hospital and Southern Hills Hospital refused the nurse-midwives' application for clinical privileges. These actions were taken despite the fact that the medical staff bylaws in each hospital permitted practice by nonphysician providers.

In October, their consulting physician had his malpractice insurance revoked by the physician-owned malpractice insurance company, State Volunteer Mutual. By the end of December, he announced that he was leaving the state of Tennessee. No other physician would agree to provide backup to the nurse-midwives. Henderson and Sizemore closed their practice on December 31, 1980, transferring 120 patients to other providers. They had been in business for just six months.

Soon after opposition to their nurse-midwifery practice became evident, Sizemore and Henderson began to discuss their problems with nursing colleagues. As members of American Nurses' Association (ANA) and the American College of Nurse-Midwives (ACNM), they asked colleagues to suggest ways to resolve their problems. The threat to nurse-midwifery services in Nashville became a cause for the nursing community. Legal action was considered, and one nurse leader challenged the support of the others by making the first contribution of $25. Subsequently, the Tennessee Nurses' Association (TNA) took a position in support of practice privileges for nurse-midwives, and TNA staff provided extensive consultation to Sizemore and Henderson in hopes of breaking the stalemate.

Extensive press coverage began in July 1980. Letters to the editor demonstrated consumer interest and support, and the case caught the attention of the national news networks. As a result of extensive local and national media attention, a group of concerned citizens formed an organization called the Consumer Coalition for Health. A town meeting sponsored by the Coalition in December 1980, just before the closure of the practice, drew 400 people. At this meeting, it was announced that the practice would have to close and that legal action would probably be taken against the hospitals, physicians, and insurance company that had forced its closure.

Political pressure was also exerted. During the week following the Coalition's meeting, Congressman (now Senator) Albert Gore, Jr, of Tennessee, sponsored a congressional hearing to investigate physician opposition to nurse-midwifery practice in Nashville and throughout the country. The hearings stimulated extensive press coverage.

The fate of the business was sealed when strategies designed to resolve the conflict with the hospitals, physicians, and the malpractice insurance company failed. It was widely believed that the hospitals, physicians, and the insurance company had joined forces to shut out the nurse-midwifery practice.

Once the initial goal of saving the business was no longer valid, new goals were considered. The new goals included plans to:

- regain the financial losses of the forced business failure
- ensure that families would have the freedom to choose childbirth options, including services provided by nurse midwives.

Henderson, Sizemore, and their advisors also decided to request a regulatory investigation by the Federal Trade Commission (FTC) and file a lawsuit against the hospitals, physicians, and insurance company.

The legal action was based on the belief that there had been a concerted effort by the Nashville medical community to restrict the practice of the nurse-midwives and their consulting physicians, thereby denying consumers access to the health care services they wanted. Review of the facts indicated that legal efforts should center on antitrust action.

An investigation of the malpractice insurance company was carried out by the Tennessee Department of Insurance and the FTC. The state insurance investigation resulted in no complaint, but the FTC investigation ultimately resulted in a consent agreement with the malpractice insurance company, announced in August 1983. Although the insurance company admitted to no wrongdoing, it signed a commitment with the FTC to engage in no unfair dealings in the future. Because of the federal jurisdiction of the FTC, the consent agreement represented a strong admonition to State Volunteer Mutual and other insurance companies throughout the country not to engage in anticompetitive behavior relative to nurse midwives.

While preparations were being made for filing the lawsuit, Sizemore and Henderson, along with their Nashville supporters, continued to tell their story. As more people learned about the circumstances of their business failure, their support increased. They were asked to speak at the national ACNM meeting in the spring of 1981. Following the presentation, their colleagues contributed $6,000 toward anticipated legal fees.

Antitrust cases are expensive because of the complexity of the issues and the length of time to bring a case to trial. It was determined that at least $50,000 would have to be raised. The Nurse-Midwifery Project of the Coalition held a public fund-raiser in the late summer of 1981. Nurses and other health professionals, political figures, the press, and consumers raised $17,000 to support the case. The money was placed in a tax-exempt fund established by the Coalition.

An antitrust lawsuit was filed in Nashville Federal Court on March 2, 1982. The plaintiffs were Susie Sizemore and Vickie Henderson, their physician colleague, Darrell Martin, and a consumer couple, Margaret and Richard Carpenter. The Carpenters' son had to be delivered in a traditional obstetrical setting because of the closing of the nurse-midwifery practice. The defendants named in the case included three individual physicians, the physician-owned malpractice insurance company, and three hospitals. Questions raised by the lawsuit included (Consumer Coalition for Health, 1983):

- Should hospitals, playing the significant role that they do in determining which options are available to consumers in any community, be held accountable for actions which have an allegedly anticompetitive motive?

- Should physician-owned malpractice companies be permitted to cancel the insurance of a physician because he or she chooses to affiliate and practice with certified nurse-midwives who may not be his or her employees?

- Should registered nurses who practice within the legal limits of their license and according to established professional guidelines be permitted the same opportunities in the free market system as those enjoyed by other health care professionals?

- Should people have the right to select the place of birth and the professionals involved in their health care?

Since the lawsuit was filed, multiple motions and schedule proceedings have been filed before the federal judge. The court dates have been changed twice, and at this writing, a new court date has not yet been set. Many depositions have been taken, including seven full days of testimony by Sizemore.

Much personal and financial support has been given to the nurse-midwives. A cookbook, *Music City Midwives and Friends*, published in the spring of 1983 by the nurse-midwifery project of the Coalition, raised $23,000. Two fundraisers in the summer of 1984 raised about $17,000. At this writing, it is anticipated that at least $10,000 more must be raised.

Sizemore and Henderson continue to practice nurse-midwifery: Sizemore in a maternal-infant care project at the Metropolitan Nashville General Hospital until August 1983, and now with Health Care Partners, Inc, where she is developing a birthing center; and Henderson in a birthing center in Delaware.

The issues in this case have created a coalition of nurses, political figures, consumers, and others who believe consumers should be able to choose their health care providers. The complexity of this case is best illustrated by the fact that it has been almost five years since Nurse-Midwifery Associates had to close its doors, and a legal resolution of the case is not yet in sight. It also demonstrates that legal action is not for the faint of heart. Such action requires an unusual degree of commitment on the part of those bringing suit because of the stress involved.

RECOGNIZING, DEVELOPING, AND PURSUING AN ISSUE

What is an "issue"? What differentiates normal day-to-day interactions from extraordinary events that require a different kind of action? How does one determine the significance of an issue? What is the price of pursuing an issue?

For the sake of this discussion, an issue will be defined as a problem, a matter of controversy, a differing opinion, or a conflict. Issues may be individual or group concerns. They may be isolated incidents of daily professional interaction, or major disputes with broad impact.

Examples of issues in the day-to-day professional lives of nurses range from individual scheduling changes to layoffs related to reduced hospital occupancy; from individual disagreement with a physician regarding patient care to challenges by medicine to the regulatory control of nursing; from determination of how to set charges for nursing service to convincing other nurses to develop new systems and organizations to deliver nursing care. Regardless of the issue, the process of analysis and action is the same.

SITUATION ANALYSIS.

The issues you select may be unique to your situation. If you are a labor organizer, you may search for strategic issues around which to organize workers. If you are an innovator of new health care services, you select which projects you will pursue. In both instances, you are selecting or creating issues to which others must respond.

Recognition.   Recognizing an issue can be equated with problem identification. First, there is the recognition that an issue exists. Then it must be defined. Staffing is often cited as an issue in hospitals, but the real issue or problem, once defined, may actually be that nurses and management are not determining patient care needs together.

Timing.   Timing is a significant factor in recognizing an issue. A project may be derailed or an issue lost because a problem is not recognized in time. By the same token, acting on a problem without careful planning may be detrimental.

Verification. Verification of facts relating to an issue confirms its existence and helps determine how or whether it should be pursued. To clarify the facts of a case, you might ask several questions: Who is involved in the issue? Are the players individuals, organizations, or both? What is the role of each player? Are they related to each other in any way? What incident(s) occurred to create the issue? What are the effects on those involved?

Chronological description of important events is another way to build a case in support or opposition to an issue. The chronology should be maintained as long as the issue is being pursued. Similarly, pertinent documents and correspondence should be collected. Recording notes in a diary will ensure that day-to-day details, which may be important at a future time, are not lost.

Scope. Situation analysis should include an evaluation of the scope of the issue. Who is involved and who will be influenced or affected by its pursuit? Are there choices about how to pursue the issue? How will strategic options affect the outcome? Is the desired outcome worth the cost of the pursuit? Are there sufficient resources available to pursue the issue? Resources can include, but are not limited to, people, time, money, and experts. What is the response of the other side likely to be? Can a settlement be negotiated?

DEVELOPING AN ISSUE.

Obviously, there are many factors to be considered in the development of any issue. As an issue grows in complexity, the factors that must be considered increase.

Players. The issue may ultimately involve more players than were initially involved. The nurse-midwives case at the beginning of this chapter is a good example. The issue appeared to be between nurse-midwives and physicians, but eventually hospital corporations, nursing associations, medical associations, an insurance company, legislators, regulatory agencies, consumers, and the press were also involved.

The players associated with an issue can be classified as advocates, adversaries, or neutral. Who can be counted on to support the issue? Will nurses or nursing organizations take a stand? Will other professional colleagues consider the issue to be credible? Is it the type of issue that will generate public support? How powerful are the advocates? Will the advocates stand together? Who will take adversarial positions? Can their reactions be predicted? How powerful are the adversaries and what kind of resources do they have? What is their cumulative strength?

Normal relationships of the players may be affected by adversarial positions regarding an issue. Will friends become adversaries? Will some people's actions be labeled as trouble-making? Will future opportunities be affected in a positive or negative way?

Some players will take a neutral position. Neutrality may promote successful mediation of a problem. It may also diffuse the position of one side or the other, if the neutral party was expected to take a more definitive position.

Public Appeal. Evaluation of an issue's public appeal is important to determine whether to seek public support. Some issues are of little interest to those outside the nursing profession. For example, it is not likely that public interest could be generated in the issue of the composition of the state board of nursing.

Public interest may be influenced by the local environment. In a community with strong unions, public appeal in a nurses' labor dispute may be significant.

The impact of public support should be considered. That impact is probably greatest when the issue captures both public and professional interest. The public's desire for less expensive health care, for example, may influence insurance companies to cover nurses' services.

The public generally responds positively to nurses. This does not mean, however, that the public knows much about nursing as a profession. Seeking public support for an issue often requires a substantial educational effort. The Nashville nurse-midwives used the press, public meetings, and film documentaries to educate the public about their practice as well as their issue.

Means of Challenge. The development of an issue should include a thorough analysis to determine how it can be challenged. Has a law, policy, contract, code of ethics, or even a constitutional right been violated? Is there any way to resolve the issue, such as filing a grievance or lawsuit, introducing legislation, creating public pressure, or simply requesting a meeting with the other party? Sometimes there are procedural requirements that must be met or the issue may be forfeited. For example, a grievance procedure may specify methods, times, and persons that must be approached in a stepwise fashion.

The ramifications of a legal or other formal procedure must also be considered. Are there precedents set by similar issues or cases? Do the contingencies of the courtroom or hearing threaten the possibilities of a favorable decision? Will a court procedure establish a favorable legal precedent for nursing? Do current legal trends favor the pursuit of the issue? Are there options to a legal challenge that are considered equally effective?

Some disputes have no basis for formal resolution. Even when there is a related contract or law, there may not be sufficient specific requirements for a formal proceeding. In those instances, personal negotiation, political influence, press contact, or public pressure may be the only recourse.

DECIDING TO PURSUE THE ISSUE

Once an issue is identified and defined, the next step is to set goals for its resolution.

Goal Setting. What are the possible solutions to the issue? Is there a win-win solution? Is there an acceptable compromise? Can an acceptable solution be negotiated?

The desired solution becomes the goal for resolution of the issue, and specific strategies are set to accomplish the goal within a given time frame. If the issue, for example, is that insurance companies do not pay for the services of psychiatric nurses, the goal may be to convince the insurance companies to add the coverage by a given date and mandate such coverage in all policies regulated by the state. Setting an achievable goal is essential to satisfactory resolution of an issue.

Risk Analysis.   The risks and payoffs of challenging an issue must be measured in the goal-setting process. What will be lost if the issue is not pursued? What will be gained if it is? How certain are those losses or gains? What are the short-term and long-term effects of either choice? The solution to any problem will produce at least one new problem. Does the value of the solution outweigh the new problem that will arise?

How objective are the decisions to pursue the issue? Often there are significant emotional factors surrounding the decision to challenge an issue. While the emotional factors should not be negated, they must be balanced with factual analysis of the cost and benefit of taking action.

How will the outcome of the issue influence the short-term and long-term goals of those involved? Will resolution of the issue occur soon? Will it, like the nurse-midwives' issue, require several years to resolve? Do those involved have the personal resources and stamina to pursue a challenge? Can they tolerate lost wages, personal and family stress, professional pressure, and public visibility?

Support Systems.   An effective support system is critical to the successful pursuit of any issue. Maintaining contact with professional association staff and leadership provides personal support and special assistance. For example, your nurses' association might provide you with:

- information, counseling, group support, or financial assistance
- a basis for a support network
- access to the press, public leaders, and political contacts.

When an issue affects the profession of nursing, an effort should be made to involve the professional associations in the problem-solving, decision-making process. Association involvement can strengthen the credibility of the issue and provide support to those leading the effort.

It is also advisable to evaluate the strengths of potential supporters. For example, some people are more effective behind the scenes, doing office work or writing press releases. Others may wish to remain anonymous, but will contribute money to a cause. The politics of developing a cadre of supporters may be as sensitive as the issue itself.

A support system can provide money as well as people. Deciding whether to pursue an issue may depend on the dollar cost to those involved. Fund-raising events, like those held for the midwives, may be necessary. A financial expert should determine if an appeal for tax deductible donations can be made. In any case, steps must be taken to record and manage funds.

Sources of official support should also be defined. When issues have legal ramifications, there are often regulatory agencies that will provide information and assistance. Such agencies include the FTC, the National Labor Relations Board, the state board of nursing, the state health department, and many others. Regulatory agencies have specified jurisdictions, and effort may be required to determine which agency has jurisdiction over the issue in question.

Political contacts may be able to direct you to the appropriate public agencies, and may assist by introducing or supporting legislation to resolve the issue. Political figures can lend credibility to an issue. Local, state, and national political figures are often approached for support on issues of concern to their constituents. For example, in the nurse-midwives' case, Congressman Gore was a valuable ally.

Pursuing the Issue.   Once the commitment to pursue an issue has been made and the goal set, the next step is to determine strategies. For each strategy, there are also tactics or action plans.

Given a set of strategic options, which is the most desirable? Who will be consulted regarding strategic options? How will the decision be made to move from one strategy to the next? Who will be responsible for strategic decision making?

Nurses involved in the issue make the decision to pursue the issue, although attorneys, consultants, association staff, and others give advice. Nurses also choose which strategies to employ.

The following illustrates the implementation of a strategy designed to expand the number of nurses concerned about an issue. A few years ago, third party reimbursement was an issue for only a few nurses. To make it an issue for the nursing community at large, a small group drafted a resolution on third party reimbursement for nurses. It was presented to the Tennessee Nurses' Association, and following its adoption, it was submitted to the ANA house of delegates. Adopted by ANA, it has become a key position of the Association.

Strategy decisions are directly tied to goals. Strategies available to nurses can be classified as professional, public, procedural, and legal. Nursing issues may require the use of one or a combination of these strategies:

• **Professional Strategies.**   Professional strategies are appropriate for issues that require a stance to be taken by nurses. The development of the third party reimbursement issue began with a professional strategy. Activities associated with a professional strategy include development of position papers, use of intra- and interassociation politics, and development of nursing support systems.

• **Public Strategies.**   Public strategies may be chosen when nurses' issues are also important to the general public. Health care, women's and labor issues often generate considerable public interest. Strategies associated with motivation of public interest include: (1) organization of citizen groups; (2) press coverage; (3) circulation of petitions; and (4) informational picketing.

• **Procedural Strategies.**   Procedural strategies use formal procedures to pursue an issue. Public hearings and public comment periods provide information about changes in regulations or legislative proposals; a grievance procedure is usually outlined in labor contracts or employment policies; and the legislative process employs formal procedures to make changes in existing laws or to write new laws.

•**Legal Strategies.** Legal strategies use the courts to resolve issues. Lawsuits may be filed when laws or contracts are violated. Choosing a legal strategy usually requires legal counsel. Good legal assistance can make or break an issue.

SUMMARY

Some or all of the strategies outlined above determine the selection of a specific plan of action. As various strategies are used, periodic evaluation will help determine if the action taken on the issue has been effective. This is particularly important if a complex issue requires a long time to resolve.

The unfinished saga of the Nashville midwives has been told for three reasons. First of all, it is important to call attention to the nursing practice and consumer issues raised by the case. Secondly, the case lends itself to study and analysis by other nurses who may wish to use the analysis of the model in responding to issues they want to address. Finally, it is important to study this case because it is inspiring and gives nurses a sense of pride in the accomplishments of their colleagues who are working effectively in behalf of the profession and health care consumers.

Chapter 17

Marketing as a Nursing Skill

Caroline Camuñas, RN, EdM

In the marketplace, a product is produced and priced to achieve certain financial goals. There is an exchange of value for value. Emphasis is on efficiency. No longer can we think of our world in terms of unlimited economic expansion, for economies are shrinking or have stabilized at lower levels. Health care has become a business and must meet business criteria. The Reagan administration has made it clear that it wants no increase in expenditures for health care, indicating that the current 10% of the gross national product is enough. As a result, intense competition for scarce resources and emphasis on cost containment programs are expanding.

Nursing has its origins in the military and the church. It has never before been concerned with economics. Traditionally nursing has been seen as woman's work done out of dedication and not for profit. Nurses have put society's needs ahead of their own. This is evidenced by: (1) the movement of the patient from the home to the hospital during World War I; (2) the switch to functional nursing during World War II; (3) the creation of the licensed practical nurse (LPN) and associate degree (AD) programs to meet society's needs for more caretakers at less cost.

Nurses did not, however, promote the baccalaureate as the entry level for professional practice at the time the federal government was investing considerable money in nursing education. Instead, organized nursing waited until economic hard times to advocate the baccalaureate as the minimal professional degree and ask for federal education funds to support this mission. From the point of view of marketing strategy, nursing missed the opportunity to promote professional nursing education when funds were available and instead selected a tough period to market its ideas.

Nurses and nursing have not always had the foresight to act in the best interest of the profession and the public. In the current economic environment, marketing expertise can provide the needed tools to provide the most equitable exchange of value for value.

205

Kotler (1984) defines marketing as "a social process by which individuals and groups obtain what they need and want through creating and exchanging products and value with others" (p 4). Communication and exchange of value for value are basic to marketing. Marketing attempts to identify and fulfill the needs and wants of consumers. This makes marketing more than just advertising to increase sales.

MARKET SEGMENTATION

The first step in marketing is to identify the groups with whom you have an exchange relationship, eg, your markets. For the nursing department of a hospital, the primary internal markets include patients, physicians, other departments such as the laundry and pharmacy, volunteers, and students. The supervisory personnel may be an important market for the staff nurses. External markets for a hospital include families, visitors, regulators, professional associations, legislators, and volunteer organizations.

An effective marketing approach divides the market into distinct groups. For example, the patient population of a hospital includes many market segments, which have specific needs, preferences, and require different services. A market approach for any one of these groups must be based upon identified goals, strategies, and tactics.

Segmentation of a market may be based upon: health problem/diagnosis; system (orthopedics, cardiovascular, endocrine); location of service (clinic, outpatient surgery); age (neonatal, pediatric, young adult, geriatric); socioeconomic status (private, semiprivate, ward); upon nursing care requirements (patient acuity, ICU, stepdown, self-care); or any of a host of other categories.

After the market is identified, detailed information about the market must be gathered. The values, attitudes, perceptions, wants, needs, and demands of the segment are studied in a systematic way. Qualitative and quantitative studies may be done if resources are available. However, the reader is cautioned about the danger of investing in poorly designed or inaccurately interpreted market research. The 1984 New Orleans World's Fair is an example of poor market research. The Fair's promotors were so caught up in the excitement that researchers found exactly what everyone wanted to hear—that the fair would be a terrific success. But the fair did not draw the large crowds the market researchers predicted, and it was a costly failure.

STRATEGY DEVELOPMENT

The next step in the marketing process involves development of strategies and tactics that will meet the market's needs. Strategies provide the guidelines needed for the attainment of goals and objectives. A strategy should:

1. state goals in terms other than maximum profit
2. outline long-range, specific plans based upon more than intuition and whim
3. influence the environment rather than just react to it
4. serve as a focus of organization effort.

The developer of marketing strategies needs to identify the limitations that will affect the outcome. Common limitations include:

1. Conflict occurs between personal, divisional, and organizational goals.
2. A strategy fails. Prediction of the future is difficult so the development of contingency plans is advised. Use of two questions can help identify alternatives:
   - What if the strategy is more successful than anticipated?
   - What if the strategy is not completely successful or is a complete failure?
3. An opportunity is lost because the marketing strategy is rigidly adhered to.
4. Communication may be secret, closed, or open.

Strategies should be evaluated when they are designed and again during and after the project. It is helpful to ask the following questions about the identified strategies:

1. Is the strategy clearly defined?
2. Does it fully exploit available opportunities?
3. Can it be implemented given the available resources and the degree of competence of the individuals involved?
4. Are the strategies consistent with the organization's goals and values as well as the market opportunity?
5. Is the chosen level of risk feasible in economic and personal terms?
6. Will the strategy stimulate organizational effort?
7. Are there early indicators that the market will respond?

MARKETING MIX: PRODUCT, PROMOTION, PLACE, AND PRICE

Marketing strategy is based upon various combinations of the elements of marketing: product, promotion, place, and price. A successful marketing mix requires one to have "the right product in the right place at the right time with the right promotion at the right price" (Ireland, 1977).

Product

Health or nursing care is a service. It is an intangible product, one that cannot easily be tried out, inspected, or tested in advance. Prospective buyers must depend upon surrogates to assess what they are likely to receive. They may look at pictures of a hospital or nursing home, consult current users, and perhaps friends who are providers (nurses), and ask experienced consumers about the quality and quantity of the nursing services provided at the facility. When prospective buyers cannot experience the product in advance, they are being asked to purchase what amount to promises—promises of satisfaction. This situation requires the consumer to adopt a certain degree of confidence in the providers' abilities.

It is difficult to ensure that consumers will continue to be purchasers of intangible products. Intangible products, like nursing care, are highly people intensive (high touch) in their production and delivery methods. A unique characteristic of intangible products is that the buyer is rarely aware of being served well. Unless there is a problem, the consumer is oblivious to the product received. For example, only when the nurse is late with the pain medication is the patient aware of the presence or absence of the product—nursing care. Consumers do not know what they are getting until they do not receive it. Then they become aware of the product which they anticipated, they dwell on dissatisfaction. Satisfaction is, perhaps as it should be, mute.

We can market nursing services effectively by using ourselves. The way we look and dress, our manner of speech, the way we work with patients, families, and health care colleagues, the degree to which we convey our understanding of a patient's health problem contribute to a positive image of nursing. It is also important for nurses to remind and show consumers of nursing care what they are receiving because buyers of intangibles, like nursing care, do not pay conscious attention to them. If the nurse explains what the patient is getting and makes him aware of the nursing care, she will be educating the consumer about the nature of nursing and will be helping to prevent the magnification of the patient's perception of any mistakes, omissions, or failures.

The nurse can make the intangible tangible by telling the patient what care he can expect to receive. Making an unspecified promise into a credible expectation requires the nurse to ensure that the patient receives the promised care. Nurses are familiar with tools for accomplishing this task: written care plans, nursing audits, and nurse-to-nurse consultations.

Like patients, physicians are consumers of nursing services. Nurses can clarify for physicians what they can expect from nurses. For example, a nurse can tell the physician that a patient can be discharged earlier than expected because of nursing interventions such as preoperative and postoperative teaching. Nurses can write articles about nursing for the hospital newsletter. These activities restate the various aspects of good nursing care and call attention to the value of nursing care.

A second characteristic of a service product is that it is inseparable from the provider. The delivery of a service such as nursing care is similar to the manufacturing phase of a product. While the assessment and planning may be excellent, if the delivery (manufacturing) is poor the patient will view the care (product) as having been poorly manufactured. As with many other intangible products, delivery and production are essentially indistinguishable.

The third characteristic of any service or product is that it is perishable. Nursing care cannot be packaged and stored for use in the future.

The fourth characteristic is that the quality of the service is highly variable and tends to resist quality control. This is because services, like nursing care, are people-intensive. The more people-intensive a product is, the more room there is for personal discretion, idiosyncrasy, error, and delay. The product depends upon the abilities, attitudes, and moods of the provider.

Promotion

Promotion is often equated with advertising. While promotion includes such tactics as advertising, publicity, and personal selling, it does more. Advertising is communication between the provider and the markets that accomplishes two key objectives: (1) it meets the market's need for a product; and (2) it enables the provider to accomplish his goal(s).

Place

Generally there are a limited number of places for nurses to practice or for patients to go for care. Often nurses will select a practice setting based upon what types of services are offered and their perception of conditions like the autonomy of nurses' practice or the collegiality and competence of fellow health professionals. Basic concerns like the safety of the parking lot and an attractive nurses' lounge affect one's perceptions of the work environment.

Patients and their families may choose a nursing home based upon its proximity to family and friends, the appearance of the facility, the appearance of food trays, the appearance of patients in a TV lounge, or the manner in which staff talk with patients. The physical environment tells about the values and attitudes as well as the production and delivery methods of the producer. The environment is part of the package of an intangible product.

Price

In the marketplace, price functions as a tool for the rationing of scarce resources. A product's price affects the demand. It can be a predictor of the demand for a good or service. In health care, however, price does not predict demand because the relationship between price and a person's willingness or ability to pay is limited or nonexistent. In many instances, individuals are covered by health insurance; "someone else" pays the hospital bill. Where coverage is not available or sufficient to cover health care costs, the need for care will usually motivate family and friends to find the money to pay for the care.

The private market can usually be relied upon to produce high quality products and services; however, the necessary conditions do not exist in the health care arena. There are three specific conditions that necessitate regulation of markets for the production of health care:

Lack of Information. Markets bring about optimal solutions to resource allocation problems if buyers have complete and accurate information about the quality of the product and how it compares with the quality of similar products. Buyers of health care often have limited or misleading information about the kind and quality of service available. Frequently they are forced to buy under stress and have no time to compare products. For example, when a child is injured in an auto accident his mother may instruct the ambulance to take him to the nearest emergency room. No thought is given to the type or quality of medical or nursing care. The mother assumes the emergency room will be able to provide the necessary care. In other instances, the consumer may have no choice because there is only one hospital or nursing home in town. The health care consumer rarely has the information necessary to make a discriminating and rational choice.

Third Party Payers.   Many health care costs are paid for by the government or private insurers. As a result, neither consumer nor provider have financial incentives to keep costs down.

Gatekeepers.   In a typical market situation, the consumer decides when to buy a product, how much to buy, and how long he will continue to be a consumer of the product. In the health care arena, it is the providers, the physician, nurse, and case worker who determine the quantity, quality, and duration of the service. The law of supply and demand, which characterizes the competitive marketplace, is not widespread in health care markets.

EVALUATION

Evaluation of results is the final marketing step. It is more readily accomplished if evaluation criteria have been incorporated into the original marketing plan. Four outcome levels can be assessed: awareness, change of attitudes, conviction, and action or behavior. Often during the evaluation process, new ideas for application of the marketing process will come to light.

CONCLUSION

Nurses and the nursing profession can meet the challenge of providing equitable, cost-effective nursing care to consumers by applying the marketing model outlined in this chapter. By developing marketing skills and applying them to their daily professional lives, nurses can successfully engage in the politics associated with influencing the allocation of scarce resources. The model presented here is applicable to the spheres of government, professional organizations, and community, as well as the workplace. Marketing is a tool for influencing in any sphere.

References

Ireland RC: Using marketing strategies to put hospitals on target. *Hospitals* (June 1) 1977; 51:53–58.
Gitel HJ: The financial feasibility study, In: *Debt Financing Capital Formation in Health Care Institutions.* Shields GB (editor). Aspen Systems, 1983.
Kotler P: *Principles of Marketing.* Prentice-Hall, 1980.
Kotler P: *Marketing for Nonprofit Organizations,* 2nd ed. Prentice-Hall, 1982.
Kotler P: *Marketing Management: Analysis, Planning and Control,* 5th ed. Prentice-Hall, 1984.
Lamb-Mechanick D, Block D: Professional membership recruitment: a marketing approach. *Nurs Econ* 1984; 2:398–402.
Sapienza AM, Kahn RA: Impacting the product: Staff involvement in a health care marketing strategy. *Hosp Topics* 1980; 58:24–27.
Shapiro B: Marketing for nonprofit organizations. *Harv Bus Rev* 1973; 51:123–32.

Vignette: **Time to Turn It Around***

Duane D. Walker, RN, MS, FAAN

Only 35 years ago, nursing was one of the two most respected of "women's occupations." In a 1947 study, nursing ranked second only to medicine in prestige (Baudler & Patterson, 1948). Now the story is different. In more recent study of women's occupations, the prestige of nursing has dropped to 91st place in a list of 123 possibilities (Temme, 1975).

What happened to the image of nursing in this relatively short period? The implications of this setback are of utmost concern to us in nursing. A negative image makes it difficult to recruit high-caliber people; it inhibits consumer acceptance and the use of nursing services; and it influences other powerful people, such as policy makers and legislators.

To be able to provide excellent nursing care—to have the necessary resources and support to do this job—we in nursing must regain and reinforce public respect. We must take every opportunity to turn around the prevailing negative image of nursing.

There is ample evidence of nursing's fallen image. You've seen the get-well greeting cards that feature a voluptuous, short-skirted, sex-object type of nurse—and the ones that picture a nurse who is dumpy-looking and carries a yard-long syringe. In contrast, you've seen the Dr Marcus Welby television physician, a man of science who not only directs patient care, but also provides nursing care in the form of preoperative teaching, psychosocial care, home care, and the like. The nurse characters in such dramas are generally placed in the background, pushing wheelchairs, answering the phone, or carrying trays. And when nurse characters are featured, they are generally shown as objects of sexual interest. Do such representations reflect the general public image of nursing? If so, they vividly illustrate that the public has little idea about what a professional nurse is and does.

Even hospitalized patients, who might be expected to have some knowledge of professional nursing, seem to know little about it. Not long ago I visited with a number of patients to see how they view nurses. Some of their comments were positive and showed some insight. These patients said that nurses "made a difficult situation (hospitalization) tolerable," "were trained to watch for changes in condition," and "made sure I got my medication on time." But many of the other patients' comments were typical of the image of nursing that is portrayed and fostered in the mass media. Direct experience with professional nurses, through hospitalization, had somehow failed to alter these patients' views.

As further evidence of nursing's negative image, look at the recruitment ads in nursing journals—the ones that refer to nursing as a "dead-end job"—and the ones that emphasize the recruiting hospital's resort-like environment as if that, not professional nursing opportunities, was important. Such ads represent a put-down of nursing by nursing itself. They are evidence that a negative media image fosters a negative self-image, which in turn diminishes nurses' ability to command public respect.

To rebuild our professional image, we must bolster our self-image as nurses. If we don't believe in our own value as members of an honorable profession and believe in

*Reprinted by permission from *Stanford Nurse*, Vol. 6, No. 2 (Spring) 1984.

professional nursing as a vital component of health care, how will we ever communicate these messages to the public?

Since research has shown that personal contact is most influential in building an image, we want to reach the public on a personal basis. And what better opportunity than when a person is hospitalized? Research has also shown that initial impressions of personal appearance, speech, and interaction style are the strongest and most lasting. Therefore, if we want people to recognize our value as nurses, we must present ourselves self-confidently as valuable members of the health care team, beginning with the first contact with each patient.

In particular, we want to demonstrate that nurses have special roles such as patient education, that nurses are empathic, that they listen to and hear the patient's and family's questions and help to find answers or offer support, and that nurses are intelligent and resourceful problem-solvers. We want to inform patients about the profession of nursing, its educational programs, career opportunities, and research activities.

These messages can be conveyed within the hospital by closed circuit television, exhibits, slide programs, and printed materials. The most important media, however, are nurses themselves in their one-to-one contacts with patients and families.

Nurses can no longer afford to miss the opportunities to turn our image around during contact with patients, the segment of the public immediately available to us. We urgently need the support of the public, and we must become much more active in communicating what we do, and its value, as we provide care.

References

Baudler L, Patterson DG: Social status of women's occupations. *Occupations* 1948; 26: 421–24.
Temme LV: *Occupation: Meanings and Measures.* Bureau of Social Science Research, 1975.

Vignette: An Evolution of Marketing in Nursing*
Gaye F. Bruce, RN

Stanford nurse recruitment has evolved from a crash marketing plan to a major image-building contribution to the nursing profession. During a four-year evolution, three distinct marketing plans have been developed, moving from a reactive approach, through a readiness plan, to the current professional image-building theme. The nursing shortage of 1979 reflected an unbalanced supply and demand ratio in most U.S. hospitals. Nurses were leaving nursing, and those who stayed in the profession "job hopped" for better salaries, benefits, and hours. Turnover rates soared, and temporary agencies sprung up everywhere. Hospitals embarked on major advertising campaigns to compete for the available supply of nurses.

At Stanford, a full-day retreat was held for nursing administrators to evaluate the needs and goals of our recruitment program in light of the shortage and turnover problem. Two major outcomes of that retreat included the following decisions. First, we would seek professional marketing assistance. Second, we would conduct a satisfaction survey of our tenured nurses to understand better: Why did they stay? What were

*Reprinted with permission from *Stanford Nurse*, Vol. 6, No. 2 (Spring) 1984.

their satisfiers at Stanford? What were their dissatisfiers? What were we doing right? What were we doing wrong?

Plan One: Crash Marketing

Because of the nursing shortage crisis, our first marketing efforts were of an urgent nature. We needed nurses now. Fast, effective recruitment was the objective we took to our newly hired advertising agency. They did a situational analysis including how our recruitment program compared to similar hospitals.

The Stanford recruitment program was of a scope, quality, and sophistication that paralleled those of other hospitals of similar size and national presence. But our program paralleled the others so closely that it did not differentiate Stanford University Hospital nursing from our competition. Most of the early recruitment ads in national journals depicted either a "happy nurse" or took a "travelog" approach, playing up the benefits of living in the San Francisco Bay Area. We were not communicating the intrinsic benefits and unique experience of a nursing career at Stanford University Hospital. Our message was not distinctive.

The situational analysis also incorporated the data collected through the satisfaction survey of staff nurses. A clear message came through in the survey. What our nurses liked was "challenge and opportunity to advance in one's career."

Following the situational analysis, our major objective of attracting nurses during the shortage was explored in terms of positioning statement, target audience, marketing strategies, and programs. The positioning statement, the image to be communicated to the target audience, must be believable and unique to the extent that no "competitive" hospital describes itself the same way. Our challenge and opportunity theme was reflective of our position that described the hospital as a "center for excellence in professional nursing."

The target audience, the specific group to whom marketing efforts are directed, may be defined geographically (local, regional, or national), by positions (clinical staff or management), or by experience (new graduates or nurses with more than two years experience). We defined our audience by two dimensions: *national*, believing we could attract nurses from across the U.S., and *clinical* as defined by our need.

Stanford sought a recruitment program that would "stand apart." The marketing agency recommended that our strategic marketing plan provide for a common look and message among all materials produced. All pamphlets, brochures, and literature should be designed to look like they came from the same hospital. Each advertising tool needed to support the positioning statement. This uniformity was expanded to exhibits and displays at conventions and job fairs. Creative pieces based on a common theme are most cost-effective to produce and have a synergistic effect on the market.

Based on the situational analysis, objectives, and strategies, the marketing and advertising agency created an image to reflect this message. They developed a bold new graphic design called "catch lightning." The message was that our nurses are challenged and opportunity is available to them. The lightning caught within the bottle symbolized challenge and opportunity—two forces intertwined. The lightning became the Stanford nursing logo. The image was dramatically different from other nursing advertising, and became easily and immediately recognizable as Stanford.

The recruitment department had been receiving approximately 35 job inquiries per month. After the new ad appeared in national journals, the number of inquiries increased to more than 20 calls per day. The ad was serving its purpose, and our marketing plan met the objective. Stanford nursing no longer had a shortage.

Plan Two: Readiness Recruitment

In sharp contrast to earlier years, the nursing shortage situation began to decrease in 1982. There were fewer jobs, less hiring, lower hospital census, nursing turnover rates declined, and vacancies practically vanished in most acute care facilities. We had moved from a state of shortage to near abundance. In reevaluating our marketing plan, we set a new objective: to create a program of readiness. We wanted a plan designed to provide flexibility, emphasizing or deemphasizing recruitment tactics as the need changed.

A new marketing plan was developed. This plan added budgetary restrictions in line with the hospital's cost-containment program, a strong new situational force. The challenge and opportunity theme was maintained. The recruitment effort was toned down. This message was developed into an ad directed to all professional nurses and was run in professional journals. It reflected the beginning of a secondary objective—to enhance the Stanford nursing image. The ad for this marketing plan, called a border ad, announced new and innovative programs at Stanford. This ad was unique in that it maintained a consistent design and could be revised to add new content as needed.

Plan Three: A Professional Image

The readiness plan had sparked positive responses from professional nurses. This encouraged a reaching out not only to nurses but to the general public to enhance the image of nursing in the public's eye. A second objective was to keep the image in readiness for a recruitment campaign should the supply of nurses drop off again.

A new positioning statement defined Stanford as a "leader and trendsetter in professional nursing practice and a source of innovative nursing programs." Two new ads were developed simultaneously. One had a message "Extend Your Reach and Yourself at Stanford" directed toward professional nurses. The other, "Nursing Touches You," was intended for the public audiences with the message "with hands that care, heal, teach, and touch."

The image ad, "Nursing Touches You," first appeared in the United Airlines magazine during the National League for Nursing Convention in June 1983. The ad drew 200 responses from all over the world. A similar ad, "Extend Your Reach," was run in professional journals and simultaneously reinforced the message to the professional nursing audience.

In addition to the professional nurse and the public, the new marketing plan has two other designated target audiences: nurses at Stanford and Stanford patients. This marketing plan delineates many projects specific to these audiences.

At Christmas 1983, all Stanford nurses received a calendar designed to correspond to our theme. The message read "This year challenge yourself with more responsibility and more autonomy. Explore opportunities to work, to learn, to build a career. Excellence through challenge and opportunity is within your grasp each day."

A series of meal tray tent cards inform patients about the expanding role of nursing. Topics include information on the clinical coordinator, nursing research, patient education, specialty care units, discharge planning, nursing supportive personnel, and clinical specialists.

A public service announcement (PSA) video cassette has been produced around our theme. The nursing logo, used in the first ad and all subsequent marketing efforts, is displayed prominently at the beginning and end to enhance visibility to the public. A local television station is airing the PSA as is our hospital's closed circuit television.

In May 1984, National Nurse Day was expanded into Stanford Nurse Week. Scheduled events included open house tours of certain areas of the hospital conducted by nurses, a health fair with exhibits and information on current health topics, and a full-day workshop on the "Image of Professional Nursing."

We've come a long way—we've changed our course as the environment has dictated and we will continue to be ready to meet future challenges in the changing health care field. Stanford's position has been established as a leader and trendsetter, and we are pleased that hospitals throughout the nation look to us to set the pace.

Case Study
Fantasy, Fact, and Finding:
A Case Study of the NURSE Inc. Suit
Against the City and County of Denver

Dody Cotter, RN, MA

It seemed simple as we sat around a table in 1973 looking at the results of the pay survey which the City of Denver used to set salaries for city employees. Credit for recognizing the disparity and inequity in the survey system belongs to the director and associate director of Denver General Hospital (DGH), Mary Lemons and Lois Cady, respectively. Denver General is one of two nursing services in the city government. The other is the Denver Visiting Nurse Service (VNS), a combined agency whose activities were directed by the city and by the private citizen board of the Visiting Nurse Association.

Lemons and Cady had analyzed the study for several years and had concluded that the survey methods of selecting key classes to compare with the community were grouped into predominantly male or female groups, and historical patterns of wage discrimination were being brought into the city pay system.

In previous years, a kind of rivalry had existed between the two nursing services. They watched each other carefully for progress one service might make in classification or benefits that the other might not enjoy. But as they came together in 1973, they set aside differences in the recognition that any effort to correct a long-standing practice would take mutual, concerted efforts from both nursing services.

Around the table were the key administrative nursing personnel of DGH and VNS. From Denver General, there were Mary Lemons, Lois Cady, and Sharon Shumway and Jean Mitchell, assistant directors. From VNS there were Margaret Lewis, director; Dody Cotter, associate director; Anne Jumper and Marilyn Shahan, assistant directors. These persons became plaintiffs as the proceedings evolved.

As we sat around the table, the sense that the survey was unfair seemed indisputable. We were all in positions that gave credibility to the effort, and we weren't afraid to work. It seemed simple. Little did we know of the seven year struggle that lay ahead.

The Fantasy

The City of Denver is bound by its charter to pay its employees the community "prevailing wage." To determine the prevailing wage, the city conducts an annual pay survey. For the survey, 716 job classes are organized into 35 pay groups. These groups (key classes) are predominantly male or female in terms of incumbent employees. An example of a key class is graduate nurse (GN I), to which all other nursing classes and health professions such as social worker and dietitian are tied. It is approximately 97 percent female.

As we looked at one class tied to the GN I, it appeared that the licensed practical nurses made $200 to $300 less per month than male job classes that required one-year posthigh school education and a license.

Knowing hard data was needed, we began the tedious task of factoring the more than 700 job descriptions in terms of required education, experience, supervisory re-

Table III-1 Plaintiffs' Exhibits: Jobs with Higher Beginning Pay Ranges and Less Job Worth than Graduate Nurse I

Job Title	Monthly Salary	% Male
Sign painter	1245	100
Plumber	1218	100
Cement finisher	1191	100
Automotive painter	1164	100
Carpenter I	1113	100
Painter I	1088	100
Tree trimmer I	1040	100
Tire serviceman I	1017	100
Auto mechanic helper	1017	100
Oiler I	1017	100
Parking meter repairman II	994	100
Graduate nurse I	929	3

sponsibility, and occupational category (an Equal Employment Opportunity Commission [EEOC] designation). We were attempting to identify comparable job worth. The next task was to determine male/female incumbency for the classes from information requested from the city. Then, actual monthly salary figures of each class were determined, including starting salary, mean in-pay grade, and median in-pay grade.

Eight nursing classes of sixteen classes were selected for comparison. These included licensed practical nurse, graduate nurse I (entry level RN), public health nurse II, graduate nurse III, clinical specialist I, public health nurse IV, associate director of nursing, and director of nursing.

The nursing classes were matched to predominantly male job classes having similar education, experience, supervisory responsibility, and occupational category and salary comparisons figured. Job worth was described by the requirements for job entry. Further factoring was done by a personnel expert who used the job description for analysis of duties. Tables III-1 and III-2 reflect the findings determined in 1974 and again in 1977.

As we analyzed the data and found the evidence of disparity that could only be explained on the basis of the sex of the incumbents, we sought help from the Colorado Nurses' Association (CNA) and asked to have their legal counsel assist us. This was not possible, and we were referred to Craig Barnes, an attorney who had successfully aided others in civil rights matters. Barnes was interested; he could see the problem. He also knew that the issue was comparable pay for comparable job worth, which would require a different application of Title VII of the Civil Rights Act. Prior to this time, this act had been used principally to resolve wage inequity between male and female workers doing the same job.

Barnes discussed alternatives with the plaintiffs. Initially the information would need to be filed with the EEOC to learn if it would pursue it. The next steps would be decided based on its ruling. The road would not be easy, Barnes made clear.

The fantasy persisted: the evidence clearly demonstrated the city pay survey system was organized in a discriminatory way, with job classes tied together not by the nature of

Table III-2   General Comparison of 100% Male and 100% Female Classes

	1974	1977
Number of 100% male classes	325	375
Mean monthly starting salary of 100% male classes	$1029.30	$1592.81
Number of 100% female classes	92	82
Mean monthly starting salary of 100% female classes	$ 817.53	$1090.77
% Difference 100% male and 100% female classes Mean monthly starting salary	25.9	46.0

the jobs, but by predominantly male or female incumbency of the related classes. The disparity for the nursing classes was $200 to $342 per month. Job worth comparisons were clearly in favor of the nursing classes. The plaintiffs believed that surely the evidence would be plain to all who reviewed it.

The Facts

Barnes insisted the data be statistically validated. George Bardwell of the University of Denver was the consultant for the statistical analysis. Armed with calculators, the plaintiffs carefully entered the salary figures and means and medians were extracted. The comparisons held in terms of statistical significance. The case was filed December 12, 1976 in Federal District Court following release by EEOC. The legal basis for the suit was Title VII of the 1964 Civil Rights Act and the Fourteenth Amendment to the Constitution.

LEGAL BASIS FOR THE CASE
Title VII Civil Rights Act of 1964: Section 2000e-2(a). "It shall be an unlawful employment practice for an employer—(1) . . . to discriminate against any individual with respect to his compensation, terms, conditions, or privileges of employment, because of such individual's . . . sex in any way which would deprive or tend to deprive any individual of employment opportunities or otherwise adversely affect his status as an employee, because of such individual's . . . sex . . . ."
Section 1983 and the fourteenth amendment: The Fourteenth Amendment mandates that no state shall "deny to any person within its jurisdiction the equal protection of the laws." Section 1983 creates a right of action against the defendants as follows:

> Every person who, under color of any statute, ordinance, regulation, custom or usage, of any State or Territory, subjects or causes to be subjected any citizen of the United States or other person within the jurisdiction thereof or the deprivation of any rights, privileges, or immunities secured by the Constitution and laws, shall be liable to the party injured in an action at law, suit in equity, or other proper proceeding for redress.

The Case

Expert witnesses were found for the suit. Resource persons in the history of nursing and its financial inequities, personnel management, and statistics were enlisted. A second attorney assisted Barnes.

Table III-3 NURSE, Inc. Income Expenses (April 19, 1975–December 31, 1979)*

INCOME

ANA contribution		$ 30,000.00
Fund-raising and donations		58,587.36
	Total	$ 88,587.36

EXPENSES

Attorney fees		52,584.47
Job worth study		6,300.00
Court costs		4,219.72
Court transcripts		1,497.15
Expert witnesses		3,065.08
Computer services		2,659.69
Printing (exhibits)		2,095.55
Audit fees		1,295.00
Miscellaneous		11,691.51
	Total	$ 85,408.17
CASH IN BANK (12/31/79)		$ 1,799.78
SAVINGS ACCOUNT (12/31/79)		6,074.13
LIABILITIES:		
Attorney fees		38,392.61
Expert witnesses		6,820.00
Computer services		1,926.94
	Total	$ 47,139.55
NET WORTH (LOSS)		($39,265.64)

*Unaudited

Costs of the effort began to mount. Barnes and others had given numerous hours without compensation. The plaintiffs had given generously of time to reduce the cost of having work done by someone else. The American Nurses' Association (ANA) had been approached early in the case, but had declined assistance at that time. As the case gained national awareness, however, and implications for other nurses became clear, ANA assisted substantially. Fund-raising began in earnest.

The 1975–1979 fund-raising efforts and the income expense statement are shown in Tables III-3 and III-4.

The Findings

The case went to trial April 17, 1978, five years after the first discussion around the table.

Presiding for the U.S. District Court for Colorado was Judge Fred M. Winner. The arguments for the case lasted two weeks. The nurses' analysis of the pay survey system was presented. The history of nursing showing occupational discrimination was described. Lois Cady described her job as associate director in terms of complexity. Judith Ives described her duties as a staff nurse.

Table III-4 NURSE, Inc. Major Fund-raising Activities (July 1975–December 1979)

	Income	Expense	Profit
Cookbooks	7,357.73	2,498.35	4,859.38
Raffle	6,029.35	1,941.55	4,087.80
Play, "A Past to Remember"	2,372.65	239.56	2,133.09
Calendars	2,920.87	1,179.38	1,741.49
Wine and cheese party	1,700.24	39.24	1,661.00
Melodrama presentation	1,418.82	395.00	1,023.82
Fashion show	1,213.10	50.00	1,163.10
Luncheon is served	307.00	37.50	269.50
Totals	$23,319.76	$6,380.58	$16,939.18

The City and County of Denver countered that their system was a model pay survey system, recognized for its merit across the county. They agreed that history had discriminated against female occupations, including nursing.

The city stated, however, that it was not its role to correct a historical pattern when supply and demand was the issue governing modern employment practices and salary scales. Nurses from across Denver, representatives of the CNA, and nurses from DGH and VNS were in the courtroom daily. For the first few days, Judge Winner's inquiry and apparent sensitivity to the issues were heartening. As the trial progressed, however, the tone changed and hope of success began to fade. On April 26, Judge Winner gave his decision, excerpted below.

This case is a case certainly of substantial importance to the plaintiffs, it is a case of substantial importance to the taxpayers of the City and County of Denver, it is a case of substantial importance to the entire community, it is a case which is pregnant with the possibility of disrupting the entire economic system of the United States of America. The case is one which states an unusual approach to employment of rates pay. It's been a very interesting case. It's been a very well prepared case. It's been a very well presented case.

We're confronted with a history which I have no hesitancy at all in finding has discriminated unfairly and improperly against women. But Congress did not, in my judgment, decide that we were going to roll aside all history and that the Federal Courts should take over the job of leveling out centuries of discrimination.

The plaintiffs here say they want their pay to be compared with other occupations. Of course they do. If that were done, it would give them more pay. But I can find nothing in the law that requires that. It would be nice for the plaintiffs. It would be completely disruptive of our way of life, and we've got enough disruptions now.

I think they have established that, by and large, male-dominated occupations probably pay more for comparable work than is paid in the occupations dominated by females.

There is another major problem in trying to apply the plaintiffs' philosophy to this case. Plaintiffs want to structure their pay utilizing a comparison to other occupations, albeit they are male-dominated occupations. I don't think the Congress of the United States intended that equality was to be such a flexible, fluctuating, impossible, imponderable thing as would result from that.

I cannot conceive of how a system could work where a group of employees' pay was to be determined by comparison with the other jobs available in that employer's economic structure.

The overall result here, in my judgment, would be absolutely chaos in the economy of the United States of America if any such program ever to be adopted.

Moreover, to establish a case of discrimination under Title VII, one must prove a differential in pay based on sex for performing "equal" work. Congress in prescribing "equal" work did not require that the jobs be identical, but only that they be substantially equal.

I expressly find that the plaintiffs failed to prove any pay differential based on sex for the performance of substantially equal work.

I expressly find that the plaintiffs here have failed to demonstrate that the difference in wages paid to the nurses and paid to unrelated occupations, whether they be male-dominated, female-dominated, or of equal mix. I expressly find that there has been no showing of any differences based directly or indirectly on sex discrimination, save and except as history has created a lower pay scale for certain occupations.

I expressly find that the City has not excluded any male from the profession of nursing based upon sex, and I expressly find that the City has not excluded any female from any other occupation based upon sex, and I expressly find that the City has made no determination as to the wages of any group based upon sex.

I have said, and I repeat, historically there has been discrimination against females. I condemn it. It's wrong. But Congress has not seen fit to try to bring it all down to date. And Congress has not said that the Courts are supposed to correct all of history. The Courts aren't qualified to do it, the Courts ought to stay out of it. And if history is that bad, the plaintiffs should direct their appeals to the Legislature, the Congress. Perhaps Congressional people are smart enough to solve it. I'm surely not.

The case was appealed to the Tenth District Court of Appeals on April 21, 1980, and received a negative ruling. The case was then appealed to the United States Supreme Court in 1980, which refused to hear the case.

The Finish

The NURSE, Inc. work, *Lemons et al vs The City and County of Denver*, was over. Seven years of grinding efforts, outstanding legal support, assistance from numerous behind-the-scenes people managing the books, handling book sales, raffles, and selling cookbooks was finished. The appeals to nurses across the country resulting in generous responses of financial support were over. Craig Barnes forgave a large amount of the indebtedness in his consistently generous way; Walter Garnsey and George Bardwell did the same. The plaintiffs took other jobs, retired, or continued with their city employment, depending on preference. The endless Wednesday and Saturday work was over. The case was finished—or was it?

In 1981 the United States Supreme Court admitted for the first time a case involving job worth. In 1984, an important court victory based on job worth was decided in the state of Washington where 15,000 public employees, mostly women, have been granted hundreds of millions of dollars in back pay and an average 32 percent pay raise to correct past wage discrimination. Four states—Minnesota, California, Washington, and Iowa—have addressed pay equity for men and women.

At the same time, the Justice Department, under the administration of Ronald Reagan, has challenged the legal victory of women who want to be paid what their jobs are worth. Ellen Goodman, national columnist, wrote:

> The assistant attorney general, Brad Reynolds, is planning to make a move on the [Washington] case. The man disputes the whole notion of comparable worth. He disputes the idea that the members of an entire job class can be victims of discrimination. If a nurse wants more money, he implies, she should become a correctional officer. (*Rocky Mountain News*, Feb 4, 1984)

Future Fantasy

When Lincoln freed the slaves, the entire economic fabric of the country was changed by the disruption on behalf of human rights. It is conceivable that nurses and other women will in time be paid what their jobs are worth, and the economy will adjust as it did when plantation owners found they would need to pay for the work they needed done.

Acknowledgments

Recognition is given to my nurse colleagues who were plaintiffs in the suit *Lemons et al vs The City and County of Denver*. These include Mary Lemons, Lois Cady, Sharon Shumway, Jean Mitchell, Judy Ives, Margaret Lewis, Anne Jumper, and Marilyn Shahan.

Deepest appreciation belongs to Craig Barnes, attorney for the suit, who believes that society and individuals can have a better lot if questions regarding human rights are asked responsibly, and to his colleagues, Attorney Walter Garnsey and George Bardwell.

To the nurses and others who quietly did the unseen, essential chores, fund-raising, bookkeeping, providing donations for the effort, go thanks for taking that wear and tear off our minds. Mildred Yingling, Ruth Ryan, Charlene Lark, and Lynn Brofman were dedicated in their responsibilities.

UNIT IV

POLITICAL ACTION IN THE WORKPLACE

Case Study **A New Day**

Case Study **Change at Bayfront Medical Center: A Case Study on the Influence of the Nurse Manager**

Most nurses confine thoughts of political action to the government sphere. The framework presented in Chapter 1 broadens the scope of politics to other spheres of influence. Perhaps none of these spheres is more important than the workplace. Nurses spend most of their time in the workplace, but exert relatively little influence there. Nurses must develop and fine-tune their political skills in the workplace if the profession is to survive and quality health care is to be provided.

Unit IV begins with a discussion of how to analyze the workplace. The author uses a marketing framework that applies the concepts discussed in Chapter 17 to the workplace. Interdisciplinary politics is discussed in Chapter 19, with the relationship between nurses and physicians receiving particular attention.

The perceived powerlessness of nurses in the workplace is often part of a destructive cycle characterized by an unsupportive work environment. Creating a more supportive work environment can often break this cycle. Chapter 20 identifies ways to create and maintain a supportive work environment. The responsibility for developing such an environment is shared by the nurse manager and the staff nurse. "A View from the Top" discusses what the top-level nurse manager can do to maintain a supportive work environment, while "Opportunities for Grass Roots Action" identifies ways the staff nurse can improve the work environment. Several vignettes are included in this chapter. "Finding Answers in Horoscopes" describes how a new head nurse gained the respect and support of an influential but wary nurse's aide, while "One Manager's Strategies for Creating a Supportive Work Environment" presents two effective strategies used by a new assistant director of nursing to change the status quo of her division. "The Nurse as Hospital Board Member" is a particularly important vignette, because few nurses sit on boards of health care institutions. Finally, "Addressing Occupational Hazards" discusses what nurses can do—and did—to create a safer work environment.

A group of individuals has greater influence than individuals working alone. Chapter 21 focuses on avenues for collective action in the workplace. "The Politics of Collective Bargaining" reviews collective bargaining and how to use it. A newer avenue for increasing the influence of staff nurses, shared governance, is described in the next section of this chapter. Following this outline of a formal system, two staff nurses describe a less complex approach to collective action—"The Staff Nurse Forum." A vignette, "Vote Yes!" describes the successful, collective efforts of San Francisco nurses to secure passage of a city referendum to make city nurses' salaries competitive with those paid in the private and not-for-profit sector.

Chapter 22 focuses on influencing the academic workplace, from both faculty and student perspectives. Nursing research in education and practice settings is recognized as a crucial tool for influencing an issue. Chapter 23 examines the politics of nursing research and suggests how the nurse researcher can develop and use political savvy to be more effective at this important endeavor.

Unit IV concludes with two case studies describing how two new directors of nursing changed their hospital departments. Both studies demonstrate the importance of understanding the structures and processes of the workplace, creating a supportive work environment, and collaborating with the nursing staff for changing the workplace.

Chapter 18

Analyzing Your Workplace

Karen Zander, RN, MS, CS

You're only as strong as the boss, the boss's boss, ...

I used to think if I was the best staff nurse I could be, I could "change the world." Then it occurred to me that *I* may think I was good, but my effectiveness and satisfaction were extremely dependent on the staff I worked with, and that, in turn, was dependent on my boss.

When I became the boss, I realized my unit's effectiveness was dependent, to a large degree, on the hospital as a whole. As a supervisor, I started to appreciate the broader picture, realizing even more clearly how my effectiveness and satisfaction depended on the nursing department's philosophy, policies, structure, strength, and collaboration with the rest of the institution.

I then began to understand the importance of the director of nursing's relationship with the entire institution, its mission, its chief executive officer (CEO), and its communication with "the outside world." Working as an internal organizational development specialist and also as a national consultant, my respect for the double tasks of maintaining operations and developing staff have multiplied. Safely and compassionately responding to the needs of patients and staff around the clock is one of the most complex, frustrating, and satisfying jobs on earth. Such is the nature of a nurse's workplace.

To influence the complex operation of any institution, one must understand the organization's political climate. Today, the health care arena is besieged with demands by government and business to contain costs. Politics, defined in this book as the allocation of scarce resources, including money, time, and space, becomes an even more important aspect of any analysis of the workplace. The nurse who wishes to better understand and influence the nature of her workplace must accept the fact that all institutions are motivated by politics and that the astute nurse can use the political system to her advantage. Developing strategies to exert influence requires an understanding of the self-interests of others: individuals, professional groups, departments within organizations, as well as the environment surrounding the organization. Nurses who use the following guide to organizational analysis will recognize the need to identify ways to develop win-win strategies to solve problems and develop the influence needed to do their jobs. The effective nurse develops and uses political skills in her daily work, especially in making an analysis of the workplace (Cavanaugh, 1985).

Analyzing the workplace is probably the oldest and most often performed function in nursing because the workplace is forever changing. At every coffee break, cafeteria line, and work party, nurses are trying to understand and master their workplace in one way or another. Every change of shift report, discussion with a patient or physician, and documentation of some aspect of nursing practice reflects an assessment of the workplace. Similarly, every employment interview, orientation class, performance appraisal, role evaluation, and exit from an organization demonstrates an action, analysis, and response to one or more components of the workplace.

Every nurse is a self-made consultant. The only difference between "official" organizational consultants and nurses in the organization is that consultants are invited and expected to make more conscious and conscientious assessments than staff. Nurses and their workplaces will only grow and prosper, however, if everyone believes that the best consultants are already working there.

There is currently an enormous amount of literature on organizational structure and design, replete with charts, diagrams, and definitions. Much has been written about the special needs of specific consumer populations and the special problems of health care and academic workplaces. The purpose of this chapter is not to repeat that information, but rather to personalize organizations from the nurse's perspective. The goal is to assist the nurse in making a practical assessment that will enable him or her to be more effective and satisfied.

Analyzing the workplace was probably the same for Clara Barton as for nurses today and the same regardless of one's specific role or agency. For a telling and rapid analysis, consider the workplace beyond the bedside (see Figure 18-1). Also, review the chain of command: the boss, the boss's boss, and so forth. For a more in-depth understanding of the workplace, proceed with a straightforward analysis of the elements of structure, process, and outcome (see Figure 18-2). Then identify your ability to influence the lives of patients, coworkers, and the surrounding environment.

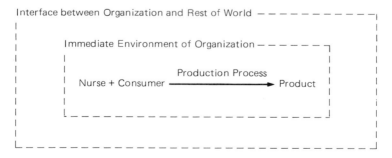

Figure 18-1   A Nurse's Workplace: The Big Picture

STRUCTURE	PRODUCTION PROCESS	PRODUCT(S) (Goals, Outcomes, Objectives)

Academia
  Courses
  Faculty
  Clinical affiliations
  Committee structures
  Application procedures
	Teacher-learner processes for
	  acquisition of knowledge,
	  skills, attitudes
	Committee work
	Advising students
		Degrees, signifying
		  achievement of specific
		  behavioral outcomes
		  BSN
		  MSN
		  DNSc
		Publications
		Research

Primary Nursing:
  Assignment & reporting
    structure
  Support systems including
    management
  Associate structure, etc.
	Nursing process via case
	  management techniques,
	  continuity of care
		Individualized outcomes
		  of nursing care based on
		  individual nursing
		  diagnoses

Operating Room
  Scrub Nurse
  Circulating Nurse
	Perioperative nursing	Patient who is physically
		  safe
		Patient who integrates the
		  surgical experience

Consultant
  Times
  Fees
  Knowledge
  Experience
	Nursing process applied at the
	  organizational level
	Project management, facilitator
	Teacher
	Mediator, arbitration
		Realistic work plan to
		  change structure or process
		Project completion
		Learning objectives fulfilled
		Conflict resolution

Figure 18-2   Examples: Relation of Product to Process and Structure

A nurse's workplace is, by definition, a place where nursing (care or education) takes place. "Nursing" entails a provider, a consumer, an outcome (product), and a production process. The production process occurs within the context of the larger milieu (environment), which includes multiple resources and their access routes. Every route to a resource entails rules and requires the use of power, influence, and political skills. Some of the resources necessary to the production process are located within the nurses' workplace, while some are beyond the boundaries of the workplace.

Ironically, analyzing the workplace should begin with outcomes and work backwards through assessments of process and structure. The key questions to use when analyzing the workplace are:

1. What is the product (outcome) of the workplace?
2. What is the production process designed to achieve the product?
3. How does the larger environment facilitate, dovetail, and impede the production process?
4. What can an individual nurse do to make the workplace work for him or her?
5. How can political skills be used to promote the nurse's goals?

THE PRODUCT (OUTCOME)

A product: (1) is reliable; (2) directs the production process and its structure; (3) creates a contract; and (4) demands accountability (see Figure 18-2). Beginning one's workplace analysis on the product (outcome) of the work eliminates confusion and distraction with the "fancier" or more obvious characteristics of a system or organization. The nursing profession has focused its development efforts almost exclusively on process and structure, rather than first defining its products and then designing structures and processes to achieve the product. "Patient care" and "nursing education" are not products—they are names for broad functions that connote many levels of process. Products are specific outcomes of those processes and the purpose of the work.

Products are the impetus for the process and reason for the structure. In other words, the product is the independent variable—it stays the same while the process may vary to adjust to certain contingencies. For instance, a nursing product for a pediatric patient was fluid and electrolyte balance; specifically, that he would not become dehydrated. His primary nurse did everything she could think of to make him drink fluids, but to no avail. She reassessed the situation and devised a game whereby the patient could color a part of a paper man based on each glass of fluid, which he could drink at any time during the shift. In exchange, the nurses would stop nagging him. The nurse and patient agreed on the ultimate product (fluid and electrolyte balance) and the process to achieve it. This example illustrates how the product—or objective—can stimulate the pulling together of divergent processes to ensure a successful outcome.

Achieving the product creates a need for a contract with the consumer. The contract can be written or implied. Use of contracts with consumers of nursing is in its infancy, sometimes used by psychiatric nurses with their patients, organizational consultants (Stevens, 1978), or by teachers with students. Attention to product-identification in the form of patient-care outcomes (knowledge, health, activity) was initiated by the Joint Commission on Accreditation of Hospitals (JCAH) (Jacobs & Jacobs, 1975). The JCAH forced nursing services to separate the product from the processes of critical and preventive management. Relative intensity measures, one system of patient classification, has further contributed to product identification (Joel, 1983). What remains is for nurses to learn how to teach and negotiate the expected products with the consumer by patient-contracting (Steckel, 1982) and assignment of accountability for guaranteeing those outcomes, ie, primary nursing.

Accountability for the product is usually the missing link in the nurse's workplace. Typically, everyone feels responsible, but no one is accountable, or accountability is at the wrong level, creating a misalignment of functions and responsibility. True accountability requires that the person who has the authority and control over the production process is answerable for the results. "Accountability, especially for outcome and not just process, is new to the profession and is more likely to be used in context with autonomous practice" (Mundinger, 1980).

Some workplaces, such as New England Medical Center in Boston, are anticipating moving beyond the assignment of accountability for specific health-related outcomes toward assignment of accountability for the financial outcomes for the primary nurse's cases. Thus, measures such as patient acuity, hours per patient day, and nursing turnover are conceptualized as variables in the larger picture; ie, nursing product-pricing.

Workplaces that put emphasis on the quality and price of products will be interested in finding the best "fit" of production processes and organizational structures. This is true whether the nurse is working in independent practice, a university classroom, or a large medical center.

THE PRODUCTION PROCESS

The production process in every nursing workplace is complex. For instance, the Visiting Nurses' Association (VNA) nurse's immediate workplace is the patient's home— simple at first glance, but complex on further analysis. The family and physical environment make up just the first level of variables, followed closely by the norms, values, and standards of the nurse's agency, plus those of the providers and other agencies in the larger community. The VNA's production process is initiated by need and referral, operationalized by visits for assessment and treatment, aided by resources, and evaluated for results.

The nursing process—assessment, planning, intervention, evaluation—could be described as nursing's first standardization of the production process (Mauksch & David, 1972). An accurate analysis of the workplace demands an assessment of the extent of *conscious* implementation of the nursing process. Nurses' abilities to independently move from one phase of the nursing process to another will be a strong predictor of success for the organization and each nurse. One must not forget, however, that the basic decisions—what the product will be and how it will be produced (the process)— are determined by those with power and influence and an ability to assess the political environment.

The nursing process transcends specific nursing roles because the critical thinking necessary to do it is at the heart of the helping process, whether the nurse is an educator, caregiver, manager, or "change agent." Do caregivers in the workplace engage in critical, cause-and-effect thinking at every level? Or, are they doing the right thing for the wrong reasons, or the best thing at the wrong time? Is there a serious and effective attempt on every nurses' part to think through a problem, or is there a routine knee-jerk reaction to situations? Unfortunately, it is true that "nurses have more opportunity to flee physically and mentally from a thought-task than other groups because there is always a patient who needs them or some other area to put their energies at the moment" (Zander, 1980). The nurse analyzing the production process should be wary of excuses for any lack of critical thinking in trying to achieve a quality product. Without an assessment of critical thinking, the analyst will be unable to evaluate the real worth of the production process.

Analysis of the nurse-patient relationship is a challenge because of the privacy and subjectivity of the interaction. What do nurses really do with patients? How much short- and long-term impact do faculty really have on students? Formal evaluation of nursing care by patients and families is just now being developed by some health care agencies (Ferguson & Ferguson, 1983). Similarly, peer evaluation is a new means of assessing the production process (Mullins et al, 1979).

Assessing the environment immediately surrounding the nurse-patient interaction is the next level of analyzing the production process. The nurse's workplace, it is hoped, contains most of the characteristics of a professional milieu (Zander, 1980). A professional milieu is an environment in which professional behavior is valued and reinforced by the majority of the people. Characteristics of this environment include:

- The patient is the primary focus.
- Professional closeness with patients is a constant goal of everyone.
- Individual, personal, and professional development is a strong motivating force. Nurse-to-nurse learning is an expectation.
- Competition is healthy rather than destructive.
- Destructive reactions are sublimated; ie, effort is made to turn the irrational into rational thought and behavior.
- There are internal and external checks and balances on decisions.
- Although each professional discipline views experiences through different conceptual frameworks, there is a striving towards unanimity and joint resolution of cognitive dissonance.
- The easiest solution is not necessarily the best.
- There is a demonstrated belief in the value of planning ahead (as opposed to reliance on luck and submission to fate).
- Quality of care is documented and intrinsic to patient care.
- Confidentiality about a patient's problems is maintained within the confines of the task at hand.
- Staff work on a task or project basis rather than an hourly time-clock.
- Attention to cost-effective policies and procedures is integrated into each person's practice.

The immediate environment in which the nurse works usually includes clinical and nonclinical staff. Analyzing the production process as it comes together from different sources is complex. One method for evaluating a workplace is the Social-Technical-Environmental Systems Analysis (STES) framework. This system was designed to "examine the relationship between the social and technological aspects of work as they relate to the environmental forces in the work situation" (Cummings & Srivastva, 1977). When applied to Pratt 4, a surgical unit of New England Medical Center, the framework and tools for STES analysis are shown in Figure 18-3.

The grass roots "action group" doing the study on Pratt 4 included physicians, nurses, and administrators who worked on the unit. Their research, sanctioned by hospital administrators, was to determine how the objectives of quality care, staff and patient satisfaction, and cost effectiveness could be met. In two-months' time, the group produced a comprehensive analysis of the production process. Some highlights are given here (McCaskey, 1983).

Technical Analysis

1. The discharge of patients was not well-coordinated. These inefficiencies disrupted other aspects of patient care beginning with the admission.

COMPONENTS	EXAMPLES	TOOLS FOR ANALYSIS
Technical System		
What work is done and how it is accomplished	• Care of patient before and after surgery • Education of students • Assignment of workers • Flow of information • Geographic work flow	• A diagram of the physical layout • A flowchart of a typical patient's progress while on Pratt 4 • Industrial engineering time studies of a staff nurse, a secretary, and a surgical intern
Social System		
The relationships among workers	• Who frequently talks to whom • How disagreements are handled • Worker's perception of the work and the roles of self and colleagues	• Interviews of 12 people in a variety of roles • Semistructured observations of people interacting
Environmental System		**Interview Questions**
External units/groups that affect work flow	• Admitting, pharmacy, labs, social service and six other departments • Nursing department outside the area of study	• What services do they provide Pratt 4? • How dependent is Pratt 4 on that service? • Who on Pratt 4 is the key contact for them? • What problems, if any, have developed?

Figure 18-3   The STES Framework Applied to Pratt 4 (Zander, 1984)

2. Nurses spent a lot of time traveling back and forth to the medication room located at the extreme end of the floor.

3. Interns, residents, and attending physicians sometimes traveled to more than ten different floors to see their patients. Improving the discharge process would allow Admitting to group a physician's patients, cutting down on travel time.

Social Analysis

1. Everybody identified communications as the number one area for improvement. Physicians were frustrated because they often could not find the right primary nurse to discuss a particular patient's care. Nurses felt the need for discussion with physicians to plan for patient care. Technicians, aides, and nurses perceived an unwritten rule against too much "upward" communication; they rarely interacted with physicians.

2. People were proud of the high quality care given on the floor, but felt it was achieved with a great effort. People came on the floor expecting "to do battle" against physical constraints and the lack of coordination among professionals.

3. The most satisfying rewards came from the respect of fellow professionals, and yet people were reluctant to reward or complement each other for a job well done. There seemed to be a fear that if one rewards someone of "higher status," such remarks would be seen as patronizing or unprofessional.

4. Disagreements were often handled through different forms of "passive avoidance." A person would demonstrate disagreement or displeasure by failing to respond to inquiries or suggestions from the other party. In addition, guilt was frequently employed, and a favorite ploy seemed to be to "put the monkey on someone else's back."

Environmental Analysis

1. The admitting process was disrupted by delays in discharging patients and also by patients' expectations of receiving a two-bed room. The creation of the new pre-admissions testing area helped expedite admission to the floor.

2. Because the discharge time was often unclear and escorts would suddenly show up to take a patient for tests, many meals were wasted. It was not possible to reheat the meals, so they were thrown away.

3. The results of the environmental analysis posed a challenge for the action group because control over policies was shared with other units of the hospital. In addition, inadequate information precluded understanding of relationships from more than one perspective. The action group must develop relations with the different services to solve problems.

This analysis of the workplace first resulted in eight proposals for change:

1. Increase communication between physicians and nurses at critical times (especially rounds) to better coordinate patient care.

2. Rearrange the responsibilities for certain tasks, yet give commensurate authority.

3. Establish collaborative practice among physicians, nurses, and administrators through a specific multidisciplinary management group.

4. Improve the discharge process by anticipating discharge dates, writing discharge orders a day in advance, etc.

5. Conduct a larger system's analysis of this unit's interdependence with lab, admitting, and pharmacy.

6. Institute standard orders for admission, beginning with the "easier" (more predictable) case types, ie, herniorrhaphy, mastectomy.

7. Switch the medication room with the more centrally located coatroom.

8. Install a microwave oven to reduce the number of wasted meals.

The analysis of this workplace is continuing. This case example demonstrates the importance of analysis at a grass-roots level and the necessity for doing something with the information. Workplaces need careful analysis and responsive action so that nurses can fulfill their goals for patient care and for themselves.

STRUCTURE AND THE LARGER ENVIRONMENT

Structure in the employing institution is concerned with span of control, channels of authority, and formal lines of communication. Theile (1983) views an organization as a tool to achieve stated purposes. Organization is defined as "the sum total of the ways in which it divides its labor into distinct tasks and then achieves coordination among them." She provides a useful analogy by equating fifteen variables that determine the uniqueness of an organization to various parts of the anatomy, stating that the "blood" is most important:

Muscle = budget, size, staff, technology

Nerves = formal and informal communication, coordination

Bones = mission, philosophy, policies, procedures, span of control

Heart = decision-making power

Blood = motivation and satisfaction of members

Organizational structure is a primary focus of nursing service directors and nursing education administrators. Developing a structure that fits the product and facilitates the production process is difficult (Mintzberg, 1981). When analyzing the workplace, do not be fooled by the advertised structure. For instance, there is rarely a pure team nursing unit in today's hospitals. It is usually some mixture of team, functional, and "volunteer" methods of assignment. Similarly, what looks on paper like a joint appointment in the academic and practice settings may actually be two disjointed, nonintegrated full-time jobs.

A final word about structure: Beware the label "decentralization." It is often used to describe a wish for more responsibility and accountability at the grass-roots level. It has often resulted in lack of any centralization of standards, policies, decisions, and education. One indication of ineffective decentralization is when people are given responsibilities without adequate preparation or continuous support. One striking example is the removal of management personnel in the name of "primary nursing" when, in fact, expert management is the main determinant for the success of primary nursing.

In analyzing structure, look for congruity between the wishes, realities, and reinforcements of the workplace. For example, if nurses want "more communication" with physicians, do they have collaborative practice "structured in" by mechanisms such as alignment of nurses' case assignments with those of physicians (Anderson & Finn, 1984)? Another example: If administration wants all shift supervisors to communicate with each other, are there mechanisms to ensure that the supervisors meet with each other on a regular basis?

The structure of the workplace should facilitate a sensible, effective, and satisfying achievement of outcomes. The same messages need to be given at all levels. Stress should be alleviated rather than generated by the organizational structure. For example, a person wanting to do a research project may feel stress about the content or outcomes of the work. The organization's procedures for reviewing proposals should not add to this stress.

The formal structure of the workplace needs to be flexible and responsive to the changing larger health care environment.

MAKING THE WORKPLACE WORK FOR YOU

Combining the elements of structure, process, and outcomes in one's daily worklife is both an art and a science. Capitalizing on the way you work with individuals in the work environment can help you make the workplace work for you.

While one's work is an expression of one's self, most nurses are employed by formal organizations. This reality often puts nurses in the position of answering to the needs of three different lines of authority: nursing, administration, and physicians. Diverse groups in hospital organizations conflict over the same basic objectives due to their own values and personalities (Rakich, Longest & O'Conner, 1982). When analyzing the workplace the nurse should be prepared to find as wide a diversity of objectives as there are lines of authority and special interest groups.

For instance, filling beds may be administration's goal, while clinicians may short-sightedly long for the decrease in pace that comes with a low census. Similarly, a nursing school's goal of teaching primary nursing may be impossible if the clinical placements in the area do not practice primary nursing. Clinical placements and pre-ceptors, beds, equipment, computer time, space, laboratory tests, and money are but a few of the scarce resources fought over when objectives in a profession, in an institution, or in a community are unclear, unshared, or poorly coordinated. Without strong leadership and commitment to an overall mission, any subgroup can sabotage the effectiveness of all other subgroups and, ultimately, of the whole purpose for organizing in the first place.

Formal organization charts are not conducive to a nurse's analysis of the use of self in the workplace because they are not subjective: "One's development is about ninety per-cent the result of day-to-day work experience" (Stewart, 1978, p 175).

Thus, a custom-made system diagram can be useful to a nurse at any level of an organization in determining a baseline for use of the self (see Figure 18-4). This per-sonal diagram can be done as follows:
1. Put your initials in the middle of the page. Using lines, arrows, or circles, draw where you place each of these persons in relationship to yourself. It may help to think of a specific day last week. Identify each individual or group by letter.

   A—Patient
   B—Patient's family
   C—Your boss
   D—Head nurse
   E—Other nursing managers
   F—Support staff
   G—Other staff nurses
   H—Nursing administrator
   I —Hospital administrators
   J —Physicians

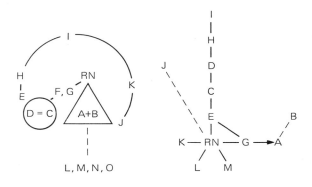

Use colors to signify quality of relationships, eg, green to signify coworker who is also a friend, yellow to signify a mentor, red to show a relationship involving serious conflict.

Note: Use your creativity to illustrate your formal and informal position, professional and political relationships in the workplace. This can help you understand the environment and plan how to exert influence and effect change. (See Chapter 10 on change.)

———— Solid line indicates direct working relationships as with fellow staff nurse

− − − Broken line indicates interdisciplinary relationship with a physician or social worker

Figure 18-4   Two Examples of Self in System Diagrams

K —Other professionals
L —Nursing associations
M—Other significant persons, eg, mentors, spouse

2. Assess your knowledge of your system
   - Where are you unsure of the connections?
   - Are there weak connections you want to strengthen?
   - What persons are key to your ability to carry out your responsibilities? Key to your satisfaction? Are they the same?
   - Where are your mentors (inside or outside the organization)?
   - Where does your influence lie? What are the political relationships? How do you think your role, responsibilities, and effectiveness are perceived by your colleagues, patients, and their families? Where do you think you would be placed in other persons' drawings?
   - Do you respect the products of your organization?

3. Which elements of your system can you change—easily, with some effort, with difficulty, not at all?
   - Can you lead, follow, or get out of the way of goals that others are working toward?
   - Where can you find the resources and supports to help you gain some positive control over your system?
   - Have you developed a way to leave your system at work? Do you seek outside influences to help you get perspective?

As your system diagram indicates, each nurse is a citizen in his or her organization and has the capacity to effect needed change. If a nurse relied only on personal resources and those of the consumer to achieve a product, she would have a clean-cut production process and a straightforward organization. To achieve production of outcomes, however, nurses require resources (manpower, technology, time, political acumen, knowledge, etc.) beyond the immediate nurse-patient relationship.

In political structure, health care institutions "differ from almost every other kind of organization" (Kennedy, 1984). The power plays are often subtle, with each major division and professional group being intensely interdependent on the other. Nurses know all too well how reliant they are on physicians, housekeeping, and pharmacy to get their patients cared for. Likewise, physicians can be the most dependent professional group in the organization because of their reliance on the services of other groups. Administrators often feel the least in control as they watch nurses and physicians go about their work in "splendid isolation" (Cleveland, 1983) from each other and from the administration.

The truth is, every professional group (and probably every group member) at times feels helpless to effect even small changes. Assuming that any one group is more powerful than others can be misleading, because power has many faces. Suffice to say, the nurse is advised to analyze the workplace in terms of the power structure and the potential for political alliances.

SHARED VISION OF THE BEST

Two landmark books about successful workplaces say roughly the same things—one about magnet hospitals (McClure et al, 1983), the other about America's best-run companies (Peters & Waterman, 1982). Both studies looked beyond structure to identify the crucial variables that separated excellence and innovation from mediocrity. The American Academy of Nursing found three phenomena common to all "magnetic" nursing environments:

- shared values from the top down and bottom up
- positive, autonomous nursing roles
- power base derived from the common goals shared by nursing and the institution.

Similarly, Peters and Waterman (1982) discovered that excellent companies were:

> brilliant on the basics. Tools didn't substitute for thinking. Intellect didn't overpower wisdom. Analysis didn't impede action. Rather, these companies worked hard to keep things simple in a complex world. They persisted. They insisted on top quality. They fawned on their customers. They listened to their employees and treated them like adults. They allowed their innovative product and service "champions" long tethers. They allowed some chaos in return for quick action and regular experimentation (p 13).

Both studies found that the key variable in magnetism and excellence in the workplace was flexibility to adjust to and create change. The workplace is a shared perception of its members, and that perception demands continued analysis so that it won't just survive—it will thrive.

Application of the tools of organizational analysis, presented in this chapter, together with change strategies, including heightened political sensitivity, will enable nurses to create magnetic work environments.

References

Anderson DJ, Finn MC: Collaborative practice: Developing a structure that works. *Nurs Adm Q* 1983; 8:19–25.

Cavanaugh D: Gamesmanship: The art of strategizing. *J Nurs Adm* (April) 1985; 11:38–42.

Cleveland R: The Pratt 4 Project (Interview). 1983.

Cummings TG, Srivastva S: *Management of Work: A Sociotechnical Systems Approach.* Kent State University, 1977.

Ferguson G, Ferguson WF: As patients see us. . . . *Nurse Manag* (Aug) 1983; 14:20–21.

Fischer R, Ury W: *Getting to Yes.* Penguin, 1983.

French J, Raven B: The bases of social power, in: *Studies in Social Power.* Cartwright D (editor). Institute of Social Research, 1959.

Jacobs D, Jacobs N: *The PEP Primer.* Joint Commission on Accreditation of Hospitals, 1975.

Joel L: Case mix reimbursement: DRGS, RIMS. *Mass Nurs* (Jan) 1983; 52:5–6.

Kennedy M: The keys to the kingdom. *Savvy* 1984; 5:47–55.

Mauksch IG, David ML: Prescription for survival. *Am J Nurs* 1972; 72:2189–93.

McCaskey M: *A Framework for Organizational Analysis: The Pratt 4 Project.* Cambridge Management Resources, 1983.

McClure M et al: *Magnet Hospitals: Attraction and Retention of Professional Nurses.* American Nurses' Association, 1983.

Mintzberg H: Organization Design: Fashion of fit? *Harv Bus Rev* (Jan/Feb) 1981; 103–16.

Morrow L: What is the point of working? *Time* (May 11) 1981:94.

Mullins AC, Colavecchio RE, Tescher BE: Peer review: A model for professional accountability. *J Nurs Adm* (Dec) 1979; 9:25–30.

Mundinger M: *Autonomy in Nursing.* Aspen, 1980.

Peters T, Waterman R: *In Search of Excellence.* Harper & Row, 1982.

Rakich J, Longest B, O'Conner T: Hospital organization, in: *Understanding Organizations.* Magula M (editor). Nursing Resources, 1982.

Small L: 10 ways to make yourself indispensible at work. *Working Mother* (July) 1982; 12–16.

Steckel S: *Patient Contracting.* Appleton-Century-Crofts, 1982.

Stevens BJ: The use of consultants in nursing service. *J Nurs Adm* (Aug) 1978; 8:7–15.

Stewart N: *The Effective Woman Manager.* Ballantine, 1978.

Theile JR: The anatomy of an organization. *Nurse Adm Q* (Winter) 1983; 7:42–45.

Zander K: *Primary Nursing: Development and Management.* Aspen, 1980.

Zander K: Use of self in the organization. *Nurs Manag* (Accepted for publication.)

Zander K: The nurse as a professional: Gaining the respect we deserve. *Nurs Life* 1985; 5:42–47.

Chapter 19

Interdisciplinary Politics

Pamela McNutt Devereux, RN, MSN

Kathleen M. Dirschel, RN, PhD

Interdisciplinary politics from a nursing perspective can be divided into two broad groups: those involving nurses and physicians, and those involving nurses and anybody else. As nurses and physicians work together in the health care setting, high-quality interaction and collaboration is essential for effective patient care. Although the nurse-physician professional relationship is not new, it has come under close scrutiny in recent years. Why are physicians and their interaction with nurses such a source of rhetoric, anger, frustration, and study? The answer is that professional relationships do not remain static. Assumptions about the appropriateness of roles, superior-subordinate, and male-female interaction have changed. Currently, interdisciplinary interaction reflects increased equality between nurses and physicians and recognition of changing professional boundaries. The rules appear to be changing, and this phenomenon is primarily a result of changes in the nursing profession and the nurse's role.

CHANGING ROLE OF NURSES

The social evolution of women's roles and the increased opportunities for professional growth have brought to the bedside a nurse who is better educated, more outspoken, more self-assured, and less willing to assume a dependent, handmaiden role. Women, acknowledged wage earners, are often heads of single-parent families and come to the workplace expecting to have input in decisions that affect them. The behavior and

---

For simplicity throughout this chapter, physicians are identified by the pronoun "he." We recognize that the number of women physicians is growing, medical school enrollment now being as high as 35% women, and that this change in gender identification will undoubtedly affect the nurse/physician relationship, so far as it is a reflection of male/female relationships.

attitudes of women, and therefore most nurses, have changed more than those of men and therefore most physicians.

In "The Doctor-Nurse Game," Stein (1968) wrote about the nurse's need to make recommendations without seeming to, so the physician could accept the advice without seeming to. The game was to mix each professional's different but equal suggestions regarding patient care without altering the hierarchy between the physician and the nurse. The nurse was responsible for significant recommendations while appearing passive. The physician, on the other hand, wanting to give the best possible care, needed to be open to the nurse's recommendations which helped him to accomplish this. Because accepting advice from nonphysicians was threatening to his dominant role, the physician received sub rosa recommendations from the nurse, making the recommendations appear to have been initiated by himself. If the game was played well, the doctor-nurse team appeared to operate efficiently. The physician was able to use the nurse as a valuable consultant, and the nurse gained some of her self-esteem and professional satisfaction from this interaction. Both the sexual identities and the traditional training of nursing students reinforced the game.

The politics involved in "the game" have changed. No longer do nursing schools promote the role of the passive, nonassuming nurse. In clinical institutions, the nursing role is more often characterized by an active, collaborative role. The practice setting demands more decision making, coordination of services, interdisciplinary collaboration, and high technology skill from nurses. The nurse does not hesitate to question the rationale behind a treatment or clarify specifics of the medical regimen. Many physicians appreciate the nurse's concerns and take time to explain or discuss what he believes should be done. It is to the physician's advantage to have the nurse understand and agree with the plan of care. The nurse may have information unavailable to the physician that will affect the patient's response. The following episode illustrates this point.

> A house officer, unfamiliar with the institution's collaborative practice model, was writing orders for his patient's treatment for the next day. Reviewing the orders, the primary nurse was confused by one of the medications. She consulted the house officer, who told her the drug was for the patient's anemia. Although familiar with the drug the nurse had never heard of its use for anemia. She questioned the physician further, and he grew impatient with her persistence and finally snapped, "Just give it because I ordered it." The nurse told the house officer she had no intention of being responsible for the administration of any medication if she did not understand the purpose. The house officer became angry and said loudly, "You're just a nurse. What right have you to question any order of mine? I am the doctor."
>
> This last exchange was overheard by the chairman of the department of medicine as he came down the hall to make rounds. He walked over to the house officer, tapped him on the shoulder, and told him quietly, "It's not just her right to question your order, it's her job. That's what we pay her for. If you don't like it, you can leave."
>
> The house officer then explained the anticipated effect of the drug on the patient's anemia, which was an experimental concept. The nurse administered the medication.

It is unfortunate that this episode had to occur to demonstrate to one physician the necessity of involving nursing in the decisions for patient care. The point here is that a nurse conscientiously pursued her responsibility and was supported by those in authority.

We don't want to replace the formerly submissive, task-oriented nurse with an aggressive, antagonistic nurse. The key is assertiveness, not aggression. The assertive nurse is confident, knows the facts, is civil, keeps ego out of the discussion, and persists in asking questions until doubts or questions are resolved (Devereux, 1981b). Other examples of new roles are demonstrated by the nurse who heads the discharge planning team, the nurse who monitors health status and change in her patients using the tools of physical assessment, and the nurse who pronounces death with equal recognition and accountability in hospices. The establishment of a Joint Physician-Nurse Committee at the National Institutes of Health (NIH) has enabled it to transfer some medically delegated functions from physicians to nursing staff (Alspach et al, 1982). The Boards of Nursing and Medical Examiners in New Jersey have established a joint subcommittee to discuss matters of overlapping practice. The addition of nurses to hospital research committees, utilization committees, infection control committees, and hospital boards demonstrates the recognition of the unique contribution made by nurses.

There would be no need for a chapter discussing nurse-physician politics if the transition in nursing roles and physician interactions were already accomplished. Obviously, it is not. The facility with which nurses are able to practice professional, high-quality, self-directed nursing care frequently depends on the individual's ability to recognize and affect the politics of the situation and the institution.

COLLABORATIVE PRACTICE

One means of fostering improved patient care is through collaborative nurse-physician practice. The ability to institute collaborative practice and its subsequent impact on patient care were the focus of a project developed by the National Joint Practice Commission (NJPC) and conducted in four hospitals from 1977 to 1980 (Devereux, 1981a).

The project sought to demonstrate that nurses and physicians could develop a cooperative, collegial, collaborative practice in a setting based on five structural elements. These elements include:

- primary nursing
- integrated nurse-physician charting
- increased nursing clinical decision making
- a unit-based nurse-physician collaborative practice committee
- a joint medical record audit committee.

The five structural elements did not originate with the NJPC. Presenting them as a single program to facilitate collaborative practice, however, was unique. Primary nursing encouraged the nurse and physician to focus their communication on a specific patient. Increased nursing clinical decision making involved the nurse in therapeutic decisions that encouraged communication between nurse and physician. Integrated charting facilitated shared communication and eliminated duplication. The unit-based joint practice committee provided a forum for discussion of unit administrative problems or patient care issues. The audit committee process reinforced that mutually determined and delivered care should be mutually evaluated for effectiveness (Devereux, 1981a).

At the conclusion of the project, nurses and physicians reported that the quality of their relationships and their collaboration had improved. A postproject, independent study demonstrated that the quality of patient care also improved. The NJPC does not claim to have invented collaboration, but it demonstrated that when a hospital endorses collaboration by implementing the structural elements that facilitate the development of communication in a patient-focused setting, the positive outcome can be a high-caliber collaborative nurse-physician practice.

Collaborative practice is not likely to occur in hospitals unless it is supported by nurses, physicians, and administrators. All must be aware of the benefits of collaborative practice and lend active leadership to its development (Adelson, 1981). A staff nurse may feel unable to influence the development of such a system, but she can discuss a collaborative practice program and encourage peers and the nursing unit leadership to look into developing unit-based communities that will foster more collegial nurse-physician practice. She can also examine her own practice and collegial relationships.

NURSES AND PHYSICIANS: THE DIFFERENCES

Despite the fact that nurses and physicians care for the same patients, there are fundamental differences in the education and practice of the two professions. If nurses are to have effective working relationships with physicians, we should look at some of the things that contribute to the differences.

Nursing's educational base is undergraduate college or less; medicine's is graduate school, often with additional science degrees. Although many nurses have baccalaureate and higher degrees, an individual can practice nursing with only two years of posthigh school education. Medicine requires at least six and usually eight years of higher education. Some physicians still perceive that nurses receive "training" rather than education, a process that prepares "task-doers," not thinkers. The most effective way to combat this perception is for nurses to demonstrate excellence in nursing practice that reflects a scientific knowledge base, innovative and thoughtful application of relevant theory, and a clear understanding of the rationale and methodology of treatment.

For example, a patient is admitted to a general medical unit for assessment of chronic emphysema and treatment of acute pneumonia. The physician orders tests and antibiotics. From the medical point of view, the care is routine and predictable. Yet the nurses need to have a thorough understanding of the pathophysiology of COPD (chronic obstructive pulmonary disease) as well as an appreciation of the challenges it poses to normal ADL (activities of daily living).

During rounds with the physicians, the nurse discusses low-energy reserves that can be exhausted by rigorous diagnostic tests, the effects of sleep deprivation and chronic high carbon dioxide levels on mentation, concern for the malnourished state of most patients with COPD, and disturbances resulting from nausea (frequently) caused by bronchodilators and other pulmonary medications. The nurse's contributions demonstrate her participation in the planning and delivery of the patient's treatment as well as her understanding of the scientific basis of her interventions.

There is a difference in both age and clinical experience between newly graduated nurses and physicians who have completed their training. The age difference between the typical new nurse graduate and a young attending physician often exceeds ten years. For example, the 20-year-old associate degree graduate takes her first position on a surgical service along with a 33-year-old general surgeon who has just completed several years of residency. Such discrepancies in age and clinical experience can set the stage for problems with nurse-physician collaboration.

Competitiveness is another aspect of differences between nurses and physicians. Entrance into medical school is very competitive, as is the matching process that determines internships and residencies. In contrast, there is not a competitive climate in nursing school, nor is there a comparable degree of competition for jobs. The medical school experience tends to create aggressive, turf-conscious practitioners. They view with suspicion the advancement of nursing into their domain through so-called "expanded" nursing practice. Nurses, on the other hand, are usually unprepared to fight for position when the arena is patient care. Their perception is that "we are all colleagues here to help each other help the patient." Nurses can diffuse defensiveness on the part of the physician by not contributing to the aggression and not competing for preeminence. They can make it clear that their concern is nursing and the patient. Success for nurses does not depend on their winning, and the physician losing.

Physicians have seen many encroachments into their practice. These encroachments threaten their prerogative to manage their patients' care. Third party payers, particularly Medicare and Medicaid, demand an accounting of what standard of care and what justification for therapeutic and diagnostic intervention was used. Utilization review departments monitor bed utilization through preadmission and postadmission certification. Antibiotic review committees review the choice of drug, dose, and duration of therapy. With DRGs (diagnosis-related groups), which determine hospital reimbursement prospectively, hospital finance departments are beginning to hold physicians accountable for extended lengths of stay and complications. It is little wonder that physicians are wary of nurses who demand to be included in decision making.

The emphasis for nursing should be on nursing. This is not as simplistic as it may sound. In emphasizing nurse-physician collaboration, there has often been too much emphasis on nurses assuming paramedical functions within the context of expanding nursing practice. We have come a long way from the "physician's handmaiden" standing ready to jump at the physician's bidding, but we need to guard against becoming merely physicians' assistants. Physicians are appropriately concerned with diagnosis and treatment. The nurses' role should focus on the patients' response to the diagnostic regimen and managing the patients' ADL while they are incapacitated. This requires experience and knowledge of the physiology and pathophysiology involved and potential complications of treatments. When making rounds or initiating discussion with physicians, the focus must stay on nursing. The physicians may focus on the diagnostic regimen, but they need to be informed and reminded of the patient's response to it. Physicians usually respect a nurse for keeping the patient's response and comfort a priority in the diagnostic and treatment program.

Another difference between nurses and physicians is their approach to the practice setting. Physicians are usually self-employed entrepreneurs. They determine who their patients are and what happens to them. Their relationship with the patient frequently predates the hospital admission and may continue after the patient is discharged. Physicians are usually involved with more than one unit or more than one hospital.

Nurses, on the other hand, are almost always hospital employees. They are responsible for patient care but accountable to the institution. Therefore, nurses spend time nursing the institution as well as their patients. Nurses do not choose their patients, have no control over admission or discharge, and generally do not see the patient before or after the hospital stay. Most nurses work on one unit, on one shift, and can become quite parochial in their perception of issues and priorities.

You see these differences when you work with an interdisciplinary committee. The physicians may not feel an obligation to attend meetings because this takes valuable time from their practice. Nurses, on the other hand, may attend because they have been directed to participate by their superiors, and they will be paid whether they are in committee or giving care on the unit. The nurses may feel that an item that concerns one unit or policy is of critical importance. The physicians may perceive the issue as less important because their practice extends beyond the hospital. Physicians may be impatient with the committee process if results are not obtained in one or two meetings. They are accustomed to independent investigation, diagnosis, and intervention in rapid order. Nurses will consider all the data, yet hesitate to impose a decision, because nurses are accustomed to taking the time necessary to reach consensus.

These differences between nurses and physicians will not disappear, so it is important that nurses acknowledge their influence on nurse-physician relationships. In caring for patients, the nurse should ask the physician what he knows about the patient's personality, family history, and previous response to illness. The nurse should remember that a physician's rounds on her unit is only one activity in a day that takes the physician to his office, the OR, several units, and possibly to other hospitals. The nurse should have her questions and observations ready for an efficient exchange of information. Although the physician's time is important, other considerations apply. For example, nurses sometimes hesitate to interject nursing concerns into rounds because they feel it wastes time. These nurses devalue their contribution to patient care and the importance of the nursing perspective. The nurse's hour-to-hour observations and interaction with the patient are invaluable to the physician when he assesses how the patient is responding to the medical regimen.

Collaborative nurse-physician relationships do not happen automatically. Being well-prepared and nursing oriented in discussions concerning patient care, presenting ideas assertively and confidently, and taking the time to understand the physicians will result in a collegial nurse-physician relationship. The nurse may also discover that physician colleagues are willing to lend their support in nursing care issues because they recognize the contribution of nursing to the quality of patient care.

Nurse-physician collaboration can expand the influence of the nursing department. Physicians are powerful because they influence the hospital's revenue by controlling bed occupancy. The physicians need nursing to implement medical regimens. It is appropriate for nurses to call on the clout of physicians in situations that influence nurses' ability to provide patient care. For example, because their movement throughout the institution provides a broad perspective, physicians can help persuade administration that a problem goes beyond a unit or beyond the control of the nursing staff.

Nurses can use the influence of physicians to promote programs or gain resources for patient care. In these circumstances, the frequently adversarial character of nurse-physician interaction is replaced with cooperative efforts to make change. Nurses may complain that there are too few transporters, or the system for assigning them is inefficient. The administration may not agree that this is a consequential issue. However, if physicians also complain that patient transport delays are affecting the OR schedule or the use of treatment rooms, administration may give the matter more attention. Unfortunately, physician influence can be frustrating to nurses who view it as a demonstration that nursing has little power in the organization. Physicians usually voice complaints to nursing but are unaware of the institutional bureaucracy that must be involved in corrective action. It is often up to nursing to direct the physician's complaint to the appropriate administrative ear. This physician's influence complements nursing organizational knowledge.

JOINT PRACTICE COMMITTEES

A good avenue for developing effective working relationships with physicians is the joint practice committee. Such committees exist under many names: patient care committee, nurse-physician relations committee, unit management, or collaborative practice committee. Regardless of the name, the goal is for nurses, physicians, and other professionals to work through a structured setting to identify and solve problems (Devereux, 1981a).

When a need for regular group interaction has been agreed upon, joint committees can be fostered by the nursing service director or by the unit head in cooperation with the unit physician. Joint committees are essential, not only to work on problem resolution, but to define professional identity and territory for each other. Joint committees serve as "release valves" when issues arise between nurses and physicians that might be destructive to their relationship. The issues can be passed to the joint committee for study and recommendation. This can diffuse a volatile issue, removing it from the realm of opposing personalities.

FOCUS ON THE PROBLEM,
NOT THE PERSONALITY

An example of the constructive intervention of the joint practice committee followed an incident that occurred between the nursing night staff and the on-call medical resident. The nurses questioned whether the resident should respond at night when called by the nurses or could send an extern (3rd or 4th year medical student). Orders written by externs could not be implemented by nurses until they were cosigned by the residents. The residents were calling the units after the externs had assessed the patient, asking the nurses to implement the orders and promising to cosign the orders on early morning rounds. The residents' approach was contrary to the policy that did not permit telephone orders. This conflict forced nurses to choose between adhering to the policy, which prohibited telephone orders, and solving a patient's problem. Nurses resented being put into a "Catch-22" situation by residents, whom they described as "lazy and unwilling to get out of bed." The residents believed that using the externs for nonemergency intervention was an appropriate extension of the available medical resources at night and provided learning situations for the externs. They thought the nurses were being inflexible and rigid in their adherence to the policy regarding telephone orders.

The collaborative practice committee took up the problem. They identified several questions: (1) When should an extern function independently? (2) Must extern orders be cosigned before implementation if the nurses are given telephone confirmation by the resident prior to implementation? (3) Were the residents sending the externs because they were busy or were they "staying in bed"? These questions were discussed and a compromise was reached. The committee determined that the resident on call should respond unless otherwise occupied with patient care. The extern may respond when the resident is busy and may write orders if the resident: (1) gives telephone confirmation to the nurse before she executes the order, and (2) cosigns the order before the change of shift in the morning. The reason for the second requirement is to prevent the passing of responsibility for getting the cosignature from one nursing shift to the next. The recommendations also led to a clarification of the entire policy regarding externs' responsibilities.

NURSES' PREROGATIVE

Discussion, collaboration, and consensus work better than confrontation. Despite new roles in nursing, the changes in clinical institutions, and the advances in nursing education, physicians are still viewed as controlling patients' care. This view is held by the patients and hospital administration. At the present time, nursing would lose in a power struggle with physicians over who had the authority to implement and manage aspects of patient care. Usually when there are changes in practice, they flow from medicine to nursing. Some see this as a positive step toward nursing accountability and authority. Others see the physician as delegating authority under the medical delegatory clause so that in effect the nurse is a dependent extension of the physician and practicing under two powers—her own license and the physician's. This implies the MD can alter or pull back this extended authority and ultimately has authority over nursing practice.

It will be a long time—if ever—before the question of who holds the final authority is settled. Ultimately, it is a legal question. In part, a way to keep the door open for nursing is to make sure that nursing practice keeps up with the changes in the health care system. This means that nurses:

• provide the "hands on" health care patients need

- maintain visibility among professionals and nonprofessionals
- get support for their changing roles from other segments of the nursing community
- seek preparation and certification appropriate for changing roles
- work much harder to educate the public about the nursing profession, what nurses do, and how that differs from what physicians do.

INTERDISCIPLINARY HEALTH CARE TEAM

The care of hospitalized patients is complex. No one individual possesses the expertise to care for patients and families in the highly technical and specialized health care field. Interdisciplinary teamwork provides an organized and unifying framework for the work of health care professions (Lowe & Herranen, 1981). Patient care, especially in large urban medical centers, requires that nurses interact continuously with social workers, dietitians, physical and occupational therapists, pharmacists, respiratory therapists, radiology technicians, and other specialists. Nurses need leadership skills to work effectively in groups while retaining the right and obligation to direct nursing care.

Frequently the team meeting is the vehicle for interdisciplinary interaction. Some team members, such as the nurses and social workers, are consistently assigned to a unit and therefore carry a regular patient caseload. Others, including medical house officers and students, rotate to a unit for a short time. Still others join in only when their particular specialty, such as occupational therapy, is required. Shifting team membership can complicate the team's ability to work effectively. Priorities, perceptions of roles, and responsibilities change along with the team members. Leadership within the team can be diluted or shifted by these transitory members. Therefore, members of the core team should not assume that everyone is working toward the same goal.

Different priorities will dictate different approaches. Even regular team members may set goals that differ from their colleagues. The physician may have a biomedical orientation and only want to discuss facilitating the diagnostic regimen. The nurse may focus on the patient's response to illness and be concerned that his diminished energy level will reduce his ability to participate in treatment. The social worker may want to discuss the prognosis and probable discharge needs so that posthospital programs can be planned. Each member of the team must recognize the validity of his colleague's point of view, so that he can work effectively with his team members on behalf of the patient.

Members of an interdisciplinary team have no authority over colleague's practice. Even if the team has a formal leader, individual professionals may resent direction. The stated goal of the team is to meet the patient's needs through joint effort, but there is also the goal of influencing other team members. Frequently, team action is intended to change the direction or stimulate the involvement of a member of the team. This is valid and should be done tactfully, but not surreptitiously. For instance, when the nurse and social worker, as the permanent team members, work together to influence or change the action of the (nonpermanent member) resident physician, such action is reasonable and often effective in accomplishing legitimate patient care goals.

DEVELOPING POLITICAL ALLIANCES

The ability to influence decisions regarding patient care and to gain support for efficient use of the institution's resources is the essence of interdisciplinary politics. Unfortunately, many nurses are not skillful at influencing the team process. One reason may be that nurses are accustomed to expressing their professional concerns to fellow nurses and physicians, but not to others. We have neglected building relationships with other professional groups such as social workers, physical therapists, and hospital administrators. These professionals work closely with nurses, yet often lack knowledge concerning the educational preparation and the different levels of nursing practice. In addition, these professional groups are altering their own practice and their relationship with nurses. In some instances, this has resulted in an encroachment on traditional nursing areas. For instance, social workers frequently assume leadership roles in case management and discharge planning, and hospital administrators are involved in making decisions about the supply and allocation of nursing resources. For these, and other reasons, it is necessary for the professional nurse to become proficient in the application of interdisciplinary politics.

How is this to be accomplished? Some guidelines for interdisciplinary interaction include:

1. Know the situation—know the patient and the problem the team must handle.
2. Know the resources available from nursing and, in general, from the institution and/or community.
3. Listen to your colleagues' concerns and plans for action.
4. Emphasize mutuality of goals shared among members of the multidisciplinary team.
5. Reinforce what is the legal practice of nursing. Work to ensure that all nurses are competent in their areas of practice and be alert to casual encroachment from other disciplines.
6. Expand the nursing goals to include those of the other disciplines that will help to build alliances in future interactions.

Despite the fact that most nurses believe they are engaged in altruistic work intended to help fellow human beings, accomplishing that in today's complex health care institutions requires political skill. Nurses' colleagues in other disciplines have their own priorities for patient care as well as for ascendancy in the health care hierarchy. To practice nursing in a professional and self-directing way requires that nurses acquire the ability to politick with other professionals.

References

Adelson B, Werner J: Fostering collaborative relationships. *Hosp Med Staff* (Mar) 1981; 10:5.
Alspach JG, Holland PV, McKeon KL: Joint physician-nurse committee ensures safe transfer of tasks. *Hospitals* (Oct 16) 1982; 56:54–55.
Devereux PM: Essential elements of nurse-physician collaboration. *J Nurs Adm* (May) 1981a; 11:19–23.

Devereux PM: Nurse/physician collaboration: Nursing practice consideration. *J Nurs Adm* (Sept)1981b; 11:37.

Lowe JI, Herranen M: Understanding teamwork: Another look at concepts. *Soc Work Health Care* (Winter) 1981; 7:6–8.

Stein LI: The doctor-nurse game. *Am J Nurs* 1968; 68:101.

Recommended Readings

Blackwood S, Ryker D: Establishing the collaborative practice committee. *Hosp Med Staff* (Mar) 1981; 10:11+.

Brown B (editor): Politics and power. *Nurs Adm Q* (Spring) 1978; 2. [Entire issue.]

Corless IB: Physician and nurses: Roles and responsibilities in caring for the critically ill patient. *Law Med Health Care* 1982; 10:72–76.

Fisher R, Ury W: *Getting to Yes.* Houghton Mifflin, 1981.

Kalisch BJ, Kalisch PA: An analysis of the sources of physician-nurse conflict. *J Nurs Adm* (Jan) 1977; 7:50–57.

Keenan J, Aiken L, Cluff LE: *Nurses and Doctors: Their Education and Practice.* Oelgeschlager, Gunn and Hain, 1982.

Mauksch IG: Nurse-physician collaboration: A changing relationship. *J Nurs Adm* (June) 1981; 11:35–38.

Mechanic D, Aiken LH: Sounding board. A cooperative agenda for medicine and nursing. *N Engl J Med* 1982; 307:747–50.

Chapter 20

Creating a Supportive Work Environment

A View from the Top

Joyce C. Clifford, RN, MSN, FAAN

Political action in the context of the nurses' work environment is generally perceived as effective communication within an organization's infrastructure, allowing the nurse to influence decisions related to nursing practice. For these relationships to occur, nursing departments must often change from centralized, hierarchical structures to decentralized and flexible structures. Successful organizational communication may also require change in the expectations and commitment of the registered nurse. From a practical point of view, anyone wishing to influence an organization must first understand the organization's mission, goals, and relationships.

THE HOSPITAL AS A WORKPLACE

Most people obtain health services within community- or ambulatory-based practice settings rather than hospitals. About two-thirds of nurses, however, practice in an acute care or chronic disease institutional setting. This fact, coupled with changes within the health care industry that promote vertical and horizontal integration of all health services, indicates that the hospital as a workplace for nurses can be used as a model for discussion. *The Report and Recommendation of the National Commission of Nursing* (1983), and to some extent the congressionally mandated Institute of Medicine Study (1983), underscore the influence the hospital setting has on the image of nursing as a satisfying, viable career choice. The need for nurses to influence the hospital industry to direct future health care decisions is great.

Organizations, like people, must respond to multiple environmental factors. Consider, for example, how the following have changed the hospital setting and subsequently the practice of nursing. Demographic information, such as the continued growth of the aged population in the United States, becomes essential when planning hospital-based clinical services within a given community. Research breakthroughs that have led to an increase in organ transplants have changed the nature of health services as have federal regulations that changed the method of payment to hospitals from a retrospective to a prospective payment system. The delivery of health services is as dependent upon the financial structure of the health system as it is upon medical technology or provider availability. Nurses must be willing to spend time reading and learning about the issues that the work organization must adapt and respond to.

Professional Autonomy and Organizational Relationships

With the development of nursing as a profession, more explicit goals have been established for autonomous decision making. These goals cut across all organizational levels. Nurse managers, educators, and direct care providers share the need for autonomy and professional recognition. As a consequence, the nursing department may splinter, and the strength inherent in a mutually goal-directed department may be lost. The chief nurse administrator of an organization must be accountable for developing a cohesive department of nursing. The administrator must establish values for nursing practice and promote a common frame of reference for patient care. The values of the nurse administrator concerning patients, families, and other disciplines will filter throughout the organization and directly influence patient care. Systems to provide effective communication between the nurse administrator and direct care provider are essential in contemporary professional practice models.

The nurse executive is responsible for integrating the professional goals of the nursing department and the managerial goals of the institution. These goals are not as paradoxical as health professionals often believe. Nonetheless, without a mechanism for information exchange and participation in program development, the staff nurse and head nurse can feel distant from the goals of the organization and the expectations of nursing administration.

Professional autonomy becomes real when standards are set, reviewed, and changed by the professional group; in other words, when nurses have control over their practice. Control of the environment for practice is the responsibility of the chief nurse administrator and the delegated nurse managers. These nurse professionals represent the standards and expectations of nursing within the broader institutional context. When interacting with other administrators and disciplines, nurse managers assume the role of educator, articulating the mission of nursing and reinforcing the way organizational decisions affect patient care and nursing practice.

Professional colleagueship develops when hierarchical relationships among nurses facilitate communication and decision making. Perceived barriers of authority, for example, may inhibit nurse managers and staff nurses from planning and developing improved systems of practice. These barriers are less evident in systems that have decentralized appropriate decision making to the practice level and have flattened their organizational model to promote unit-based leadership and authority. A fragmented approach to patient care dilutes individuals' professional autonomy and accountability.

Primary nursing supports planning of care by individual nurse professionals. Through the concept of 24-hour accountability, associate nurses learn the art of negotiating with the accountable primary nurse if they seek a change in the plan of care. Such behavior is not evident in other systems of care delivery. In addition, when nurses are not directly involved in planning for and evaluation of specific patients, they are deprived essential information needed to build collaborative relationships with other disciplines. Clinical competence, effective communication, and information sharing are essential ingredients for political action in the workplace.

THE NURSE MANAGER

Contemporary nursing practice models have redirected the nurse-professional to full patient care and have invested the head nurse with authority as a manager within the hospital. The quality of head nurse leadership is one of the most critical factors in promoting growth in a hospital organization for nurse professionals. Through the head nurse, staff nurse leadership will be developed, assuming that nursing administration views leadership as an integral part of the professional role. Head nurses' responsibilities include selection, and when necessary, elimination of staff, as well as development of staff in the practice area. Such responsibility results in a mutual level of commitment between the head nurse and staff nurse.

The opportunities to establish positive relationships on all levels of the nursing hierarchy are infinite. Sometimes the most productive meetings are informal coffee or lunch meetings. These can be planned in advance or may occur spontaneously. The positive impact of meeting others within the organization on a personal basis cannot be underestimated. Professional colleagueship and respect between nurse managers and nursing staff will occur when philosophical direction, goals, and limitations are shared.

Failure to respect or recognize nurses may lead to further breakdown in institutional relationships. In some instances, nurses have sought unionization as a way of achieving improved status within their hospital or agency only to be further disillusioned by the inability of a union contract to negotiate respect or supportive collaborative relationships. Negotiation with nurses in the union model limits the ability of staff nurses to work in a collegial fashion with institutional administration. Other avenues for seeking change in an organization should be chosen if full professional practice models are desired. (See Chapter 21, "Contrasting Politics: Hospital Bureaucracy and Shared Governance.")

Similarly, petitions or group-signed letters to the nurse administrator, hospital administrator, or even the board of trustees often fall short of the group's intentions. The receiver of such a letter frequently concentrates on the process rather than on the content or issues raised, and the response may be defensive rather than constructive. Individual, well-written letters, expressing concern regarding a particular situation, are likely to receive a more positive response. Before either avenue is attempted, however, the nurse should feel confident that efforts to communicate through all established organizational channels have been attempted. Frequently, nurses fail to understand that simply calling for an appointment to meet the chief nurse executive or manager is within their power. The role of nursing administration must be viewed as a facilitator, not a barrier, to practice.

Nurses should always expect that problems can be solved, and the system should be designed to fulfill these expectations. Decentralized, open systems will allow many practice issues to be resolved at the unit level. Not all clinical issues need to proceed through a hierarchy for resolution. For example, when nurses come across issues of concern related to the practice of another, be it a physician, nurse, or other health professional, a legitimate process should be followed. The first principle is, of course, to be knowledgeable and sure of your facts. Second, courtesy dictates that you confront the individual first. Often confrontation will rectify the situation, but all organizations have mechanisms for appropriate escalation of practice issues.

There are some general principles for such circumstances. First, an individual's right to privacy must be protected. The intent of the process is to change a practice or situation, not to harm another person.

As an issue moves to other levels in the organization, trust must be placed in those who must now resolve it. It is important to understand that others may need time to resolve the issue, and they have the right to develop their own process. Often, an unstated question, but an important one, is "must you know how I have solved this issue or can you trust that it will be solved?" The person escalating the issue must judge whether the issue is falling on responsive or unresponsive ears. Knowing the organizational structure and philosophy will provide direction in either case.

PARTICIPATION

Control over nursing practice in hospital organizations requires a high level of staff involvement, particularly in committee activities. Each institution will have its own committee structure and process for membership selection. Nurses should receive information related to the standing committees of the nursing department. What is each committee's charge? How are members appointed? Will participation on committees help fulfill responsibilities associated with the advancement program or clinical ladder in the nursing department? What happens to the minutes of committee meetings or the results of committee activities? All these questions are important in understanding the organization's commitment to shared governance and professional autonomy.

The chairperson of the committee should develop expectations for committee participation and evaluate individual participation. This way, the professional work of committees will move forward and a valuable committee appointment is less likely to be wasted on an uninterested staff member.

Through committee appointments nurses can earn another level of respect from their peers and managers. For the nursing department, committee involvement offers additional mechanisms of recognition that can be rewarded through a level of practice program.

Committees and task force activities are essential to ensure participation of nurse professionals in the design and evaluation of the nursing care system. Committee membership by nurses should extend beyond the nursing department to representation on hospital-wide and interdisciplinary committees or projects. This involvement promotes collegial relationships and professional identity for nursing.

Today's health care requires considerable interdisciplinary coordination and collaboration. Effective collaboration is more likely to occur if relationships are developed before adverse issues occur. The work climate must be supportive of such practices, and committee work needs to be integrated into practice. Nurses must value and be willing to share their experience in groups.

SUMMARY

The benefits for nurses who seek ways to influence the direction and decision-making processes of an institution extend beyond self-satisfaction as professionals. The institution and nursing department gain a level of expert resource crucial for today's complex and fast-changing health care environment. An essential component in this process is the development of a common philosophy of nursing that can be actualized and supported in the practice system and used by individual nurses as a framework for participation as active, involved nurse professionals.

The structure of the nursing service department should facilitate the work of the direct care provider, ie, the staff nurse, and support the goal of the hospital to provide quality patient care. When organizational structures form a network of advocacy for patient and care provider, the nursing management and clinical practice staff come together in a professionally accountable relationship that benefits patients, nurses, and the institution. This relationship establishes a common power base and enhances the potential for parity in decision making.

Individual nurse professionals must accept accountability for their own practice. At the same time, head nurses must provide strong managerial and clinical leadership for the staff nurse. Collegial relationships with other disciplines will grow as nurses develop a broader-based knowledge of health care issues. As this occurs, the professional identity of nursing will be enhanced, and the organizational influence of the nurse will increase.

References

Institute of Medicine: *Nursing and nursing education: Public policies and private actions*. National Academy Press, 1983.

National Commission on Nursing: *Summary report and recommendations*. American Hospital Association, 1983.

Opportunities for Grass-Roots Action

Susan W. Talbott, RN, MA, MBA

The complexity of health care makes work environments stressful for many nurses. Many staff nurses complain and wait, often in vain, for "someone to do something."

Quality of life in the workplace concerns many nurse administrators, but is of even greater concern to the thousands of nurses who staff units day and night in hospitals and nursing homes.

If you listen to staff nurses talking about their work you hear a lot of griping. The complaints are familiar: short staffing, too much overtime, inadequate continuing education opportunities, poor salaries, too much paperwork, absence of collegiality among health professionals, lack of child care facilities, or too much shift work. A landmark study (Wandelt, Pierce & Widdowson, 1981) documented these complaints, stating that ". . . dissatisfaction stems from the work setting rather than nursing practice" (p 73).

If nurses leave nursing because workplace conditions interfere with their ability to practice nursing, what can be done? This section outlines how staff nurses can take action on their own behalf. Staff nurses can and must contribute to the creation and maintenance of a supportive work environment.

The politics of work deserve careful examination, for after all, people are political. Consider how you and your peers get along. Are you thoughtful and considerate of one another? Do you pitch in to help another nurse without feeling put upon or angry? Despite the fact that nursing is a humanistic profession and nurses are in the "nurturing business," we often fail to nurture ourselves or our colleagues.

TEAM BUILDING

Nurses who feel isolated from their peers and lack a sense of professional accomplishment often become chronic complainers. A "problem" nursing unit often has a number of frustrated, demoralized nurses. One way to turn chronic complainers into productive problem solvers is to develop a team approach on the nursing unit. By this we do not mean team nursing, but a unity of purpose that successful work groups seem to have (McGregor, 1960).

A group of staff nurses can improve attitudes on the unit by developing team-building skills. The first step is to assess the way the work group functions. This can be done in a number of ways.

Get together with a few colleagues and ask yourselves some questions. Your discussion should give you some ideas about what problems need attention:

- Has the unit's productivity been decreasing?
- Has the number of complaints and grievances increased?
- Is there evidence of hostility or conflict among staff members?
- Have there been mistakes due to poor or incomplete communication?
- Are staff dependent on the head nurse, or hostile toward him or her?
- Are patients complaining about poor nursing care?
- Could staff meetings be more effective?
- Is there apathy among the nursing staff?

If you find many "yes" answers to these questions, then you and your work group may want to consider developing a formal team-building program with your head nurse and possibly an inservice education instructor.

Cohen and Ross (1982) describe a team-building program designed to build cohesiveness on a nursing unit. Dyer (1977) has developed a more thorough evaluation of the unit work group.

BRAINSTORMING

Another approach to problem solving is brainstorming, a technique that stimulates and captures creative thoughts. You might suggest using this approach in a staff meeting. Some guidelines for brainstorming include (Talbott & Webster, 1984):

- Schedule an adequate amount of time.
- Let people know ahead of time the purpose and topic of the meeting so they can do some thinking in advance.
- Review the following four rules before brainstorming:
  1. Rule out criticism: withhold judgment, analysis, and evaluation until the second phase of the session.
  2. Think freely. Accept even "wild" ideas.
  3. Encourage quantity. Try for the maximum number of ideas. Maintain a rapid pace.
  4. Build on other ideas. Seek combinations, embellishments, and improvements.
- Use a flip chart, blackboard, or tape recorder to capture ideas.
- Encourage all participants to contribute, but do not press quiet group members.
- 2nd phase: Evaluate the ideas the group generates, asking the following questions:
  1. Can it be done?
  2. Will it be useful?
  3. Will it work?
  4. Will it be valued?

SUPPORT GROUP

Another way nurses can foster their professional growth is to start a support group. This is a type of self-help group for learning together and supporting others in professional development. A support group offers a variety of learning modes. Nurses might take turns presenting information on clinical topics. This teaching-learning model is appropriate for a professional support group. Another way a self-help group can foster professional growth is by encouraging individuals to present problems they would like assistance in solving (Kirschenbaum & Glaser, 1978).

NETWORKS

Networks of professional colleagues can improve the quality of work life. Share a meal with a colleague you do not see often, or arrange to meet another nurse at a nurses' association meeting. Informal professional relationships can be rewarding, and it is politically wise to expand your horizons beyond your unit. (See Chapter 15 for more on networking.)

RELATIONSHIP WITH SUPERIORS

A boss can make or break your day. How is your relationship with your head nurse or supervisor? How often do you meet with her on a formal or informal basis? Are you satisfied with your evaluations? If not, here are some actions you might consider:

- Before your next evaluation tell your boss you would like to do a self-evaluation using the evaluation form she will also use and then compare yours with hers. Ask her if she will help you use the results of the mutual evaluation to set goals for your professional development for the next year.
- Keep notes on your own performance. Ask a colleague to help you evaluate the care you plan and give to a particular patient. Try using the teaching-learning model referred to above.
- In between formal evaluation meetings with your boss, arrange for frequent "how am I doing" meetings. This helps busy people keep in touch and can prevent unwelcome surprises at your formal evaluation session.

One way to earn the respect and appreciation of the boss is to volunteer to help with a task. For example, if a new procedure needs to be written, offer to do it. You will learn something while you engender her gratitude. When students come to the unit, offer to be a preceptor. Find things to do that will benefit your professional growth and your peers and the unit.

While you are thinking of ways you might assist your boss, you might give some thought to what her job entails. Often we think we could do the boss' job better, but then upon reflection realize that the scope of his or her job is different from ours.

Staff nurses can find creative ways to turn problems into opportunities, for themselves, their patients, colleagues, and profession. Join with colleagues to find ways to improve the quality of your work life. Judicious application of political wisdom and humanity will enable nurses to individually and collectively make a difference.

References

Cohen MH, Ross ME: Team building: A strategy for unit cohesiveness. *J Nurs Adm* 1984; 12:29–34.

Dyer W: *Team Building.* Addison-Wesley, 1977.

Kirschenbaum H, Glaser B: *Developing Support Groups.* University Associates, 1978.

McGregor D: *The Human Side of Enterprise.* McGraw-Hill, 1960.

Talbott S, Webster R: *Brainstorming.* (Workshop material.) Nurse Management Institute, New York, 1984.

Wandelt M, Pierce P, Widdowson R: Why nurses leave nursing and what can be done about it. *Am J Nurs* 1981; 81:72–77.

Vignette: The Nurse as Hospital Board Member
Elizabeth Dorsey Smith, RN, EdD, FAAN

A trustee of a voluntary organization holds fiduciary responsibility for the institution or agency. The board of trustees is responsible for the operation, planning, and mission of the institution, including clinical practice. In addition, trustees are expected to contribute financially to the institution.

All aspects of the daily activities of the agency—budgeting, care delivery, and personnel—are ultimately the board's responsibility. The board must exercise its accountability by hiring competent physicians and a chief executive officer (CEO). Unless nurses are self-governing (an arrangement that has only recently received attention in the nursing community and is still rare), they are employees of the institution and are usually not hired directly by the board. Therefore, although the nurse manager accepts responsibility for hiring competent nurses, the board remains accountable.

In general, boards of trustees are composed of lay persons with a variety of business skills—eg, lawyers, accountants, personnel officers, managers, investment brokers, real estate experts, and public and community relations experts.

Corporate boards of directors and boards of voluntary organizations have traditionally been composed primarily of men. This is significant because of the concepts of power and volunteerism. Women have traditionally served in large numbers as direct service volunteers. Men have served as policy makers in powerful decision-making volunteer positions as trustees. Women have come slowly to boards, often through the community relations route rather than the search for professional skills. This is changing as more women enter the job market.

Within the past ten years, the Joint Commission on Accreditation of Hospitals (JCAH) has recommended that physicians be appointed to hospital boards. Women and nurses have been underrepresented on hospital boards. The American Nurses' Association is not a member of the JCAH board of commissioners, which may be a factor.

Most boards are self-perpetuating—that is, they select and elect their own replacements. Therefore, if nurses wish to become board members, they need to get to know present board members. They must bear in mind that trustees are the embodiment of management.

My experience in becoming appointed to the board of trustees of a 300-bed community hospital began at a social occasion when an old friend consulted me about trends in nursing's image. I was surprised by the questions. A year later, this same friend asked me to join the board of trustees. I was startled, because I did not know he was involved with the hospital in any capacity. After a careful study of the annual reports and discussions with others in the community regarding the hospital, I accepted the appointment with the understanding that I was volunteering approximately three to six hours per week, generally in the evening for meetings and other activities. As I became a more seasoned board member, the time commitment escalated.

The primary reason I was asked to join the board was to be a consultant for nursing. Initially I was involved with personnel matters, capital budget approval, educational efforts, and inspection of the physical plant. As time went on, I became involved with efforts to represent the board on the search committees for the chief of service of a major medical department and for a new chief executive officer. I did not have primary responsibility for matters involving physicians in a dispute with the hospital, the operating budget, real estate, and public relations.

During my tenure, one contribution I made was to have the director of nursing invited to attend board meetings, as her colleagues on the senior management level did. All the other managers who had previously attended were men. Her presence opened up direct communication between nursing and board members. No one else, neither administration nor medicine, should articulate nursing to board members. For example, when a shortage of OR nurses occurred, many physicians doubted this scarcity because it was a new phenomenon. The director of nursing was asked to update the surgeons and board members about the nursing shortgage nationally and in our community. This forum stimulated the development of a program to respond to the shortage.

The experience of being a hospital board member was educational and rewarding. If nurses are to influence the operations of health care institutions, they must make sure the profession is represented in the boardroom. While cultivating nonnurse advocates is essential to ensuring such representation, appointment of nurses to boards can do even more to further the image of nursing as well as its mission.

References

James J: Becoming a health care agency trustee. *Nurs Manag* (Mar) 1984; 15:17–19.
Smith ED: Nurses in policymaking and volunteerism. *Nurs Health Care* 1983; 4:135–37.

Vignette: Finding Answers in Horoscopes
Helen M. Archer-Dusté, RN, MSN

I have found that the best way to foster a supportive work environment is to establish myself as a credible clinician. Compassion, competence, and conscientiousness are the hallmarks of credibility. Physicians, nurse colleagues, ancillary staff, and nurse managers are willing to recognize the opinions and views of one who is known as "a good nurse." Clinical excellence forms a strong power base.

The second most valuable skill is clear communication. The nurse who can conceptualize a problem or idea, outline alternatives for action, and articulate those thoughts will usually draw greater attention. It is important to feel comfortable raising issues with persons at all levels within the organization.

Lastly, relating to coworkers as individuals can do much to eradicate potential barriers and foster cooperation. Sincerity in asking about someone's children, how their vacation trip went, or expressing sympathy at a family tragedy will strengthen the human bond between yourself and your coworker.

A few years ago, I learned the value of this approach. I had transferred from the trauma intensive care unit to a medical-surgical unit. Resentment arose as I quickly moved to a charge nurse position on the unit. This was most openly expressed by Mrs H, who had worked for 40 years as a nurse's aide at the hospital. She lost no time in impressing upon me that she knew more about the system, and that any newfangled ideas I might have about patient care would be ignored. Racial factors added tension to the situation.

I had two options: (1) to attempt to obtain her compliance unilaterally or, (2) to establish rapport and cooperation more gradually. I chose the latter approach, but wondered what I could find in common with Mrs H. How could I get to know her without appearing insincere?

The daily newspaper horoscope provided the answer one morning during a coffee break. Mrs H's daughter is a Leo, as am I. I soon became Mrs H's "white daughter," and she would scold me or tease me about the horoscope for each day. We became close, and were able to cooperate in the workplace.

Once reluctant to follow through on my suggestions, Mrs H. began to volunteer positive ideas. The sense of teamwork grew. Through the next two and one-half years, a friendship blossomed. My expectations of Mrs H's performance were higher, and she met the challenge. When I left the unit, Mrs H, beaming with pride and misty eyed, wished me well, saying, "You're the best. We are going to miss you." Differences in culture, age, race, and educational preparation were transcended by the common bond of humanity.

Vignette: One Manager's Strategies for Creating a Supportive Work Environment
Donna Costello-Nickitas, RN, MA

I joined the nursing administration staff at a large New York City hospital, as an assistant director of nursing when I was fresh out of graduate school and twenty-eight years old. I was the youngest nursing administrator in both age and experience, and I had never worked at this hospital before. I was enthusiastic and full of ideas. My colleagues welcomed me, but made it clear that I would have to learn "their way" of nursing management to survive.

I set out to manage a 210-bed clinical service with over 200 employees, including 2 critical care units, 9 general care units, 1 day hospital unit, 6 nursing supervisors, 11 head nurses, 80 staff nurses, 60 auxiliary nursing staff, 2 office clerks, and 11 ward clerks. I was counting on my experience in the military to help me administer this complex division.

Effective operation of this service, which was larger than many community hospitals, required a cohesive leadership team. Developing such a team was a priority, because the management group I was to lead was divided by personality conflicts; power struggles; and continual battles for scarce resources, including personnel, supplies, and equipment.

My initial observation of the nurse managers in my division revealed that most relied upon personal connections within the hospital to obtain the supplies they needed for their units. Several nurse managers explained to me that their ability to manage was not based on what they knew, but whom they knew. For example, when a head nurse discovered her unit did not have an adequate supply of syringes to give morning medications, she would call her friend, a department head in central supply, and ask for a special delivery. The routine use of requisitions to obtain supplies seemed to have ceased.

In another instance, a nurse manager used manipulation to obtain isolation masks and gowns. When supplies grew low, she would call the hospital epidemiologist, warning him of a potential breakdown in isolation technique due to a lack of supplies. Such a call invariably resulted in a quick delivery of the needed supplies.

While these informal exchanges were appropriate at times, the failure to document inadequate supplies perpetuated the problem. Many nurse managers believed their strategies were valid. They reminded me that they had years of experience, and were content to manage business as usual.

The Challenge

Positive change in nursing management and patient care was needed in three key areas. I devised strategies to:

- overcome the lack of cohesion among the members of the top management group
- promote respect for clinical expertise among all nurses in the division
- encourage use of more effective management techniques.

I consulted with former professors and more experienced nurse managers and determined that, among other things, I would: (1) set up regular meetings with the supervisory staff at which I would serve refreshments; and (2) establish regular patient rounds on each unit. These two strategies were designed to improve communication among staff, managers, and myself.

Regular Meetings: Small, Frequent Feedings

Weekly supervisory meetings promoted harmony and reduced hostility among members of the nursing management team. By meeting face-to-face and discussing the problems and needs of each clinical unit, all supervisors had an opportunity to air their concerns. Individuals seemed to feel less alone when each of them could express frustration and seek the support of peers.

I provided coffee, tea, and bagels at these meetings, indicating that I cared about the participants and their needs. I was pleased when I discovered that the supervisors soon set up similar meetings for head nurses they supervised.

Sight and Sound: Be Visible and Listen Carefully

To get acquainted with the staff and to learn more about each clinical unit, I made frequent patient rounds with supervisors. Gradually head nurses and staff nurses began to approach me. They asked for help in solving patient care and supply problems. They asked for advice on how to cope with such things as continual staff shortages and complaints about housekeeping service. Being visible and listening sent a deliberate message to my staff: I am part of your team, and I am concerned about you, your patients, and your problems.

Clear Messages: Two-Way Communication

The majority of my time was spent communicating the goals and objectives of the division to the staff. I took whatever time was needed to ensure that my staff received adequate information and instructions. They understood what was expected, what authority they had to accomplish their work, and when it was to be completed. The success of this strategy was reflected by a general improvement in staff performance and morale.

By keeping channels of communication open, staff received important information and were able to convey their ideas and exert influence appropriately. Their input, interpretations, and critique on policy, procedures, and protocol were solicited and valued. An exchange of ideas and brainstorming sessions concerning unit and division problems generated a variety of solutions to age-old problems. Staff morale improved with each staff member's idea that was implemented. Efforts to improve communication between myself, the leadership group, and their subordinates were based upon the philosophy that honest, open, and direct dialogue promotes team work, high productivity, and group morale. The staff became active participants in creating and maintaining a supportive work environment.

Vignette: Addressing Occupational Hazards
Diane J. Mancino, RNC, MA

Nurses are applying basic principles of political action to improve the quality of their occupational environment. Realizing that grass-roots involvement can promote change, nurses are collectively taking steps to identify and prevent health problems related to environmental factors in their workplace.

Examples

After oncology nurses at a large New York City metropolitan hospital found that chemotherapeutic drugs were producing mutagenic activity in the urine of nurses mixing and administering the drugs, the nurses insisted that management provide for safe mixing and administration procedures. When management refused, the nurses en masse stopped mixing and administering the drugs and said they would not do so without the proper protection. Now, the pharmacy prepares the medications using procedures recommended by the National Cancer Institute.

In another situation, also at a metropolitan New York City hospital, nurses reported their hospital to the Bureau of Radiation Control for violating the New York City Health Code, which states that women of childbearing age are not to hold patients during radiographic procedures. The nurses, who worked in a neonatal intensive care unit, were requested to steady infants during x-rays. Even after fines were incurred for the violations, the hospital continued to insist that the nurses hold the infants. After a court battle, the judge found the hospital in violation of the New York City Health Code and instructed the hospital to abide by the law. The hospital now uses restraints to steady the infants.

Guidelines for Rectifying Hazards of the Workplace

Three nurses who met during a nuclear power plant protest got together later to discuss what nurses should do to protect people from unhealthy effects of environmental pollution. These nurses started a national organization, Nurses' Environmental Health Watch (NEHW), which has attracted attention from nurses all over the United States, Europe, and Canada. The group's goal is to educate nurses about environmental health issues, including hazards of the workplace. The organization has assisted nurses in their efforts to identify and rectify these hazards.

In response to inquiries about where to begin to rectify a workplace hazard, NEHW recommends the following steps:

Step 1. Once a hazard has been identified, check the hospital policy book and determine if hospital policy is being implemented.

Step 2. If there is a correct, safe hospital policy that is not being used, bring it to the attention of nursing management and have the policy enforced.

Step 3. If there is no policy or the policy is outdated or inadequate, research the topic (include a thorough search regarding laws and regulations that may be appropriate) and draft a policy statement documented with your research findings.

Step 4. Present the policy statement to the appropriate nursing department or committee (ie, safety committee, committee on hospital policy and procedures, or the risk management officer). Document all correspondence and keep copies of everything. Send copies of correspondence to the director of nursing, chair of the board of trustees, and the chief executive officer of the hospital. If you are represented by a collective bargaining unit, consider involving union leaders. Seek support from your peers and colleagues. Keep your agenda objective and document your facts.

Step 5. If change cannot be negotiated within the institution, you may seek assistance from government agencies such as the Occupational Safety and Health Administration or the National Institute for Occupational Safety and Health. In addition, agencies that focus on a specific aspect of hospital safety, such as the Food and Drug Administration Center for Devices and Radiological Health, can be contacted.

Step 6. Once the change has taken place, share the information. Write about it, talk about it, and reach out to your peers who may be facing similar situations. If the change did not take place as anticipated, you may want to seek outside consultation to determine a new strategy.

Step 7. Become an expert by continuing your education, take courses that address occupational safety and health, and apply the information to your own work situation. NEHW has publications and presents workshops on this and other topics.

Involvement requires an awareness of the dynamic nature of health and illness and courage to address unpopular issues.

Chapter 21

Collective Action for Change in the Workplace

The Politics of Collective Bargaining

Mary E. Foley, RN, BSN

This chapter introduces nurses to the politics of collective action through collective bargaining in the private sector. It includes a brief review of nursing's history in collective bargaining; the role of the union and the professional nursing association in organizing nurses; the essential components of collective bargaining and how to influence them; and the outlook for collective bargaining in light of the current political, legal, and economic environment. The myriad of local and state laws that govern the public sector make it impossible to generalize about the bargaining process in that sector and will not be dealt with here.

For purposes of this chapter, collective bargaining is defined as a struggle for power in which the opposing parties, such as the employer and the collective bargaining agent, rival and manipulate each other in an effort to improve and advance their respective positions. In the health care setting, the broadly defined bargaining objectives include: "(1) to protect the economic position and personal welfare of the worker; (2) to protect the union's integrity as an ongoing institution; and (3) to recognize the outer limits imposed on collective bargaining outcomes by the economic conditions of the industry and the employer and by the climate of opinion" (Stern, 1982, p 11).

NURSING'S LABOR HISTORY

The first nursing association to represent nurses was the California Nurses' Association. The desire to organize collectively, which came from within nursing, was forced by the conditions of the workplace and proceeded with or without legal sanction.

There is some belief that the employers in California saw the alternative—trade unions—and opted for the "lesser of the evils" by cooperating with the California Nurses' Association (CNA) proposals of the 1930s and 1940s. Nursing's history in the bargaining arena predates the earliest labor law, and existed in a period when little protection was offered the hospital worker.

Other major events in nursing's labor history include the following:

1913   The California legislature extended the "8-hour" law to "pupil nurses." Most hospital work at that time was performed by pupil nurses, with 12- or even 24-hour shifts.

1919   Formation of the Union of Stewards and Nurses. A small number of civil service employees in San Francisco registered under the Federation of Labor to improve working conditions. This union met with disapproval from the California State Nurses' Association (now the California Nurses' Association) because of its trade union affiliation.

1937   The American Nurses' Association's (ANA) official statement did not recommend nurse membership in unions at that time and concluded that "in their professional organizations nurses have the instruments best fitted and equipped to improve every phase of their working and professional lives" ("Nurse membership," 1937, p 766). Problems identified at that time included: hours, working conditions, economic security, health, increased and improved services to the sick, reasonable patient load, staff preparation and education, and graduate and undergraduate education.

1946   Trade union nurses in Southern California went on strike. This led to a call for collective bargaining for nurses by a qualified and professional staff, provided by nursing organizations to allow "collective nursing action." The hospitals also called for reasonable negotiations with nurses on matters affecting their livelihood, with the expressed purpose to prevent "unionism."

July
1946   The first hospital contracts with the California Nurses' Association were signed covering salary and employment conditions for staff and supervisory nurses.

November
1946   An ANA resolution affirmed that state and district nurse associations were entitled to act as exclusive agents of their memberships in the important fields of economic security and collective bargaining, and at the same time emphasizing that "under no circumstances would a strike or the use of similar coercive measures be countenanced" (ANA activities, 1946).

More discussion of the significance of strike/no-strike policies will follow. Most contracts throughout the nation included no-strike language through the 1960s and 1970s. Table 21-1 highlights the history of labor law in this country.

Table 21-1   A Review of Major Events in the History of Labor Law

1935	Passage of the National Labor Relations Act, also known as the Wagner Act: Allowed private sector employees to organize for the purpose of negotiating terms of their wages, hours, and working conditions.
1947	Taft Hartley Amendments of the National Labor Relations Act: Placed specific restraints on unfair labor practices by unions.
1947	Tyding Amendments: Exempted the nonprofit health care industry from the National Labor Relations Act.
1974	Repeal of the Tyding Amendments: Extended the National Labor Relations Act to employees of the nonprofit health care industry.

SHOULD NURSES ORGANIZE?

Nursing has been and to some extent remains embroiled in a debate about whether professional nurses should organize for collective bargaining. That debate stems from the desire to identify nursing as a profession.

A profession is a body of people who have pursued a long period of specialized education to prepare for service to society and generally enjoy one-to-one relationships with their patients. Because of their expertise and the value of their service, professionals are granted a measure of autonomy in their work. This autonomy permits independent judgment and decision making using a theory base obtained through study and practice.

Most nurses, however, are employed by hospitals, nursing homes, or other bureaucratic institutions. As such, they do not enjoy self-employment, or the professional-patient relationships that characterize most professions. As employees accountable to an institution, nurses lose control over their practice and working conditions. Usually, they have had little or no orientation to labor practices and procedures or organizational theory.

Conflict inevitably results from the differences between the professional role in patient care and the productivity and resource utilization techniques imposed by management. In addition, nurses are no longer immune to job security issues. As cost containment becomes the watchword of hospital management, layoffs of nurses and increased workloads have occurred and may continue.

A study conducted by a Kansas City employee and labor relations consulting firm tried to define why hospital employees and nurses joined unions, and how union organizers garnered their support. The study was intended for use by hospital managers to define strategies to eliminate the need for outside representation for professional nurses. Their conclusion speaks for itself—"A myth widely subscribed to by hospital management is that big powerful unions organize professional nurses. In fact, unions do not organize nurses; professional nurses organize themselves. They do this because administrators and nursing supervisors fail to recognize and address nurses' individual and collective needs" (Stickler & Velghe, 1980, p 14). In addition, a study from the University of California, Berkeley, found that nurses who engage in collective bargaining believe it is the only solution to a management-employee power struggle. They conclude that nurses decide to unionize because of their "inability to communicate with management and their perception of authoritarian behavior on the part of management" (Parlette, O'Reilly, Bloom, 1980, p 16).

Nursing has used collective action to its benefit, achieving professional goals through lobbying efforts in the political arena. Many nurses support collective bargaining in the workplace as a way to control their practice by redistributing power within the health care organization. Virginia Cleland (1981) stated, "The power bestowed upon the nursing profession should derive not from the hospital administrator's benevolence, but rather from the public's view of the value of services provided by the practitioner" (p 17). Ada Jacox (1980) has criticized nursing departments that fail to acknowledge that nurses are professionals. In her view (and the author's) the authority for nursing practice must rest within the profession. She suggests that collective bargaining through the professional organization may be a way for nurses to achieve collective professional responsibility.

WHO SHOULD REPRESENT NURSES?

Nurses are professionals, yet they are also hospital workers. So, who should represent nurses in the workplace? Many labor organizations have tried and are still trying to represent nurses. Meatpackers, paperhangers, longshoremen, teamsters, Local 1199 AFL-CIO, the Service Employees International Union, the Association of Federal, State, County and Municipal Employees (AFSCME), and the American Federation of Teachers (AFT) are among the competitors.

Some of these unions offer organization, great resources, and lengthy experience in labor relations. Traditional unions, however, are reluctant to become involved in worker control issues—control of practice that many nurses seek when they pursue collective bargaining—and often focus only on wages and benefits. Even if unions are generally willing to negotiate those concerns, nurses may find themselves competing with other units within the union and perhaps being overruled by other union constituencies. Decisions affecting nursing issues may be made by nonnurses and a predominantly male population. In fact, there is no legal requirement that a union include its members in policy formulation. A union may make a determination for the good of the union even if the position is adverse to a particular segment or group the union represents (Silverstein, in Eldridge and Levi, 1982).

If nursing goals are to be consistent nationally and be set by nurses, nurses must represent themselves. As Jacox and Cleland and many other nursing leaders have stated, the professional association has the means and responsibility to represent nurses. The national professional organization for nursing is the ANA with its constituent units, the state and territorial nurses' associations. Through its economic security programs, ANA recognizes state nurses' associations as the logical bargaining agents for professional nurses. These professional associations are indeed multipurpose; their activities include economic analysis, education, nursing practice, research, collective bargaining, lobbying, and political action.

The ability of the professional association to represent nurses has been questioned in a 1985 NLRB ruling. In 1977, North Shore Hospital protested its nurses electing the New York State Nurses' Association as their bargaining agent. At question was the presence of supervisors within the nursing association's organizational structure. The NLRB ruling in favor of the hospital may necessitate restructuring the professional association to remedy the appearance of conflict of interests between the management members of the association and the staff nurses represented by the collective bargaining unit of the association.

If the ANA and state nurses' associations are logical bargaining agents for professional nurses, why are so few joining associations and even fewer pursuing collective bargaining? Studies of organizational behavior have demonstrated that most persons join an organization only in response to a particular incentive or when coerced. Otherwise, people will "free ride"—enjoy whatever collective goals are obtained without helping to pay for them (Olson, 1977).

Collective bargaining by state nurses' associations usually occurs in states where there is significant union activity. Fewer than one-half of the state nurses' associations engage in collective bargaining. Some state associations have left the arena because of external pressures: challenges by competing unions, excessive resistance by employers, or state policies that make unionization difficult, such as right-to-work laws. Some have chosen to cease bargaining activities in response to internal organizational pressures. The cost of collective bargaining can be high. The financial and staff commitments may be viewed as excessive.

Philosophical conflicts regarding the benefits and risks of professional association bargaining have also led some state associations to abandon the role. Some state organizations have hoped that suspension of bargaining activities would increase membership. Two states that have dropped collective bargaining, Wisconsin and Connecticut, have not shown appreciable membership gains. This leads back to the question, is it the spectre of collective bargaining that causes membership problems, or is it the "free ride" phenomena? How will collective professional goals be achieved if so many nurses depend on the time and finances of so few? Of the 1.6 million professional nurses in the United States, only 125,000 are organized by their state nurses' association. A more aggressive effort by the national and state professional associations is needed to address the collective needs of employed nurses and to lead a stronger alliance.

ELECTING THE COLLECTIVE BARGAINING AGENT

Nurses in the private sector are now guaranteed protection if they seek a collective bargaining agent. Once a drive for such representation is under way, and 30 percent of the employed nurses have signed cards signaling their interest in representation, the employer is prohibited from engaging in antilabor action, including firing the organizers, refusing to allow dissemination of union information in the workplace, and ignoring the request for a vote of the workers for full representation by the union as collective bargaining agent. A vote is then taken, and 50 percent + 1 of those voting selects the agent.

An employer may elect to recognize the agent (this usually occurs only if a large majority supports the union) and choose to bargain in good faith on matters concerning employee working conditions. This is seldom the case, however, because employee requests may be appealed to the National Labor Relations Board (NLRB) by the employer. Before and during the appeal, other unions may intervene and try to win a majority of votes.

Arguments are made before the NLRB, as to why, by whom, or how the nurses are to be represented. For example, the hospital may raise the question of "unit determination." The original intent of the policy interpretations of the labor law was to limit the number of individual bargaining units an employer or industry would have to recognize as representing any single unit or group of workers yet allow for distinct groups of employees who may have a legitimate need for separate representation. By raising the question of unit determination, an employer can try to lump employees into a single bargaining unit (or numerous units) depending upon his strategy of how best to weaken the union's power base. Nurses have usually sought an all-RN unit and until recently have been supported by the NLRB, thus avoiding the dilemma of professional nurses being lumped in with other health care workers seeking representation. In 1984, however, the NLRB ruled against unit determination in the case of nurses at St. Francis Hospital in St. Paul, Minnesota. The board ruled that there was not sufficient "disparity of interests" for nurses to have a bargaining unit separate from the other professional staff. In all professional units, nurses are included with respiratory therapists, social workers, physical therapists, librarians, pharmacists, and the like. These determinations jeopardize representation of nurses by a nursing organization because it is less likely that the nursing organization will be the elected agent. Subsequent to the 1984 NLRB ruling, the Minnesota Nurses' Association (MNA) lost its bid to be the bargaining agent for an all-professional unit at St. Cloud Hospital after the NLRB had ruled against MNA representing an all-RN unit at the hospital (Nurses association loses, 1984). If it is to compete for representing "all professional" units, the nursing associations must decide how to accommodate nonnurse membership.

Nurses represented by a bargaining agent can vote to drop or change (decertify) that agent by a similar campaign of signatures (30 percent) of the affected members, followed by a vote, again requiring a 50 percent + 1 vote in a unit-wide election. While the election process may ensure fair representation and the agent's accountability, election campaigns can be destructive and diversionary when initiated for nonconstructive reasons.

WHAT A CONTRACT CAN DO

Generally speaking, what can a union contract do for a hospital? A recent study of 36 hospitals nationwide with long contract histories illustrates the positive effects a union can have: (1) unions stimulate better hospital management by fostering formal, central, and consistent personnel policies with better lines of communication; and (2) unions "force" improvements in the workplace so that recruitment and retention become easier (Juris & Maxey, 1981).

Wages are the foundation of a contract. Wages are the remuneration one receives for providing a service and reflect the value put on the work performed. One author decries nurses for accepting substandard wages. She claims that nurses "are doing themselves and their profession a disservice to let the public think they are worth only $6.78 an hour . . . society values . . . services according to how much they pay for them" (Gideon, 1980, p 1202).

Nursing wages have increased. In 1981, in metropolitan areas nursing salaries ranged from $8.26 an hour in Atlanta, Georgia, to $11.46 an hour in San Francisco and Oakland, California. An ANA review of contracts negotiated in 1984 found salaries ranging from $12.35 an hour in California to $9.42 in southeastern states (Annual Review of Nursing Salaries, 1984). The average annual salary for a 40-hour week general duty staff nurse was $17,802 in 1982, or a 35.4 percent increase since 1977, when the average annual salary was $13,152 (*Facts About Nursing*, 1982–83). (Although nursing salaries have improved, there is debate as to whether they reflect what nurses are worth; see "Comparable Worth" section and Chapter 3.) Between 25 percent to 40 percent of all nonnursing labor contracts negotiated during 1982–1983 contained either a wage freeze or wage concessions. Hospitals are facing increasing financial constraints, and labor is often targeted as an area where costs can most easily be reduced.

Job security is an objective of collective bargaining. Once nurses have obtained the desired wages and negotiated benefits, their next concern may be how to maintain satisfactory employment status. While a variety of job security provisions can be found in different contracts, the specific conditions of employment in each require the governing policies of the individual hospital not conflict with or exceed the requirements negotiated. New positions must be posted and awarded to eligible nurses within the bargaining unit.

Nurses who remain on staff at an institution accrue seniority rights. These rights arise from the ethic of rewarding permanent employees for their service, viewing these employees as assets. Seniority language in a contract provides that senior nurses accrue more vacation time and have preemptive rights to bid for time off, new positions, or relief from shift rotation requirements. In the event of a staff layoff, "the last hired become the first fired," protecting senior nurses. Seniority may be applied hospital or unit wide, and transfers and promotions must accommodate the most senior, qualified nurse. The absence of seniority language in the Minneapolis–St. Paul contracts was the key reason for the 1984 strike by registered nurses.

Grievance mechanisms, sometimes explicitly spelled out in each contract, are the backbone of any agreement. A grievance arises out of different interpretations of a contract, often in relation to job security (a union priority), job performance, and discipline (a management priority). Grievance mechanisms attempt to resolve the conflict at the level closest to the parties involved. The employer, the employee, or the union may issue a grievance. Nurses covered by contracts should be afforded representation rights at any meeting or hearing they feel may lead to disciplinary action. That representation can be provided by a coworker, the elected nurse representative, or the labor staff.

If the grievance mechanism does not resolve the issue, and all steps are exhausted by the parties without satisfaction, some contracts allow for referral of the issue to arbitration. A knowledgeable but neutral arbitrator acceptable to both parties (union and hospital) will be asked to hear the facts in the case and issue a finding. In preagreed, binding arbitration, the parties must accept the decision of the arbitrator. For example, some hospital contracts require all discharges (suspensions and terminations) to be brought to arbitration. When a nurse is suspended, the case is presented to an arbitrator chosen from an established list of arbitrators. Based on the facts presented, the nurse could be reinstated, perhaps with back pay, remain suspended, or be terminated. If the contract states it is a final and binding decision, there is no further contractual avenue for either party to pursue.

Arbitration has also been used to resolve issues of integrity of the bargaining unit's work. As more supervisory categories are designed, more nurses are exempted from the unit. Many still perform nursing functions, however, and there have been arbitrations to decide if they are still eligible for bargaining unit coverage. If not, they must stop taking patient care assignments that reduce the work available to the bargaining unit nurses.

Mediation, arbitration, and fact-finding have all been used in conflict resolution in contracts. There is strong support for using these methods in contract negotiations, yet the hospitals have resisted them. Nursing has usually fared well when contract enforcement issues have gone before a neutral third party, and facts, not power or public relations, have determined the outcome.

ELEMENTS OF A SOUND CONTRACT

Membership. The inclusion of union security provisions is an essential element of a sound contract and one of the defined goals of collective bargaining (union integrity). Enforcement of membership requirements, collection of dues, and access by the union to the members are areas directly negotiated in individual contracts or side letters of agreement. The type of membership requirements negotiated can affect the strength of the unit and its financial base. In open membership, there is no obligation to belong— an invitation to free riders to get benefits without contribution. Obviously, a union will try to negotiate a more secure base. Closed shops, which require prospective employees to join the union or association before they may be hired, are illegal. A modification of the closed shop is the agency shop, in which new employees are given a period of time during which they must become a member of the union.

If a new employee refuses to join (or pay an equivalent amount of money for services without joining), the employer is supposed to dismiss the employee. Employers are reluctant to enforce these provisions because of their general noncooperation with the union and because it increases employee turnover. Modified membership requirements may be a middle position—those who are members of the bargaining unit at the signing of a contract must remain members and newly hired nurses must join. A current negotiating goal for many association contracts is to increase membership obligations by negotiating agency shop clauses, mandating membership once employed.

Practice Issues. The essence of the professional nurse contract is control of practice. For example, nurse councils or professional performance committees provide the opportunity for nurses within the institution to meet on a regular basis. These meetings can be sanctioned by the contract. The elected staff nurse representative may, for example, have specific objectives: to consider the professional practice of nurses and nursing assistants; to work for improved patient care and nursing practice; to recommend ways and means to improve patient care; to make recommendations to the hospital in which, in the opinion of the committee, a critical nurse staffing shortage exists; and to consider elimination of hazards in the workplace.

The nurse committees should have a formal relationship with nursing administration. Regularly scheduled meetings with nursing and hospital administration can provide a forum for discussion of professional issues in a "safe" atmosphere. Many potential contract conflicts can be avoided by discussion before contract talks begin or grievances arise. Ideally, physicians should be a part of these forums; joint practice language has been proposed in some contracts. If a difference of opinion occurs between the nurse-hospital committee, a review can be conducted at the request of either party by outside reviewers representing both parties.

Educational Leave.   Paid time off for educational purposes appears in many nursing contracts. In states with mandatory continuing education requirements, paid educational leave has lessened the financial burden of fees and absence from work. Expanded interpretations use these days for conference and professional meetings. Clinical nurse specialists in a major New York hospital have negotiated educational sabbaticals.

Objection to an Assignment.   The right and means for a nurse to register objection to an assignment are essential. Professional duty implies an obligation to complete an assignment despite disagreement with it. Nurses cannot abandon their posts without risking disciplinary action. Some contracts and national proposals endorse refusal when the assignment could violate patient protection language of the state nurse practice act. An assignment-despite-objection report is submitted to nursing administration and the bargaining agent simultaneously, officially registering the complaint. Constructive follow-through may improve the situation in the future, serving as a basis for a grievance and/or negotiated change in the contract. It also gives vent to frustration and anger and can turn a bad experience into a positive effort.

Inadequate staff, poorly prepared staff, high patient acuity, and excessive use of registry personnel are all common nursing complaints. In 1981, at the peak of the highly publicized nursing shortage, many nurses abandoned staff positions and joined registries, or temporary staff agencies. It was not uncommon for the majority of a floor or unit staff to be agency employees. These staffing patterns placed a greater burden on the skeleton staff of regularly employed nurses. Supervising nonoriented, temporary personnel, who viewed care in terms of eight-hour assignments, was demanding, demoralizing, and disturbing. Numerous written complaints were filed by the bargaining unit nurses in California, and in 1981, the California Nurses' Association (CNA) successfully negotiated contractual language that addressed registry use. A registry committee was formed by CNA and the hospitals to examine policies in the institutions. The commitment to develop and maintain functioning hospital float pools was renewed. Emphasis on recruitment and retention efforts led to the clinical ladder concept, which recognizes the value of a regularly employed, experienced nurse.

Documentation and written complaints by nurses employed in these contract hospitals gave weight to future bargaining positions. In Canada, the Ontario Nurses' Association succeeded in negotiating professional responsibility clauses: if nurses believe their work is handicapped by excessive patient loads, they can make a complaint before a committee of three registered nurses.

Staffing. Staffing requirements are mandated, in part, by applicable agency standards, ie, Medicare patient coverage, state health department licensing requirements, and the Joint Commission on Accreditation of Hospitals. However, a standard that outlines patient ratios does not address the issue of what qualifications the nurse must have. As technology in the hospital specialty care units increases, extra education and experience become a requisite.

The 1974 Bay Area (California) strike was the result of a nurse/hospital standoff on staffing issues. Management resisted professional association and nurse review of staffing and specialty area qualifications. After a 21-day strike involving 42 northern California hospitals and clinics, the final agreement included these key provisions: (1) staffing systems must be clearly spelled out, and the bargaining agent must be made aware, in writing, of any changes; (2) new employees will not be counted as staff while they are being oriented; (3) the hospital will not, except in emergencies, assign an unqualified nurse to the intensive care unit, respiratory care unit, burn unit, postanesthesia recovery room, intensive care nursery, or renal dialysis unit; and (4) the hospital will provide specialty unit staff prepared through inservices or other programs for nurses on staff, and will use a pool of qualified regular and short-hour nurses.

Management wants to maintain the prerogative in decisions such as staffing. The Michigan Nurses' Association's (MNA) "shared responsibility" proposal takes a combined approach. It acknowledges that patient care is a priority and that nursing and management share responsibility to provide the best care possible, guided by agency standards, nurse practice acts, and nursing practice codes. The MNA also recommended "right of management" clauses, reaffirming management's right to determine staffing patterns, qualifications, and unit openings or closings only in direct response to public need rather than its needs (Cleland, 1981, p 20).

Retirement. Most pension or retirement programs for nurses have either been the Social Security system or a hospital pension plan. Individual retirement accounts (IRA), which are transferable from hospital to hospital in case of job change are relatively rare and can be a topic for negotiations. In fact, the ANA has considered a national pension plan to which a nurse could contribute through her lifetime of employment, irrespective of geographic location or hospital moves. This plan may well be complicated by conflicting state laws governing pension plans. Language dating to 1976 appears in California nursing contracts mandating employer contributions to individual retirement accounts for each nurse with immediate vesting (eligibility for access to the fund) and complete portability for the participants.

Mobility in nursing has been one of its most attractive benefits, but long-term retirement monies are lost with each move. Pension programs should be looked at not as a reward for continued service, but as a basic protection earned by employees as part of their benefit program. With financial cutbacks in the hospital industry, retirement plans are in danger of being targeted as givebacks in negotiations.

Health Hazard. Nurses are using contracts to safeguard against the health hazards and unsafe working conditions in the workplace. As more is known about the dangers of substances used in hospitals, the contract may be an even stronger tool. Right-to-know provisions (knowledge of where and what a substance is and how to use it safely) and job security in the case of reassignment can be written into the contract. These agreements have been successfully negotiated in contracts in the District of Columbia and Illinois, and nationally, the ANA is urging the Occupational Safety and Health Administration (OSHA) to extend hazardous substance information to health workers. Some state associations, such as the Minnesota Nurses' Association, are proposing or endorsing worker information legislation at the state level.

CLINICAL LADDER

The clinical ladder (Wieczorek, 1982, 1983; Huey, 1982), or career ladder, has a definite place in collective bargaining agreements. There is a proliferation of clinical ladders, usually addressing clinical, educational, or administrative nurses. (In San Francisco, a clinical ladder was negotiated for a seven-hospital master agreement in 1983. While implementation has been slow, the language is in place to build upon.) For the clinical nurse in a traditional employment setting, there may be little to look forward to once tenure increases are exhausted and maximum benefits are reached. The nurse with accumulated experience and expertise may become frustrated. A clinical ladder can provide an avenue for that nurse. If qualified through judgment of competence, a nurse could move up a clinical ladder that rewards expertise. A clinical promotion gives the intrinsic rewards of achievement and career satisfaction. The extrinsic rewards are compensation and recognition commensurate with the position. The reports of the National Commission on Nursing (1983) and the Institute of Medicine (1983) both cited the career ladder as a positive career retention tool.

COMPARABLE WORTH

Comparable worth, or pay equity, has emerged as the key compensation issue of the 1980s. Women earn substantially less than men ($.62 for every $1) because women do different work than men do. Historically, women have been clustered in a few job classifications, which they dominate. These jobs tend to be low paying. Census data shows that women predominate in only 20 out of 427 occupations (O'Reilly, 1982). Movement of women into nontraditional jobs has not occurred despite the Civil Rights Act. The Equal Pay Act prohibits pay differentials only when men and women do equal work using equal skills under similar conditions. Neither of these laws consider the outcome of the work and its value.

While many attribute the relatively low wages paid RNs to the fact that nursing is a female-dominated profession, the issue of market forces should be considered as well. Schramm (1982) states that low wages for nurses are related to the fact ". . . that the nursing labor market is not a properly functioning, purely competitive market, but is a monopsonistic market, which means there exist only a few firms who employ the majority of nurses" (p 52). In most communities the local hospital is the primary employer of nurses. Because the employer, the hospital, does not have to compete with others for the available pool of nurse employees, the employer is free to set a relatively low wage, usually just above that paid to aides or licensed practical nurses (Yett, 1975). Indeed, Schramm indicates that hospitals appear to be hiring nurses to do the work of aides because it does not cost that much more in salaries and benefits, and there are actual savings due to lower turnover and training costs for nurses as compared with aides. Schramm reviews a variety of solutions to the problem of artificially low wages for RNs, including the collective bargaining process. (See Chapter 3 for further discussion of the issue of comparable worth.)

In 1982, nurses in San Jose, California, went on strike on a comparable worth plank. Myra Snyder, RN, EdD, executive director of the California Nurses' Association, believes that the strike was a success, even though comparable worth never received bargaining consideration. The strike attracted national attention to the comparable worth issue, and occurred just as the economy was beginning a serious downturn. She believes collective bargaining is indeed an appropriate way to address pay equity and predicts there will be continued progress on the issue (Snyder, private interview, 1984).

Nursing is in the vanguard of female-dominated occupations with the means and desire to push for wage equity. Professional nurses must use their lobbyists, legal resources, and bargaining agents in a unified, rational effort to achieve equal pay for comparable worth.

NEGOTIATIONS

The principles of successful negotiations are difficult to delineate. Nurse negotiators are elected by their peers, and must represent a diverse population (a multitude of specialty areas, educational backgrounds, and practice needs). Nurses have little or no introduction to labor practices or procedures while preparing to become a nurse, and lessons are learned on the job. Even more foreign to nurses may be the other factors that affect negotiations—power, politics, economics, and competition.

Negotiations are held at the outset of a new contract and at the expiration date of a contract. The nurses within the bargaining unit elect a negotiating team to represent them at the negotiating table. The nurses may be assisted in the negotiations by labor staff, skilled negotiators, economists, and/or legal staff.

The ideals of professional goals and practice needs have a place at the negotiating table, but the personnel directors, hospital administrators, and hospital lawyers have difficulty relating to the discussion of practice. The nursing directors are usually in the wings, only to be brought to the table at the discretion of the administrators.

What nurses may want, and what nurses can achieve during negotiations may be worlds apart. While a survey of the nurses may lead to a "wish list," it must be pared down to only those issues that are of greatest importance to the whole and have the most chance of surviving. Impressing on nurses these difficulties of the negotiating process may lead to a sense of nonrepresentation of individual needs.

Administration of a contract throughout the life of the contract (handling of grievances, representation of the nurses, implementation of programs or committees within the contract, and membership requirements) will affect the negotiations. If problems have arisen and patterns are documented, there is justification for proposing changes at the negotiating table. If senior nurses have been laid off or given less work, language to prevent those practices may be negotiated.

Dissatisfaction with the bargaining agent may lead to unsuccessful negotiations, even loss of a contract, if allowed to surface at the negotiating table. The perceived power of the bargaining agent determines success during negotiations. In nonmandatory membership contracts, the agent's effectiveness is seriously weakened if only a handful of nurses have maintained membership within the bargaining unit. A disgruntled negotiating team will convey their disunity to the management negotiators. And a bargaining unit unwilling to attend meetings in large numbers or give votes of support to the negotiating team will seriously undercut the achievable goals of the negotiations.

STRIKES

Just what can nurses do in the face of a standoff during contract negotiations? The options now are quite different from just 15 years ago, when a greater sense of powerlessness prevailed. Despite the threats of sickouts, walkouts, picketing, or mass resignations, the employer still had an effective power base. While threats of group action attracted public attention, they had little effect on employers because nurses maintained a no-strike policy. As negotiations became more difficult, it was apparent that nursing was in the weaker bargaining position. But nurses were changing, and a new militancy was emerging. For example, work stoppages were widespread during the 1966 CNA negotiations in the Bay Area. In August 1966, the CNA Board of Directors voted to reverse the no-strike policy, stating that CNA, as the bargaining representative, "will take all necessary steps, including economic action where necessary, consistent with the law and nurses' professional responsibilities" ("No Strike Policy . . .", p 1897). In 1966, the Pennsylvania Nurses' Association adopted the same position. The ANA responded to these actions of state nurses' associations and, in 1968, reversed its 18-year-old, no-strike policy.

Strikes do represent a last resort effort, used only after every other recourse fails. Many nurses are uncomfortable with the idea of abandoning their patients. It runs counter to the service ideal. It is important for nurses who contemplate striking to discuss plans for patient care with nurses who have previously conducted strikes.

Certainly, nurses who choose to strike are taking their appeals to the street, hoping for positive public sentiment. When an impasse is reached in hospital negotiations, national labor law requires issuance of a 10-day notice of intent to strike. In the public's interest, every effort must be made to prevent a strike. Mediation is mandated by the National Labor Relations Act, and a board of inquiry to examine the issue may be created prior to a work stoppage. The hospitals are supposed to use this time to reduce the patient load and to slow or halt elective admissions and surgeries. In the meantime, the nurses' strike commitee will develop schedules for coverage of emergency rooms, operating rooms, and intensive care areas. This coverage is to be used only in the case of real emergencies. In some strike settings, a nurse committee would have to review each request for nurse staffing to verify that there was an emergency. Wages paid to those nurses are often added to any supportive funds raised for the striking nurses. This method of patient care coverage should satisfy nurses troubled by the strike scenario.

NURSE UNITY

Nurses organized by collective bargaining agreements in hospitals and the community have common interests. Areawide nurse councils provide an opportunity to share experiences and ideas beyond the sphere of one hospital. Newsletters that are specifically geared toward the bargaining units can keep nurses abreast of the latest contract gains or grievances. They can also alert nurses to new or emerging concerns. A recent example was an article in a staff nurse newsletter alerting nurses to the dangers of working with chemotherapeutic agents. This alert preceded widespread dissemination of the guidelines in clinical publications.

Worker solidarity and loyalty are associated with the ability to achieve objectives important to the worker. Union membership beliefs are a key to the power of the union, and an indicator of the degree of support a union will be given (Beletz, 1980). A union of professional nurses must accommodate the gamut of practice areas and educational backgrounds in nursing. While there cannot be complete satisfaction with every position taken by the union, if dissatisfaction is frequent and widespread, support for the union will erode. Keeping a union relevant and honest is up to its members. The Beletz study, however, showed a disappointing lack of self-education by nurses with respect to collective bargaining. This study also found that nurses represented by their professional association perceived it as less successful than other hospital bargaining agents, despite studies that refute those impressions.

EMPLOYER TACTICS

There is now a strong antiunion sentiment in this country, and the 1980s are providing ample opportunities for management to regain the right to rule the roost. Though hard to define, the disdain for unions seems to stem from a general dislike of having anyone observe or judge how management does its job. As was observed in the discussion on the organization of hospitals, the business principles of productivity and efficiency can clash with the practice of professional nursing care.

The National Labor Relations Act prohibits certain unfair labor practices once organizing in a hospital begins. An employer cannot engage in interference, domination, discrimination, or refusal to bargain. Nevertheless, there are ample opportunities for hospital management to hamper or "bust" a union.

Before 1983, Medicare allowed hospitals to include antiunion expenses in their bills. Hospitals, like private industry, have hired high-priced, antiunion "industrial relations" firms to coach management in techniques to quickly detect prounion sentiment. Although within the letter of the law, this practice demonstrates the fine line between legal and illegal activities. During the 1982 nurses' strike, the San Jose hospitals employed one such firm at great expense to the hospital to diffuse the strike and defeat the union. One wonders why that same money was not used to compensate nurses, to improve working conditions, or to introduce positive approaches to shared governance (Porter-O'Grady, 1984) and conflict resolution.

Hospitals can employ a number of measures to diminish the impact of a work stoppage by registered nurses. One organizational tool is reshuffling the levels of nursing administration to increase the layers of nurse managers. The traditional charge nurse is given a midlevel management title, which necessitates her removal from the bargaining unit as a supervisor. This cushions the hospital in the event of a professional nurses' strike by making more management-level personnel available to give nursing care.

If a strike is called because of an economic impasse, the employer is permitted to replace those nurses on strike. (The employer, however, is not entitled to replace employees when a strike is called over unfair labor practices.) A whole cadre of nationally mobile scabs (workers who cross a picket line to break a strike) has been flown from striking hospital to striking hospital to keep the hospitals operating. The ANA has called for formal sanctions against the agencies which provide these strike-breakers, and files are being developed in anticipation of unfair labor practice charges. As the market for nursing positions becomes tighter, nurses who strike may indeed find themselves without jobs, as did the striking air traffic controllers.

Employers are using new bargaining trends to squeeze the labor sector. Give-backs are increasing, in which previous gains in contracts are reduced or removed. Health insurance coverage and pension plans constitute two identified targets. Another popular tactic is to create a two- or three-tiered contract that gives new hirees less in wage formulas or benefits. This weakens a union by dividing contract workers.

Nurses who perceive their professional association as unable to help them compete in the workplace, or who have a limited affiliation with the professional association, will select a competing union, if given the opportunity. Organizing drives in a hospital takes time and money, and it has been apparent that the parent national trade unions such as United Federation of Teachers, 1199, and AFL-CIO have underwritten many attempts to organize nurses. In an era of externally induced labor difficulties, the unions have begun to recognize the futility of aggressive competition. This by no means implies noncompetition among the unions, but there is an obvious move for hospital unions to combine their strengths to withstand employer and government erosion of union status. They do not advocate formal merging, but they acknowledge the united front. Respect for the work done by another union and careful observance of work stoppages by either party can lead to mutual respect. One hospital workers union was instructed during 1983 nursing negotiations to respect the nurses' picket lines if a strike was called. To reciprocate, nurses joined hospital workers' picket lines when their union called for a strike. There have also been suggestions for simultaneous negotiations, with contract expirations for all bargaining units in a hospital coinciding. In the event of impasses, work stoppages could have a significant impact on an employer.

WHAT LIES AHEAD

The widespread shortage of nurses of the 1960s and 1970s is over and has been re-placed by the maldistribution of nurses by location, type of nurse, and work setting. Other than the persistent maldistribution of nurses in some inner city and rural areas, hospital positions are generally filled. In fact, there are now hiring freezes and layoffs as hospitals adjust to prospective payment systems. An index of nationwide trends in nursing employment found a 33 percent decrease in advertising from February 1982 to February 1983 (*Facts About Nursing*, 1983).

There is serious concern among the nursing community that in the interest of cost containment, hospitals will reduce the amount of money available to deliver nursing care. Serious deterioration of staffing patterns will result. There is also concern that hospitals will attempt to economize by substituting less qualified personnel for the de-livery of care. The ultimate irony would be for the hospitals to adopt any of these personnel-related, cost-cutting mechanisms, since it is extremely unlikely that in the long run the care would become more efficient. Studies confirm the cost and quality benefits of staffing with professional nurses and professional nurse coordination of an-cillary personnel (Halloran, 1983).

Hospitals are already reducing nursing staff, both in real numbers and in making nurses responsible for more nonnursing functions such as transport, clerical duties, and cleaning. Some hospitals want to employ new graduates in place of veteran nurses. It can only be assumed that the hospital expects the new graduates to accept lower sala-ries, be more easily shaped in the image the hospital wants, and be less likely to be affiliated with a union or nursing association. From a job security standpoint, seniority language will provide division of the available work among the most experienced nurses. This does not address the question of who determines how much work there should be, but will permit a fair policy that will retain the skills and the voice of the experienced nurse.

An equally ominous trend in the health care industry is the growth of the corporate-owned, chain-operated hospital. The for-profit hospital is not new, but hospital chains owned and operated by sizable corporations have appeared since the 1960s. The corpo-rations claim that they can operate a hospital at 30 percent to 40 percent less than the nonprofit hospitals. They are unique in their ability to raise capital funds. In the for-profit hospital, as in no other, is the stated intent of high patient selectivity. Hospital management in the for-profit sector makes no secret of its desire to care for the well-insured, private patient, shuttling the indigent and aged to voluntary hospitals.

There is no indication of any role for the key providers of care—the nurses—in corporate policy making. Nurses must be attuned to the proliferation of corporately owned hospitals and strengthen themselves in anticipation of more conversions.

The Reagan Administration has set an antiunion, promanagement tone, blatant in its disdain for organized labor. The National Labor Relations Board (NLRB), the quasi-judicial agency that arbitrates labor-management disputes, has been on an ag-gressive, conservative-backed program to reverse previous NLRB precedents consid-ered prounion. As of December, 1983, Reagan appointees had gained a majority on the NLRB, and the chair, Donald L. Dotson, was an outspoken union antagonist.

Also at issue is the backlog of cases before the NLRB, capped at 1,700 by early 1984. The backlog and long delays prior to hearings weaken union organizing, because the worker at risk for unfair labor practices by the employer is virtually unprotected for long periods of time. The decision that an employer can ask employees about their union sympathies as long as it isn't coercive further weakens workers' rights. Coerciveness is indeed in the eyes of the recipient, and such questions in an employment interview can seriously jeopardize its outcome.

In the beginning of this chapter mention was made of the 1985 NLRB ruling against the New York State Nurses' Association at North Shore Hospital because of the inclusion of managers as members of the association. This finding may put at risk, even in nonbargaining areas, nursing associations as collective bargaining agents. It is predicted that nursing associations will have to go beyond their present efforts to insulate collective bargaining activities from the challenges sure to follow. Proportional governing bodies may grow in popularity and could be a boon to staff nurse participation in organizational direction setting. The ratio of staff nurse members in the organization would match the ratio of staff nurses on association governing bodies.

Another agency influenced by the Reagan administration is the Equal Employment Opportunity Commission (EEOC), an arm of the Department of Labor. By late 1984, over 200 sex-based wage discrimination cases awaited consideration by the EEOC. At question, in part, is whether the EEOC has jurisdiction over sex-based wage discrimination. Indeed, there has been every indication, official or not, that the EEOC does not intend to pursue wage discrimination claims.

Another antilabor influence is the nationwide restriction of bargaining activities imposed on nurses employed by the Veteran's Administration (VA). Following two recent decisions by different circuit courts of appeal, the VA has limited the scope of what is negotiable. These limits essentially gut the intent of a collective bargaining agent and have led, at least in Southern California, to disruption of representation by the California Nurses' Association.

Nurses who are not organized for collective bargaining purposes should examine their work setting. If collective bargaining could improve the lines of communication and management authority, benefit packages, or practice controls, contact the state nurses' association and explore the possibility of an organizing campaign. Organizing and retaining nurse interest in collective bargaining is a serious and strenuous undertaking. What is important, though, is the collective nature of such organizing, and the benefits and protections received by all nurses strengthen nursing and reduce the pressures on each nurse.

The multipurpose functions of the professional nursing association will preserve the future of nursing. This chapter cannot stand alone, nor can the nurses in the workplace stand alone if they are to offset the forces that negate contributions of nursing. Political action and lobbying, research, and education are necessary to further the cause of nursing and the public. Nursing education must accept responsibility for preparing students at entry and advanced levels to participate in the politics of the country and the health care industry. Collective action must be promoted by words and actions. Educators who shun the nursing organization do their students and the profession a great disservice. Nursing administrators also must affiliate themselves with the nursing community. The time for a "we" and "they" mentality is over, for there will be no "we" if every nurse or group of nurses tries to stand alone. And practicing nurses must overcome the isolation of their unit or individual shift. Let us unify our skills, knowledge, and numbers to succeed.

References

American Nurses' Association activities. *Am J Nurs* 1946; 46:728–30.

Annual salary review: A national roundup of 1984 nursing salaries, plus a forecast for 1985. *Am J Nurs* 1984; 84:153.

Becker E, Sloan F: Union activity in hospitals: Past, present, and future. *Health Care Financing Rev* 1982; 3:1–13.

Beletz E: Organized nurses view their collective bargaining agent. *Superv Nurse* (Sept) 1980; 11:39–46.

Benner P: From novice to expert. *Am J Nurs* 1982; 82:402–7.

Brett J: How much is a nurse's job really worth? *Am J Nurs* 1982; 82:877–81.

Cleland V: Taft-Hartley amended: Implications for nursing—the professional model. *J Nurs Adm* 1981; 11:17–21.

Eldridge I, Levi M: Collective bargaining as a power resource for professional goals. *Nurs Adm Q* 1982; 6:29–40.

Facts About Nursing. American Nurses' Association, 1982–1983.

Gideon J: Unions: Choice and mandate. *AORNJ* 1980; 31:1201–7.

Halloran EJ: RN staffing: More care-loss cost. *Nurs Manag* (Sept) 1983; 14:18–22.

Huey FL: Looking at ladders. *Am J Nurs* 1982; 82:1520–26.

Institute of Medicine, Health Care Services, Nursing and Nursing Education Committee: *Nursing and Nursing Education: Public Policies and Private Actions*. National Academy Press, 1983.

Jacox A: Collective action: The basis for professionalism. *Superv Nurse* (Sept) 1980; 11:22–24.

Juris H, Maxey C: The impact of hospital unionism. *Mod Healthc* (Dec) 1981; 11:36–38.

McCarty P: Monograph describes progress in women's fight for equal pay. *The American Nurse* (Mar) 1984; 16:1, 15–16.

News and background information: *Labor Rel Rep* (May) 1984; 116:11–12.

No strike policy set aside in California. *Am J Nurs* 1966; 66:1897–1903.

Nurse membership in unions. *Am J Nurs* 1937; 37:766.

Nurses association loses in election in unit based on disparity of interest test. *Health Labor Rel Rep* (Nov 12) 1984; 1.

Olson M: *The Logic of Collective Action*. Harvard University Press, 1977.

O'Reilly C: Comparable worth: Issues and perspectives ending sex discrimination in wage setting. Pages 150–55 in: *Proceedings of the Thirty-fifth Annual Meeting of the Industrial Relations Research Association*. University of Wisconsin, 1982.

Parlette GN, O'Reilly CA, Bloom JR: The nurse and the union. *Hosp Forum* (Sept–Oct) 1980; 23:14–15.

Porter-O'Grady T, Finnigan S: *Shared Governance for Nursing: A Creative Approach to Professional Accountability*. Aspen Systems, 1984.

Shramm C: Economic perspectives on the nursing shortage. In *Nursing in the 1980s: Crises, Opportunities, Challenges*. Aiken L (editor). Lippincott, 1982.

Stern E: Collective bargaining: A means of conflict resolution. *Nurs Adm Q* 1982; 6:9–20.

Stickler KB, Velghe JC: Why nurses join unions. *Hosp Forum* (Mar) 1980; 23:14–15.

Wieczorek, RR et al.: A Clinical Career Pathway, Part 1. *Nursing and Health Care* (Dec) 1982; 3:533–35. Part 2, *Nursing and Health Care* (June) 1983; 4:318–21.

Yett D: *An Economic Analysis of the Nursing Shortage*. Heath, 1975.

Contrasting Politics: Hospital Bureaucracy and Shared Governance

Timothy Porter-O'Grady, RN, EdD

Nursing has struggled to survive as a profession within bureaucratic institutions. Sixty-one percent of American nurses work within hospital institutions (Rowland, 1984). Therefore, the vast majority of nurses operate within the constraints of bureaucratic governance systems.

BUREAUCRATIC STRUCTURE

The characteristics of a bureaucratic structure have remained essentially unchanged from those defined by Frederick Taylor (1911). The descriptors for the bureaucratic organization are: hierarchical, controlling, vertical communication channels and defined authority base, structured organizational chart, administrative governance, pyramided levels of accountability, and a strong policy base. All efforts must support the bureaucratic organization and provide for its integrity. To survive, the worker must operate within these constraints.

The problem is, however, that those definitions that most clearly articulate nursing professional practice—consultive, collaborative, having a scientific base of knowledge, judgment rendering, having a lateral communication network, developmental, standard-centered, having measurable practice and interdependent relations—generate entirely different needs and behaviors than those associated with the bureaucratic organization. The struggle has been to bring the characteristics of bureaucratic organizational design and those of professional practice together. The struggle has been rife with difficulties.

Power Structure

In the bureaucratic organization, the power structure is generally defined within the context of individual authority. The authority for decision making and problem solving rests with identified individuals, usually within management. Functions are clearly separated. There are those that manage and those that are managed. Therefore the managed must perform or carry out obligations determined for them by the manager. There is also a clear differentiation between management accountability and worker accountability. The bureaucratic organization is structured on the manager's accountability to see that work results in some measurable output. The individual accountability for defining, outlining, and specifying the work rests with the manager, not with the individual who does the work.

Task Orientation

Since bureaucratic organizations focus on production and productivity, much of the activity that is valued is task centered. Completion of specific tasks results in some measurable output. In the case of nursing practice, the number of nursing tasks that are accomplished in a day is equated with positive, patient outcomes. Therefore, the focus of the worker is narrowed to those tasks the institution values and believes are essential to facilitate the output of the organization. Often the tasks themselves have been determined and outlined by others than those who must carry them out. For example, physicians provide the medical framework that determines many tasks that are carried out by nurses. Regardless of how carefully nursing identifies its own characteristics in relationship to these tasks, the primary motivation, construction, and obligation of the institution in a bureaucratic framework falls within the administrative and medical models. This is a key nursing concern about hospital bureaucracies.

Nursing Within a Bureaucracy

The bureaucratic hospital leaves the individual worker—in this case the professional nurse—with few opportunities to influence the mission, goals, and objectives of the institution. In fact, the professional nurse becomes a part of the process of fulfilling goals and objectives determined by others, specifically the managers who oversee the bureaucratic framework. The nurse becomes a part of the process, rather than a key contributor to the establishment of the organization's agendas, policy, planning, and productivity—all roles currently assumed within the management context.

Within the bureaucratic structure, which most hospitals represent, individual nurses experience impotence and isolation. They have little or no control over the circumstances of their practice, the direction of the institution, the key decisions that affect patient care. They are rarely placed where they can use their position, power strategies, negotiation skills, and special knowledge to make needed and appropriate changes in the structure that governs their work. Their only option is to work with key management individuals to whom they report to make significant systems adjustments.

In this relationship, professional nurses operate in a "Catch-22" situation. They can identify the concerns, issues, processes, and constraints in nursing practice and undertake action to correct them. Because of location in the organization, however, they are distanced from the power positions essential in making changes to improve nursing practice. The bureaucratic structure supports this daily frustration in hospitals across the nation, regardless of the goodwill of those who hold management positions in the bureaucratic structure.

The individual nurse is continually subject to the conflict between bureaucratic needs and professional delineations. The dissonance produced by this conflict fosters powerlessness in the nurse and diminishes the interaction between practitioner and manager. It limits colleagueship and collaborative relationships. It prevents nursing accountability, maintaining the "us/them" conflict between manager and nurse. It also focuses attention on task rather than accountability for nursing practice.

SHARED GOVERNANCE

In a shared governance organizational framework, the principles and rules provide a decision-making framework that articulates the best interests of nursing. Shared governance describes a political, social, and organizational framework that permits:

- consensus decision making;
- sharing accountability among professional practitioners for issues related to professional practice and its outcomes;
- full participation in determining and influencing the goals and objectives of nursing practice in the institution;
- development of collaborative structures based on relationships rather than organizational locations. Collaboration and interaction assures peer interaction and communication across all clinical specialties;
- movement of control of decision making from central management to the nursing staff as a corporate body. (Decision-making processes are centered on the professional nurses' practice);
- an articulation of the practice of nursing and its impact on the mission of the institution. This is expressed not only in clinical practice, but in governance activities that affect the institution (Porter-O'Grady & Finnigan, 1984, pp 75–105).

Shift in Power

Shared governance shifts organizational power and requires a major commitment by the organization and its leadership. Nursing administrators must recognize the political reality that means the broader the power base, the stronger the power. When the power in the nursing division of an institution rests with key individuals, that power does not necessarily extend beyond those individuals. When the power of an organization, however, is spread throughout the organization and a larger number of individuals share in it, that power is broader and has stronger implications for the institution. Shared governance recognizes that reality and uses it in the best interest of the institution and professional nursing practice.

A Model for Shared Governance

Consensus models facilitate interaction essential for professional practice and organizational decision making. In shared governance, there is individual accountability for defining the roles, responsibilities, and mandates. Accountability is more uniquely experienced by nurses when they participate in decision making and practice knowing that peers share in practice decisions.

The professional nurse plays an individual and collective role in creating, maintaining, and, at times, expanding the power base. Nurses feel stronger ownership of the outcomes of decisions made by the staff through its governance structure. This ownership of decisions provides stronger commitment to the roles and responsibilities of nurses. When decisions, rules, mandates, and processes have been outlined by peers, and the quality assurance and compliance mechanisms have been structured by those peers, ownership of their outcome can be more broadly spread among the professional staff. The system begins then to reflect those professional characterizations that identify the collaborative, communicative, and interactive professional practice. Since these professional behaviors are evident in the political and power arena, nurses become more visible in the practice environment. In comparison with the traditional bureaucratic organizational framework, shared governance enhances the potential for nurses to experience successful collaborative relationships.

Outcomes of Shared Governance

The ultimate result for the practitioner is an altered professional self-image evidenced not only by the opportunity to participate, but by the expectation that governance will be provided by peers through an organized, defined, shared governance framework. The demand of shared governance, on the other hand, is that it depends on the individual nurse for success. Solving problems, identifying options, taking action, undertaking corrective behavior, and improving practice no longer rests with management, but with the professional nurse, individually and collectively with peers. The political, social, and practice opportunities for nursing are expanded.

Much of politics is related to the image projected to those whose view is significant to an individual's or group's success. One of the major historical problems in nursing has been the dissonance between what nursing believes and what nursing practices. Shared governance changes the self-image of nurses by providing broader participation and responsibility in governance. The individual assumes activities beyond clinical care as a part of professional practice. While patient care is the central component of nursing activity, it is not the full scope. The largest portion of nursing activity may occur someplace other than at the bedside. Is it not as significant to be involved in legislative, political, social, and institutional affairs that influence the practice in the institution as it is to do "hands-on" nursing care? Shared governance demonstrates the key positioning, independence, capability, and power of nursing within the health care arena. The obligation for assuring that this occurs, however, lies within the institutional framework and the value system of nursing practice. When the governance structure is in place and operating effectively, representing the best interests of nursing and patient care, a stronger position of power and accountability exists. This situation also creates some internal demands.

When the practicing nurse assumes control and authority for her practice, major political and social changes, led by nursing, will be successful. The adoption of shared and self-governing strategies can foster such change.

References

Porter-O'Grady T, Finnigan S: *Shared Governance for Nursing.* Aspen Systems, 1984.
Rowland H: *The Nurses Almanac.* Aspen Systems, 1984.
Taylor F: *The Principles of Scientific Management.* Harper and Brothers, 1911.

Nonunionized Collective Action: The Staff Nurse Forum

Norma L. McKay, RNC
Walter A. Lumley, RNC, BSN

In 1982, the staff nurses at Philadelphia Veterans Administration Medical Center (PVAMC) were not unionized. Our main objection to unionization was that it would not allow professional nurses to regulate their own practice. We wanted to be part of decision making, and we wanted to practice knowing that the nursing administration was backing us. Poor morale, however, was causing us to look for some means of bargaining.

Historically, staff nurses have viewed administration as "the enemy." If nurses had unionized, the "us against them" attitude would have remained, and nothing would have been solved. We needed a new approach.

PVAMC is a 479-bed facility with full outpatient services and two medical school affiliations. This dual affiliation was the source of many problems. Because of the rapid turnover of medical and surgical staff, including students, residents, and interns, the nursing staff had to deal with new physicians as often as every three weeks. Since this is a government hospital, the rules and regulations differ from private sector hospitals. Because the physicians were from different schools, the medical ideologies were also different and many times conflicted with hospital policy. This put staff nurses on the firing line, and many of us quit. Frustration with hospital and nursing administration was also a major problem.

In defense of the administrators, 1982 was a year of transition for the hospital's administration as well. Many nurses became discouraged because they did not have the stable administration they needed. Because of this, many nurses made only half-hearted attempts to solve problems. Soon the method of dealing with problems became grumbling and complaining, symptoms of our sense of powerlessness. We needed a way to constructively channel nurses' energies and alleviate the tension and frustration that were leading to staff dissatisfaction. Nurses needed a greater role in decision making at the medical center, particularly with regard to issues that concerned patient care and the nurses' own professional standing.

Our chief of nursing service set up a series of workshops with a nursing consultant in an attempt to solve some of these problems. These workshops led to consciousness raising with regard to nurses' professional authority, autonomy, and accountability.

THE IMPETUS FOR CHANGE

The workshops had a positive effect. Within a few weeks informal meetings were started among staff nurses. In the next three months, another set of classes was held, and more staff nurses began to attend the meetings. Discussions at these meetings concentrated on communication.

To give the meetings some structure, staff nurses elected officers, and each nursing unit elected a representative. In time, the newly formed group was called the Staff Nurses Forum (SNF). Because communication was the issue, the first few meetings focused on staff nurses' need for a way to get policy information firsthand. To this end, we nominated and elected a representative to the nursing executive board, a group of upper-level management personnel from the nursing department, which establishes nursing policy and sets standards for care. The nursing administration accepted the representative, and for the first time a staff nurse had input.

With this success, we decided to obtain a more legitimate status for the SNF by requesting on-duty time for meetings. What we received was more than we expected. We not only obtained the time requested, but also a permanent meeting room and compensatory time for anyone who attended the meeting on their own time. The SNF was off to an excellent start.

ACHIEVING GOALS

Our first goals were set in the summer of 1982. They were three simple, short-term goals—or so we thought:

1. develop a safer environment in our parking lot
2. improve the staff's access to inservice education
3. create space for a nurses' lounge.

Our first goal was met quickly. After a SNF meeting where parking lot safety was the main topic, we drafted a memo to the hospital director through the chief of hospital police. This memo listed the number of cars stolen or damaged. We made suggestions to improve lighting, to increase police patrols, and to trim the trees that blocked the view of the surveillance TV cameras. This memo resulted in increased patrols by police during the day, new lighting in the lot, and the large trees being trimmed. The hospital director instructed the police to provide escort service to all personnel leaving the hospital after dark.

Our second goal of making nursing education more accessible was handled within nursing service. Our inservice education department does an excellent job with mandatory classes, but it is unrealistic to expect it to provide all the education needed for each nurse. To remedy this, the SNF started a cassette library for nursing personnel. Staff nurses in specialty areas were asked to tape an inservice lecture on their specialty, ie, nursing care of the diabetic, hypertensive, dialysis, or critical care patient. These audiotapes were kept on a centrally located nursing unit. Nursing service personnel could sign out a tape for inservice on the unit or for personal use. The SNF also provided information on the use of the hospital library including the MEDLINE computerized literature search, and shared pamphlets on pending workshops and patient education materials. Our biggest problem was convincing staff nurses that they could have an inservice program whenever they had time. At each SNF meeting, the officers stressed compliance with the nursing office memorandum regarding monthly inservice, which these tapes would satisfy.

Our third goal of creating a nurses' lounge met with what can be best described as passive aggression, not by nursing service, but by hospital administration. The hospital administration did not know how to handle the SNF. Should they treat the SNF as a bargaining unit, a threat, or a wayward child? Our first break came when the hospital director agreed to meet with the SNF officers. After the meeting, our course was set. We knew we had to dispel the perceived threat. For the next year, we concentrated on developing support within the nursing service department and the hospital.

DEVELOPING SUPPORT

There are many ways to develop support. We decided to begin with basic interpersonal techniques. If the work atmosphere is congenial, support is easier to obtain. A hand-shaking campaign was launched. Nurses were asked to shake the hands of administrators, new physicians, or other personnel who entered their unit. Any meeting with hospital officials was preceded and ended with a handshake. This was hard for many women. Nurses were encouraged to practice with each other until they developed the skill of shaking hands. When they finally began to shake hands, the treatment they received proved to be more professional and reinforced the behavior.

In March 1983, the SNF took on the task of bringing departments together at social occasions. We planned to raise money with a cake sale, a flea market, and a food festival. The money raised from the cake sale was used to fund a celebration for National Nurses' Day. The flea market and food festival were used to sponsor a hospital-wide picnic in August 1983. These activities took many hours of planning, but the benefits are evident today. The social activities provided an opportunity for networking by SNF members. Cooperation between staff nurses and other departments has increased. Problems among departments are now solved on a professional basis. Complaints are minimal and viewed as constructive criticism.

The officers of the SNF were also active in developing liaisons with hospital police, the engineering service, the building management (housekeeping) service, and the medical administration (clerical) service. These liaisons provided an unofficial pathway in an official government agency. A problem can be unofficially discussed with a service chief before the official steps are taken. For example, the hospital carpool spaces were being used by persons who did not meet the criteria for them. Many nurses who wanted to carpool were unable to obtain a space. Filing formal complaints in the past had been futile. The SNF vice-president and the hospital police chief began informal discussions about how nurses could help the police monitor the situation. In a bureaucratic setting, what seems easy is usually complicated. Every special interest group in the hospital was blaming the police for not managing the parking lot more closely.

The nurses found out that the police were understaffed and that the requests for additional staff had been unanswered. The SNF sent memos to the hospital director supporting the police, and documenting the date, time, and license number of illegally parked cars. Dates and times when nurses had to leave the hospital at night without proper escort were also noted.

The official results of this unofficial collaboration included:

1. Two additional hospital police officers were hired.

2. Carpool spaces were reassigned. Applicants had to provide: (a) proof of address; and (b) proof of shift assignment. (All carpool people must be on the same shift.)

3. Parking spaces were provided for subcompact cars, increasing carpool spaces from 47 to 60.

4. The parking lot, which was full by 7:15 am, now had empty spaces at 7:45 am.

The police got what they needed, and the SNF got the parking problem solved.

Another example of the SNF's collaboration with other departments involved meetings with the chief of building management service to streamline the procedure to identify poor employee performance and to establish a mechanism to commend good performances of his personnel.

In other situations, nursing administration's assistance was elicited to develop formal policies to rectify problems the SNF had identified involving other departments. One such policy was developed in response to nurses being required to move large furniture as the hospital was remodeled. When informal communication with the appropriate department failed, the SNF enlisted the formal assistance of the chief nurse. A policy was written to discourage this practice.

FORMULA FOR SUCCESS

In all areas where change was needed, the SNF adopted the same approach. All plans for securing change included the following:

1. A professional presentation by a staff nurse officer to the official or body who could effect change.
2. Presentation of all the compiled facts.
3. Presentation of requests with two to four options from which the official could choose.
4. Another staff nurse in attendance to the meeting to corroborate what was said.

The following example illustrates how these principles were followed. A four-bed room on several nursing units had a door that was blocked open by an extra bed. This bed had to be moved to close the door in the event of a fire. All previous attempts to rectify this situation were answered with, "The bed must stay—nurses must be aware of the need to move the bed in the event of an emergency."

Presentation of Facts

This four-bed room occurs on 18 nursing units. Permanent removal of 18 beds is unacceptable because of patient needs. A potential hazard exists, however, in the event of an emergency. Personnel and patients could be endangered.

Recommendations and Options:

1. Move a bed out of each room.
2. Remove the door and install a new one that would open into the hallway.
3. Rearrange the furniture in the room to allow the door to be closed.

This information was presented to the hospital director and the nursing executive board by the SNF president and executive board representative.

Results. Option #3 was accepted. Beds were moved, and a potential hazard was averted. A systematic approach corrected the problem.

It has been said that nursing is in trouble because of a lack of unified effort from all nurses. To many, the answer is unions. To the staff nurses at PVAMC, it means that nurses must begin to work together using their professional knowledge of interpersonal relationships. We deal well with sick people, and we must learn to deal as well with healthy people. The SNF strives to channel random griping into effective change.

Certain guidelines are followed. They include:

1. Channel all complaints and/or problems through proper channels first.
2. If this fails, attempt informal contact and seek a mutually beneficial plan for change.
3. Develop a staff nurse task force of interested nurses to collect information on the situation under consideration.
4. Brainstorm in open forum to identify several options to be presented.
5. Have SNF officers look at options and decide:
   a. Which should be presented and in what order?
   b. Is the time ripe for change in this area?
   c. If we lose, how can the SNF turn the loss into a positive action?
   d. Who must be contacted?
      – formally
      – informally
   e. Who can we enlist in the fight?
      – medicine
      – engineering
      – nonprofessional union representatives
      – police
      – others

If the SNF decides to take on a project and the time is right, then an all-out effort is made to solve the problem. If the time is not right, however, the project can be put on hold and brought up at a better time. This is sometimes perceived by the general nursing population as inactivity. The officers must strive to educate the general staff nurses about planning for change.

THE FUTURE

The SNF at PVAMC is now several years old, and the primary goal to improve unity among nursing personnel has been accomplished. Complaining is still evident, but a mechanism for support is in place. Nurses know they can make changes.

Vignette: Vote Yes!

Helen M. Archer-Dusté, RN, MSN

In 1981, the City and County of San Francisco had multiple vacancies in acute care, public health, and long-term care nursing positions. In the spring of that year, the staff nurse negotiating committee brought the issue of understaffing to the bargaining table. This committee represented nurses from all of the city's health facilities and programs. Competitive salaries and benefits became the focal point of that year's negotiations.

An aggressive public relations campaign and a threatened strike strengthened the staff nurses' position. The city negotiating committee found its hands were tied by the salary standardization provision of the city charter. Under this clause, a benchmark is established for each occupational grouping after a survey of compensation for other public and private employees in that occupational group. Using this method, professional nurses consistently received lower compensation than the average when compared with other nurses in the Bay Area.

During the final negotiation sessions, a deal was struck. The nurses agreed to accept the maximum increases the city could offer under the current restriction, but with the proviso that the board of supervisors and the mayor would sponsor a charter amendment referendum on the November ballot. In addition, an inhouse recruitment and retention committee was established. After much politicking, the contract was ratified.

The charter amendment became the new focus for the emerging coalition of staff nurses. A strategy committee was convened in August, and the staff nurses requested seed money from their collective bargaining agent. An experienced campaign organizer was retained. The city's fire chief was invited to serve as the campaign's honorary chairman. This partnership proved invaluable; nurses were now viewed as being in the company of firemen and policemen. Firemen and policemen had been removed from the charter restrictions years before and bargained independently with the city.

The city attorney's office drafted the language for the charter amendment and the ballot proposal. The strategy committee approved the final ballot proposal that provided for removal of the registered nurse classifications from the salary standardization mechanism and setting of a new salary survey mechanism to look at the highest salaries and benefits paid to registered nurses in the Bay Area. Nurses and the city would then be able to negotiate up to this new ceiling of the highest compensation for comparable nursing positions throughout the Bay Area.

Now began the tedious work of fundraising and campaigning. The campaign theme was developed: "Quality health care: You're worth it." T-shirts, bumper stickers, and buttons were printed and distributed. Several strategies for approaching the public were successful. A blood pressure screening booth at the fire department's open house provided both a service and an opportunity to highlight the roles of city nurses. Leaflets encouraging a "Yes" vote on the proposition were distributed at all major shopping centers. Interviews and special focus news articles were developed and ran for approximately four to six weeks prior to election day.

In San Francisco, propositions, like candidates, can collect endorsements. We received tremendous support from Democratic organizations and ethnic groups, many of whom use the city's health facilities for their primary care. We did not win the endorsement of the major newspapers, the San Francisco *Chronicle* and the San Francisco *Examiner*. This was considered a blow to our potential success. We did get the endorsement of all the neighborhood newspapers and *The Progress*, a citywide paper that reports local news. We also obtained endorsements from the mayor, several members of the board of supervisors including its president, many well-known San Franciscans, and the California Nurses' Association.

Fund raising efforts focused on contributions from nurses, physicians, and pre-selected contributors in the community. A cocktail party was held for San Francisco General Hospital (SFGH) attending physicians who made average donations of $50 to $100 each. A raffle was held for all hospital employees. The mayor donated her contributor list and a special mailing was also done to all SFGH volunteers and prior donors. Finally, the head nurse group loaned us a lump sum of money, and individual nurses donated regular contributions.

Of particular concern was the large number of San Franciscans who don't use municipal health facilities as their primary care provider. This group also tends to be the homeowner-conservative group who votes regularly. They could make or break our campaign. A direct mail campaign to all San Francisco homeowners was done. The mailing highlighted the trauma center at SFGH and the nurses' roles on the trauma team. It was, quite frankly, the only service that many of this group of citizens could imagine getting from the city's health system. The message was the same: "Quality health care: You're worth it."

Election day came. No predictions could be made, though many experienced campaigners said we would lose. We won by a slim margin. Nurses are now free from the charter restrictions and bargain independently with the city. The salaries and benefits offered are now the second highest in the Bay Area.

The sense of power that this experience gave to each of us on the strategy committee has lingered. Many of us have gone on to address other concerns within the nursing organization. Staff nurses can have tremendous impact on the nature of their work environment through creative use of the political process.

Chapter 22

When the Workplace Is Academia

The Faculty Perspective

Sr. Rosemary Donley, RN, PhD, FAAN
Sr. Mary Jean Flaherty, RN, PhD

What political skills do deans and faculties of nursing need in the academic workplace? This chapter will explore the human and material resources available to schools of nursing in colleges and universities. Several principles have influenced the development of the ideas presented in this chapter.

1. The dean and the faculty of nursing cooperatively shape the image and define nursing as an academic discipline on the campus.
2. Nursing shares certain publics with the university. Neighboring communities, prospective students and families, boards of directors or trustees, accreditors, and representatives of various levels of government are important constituents in the academic workplace. Schools of nursing, however, also relate to other elaborate, specialized networks in hospitals, health agencies, state boards of nursing, and in professional and specialized associations. This complex array of "significant others" critically influences the development and expenditure of human and material resources within schools of nursing. The second set of public relationships is not well understood within the larger academic community.
3. Any serious discussion of political life within academia must consider the organizational structure of the university and nursing's place within it. In theory, an autonomous school of nursing, located on the main campus with the president, is more visible and powerful than a department or division of nursing located on a branch, professional, or health science campus.

4. Academic nursing is challenging because it bridges the political minefields of academic and clinical worlds.
5. Attention to political strategies within the academic workplace will improve nursing education and the care of patients and clients.

THE WORKPLACE

The academic workplace, described by these principles, is a two- or four-year college or university that offers a nursing program. The nursing unit may be a department, a division, or a school housed within a four-year liberal arts college, a junior or community college, an academic health center, a health science campus, or a university. Its sponsorship may be private or public. If private, it may be religious or secular in its organization. If public, it is operated by some level of government, usually the state or county. The nursing program may be associate degree, undergraduate (upper division or four year), or graduate. The school of nursing may be the only health-oriented program on the campus, one of several schools of the health professions, or one school of an academic health center. This discussion will not address hospital nursing programs.

The first political task of the dean and faculty is to analyze the place of nursing within the structure of the parent institution. The placement of nursing within the academic constellation is the most critical variable in the development of any strategic political plan. If data derived from an organizational analysis show that nursing is buried in an academic bureaucracy, the first, although by no means the easiest task, is to free nursing from the shackles of schools of medicine, departments of community health, or schools of education. Institutional reorganization may consume the tenure of several deans. However, unless faculties of nursing have direct access to academic decision makers and fiscal officers, their energies are diverted from nursing education and research.

THE PLAYERS

Any good analysis of the political world of academic nursing includes a description of the characters. Faculty, students, administrators, and support staff are the players in the academic workplace. Universities have well-established academic roles and hierarchies. These medieval patterns compete with less formal educational systems in American universities and colleges. One sign of the formal structure within universities is rank (instructor, assistant professor, associate professor, and professor). Initial appointment to faculty rank and subsequent promotion and tenure are contingent upon evidence of appropriate education and earned degrees; professional experience; good teaching; scholarly research productivity; and public, professional, and academic service. Each institution develops written and unwritten policies about the nature of the academic evidence, the weight assigned to each broad category, and the attention given to each line of the faculty member's curriculum vitae.

APPOINTMENT AND ADVANCEMENT

It is generally accepted that the traditional rank order of research and scholarly productivity, teaching, and service represent the criteria for appointment and advancement among academic nurses (Chater, 1983). Because scholarship, as represented by doctoral and postdoctoral study and research, has not characterized the nursing profession, nurses enter academia older, less prepared, and less socialized than their colleagues on the faculty.

The "publish or perish" requirement has particular meaning to nursing faculties. Many nurse faculty members are seeking academic credentials and building research track records. A national survey of baccalaureate and graduate faculties reveals that only 24 percent of nursing faculty hold doctoral degrees (AACN, 1983). The typical faculty member teaches basic students and spends at least twelve hours a week in clinical education in addition to other teaching, advising, and committee responsibilities (Dienemann, 1983). This picture of the modern Florence Nightingale does not resemble the philosopher-king, scholar-teacher immortalized by Plato. Discussions of political strategies and plans, however, must attend to the real players. Most contemporary members of the academic community are overachievers. Like women of all ages, nurse faculty try to prepare themselves for roles that have been thrust upon them. Usually they also provide for others rather than receive friendly support (Sheehy, 1976).

A major task of deans and senior faculty is to develop a blueprint for scholarly development for nurse educators. Scholarship requires the appointment of a competent, doctorally prepared faculty of an appropriate size and continuing negotiations about teaching loads, committee responsibilities, and student advising. Success in these negotiations may be the difference between mediocre education and academic excellence. In all these conversations, nurses as newcomers to academia and as women are in double jeopardy.

National studies criticize traditional disciplines for their slowness in promoting and tenuring qualified women (Baldridge et al, 1978). Because influential positions are given to senior faculty, tenured associate and full professors, academic nursing is several years away from having its members possess academic security. Although the literature bemoans nursing's failures in academia, it should be noted that there are 936 accredited nursing programs (ADN, BSN, MSN) in American colleges and universities (Vaughan, 1983). Nurses, the academic leaders of these programs, sit with other senior faculty on policy committees, councils, and forums.

ACADEMIC COALITIONS

The logical question of the political analyst is, "How does nursing gain more academic prestige within the system?" In an interesting comparative study of schools of nursing and faculties in eight professional schools and two departments in schools of arts and sciences, Dienemann (1983) found that the allocation of academic resources flows along traditional academic power lines, and that those nursing schools that earn high marks in research and educational grant procurement, alter the distribution of power within their institutions.

Equally provocative is the transcript of the 1983 meeting of the American Academy of Nursing. In a discussion of the merits of legislation to establish the National Institute of Nursing (NIN) at the National Institutes of Health (NIH), nursing's elite from education and practice debated the critical number of doctorally prepared researchers and the difficulties nursing would face in the NIH halls of science (American Academy of Nursing, 1983).

As nurses struggle for parity in the "halls of ivy," they face similar conflicts in the informal power coalitions. In an academic institution known to the authors, a small group of male administrators and senior faculty eat lunch together in the faculty dining room. The "lunch table" has become a symbol of the place where decisions are made. Being welcomed as a colleague on biomedical research campuses or eating lunch at "power tables" are examples of the symbols of membership in informal hierarchies within academia. As nurses struggle for presence as well as place, it is important to remember that credentials, money, or position alone do not entitle persons to membership in "the clubs," the informal political networks (Welch, 1980). This observation is as relevant in academia as it is among country club sets. Faculty who aspire to leadership in academic settings must earn credentials and acceptance. The acquisition of proper credentials—terminal degree, professional recognition of clinical knowledge and expertise, and broad-based clinical and educational experiences—is relatively straightforward. Acceptance in an academic community is another matter. How do academic nurses gain acceptance? Membership may be tied to seniority. For while universities have been around a long time, nursing became an academic discipline in 1919. The nurses prepared in the first university program, however, did not earn baccalaureate degrees (Dolan, 1973). Other explanations for nursing's invisibility in informal networks direct attention to the formation of political alliances. Leininger (1977) describes how faculties align themselves around intraprofessional issues as "amity-enmity complexes." Traditionally, schools of nursing and social work have emerged as allies, while medicine, dentistry, and pharmacy schools line up on the other side. It is significant that the antagonists are female- and male-dominated professions. It is also of consequence that in the paradigm outlined by Leininger, nurses are on the opposite side of the traditional power curve.

Timing is another factor to be considered in the study of academic coalition building. Acceptance within the academic community takes on new meanings during periods of ideological, financial, or organizational change. College administrators are planning for declining enrollments (Baldridge et al, 1978). Liberal arts colleges admit students who want to learn marketable skills as well as critical thinking. While health careers are still important to women, female students interested in health careers now choose among pharmacy, medicine, and nursing. These three trends indicate that academics in general, and schools of the health professions in particular, are in flux. Deans and faculties of nursing can use this period of transition to establish or solidify positive coalitions; articulate the goals of nursing with those of the college/university; develop mentor/consultant relationships with administrators and other academic deans; and participate in the academic and social life of the university community.

Another way of discussing coalition building is to examine networks. Perusal of the women's literature reveals that mentoring, sponsorship, and network building cross institutional boundaries (Kleiman, 1981). It is often said that nurse faculty are "buried" in schools of nursing, and that tunnel vision and introspection plague the profession.

Deans and senior faculty can reorient the faculty toward a more cosmic outlook. Prestigious faculties in successful schools of nursing have interdisciplinary, national, and international orientations. They are leaders on their campuses and in their disciplines. They exert influences on policies and programs.

Several years ago, when Hildegarde Peplau was president of the American Nurses' Association, she noted that nurses win battles for patient care at the bedside and lose them at policy tables (Peplau, 1971). This observation suggests that nurses identify major critical issues but choose parochial and individualized means to solve problems. Concerns about patient care or nursing education transcend individually oriented solutions and demand reform in social, political, and economic systems. Legislative awareness and political action are radically different approaches to advancing nursing's agenda. One striking observation about deans and faculty is that their political activity and influence are directed outside their schools and institutions. Modern nursing faculties are concerned more with changing nurse practice acts than teaching their texts. Progressive deans recognize that political action is a key to their relationships with the legislators. Student loans and traineeships, money to begin graduate programs, support for nursing research, and practice rights for nurse practitioners and midwives are illustrative of issues that require political action. Not only are nursing faculties mobilized to explain their positions in the chambers of legislators and Congress, but legislative and policy courses are part of nursing curricula.

RESOURCE ALLOCATION

No discussion of political activity can overlook the allocation of resources: space, money, equipment, and educational support services. Nursing's success in academia flows from the ability of its leaders (deans and chairpersons) to win some of the political battles over resource allocation. In these skirmishes, academic nursing does better if it has a recognized power base. Territorial ownership is associated with identity, survival, status, and prestige. In fact, when there are significant territorial differences between the school of nursing and other academic units, it becomes difficult for the dean to play in the academic power-authority arena (Leininger, 1977).

Space is accepted as a given until it becomes a personal issue, for example, when offices are divided to accommodate two or more faculty, or when university or nursing space is given to other more aggressive schools. We have observed the "hunting space syndrome" in hospitals, colleges, and universities. These casual walk-throughs "mark" space to be conquered in overt or covert battles. Leininger (1977) notes that this first appeared in schools of nursing during the sixties after federal monies became available for the construction of new nursing buildings. Prior to this period, other disciplines were not envious of the leftover and vacated spaces that had been delegated to nursing schools. Even if nursing did not need to protect its space from academic predators, changes within practice and education would force deans and faculties to acquire new space and to reexamine decisions about space allocation. For example, professional and personal goals to improve teaching and practice require the use of modern technology such as personal computers. Graduate students need seminar and/or conference rooms. Faculty and students need quiet places to analyze and discuss research data.

Nurses are good at improvisation. Power questions, however, are not about the cleverness of nurses in managing with less than desirable space. Rather, power is the ability to assert claims of ownership and to negotiate within academic power structures to advance nursing's agenda and goals. Larsen (1983) suggests that problems develop with effective nursing leaders in health agencies and schools of nursing because of gaps in understanding structures of power, opportunity, and education. Static curricula are one result of insufficient political knowledge and skill (Leininger, 1977).

A recent study funded by the W. K. Kellogg Foundation examined the role of the school of nursing in a health center. Allocation of space was designated as one of five most important areas of concern and one of the five most troublesome areas. This designation was given by deans of nursing schools and administrative officers in the health center (Morris et al, 1983). In hospitals, unresolved conflicts result in competition for "the best" clinical units among various faculties of nursing and arguments about rooms for clinical conferences and storage space for valuables, books, and clothing. In some settings, these arguments include access to special space (carrels, lockers, and study rooms) in health center libraries. Lack of space for faculty and students results in frustration and hostility in already overcrowded nursing stations and hallways. These territorial battles alienate faculty and students from their colleagues in practice.

Long-range planning for student placement in clinical agencies is essential for good working relationships and the accomplishment of educational goals. Sometimes deans and chairpersons must become involved. However, faculty members can bring major leadership to these discussions by knowing their students well, identifying their needs in clinical areas, and negotiating early with appropriate agencies.

Socialization of faculty members in "space psychology" is a complex matter because it places nurses in the complicated organizational systems of health centers, other health agencies, and universities. Senior faculty members can provide expert mentoring for younger faculty if the organizational climate of the school and its clinical agencies promote the value of such relationships.

Salaries

Another resource associated with power and status is salary. The American Association of Colleges of Nursing (1983) is the source of salary data for academic nursing. Its data, reported yearly, reflect differences by rank, type of school, location, and length of contract (academic or calendar). These data permit intraprofessional comparisons and give deans a national data bank to use in local negotiations. They do not tell deans or faculties where nursing faculty stand in their own institution or city. If the school of nursing is within a public institution, salaries by rank and school are public information. Private schools are more protective of salary data. Usually the dean or faculty in these schools know salary ranges by rank within and among schools. Pfeffer and Moore (1980) suggest that resource allocation, of which faculty salary is an important component, flows from enrollment and from "power shares." In their formulation, power shares include grants, faculty sex mix, faculty rank, and enrollment. Schools perceived to have power find that their faculties are better paid. In all discussions of academic salary, it must be remembered that salary lines in the budgets of schools of nursing are contingent upon the number of faculty, their rank, and the number supported by research and training grants. Schools of nursing have more than their shares of junior faculty. These junior members struggle with academic status, lower salaries, and fewer opportunities to improve their income and status through the acquisition of research grants.

Most savvy deans and faculty recognize that research productivity and grantsmanship are the keys to breaking into power circles. Few academic nurses, however, have strategized to achieve power and resources through the creative use of clinical and hospital appointments. If comparisons are drawn between faculties of medicine and nursing, it is clear that the resources given to medical schools flow more from research grants, educational contracts, and clinical practice plans than from tuition incomes. While academic nurses who provide patient care or consultation cannot charge directly for their services, nurse administrators and faculty need to explore new ways in which nurse clinicians can take more active roles in nursing education, and faculty can assume more responsibility for practice. It was suggested earlier that hospital and health agency liaisons might be used to support clinical scholarship and research. Faculty practice plans can also augment academic salaries. This option is not available to the faculties of arts and sciences. The opportunity to expand the clinical authority and responsibility of nurse faculty and to bring practice and research into the educator role gives nurses a unique opportunity to advance in the academic world.

Support Services

Other factors to be considered in resource allocations are euphemistically called "support services." This phrase includes secretarial services, access to word processing equipment, photocopying cards, computer time, research or teaching assistants, library resources, statistical advice, and editorial assistance. As a rule, schools with large enrollments and research grants capture more support services (Hennings et al, 1974). Failure to make educational and research support available, however, creates an academic "Catch-22." Without support services, it is difficult to recruit students and to compete successfully for research grants and educational contracts. Yet schools and faculties who lead in enrollment and research productivity also capture most of the "support services" on campus.

CONFLICTING VALUES

Political activity cannot be explained by examining structures and roles. It is important in any political analysis to examine the values operative in the workplace and the norms that motivate nurses. Relative newcomers to academic life, many nurses maintain strong bonds to their practice careers.

Concerns with status, tenure, science, and creativity conflict with traditional nursing values such as caring, service, and giving to others. Batey (1983) argues that self-expressive values have been more strongly associated with academic nursing, and humanitarian norms identified with nursing service personnel. While this dichotomy may be too extreme, beliefs about what is important influence decisions and career tracks. It is possible to find anecdotal support for Batey's position as service-based nurses seek the recognition and status associated with adjunct or clinical appointments in hospitals or health agencies, and nursing faculty seek joint appointments in practice sites. Values about self-promotion and service to others can be reconciled and shared. If they are unresolved, they create ambiguity in the work place. Ambiguity and guilt-ridden role negotiations interfere with full achievement of primary and secondary goals.

Confusion about academic values and service norms are not only evident in associate professors and chiefs of services but also appear when junior faculty and staff share roles or change their places of employment. Several years ago, a clinically competent and talented young nurse was recruited from a specialty practice area by a school of nursing in a large medical center hospital. Her responsibility was to orient and educate young students in the clinical specialty unit. Her motivation for the change in position was mixed. She was interested in advancement and saw an academic appointment as an important step in her career. She also believed that patient care in her specialty would be enhanced if students learned from a nurse who was clinically experienced. Transition from a hospital nursing service to academic nursing meant a change in status, weekday hours, and some independence and flexibility. Conflict in values arose when the new clinical instructor first appeared on the unit in a lab coat. She was immediately labeled the "lab nurse." To her, the lab coat symbolized freedom of place and time. The new instructor was not bound by a routine schedule or nursing unit boundaries. To her former colleagues, however, the white coat symbolized alienation from the clinical field. The new faculty member was unable to negotiate access to the clinical resources on the specialty unit. This true story is important for its symbolic display of values that caused disruption in an important colleague relationship.

Negotiation around values is less discussed in the literature than negotiation for power and position. Yet consensus about beliefs and the norms that influence action is more central than agreement about nursing's place within power structures.

Successful political action results in the power to make decisions about resource allocation (Donley, 1979). Nurses who seek power in academic settings need to clarify why they want this power. If promotion and tenure become an end rather than a means, academic nurses may have little to say in public arenas. If, however, the discovery, advancement, and dissemination of knowledge is the end, then tenure becomes a means to promote the well-being of others.

References

American Academy of Nursing: *Forum Discussion on the Institute of Medicine.* AAN, 1983.

American Association of Colleges of Nursing: *Report on Nursing Faculty Salaries, 1983–1984.*

Baldridge J et al: *Policy Making and Effective Leadership.* Jossey-Bass, 1978.

Batey M: Structural considerations for the social integration of nursing. Pages 1–12 in: *Outcome: Making It Work.* Bernard K (editor). American Academy of Nursing, 1983.

Chater S: Faculty practice considerations in academic health centers' schools of nursing. Pages 59–65 in: *Structure to Outcome: Making it Work.* Bernard K (editor). American Academy of Nursing, 1983.

Dienemann J: *Power Sharing in Universities: The Case of Nursing.* (Dissertation.) The Catholic University of America. Washington, DC, 1983.

Dolan J: *Nursing in Society: A Historical Perspective.* 13th ed. Saunders, 1973.

Donley R: A nurse's experience in Washington. *AORN J* 1979; 29:1270+.

Hennings CR et al: Structural considerations of intraorganizational power. *Adm Sci Q* 1974; 19:22–44.

Kleiman C: Does sisterhood stop at the top? *Ms* 1981; 9:100.

Larsen J: Leadership, nurses and 1980s. *Adv Nurs* 1983; 8:429–35.

Leininger M: Territoriality, power, and creative leadership in administrative nursing contexts. Pages 6–18 in: *Power: Use It or Lose It.* National League for Nursing, 1977.

Morris A, Hasting D, Crispell K: The role of the nursing school in the academic health center: Report of a study. *J Nurs Educ* 1983; 22:152–60.

Peplau H: Speech to Pennsylvania Nurses' Association, District 6, 1971.

Pfeffer J, Moore W: Power in university budgeting: A replication and extension. *Adm Sci Q* 1980; 635–53.

Sheehy G: *Passages: Predictable Crises of Adult Life.* Dutton, 1976.

Vaughan JC. Educational preparation for nursing—1982. *Nurs Health Care* 1983; 4:460–64.

Welch M: *Networking: The Great Way for Women to Get Ahead.* Harcourt Brace, 1980.

The Student Perspective

Helen M. Archer-Dusté, RN, MSN

Being a new student can be exhilarating. The challenge of learning, mastering new skills, and broadening one's perspective proves stimulating to most students. True learning is cultivated in environments where academic freedom prevails. Yet many academic institutions have become bureaucratic, with rules and regulations abounding. The student can easily become tangled in a web of confusion, leading to disillusionment and a sense of powerlessness. This chapter explores survival strategies the student can use for negotiating in the academic organization. First, the history of American nursing education and the evolution of the students' rights movement will be discussed. This will be followed by a pragmatic overview of action steps that build skills in academic survival.

AMERICAN NURSING EDUCATION

The first American training school for nurses, patterned after the Nightingale system, opened in 1873. The evolution of schools of nursing can be attributed to public demand for improved patient care. The dual purpose of the training of better nurses and the provision of an expanded nursing service within hospitals were best met by long working hours and excessive responsibilities for students. It was an apprenticeship method supplemented with occasional lectures (Bullough & Bullough, 1978).

The first lasting university-affiliated program began in 1909 at the University of Minnesota. The early establishment of university affiliation was championed for several reasons: (1) to enhance the leadership skills of nurses; (2) to strengthen student entrance requirements; and (3) to foster increased recognition and, in turn, endowment of nursing education (Bullough & Bullough, 1981).

Nursing education was further shaped by three commissioned investigations. The first, the Goldmark Report (Committee for the Study of Nursing Education) in 1923 called for: (1) increased financing of nursing education; (2) a reduced work week for student nurses; (3) separate governing boards for training schools; and (4) a change in focus from serving patients to educating students. The Burgess Report (1928) cited the need for standardization of the size and caliber of training schools, laying the foundation for accreditation. In 1948, Brown voiced the need to mainstream nursing education into institutions of higher learning.

Educational preparation is now available in a variety of settings, ranging from hospital-based diploma programs to entry-level master's and doctoral programs. Despite this diversity, common underpinnings are evident. Nursing education remains largely unendowed and underfinanced, especially when compared with other professional schools (Grissum & Spengler, 1976). A hierarchical structure prevails; a legacy that has fostered powerlessness in deans, directors, and faculty. Isolation from other disciplines has been the norm. Academic freedom and inquiry are relatively new concepts in nursing education. This history reflects the evolution of the profession from powerlessness and subservience to an emerging stature of power and self-definition.

THE STUDENTS' RIGHTS MOVEMENT

Prior to the 1960s, academic institutions functioned independently in the creation of rules and regulations affecting students' academic and private lives. "In loco parentis," the concept of schools acting in place of a parent or guardian, prevailed. Dissatisfaction with this led to several legal challenges by students. The courts began to point the way to an environment of open participation by students and faculty in academic life. This process has been reinforced by the changing characteristics of the student population and recent legislation (Limandri, 1981; Niedringhaus & O'Driscoll, 1983; Pollok et al, 1976).

Three fundamental rights were supported by the courts: freedom of expression (the First Amendment), the right to due process (the Fifth and Fourteenth Amendments), and freedom from illegal search and seizure (the Fourth Amendment). As a result, students began to be recognized as citizens first, and students second (Pollok et al, 1976).

In 1968, the American Association of University Professors and the National Student Association issued the "Joint Statement on Rights and Freedoms of Students" that elaborates upon these fundamental rights and academic freedom (American Association of University Professors et al, 1968). The National Student Nurses' Association adopted a students' bill of rights in 1969, and in 1974 authorized its implementation in schools of nursing (Blakely, 1975). The document outlines the rights of students including freedom to learn, the right to have a voice in curriculum determinations, freedom from prejudicial and capricious treatment, the right to privacy and to participate in academic policy making, and the right to due process (NSNA, 1975).

The American Nurses' Association also advocates student participation in its *Standards for Nursing Education* (1975):

1. Students participate with faculty in the identification of learning needs, in the evaluation of performance, and in evaluation of learning experiences.

2. Expected outcomes are explicated and communicated to students.

3. Systematic inquiry characterizes all learning opportunities provided for students.

4. Administrative organization assures student participation on committees involved with student welfare or rights.

Accreditation criteria of the National League for Nursing (1977a, 1982b) address the role of students:

> Students' rights and responsibilities are established and available in written form and are implemented through student-faculty-administrative relationships.
>
> 1. Exercise of the liberty to discuss, inquire, and express opinions is encouraged.
> 2. Channels for the receipt and consideration of student views and grievances are clearly defined.
>
> Although ultimate responsibility for the development and conduct of the educational program(s) in nursing rests with the faculty, channels are provided for student involvement in:
>
> 1. The development of criteria for admission, progression, and graduation.
> 2. Curriculum planning and evaluation.
> 3. Evaluation of teaching effectiveness and faculty selection and promotion.

The students' rights movement brought about much needed change in the atmosphere and policies of academic institutions. Students have moved from an adversarial stance to one of partnership with faculty and administrators. The provision for exchange among all members of the academic community is essential to active, responsible learning.

STRATEGIES FOR ACTION

With the appearance of this new partnership, the onus is now on the student to participate actively in academic life. Common concerns of students are: relevancy of the curriculum, fairness in grading, preparation and skill of the faculty, changes in the curriculum, administrative rules, and policies regulating student campus life.

The first process to be initiated is that of organizational analysis. What are the structure and the dynamics of the organization? Where do formal and informal accountabilities exist? What formal provisions for student participation are evident (ie, student government, membership on academic committees, liaison positions)? How receptive are key individuals, especially the dean or director, to individual student input? Who are the most vocal faculty? In whom do students appear to have a willing listener to hear concerns? One can glean this information from official school publications, conversations with other students, and interaction with faculty. Understanding the nature of the particular organization can strengthen one's involvement and potential for securing change.

Of equal importance is identifying a mentor. This person may be an assigned faculty advisor, another faculty member with whom one shares interests, or an upper classman. Mentorship has been discussed in detail in the feminist and professional literature (see Chapter 14). It is well recognized as a crucial component of success. The experience, wisdom, and reasoning of another can be tapped as a resource by the novice. The mentor can serve as a sounding board for both immediate issues regarding curriculum plans or course objectives, as well as those related to future aspirations.

Developing a network with other students can prove invaluable. Common concerns can be identified, joint grievances voiced, and corrective strategies planned. Fostering mutual support can enhance one's ability to cope with stressors. Networking can take the form of informal coffee sessions or planned support group meetings with a facilitator. School chapters of the National Student Nurses' Association provide the structure for such interactions. Participation beyond the school in state and national meetings and committees broadens the student's perspective and resources. Awareness of issues that affect all nursing students may have bearing on issues within one's own campus.

Academic rules and curriculum plans are now developed with student input. The opportunities for such input are limitless: membership on admission and curriculum development committees; completing evaluations of course content and instructors; membership on joint faculty-student-administration committees; participation in interdisciplinary committees of the parent institution; serving as a student representative to the academic senate, the board of regents, or board of trustees; and membership on special advisory committees on affirmative action, the status of women, or the disabled.

All of these ideas are proactive in nature. Selecting one or more of them for participation will empower the student in the academic community. Theoretically, open exchange among members of the academic organization precludes the escalation of conflict. This is not always realistic. What does one do when conflict arises?

Due process protects individual rights and liberties. The Fourteenth Amendment to the U.S. Constitution outlines the right to due process:

> . . . Nor shall any state deprive any person of life, liberty, or property without due process of law, nor deny to any person within its jurisdiction the equal protection of the laws.

Applied to academic life, due process assures that the student has a right to be notified of impending action and has a right to a hearing prior to severe disciplinary action being taken. It also implies that fairness and reasonableness have prevailed. Explore the facts and precedents related to the current situation. Discuss it with fellow students or faculty if appropriate. Approach the individual involved and attempt to negotiate one-to-one about the issue.

If the issue is significant, file a formal grievance through the process outlined in the school's handbook. If no grievance procedure is delineated, secure a copy of the guidelines for grievance procedures developed by the National Student Nurses' Association. Elicit the support of the student association and explore whether the concern affects more than one student. Above all, avoid overreaction or hyperbole in the discussion of the issue. Clarity, explication of the facts, and level-headedness will afford one greater respect and potential success.

Most conflicts between faculty and student can be resolved internally, either by formal or informal mechanisms. Should the institution fail to comply fully with due process, a civil proceeding can be initiated by the student. While the courts have been reluctant to address many of the questions related to rights in academic settings, proof of lack of due process has consistently resulted in rulings favorable to the student.

SUMMARY

We have explored students' rights strategies for survival in the academic organization. Active participation in the organization is the key to academic survival.

References

American Association of University Professors et al: Joint statement on rights and freedom of students. *AAUP Bull* 1968; 54:258–61.

American Nurses' Association Commission on Nursing Education: *Standards for Nursing Education*. ANA, 1975.

Blakely W: NSNA adopts guidelines for grievance procedures. *Imprint* 1975; 22:49+.

Brown EL: *Nursing for the Future: A Report Prepared for the National Nursing Council.* Russell Sage Foundation, 1948.

Bullough B, Bullough V: *The Care of the Sick: The Emergence of Modern Nursing.* Prodist, 1978.

Bullough B, Bullough V: Educational problems in a woman's profession. *J Nurs Educ* (Sept)1981; 20:6–17.

Burgess MA: *Nurses, Patients, and Pocketbooks.* Committee on the Grading of Nursing Schools, 1928.

Committee for the Study of Nursing Education: *Nursing and Nursing Education in the United States.* Macmillan, 1923.

Grissum M, Spengler C: *Womanpower and Health Care.* Little, Brown, 1976.

Limandri BJ: Academic procedural due process for students in the health professions. *J Nurs Educ* (Feb)1981; 20:9–18.

National League for Nursing: *Criteria for the Appraisal of Baccalaureate and Higher Degree Programs in Nursing.* NLN, 1977.

National League for Nursing: *Criteria for Evaluation of Diploma Programs in Nursing.* NLN, 1982a.

National League for Nursing: *Criteria for Evaluation of Educational Programs in Nursing Leading to an Associate Degree.* NLN, 1982b.

National Student Nurses' Association: Student bill of rights. *Imprint* 1975; 22:49–68.

Niedringhaus L, O'Driscoll DL: Staying within the law: Academic probation and dismissal. *Nurs Outlook* 1983; 31:156–59.

Pollok CS, Poteet GW, Whelan WL: Students' rights. *Am J Nurs* 1976; 76:600–03.

Recommended Readings

Ashley JA: *Hospitals, Paternalism, and the Role of the Nurse.* Teachers College Press, 1976.

Chaska NL (editor): *The Nursing Profession: A Time to Speak.* McGraw-Hill, 1983.

Heinert J: Why student rights? *Imprint* 1975; 22:48+.

Levine AH: *The Rights of Students.* Avon Books, 1973.

Ozimek D: Rights and responsibilities of students and faculty. *Imprint* 1982; 29:50+.

Chapter 23

The Politics of Nursing Research

W. Carole Chenitz, RN, EdD

Research is the systematic study of phenomena to generate knowledge. The purpose of research is to create or test knowledge.

In nursing, phenomena for study are based on the definition of the profession (Brink, 1983). In 1980, the American Nurses' Association (ANA) proposed that "nursing is the diagnosis and treatment of human responses to actual and potential health problems" (ANA, 1980). Nursing research, then, is the systematic study of human responses to health problems and their treatment. The purpose of research in nursing is to improve health care. To effect a change in health care, nursing must exert influence. Since politics is defined as "influence," nursing research is a political activity and has political implications. In this chapter we will examine the political nature of research at two levels.

The influence that nursing, as a discipline, has on health policy and the delivery of health care at national, state, and local levels is a result of many factors. Some major factors are image, organization, power base, and knowledge. Knowledge and the generation of knowledge depends upon research activity. The first part of this chapter will focus on the history and development of nursing research as a politically important endeavor.

While being a source of influence itself, research depends upon influence to obtain necessary human, financial, and other resources. Individuals and small groups of nurse researchers engage in politics with other nurses, researchers, technicians, and institutions such as schools and hospitals, private and public organizations, and government agencies. The second half of this chapter focuses on politics for the nurse researcher.

307

NURSING RESEARCH

The development of nursing research has encountered many problems and obstacles. Of this evolution, Stevenson (1979) notes:

> Despite slowness of growth, uneven quality, minimal quantity, questionable relevance, and disappointing lack of impact on nursing practice, it (research) has evolved. One would be hard put to deny that fact (p 38).

Research as a function for nurses dates back to Nightingale. Florence Nightingale kept accurate, detailed, and thorough descriptions of patient care in Crimea. She recorded and analyzed case studies and presented detailed statistical accounts. Nightingale used her descriptions of patient care, analysis of case studies, and statistics to influence change in health care based on research. She urged others to continue improving care of the sick through research (Grier & Grier, 1978; Knopf, 1978).

While Nightingale's advocacy of nursing research was ignored for the next half century, there were enormous changes in medical and health care. Hospitals, once isolated death houses, were now community institutions for cure and recovery. Finally, the growth of modern American nursing to provide care for the sick in hospitals was accomplished by the creation of hospital schools to train nurses.

In these schools, nursing education was based on an apprenticeship model. Nurses learned while they worked. Even during school, delivery of services was more important than formal education of the novice nurse (Ashley, 1976). Research in nursing was conducted predominantly by nonnurse social scientists. Nursing was considered a national resource of which an adequate supply was needed, particularly during times of war.

By the 1960s, advances in science and technology had affected all of health care. A broader knowledge base for nurses was required to transfer basic principles of science to the new technology. The development of allied nursing personnel after World War II, the relative scarcity of registered nurses, the increased technology in hospitals, and the rapid specialization and subspecialization of medicine meant that nurses were managers, teachers, and counselors as well as clinicians. At the same time, the social sciences had an impact on nursing. As Abdellah noted, "The social sciences challenge our ritualistic preoccupation with the prescribed physical care of the patient" (Abdellah & Levine, 1971, p 13).

In addition, sociopolitical events and ideologies of the times, ie, the Vietnam War and the civil rights and women's rights movements, sensitized nurses to problems in the health care system. Efforts to make change increased awareness of the relative political powerlessness of nurses, the largest group of health care workers. With awareness of powerlessness came the realization that change in health care could not be effected without changing nurses, nor could change be effected by nurses who were educated solely to meet the needs of the existing system of care.

This process of sensitization, awareness, and realization developed with close self-examination of the discipline. Nurses raised questions: What is the mission of nursing? What are the needs of people for nursing? What is our contribution to health care?

How can we best meet the needs of patients? Can people have direct and/or more equal access to nursing services? These questions presented no ready answers but generated discussion about control over nursing and the power needed to effect change. Issues of control and power lead to a course of action—the professionalization of nursing. As it has for other professions such as medicine, law, and religion, professional status for nursing would define its mission to society and create a system to fulfill that mission.

In 1965, the ANA position paper on entry into professional practice set forth the course of action that would lead to professionalization and change. By 1985, entry level for a professional nurse would be the baccalaureate in nursing. Other educational preparation would be considered "technical." Leaders in nursing concurred with Russell that "professional practice today calls for individuals who have a wide range of knowledge, keen intellect, and clarity of vision concerning human values" (Russell, 1960).

Universities offered the education that would provide nurses with a wide range of knowledge. By the time of the 1965 ANA position paper, a change in nursing education had begun. However, the movement from service to educational institutions, from apprenticeship to academia, and from a discipline to a profession had major obstacles. A basic characteristic of a profession, the possession of a body of knowledge in service to society, was lacking (Wilinsky, 1964). Nursing practice and education based on dogma, tradition, trial and error, and intuition did not stand up as a body of knowledge in universities. Only scientific knowledge developed and tested by research would provide this basic professional characteristic.

In the 1960s, nurses found themselves following the path blazed by Nightingale 100 years before. Theories about nursing were generated and nursing research was nurtured and developed. In this early stage, a philosophical ideology of "the patient as person" was espoused by nurses. As technology and specialization divided the patient into anatomical parts and systems, the social sciences increased nurses' awareness of the human side of technology. The patient was seen by nurses as a person with biopsychosocial needs that had to be addressed to reduce or prevent health crisis. Abdellah wrote, ". . . no single concept has greater significance for nursing research than that of viewing the patient as a person . . . research is needed to spell out the nurses' role in the electronic age and to protect the patient from becoming a part of the automation" (Abdellah & Levine, 1971, pp 11–12). Research in nursing would increasingly humanize health care. The driving force behind the development of nursing research was the belief that research could assist in developing a body of knowledge, and generate a science of nursing and theories about nursing that would establish the professional status of the discipline and enable nurses to have impact on the delivery of care and fulfill the nursing needs of clients.

In 1974, the ANA house of delegates passed a resolution:

WHEREAS, nursing lacks significant influence, power, and prestige because of its inability to specify its contribution to health care; therefore be it

RESOLVED, that the American Nurses' Association make a concerted effort to build a public image of nursing research as an essential contribution to knowledge in the health care field.

Downs notes, "the preceding statement points out other interesting and often ignored features associated with an increase in research activity: the close link between the use of scientific methodology and the establishment of professional credibility, influence, and power; and the ability to create and foster a new public image" (Downs, 1979, p 68).

The development of nursing research is intertwined with the professionalization of nursing, credibility, and public image. Through research, power and influence by nurses could be realized. The scope of nursing's influence and power is related to the image and credibility of the discipline.

Nursing research is a political activity because the knowledge generated by research is essential to professionalization. The image and credibility attributed to a professional group empowers that group to influence health policy and health care.

New Directions for Research

Over the last decade, research in nursing has seen quantitative and qualitative growth. There are three journals devoted to reporting nursing research. Clinical journals carry regular reports on research, and international, national, regional, and local research conferences for nurses abound. Research as a discipline is taught in undergraduate programs, and graduate students are expected to conduct a research project.

A 1984 report on nurses with doctoral degrees provided data on 3,650 nurses, or 3 percent of all practicing nurses. This group represents a cadre of "independent investigators prepared for scientific inquiry of phenomena relevant to nursing" (ANA, 1984, 1981).

As a result of the growth and development of research in nursing, interest in funding for nursing research has increased. The federal government is the largest sponsor of research. Hence, funding of nursing research at the federal level is a concern for the discipline. At present, the Health Resources Administration Bureau of Health Professions Division of Nursing, a branch of the U.S. Public Health Service (USPHS), is the agency primarily responsible for the allocation of federal funds for nursing education, research, and demonstration projects. Since the research funds within the Division of Nursing are limited, funding for nursing research by other agencies in USPHS is a current issue.

Funding of nursing research by federal agencies other than the Division of Nursing generated a major project conducted from 1981 to 1983 by Joanne Sabol Stevenson for the ANA in cooperation with several agencies of the USPHS. The purpose of the project was to "facilitate the review of draft proposals written by nurse researchers." Recent doctoral graduates were contacted, and 111 proposals from 106 investigators were submitted. The investigators were given feedback on their proposals from several agencies of USPHS. An analysis of the staff reviews at these funding agencies showed the proposals had four major focuses: studies of care (as opposed to cure); family as the unit of health care; interpersonal processes; and health promotion. These focuses are not new in nursing and represent priorities identified by the ANA Commission on Research in 1981 (Stevenson, 1983). Yet, these areas fell outside the interest, and hence, funding priorities of any agency within USPHS except the Division of Nursing. The implications of this finding is summarized by Stevenson: "This latter discovery has policy implications for the future development of an appropriate home for nursing research and the development of a stable and dependable funding base for nursing research" (Stevenson, 1983, p 7).

Currently, an effort has been launched at the national level by the ANA to create a National Institute of Nursing. This movement was generated by the desire within the discipline to achieve adequate funding and recognition of nursing science.

THE INDIVIDUAL INVESTIGATOR
AND THE POLITICS OF NURSING RESEARCH

Brooten (1984) summarizes the lessons she learned about the politics of nursing research. The first lesson was learned when a physician denied her access to his patients because she had failed to share her study with him before showing it to some of his colleagues. The lesson: "To avoid trouble . . . make every attempt to share proposed work equally with all clinicians if there is any chance you might be requesting access to 'their' patient" (p 318). The second lesson was learned when an up-and-coming young physician, who seemed envious of her research commitment, decided to be a roadblock to another study she was conducting. Lesson Two: "Pay attention to possible resistors who may limit access to the patient population and solicit their suggestions and comments." Her third lesson came when, much to her surprise, her colleagues on the institutional nursing research committee proved to be as difficult and obstructive as the physicians. Thus, Lesson Three: "The same process of neutralizing resistance has to be done with nursing colleagues."

Nurse investigators engage in political activity from the time they conceive of the problem to its completion. Political activity occurs on two levels: the content level and the technical level.

At the substantive or content level, the investigator pursues information and persons knowledgeable about the phenomena under study. Clinicians and researchers from many disciplines may need to be contacted or consulted about the question under study. For example, if a study about individuals' adaptation to genital herpes is contemplated, the nurse investigator must review published and unpublished reports, talk to clinicians, contact other investigators who can provide unpublished information that may be critical to the study, and work with technicians, statisticians, and other specialists. The investigator who is wise will recognize the political nature of such activities. The relationships and networks the nurse researcher builds with other researchers can influence her access to information and other resources.

The researcher must have knowledge about the phenomena under study to gain access to institutions. It is not unusual for nurse investigators to be questioned and challenged about the content of their study by members of institutional review boards or administrators. For example, a nurse investigator studying the effects of a cancer chemotherapy agent on quality of life must be able to speak knowledgeably about this agent and others, their effects, issues for oncology nurses, and quality of life for cancer patients. This investigator may be obliged to speak on these topics to nurse clinicians, administrators, physicians, and funding agency representatives, to name a few. Knowing the biases, special interests, and priorities of people who will be making decisions about the investigation can help the nurse researcher prevent or effectively handle obstacles that can arise. In addition, the nurse investigator must interact with a variety of people from different backgrounds to get necessary technical assistance.

For example, all nurse investigators need information about how proposals are reviewed by the Committee on Human Research. The Committee on Human Research is one type of institutional review board. The Committee on Human Research may be a subcommittee of a larger research and development committee in an institution (Robb, 1981). In a broad sense, institutional review boards (IRB's) are concerned with the initial review of a project. IRB's may be responsible for: 1) the protection of human subjects; 2) the review of the scientific aspects of research; and 3) administrative issues that will effect the implementation of research in a setting, such as resources used. The scope and focus of the IRB will depend on the institution. IRB's are most often composed of physicians, key administrators, other health care personnel and representatives from law, ethics, and the public. If nursing is represented on the IRB, it is most likely through the Director of Nurses. Nurse investigators seeking IRB approval must have the approval of the Department of Nursing and the head of the department in which the study is to be done. The approval of these persons in the institution produces supporters for the project on the IRB. The Chief of Staff is another key person in medical centers. Often, their approval is sought indirectly for the project by the Director of Nursing. Informal contacts and review by these persons allows them to raise questions about a potential project that can be answered prior to a formal review. Study procedures can be modified or clarified through this informal review that will facilitate approval at the formal IRB level. Supporters for the project can be secured in the agency.

To submit a proposal for review by this group, the investigator needs to know how long the review takes, what forms to complete, number of copies needed, different types of review, and who sits on the committee. An investigator not aware of the criteria may needlessly submit 15 copies of a proposal with appendixes for a study that may be eligible for the expedited review process. A committee may skeptically regard a researcher who is not aware of basic criteria. On the other hand, a researcher who complies perfectly with the criteria for proposal review can find herself frustrated when a powerful member of the committee, whom the researcher had not consulted prior to the review, finds a spurious objection to the study.

Like members of any committee, those on the IRB have personal and professional beliefs and values and are influenced by events and the times. Nurse investigators need to be aware that the conduct of research in nursing is relatively new (comparatively speaking). Research by nurses may be unheard of by some IRB members. In the review, it may be necessary for the nurse investigator to teach these members about research in nursing. Acting defensively or with personal sensitivity are to be avoided. The researcher strategically uses a scholarly, educational approach.

Formal and informal contacts with IRB members and administrative personnel can also be a valuable source of funding and funding information. For example, bequests and gifts are often made to hospitals. These gifts may have special requests by the donor, such as, geriatric research. Members of the IRB can alert the nurse investigator of these sources of funds and facilitate application for funding.

Research is thus an endeavor which, contrary to popular thinking, requires human interaction. For the individual researcher, this is what makes nursing research political.

The Nurse Investigator
and the Research Process

The basic essentials for research are: time, money, consultants and technical advisors, and an administrative structure that supports research. For nurse investigators to be successful, these essentials must be negotiated within an institution.

Most nurse investigators are educators or clinicians. Few nurses have full-time research positions. Most are employed in schools of nursing, hospitals, and other health care facilities. Therefore, the first political issue facing nurse investigators is perception of the nurse as investigator by herself, nurses, other professionals, administrators, and patients. The shift from a clinical or educational function to a research function is not easy. It is essential, however, if the nurse is to successfully assume a research role. There are few mentors or role models for researchers, and hence, nurses learn the research role through experience and trial and error.

A basic element in this role shift is whether the research role is valued. If it is not, there will be little motivation and commitment to conduct research. Werley (1974) notes that "nurses are concerned about 'doing' for the patient and apparently feel the need for immediate gratification to be obtained from patients. Delayed gratification, which is usually the case in research, seems to be held in less high esteem. The same might be said in regard to teaching and the more immediate gratification from students" (p 143). In this author's experience as a researcher and consultant to other nurses, the process of role shift and identity transformation cannot be ignored. Ultimately, the nurse clinician or educator can become comfortable in the role of investigator, usually during the course of the research process.

The next political issues are structural, such as: administrative policies for research by nurses employed in an agency; time; funding; and consultants or technical advisors. It is important to recognize that one or more of these may be lacking in an agency. The most common problem faced by nurses is lack of time to conduct research. Often, release from all or part of one's current responsibilities is not possible. Time becomes a political issue that must be negotiated. Release time may be nonnegotiable within an institution. The investigator will then need to work around the issues; this can try one's motivation and commitment to a project or the entire research process. A nurse may well ask herself, "Why am I doing this? No one seems to care. Why do I care?" This point is critical, may arise often, and cannot be ignored. The original motivation to conduct research can often supply the impetus to get over the immediate obstacle. Contact with other nurses and support from investigators from other health care disciplines can also be helpful. Interaction with other researchers can relieve researcher fatigue, decrease loneliness, and provide ideas for present and future ways to facilitate research in a given institutional structure. It is politically wise for the nurse investigator to reach out to other research-minded nurses for support.

Some strategies used by nurses to obtain structural support for research within institutions are: establishing a research committee; supporting graduate student research or graduate programs in the school of nursing; getting technical advice and research consultation from staff outside the discipline of nursing; using educational funds offered by the agency to attend research conferences, workshops, or classes; and developing contacts among local institutions to facilitate research among nurses.

Individual nurses may form research teams and divide up the work among several people. Nurses can plan projects that are low in cost (such as surveys), find non-nurse technical advisors on staff, and use time allotted for continuing education to take courses on research. Other strategies that can be used are to allocate personal time for research and seek institutional, professional, or private funding sources to pay for assistance and consultation.

CONCLUSION

We have examined the politics of nursing research for the discipline and the individual nurse. We have identified the conduct of research within nursing as a political issue. Research provides knowledge necessary to improve practice and achieve professional status. Through research, nursing can improve care of persons in need of health service and affect policy that directs the way health services are provided. For the nurse investigator, research is an ongoing process of acquiring content and technical knowledge and information. The researcher must interact with individuals and groups to carry out the study. Political wisdom is an integral part of the research act.

References

Abdellah FG, Levine E: *Better Patient Care Through Nursing Research.* Macmillan, 1971.
American Nurses' Association: *Social Policy Statement.* ANA, 1980.
American Nurses' Association: *Directory of Nurses with Doctoral Degrees.* ANA, 1984.
American Nurses' Association, Commission on Nursing Research: *Guidelines for the Investigative Function of Nurses.* ANA, 1981.
Ashley JA: *Hospitals, Paternalism and the Role of the Nurse.* Teachers College Press, 1976.
Brink P: What is nursing research? (Editorial.) *Western J Nurs Res* 1983; 5:113–14.
Brooten DE: Making it in paradise. *Nurs Res* 1984; 33:318.
Downs FS: Clinical and theoretical research. Pages 67–87 in: *Issues in Nursing Research.* Downs FS, Fleming JW (editors). Appleton-Century-Crofts, 1979.
Grier B, Grier M: Contributions of the passionate statistician. *Res Nurs Health* 1978; 1: 103–9.
Kopf E: Florence Nightingale as statistician. *Res Nurs Health* 1978; 1:93–102.
Robb S: Nurse involvement in institutional review boards: The service setting perspective. *Nurs Res* 1981; 30: 27–30.
Russell CH: . . . on a liberal education. *Am J Nurs* 1960; 60:1485–87.
Spross JA, Kilpack V, Marchewka AE: Committee evolution in a medical center. *Nurs Res* 1980; 30:30–31.
Stevenson JS: Support for an emerging social institution. Pages 39–66 in: *Issues in Nursing Research.* Downs FS, Fleming JW (editors). Appleton-Century-Crofts, 1979.
Stevenson JS: *New Investigator Federal Sector Grantsmanship Project: Final Report.* ANA Cabinet on Nursing Research, 1983.
U.S. Department of Health & Human Services, Public Health Service, Health Resources & Services Administration: *The Registered Nurse Population: An Overview from a National Sample of RNs.* November, 1980.
Werley HH: This I believe . . . about clinical nursing research. In: *Action in Nursing: Progress in Professional Purpose.* Lysaught J (editor). McGraw-Hill, 1974.
Wilinsky HL: The professionalization of everyone. *Am J Sociol* 1964; 70:137–58.

Case Study
A New Day

Anne M. Barker, RN, MSN, CNAA

Each nursing director brings to his or her position of leadership a philosophy of nursing and administration. As a new director of nursing in a 479-bed medical center, I brought a belief that a decentralized organizational structure was best for managing a clinical service. Decentralization is based on the concept that the decisions regarding patient care and the management of the nursing unit are best vested in head nurses and staff nurses. I assumed my position at the height of the nursing shortage. The medical center was faced with bed closures and a dissatisfied nursing staff. Reducing conflict between the professional nurse and the bureaucracy through decentralization of the service was essential to build a satisfied, competent staff.

I began by analyzing the people and the formal and informal power structure. I identified individuals I would need to support the changes I planned. They included the medical center director, the chief of staff, nursing middle managers, head nurses, and the nursing staff.

When I interviewed for the position of director of nursing, I was forthright about my philosophy of nursing and administration and my beliefs about decentralization of nursing services. I viewed the interview process as a time to determine if my goals and the institution's mission and goals were congruent. I needed assurance that the director and chief of staff would support my plans and goals. I determined at this time that these two key individuals would support a major innovation in the nursing service. My perception proved to be a realistic one, and only an occasional update of "this is where we are headed and this is the progress made so far" was needed to ensure their continued support and involvement in the process.

Strategies for Gaining Nurses' Support

Gaining support within nursing was not as easy, because these were the individuals who would be most affected by the changes in policies and procedures. Support was mixed, so I used a variety of strategies. First of all, I voiced my beliefs and ideas to all levels of nursing and analyzed their responses as individuals and as groups. I listened to their complaints, to what they believed would work or would not work, and to what they believed the organizational value system was.

I learned from this process who wanted change, who wanted to maintain the status quo, and who had formal and informal power. Head nurses, staff nurses, licensed practical nurses, and nursing assistants (the first-line staff and the ones who felt powerless to effect changes) voiced the need for change, especially in time scheduling, staffing, and accountability for practice.

"Decentralization" became a buzz word, meaning both a flattened organizational structure and each nursing unit being responsible for its own staffing. When making short- and long-term staffing projections and when rewriting policies, I made decentralization the common, although not always agreed upon, goal.

Team Building

Some head nurses and supervisory personnel would not adopt decentralization as a mutual goal for the service. Because I believed that some individuals would thwart changes, I decided that changes in some key people within the nursing organization were needed. It was necessary to bring in new people whose ideas and philosophies were similar to mine to provide support and suggest creative ways to implement change.

This strategy's weakness was its tendency to alienate "old" staff. The staff needed to feel their input and ideas were valuable. For example, an orientation ward had been instituted several years before my arrival. Due to a large turnover of new orientees, as well as my belief that this arrangement was contrary to the philosophy of decentralization, I wanted to reorganize the orientation program and have staff oriented on the ward to which they were assigned. I listened to the individuals who had been employed since the initiation of the orientation unit. They were able to tell me why the ward had been started and why orientation on each individual unit had failed. As they shared this information with me, they realized that many of the stable staff nurses who had been present at the time the unit was started were now head nurses or had retired, and that the orientation ward was no longer the best method to orient new staff. I believe all organizations have a history that must be understood and respected if changes are to succeed.

Timing

Changes were introduced gradually. For almost a year, I made few noticeable changes. Members of the staff began to tell me they were willing to be responsible for staffing their units. I sensed it was time for a policy statement on staffing, calling for significant changes. The document was labeled "Staffing: Phase One," to convey the message that future changes would occur. This satisfied two groups—those who wanted immediate change, and those who had lost power and were resisting change.

Task Force

Task forces of five to seven people were formed to tackle changes and implement new programs. Members of these task forces had to be carefully selected. People with both formal and informal power who resisted change had banned together. I placed these individuals on task forces along with people who desired change. Those with similar vested interests were not placed on the same task force. This strategy served three purposes: (1) it broke up pockets of resistance; (2) it encouraged active participation in the decision-making process by some of these individuals; and (3) it enhanced the nurses' acceptance of the task forces' recommendations as being unbiased.

Consultants: Agents for Change

Use of outside consultants proved to be an excellent change strategy. The consultants worked with staff nurses and head nurses, providing new knowledge and skills and support in a time of uncertainty. This support helped to decrease resistance to change and establish a trusting relationship with me.

One consultant was hired to assist the head nurses in identifying and solving problems. Through educational workshops, the head nurses learned to focus on problems and to work as a group to solve them. The head nurses and I spent one day at a retreat where we learned about each other as individuals and discussed our mutual goals and expectations. This proved to be a significant turning point in lessening resistance to change and in establishing a mutually trusting relationship.

As a result of work with their consultant, staff nurses formed a group called the Staff Nurse Forum (SNF) (see Chapter 21, "Creating a Supportive Work Environment"). This group, supported by me, has been one of the most effective means of implementing change. One theory states that change occurs as a result of persuading from the top and pushing from the bottom. The SNF has been a fine example of this. Because my primary concern as the new director of nursing was to provide a satisfying environment for the practice of professional nursing by the staff nurse, and because resistance to this goal was coming from middle managers, the forum served to "push from below" on many issues such as scheduling, staffing, and clinical practice.

Lessons Learned

Over the past three years, I have learned, not always easily, many lessons about leading a nursing service and effecting change. A brief discussion of some political considerations follows.

The nursing leader must articulate and promote a nursing philosophy and a value system. This is the leadership function of a manager. Without a value system and goals consistent with those values, the service may be managed but will not grow.

A working knowledge and understanding of the history of the organization are essential. If you hear, "We tried that before and it didn't work," then you must explore why. By finding out why something didn't work in the past, you may decide not to make a particular change, to modify your plan or to help people recognize why something might work under present-day circumstances.

An analysis of the people in the organization, within nursing and in other departments, is essential. You should determine who has formal power and how they exercise it. A more difficult task is determining who has informal power and how it is used. When you have identified people with influence, you can focus your attention on selling them your plans and decisions. Also, if these individuals introduce ideas and announce change, resistance will be lessened.

Communication with all individuals in the organization is essential. Honest, open sharing of values and goals and effective listening cannot be stressed enough. Further, the director of nursing must be able to elicit and accept constructive criticism and advice from all levels of personnel.

Throughout the past three years I have found that reading both "classic" articles and current literature on management and nursing administration has helped me to look at problems objectively and seek creative solutions. These readings have also helped me develop my own role within a political environment.

One of the most difficult lessons to learn is that change takes time. There are many reasons for this, but the need to introduce change in increments and to time it appropriately are among the most important factors. People simply need time to accept new ways and to be assured that changes are positive. Consensus for change must be achieved; too powerful an opposition will assure failure.

The director of nursing must also know what data will be used to measure her success. In this situation I was evaluated by two sets of individuals who used some similar and some different measures of success. The director and chief of staff were interested in the number of RN vacancies and the number of beds closed. Therefore, it was important to inform them of recruitment activities and staffing statistics. On the other hand, the nursing staff measured success by the number of times they were pulled to other units and by the number of personnel who were available to care for patients. It was important to remind them that "floating" had decreased by 75% and to share staffing statistics. Although these data were important to me as well, my measure of success was a decrease in turnover.

Status of Decentralization

Today the nursing service is decentralized. Each unit is responsible for its own staffing. Nursing middle managers are available to assist staff in securing help from a centralized float pool on some occasions. The organizational structure has been flattened by eliminating the supervisory level. Head nurses report to one of three assistants. Each nursing unit is given the authority to experiment with various models of time scheduling and organize their system of delivery of nursing services as they deem appropriate within the philosophy, goals, and values of the nursing service.

Case Study
Change at Bayfront Medical Center:
A Case Study on the Influence of the
Nurse Manager

Joan O'Leary, RN, EdD

Bayfront Medical Center in St. Petersburg, Florida, was a former city hospital that had been turned over to a nonprofit corporation. It was the hope of the board of directors that the hospital could be managed at a standard above average for the community.

I was hired as the director of nursing for the hospital and came convinced that motivated nurses could provide a higher quality of service to patients. When I arrived, functional nursing was in place on some units, and team nursing in place on others. There was a staff of 400—21% were registered nurses, and the remainder licensed practical nurses (LPNs) or nonprofessionals. The attrition and turnover rate of RNs was at an all-time high. Morale was at an all-time low. There was one master's-prepared nurse, six baccalaureate nurses, and the remaining nurses were diploma or associate degree graduates. LPNs were in charge on the 3 to 11 and 11 to 7 shifts, and nursing assistants were providing most of the direct patient care.

The patient census reached all-time highs during the winter months (at times over 100 percent). During the hot summer months, it dropped to 60 percent. Staffing and scheduling were major problems for the nursing office. Previous directors of nursing had stayed about a year, and then moved on.

There were a number of proprietary hospitals in the area, and they were actively recruiting physicians to admit patients to their hospitals.

My goals were to develop an organization that would be regarded throughout the country as an outstanding nursing clinical campus. The second-line supervisors I first met represented a core of loyal, supportive employees. All had stayed with the organization through thick and thin. They were personally involved and committed to the overall belief that quality nursing care can make a difference in the achievement of excellence in an institution. Not only were the employees supportive, but the president and many physicians openly welcomed me as well.

Adversity can bring cohesive action and make petty problems unimportant. During that first year, all worked together. In retrospect, many of the things my administration was given credit for might have been attributed to my arriving at the right moment. Much of the eventual success of Bayfront Medical Center resulted from the effective action of people around me.

Implementing Primary Nursing

There was an overall commitment to a philosophy of care that one nurse should be responsible and accountable for patient care over a 24-hour period. Through small group meetings and over many cups of coffee, this philosophy was communicated to everyone involved in the change to primary nursing care. The president, Mr. Ken Swanson, was willing to take a gamble that primary nursing would improve patient care and thus supported my philosophy.

Mr. Swanson allowed me to present the philosophy of primary nursing at the Board of Trustees meeting. I knew that when attending a board meeting, a presenter should:

1. Know the agenda ahead of time and be prepared to provide members with an objective analysis of the situation. Do not get defensive and arbitrary; but be objective. No one is always 100% right, and the same goes for being wrong.
2. Routinely request time to present the current status of activities. Use quality audiovisual media—overheads, slides, and handouts—to state points.
3. Be brief, concise, and to the point.
4. Allow time for questions and identification of future problems and concerns.
5. If possible, allow others to participate in these meetings. The knowledge base they represent can be invaluable. Do not take all the credit.

The Board of Trustees medical staff gave full approval for implementation of he pilot unit.

After everyone had been informed, a pilot unit was identified. A head nurse, Neoka Marple Apple, and a staff nurse, Cecilia Ponath, expressed interest in trying primary nursing. They were risktakers. They initially learned about primary nursing from me, and then began reading about the system. The associate director of nursing, Ethel Hill, also attended many meetings. Ms. Hill was in her sixties and had an enthusiasm and vibrancy unlike many her age. She knew that only 20 percent of the staff were registered professional nurses, but her comment as she reviewed the staffing and scheduling sheet was: "Why not—anything is better than what we have."

The nursing unit for which Ms. Apple was responsible was a medical/surgical floor of 40 beds. The hospital had been built in the 1940s with the traditional central nurses' station and three long wings.

The first week, Ms. Apple divided her unit into two wings. The long wing was team nursing, and the short wing was primary nursing. The short wing had twenty beds, so Ms. Ponath became the primary nurse for ten beds, and Ms. Apple the primary nurse for the other ten beds. They focused on working with their patients and families to assess and plan care. The other wing's nurses functioned as usual, commenting at times that they were lucky because they didn't have to stay in the patient area all the time. I made rounds frequently, visited with patients, and provided support and encouragement, as did Ms. Hill.

Shortly after beginning the pilot unit, the president visited my office. His comments were, "I am flooded with letters of praise about the pilot unit. Never in all my years have I She was having difficulty with room scheduling. Patients, readmitted after discharge from the pilot unit, were requesting the same room and same primary nurse. This unit had traditionally functioned at about 80 percent occupancy. Physicians were also requesting that their patients be admitted to the primary nursing unit. Suddenly we were having to cope with too many patients.

The nursing administrative team, the president, and the human resource development department had a meeting. We were excited about the success of this unit and planned a house-wide, full-year schedule for implementation.

The human resource department, committed to primary nursing care, set up a 12-hour educational program for the nursing staff. Nursing assistants, licensed practical nurses, and registered nurses were included. All of the staff were considered part of an exciting adventure, and were considered members of the hospital family.

At the conclusion of the educational series, some of the staff became so excited about the change that they volunteered to assist in rewriting their job descriptions. All of the job descriptions were written off duty, on everyone's own time.

The Unit Secretaries recommended that one individual on each floor be identified as a unit aide. This individual would support the primary and associate nurses, providing nonnursing functions and supplying the units, thus freeing the nurse for patient care.

The other wing was the next unit to volunteer to move to primary nursing. In the beginning, the staff had commented negatively about the system, but saw the pride and excitement of the pilot unit, and told the nursing office they wanted to be next in line to give primary nursing care.

We had a problem: only 21 percent of our staff were registered professional nurses. We did not have enough primary nurses or even enough nurses.

Over the years, attempts to recruit new graduates and retain staff had met with poor results. The implementation of primary nursing had improved retention, but we needed registered nurses.

As a nursing administrator, I had always been committed to students. I telephoned universities throughout Florida. I said to deans and faculties, "What we are doing at Bayfront Medical Center is an extension of what you have been doing for two or four years. The philosophy of nursing care that you include in the curriculum—the nursing process, the practitioner role, and the change process—is what we are putting into practice at our hospital. Send us your students. Allow them to practice what you have been teaching."

One of the calls was to the University of Florida. Dr. Blanch Urey, then dean of the College of Nursing, said she had some senior students who could spend three months at Bayfront, if I would act as mentor and if the preceptor was an experienced registered nurse. The students could receive university credit for the experience. Dr. Urey asked if I would come to Gainesville. Although it was a four-hour drive, I was so committed to establishing a preceptor program, that I agreed. During the meeting, Dr. Urey said, "Joan, never has a nursing administrator pounded on my door, asking for students. Usually hospitals shudder when we make calls for placement. I will provide you with two students, and we will go from there." These students were assigned to Ms. Apple and Ms. Ponath and today, 10 years later, they continue to work at Bayfront.

Now after five years, over 16 universities are affiliated with Bayfront in preceptor programs. We became the clinical campus for the southern region of the country.

While the administrative staff was pushing the nursing staff to implement primary nursing, students were pulling staff along with them. The students' presence at Bayfront was a supportive and critical element in the success story. At Bayfront, primary nursing bridged the gap between education and service.

Strategies for Change

The most influential person in effecting change in nursing care delivered in a hospital is the director of nursing. One of the primary obligations of this position is to develop staff to their highest potential. A democratic environment allows every individual to be imaginative, creative, knowledgeable, and heard. Ideas and opinions should be listened to, and individual recognition freely given. People need time for value clarification and the settling in of goals. If a conflict in values occurs, management must allow it to be expressed. A professional, given an opportunity for self-fulfillment, will seek and accept responsibility for self and others. Self-respect grows in this environment.

We in nursing should make an effort to understand the needs of our staff, not only from our point of view but from theirs. Only then can groups work to attain goals. The axiom "know thyself" is important for all staff, but becomes a commandment for the director of nursing. A successful leader and manager in nursing must be comfortable in that role.

To be effective the nursing administrator needs:

1. self-understanding
2. expert knowledge
3. a warm personality
4. knowledge of the social system in the hospital
5. a knowledge of power
6. the ability to develop a logical, step-by-step process to change a system.

It is up to every nursing administrator to determine a philosophy of nursing. There is no "right" style, and style may change, depending on the situation. The administrator should approach the role in a statesmanlike manner with vision and the capacity to communicate that vision, not only to those above, but to those below.

POLITICAL ACTION IN GOVERNMENT

Chapter 31   Educating Nurses for Political Action
Teaching Policy and Political Process

Legislative and Political Internships and Fellowships

Case Study   Putting It All Together

Unit V examines political strategies in government, beginning with local government in Chapter 24. Nurses' involvement in local politics has received little attention in the nursing literature. Nurses have greater access to influential citizens and legislators on this level of government than on the state or federal levels and can do a great deal to influence local health policy decisions. The reader unfamiliar with the structure and processes of government should begin by reading Chapter 25. It explains the workings of any government through state government.

Chapter 26 describes the federal government. The authors discuss their years of in-volvement with legislation and regulations associated with the Nurse Training Act. They describe how the different branches of government can exert influence on the same issue.

One of the ways to influence the governmental sphere is through political appoint-ments. Unfortunately, few nurses seek volunteer or paid appointments as a means of influencing health policy. Chapter 27 examines the different kinds of political appoint-ments and strategies for getting appointed. Two nurses describe their political appoint-ments. One is the first woman to head the Health Care Financing Administration, an agency with the third largest budget in the federal government in 1985.

Chapter 28 examines political parties and clubs from the perspectives of two nurses who have held elective offices in their parties and have used their influence to further nursing and health care.

The legislator is an important player in the sphere of government, and his or her influence may extend to the other spheres. Developing a good working relationship with legislators is imperative for nurses who want to influence legislation, their work-place, or their local community. Chapter 29 discusses how to build such a relationship from the perspectives of three nurses in different positions: a state legislator, a Con-gressional staff member, and a lobbyist for a national nursing association. They provide the reader with strategies for communicating with legislators, including how to write and prepare testimony to be presented at governmental hearings. The editors caution the reader that this final section on testimony is included because nurses need to do more of it; however, readers are advised to prepare and deliver testimony in coopera-tion with their nurses' association(s) whenever possible.

Although 1984 saw the first woman vice-presidential candidate nominated by a ma-jor political party, women and nurses have not yet maximized their potential influence as voters and campaigners. Chapter 30 presents strategies for voter participation from registration to campaigning written by the nurse who has developed a national network of nurses to coordinate Congressional lobbying and electioneering activities for the ANA. The chapter concludes with the stories of two nurses who have run for elective office.

The importance of educating nurses to influence government is conveyed in Chapter 31. The first part of the chapter will help those who want to develop undergraduate and graduate courses and programs in politics and health policy. The second part of the chapter discusses the legislative and political internships and fellowships that nurses can apply for or create on the local, state, and national levels. It includes vignettes by nurses who have held internships and fellowships, including one whose fellowship took her to the White House.

Unit V concludes with a case study that demonstrates how strategies for influencing the governmental sphere interrelate and overlap with the other three spheres. It is the story of Michigan nurses who developed and used their influence to further the welfare of the profession and the health of the consumer.

Chapter 24

Local Government

Clair B. Jordan, RN, MSN

More than ever before in our history, local governments are spending more money, employing more people, creating a greater impact on our lives. The 1960s and 1970s, characterized by a trend toward "national domination," concentration of power in the federal government and decline of local authority, have come to an end.

Local governments are growing and encompassing a wider range of services to meet new demands such as pollution abatement, slum clearance, public housing, urban renewal, mental health programs, highway construction, and care for the indigent. Older activities have continued, such as regulating relations between the sexes (marriage, divorce, and alimony) and punishment for criminal behavior. Virtually every area of our lives is touched by local government.

WHY NURSES WANT TO BE INVOLVED

The registered nurse will find few facets of the health care delivery system untouched by local government. For all practical purposes, local government can be defined as the governance of the counties, cities, townships, and schools. While the specific role of state and local governments in promoting health is not easy to define, more local governments are deeply involved in health matters. Over 1,600 hospitals are operated by cities, counties, or city-county combinations. Public health services reach citizens through local agencies every day. Full-time staff are found in most county health services. Larger cities have a health agency separate from the county (Grant & Nixon, 1975). In addition, local health departments exercise powers of governance with respect to quarantine, vaccination, inspection of products and premises, and elimination of unsanitary conditions. Cities are also developing departments for emergency medical services and special services for the elderly.

Health care is a major component of the local government today. Nurses concerned about professional issues, quality of care, and public well-being of consumers often find their first conflict will be with one of these local forms of government. To solve the conflict, the registered nurse needs to understand the historical development of local government, some of its operational policies, and some of its political quirks.

Besides the use of local governments to solve professional concerns, the registered nurse may want to use the local government system to develop political prowess. Local governments make a significant contribution to the training of national leaders, both legislative and judicial. Many a legislator has reached Congress via a county courthouse. Nurses will find that using local government to learn political prowess has many advantages. The opportunity is close at hand and does not involve travel. The leadership is more accessible and might be a neighbor. Often issues are easier to understand because they involve local problems and concerns.

THE STRUCTURE AND FUNCTIONS

City Government

Cities have a long history of independence and self-government. Early in the Middle Ages, European cities received crown charters, which established them as separate and independent entities. In America, this tradition continued. Early American cities sought charters initially from the British crown and later from the state legislature (Kraemer, Crain & Maxwell, 1975).

City government lacks the geographic coverage of state and county governments and is only applicable to an area within the boundaries of the other entities. Municipal corporations usually come into being when a community desires certain services or controls not normally provided by other units.

American cities are incorporated under charters that provide for boundaries, governmental powers and functions, methods of finance, and election and appointment of officers and employees. Municipal charters, to a large extent, consist of laws that have been adopted by legislatures or local provisions (local elections). Some city charters, such as New York City's, are voluminous, running to several hundred pages.

Almost every American city charter provides for one of three forms of city government: mayor-council, commission, or council-manager. Nurses should establish what form their cities have. Literature describing the function and structure of specific cities and local government in general is available from your local League of Women Voters.

Mayor-Council.   The mayor-council form (Figure 24-1) is the most common in large cities. It was popular on the East Coast during the early years of our nation and moved westward with migration. The city council, with legislative power, is elected at large or by wards or districts of the city. A mayor, elected at-large, participates in the legislative functions with the council and acts in an executive capacity with power to hire and fire department heads and develop budgets. There are adaptations of this form; some weaken the position of the mayor.

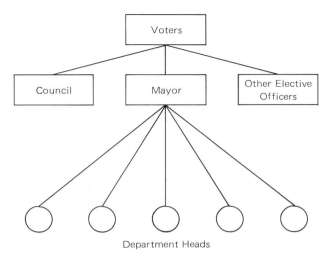

Figure 24-1   Mayor-Council Form

Commission.   The commission (Figure 24-2) is the second basic type of city government among American cities. It got off to a dramatic start in Galveston in 1901. After Galveston's disastrous storm and tidal wave in 1900, entailing a great loss of life, the mayor-council government could not cope with the urgent problems. A group of businessmen secured approval of a new charter, which provided for government by commissioners. All legislative and administrative power was concentrated in five persons, with one designated as mayor. Together, the commissioners served as the legislative body and each served as head of an administrative department.

The simplicity of the form, coupled with its success in Galveston, gave it a quick start. By 1917 over 500 cities had adopted commission charters. In this form of government, a small commission, elected citywide, serves as the legislative body. Each commissioner serves as head of an administrative department.

Council-Manager.   The newest form of city government is the council-manager (Figure 24-3). Saunton, Virginia was the first city to use the term "manager" in 1908; and Sumter, South Carolina in 1912 became the first city to operate under a charter providing for a council-manager form of government.

This form combines municipal legislative and policy-making powers in a small elective council and concentrates administrative authority in a manager selected by and responsible to the council. While a mayor is usually selected, either by voters or council membership, he or she is not the administrative head as in the mayor-council plan. Responsibilities usually include presiding over council meetings, representing the city on formal occasions, and participating in the policy making.

The characteristics of the council-manager form of government include a small elected council with legislative and policy-making powers, which employs a city manager, who serves at the discretion of the council.

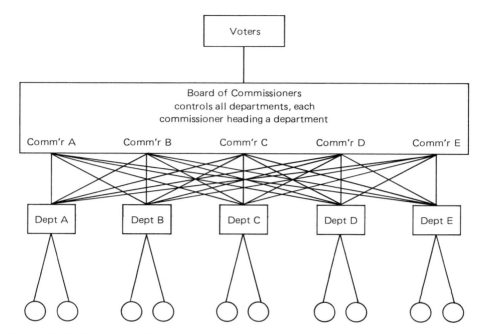

Figure 24-2 Commission Form

County Government

County government is the oldest form of local government in America. The concept of county government originated in medieval England when a county equivalent was called the shire. Today's county sheriff derives his/her title from the word shire—meaning chief officer of the shire. Settlers from England brought this concept of government with them when they migrated to the United States. While acceptance of county government was not great on the East Coast, it was and still is the most important local government below the Mason-Dixon line. Except for Connecticut, Rhode Island, and Alaska, all states are divided into counties. In Louisiana, the state is divided into parishes rather than counties. The population of a county can vary from 160 individuals, as in Loving County, Texas, to millions, as in Los Angeles County, California. The area of a county varies from 24 squares miles in Arlington County, Virginia to 20,131 square miles in San Bernardino County, California. The 3,044 counties are distributed among the 50 states, with an average of 65 per state (Grant & Nixon, 1975).

County government is a creation of state government. Citizens could not be expected to travel to the capital to conduct business with the state, so counties were designed as geographically accessible units of state government. They became community centers. The competition among communities hoping to be designated the county seat was great in this country's development. At stake were such outcomes as the county fair, with increased retail trade and greater prestige.

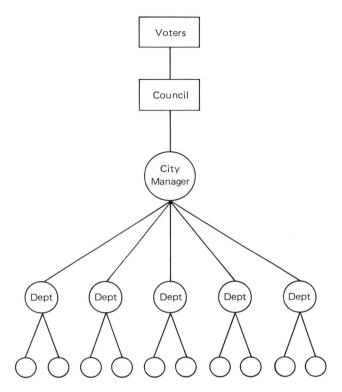

Figure 24-3 Council-Manager Form

Counties, unlike cities, are not incorporated. As a rule there is no chief executive such as a mayor or city manager. The governing authority usually is a body of elected members with the title of "board," "court," or "commission." The size of the governing board is usually 3 or 5 members, but may extend upward to 30 or more members.

County boards differ greatly in operations, but it is possible to type them in the following ways:

- Boards of commissioners (approximately two-thirds of all counties)
- Boards of township supervisors responsible for the township and the county
- Judges and justices of the peace who serve the county and act as judicial officials
- Judges and commission boards, which are mixed bodies

The county board serves both as a policy-making and an administrative body, usually appointing the head of highways, construction, and management of properties. The county may have regulatory jurisdiction over various matters—such as county hospitals. The largest single source of income for counties is the property tax.

School Boards

Public schools were accepted institutions in the North by the early 19th century but were not established in the South until after the Civil War.

About one-fourth of the nation's citizens are enrolled in schools or colleges. A high percentage are enrolled in state or public systems of education. Public education, which involves the governing of schools and their financing, is a complex political entity. While some states have attempted to remove schools from politics by having elections of nonpartisan school boards, these elections are often hotly contested races, denoting the power school boards may have in a local community.

In general, the basic decision-making and financial arrangements for education are established by the state through its constitution. Most states have, in addition, some form of a board of education, which is usually appointed by the governor but may be elected. This body approves organizational plans, develops budgets, and contracts for the purchase of textbooks. It also establishes standards for public schools and adopts plans to meet the educational needs of the state. Generally composed of laymen, the board selects a principal executive officer.

Most routine decisions are made by local school boards. This local body usually employs the teachers, approves textbooks from lists of state recommendations, adopts the local budgets, sets the tax rate, and maintains the public schools. School board members are usually lay individuals who have leadership skills and interest in the school system. A common practice of school boards is to appoint special committees on a variety of subjects. One of the committees appointed may be on the health and physical well-being of school children. This body can advise the school health program.

NURSES' ACCESS TO POWER

Nurses will most likely have their first association with their local government either through their employment or as a citizen desiring certain services. Nurses who have decided to influence the local system through politics will need to decide—do they wage their campaign alone, or do they work through a preexisting organization or structure.

Influencing Local Government Alone

Nurses may not have access to a local district nurses' organization or support group and may choose to influence the system alone. If a nurse is going to do this, a number of items need to be kept in mind:

1. Find a mechanism to secure information on the issue as well as the operations of the level of government involved. Simply finding out dates and times and usual protocol for meetings may be a chore. A nurse may try to talk with an insider of the local government, who may be friendly on the issue and share information.
2. Establish oneself as a "legitimate person" who should be trying to influence decisions. This is much easier when an individual works through an organization that

already has a credible reputation. The nurse may wish to have personal reference letters from recognized community leaders to improve her credibility and recognition.

3. Demonstrate that the issues one is bringing to the local government's attention are important to a number of citizens or nurses. This can be done by support letters, testimony, or the collection of names on a petition.

Choosing an Interest Group

When selecting an interest group, be aware that certain characteristics of groups give them more or less strength. These include:

1. Size: The number of members (potential voters) increases its power.

2. Cohesion of membership: Sometimes as groups grow, public disunity occurs, reducing the strength derived from the numbers of members.

3. Geographic distribution: If the membership is representative of a large and varied area, it expands the power. One neighborhood association approaching the city council about the quality of emergency medical services will not have as great an impact as will a coalition of representatives from each neighborhood association.

4. Status: While this characteristic is intangible, it usually relates to the prestige of the group. Representatives of the banking association will usually have more status than an unknown group. Status groups are usually committed to working within the system. Leaders within the system tend to reward only those groups that work within the system.

5. Leadership: A power-based group has a centralized, tightly knit organization that concentrates authority in the top leadership. This enables the organization to take public stands, negotiate problem areas, and outmaneuver opposition groups without time delays.

6. Program: A pressure group's issue or concern is in line with the public beliefs. If the group's issue fits the community's prevailing beliefs, it will be more successful.

7. Political environment: If the characteristics of the local community and the pressure group are alike, the pressure group will have greater power. If 80 percent of the townspeople are registered Democrats, and the pressure group has a democratic base, it will have more strength (Grant & Nixon, 1975).

Tools of Interest Groups

Interest groups use a variety of approaches to affect local politics. Many of the tools used at the local government level are also used at the state and federal levels. While most groups have developed their operations from the grass roots up to other levels, nursing has tended to develop political sophistication at the federal level. Other chapters will describe nursing's political action committees and governmental affairs committees at the state and national levels. Few of these activities, however, have been used at the local level by nurses. Local government represents one of the last frontiers for organized nursing.

Local Nursing Governmental Affairs Committees. One of the greatest needs nurses have is to know what is going on and when action on behalf of nursing is called for. District nurses' associations, which are constituents of state nurses' associations, often have local governmental affairs committees or legislative committees that augment activities of the state organization in influencing state policy. These local committees could also cover local government as well. Activities that would ensure nursing input and involvement include:

- *Monitoring meetings.* To understand the local issues, personalities, and power plays of local politicians, nurses need to plan on routine monitoring of city council, county commissioner, and school board meetings. Publications prepared by the League of Women Voters can guide nurses on how to get to know their county and community through self-study.
- *Developing nurses' positions on health issues.* Local governmental affairs committees can identify issues where nursing input and the development of an official position are needed. For example, if a nurse monitoring the school board meeting notes an incorrect stand on quarantining students with lice, the nurse may wish to go back to his or her original group and develop a position on the best method of handling school children with lice. This position could be shared with the school board as the advice of a profession interested in the community.
- *Monitoring officials' performance on health issues.* The local governmental affairs committee can keep an ongoing tally of city, county, and school board officials and how they respond on health issues and to nurses' concerns. This information is important at election time.

Participation in the Election Process

While nurses have formed political action committees (PACs) to participate more fully in the electoral process at the national and state levels, few PACs exist for nurses to participate in local elections. As a general rule, federal laws govern federal PACs and federal elections, state laws govern state PACs and state elections, and local city/county ordinances govern local PACs and local elections. Occasionally, state PAC laws will require that local PACs report their activities to the state level. Nurses forming a local PAC should consult a local attorney for formation and reporting rules.

Local nurses' PACs would have activities similar to the state and federal PACs. They would:

Gather Information. For all candidates running for local office, information could be secured from incumbent voting records, newspaper clippings, and conversations with the candidates. Nurses may wish to host a candidates' night where candidates running for a city council seat would come and discuss the city hospital, local health department, and other items of interest to nurses. This forum provides nurses with excellent access to the candidates and promotes an image of nursing as an organized, interested body of professionals.

Endorse Candidates. The local nurses' PAC would go on public record as supporting a certain candidate. The criteria for deciding on a specific candidate would be up to the local nurses.

Organize Work-Banks for Candidates. The local PAC would organize nurses to work in the candidate's campaign doing such tasks as staffing phone banks, putting out yard signs, and canvassing local neighborhoods. Nurses might also host local neighborhood socials where candidates visit with individuals in their homes. The emphasis in campaigning for local candidates is less sophisticated advertising and more local contacts with citizens.

Establishment of Nurses as Experts on Health Issues

If the community is small, the nurse may already be viewed as a health expert. Many nurses in small towns find their advice is important to local citizens who have fewer health resources than in larger areas. If this is the case, the nurse may simply let her community officials know she or he would be glad to serve on any special task forces or offer help on any health problems or issues. If the nurse resides in a larger city, however, the process may be more cumbersome. The nurse may have to work up the hierarchy by serving on: (1) boards and commissions; (2) speaking up at public hearings; and (3) responding to health issues in the media. Many large cities have special staff assigned to keep up with appointments to commissions, task forces, and boards. Nurses wanting appointments should contact the mayor's office for direction to the appointments assistant. These individuals will provide a list of upcoming appointments and qualifications desired. Nurses should be prepared for fierce competition and do homework on the position wanted. The most important thing nurses can do to establish themselves as experts is to offer advice that dramatically solves a city or county health problem, especially one that saves taxpayers' money. (See Chapter 27 for guidelines on how to get nurses appointed to paid or volunteer positions.)

Involvement of Nurses in Community Coalitions

Local nursing organizations can increase their political strength by forming coalitions with other groups. A coalition is a group of organizations that share a common interest in a single issue. The groups that nursing might form coalitions with are as numerous as the issues that might be addressed. If a coalition is to increase nursing's power, however, it should involve groups as strong or stronger than nursing.

Some ideas for coalition building (also see Chapter 15):

- The best way to start a coalition is to call an informal meeting for individuals to explore an issue and identify mutual concerns.
- Each member should contribute to the coalition and have equal vote in the activities.
- The best way for a coalition to function is to limit discussion and activity to the major issue—and not offer the opportunity for side-line disagreements.

Electing Nurses to Community Leadership Positions

The ultimate strength for nursing lies in electing nurses to local official positions. Running for and holding an elective office is the highest form of political participation. The larger the area, however, the more acquaintances, influence, determination, and money it takes to stage a successful campaign. Nurses will need a long-term strategic plan for election of nurses. Nurses may wish to contact the National Women's Education Fund for guidebooks on electing a candidate. Some general start-up hints might be (also see Chapter 30):

- Know and work closely with the neighborhood party precincts or clubs (the basic units in the political structure). These groups often respond early with support for individuals running for office.
- Begin to identify and groom potential candidates in the nursing population for leadership.
- Stay in close contact with incumbents so nurses will be among the first to know a nonincumbent position will be upcoming.

EXAMPLES OF NURSES INFLUENCING LOCAL GOVERNMENT

Nurses are influencing and filling a variety of public offices at the local level of government. Unfortunately, there is not a systematic way to keep track of their successes or to evaluate their methods. This is the story of how some nurses gained political strength through their district nurses' association.

RN Appointment to City Hospital Board

In the mid-1970s, nurses employed in city-owned hospitals and other nurses in the community became concerned about the hospitals' attitudes and practices in regard to nursing. Attempts by the nurses to influence the administrative level of the hospital had not been successful. Although they approached hospital board members, they found them ignorant about standards of care. Upon further investigation, the nurses discovered that the mayor appointed to the hospital board community leaders who supported his candidacy. The nurses tucked this knowledge away and waited.

The next mayor's race emerged as a heated battle between two nonincumbents—a young attorney sympathetic to the nurses' concerns about the hospital and an older physician who tended to be paternalistic. Through their district nurses' association, the nurses debated pros and cons of their action and, two weeks before the election, went to the city offices and filed papers to form a local nurses' PAC. Their next step was to call a press conference on the steps of city hall and through the PAC endorse their first candidate for mayor—the young attorney who was sympathetic to their concerns.

The two ensuing weeks were difficult for nurses. They did as much canvassing, telephoning, and sign-making as possible for their candidate. At the same time, they had to withstand heavy criticism from the medical community. Election night, however, gave the nurses something to celebrate. The young lawyer pulled ahead by two hundred votes.

As one of his first actions, the new mayor appointed the first registered nurse to serve on the city hospital board.

City Nurses' PAC Elects New Sheriff

County health department nurses had a long history of providing health services to occupants of the county jail. As they worked with prisoners who were suicidal and had other major psychological problems, conflict arose. The elected county sheriff and the nurses disagreed over who was in charge of the prisoners' health care. The sheriff believed he had ultimate responsibility and did not wish interference from "a bunch of female nurses." The sheriff expelled the nurses from the jail and hired ex-corpsmen to provide health services. The nurses found little support from the county commissioner's court where they took their appeal. The commissioners felt they had little say over the sheriff.

The nurses were concerned about the quality of care and its legality. They made their concerns known.

As election time approached, the nurses were consulted by a candidate for sheriff who knew of the nurses' problems with the current sheriff. The candidate was asked to speak at the nurses' local district meeting. He was endorsed by all the nurses present. The nurses set to work campaigning for an office which two years previously they had hardly noticed.

The new sheriff won his election over the incumbent, and residents of the city jail once again received physical and mental health services from registered nurses.

School Nurses Form Coalition to Remove Vending Machines

School nurses in the junior high schools were concerned about the nutritional status of students who ate lunches from vending machines located near the school cafeteria. Attempts to inform administration about their concerns did not meet with great success. One school nurse, meeting with the local PTA chapter on another issue, casually mentioned her concern. Parents immediately offered their support. A brief meeting was called with the school nurses, PTA, and the president of the local dental society. The mission of the group became to convince the local school board, using statistics and expertise, that the vending machines offered an unhealthy alternative to lunch and should be removed.

The school board agreed to a 45-minute presentation from the coalition. At the conclusion of the group's statement, the school board voted not only to remove the vending machines but also to invest money in a salad bar and popcorn machine for the lunchroom cafeteria.

RNs Advise City Council on Establishing a New EMS System

Registered nurses were pleased to learn that the city council had voted to institute a city-wide emergency medical service (EMS), but were startled to see the newly appointed director announce on local television that he would not employ RNs because they knew nothing about emergency care. The nurses were aware they had a major problem on their hands, not only because of the director's attitude, but because they would not have a sound mechanism for solving the coordination problems they foresaw between the new EMS system and cooperating emergency rooms. The local district nurses' association formed a committee to develop suggestions for nurses working with the EMS department. After surveying other EMS systems in the state, the nurses' association appeared before the city council and addressed their concerns about the service and recommended the establishment of a nurse advisory council to the EMS. The mayor and council responded by appointing a quality assurance committee to the new department with a permanent position being designated for a registered nurse.

CONCLUSION

These examples demonstrate the influence nurses can and should have on the local government. As the societal trend towards decentralization continues, the local government will play an increasingly important role in the health and welfare of the nation's citizens. Nurses have valuable expertise, which local governments need if they are to fulfill this role in a humanistic and competent manner.

References

Banfield EC: *City Politics*. Harvard University Press, 1967.
Grant D, Nixon HC: *State and Local Government In America*. Allyn and Bacon, 1975.
Kraemer R, Crain E, Maxwell WE: *Understanding Texas Politics*. West, 1975.
League of Women Voters: *Know Your County*. League of Women Voters, 1974.
Peterson GE: *Cities in Crisis: Taxes, Budgets and Services*. League of Women Voters, 1978.

Chapter 25

State Government

Mary N. Long, RN, BSN
Diana J. Mason, RN, MSN

Professional nurses have a long history of involvement in state politics. During the late 1800s, the Nurses' Associated Alumnae of the U.S. (forerunner to the ANA) concluded that if nurses were to be recognized as professionals, they had to develop legislation on a state-by-state basis to establish standards for nursing practice and protect the public. The state nurses' associations were organized and provided the leadership to lobby for enactment of nurse practice acts, usually in the face of opposition from the medical community. The state nurses' associations established special legislative committees, whose members served as lobbyists. These committees developed specific information for the public and legislators concerning the need to pass licensing laws for professional nurses and establish state boards of nursing responsible for the regulation of nursing practice (ANA, 1982).

Today, nurses continue to refine state legislation that defines and regulates nursing practice. Nurses' involvement in state government, however, is often criticized for being too self-interested. Indeed, nurses are recognizing that they have a significant role to play in shaping health policy in their communities. With the development of the New Federalism since 1980, the states have increased control over the allocation of federal monies and developed policies for health and social services. Nurses need to expand their understanding of state governments and increase their political power at this level to influence health policy development and resource allocation and assure proper state regulation of nursing practice. This chapter reviews the structure and process of state governments and gives examples of nurses influencing state government activities.

Mary Long wishes to acknowledge Julia Gould and Carole West, who assisted her with this chapter; the late Georgia State Representative Sidney Marcus, a friend of nursing in Georgia and a special man who cared about all the citizens of Georgia; Sharon Adams, a good political friend; and Demetrious Mazacoufa, the Georgia Nurses' Association's lobbyist.

ROLE OF STATE GOVERNMENT

The federal constitution reserves certain powers for the states and contains some provisions to protect the states. For example, the federal government will protect states against foreign invasion and assure each state of equal representation in the U.S. Senate. Initially the states provided the basis for a decentralized system of national governance, because they had tremendous power and responsibility. With the depression in the 1930s, however, the states were unable to provide for the health and social welfare of their unemployed citizens, and they appealed to the federal government for help. Ushering in the New Deal, President Franklin D. Roosevelt increased the power of the federal government in determining health and social policy and in financing the programs (Piven & Cloward, 1971).

The federal government continued to play a dominant role in health and social policy, with another expansion of programs in the 1960s with President Lyndon B. Johnson's "war on poverty." As federal health and social programs expanded, centralized governance became the target of public concern. In 1980, President Reagan was elected on a platform that promised to curb federal influence and the growing federal deficit. Reagan consolidated monies for health and social programs into block grants that the states could use to meet their needs as *they* determined them.

The states have retained their original right to legally define and regulate the professions. Subtle differences in nurse practice acts among the states can translate into nurses having broad prescriptive power in one state and no such power in another (Bullough, 1983).

The structures of state governments vary. Some of these variances have been outlined for easy reference by Archer and Goehner (1982). If you are unfamiliar with the structure of your state government, refer to this source or contact your state capitol or the League of Women Voters in your community. The League frequently publishes a directory of state representatives with contact information and a synopsis of the government's structure and process in a particular state.

Legislative Branch

The legislative branch of the state government is responsible for lawmaking.

Houses. Except for Nebraska, which has only one body, the state legislatures, or general or legislative assemblies as they are sometimes called (New Hampshire uses the term "general court"), are bicameral (two chambers). One house is based upon equal representation and called the senate. The other is larger, composed of members representing a specified number of constituents, and is referred to as the assembly, house of delegates, or house of representatives.

Many battles have been fought over how the districts of these bodies should be demarcated, particularly after a census identifies population shifts. The reapportionment of districts can dramatically affect the distribution of political power within a state and influence public policy. In 1962, the U.S. Supreme Court ruled on the "one man, one vote" issue. This was based on a Georgia case challenging the geographic system of representation that prevented the formation of a voting bloc of blacks in sufficient numbers to elect a black candidate to state office. Under this ruling, redistricting must demonstrate an intent of fairness. If this intent is suspect, the boundary lines of a district can be challenged in court and redrawn if shown to be unfair.

The political party with the largest number of seats in a particular house is considered the "majority" party. Since legislators frequently vote along party lines, the majority party has the potential to wield power over what legislation gets passed and what doesn't. If one political party is in the majority in both houses of the legislature and the governor is of the same party, that political party's power can become enormous. In any case, the "majority" and "minority" party leaders in each house are important players in the legislative process. They work at developing a cohesive party stand on issues. If a third party reimbursement bill for nurses is in the Republican-controlled senate and the chief sponsor of the bill is a Democrat, it could become a partisan issue unless nurses ensure that the bill has sponsors from both parties.

Both houses meet individually as formal bodies in regular or special legislative sessions. The regular sessions vary by state in starting date and length. Most states have annual sessions, although several meet biennially, in which case bills that are introduced the first year may carry over to the second year of the session. Special sessions may be called by the governor or a majority of the legislature.

Knowing the schedule of your state legislature is important in terms of timing your activities. For example, if you know that although the legislative session starts in January, the budget has to be approved by March 31, timing a lobbying effort for a bill on third party reimbursement of nurses for the end of March would be unwise, since the legislators will be preoccupied with the budget and have little interest in your bill. On the other hand, if the legislative session ends on June 15, and the insurance committee has not acted on your bill by June 1, you will know that intense lobbying is needed to allow enough time for the bill to be voted out of committee and sent to the entire house for a vote.

Frequently a large number of bills requiring action accumulate toward the end of the session. This could be to a bill's advantage. Since legislators are human, they do not relish the notion of an extended session and may act quickly on bills that would have evoked hours or days of debate if brought to the house for a full vote earlier in the session. Such timing considerations can be used to one's advantage.

Committees.   Each house has standing committees usually established by the rules of the houses. These committees refine legislation before it is brought to the full house for a vote. The committees may meet between legislative sessions as well as during the regular session. Interim or ad hoc committees may be created by the legislature to research and formulate legislation on a particular subject. States vary in the names and numbers of committees. (North Carolina has the largest number in both houses.) Contact your state capital or state nurses' association to find out what committees in your legislature deal with health and social matters.

Other committees important to nursing practice are education and insurance. In most states, the health or education committee considers all legislation that would affect the professional practice acts. If the podiatrists wanted to alter the nurse practice act to make nurses responsible for executing podiatrists' orders, the bill would most likely originate in either of these committees. The insurance committee considers health insurance legislation, including bills covering third party reimbursement of nursing services. The "ways and means" committees are extremely important. Any bill with fiscal implications will undoubtedly have to receive this committee's approval before going for a full house vote.

The chairpersons of these committees can be powerful figures. They are usually appointed by the lieutenant governor, speaker, or majority party leader of each house. Thus, if Republicans hold the largest number of seats in the senate, all senate committees will be chaired by Republicans. A strong chairperson usually controls the committee's agenda and process. For example, the chairperson decides when a particular bill will come up for a committee vote and can influence how the committee votes. One legislator on a state assembly education committee told a nurse constituent who asked about the legislator's position on a nursing bill on entry into practice that he voted however the committee's chairperson (who was of the same political party) told him to vote. This does not mean that this nurse should not continue to court the legislator. In this case, however, a long-term multifaceted approach to developing a working relationship with her legislator was necessary. The issue at hand demanded that she expand her immediate lobbying efforts to include the committee chairperson.

Most of the work of the legislature is carried on through the committee process. Committees in either house do not report or act on all bills, and public hearings are left to the discretion of the committees. Hearings are usually held for one of two reasons: to obtain information on complex issues before formulating or acting on a piece of legislation; or to elicit public support for a legislator's pet bill. In one state, the chairperson of the assembly education committee had his own idea as to what was needed for legislation affecting nurse practitioners and the "entry into practice" issue. His views were in opposition to those of the state nurses' association. He knew that support from the public and medical community would be necessary to pass his legislation. He held hearings across the state to appear to be gathering data to develop unbiased legislation. Hidden agendas can abound in any political arena.

How a Bill Becomes Law. (See Chapter 29 for a more detailed discussion on "Communicating with Your Legislator.") The idea for a bill may come from an individual legislator, nurse, lobbyist, the governor, committees of the legislature, or anyone. For it to be considered by the state legislature, however, a bill must be drafted and have a sponsor in each house of the legislature. Frequently legislative aides or committee staff members will help nurses who want to develop an idea into legislation. The legislation also can be drafted privately and given to a friendly legislator, who will be the chief sponsor of the bill in his/her house and will work for its passage.

Bills are often difficult for the lay person to understand, since they are written in legal language and form. Nurses often rely on interpretations by the nurses' association. Sometimes it is helpful to see the original language so you can argue more effectively for or against the bill with a legislator or the public. The lobbyist for your nurses' association can help you to analyze a bill; or refer to Archer and Goehner (1982) or Bagwell and Clemens (1985) for a sample bill with an accompanying analysis.

Since bills must be introduced separately in each house, a sponsor is needed from each. Cosponsors from each house will also be sought. Cosponsorship by a variety of respected legislators from both parties is essential. Cosponsorship only by members of the minority party can create a winless partisan struggle. Seeking cosponsorship should arise from a collaborative effort between the bill's chief sponsor and the nurses' association. Cosponsorship of a bill shows a commitment of support from an individual legislator and serves to influence other legislators to support the bill. Individual nurses lobbying their legislators should note whether the legislator is one of the bill's sponsors and, if not, ascertain from the nurses' association whether it would be desirable to have this legislator "sign on" to the bill.

After a bill has its sponsors, it is introduced in each house by the bill's sponsors and a number assigned for each house version. Thus, the senate version of a mental health service bill is assigned one number (prefixed by an "S"; ie, S.4123), while the assembly version, which may or may not have the same text as the bill introduced into the senate, is assigned another number (prefixed by an "A"; ie, the assembly version of S.4123 may be A.7279).

The bill is then referred to the appropriate committee by the presiding officer of each house. Thus, the mental health service bill may be assigned to the health committees in both houses. Or, the bill for third party reimbursement for nurses would be assigned to the insurance committees. The bill could be assigned to a subcommittee, which would recommend action to the full committee. This usually occurs with committees that consider a large number of diverse bills, such as insurance or health committees.

At this point, public hearings may be held on the bill. It is crucial that nurses participate in such hearings in a coordinated fashion. If you know that hearings are being held in your city on the mental health services bill and you have some data and expertise in this area, you should contact your state nurses' association and volunteer to testify. The association staff can help you prepare written testimony and advise on speaking before the hearing committee.

With or without public hearings, the subcommittee, and then the full committee, can do one of several things with the bill. It may be amended, defeated, tabled or held, or passed and sent to another committee or to the house for a floor vote. Many bills die in committee because there is not enough support for their passage, and legislators don't want to go on record as having voted against a bill backed by some of his or her constituents.

When a bill is at the committee level, nurses need to lobby their legislators who may sit on the committee. It is also important to lobby the committee's chairperson, even if the nurse is not in the chairperson's district. Usually legislators do not pay attention to nonconstituent input unless it comes from an organized group or a powerful individual. Committee chirpersons, however, have a responsibility to all citizens for the committee's deliberations, and as such, should be lobbied by nonconstituents who want action on a bill.

Contact should also be made with the powerful president of the senate and the speaker of the house, who oversee the deliberations of their respective houses and can change the formal process of handling a bill if desired. For example, recently in one state, a Democratic assemblyman was committed to securing third party reimbursement for nurse-midwives but knew he would have great difficulty getting the bill through the Senate Insurance Committee. The committee was chaired by a Republican senator who was backed by and loyal to the medical and insurance communities, both of which opposed the bill. The assemblyman, as the assistant majority leader of the assembly, made a deal with the senate majority leader, whereby the latter directed the midwifery bill to the senate floor for a full house vote, bypassing the Senate Insurance Committee. The assemblyman attributed the bill's enactment to this single move, since it spared the Senate Insurance Committee chairperson from having to publicly choose between party loyalties and campaign support.

While the bill is in committee, factual information should be shared with legislators about the pros and cons of the legislation. With concern over cost-effectiveness of government actions, it is imperative that nurses provide data about the fiscal impact of any bill and show cost savings where possible.

If the bill is passed by one committee, it may go to another before reaching the full house for a vote. It is routine for bills with fiscal implications to be considered by the ways and means committee and for most bills to go to the rules committee.

If a bill passes through the appropriate committees, it will be called by the speaker or president of the senate, read by the clerk, and discussed by the bill's sponsor. The sponsor will then yield the floor for questions and debate. In Georgia, the legislation may be amended on the floor by another legislator as many as twenty times. Sometimes amendments are added to a bill to render it useless, or unrelated amendments may be added to force supportive legislators to vote against it. If amendments pass, they are added to the original bill. If the legislation fails, the sponsor may put the legislators on notice that he or she will ask for a motion to reconsider the bill.

A bill must pass both houses. As stated previously, there may be two different versions of the same bill. If this is the case, a conference committee with members of both houses will work out one version of the bill acceptable to both houses.

Once the bill passes, it goes to the governor for his or her signature within a certain time. The governor can also veto the bill or return it to the legislature with recommendations for amendment. In some states, the governor may not want to endorse or veto the bill and can let it become law by not signing it within a specified time (after 10 days). If the governor fails to sign a bill and the legislature adjourns before the ten days are up, the bill does not become law—a "pocket veto."

Although bills can be passed by legislatures by a simple majority, most states require a two-thirds majority vote to override a governor's veto. Although difficult, this is not an impossible achievement. In 1976, the governor of Missouri vetoed a progressive nurse practice act that the nursing community had worked hard to get passed in the legislature. Through a well-organized effort, the nurses were able to secure the first override of a Missouri governor's veto in 138 years (Missouri nurses' efforts, 1976).

Executive Branch

Many nurses are unaware of how the executive branch of state government affects them. As the branch of government responsible for the administration of the government and its laws, it can be of great importance to nursing and health care.

The Governor is the chief executive officer in each state as well as the leader of his or her party. However, his or her duties touch on all three branches of state government.

As stated earlier, the governor holds veto power over all bills passed by the legislature. By being party leader, the governor can also introduce bills and move them through the legislature with relative ease when his or her party is in control of the legislature.

The governor's fiscal and program priorities are usually outlined in a "state of the state" address at the beginning of each year. (This speech is printed and available to the public.) The governor's budgetary recommendations will influence the allocation of monies to health care services, research, and education. The budgetary process varies from state to state, so that nurses should learn about their state's process and participate in it.

In many states, the governor also appoints heads of government departments such as health and welfare agencies. There are several states, such as Maryland, Kansas, and Michigan, where nurses have been appointed as the directors of the health and human services departments. The positions these nurses hold make a significant difference in the health care of citizens and the status of nurses employed in state health care institutions. In Wisconsin, Barbara Nichols, past-president of the American Nurses' Association, was appointed to the state cabinet-level position of Secretary of the Department of Regulation and Licensing. Other nurses have been appointed to commissions or task forces on health concerns such as domestic violence, teenage pregnancy, and aging. Such groups are important because they recommend policy to the governor and serve as a forum for nurses to network with other influential citizens and demonstrate their expertise and concern for health issues.

To receive such an appointment, a nurse must be known to the governor or his or her associates. In one state, some nurses who had worked closely with the state's Division for Women gave the division's director resumés of nurses qualified for appointment by the governor to serve on various state boards and commissions. Frequently, appointments are made because the individual worked in the governor's or other top official's campaign. Also, some state nurses' associations are asked to submit names of qualified applicants for consideration. Ask your state nurses' association for a list of nurses who hold state appointments to volunteer boards, committees, or commissions.

Several years ago, a state department head decided to remove all chief nurses in the Georgia State Health Department at the local county levels. The state nurses' association opposed this plan. Because the public health nurses were prohibited from lobbying, the state nurses' association lobbied for them, informing legislators why it was important to keep registered nurses in leadership roles at the local level. As a consequence, the state and local district chief nurses retained their positions.

The Lieutenant Governor takes over for the governor when the latter resigns, dies, or temporarily leaves the state. He or she is often nominated and elected separately from the governor, particularly in primary races, and can be a potential candidate for the governorship. The lieutenant governor usually presides over the state senate, and should be lobbied by nurses interested in getting legislation passed through the senate.

The Attorney General heads the state's legal department and serves as the legal adviser to state boards of nursing when there is a need to clarify laws that affect nursing practice. In addition, the attorney general can prosecute cases of discrimination that violate state laws. This may be an important forum for nurses fighting for equal pay for comparable work.

The Secretary of State is responsible for enforcing state laws; supervising elections; granting charters to corporations; and, of importance to nursing, administering the various examining boards and the registration of state political action committees. The state board for nursing is accountable to the secretary of state, although in most states, the members of the board are appointed by the governor and approved by the senate.

North Carolina represents an exception to this process, being the first and only state to have its state nursing board elected by the state's registered nurses. Several years ago, nurses in North Carolina decided that their practice act needed revision. Several institutions were allowing unlicensed personnel to provide professional nursing care, including medicating patients. The North Carolina Nurses' Association formed coalitions with other nursing groups to develop legislation that would halt these practices. They were also instrumental in adding an amendment that would allow members of the North Carolina Board of Nursing to be elected by nurses rather than appointed by the governor. This precedent-setting law may encourage other state nurses' associations to try to gain greater control over who sits on their boards of nursing.

Actions of various state departments need to be monitored by nurses. These departments are responsible for interpreting the laws, writing regulations based upon the laws, and seeing that the regulations are followed. Thus, the regulatory process is just as important to monitor as the legislative process. The staff of the state departments are important persons with whom the nurse should become acquainted. Although in their positions longer than legislators, they are likely to be just as unfamiliar with nursing.

While cultivating relationships with the staff of departments and educating them about nursing are probably the most important ways to influence the regulatory process, the public usually has the opportunity to shape regulations through hearings and written comments. The public is often required to be notified of a specific time period, prior to the final adoption of regulations, when written comments will be considered. While this public notice is provided in standard government publications, it is seldom given other publicity. Changing regulations after they have been drafted is difficult though not impossible. Regulations can be changed by the executive branch or challenged through the judicial system.

The department of health is of obvious importance to nursing. The state commissioner of health, appointed by the governor, has great influence over the regulations developed to implement health laws. For example, in one state, the public health code states that physicians are required to do admitting histories and physicals on all patients admitted to a public hospital. In some public hospitals, nurse practitioners were doing these histories and physicals on psychiatric admissions. To restrict the practice of nurse practitioners, the health department began to enforce this code by issuing citations to hospitals using nurse practitioners in this capacity. As a result, some of the hospitals stopped hiring nurse practitioners, and others replaced them with physician's assistants.

Another department of importance to nursing is the education department, which governs the credentialing of nursing education programs in a number of states. In addition, some education departments, under the direction of a board of regents or state board of higher education appointed by the governor, oversee the writing and enforcement of regulations that govern nursing practice.

One department that has taken on greater importance to the nursing community in recent years is the insurance department, which regulates the insurance industry. In a growing number of states, insurance laws have been altered to provide reimbursement for nursing services. The regulations that the department develops to interpret and implement such legislation require scrutiny by the nursing community. What appeared to be a progressive reimbursement law could be rendered useless by insurance department regulations that restrict or encumber its implementation.

Besides departments mandated in the state constitution, a state may have other statutory commissions, agencies, and authorities, whose heads are appointed by the governor. The heads, members, and paid staff of these bodies often develop policies that affect nursing practice. Consider this example.

The plight of nurses who work in state mental health facilities is a major political issue in many states. In one state, the lieutenant governor commissioned a blue ribbon committee to investigate a facility reported for patient abuse and a death.

Upon completion of the investigation, the Senate staff requested assistance from the state nurses' association. A position statement was presented by the latter outlining the roles and functions of nurses employed in state institutions and the need for leadership at the state level. The need for professional registered nurses to supervise other nursing personnel, to collaborate with other health professionals, and to govern their own practice was clearly delineated. The position statement was shared with the commissioner of health, the director of mental health, and the administrative nurse in the state facilities.

The state mental health facilities were threatened with loss of third party reimbursement unless improvements were made in patient care. At this time, the state public health commissioner contacted the association president for additional assistance. The president called a special meeting of interested nurses employed in state mental health facilities to share their concerns with legislators and nurses.

The lieutenant governor's blue ribbon committee called a special meeting and requested testimony from the institutions as well as from the nursing community. The staff of the blue ribbon committee reviewed the recommendations from the state nurses' association and presented them to the special committee, which accepted them.

Since that time, the state nurses' association has worked with nurses in the institutions to disseminate information. Nurses have gathered data on salaries and nursing practice concerns and worked with the families of the patients, the American Red Cross, and the Mental Health Association. The commissioner has recommended that salaries of nurses employed in mental health facilities be a priority in his budget. Nurses in this state have been able to use their political clout to improve and upgrade the status of nurses employed in several state institutions.

Judicial Branch

The judicial branch of state government interprets and applies the law by adjudicating issues in controversy. There are a variety of courts that serve this purpose, as specified in the state's constitution. In Georgia, there are the state supreme court, court of appeals, superior courts, probate courts, and justice of the peace courts. In addition, the general assembly has created courts with county and citywide jurisdiction.

All lawsuits that affect nursing are handled by the courts. Although some of the judges are appointed, many are elected. In either case, but particularly the latter, nurses can influence who may preside over a future court case affecting their practice. Two recent examples include the Missouri Supreme Court decision that nurse practitioners in that state were practicing in accord with the intent of that state's revised and progressive nurse practice act; and, in Tennessee, a state court is scheduled to hear a case in which nurses' rights to practice midwifery were blocked by hospitals and a physician-owned insurance company.

NURSES IN ACTION

Nurses in Georgia have been politically active for many years. This is one of their success stories.

In 1980, a state senator introduced an amendment to the Medical Practice Act, which placed one aspect of nursing practice under its auspices. Obviously, this was of great concern to nurses in Georgia.

At the time, I (Mary N. Long) was chairman of the Georgia Nurses' Association's Legislative Committee and responsible for communicating the impact of this amendment to the association's members and the public. I called a meeting of the committee and invited other interested nurses to participate. A statement regarding the amendment and the date and time of its introduction in the Georgia Senate was developed and disseminated by mail and telephoned to the Georgia Nurses' Association leadership in each area of the state. The leadership in turn contacted institutions, agencies, schools of nursing, and other places where nurses were employed. Nurses were asked to come to the state capitol when the amendment was to be presented. A time and meeting place were designated. Those who could not attend were asked to send telegrams or make telephone calls to their senators.

On the day of the hearing, more than 300 nurses assembled at the state capitol. Each nurse was given the position statement that the association had developed. Nurses were asked to call their senators out of session and discuss the amendment with them. You can imagine how surprised legislators were to see nurses, their constituents from 30 to 200 miles away, at the capitol. We were successful. The author of the proposed legislation stood on the floor of the senate and withdrew the proposal.

State nurses' associations continue to take the leadership in monitoring and participating in local and state political processes. Several associations have developed visitation programs for nurses during the legislative sessions. The visitation program allows nurses to visit the capitol, speak with their legislators, and be oriented by the association's lobbyist or others to the activities of the state government.

The voting records of legislators on nursing and health care issues should be published in association newsletters. Voting records are usually available in the clerk's office of each state legislature.

In Georgia and New York, as in many states, the nurses' association hosts a social event during the legislative session. Nurses, legislators, and special guests are invited to attend a large reception in a location close to the capitol. Key individuals from the state government are invited, such as commissioners of health, secretary of state, secretary of examining board, and boards of nursing and staff.

Also in Georgia, special efforts are made to work with nursing specialty organizations to use their members' expert testimony and to develop a unified presence. The specialty organizations contribute financially to the Georgia Nurses' Association to aid the efforts of the association during the legislative session for mutual gain.

Of course, access to legislators is greatly influenced by the extent of constituents' involvement in candidates' campaigns. Although nurses' associations participation in partisan politics is limited, they can form a political action committee (PAC) that can endorse state candidates, make political contributions to key races, and coordinate nurses' participation in campaigns. These activities are an essential part of developing nursing's political influence on the state level. A growing number of state nurses' associations have such PACs that need your support.

CONCLUSION

The state government is an important political arena for nurses because of the shift in power from the federal government to the states, the state's role in the development of health policy, and its jurisdiction over the professions. An understanding of the structure and workings of the state government is necessary if nurses want to influence the legislative, executive, and judicial processes. While this chapter has provided a general description of state governments, the reader is encouraged to acquire a thorough understanding of the specifics of his or her own state government through publications and personal involvement. The state nurses' association is the primary means for nurses to develop and exercise their political power in this important sphere of influence.

References

American Nurses' Association: *One Strong Voice*. ANA, 1982.

Archer SE, Goehner PA: *Nurses: A Political Force*. Wadsworth, 1982.

Bagwell M, Clements S: *A Political Handbook for Health Professionals*. Little, Brown, 1985.

Bullough B: Prescribing authority for nurses. *Nurs Econ* 1983; 1:122–25.

Meredith JC, Myer L: *Lobbying on a Shoestring: How to Win in Massachusetts . . . and Other Places, Too*. Poverty Law Center, 1982.

Missouri nurses' efforts win override of veto of nurse practice act amendments. *Am J Nurs* 1976; 76:461.

Piven FF, Cloward RA: *Regulating the Poor: The Functions of Public Welfare*. Vintage Books, 1971.

Chapter 26

Federal Government

Gretchen A. Osgood, RN, MA
Jo Eleanor Elliott, RN, MA, FAAN

The year 1984 marked the twentieth anniversary of the passage of Public Law 88-581, the Nurse Training Act of 1964. This is the most significant federal legislation in support of nursing ever enacted in peacetime. During this period, nurses have learned that politics is the art of getting things done, and the Congress and the executive branch have become mindful that nurses are a force to be reckoned with. At local and state levels, nurses have been more active in discussing and taking positions on nursing and health-related issues that require legislative action. These views and recommendations are channeled, generally through professional organizations, to legislators at appropriate levels of government. This chapter describes in general terms governmental processes at the federal level in support of nursing and suggests ways in which nurses can influence change.

THE FEDERAL ROLE IN PUBLIC HEALTH

At the outset, it is important to remember that the United States is a federation of 50 states. Framers of the Constitution vested powers of governance in states, leaving to the federal government only those responsibilities that transcended state boundaries and interests. The federal government's activities in the health arena are derived principally from broad phrases in the Preamble to the Constitution outlining the purposes of government and the intent to "promote the general welfare." Subsequent interpretations of this phrase by the Supreme Court, together with specific responsibilities assigned to the federal government such as the power to regulate commerce among the states, form the basis for federal intervention in the public's health. These authorities are so broad that they would seem to permit the Congress, as the nation's lawmaking body, to pass legislation touching on every issue involving the nation's health.

In practice, however, the federal role is limited to actions requiring bold initiatives or continuing attention to alleviate problems of nationwide concern. The present federal commitment to providing for the nation's health is rooted in the aftermath of the Great Depression of the 1930s when local communities and states were no longer able to cope with the problems of unemployment and its attendant social consequences. Recognizing that preserving the health of the citizenry was essential to rebuilding a sound economy, Congress enacted the Social Security Act of 1935, providing for care of the indigent and infirm elderly. Amendments to the Act in 1950 and the enactment of Medicare and Medicaid legislation in 1965 further expanded federal responsibilities in the health arena, not only for payment for health care but also for insuring that the services for which payment was authorized were available and of good quality.

GROWTH OF NURSING LEGISLATION

Since nurses constitute the largest single discipline of health care providers, the adequacy of their numbers and quality of their services were legitimate federal concerns. Soon after the end of World War II, there was evidence that the nation's need for nurses outstripped the supply, qualitatively as well as quantitatively. The population had grown, and changes in demographic characteristics required intensifying services to individuals at both ends of the age spectrum. Advances in medical science and the application of new technologies and treatment modalities resulted in rising rates of hospitalization. Increasing coverage of the population by voluntary health insurance plans and by publicly supported medical care programs enabled more people to use and finance needed care. At the same time, nursing education was undergoing major changes as the locus for programs began to shift from hospitals to academic settings, compounding the already critical problem of insufficient numbers of well-prepared faculty. In the spring of 1961, the surgeon general of the United States Public Health Service appointed a Consultant Group on Nursing to address the complex issues contributing to the shortage and to advise him on the appropriate role of the federal government in assuring adequate nursing services for the nation. The Consultant Group's report, "Toward Quality in Nursing, Needs and Goals," became the cornerstone of Public Law 88-581, designated the Nurse Training Act of 1964. The law added Title VIII, Nurse Training, to the Public Health Service Act.

This excursion into history is important for understanding the context in which changes in the legislative authorities have been made since 1964 and particularly for understanding the position taken by the Reagan administration with regard to federal support for nursing. The provisions of the Nurse Training Act of 1964 constituted a frontal attack on a pervasive national problem. When legislative authorities were extended and revised in 1968, 1971, 1975, 1979, and 1981, modifications were made in response to changing health needs. For example, improving access to health care at an affordable cost became a priority in the 1960s and led to provisions in the law supporting the training of nurse practitioners. Parenthetically, the interest of the profession in nurse practitioner preparation centered on expanding the nurse's role in assessment and management of patient care and improving the quality of care; the interest of the administration and the Congress focused primarily on providing services in inner cities and rural areas where medical services were in short supply.

Legislative authorities were also modified during the 1960s and 1970s to address the issue of underrepresentation of minorities in the nursing work force. This initiative was seen both as a means of increasing the nurse supply at a time when enrollments in schools of nursing were tapering off and as an action consistent with other Great Society programs aimed at increasing opportunities for education and gainful employment. It was also hoped that individuals recruited from inner-city areas would return to work in these communities.

DEFINING THE FEDERAL ROLE

Federal support proved to be an important instrument in increasing the supply of registered nurses. Despite the increases, it was generally accepted that the shortage of nurses was a persistent problem. Controversy between the administration and the Congress focused less on the existence of a shortage than on the appropriate federal responsibility in alleviating it. Congress has been strongly inclined to extend legislative authorities emphasizing provisions that would increase the supply of nurses to provide primary care or to serve in leadership capacities as teachers, administrators of nursing services, or as expert clinicians, or that would rectify problems of specialty or geographic distribution. On three occasions, presidential vetoes of nurse training legislation were overridden. The position of both Republican and Democratic administrations over the past ten years has been that, given the federal investment of some $89.7 million, states and the health care industry should assume a more prominent role in maintaining the supply of nurses or subsidizing the cost of further increases. They further believe that federal support should be limited to areas amenable only to federal intervention or to actions that can serve as a catalyst to the nonfederal sector.

Efforts to curb federal spending are almost certain to continue, and competition for scarce budgetary resources will be increasingly keen. Nurses should not be lulled into complacency, anticipating that past successes in obtaining federal support will continue, nor should they assume that federal intervention is necessarily appropriate in resolving issues in education and practice. Far greater attention needs to be paid to sorting out the respective responsibilities of states, the private sector, and the profession and to collaborating on strategies that will be responsive to the issues.

To identify the federal role in support of nursing and to use federal resources wisely, nurses need to be informed about the priorities of the administration, the interests of the Congress, and how to use federal processes effectively. The powers of the federal government are vested in three branches: the executive, legislative, and judicial. The executive branch of government, headed by the president of the United States, represents the political party in power. All federal employees, whether in career service or appointed by the president, must support the position taken by his administration— a principle that applies in most public and private organizations. Not infrequently, the nursing community mistakenly expects its professional colleagues in government service to publicly espouse positions taken by the profession even when they are contradictory to those taken by the administration. When professional judgment is at variance with an administration position, however, there is usually room for negotiation. Channels of communication are generally open to exchange views, and operating programs such as the Division of Nursing have the responsibility for transmitting information that will shape policy decisions through the governmental system. An effort is made to provide legislative advice, for example, that is both professionally sound and consistent with the general position taken by the administration as stated in the president's health message or in directives or policy statements.

Similarly, the Division of Nursing makes and justifies recommendations on the allocation of resources, identifying needs of national concern that require federal action. Some years ago, for example, the Division of Nursing, together with national and state nursing organizations, recognized the poor incidence of success of graduates of foreign nursing schools in meeting state requirements for licensure. The concern was shared by immigration authorities, who were issuing visas to nurse immigrants as fully qualified nurses only to discover that they could not meet legal requirements for practice. The Department of Labor was also concerned that continuing to approve visa petitions for nurses as a category of workers in short supply could eventually deprive U.S.-trained nurses of employment opportunities and depress salary scales for nurses in this country. The profession was concerned that the inability of foreign nurses to meet the legal requirements for practice seriously jeopardized the safety and quality of care. Information about the extent of the problem was fragmented among federal, state, and voluntary agencies. The role of the Division of Nursing, as an agency of the federal government, was to initiate, promote, and support measures to help insure that these nurses met recognized qualifications for practice.

Accordingly, the Division held conferences to explore the problem, studied applicable immigration laws and nurse practice acts, surveyed state boards of nursing to obtain a data base on foreign nurse graduates, and contracted for the development of a plan for the establishment of a preimmigration screening procedure for foreign nurse graduates. These efforts culminated in the establishment of an independent Commission on Graduates of Foreign Schools of Nursing, which has successfully administered a preimmigration examination in English language proficiency and nursing knowledge in five subject areas. It has also established procedures that reasonably predict the ability of these nurses to meet licensure requirements.

THE LEGISLATIVE BRANCH

The legislative branch is the lawmaking body in the federal government. Legislative proposals, referred to as bills, can be introduced only by a member of the House of Representatives or of the U.S. Senate, but ideas for legislative action can be put forward by an individual, a professional or voluntary organization, a department of the executive branch or the president himself, a member of Congress, or staff of a Congressional committee. The first step in translating an idea for legislation into law is the drafting of a bill in suitable legislative form and language for introduction to the House or Senate. Most organizations and all executive departments have legal counselors with knowledge and experience in drafting of legislation. Once a bill is introduced, it is given a sequential number, usually preceded by "H.R." for a House introduced bill and "S." for one introduced in the Senate. Thus, S.2559, Nurse Education Amendments of 1984, indicates that 2,558 other bills have been introduced in the Senate during the two-year 98th Congress, which began in January 1983.

Clearly, nursing matters have keen competition on the Congressional agenda. Bills dealing with similar proposals are often under consideration in both Houses at the same time, and 1984 was no exception. A bill to modify and extend the nurse training authorities was introduced in the House (H.R. 5602) and Senate. Both the Senate and the House bills represented initiatives of members of the Congress, although the bill was vetoed by the president. Although the Nurse Training Act of 1964 in its initial form was drafted by the administration and introduced into the Congress at its request, legislative proposals of succeeding administrations have tended not to thrive in Congressional climates that have supported more vigorous assistance for nursing.

The second step toward enactment of legislation is referral to the committee having jurisdiction over the particular subject matter. Committees may have subcommittees to deal with specific areas of jurisdiction. In the House of Representatives, nursing legislation is referred to the Committee on Labor and Human Resources. Committees may take several types of action: they may refuse to consider the bill; they may make minor or major modifications; or they may approve the bill and send it to the floor of their respective body. Committee consideration usually consists of four activities: hearings, mark-ups, voting, and reporting. Unless a bill is rejected outright, hearings on the bill are scheduled to provide a permanent public record of the position of committee members, organizations, individuals, and executive agencies on the proposal. Committees may request organizations to supply witnesses, or individuals or organizations may request the opportunity to give testimony in support of or in opposition to the proposal.

Hearings are followed by "mark-ups," in which modifications are made in the content of the legislation or in the sums of money authorized to carry out proposed activities. Strategies employed during mark-ups to facilitate or inhibit reporting of a bill to the full committee or to the floor of the House or Senate are as limitless as they are fascinating. In 1964, for example, the administration bill included authorization for support for all types of nursing education programs leading to professional nurse licensure. At a time when diploma programs of nursing saw their future threatened by the debate in the profession over what constituted basic preparation for professional practice, and when the number of nursing programs in academic institutions was increasing, the American Hospital Association exerted pressures that resulted in providing institutional support to diploma programs. This promoted their development and prevented further attrition by defraying a portion of the cost of training students whose enrollment could be reasonably attributed to the provisions of the Nurse Training Act. Suffice it to say that compromises reached in mark-up sessions may strengthen or weaken a bill or significantly alter its character. When bills have been substantially modified, they are often rewritten as a "clean bill" and assigned a new number before being sent forward for further action.

Preparation of a report summarizing the intent of the bill, explaining modifications, especially in relation to existing legislation, and discussing the views of the committee is the final step in committee action. Reports are intended primarily to prepare legislators for voting on a bill, but they serve the additional and useful purpose of providing the executive branch with information on legislative intent, which is essential to implementing a bill once it is enacted.

The next step in the procedural journey is floor action. House and Senate bills are sent to their respective floors where they are debated and sometimes amended before final passage or defeat occurs. If both Houses of the Congress have voted favorably on bills addressing a single topic, any differences between the two versions must be resolved before the bill can be sent to the president for action. If necessary, a conference may be held between House and Senate members to reach agreement on disputed provisions.

When a bill has been approved by the House and the Senate in identical form, it is sent to the president for signature. The president has ten days, Sundays excepted, to act upon the bill. He may sign the bill into law, in which case it is delivered to the administrator of the General Services Administration for assignment of a serial number preceded by the letters P.L., standing for public law, and the number of the Congress in session. If the president chooses to veto the bill, he returns it, together with a veto message, to the House where it originated. Vetoed bills can become law by a two-thirds vote by each House of the Congress. If the president does not sign the bill within the ten-day period, it becomes law unless Congress has adjourned; in which case, the bill dies.

NURSES CAN INFLUENCE LEGISLATIVE PROCESS AND OUTCOMES

Throughout this process, there are opportunities for nurses to influence the course of events. Members of the House and Senate depend upon their constituencies for feedback and are responsive to the people they represent. Nurses, like individuals from other walks of life, are quick to register complaints with legislators or to request their support or opposition to bills being considered. It would be even more effectual for nurses to keep legislators informed about accomplishments resulting from federal support. For example, recipients of grants to establish programs of advanced nurse training should let their legislators, as well as members of committee and subcommittee staffs, know how such programs have increased the number of nurses in leadership positions. Similarly, nurses who have received professional nurse traineeships or other types of support for advanced study should tell their representatives how federally assisted training has extended their knowledge and enabled them to function more effectively in the roles for which they have been prepared. Sustained interaction emphasizing positive results of federal support can be a powerful tool in generating continued Congressional support for nurses and nursing.

THE EXECUTIVE BRANCH

The executive branch is responsible for administering laws passed by the Congress. For legislation in support of nurse training, the Department of Health and Human Services is assigned responsibility for implementing the legislation. This responsibility is further delegated to the Division of Nursing of the Bureau of Health Professions of the Health Resources and Services Administration. The Division of Nursing is the operating program unit with knowledge and expertise in this subject matter area.

Probably the most important step in implementing legislation is developing regulations that have the force of law and that clarify or define terms used in the law, interpret areas not specifically addressed in the law itself, or establish criteria as required by law. For example, one of the nurse training authorities authorizes support for programs to increase nursing education opportunities for individuals from disadvantaged backgrounds, "as determined in accordance with criteria prescribed by the Secretary." These criteria have been specified in the regulatory process. Terms such as "primary health care" also have been defined in regulations for purposes of administering the nurse practitioner training authorities. When the law has stated that special consideration shall be given to certain types of applications (for example, applications for traineeship programs that include nurse practitioner training), regulations have specified how grants will be awarded to carry out the legislative mandate. Legal advice and assistance are indispensable in development of regulations that are fair, legally defensible, and capable of being administered. In short, regulations lay out for the nursing community and the public the ground rules for carrying out the letter and spirit of the law.

Regulations are published in the *Federal Register*, published daily and circulated nationwide. The initial publication may take several forms, such as Notice of Proposed Rulemaking (NPRM) or Interim Final Regulations. Public comment is invited, generally for a 30- to 60-day period. Every comment is reviewed, and those addressing particular issues are considered together in preparing the Administration's response and final decision regarding the points that have been raised. Most academic settings and service agencies assign someone to review the *Federal Register* for notices affecting programs that they administer or areas in which they have an interest. Nurses can and do use the public comment period to register their concerns about proposals for implementing legislation.

The last step in the regulatory process is the issuance of final regulations. The complexities of obtaining concurrence on regulations from numerous program units, offices at various levels of the Department, and other federal agencies often prolong the publication of final regulations for months. Meanwhile, regulations in draft form are used in the development of guidelines that provide detailed guidance for prospective applicants for federal support.

BUDGET FORMULATION

No description of federal processes would be complete without a general discussion of the ways in which budgets are formulated, and how funds are appropriated by the Congress and administered by the executive branch. Budget formulation is begun many months in advance of the federal fiscal year, which extends from October 1 through the following September 30. During the month of January preceding the beginning of the next fiscal year, the president issues his budget message and transmits his budget to the Congress. Requests for funds for each of the programs authorized by legislation and administered by the operating program, in this case the Division of Nursing, must be consistent with the position taken in the budget message and must not exceed the level of funding specified in the authorizing legislation. In recent years, the amount requested for nursing programs specified in the president's budget has been significantly less than the amounts authorized in the legislation. When new legislation is being considered in the Congress, as was the case in 1984, budget formulation is particularly difficult. Based on past experience and professional judgment, one can expect legislation to be enacted that will continue programs already under way. However, program units in the executive branch are obliged to limit their requests for funds to amounts specified by the president and monitored by the Office of Management and Budget. Marked differences between the Congress and the executive branch as to the expected level of support for nursing compound the problem of planning, both within the federal establishment and in the nursing community.

The House of Representatives initiates action on all appropriation bills. Bills dealing with particular subject areas are referred to subcommittees of the Appropriations Committee. In the House of Representatives and in the Senate, appropriations for nursing are considered by the subcommittees on appropriation for Labor and Health and Human Services. These subcommittees conduct hearings with witnesses from the public and from federal departments that administer the programs under discussion. Nurses, individually or as members of professional organizations, can influence the views of their representatives regarding the types and levels of support they believe necessary for nursing. On the basis of their testimony, a review of the Administration's budget proposal, and the judgment of subcommittee members, an appropriations bill is drafted for submission to the full committee which, in turn, sends the bill to the floor of the House for debate, modification, and a vote. The bill then goes to the Senate. If the Senate makes changes in the House bill, the bill is returned to the House for reconsideration and a vote. Disagreements must be resolved through a conference committee consisting of both House and Senate members, and both Houses must vote favorably on an identical bill before it is sent to the president for signature. On several occasions, action on an appropriation bill has not been taken by October 1, the beginning of the new fiscal year. To avert disruption in carrying out programs, Congress passes a continuing resolution providing funds for a designated time period at several possible levels, such as those in the appropriation bill being considered or the current year's operating levels.

CONCLUSION

Understanding federal processes is the first step in using them effectively. Nurses must also be informed about general issues debated in newspapers and in the media as a basis for understanding political realities. If possible, they must deal with divisive professional issues privately so that they speak with one strong voice in the public arena. The strength and vitality of nursing flow from the corporate commitment of informed and dedicated nurses.

References

Aiken LH(editor): *Nursing in the 1980s: Crises, Opportunities, Challenges.* Lippincott, 1982.

Davidson RH, Oleszek WJ: *Congress and Its Members.* CQ Press, 1981.

Dodd LC, Oppenheimer BI (editors): *Congress Reconsidered.* CQ Press, 1981.

Dove RG: *Enactment of a Law: Procedural Steps in the Legislative Process.* Document No. 97-20, 97th Congress, 2nd session. U.S. Government Printing Office, 1982.

Hanlon JJ, Pickett GE: *Public Health Administration and Practice.* Mosby, 1984.

Kalisch PA, Kalisch BJ: *The Federal Influence and Impact on Nursing.* HRP 0900636. National Technical Information Service, 1979.

Oleszek WJ: *Congressional Procedures and the Policy Process,* 2nd ed. CQ Press, 1984.

U.S. Department of Health, Education, and Welfare, Division of Nursing: *Toward Quality in Nursing, Needs and Goals: Report of the Surgeon General's Consultant Group on Nursing.* Public Health Service Publication No. 992, 1963.

U.S. Department of Health and Human Services, Division of Nursing: *Survey of Foreign Nurse Graduates.* HHS Publication No. (HRA) 76-13, 1976.

U.S. Department of Health and Human Services, Division of Nursing: *Nurse Supply, Distribution and Requirements: Third Report to the Congress.* HHS Publication No. (HRA) 82-7, 1982.

Chapter 27

Political Appointments

Getting Appointed

Susan W. Talbott, RN, MA, MBA

Nurses are realizing that one of the greatest opportunities to influence health policy comes through a political appointment. There are a wide variety of paid and volunteer positions in federal, state, and local government filled by political appointment. The president, governors, and mayors appoint individuals to cabinet posts (such as the appointment of Barbara Nichols, RN, past-president of the ANA, as Secretary of Wisconsin's Department of Regulation and Licensing) and to head agencies such as the health department. These are full-time, paid positions for which the candidate must have particular credentials. Citizens who are appointed to serve on commissions and task forces are usually volunteers, and their work is part-time.

It is important for nurses to seek and receive political appointments. The most obvious reason is so that nurses, rather than hospital administrators or physicians, can present nursing's point of view on health policy and service development. If there is no nurse on the health planning commission, and in at least one state that was the case, how will critical information about nursing care and nursing practice be conveyed to those who are doing health planning?

Another reason nurses should seek appointments is to offer their expertise on a particular subject. When a city task force on school health is convened, shouldn't there be a nurse with expertise in this area serving on the committee? Nurses are experts in many areas, and the public will be better served if nurses' knowledge and skills are available through their appointment to paid or volunteer posts.

Nurses who serve on public bodies, such as a commission on mental health or as a paid commissioner of health, have an opportunity to not only influence public policy, but also to convey to their colleagues and the public at large a positive image of nursing. Nursing still suffers from the handmaiden image in many circles. As political appointees, the nurses have the opportunity to educate coworkers and the lay public about modern nursing.

At the same time nurses are contributing their expertise and working to improve the profession's image, they also have the opportunity to expand their networks. For example, when I attend meetings of the New York Governor's Commission on Domestic Violence I have access to important city and state employees. Often the governor's director of the Division for Women, a cabinet appointee, attends the meetings. When the nursing association's third party reimbursement bill was coming up for a vote, I asked her to lobby the governor on behalf of the bill. Representatives from every state office attend Commission meetings. By getting to know each commissioner's designated representative (health department, social service, labor, etc.), I have indirect access to both information and individuals in these various state offices.

Often legislators with particular interest in the work of the Commission attend meetings. They and their staff are readily available for informal lobbying about nursing issues. These kinds of relationships, however, must be "two way." Just as I feel free to ask a legislator to help with a nursing bill, I am careful to inquire if he needs help from the nurses' association on an issue he is working on. If help is needed, then I alert the nurses' association and urge their support.

Politics are people. Our relationships with others in all spheres can either promote or hinder the profession's growth and development. The personal contacts nurses can make at the same time they are doing the business of the group to which they have been appointed represent opportunities for image building, favor asking, and exertion of influence.

HOW TO GET POLITICAL APPOINTMENTS

There are a number of ways to put yourself in a position to receive appointments.

1. Begin to do volunteer work in political campaigns or in local offices of government. You can prove your worth and gain notice by doing good work.
2. Identify an area of expertise you think would be valuable to share. For example, if you are an expert in the care of the chronic mentally ill, you may be in demand because cities, counties, and states are faced with problems in planning and delivering care to this population.
3. Obtain information about the commission, task force, board, or committee of interest to you. What is the purpose of the body? Who makes the appointments (the public official and the staff involved)? Who are current members? What are the formal and informal qualifications for appointment to the body?
4. Particularly if one of the qualifications for membership has to do with organizational affiliation, submit your curriculum vitae or resumé to your state and district nurses' associations with a cover letter explaining your expertise and willingness to have your name submitted to those in government who ask for names of individuals to serve in either a volunteer or paid capacity.

5. Regardless of whether the appointment is based on organizational affiliation, review your personal telephone book and identify a list of influential well-connected individuals who might also help you arrange interviews or speak in your behalf to those who make recommendations for or actually make the appointments. Arrange a meeting with your local, state, or federal elected representatives and ask their help in getting your name and credentials presented to the right person.

VOLUNTEER POLITICAL APPOINTMENT: THE STATE LEVEL

I was appointed to the governor's Commission on Domestic Violence because I knew the health commissioner. I had not been seeking an appointment, and my nursing expertise and political activity on behalf of the governor were secondary factors in my selection. I was not an expert in domestic violence and had not done anything more than register as a member of the governor's party and vote for him. What brought my appointment was the health commissioner's recommendation. He trusted me personally and knew I was a hard and competent worker with statewide networks among health professionals. At the time, the Commission was in need of a person to chair a new committee on professional education, and he felt that I would be a good candidate for the position. I was interviewed by a member of the governor's staff. Then my credentials were assembled and submitted to the governor for review and approval. I have worked hard on the Commission and have taken advantage of the opportunities to expand my professional networks and influence on behalf of nursing. I have learned a great deal and enjoyed my work.

PAID POLITICAL APPOINTMENTS: THE FEDERAL LEVEL

In recent years, several nurses have been appointed to prominent positions in the federal government. Two have written about their experiences for this book.

Carolyne K. Davis, former head of the Health Care Financing Administration, talks about her appointment and influential position in the Reagan administration. Sheila Burke, a member of Senate Majority Leader Robert Dole's staff, writes about her role on the Senate Finance Committee (see Chapter 29).

The Federal Level

Carolyne K. Davis, RN, PhD

Each political party has a basic platform of policy issues that are shaped during the debates at the national conventions that nominate the presidential candidates. Once a political party is elected into office, there is a need to place people in key positions in the executive branch who are knowledgeable about the party's policies and can interpret these policies to both the general public and the career civil servants. Thus, whenever a new president is elected, a number of policy positions in the federal sector change personnel to accommodate the need for informed individuals who endorse the party platform and can help to shape policies in the new administration. Generally these positions are heads of agencies or their deputies.

The executive branch now has about 2,323 positions designated as Schedule C or political appointees. These positions are always cleared and endorsed by White House personnel. Although individuals selected are almost always from the same party, there are a few appointees from the other major party whose competence and endorsement of fundamental policies is congruent with the president's. The key criteria for selection is knowledge in one's field, competence in management, and endorsement of the president and his key policies.

I have been asked many times by my nursing colleagues how I got to be a political appointee, and what it is like to work within the government in this type of role.

In the late 1970s, I became active in nursing's struggle to keep federal monies for undergraduate and graduate education and for research. As a result, I became an active supporter of our local Republican Congressman Carl Pursell. In his 1978 and 1980 reelection efforts, I organized the nurses in his district to work for his reelection. We held fund raisers, spent hours addressing envelopes to raise campaign contributions, provided coverage of his campaign office to answer telephones, and helped with the many small tasks required to keep a campaign flowing smoothly. We even passed out campaign literature prior to football games. I did several radio announcements and press interviews on his behalf and worked with his press office in developing material specifically targeted to health care providers.

After the 1978 election, I continued to work with the Congressman and his Washington staff. Because he is an active member of the House Appropriations Subcommittee Labor/HHS/Education, I provided briefing papers on health-related topics. At the request of another Congressman from Michigan, David Stockman, former director of the Office of Management and Budget, I worked actively to defeat the hospital cost-containment legislation proposed by President Carter. During this process, I became acquainted with Congressman James T. Broyhill from North Carolina, ranking Republican on the House Energy and Commerce Committee, and Congressman Robert Michel from Illinois, a key House Republican and currently House Minority Leader. As I worked with these Congressmen, I grew more experienced in the development of health policy and the political process. During the 1980 presidential campaign, I worked for the election of President Reagan as well as Congressman Pursell's reelection.

As a nurse and registered Republican, I was asked by several people to submit my credentials for consideration for a political appointment in the Reagan administration after the election in November 1980. Because of my activities in the Republican party and my personal experiences working with the Congressmen on health policy issues, I was fortunate to be cosponsored by Congressmen Michel, Broyhill, and Pursell. Each of them wrote letters and made telephone calls on my behalf.

President Reagan is a strong supporter of the appointment of minorities and women to key administration positions. In his first two years in office, he has selected women to fill over 1,200 high-level policy-making positions in the executive branch. I was tapped in January of 1981 to become the first woman to administer the agency within the Department of Health and Human Services that has responsibility for shaping Medicare and Medicaid policies. The Health Care Financing Administration (HCFA) is responsible for payments for the health care needs of 50 million elderly, disabled, and poor Americans. HCFA has the third largest agency budget within the federal government (behind the Defense Department and Social Security Administration), totaling $86 billion in 1984 and over $95 billion in 1985.

Political appointees are often called upon to represent the administration's position on public policies to Congress and the general public. All political appointees must have special security clearances with a background check. This is done by the Federal Bureau of Investigation. One's acceptability and commitment to the party's policies are checked by personal interviews and references from state and local political party members.

As HCFA administrator, I managed the agency and its 4,000 employees and dealt with the varied and volatile issues that are part of any large bureaucracy. The necessity to reduce our overall inflation rate, especially in health care, where inflation has continually outpaced the Consumer Price Index by double or triple, has generated an intense interest in both Medicare and Medicaid.

In my position, I reported directly to the secretary of the Department of Health and Human Services, as do all the other assistant secretaries. An important part of the job is clarification of the intent behind specific policy recommendations or decisions. Congressional committee hearings provide for interpretation of our policies to Congress. Sometimes HCFA represents the administration's position and sometimes we were joined by a colleague from the Department of Health and Human Services. Sometimes the administration is represented by Secretary Margaret Heckler, and we attended as support personnel, having briefed the secretary on specific details of the issues the hearing would cover.

Sometimes I was asked to prepare briefing documents on special areas of Medicare and Medicaid of interest to other key administration officials. Occasionally I briefed key White House personnel and even joined Secretary Heckler as backup support when issues of critical concern regarding Medicare and Medicaid were discussed in Cabinet meetings with the president.

Special interest groups working through the White House Public Liaison Office sometimes request briefings on specific issues. One learns to present key elements in a succinct fashion because, as part of a team, one usually has only ten to fifteen minutes.

At our level in government policy-making, we were expected to represent the administration in meetings with professional groups in the United States as well as overseas. As a symbol of the administration and its policies, one is required to keep up to date on current issues of concern to the various constituencies. As one of the women appointees in this administration, I was keenly aware of the role of educating people about the status of women's issues as well as health policy issues. Background briefings by White House personnel were conducted frequently on specific issues to enable us to have a broad understanding of the president's policies in key areas outside our sphere.

Extensive briefing materials must be read and clarified through personal interaction with others in the government before representing the United States in meetings abroad. I believe it is during these meetings with other nations that one truly realizes the enormous responsibilities of one's position. Interpreting U.S. policy to delegates from other countries and listening to them interpret and clarify their government's positions makes one realize that what is said or not said is important. Likewise, actions are scrutinized at all times since you are the official U.S. representative and have been empowered by the State Department to speak to our nation's policies relative to health care.

One is equally subjected to the same visibility at home. It is impossible to go anywhere or do anything without realizing that one is representing the executive branch at all times, even on those rare occasions when one is not at work. As a political appointee at the assistant secretary level, I was always on call for the Secretary of Health and Human Services and those in the White House who make broad policy decisions. Thus, the carefully constructed schedule for the day or week is subject to constant change to meet the needs of those in higher policy-making areas. One learns to be adaptable, recognizing that demands on one's time are frequently controlled by others.

As a symbol of the administration, I was often called upon to do radio, press, and TV briefings or appearances to inform the public of new policies or interpret and clarify issues of interest. With the recent concerns over the enormous growth in Medicare and Medicaid expenditures, my agency was constantly in the public eye. HCFA maintains a public affairs office whose major responsibility is to clarify and interact with the media on a daily basis. It provided briefings and background documents for my use before media interviews and other public appearances.

Travel was an essential component of my responsibilities because it was important to address key national groups such as the American Hospital Association, Federation of American Hospitals, physician and nursing organizations, and other providers of health care services. Formal speeches were usually followed by questions and answers to clarify the administration's policies.

Because of the workload in the office, it was impossible to be away for long because the essential activities of the central office could be delayed. My travel was usually limited to attending the meeting briefly to give a speech, meet with key leaders, and then return to Washington or to my next speaking engagement. While I criss-crossed America in my 56 months as spokesperson for HCFA policies, most of my time was spent in meetings with community leaders, press conferences, and keynote speeches with almost no time for sightseeing or meeting with friends. One is always on call and may have to return to the office because of an unforeseen crisis. Whenever I traveled, I was in touch with my office at least twice a day and spent at least an hour of the day in conference calls with my key administrative associates in the central office to keep in touch with late breaking developments and give directions regarding policy interpretation. I learned it was difficult to be away more than two or three days at a time.

As a nurse, I believe I was one of two appointees in this administration (Judi Buckalew, White House liaison, is the other one and the first nurse to hold such a high level position in any administration). Because of this, I tried to accept a few more speeches to nursing groups than one normally would in this position. I sometimes spoke to state and local groups rather than limiting my appearances to national groups, because I believed it was important to encourage other nurses to think about moving into policy-making positions within state and federal government.

One of the most difficult adjustments that I had to make in this policy-making position was to recognize that every decision I made was somehow leaked to the general public. In Washington rumors abound, and frequently time is spent reassuring people that either a policy decision has not yet been made or it has not yet been approved by the secretary. Likewise, under the Freedom of Information Act (FOI), one's daily appointment schedule, travel schedule, and expenditures are subject to FOI by anyone who requests them. Personal financial status is reviewed once a year, and we were required to submit an updated statement that listed any gifts over $40 or any expenditures on our behalf of more than $250 by any organization. Because of potential conflict of interest, strict ethical codes usually forbid my accepting any gifts.

If you are interested in a political appointment, you must acquire a sound knowledge base of not only nursing but also health care policy. You must be willing to devote extraordinary time and attention to the job. My days were 14 hours or longer every day, including weekends, with a few 17 or 18 hour days each week. With such a grueling schedule and emotional pressure to correctly interpret administration policies as well as lead one's agency, it is little wonder that many political appointees resign after an 18- to 24-month schedule of government service. Burnout occurs in these positions. The stress of the position and its responsibilities are enormous, yet the rewards are worth the sacrifice in time and money.

The recognition of successes and the power and influence that one wields in the political sphere regarding policy decisions make for interesting discussions with other top level people in all professional areas of health care. Credibility with one's public and one's employees is important in accomplishing the job. That means a willingness to listen to the concerns voiced by all sectors before making critical decisions. Gaining the endorsement of the White House, the Office of Management and Budget (OMB), and Congress takes time and many meetings in order to clarify the rationale for decisions.

Most important of all is the opportunity to serve one's country and one's president to achieve a common purpose. To have a small part in shaping history is worth the emotional and physical stress of the position.

Lest anyone think a political appointment is a glory trip, remember that the decisions one makes have an impact on many Americans—in my case, the 50 million Americans who depend on Medicare and Medicaid to pay for their health care services. HCFA has the responsibility to work with 50 state Medicaid programs and supervise the intermediaries and carriers such as Blue Cross and Blue Shield. Decisions I made will also impact on 7,000 hospitals, 450,000 physicians, 1.6 million registered nurses, and many other providers of health care services. It was an awesome responsibility, but one that was made easier for me because as a nurse I learned the basic skills of management and working with people.

If you aspire to an appointive position in government, begin now to work with your political party. Help to shape its policy platform issues and put yourself in a position to be considered for a political appointment. Only if you have the knowledge of your profession and credibility from working within your party's philosophical platform can you hope to attain such an appointment, because a political appointee is the president's representative.

For those who would follow my footsteps into the public arena of health policy development as a political appointee, I suggest several steps:

1. Become actively involved in your own political party. While nurses may not have a large amount of dollars to contribute to campaigns, most campaigns need people to carry out the work assigments as much, if not more, than financial support.

2. Expand your knowledge and expertise beyond nursing to encompass broad health policy issues. Study your party platform on health care issues to see if your viewpoints in the major areas are congruent with the philosophy of the party.

3. Actively comment on public policy issues and make your position on these issues known to members of Congress and the administration. Be concise and always look at the pros and cons of any issue. A single-minded viewpoint is not helpful, since you must know the opposition's point of view, articulate it, and be able to counter its arguments. Offer to give expert testimony at Congressional hearings.

4. Be prepared to make a significant commitment of time and energy to become recognized and valued for your expertise.

5. Most political appointees have positions offered to them in Washington. Be prepared to relocate if offered the opportunity.

I am grateful to President Reagan for inviting me to be a member of his executive team and proud that a nurse was given the opportunity to help shape health policy at such a high level in this administration. It speaks well for President Reagan's respect for nursing and represents a key breakthrough for nursing. I hope nurses will continue to occupy such positions in the future.

Chapter 28

Political Parties and Clubs

Political Parties

Cathy Chapman Hughes, RN

The founders of the American Government did not envision a political party system. Leaders, including Washington, Jefferson, and Adams, feared that political parties would be a divisive force in the new nation. They assumed that most Americans had left Europe to seek religious or political freedom and would not desire conflict in the affairs of government.

The authors of the Constitution provided for three separate branches of government: legislative, judicial, and executive. Each branch has specific functions, but overlapping responsibilities create a system of checks and balances. After ratification by nine of the thirteen states, the new government, a federation of states, became operational; and thus the leaders who wrote the Constitution and promoted its ratification were called Federalists.

When George Washington was unanimously elected president in 1789, he did not run as the candidate of any political party, and he had no opponent. Following the ratification of the Constitution and Washington's election, it became evident that a system for running the government was needed. Many problems faced the new government, including the need to pay off the Revolutionary War debt.

Alexander Hamilton, Washington's Secretary of the Treasury, helped to build our two party system by creating a strong financial base for the new nation. The Federalist program, supported by Hamilton, created a National Bank and instituted taxation to raise money to reduce the national debt, including repayment of the war debts.

Wealthy individuals favored Hamilton's approach; they regarded the National Bank as a source of business capital they could use to increase their personal wealth. Opposition to the Federalist program came from farmers, craftsmen, and others who felt that they would not benefit from Hamilton's programs. Out of this opposition grew the Republican party (the forerunner of the Democratic party). It was supported by individuals who favored decentralization of power and an economy that benefited farmers and small shopkeepers. Thomas Jefferson, like Hamilton, deplored the idea of political parties, but he did not want to see America ruled by members of the wealthy upper class. As a result, between 1793 and 1796, Jefferson helped organize the first state and local party organizations and, in 1800, the fledgling Jeffersonian-Republican party organized around Jefferson's candidacy for president.

Ultimately, political leaders realized that a single party system would not be useful. Indeed, the Federalists recognized the right of the Jeffersonian-Republican party to exist and acknowledged that efforts to prevent the development of a two-party system would be more divisive than the two-party system itself.

By 1820, the Federalist party ceased to exist, and the Jeffersonian-Republican Party split into the Democratic-Republicans and the National Republicans. Subsequently, the Democratic-Republicans shortened their name to the Democratic party, the name used today. The National Republicans evolved into the Whig party, which existed until the Civil War.

Between 1820 and 1840, the Democratic party was reorganized and became the "party of the people." In 1828, Andrew Jackson, a Democrat, became the first president of the United States who was neither highly educated nor a member of the upper class. The common man felt that the depression of the 1820s was the fault of the ruling class and that Jackson and the Democrats offered an alternative. Jackson's election shifted political power away from control by the wealthy so that average citizens had a greater voice in government. It was during this period in history that the number of elective offices grew and the system of convention nomination for president and vice-president developed.

Political parties continue to be an important part of American society. A vehicle for people with common ideologies to influence the direction and policies of government, they are essential to the well-being of a democracy.

THIRD PARTIES

Abraham Lincoln's election in 1860 is the only time in United States history that the candidate of a third party has won the presidency. The members of the two major parties, the Democrats and Whigs, were split over legislation that would allow territories and new states to choose whether they would permit slavery. This split opened the door for the development of a third party—the Republicans. They supported legislation that would prohibit slavery in newly settled areas, but would allow slavery to continue in southern states. The Republicans were able to elect their candidate, Lincoln, by garnering the votes of disaffected members of the Democratic and Whig parties.

Other third party presidential candidates have emerged around the central issue of race since the Civil War, but only George Wallace, the American party candidate in 1968, has ever won a significant number of votes: 13.5% of the popular vote.

It is difficult for third party candidates to win because, while both major parties include a wide variety of people with diverse opinions, they can achieve consensus on major issues. This leaves only radical or secondary issues around which a third party can coalesce. In addition, state election laws discourage third party candidates. For example, each state determines the number of members a party must register before its candidate can appear on the ballot. In 1980, when John Anderson ran as a third party candidate, he was not able to get on the ballot in some states because he did not have the required number of signatures. However, he did win a sufficient percentage of the popular vote that his candidacy may have caused Jimmy Carter to lose the election.

Third parties have contributed to our system because they have forced the major parties to arrive at a consensus on issues that otherwise might have been ignored. Among the more enduring third parties are the Prohibition party (1869), the Socialist Labor party (1876), and the Communist party (1919). Whatever its ideology, the major parties and the third parties exist to provide electable candidates who will support the party's platform.

SINGLE ISSUE GROUPS

A trend that has received both praise and criticism is the rise in single issue groups. These groups are formed to promote single issues, rather than a global ideology. For example, many nurses participate in the activities of groups that support the nuclear freeze movement, such as the Nurses' Alliance for the Prevention of Nuclear War. Others work for a myriad of environmental protection organizations, including Nurses' Environmental Health Watch.

Single issue groups are important because they focus attention on critical issues and help educate the public about these issues. In many cases, especially on local issues, single issue groups can facilitate the resolution of a problem. Single issue groups are often coalitions made up of individuals or groups that are like-minded on one issue but may have diverse opinions on other issues.

Choosing a candidate for political office on the basis of a single issue is often difficult because the single issue candidate may not have developed positions on other key issues. Moreover, some critics contend these groups are splintering the efforts of the major political parties, which address a myriad of issues based upon an ideology. The question becomes, should government base its actions on pressure from special interest groups or on a consistent social ideology? Our society is still grappling with the answer.

PARTY ORGANIZATION

Each state Republican and Democratic party has a written organizational plan. The local unit of each state party is called the caucus or precinct. Its size can vary from a few blocks in an urban area to several square miles in rural areas. Caucuses usually meet annually to elect committee officers. They may also elect members of a municipal committee or delegates to a county convention, depending upon the state party system.

County officials serve as the link between the local caucuses and the state party officials. County committees usually hold regular meetings and elect members to represent them on the state party committees, raise money, and maintain a headquarters. County party organizations can be powerful political groups.

PARTY ACTIVITIES

Since every registered party member (Democrat or Republican) can attend the local caucus meeting of his party, this is a good place for the novice political activist to become involved. The nurse who wants to learn more about politics can volunteer to work in a variety of caucus activities including:

1. voter registration drives
2. get out the vote campaigns during elections
3. campaign activities of party candidates
4. caucus study groups that examine party organization and platform and reviews candidates' positions on issues

Political parties are most active during the even numbered election years when congressional and/or presidential elections occur. Volunteers are needed for all types of activities. To win elections, a party must get its message to the voters and then convince them to vote for the party's candidates. Several steps are involved in this process:
Before election day:

1. voter registration drives
2. telephone banking (calling registered voters to urge them to vote for the party candidates)
3. door to door canvassing to determine voter opinions
4. distribution of literature that presents the party's candidates for office

On election day:

5. distribution of campaign literature at polling places
6. phone banking reminding voters to vote
7. providing transportation and babysitting service
8. poll watching (to ensure that voting process is carried out according to the election laws)

Candidate selection is an important party activity. Individuals can have a role in candidate selection at the grass-roots level by participating in the Democratic or Republican party at the local or state level. Nurses who want to influence selection of candidates should join and take part in the activities of their local Democratic or Republican club, caucus, or precinct. Most candidates who attain high political office began their political careers on a local level with the backing of their precinct, caucus, or political club. Once candidates get on the ballot, they face a race in a primary or the general election. In the primary election in most states, one can only vote for candidates of the party to which the voter in registered.

Although political party activity decreases after major elections, local clubs often work for candidates in town, city, county, and state elections. In between elections, party activity centers around auxiliary organizations such as party organizations for women and young adults. The Republican and Democratic women's groups each sponsor clubs in all states. One of the purposes of the women's organizations is to provide political experience for women. The clubs offer seminars, workshops, and opportunities for experience that women need to be party leaders or to run for public office. The primary purpose of the women's clubs is to further the goals of the political party through activities such as fund-raising and recruitment of new members. In some local Democratic and Republican clubs there are also groups for men, although these are not organized on a state or national basis as are the women's groups.

The Young Republicans, organized nationally in 1931, have 1,700 local chapters and offer political training and experience for people 18 to 40 years old. The Young Democrats offer similar experience for Democrats 18 to 35 years old in 2,000 local chapters. In addition, many college students belong to Democratic and Republican clubs on their campuses. The College Republicans are organized on a national level, while the College Democrats have state-wide organizations.

In some communities, there are party organizations for teenagers. Although many clubs do not have formal teen groups, young people are encouraged to participate in regular Democratic and Republican club activities.

The newest auxiliary organization is the Senior Democrat's Club for men and women over 60. At this writing, North Carolina has the only Senior Democrat's Club with a state organization, but they are growing at the local level in many states. The Senior Democrats want to ensure that the Democratic party has candidates concerned and knowledgeable about the needs of senior citizens.

MAJOR ELECTIVE POSITIONS

Members of a political party can seek election to two major positions: the platform committee at the state and national level, and delegate to the national party convention where the party's presidential and vice-presidential candidates are selected and the party platform is determined. The party platform outlines the party's programs and ideas. The party's candidates are supposed to promote the platform during the campaign and work to implement it after the election. Often the platform committee makes headlines when there is an internal split over a "hot" issue. For example, at the 1984 Republican convention many Republican women spoke out against the party because it refused to include ERA as a plank in the party platform. Geraldine Ferraro was conspicuous as the chairperson of the Democratic platform committee.

The delegate selection process varies from state to state, but in all states it begins with participation at the annual caucus. Individuals elected to state or national office have demonstrated their competence and commitment by their work with their party.

OPPORTUNITIES

Involvement in political parties can provide nurses with a variety of opportunities for personal and professional growth. They provide a vehicle for exerting influence in local, state, and national communities. In addition, the parties need the expertise of nurses to help develop positions on health and social issues. The parties also offer opportunities for leadership roles.

The following describes my experience of working with a political party.

MY POLITICAL EXPERIENCE

In May, 1971 I began my career as a staff nurse in a large county hospital. Like most new graduates, I was idealistic and believed I could use the knowledge I had gained in nursing school to help people.

Reality shock soon set in. There never seemed to be enough staff or time to provide the nursing care I thought patients needed and deserved. At times I felt alone or that I had failed. I felt that way because I realized I could do little to influence the decisions that affected my practice. The hospital hierarchy left little decision making to the nurse. As a staff nurse, I received little support or incentive to deliver nursing care as I had been taught in school. Despite my feelings and the realities of the workplace, I was still idealistic and believed the principle that one person can make a difference. I was sure I could find a way to improve the system.

Politics: Change the System

The solution I sought came when I realized that I had a chance to effect change by using the political process. I view politics as the process by which decisions are made on how to divide up scarce resources. For example, elected officials decide how much money will be allocated for the county hospital, the prison health program, and day care centers. Each voter helps to decide who will divide up the resources within the community.

The next major revelation for me was that elected officials are people like you and me who hold office because people like us have voted for them. To have constituents continue to vote for them, politicians must be responsive to the electorate's needs and wishes. As nurses, we are not only voters, we are experts—we have knowledge that can help politicians make informed decisions about nursing and health care issues.

These ideas did not occur to me in an orderly way, but in retrospect I think that my understanding that elected officials are approachable is what motivated me to get involved in politics. Often, when I talk to nurses about the need for them to communicate with elected officials, I have to convince them that they need not be in awe of them. I urge nurses to be respectful of elected officials' positions, but at the same time to recognize that they are human beings like the rest of us.

Getting Involved

How do you get started? Read the newspapers and talk with political activists before you decide which party has positions compatible with yours on issues important to you. Then choose a candidate whose positions reflect your opinions on key issues and call his campaign headquarters to volunteer. Describe the skills you have and when you are available. There are numerous jobs in a campaign that do not require specific skills, although nurses' communication skills can often help candidates get their message to voters through telephone campaigns or door-to-door canvassing.

In 1972, when I first became politically active, I worked for the only candidate I had met—Senator George McGovern. He had been a speaker at a convention of nursing students, and I shared his commitment to world peace. While I continued to be concerned about nursing and health care issues, I decided to work in the McGovern campaign because I believed in him and was not yet ready to pursue my dream of running for a political office myself.

While working for Senator McGovern, I met other Democratic candidates and elected officials. Later, I joined the Democratic Women's Club and became involved in local and state Democratic activities. I learned that the state legislature had great influence over issues that affect nursing practice. This knowledge of the system and its effect on nursing led me to work for candidates for the state legislature who shared my concerns about health issues. In 1978, I was appointed to the steering committee for Mecklenburg County Democratic state house candidates.

A Real Nursing Issue

In 1977 the state legislature passed sunset legislation that mandated review of the North Carolina Board of Nursing in the 1981 session. The Board of Nursing would be terminated if renewing legislation was not passed in 1981. The North Carolina Nurses' Association (NCNA) began to organize nursing groups to review this proposed legislation revising the Nurse Practice Act. In 1980, after three years work, these groups proposed a revision of the act. NCNA then organized nurses to lobby for its passage. I knew many state legislators, so I lobbied them before and during the legislative session. The efforts of organized nursing in North Carolina paid off, for the new Nurse Practice Act was passed in May, 1981, giving North Carolina nurses the first Board of Nursing in the country elected by practicing nurses.

As a result of the passage of the Nurse Practice Act, many more nurses recognized the importance of the political process to the nursing profession. During the 1982 elections, more nurses were active in local and state campaigns.

Participation in the Professional Association

NCNA's awareness of my political activism led to my being asked to chair NCNA's Political Action Committee (PAC) during 1982–83. During my tenure, PAC contributions increased 300%. Nurses demonstrated their understanding that legislative and political involvement also requires financial commitment. My experience as PAC chairperson broadened my understanding of how nurses can participate in politics and reinforced my belief that our profession's growth is dependent upon expansion of the influence of nursing PACs along with legislative initiatives.

Candidate for Office

Near the end of my term as PAC chairperson, I was invited to run for the first vice-chairperson of the Mecklenburg County Democratic party. I decided to run because of my commitment to work for Democratic victories in 1984. For example, I knew that the race for the U.S. Senate between Senator Jesse Helms and North Carolina Governor Jim Hunt would be among the most important in the country. Furthermore, I knew that the success of statewide Democratic campaigns would increase if the county party organizations could be made more effective, and I wanted to help.

The Process: My Election

In North Carolina, county officers are elected by the precinct delegates to the county convention. It is desirable to have information about your candidacy read at each precinct meeting before the county convention, but I did not decide to run until after the precinct meetings were held. So, I spent the four weeks before the county convention telephoning precinct officers, elected officials, and auxiliary organization officers to inform them of my candidacy and to ask for their support. I developed a brief statement that outlined why I was running and why I believed I would be an effective first vice-chairperson.

In addition to my telephone campaign, a small committee was organized that included a county commissioner and a city council member. It made calls supporting my candidacy, and also wrote a letter, signed by twenty supporters, describing my qualifications. It was sent to all county precinct officers asking for their vote.

Following my whirlwind campaign, the elections for county leaders were held at the spring county convention. Short nominating and seconding speeches were made for me by the county commissioner and city council member who served on my campaign committee. During the two minutes I had to address the voters, I outlined why I would be a good first vice-chairperson. I won!

I believe I was elected because I had been an effective volunteer in so many Democratic party activities during the prior twelve years: the Democratic Women's Club (local, district, and state), and the Young Democrats. Additionally, the Democratic leadership knew about my leadership of the NCNA PAC and my contributions to getting the new Nurse Practice Act passed by the legislature. Having a good reputation and a cadre of hard working supporters makes winning elections easier.

Democratic County Official

My power as first vice-chairperson is based upon timely information I receive from the state Democratic party leaders. For example, I often know about important local events or what is going on in Raleigh (our capital) before others. Because knowledge is power, my tenure has been a heady experience. I enjoy feeling sought after for information and opinions—until I am brought up short by an individual who blames me for any problem he or she has with the Democratic party.

My responsibilities as first vice-chairperson are determined by the chairman. I have been appointed editor for the Mecklenburg *Democrat*, our county newsletter. Additional responsibilities include attending meetings of both the county and district executive committees. I also help to maintain the local party headquarters. During elections, party officers are invited to attend candidate fund-raising events, and generally we have to pay a fee just like everyone else. In addition, officers are expected to sell tickets for state party events and are asked to contribute to the state's sustaining fund, which helps support county party activities.

Another Race

In February 1984, ten months after being elected to first vice-chairperson, I decided to run as a Jesse Jackson delegate to the National Democratic Convention (NDC). The first step was to alert my friends and ask them to support my candidacy at the March, 1984 precinct meetings where delegates to the county convention would be chosen. Subsequently, at the April county convention, delegates were elected to attend the 9th district convention in June, 1984 where the national delegates would be selected. At the district convention, five delegates and two alternates to the national convention were elected. While I lost at the district level, the Jackson campaign nominated me as a pledged party leader, and I was elected at the state convention. I became one of the 88 delegates and 29 alternates from North Carolina at the National Democratic Convention in July, 1984. (The process by which convention delegates are selected is complex. Consult your party's headquarters for detailed information.)

CONCLUSION

Political parties are an essential part of American society. They influence who gets elected to what office and by doing so, have enormous impact on the country's policies and laws. Numerous opportunities exist for the individual citizen to influence the positions and practices of the parties. My experiences as vice-chairperson of the Mecklenburg County Democratic party and as a delegate to the 1984 Democratic national convention have made lasting impressions on me, especially the role nurses must play in this part of our country's political process.

My professional growth and development has been enhanced by my legislative and political activism. I believe that my colleagues and I have collectively made a difference in the quality and quantity of health care available to citizens in North Carolina.

Political Clubs

Ann Marie McCarthy, RN, MA

WHAT IS A POLITICAL CLUB?

Defining a political club is like trying to define a nurse. There are many kinds of political clubs, and each has its own unique quality. However, all political clubs have some common qualities: all members are of the same party, and most members live in the geographical area of the club's jurisdiction. Their purpose is to endorse and support the public officials representing that area. These public officials serve at the local, state, or federal level in either the executive, legislative, or judicial branches of government.

Clubs are organized much like any organization. They have a president, officers, a board of directors, or executive committee. These individuals set policy and direct club activities. They are assisted by the work of standing and ad hoc committees including fund-raising and community affairs.

CLUB'S INFLUENCE OR POWER

Clubs often have considerable influence in their local community. If the local political club has supported a public official, this politician will usually respond when the club requests help. For example, one of New York City's Public Health Centers is in my community. For fiscal considerations, many health centers were closed down completely or forced to reduce their services drastically. Our health center was saved with only minimal service cutbacks. This was in large part due to the leverage of our club (Chelsea Reform Democratic Club) resulting from actively supporting the public officials involved with the decision to keep it open. We had supported the Councilman-at-large who was on the council's health committee, and our city councilwoman had the most seniority and considerable influence within the council and with the mayor. Also involved with the decision were the borough president, the City Council president, and the city controller. Our club had supported all three in their campaigns.

Another example of our club's influence in the Chelsea community is our successful effort to save a women's center, located in a city-owned building, a former firehouse no longer needed by the city. In 1973, with the city's encouragement and support, the women's center took over this building. At that time, Chelsea was not a valuable real estate area. Now it is considered one of the prime places to live and work, and the city wants that property back. Over these ten years, the women's center has offered free, or at a minimal cost, such services as alcoholic counseling, wife and child abuse protection, rape counseling, and job counseling. With the help of our councilwoman, our club convinced the city that if this center was closed, the women it served would not get help and might have to go on public assistance, which would cost the city more money. The city agreed and, with a reasonable increase in the rent, the center remained open.

In the political arena, the club serves as the community's political operations center. It is where "the nuts and bolts" of campaigns take place. Regardless of whether the race is for an executive, legislative, or judicial position, the political process is similar. Any Democratic candidate seeking the club's endorsement appears before the club's membership. If the membership endorses the candidate, it actively works to get that candidate the most votes in the club's area. This may be done by getting the necessary signatures on the candidate's petitions, holding receptions or fund-raisers for them, or distributing their literature.

Obviously, there is more direct communication between the club and the candidate in a local race. In a race for governor or U.S. senator, there usually is no personal contact between the club and the candidate. However, if it is a contest for a seat in the state senate or assembly or in the city council, that candidate campaigns in person.

Where a political club exists, candidates usually do not ignore the political club process. Some run even though the club does not endorse them. Usually, they lose.

In the race for judicial office, each city or state elects or appoints judges for family, civil, criminal, and state supreme courts. Whether the judge is elected or appointed varies from city and state. If the judge is elected, the club endorses and campaigns as they would for any candidate running for executive or legislative office.

Many people, especially members of the press, view the club structure as a relic. With sophisticated telecommunications, the political club's influence on the electorate's decision to vote for candidates, especially those at the top of the ticket, has diminished.

Even when the contest is for U.S. president, however, the club still plays a role. A presidential candidate needs sufficient petition signatures to appear on the state's primary ballot. In the 1984 New York State presidential primary, the names of the delegates for the national party convention appeared on the ballot along with the presidential candidate they were supporting. The majority of these delegates were club participants.

The club still plays a pivotal role in a top race such as the one for governor. An example was the 1982 gubernatorial race in New York State. The leading politicians, press, and large financial contributors favored Mayor Edward Koch in the Democratic primary. The political clubs supporting Mario Cuomo were able to reverse this by an intense, well-organized grass-roots effort. Cuomo and his family appeared at political clubs, shopping markets, and senior citizen centers. Club members volunteered many hours of campaign work such as distributing his literature and making phone calls. Governor Cuomo's victory enhanced the political clubs' esteem and made the political analysts take note of the valuable contributions of clubs.

WHY NURSES SHOULD JOIN POLITICAL CLUBS

I believe nurses should join political clubs. It is important for public officials to see nurses take an active role in the political process.

Often on television, in movies, plays, and books, our public image is less than positive. If intelligent and sophisticated nurses join a political club, they will give other club members a positive view of our profession.

There must be a greater awareness among nurses that legislation must be voted on by elected officials in a governmental body. You can have the greatest resolution passed by a state nurses' association or the American Nurses' Association, but unless the message is conveyed to the elected politicians, it is all for nothing.

Membership in a political club provides better visibility and communication between nurses and local politicians, but it also gives nurses contact with their legislative assistants. Legislators depend on assistants to keep them informed of community and individual concerns. The legislative assistants actually draft most of the bills. If nurses make a favorable impression on them, they can move nursing concerns from the "back burner."

Legislators sometimes comment that nurses are not concerned about the political process unless it directly affects the nursing profession and that nurses do not form coalitions with groups that support similar legislation. We are perceived as isolationists or as having narrow interests. The political club supports legislation concerned with many areas—housing, sanitation, public safety—as well as health issues. By joining clubs, nurses will begin to be perceived as having other concerns besides nursing and demonstrate to politicians that we can work with other groups on issues of mutual concern.

Usually politicians do not receive many letters or phone calls about health related issues, unless there is an imminent crisis like the closing of a local hospital. Most legislators receive more mail about crime, sanitation, housing, and transportation. Unfortunately, many people don't think about health related issues until they get sick. By joining political clubs, nurses can help sensitize their fellow club members to the importance of health legislation.

MY CAREER AS A DISTRICT LEADER

My career as an official of the Democratic party began in 1979 when I was elected district leader from the Chelsea section of Manhattan. As a district leader, my approval was sought by anyone running for public office, from city council candidates to aspiring U.S. senators. I judged candidates on their overall records, which included their thoughts on health issues and nursing concerns. The population of Chelsea is approximately 125,000 people with about 65,000 registered voters; 92 percent are registered Democrats.

With the exception of two years when I taught nursing in Iowa, I have been a member of the Chelsea Reform Democratic Club since 1972. While club president from 1977 to 1979, another club member and I coordinated the Chelsea Drive to "Save the Village Nursing Home." We raised $40,000 by contacting local merchants, block associations, tenants' associations, and other community groups. When the assembly district leader decided not to run again, I was asked by the club membership to seek the Democratic district leadership.

I received the official endorsement of my club and the elected public officials representing my area. I distributed literature and posters on my candidacy, appeared before community groups, and met voters at street corners and supermarkets.

The district leadership is a nonpaying job and supposedly part-time. It can become expensive because much of the political business and networking occurs at fundraisers. So while a district leader, I also worked full-time as a nurse.

My official responsibilities were varied, but included the endorsement of candidates for office and the organization of support to help candidates get elected. Anyone running for office, whether for executive, legislative, or judicial office, who represented or served the Chelsea area, sought my endorsement and support.

As a district leader, I was a member of the executive committee of the New York County Democratic Committee. The committee is made up of forty male district leaders and forty female district leaders. The committee decides which candidates will receive endorsement. I was responsible for becoming knowledgeable about my candidate so that I could speak intelligently for him or her in Chelsea. I would often accompany the candidate and introduce him or her to the voters.

I was expected to be a community leader as well as a political leader. Theoretically, my responsibilities were only political. The majority of voters voted for me, however, because of my community leadership; that is what they can observe firsthand.

Some of the activities I participated in as a district leader included:

- Actively supported the Chelsea Coalition on Housing. This group tried to protect tenants in their basic housing needs, ie, heat and hot water. Whenever possible, I would accompany tenants to court.

- Served as Conference Chairperson for two years on the Board of Directors of the Chelsea Interagency Council. In one of those years the topic was "Resource for Health." I invited such groups as the Visiting Nursing Service to speak to the group.

- Led the fight to prevent a massage parlor from being opened. This would have been in the heart of Chelsea's residential area, in close proximity to schools and churches.

- Active participation in the Chelsea Neighborhood Association. This was a coalition of neighborhood groups that successfully prevented the U.S. Postal Service from building a large vehicle maintenance facility in Chelsea. We were concerned with the environmental hazards of this facility.

- Active participant in my block association.

- Member of the Community Planning Board for two years. Served on the Housing, Waterfront, and Health and Social Service Committees for one year.

As a district leader, I had considerable influence with public officials. I also served as the liaison between the community and the legislators. I would keep the legislators informed of local concerns and similarly would bring back information and advice from the legislators to the citizens.

This was true not only for issues and projects, but on the personal level as well. For example, I informed the legislator when a constituent died or was sick. When a community member was unemployed, and I heard about a job opening with the city or state, I would suggest that person to the legislators.

I believe in the holistic view of life. I never thought I was wearing three separate hats as a nurse, a community leader, and a political leader. They were three corners of the same hat—independent but interrelated. Perhaps the best example of this was my involvement with keeping a local hospital open. I had supported the Manhattan borough president in his reelection bid. In return, he appointed me to the local community board. The chairperson of the community board knew I was a nurse and asked me to become chairperson of the Health and Social Service Committee.

A hospital, located in mid-Manhattan, was facing bankruptcy and possible closure. My committee took an active role in keeping the hospital open. We solicited the help of our state senator and assemblyperson who obtained a better medicaid reimbursement rate from the State Department of Health. Although the hospital has had to cut some of its services, the most needed services (emergency and ambulance) are functioning well.

My immediate goal is to become a lawyer and eventually run for elective public office, preferably for U.S. Congress. As a district leader, I have gained valuable experience and contacts that will serve me well when I run for political office in the near future.

Chapter 29

Communicating with Your Legislator

A Legislator's Perspective

Marilyn Goldwater, RN

> Men in general judge more from appearances than from reality. All men have eyes, but few have the gift of penetration.
>
> —MACHIAVELLI

> Things are seldom as they seem, skim milk masquerades as cream.
>
> —W.S. GILBERT (HMS PINAFORE)

Whether you take your political philosophy from Machiavelli or from Gilbert and Sullivan, you will probably draw the same conclusion. In communicating with politicians, perceptions aren't everything; they're the only thing.

As a nurse who has worked both sides of the political fence, first as a community activist and then as a member of the Maryland General Assembly, I have learned that perceptions are often more potent than reality. Perceptions are what we deal with every day in the legislature—perceptions of each other, of the people who come to us to press their causes, of issues, and of the impact those issues are likely to have on our constituents.

We also rely on perceptions when the time comes to lend or deny our support to a proposal. Without sufficient time to study the countless requests and proposals that are constantly placed before us, we find ourselves relying on impressions, reputations, and appearances. What is this group's track record? Can we trust their information? Whom do they claim to represent? Is their lobbyist trustworthy? Can we count on their continuing support once we take on their cause? How about later on, in our reelection campaign? Could they be potential allies in a legislative battle we may want to mount? Whom will I please or alienate by taking on this cause?

From the legislator's viewpoint, the perception of each issue or cause boils down to the age-old question: What's in it for me?—and by implication, what's in it for my constituents? As an advocate of a nursing or health care issue, you should be prepared to answer with specific data and examples, so that the legislator sees immediately the many interests she or he has at stake.

While it would be inappropriate to offer an envelope of cash or promise support in the next general election in return for your legislator's support, you can offer reliable information and your hard work, which will establish you or your group as an invaluable resource. You can also offer your help or your organization's help in disseminating information and drumming up support for your proposal in the legislature and in the community. If there's one thing an overworked, understaffed, and overextended legislator can't resist, it's a politically attractive, sound proposal backed by good supporting data and an army of volunteers.

NURSES AND LEGISLATORS

Most legislators have a great deal of respect for nurses, having observed them as conscientious people who do their homework before they come to testify and as advocates for health care. But they know little about the nurse's role in today's health care delivery system. Hence, they are not aware of the nurses' qualifications as spokespersons or authorities on health care in general. Legislators also don't distinguish among nursing specialists or organizations. For the average legislator, a nurse is a nurse.

Although many nurses don't belong to a state or national organization, and some belong only to specialty groups, the legislators perceive that the national, state, or district association speaks for all nurses. There is a good reason for that perception. It is much easier for a legislator to work on the assumption that one organization represents most nurses' interests than to deal with the myriad of specialty groups of nurses—or of any profession, for that matter.

Unfortunately, legislators don't perceive nurses as particularly active in political campaigns. Nurses are perceived as similar to many other women professionals: women are seen as nurturers, not influencers—helpers, not powerbrokers.

How can nurses change that perception and thereby strengthen their political leverage? One way is by becoming more politically aware, more politically active, and by raising their own political profile and that of their organization. The more aware and active one becomes, the more skillful and effective a communicator and advocate one can be.

Two examples from my own experience illustrate this point. In 1976, members in one district of the Maryland Nurses' Association decided they needed to develop a closer rapport with their local legislators. The executive board began meeting their legislators *before* the legislative session for an informal, dutch treat dinner to discuss issues of concern to them and to get to know their representatives better. That event has since grown into an annual tradition sponsored by the district association and now includes the county elected officials as well as the state legislators. Nurses and elected officials share valuable information, air their concerns, and cement relationships. Once the session begins, and the nurses and legislators find they need to work with each other on an issue, they already have established a basis for communication.

These meetings fill two important needs: the need for nurses to know legislators before a problem arises and the need for legislators to see nurses as reliable, valuable sources of information. The practice has been duplicated in all the districts in our state with great success, and is an example of successfully maintaining channels of communication with one's legislator.

The successful effort to enact third party reimbursement legislation is a second example of how to practice political activism. Before the General Assembly even held hearings, the nurse practitioners and nurse midwives supporting the proposal had been visiting their legislators. They explained the proposal, supplied necessary information, answered questions, and offered to provide more information as opponents raised questions and objections.

When the General Assembly held hearings, each nurse testified on an aspect of the proposal that she knew well. At the close of the hearings, these nurses made information packets available to the legislators and visited them again. They were superbly organized.

My colleagues' perception of the nurses' efforts was favorable. They noted how much they had learned during the process, and how well organized the nurses were. They commented on how useful and critical the nurses' information and preparation were. As a result, these nurses were perceived as politically astute, active, and valuable. If these nurses were so well organized on this issue, the legislators reasoned, they undoubtedly represented excellent potential to be tapped later. Those nurses didn't have to prove themselves again. They had established themselves as effective communicators and gained a strong foothold in the political arena.

It is a political fact of life that in every legislative battle there are not two, but three sides: those who support you, those who oppose you, and those who need you to help make up their minds. As nurses who not only want to influence the health care delivery system, you must learn how to help the first group, fight the second, and persuade the third. Whether you do it by contributing one hour or ten to a legislative initiative or political campaign or one dollar or fifty to the candidate of your choice is not important. What is important is that you do something. If you do, you will find that when the campaign or legislative battle is over, and your candidate or legislator has won, you can ask for positions on boards and commissions as your political due. You will also find that the next time you come to Annapolis, Sacramento, Columbus, or Albany seeking our support, we as legislators will have a clearer notion of what's in it for us.

Congressional Staff Perspective

Sheila P. Burke, RN, MPA, FAAN

Many political aspirants and newcomers approach people in government and the system with awe, thinking that there are complex formulas and theories that must be understood before change can be made. This is a fundamental error. The key to government and its system is people—what makes them "tick" and what value systems they and their compatriots live by.

—Pamela Maraldo, RN, PhD (1982)

People are the source of power in Washington, because they are the source of information. As a result, access to people is a critical aspect of any political action. Access generally comes, however, only after one has developed personal relationships with those in power, so that communication can flourish. If one is to be truly involved in the legislative and political process, these relationships must be developed with both legislators and members of their staff. Of course, the closer and longer the relationship, the better.

Like many other organizations, Congress has, in recent years, made increasing use of professional staff. Staff members on committees and on the personal staffs of senators and representatives make up what some believe to be a congressional bureaucracy. Little is known about this group because they are, in large part, an anonymous community.

The Appropriations Act of 1856 authorized the hiring of a clerk for the Senate Committee on Finance, a clerk for the Senate Committee on Printing, a clerk for the House Committee on Claims, and a clerk for the House Committee on Ways and Means. This act is believed to have been the first to authorize the employment of staff for congressional committees. It was not until 1885, however, that each senator was authorized to hire a clerk at about $6 per day.

The Legislative Reorganization Act of 1946 resulted in a marked change in congressional staffing. Following the passage of that act, staffs began to grow at a rapid rate. By 1976, the legislative branch employed over 38,000 persons, including 3,000 committee staff members, approximately 10,000 personal staff members, and 17,900 in support agencies such as the Library of Congress (Jox, 1977). Since that time, staffs have grown even larger. For example, the staff for the Senate Committee on Finance increased from 6 in 1960 to 52 in 1984. In addition to the growth in numbers, staff responsibilities have also changed, although not as dramatically.

Legislative aides have significant influence on congressional decision making since their expertise and judgment are often critical to their employer. For instance, staff exercise a certain amount of control over communications into and within a committee and personal office. They participate in identifying issues and developing legislative positions. They conduct research, gather background data on specific legislative matters, and draft legislation. They prepare testimony, speeches, floor statements, explanations to constituents, and reports. They brief members on pending legislation and, most importantly, they are expected to offer their opinion and act as a sounding board for senators and representatives (Jox, 1977).

This system that provides such extensive responsibility to both personal and committee staff members does have a rationale. The reason for having staff is similar to the reason for congressional committees: Congress is best served by specialists (those assigned to certain committees) with the majority accepting the expertise of a few on most issues. Congress needs staff, just as it needs specialist members, to help it evaluate the flood of materials from the outside.

PERSONAL VS COMMITTEE STAFF

In deciding whom to contact in Washington you must understand the different responsibilities of the two key types of staff. The personal staff on both the House and Senate sides are guided by the particular senators' and representatives' political attitudes and ideology, the needs and concerns of the state or district that member represents, the member's interests, and the organizational realities of their office. Personal staff handle constituent problems such as casework and projects, requests for information, correspondence, and visits with constituents and special interest groups.

The responsibilities of the committee staffs are more difficult to categorize. Committee staff are primarily involved with the drafting of legislation, oversight and investigations, and dealing with lobbyists. Administrative, research, correspondence, and some press functions are also performed (Jox, 1977).

Committee staff can be responsible to the chairman of the committee or the subcommittee and work in large part for that person, reflecting his or her views; or alternatively, they can also be more bipartisan in nature, available to work with any member of a particular committee. Generally, committee staff are viewed as the technical experts and are often the most useful source of information. They are also considered the most influential in determining the outcome of legislation.

All staff, both personal and committee, differ in the degree of latitude they are given for independent action and in their willingness to provide information for legislative initiatives. Some view themselves as advocates seeking facts to justify preconceived preferences. Others try to be objective, but are still active fact finders. And some see themselves as neutral intermediaries whose job it is to sift contrary arguments and explain them to members (senators or representatives) in ways that make the policy options understandable (Malbin, 1976).

NURSING INPUT

Given the wide range of responsibilities of the staffs of senators and congressmen and congresswomen, it is understandable why nursing must provide input on issues of concern. There is no master bulletin board in Washington where people can look to see what important issues will be coming up on the Congressional agenda. If you don't have good friends in the right places, you won't even know when a bill is likely to come up for consideration, let alone have input into its content. As some nurses have learned, you may not even be scheduled to testify on a bill of importance to you if you have not gotten to know the staff person doing the scheduling.

The nursing press is constantly recounting stories of the influence of nursing on the policy process. Much of this influence has come through the wise, thoughtful, and planned development of relations with staff members. This is, of course, true on not only the federal level, but also on the state and local levels.

An excellent example of how the system can work on the federal level took place during the 1983 consideration of the regulations implementing the new Medicare hospice benefit. Our office was in constant contact with not only the official representatives of organizations serving as spokespersons for the hospice industry, but also with nurses in home health agencies whom we had come to know and trust over the years. Colleagues of mine from Tennessee were particularly concerned with the consent form to be signed by patients, waiving their rights to traditional Medicare coverage. Changes were made in the regulations as a direct result of their input.

On the state level we have seen an increasingly large number of legislative successes as the result of nurses' involvement. The increase in coverage of the services of nurse midwives under state Medicaid plans is probably one of the best examples.

When communicating with staff, know what you are talking about, and don't attempt to deceive. No one expects you to tell everything you know, but what you do offer should be truthful and accurate. One attempt to mislead may end an excellent relationship that you may have taken months or years to establish (Constantine, 1984).

Remember that congressional staff are human. They can be personable, pompous, professional, or prima donnas. Being so close to power can affect people in different ways. There are those who perceive themselves as being almost as important as' the senator or congressman for whom they work. At the same time, there are many trying to do a professional and accountable job—but in a political context that requires an ability to balance legitimate competing or conflicting interests. It is always important to remember that they need your help to the same extent you need theirs.

Lobbying Demystified

Sally Austen Tom, RN, CNM, MS, MPA

There is a one-liner in Washington that goes, "Lobbyists are the only people in Washington who are honest about what they do." Our purpose as lobbyists is to influence the outcome of governmental decisions, but an air of mystery seems to cloak the public's perception of how we do this. Lobbying is not making secret deals in smoke-filled rooms, using a mysterious process, or passing money under the table to buy votes.

Despite the large number of paid lobbyists in Washington and in state capitals, the majority of lobbyists across the country are citizens who individually, or in groups, talk to their elected or appointed officials. The most powerful and fundamental type of lobbying occurs when citizens who have firsthand experiences and personal involvement in issues come together and tell their story to people in government. One certainly does not have to be paid or live in a capital to be an effective lobbyist.

The effectiveness of citizen-lobbyists, particularly those who work together in coalitions, was demonstrated in 1983–1984 in Nebraska. A young woman, who moved to Nebraska during her first pregnancy, discovered she could not continue to receive nurse-midwifery care because Nebraska had not yet legalized nurse-midwifery practice. She resolved to change the law, formed a coalition that grew to 700 members, and worked with a state legislator to draft a bill. The Nebraska nurse-midwifery practice act passed in early 1984 the first time it was introduced during a short session of the legislature. One concerned citizen made this happen by taking the first step of speaking from her personal experience and organizing her fellow Nebraskans to work for this specific goal.

PRINCIPLES

Lobbying is, simply, two-thirds teaching and one-third selling. There are general principles that guide lobbying on both the individual and organizational levels. These principles take the mystery out of lobbying and make it interesting and fun. Many of the skills nurses use in their everyday professional practice are easily transferred from the hospital to the legislature.

The most important asset a lobbyist has is her credibility, ie, her reputation for providing solid, accurate information. No legislator or staff person will trust a lobbyist again if she has given him or her information that is later discredited publicly by the advocates of another side of an issue. Just as a nurse cannot lie to patients and retain her interpersonal effectiveness, a lobbyist cannot mislead legislators with inaccurate information or exaggerate the validity or importance of her data.

A lobbyist, just like a nurse doing health education, must put information together in a clear and concise fashion, placing the most important information or argument in favor of her position first because she might not have the chance to make the second argument.

A lobbyist, again like a nurse teaching a patient about a health condition, must pick the right time to present information. For instance, a good lobbyist does not visit a legislator on the day the government's budget must be completed to talk about a bill to be introduced in two months. A good lobbyist visits legislators and staff when the legislature is not in session to make long-range plans and begin drafting legislation.

A lobbyist must be enthusiastic about his or her issue to move others to care about the issue. The merits of an issue are not always sufficiently compelling to change votes. Legislators have to know that the lobbyist and the people he or she represents care about the issue, as well as why they care about the issue.

A lobbyist must know the basic processes and timing of the legislature or regulatory agency. This does not mean that lobbyists have to be political scientists. (A review of Chapters 24, 25, and 26 in this book will serve the beginner well.) Everyone learns the nuances of parliamentary procedure as they go along.

To succeed in the legislative arena an organization must have a well-identified goal and clearly understood strategies for reaching that goal. Organizational plans for lobbying should take into account several realities about political processes:

- The work of advocating for a change in laws is best begun with the drafting of the bill and when the bill is first in committee. Citizen-lobbyists can pull their ideas together, find a sympathetic legislator, and follow a bill from its inception to passage. It is much more difficult to change the course of a bill once it has been voted on at any level of the legislature—subcommittee, committee, House, or Senate.

- On the other hand, it is easier to stop a bill than to pass one. Most of the bills introduced in the Congress or the state legislatures never even receive committee consideration.

- The work of advocating for a change in the law does not end with a victory in the legislature. Lobbyists must follow their new law as it makes its way through the executive branch, including signing by the governor or president, promulgation of regulations, and enforcement of the law.

- An organization must have a long-range perspective and lots of patience to achieve its goals. After the Congress passed the law requiring Medicaid to reimburse nurse-midwives in 1980, two years passed before the federal regulations were issued, and some states had not implemented the law even by the end of 1985. This pace is not an unusually slow one, particularly when one takes into account the large number of bureaucracies involved and the delays caused by the changes in the federal admin-istration in 1981.

- Both organizations and individual lobbyists must be willing to give the credit to others for victories secured largely as a result of the organization's or individual's work. Legislators need the sunshine of public approval and the chance to win votes; lobby-ists need to succeed in their goals.
- Organizations have to be willing to work in coalitions with other organizations to maximize political clout and resources. Territoriality about an issue or bill is usually not a helpful impulse.

Lobbying in many ways is like assessing a patient and utilizing one's best skills in psychosocial interactions. As with managing a patient, it requires insight into hu-man behavior, some theoretical perspectives, and above all, the ability to be flexible when factors completely beyond your control influence the outcome. Lobbying is an almost always interesting, usually congenial, and decidedly challenging endeavor.

Strategies for Individual Nurses

Sally B. Solomon, RN, MSN, CPNP

> For the remainder of this century, the most worthy goal that nurses can select is that of arousing their passion for a kind of political activism that will make a difference in their own lives and in the life of our society ("Election 1984," 1984).
>
> —Peggy Chinn, RN, PhD, FAAN

This section focuses on guidelines and strategies for individual nurses to communicate with their legislators and participate in the political process. It summarizes recommen-dations from the previous sections and provides additional information so that nurses can convey their political concerns in a most effective style.

DOING YOUR HOMEWORK

To be successful in the political arena, a certain amount of preparation or homework is needed. This is true for letter writing, personal contacts, preparing testimony, and rallying support.

An individual nurse or representative of a nursing special interest group must first learn the history and background of a particular topic or piece of legislation. One of the best ways of doing this is to contact an organization likely to be involved with the issue. Meet or speak with their government relations staff and ask what written infor-

The editors thank Sally B. Solomon for coordinating this chapter.

mation is available. One would also want to know where they are targeting their legislative actions and how one can be kept up-to-date (mailing lists, membership, publications, etc.). It is important to know what the most recent strategies are so that one's own efforts will be the most expedient and will not conflict with or jeopardize whatever lobbying has already taken place. Sometimes copies of written testimony can be obtained from the organization and are good sources of data and information.

Many organizations, such as the League of Women Voters (LOWV) or Planned Parenthood, sell brochures on the structure and process of specific cities, counties, or states. They also publish directories of the elected officials in these specific locales, which include the officials' names, addresses, telephone numbers, and other information.

One should be familiar with a legislator's political background, such as party affiliation, years in office, year due for reelection, committee memberships, and what issues the legislator is known to have championed. This information is routinely available from the legislator's local office and can also be ascertained from your local, state, or national nurses' association or a nurses' political action committee (PAC).

Knowing whether a nurses' PAC has endorsed the legislator as a candidate in past or future elections and what the legislator's stand has been on other nursing or health care issues is also important. It is always wise to thank the legislator for previous legislative support and to cite examples of how the legislator's actions have affected constituents—whether they be health care providers or consumers.

Finally, if dealing with a specific piece of legislation, one should be prepared as much as possible, with cost implications. In these days of budget deficits and fiscal restraint, cost-effectiveness carries a lot of weight, and legislators are less willing to commit themselves to increased allocations without knowing financial implications. Financial data can range from aggregate cost data to examples of savings or expenses for an individual consumer or provider.

WRITTEN COMMUNICATION

In writing to a legislator, several key points will make for more effective communication. Letters should be typed and include an inside or return address, preferably indicating that the writer is a constituent of the legislator's district. Be sure to state that you are a nurse and if pertinent, include your position, place of employment, and any other relevant data (ie, identify yourself as a nurse-practitioner, having a special interest in long-term care, working with diabetics, or holding a position with a nursing association). If the legislation has been assigned a bill number, it is important to refer to the number in your letter. If you know that the legislator sits on a committee that will be dealing with the bill, make reference to the committee as well. State your stand on the bill and give one or two examples of the significance of the legislation—either pro or con. Letters should be concise and need not resemble term papers in their thoroughness. Remember that all the authors of the previous sections described how legislators and their staff are approached on a multitude of issues. Hence, brevity is essential. If appropriate, offer your availability or expertise in the event that additional information is needed.

Tips for Visiting Legislators

1. Call ahead to make an appointment whenever possible. Ask to meet with the senator or representative. If the member is not available, ask to meet with the staff person who handles health issues.

2. Prepare in advance. Know the background of your representative and the history of the legislation you're discussing.

3. At the beginning of the visit, introduce yourself and state what you want to discuss. Specify the issues and bills.

4. Ask the legislator what her or his position is on the issue or bill.

5. Many legislators and staff might not be familiar with nursing practice or legislative concerns. Be prepared to explain them in basic terms. If possible, be prepared with facts about nursing practice in your state or district.

6. Ask if she or he has heard from others who support this issue or bill. Ask what the supporters are saying.

7. Ask if she or he has heard from opponents. Ask who the opponents are and what their arguments are.

8. Offer to provide additional information, if you don't have data at hand; but don't make promises you can't keep. It's better to admit you don't know than to promise and not deliver or to convey erroneous information.

9. Follow up with a thank you note and share your reflections on what you felt about the visit.

10. Keep a written record of the visit for your files and, if possible, notify government liaison staff at a professional nursing organization, so that they can follow up with the legislator.

11. Spend time with your legislators even if their position is not in agreement with yours. You can lessen the intensity of their positions and maintain contact for subsequent issues.

Mailgrams and telegrams can also be sent for urgent matters. Details on letter-writing and dispatching telegrams are provided in "Tips for Writing Legislators" on the following page.

MEETINGS

Meeting with a legislator requires additional preparation. Appointments should be made in advance by phone or by letter; dropping in is never desirable. When you make the appointment, identify the bill(s) or issue(s) you wish to discuss. It is customary for a staff person to be assigned to meet with you, unless there is a particular reason to meet the legislator in person. Find out the name (including proper spelling of the

Tips for Writing Legislators

1. Use your own stationery, not hospital or agency stationery. A letter is better than a postcard or telegram. Use your own words. Form letters are not as effective as original ones.

2. Identify your subject clearly. State the name of the legislation you are writing about. Give the House or Senate bill number, if you know it.

3. Be brief, giving the reasons why you are for or against the legislation. Explain how the issue would affect you, your business or profession, or what effect it could have on your state or community.

4. Know what committees your legislators serve on and indicate in the letter if the bill is being brought before any of those committees.

5. Sign your name with "RN" after it. Be sure your correct address is on the letter as well as the envelope. Envelopes sometimes get thrown away before the letter is answered.

6. Be courteous. A rude letter neither makes friends nor influences the legislator. Be sure to express your appreciation for work well done, a good speech, favorable vote, or fine leadership in committee or on the floor.

7. Timing is important. Try to write your position on a bill while it is in committee. Your senators and representatives will usually be more responsive to your appeal at that time rather than later on, when the bill has already been approved by a committee.

8. Limit your letter to one issue and don't write more than once or twice on the same subject.

9. Keep a copy of all correspondence for your files.

10. Address written correspondence as follows:

    U.S. Senator
    Honorable Jane Doe
    United States Senate
    Washington, DC 20510

    U.S. Representative
    Honorable Jane Doe
    House of Representatives
    Washington, DC 20515

    Dear Senator Doe: Dear Representative Doe:

    The same format applies to state and local officials.

11. Mailgrams, which take two days, and telegrams, which are faster, can both be ordered through Western Union's toll free number: 1-800-325-6000.

name for future contact and follow-up) of the legislative assistant who deals with health issues and be prepared to meet that person.

Keeping in mind the power of perception and of first impressions, dress appropriately. Remember that politicians tend towards conventional dress. One word to the wise—if you visit several legislators in one day at the capitol, wear comfortable shoes.

If possible, have some type of written information available. This is not essential, but can be helpful. Fact sheets from a nursing organization, data you have collected on your own, pertinent articles, or brochures describing your organization are some examples of possible instructional material. Similarly, since your visit will be limited to 10 to 20 minutes, leaving handouts that summarize information you could not cover is a good strategy.

Plan in advance the items you wish to cover and prioritize them. The impact of urging support for a particular issue is lost when diluted with several other issues. If visiting with other nurses, delegate one person as spokesperson for each visit so that there will be continuity to your discussion. Let that one person be responsible for handouts, introductions, moving the agenda, and any necessary follow-up.

A few comments on communication techniques are in order. The unwritten protocols for lobbying and politics follow the same conventions as other social situations. This means that before one employs a heavy-handed lobbying approach, it is necessary to develop a rapport with the legislator or staff and gain their trust. One needs to get a sense of who they are and what they already know about nursing or other particular issues. This must be an ongoing part of successful lobbying, not just part of the initial encounter. To bypass or ignore this step can minimize the effectiveness of even the most skillful lobbyist's technique, because the most important concept—credibility—has not been established.

Finally, it is important to follow up on all communications, whether they were letters or personal meetings. Follow-up is best done by a letter, thanking the person for his or her time and if applicable, including any additional information promised during the visit. To develop a reciprocal relationship, contact with staff or legislators should be maintained periodically, at least every six months. It is best not to wait for crises or problems in communication to plan meetings with these people. It is preferable to maintain regular contact and acquaint oneself with the broad spectrum of health care legislation.

In conclusion, communicating with your legislator should be an ongoing endeavor. Since legislators are human, they respond well to considerate, thoughtful communication. With nurses' skill in interpersonal relationships, we have the potential to be effective at shaping health policy through influencing legislators.

References

Constantine J: An insider's view on lobbying congressional staff. *Caring* (March) 1984; 3:44.

Election 1984: Nurses are making a difference, brochure. CE program sponsored by the DC-PAC, 1984.

The Emergence of Nursing as a Political Force. National League for Nursing, 1979.

Jox H, Hammond W, Webb S: *Congressional Staffs. The Invisible Force in American Lawmaking.* Free Press, 1977.

Malbin MJ: Congressional staffs—growing fast, but in different directions. *Natl J* (July 10) 1976; 8:958–65.

Maraldo P: Politics: a very human matter. *Am J Nurs* 1982; 82:1104–5.

Writing and Presenting Testimony

Sally B. Solomon, RN, MSN, CPNP

Presenting testimony at hearings is an important part of the political process since it is a formal mechanism for directly communicating with legislators on key issues. It has received less attention from nurses than have other, more widely publicized components of grass roots lobbying. The importance of testifying cannot be minimized, however, as illustrated by the numerous hearings held each year and the many organizations and individuals who use hearings to express their points of view.

Presenting testimony requires skills that can make the difference between merely going through the motions of testifying and being successful political players. The wide public exposure characteristic of hearings makes it important that testimony be delivered smoothly and with expertise to convey a positive image of nurses to the committee holding the hearings and to the public.

Professional organizations usually have staff to follow legislative issues and prepare testimony. Whenever possible, consult the professional nurses' associations to see what their official stand is on an issue and what actions they have taken so far, including intentions to testify. If you need to prepare testimony on your own, you will find the resources of the professional organizations useful. If more than one nursing organization plans on testifying, consider preparing a joint statement or having one witness from each organization submit a written statement. A public display of unity on behalf of nursing can be beneficial in promoting public policy of importance to the profession.

THE FIRST STEPS

Hearings are held by committees of national, state, or local legislatures. Being kept informed about hearings is the first and perhaps most important step and requires some planning.

If there are committees or subcommittees that routinely deal with nursing and health issues, you should be on the committee's mailing list so that you can receive announcements of upcoming hearings. This, of course, implies that you are familiar with the jurisdiction and membership of certain legislative committees and can identify committees likely to hold hearings on issues relevant to nursing.

It is the responsibility of individual nurses or organizations to be sure they are kept informed of hearing dates and topics. If you know a committee will hold hearings on a particular subject, write the chairman asking to be notified when the hearings will be scheduled. Be sure your requests to be notified about a particular hearing are submitted in writing, since it is not customary for staff to notify agencies or individuals about scheduled hearings without written requests.

You must also assess the importance of a hearing relative to your organization's priorities and objectives. Presenting testimony at every hearing of the slightest relevance

Guidelines for Presenting Testimony on Legislation *

Some 20,000 bills are introduced during the two-year course of a congressional session. As few as 500 may be signed into law, but many more are the subject of hearings. The following suggestions are intended to be of assistance in preparing testimony for public hearings.

THE DO'S

Do— Become familiar with the jurisdiction of legislative committees, their subcommittees, and their membership.

Do— Identify bills that would have the most impact in the program areas that are your responsibility. This will require an evaluation of your priorities.

Do— Consult other professional nursing organizations to coordinate your efforts and energies.

Do— Write the chairman of the subcommittee or committee who will chair the hearing and ask to be notified when hearings are scheduled.

Do— Find out the "ground rules" applicable to the hearing, ie, time limitations, length of testimony, number of copies of printed testimony, the deadline for submitting advance copies of testimony, etc.

Do— Prepare testimony, in accordance with the "ground rules," that agrees with approved policies of your parent organization.

Do— Select a witness knowledgeable in the subject area who will abide by the time limitations.

Do— Notify your elected representatives of your appearance, especially if they serve on the committee or subcommittee holding the hearing.

THE DON'TS

Don't— Request the opportunity to present oral testimony on bills of marginal interest.

Don't— Request the opportunity to present oral testimony on bills if a written statement to be inserted in the printed record of hearings would suffice.

Don't— Guess at the answer to a question. Ask to submit the requested information at a later date.

Don't— Fail to follow up on your oral testimony with copies to colleagues who could add to the arguments in behalf of your recommendations.

to nursing would be too time consuming. Weigh each situation carefully and don't request the opportunity to present oral testimony on bills if a written statement inserted in the printed record would suffice.

Once notified of the hearings, follow the instructions for submitting testimony. They

---

* Adapted by Sally B. Solomon, RN, from Government Relations Pamphlet No 3 of the National League for Nursing.

can vary markedly for each committee and for each hearing. Some committees require an outline summarizing major points of the testimony. Others prefer to review applications for presenting testimony or the actual testimony itself before making the final decisions as to which organizations will appear. Each committee has a different format for length, typing specifications, and the number of copies of the written testimony to be submitted in advance. Being familiar with these guidelines can help you avoid problems or surprises later on.

WRITING THE TESTIMONY

Draft the written testimony first and then excerpt key points that will be included in the oral statement on the day of the hearing. Before writing the testimony, you should be clear about the intent of the hearing. Often hearings are held on a specific bill that is being drafted or has already been proposed. In these cases, nurses should be familiar with the bill and state their views for or against it. In other instances, hearings are held on a general legislative issue, not necessarily in bill form. This is usually a more difficult situation since the parameters of the hearings are less clearly defined.

The intent of the hearings will also influence the style used in writing the testimony. Fact-finding hearings differ from hearings on a specific bill. The former requires a more objective approach, focusing on what has transpired around an issue. In the case of a specific bill, you should make a convincing argument in favor or against legislation. The language and tone used may need to be different to convey a certain point of view. Always try to be as logical and concrete as possible. Hearings are not the place to air personal gripes and complaints.

In writing the testimony, you should keep several points in mind:

- Whenever possible, include recent statistical data and cite specific examples to substantiate your major points. Rhetoric without documentation is not effective.

- Discuss the issue with nurses and other health professionals, as appropriate, to ensure that you have a full grasp of the topic. If possible, review previous testimony on the same issues to be as well prepared as possible.

- Consult with key constituents of your organization to be sure that your testimony agrees with organizational priorities and current thinking.

- Include in the first part of the testimony a description of your organization, its membership, and why the hearings are important to your organization's activities, as illustrated in the following example:

Mr Chairman, I am Dr Louise Fitzpatrick, dean of the School of Nursing at Villanova University. I am speaking today on behalf of the National League for Nursing (NLN) and the American Nurses' Association (ANA). NLN is the nationally recognized accrediting body for nursing education and one of the largest coalitions of health care professionals, practitioners, and consumers dedicated to providing quality health care. It includes 2,000 agency members and 17,000 individual members residing in constituent leagues throughout the country. ANA represents 185,000 registered nurses through 53 constituent state nurses' associations.

We appreciate the opportunity to present our views on the subject of Medicare's role in the financing of nursing education. Members of both organizations have a strong interest in maintaining high standards of nursing education so that patients, many of whom are Medicare recipients, can receive the best nursing care.

SELECTING A WITNESS

For organizations, the person writing the testimony is often not the person who will testify. Whenever possible, select a witness who is from the district represented by the chairman of the committee or by another committee member. Always select a witness knowledgeable in the subject area who is a good public speaker. The witness's familiarity with the subject will augment the delivery and help with responding to impromptu questions. All witnesses, no matter how seasoned, should be briefed about the legislation and the committee's record on the issue. If you are chosen as a witness, be sure to notify your elected representatives of your appearance, especially if they serve on the committee holding the hearings.

PRESENTING TESTIMONY

Presenting testimony is like staging a theatrical production. It requires setting the scene (writing the testimony), selecting the actors (choosing a witness), and rehearsing the script (briefing the witness). The quality of the final production is still dependent on the director (the committee chairman), how well prepared the actors (the witnesses and committee members) are, and how they relate to each other. A few guidelines can make for a smoother production.

First, be sure that the oral statement is succinct, outlines the key features of the written testimony, and can be presented within the time period specified by committee guidelines. Even though it is helpful to have a prepared oral statement, the most effective witnesses speak spontaneously and not word-for-word from a prepared text. If a prepared statement is read, try to interject some parts that are more spontaneous, such as a personal anecdote or summary comment.

Even while reading from a prepared statement, witnesses should establish eye contact with the committee members, especially the chairman. Hearings can be tedious proceedings for members and any efforts at easing the routine are appreciated and make the presentation more effective.

At one memorable senate hearing on nursing education and research, several expert nurse witnesses read their prepared texts. The final witness, a nurse researcher, managed to engage the committee chairman in a dialogue regarding the importance of infection control in nursing practice. Her statements stood out from the others and had greater impact on the senator, mainly because she had taken the risk of speaking spontaneously and had not depended on a written text. Not every witness can do this, but the more natural and relaxed the presentation, the better.

The witness will usually be asked questions after presenting testimony. Try to contact a committee staff person when submitting the written statement to see if you can suggest or submit certain questions or if you can review the questions in advance of the hearings. Knowing the questions beforehand helps alleviate what can be a tense situation for the witness.

If not prepared to answer a question, do not guess. It is perfectly acceptable to say that this is an area you are not familiar with, but you would be glad to look into the matter and submit a written statement for the record. Be sure you follow through by calling a committee staff person after the hearing and asking what their procedures are for such circumstances.

FOLLOW-UP

After the hearings, submit any information that was requested during the hearings to the appropriate committee staff. It also helps to circulate copies of the written statement to persons interested in the topic, such as membership groups, other organizations, other legislators, or the press.

Publicizing and reporting on the hearings in professional journals are also important to educate members and to let them know of the organization's involvement in legislative activities. Be sure to thank the witness and any staff who were instrumental in facilitating your involvement in the hearings.

SUMMARY

Every hearing is different, depending on the committee guidelines and the interaction between the witnesses and the committee members. Being well prepared and presenting succinct testimony is half the battle. Exhibiting self-confidence and being able to deal with uncertainties and unpredictable questions are also part of the process. These skills can be acquired through practice and experience.

Chapter 30

Voter Participation and Campaigning

Patricia Ford-Roegner, RN, MSW

Often I am asked if nursing and politics blend together. That's easy: of course, they do. The two professions have numerous similarities. Novices in their first political campaign soon realize teamwork is essential to getting the job done. Resources are always limited, and time is much too short. There are never enough people, and the telephones never stop ringing. Organization, as well as money, is the key to success. If a nurse were to tell me none of this sounded familiar, I would know she had never practiced nursing. Nurses make excellent campaign staff. And thousands of nurses are doing just that all over this nation. (See Appendix D, "The Hatch Act," for discussion of what the nurse employed by the federal government can do in terms of political activity.)

VOTER REGISTRATION: THE RIGHT TO VOTE

The first political act that each nurse can do is register and vote. We can make sure that our family, close friends, and colleagues are registered to vote and do vote.

Do those votes count? Congressional elections are often won by those 2,000 votes you just registered. In 1982, for example, the Nurses Coalition for Action in Politics-endorsed candidate Peter H. Kostmayer beat Congressman James Coyne by just over 2,000 votes in that Pennsylvania race (Barone & Ujifusa, 1984). Today, there are an estimated 47 million unregistered eligible voters in the country. Thirty million women are not registered to vote, and millions more do not vote in each election. Fourteen million young people between the ages of 18 to 24 are not registered. Voter registration is promoted by numerous organizations. Close political races can be won or lost by getting out the vote. For example, in 1982 in Missouri nurses worked hard to elect Harriet Woods, who was endorsed by N-CAP, for the U.S. Senate. The race was lost by less than 2 percent or fewer than 26,000 votes out of 1,543,505 votes cast.

The same year in Illinois where State Nurses Active in Politics in Illinois (SNAPI), the political action arm of the Illinois Nurses' Association, endorsed Adlai Stevenson for Governor, both he and Governor James Thompson received 49% of the vote. Stevenson lost by 5,000 votes in an election when the total votes cast numbered more than 3,600,000 (Barone & Ujifusa, 1984). Your vote does count.

When you and the five friends you take with you (never miss an opportunity to organize) register to vote, pick a party affiliation. While some may believe registering as an independent is a political statement, in most states, party registration is the only way you can vote in the Democratic or Republican primaries. It is in the primaries that you have your greatest opportunity to select a candidate of your choice. It is critical to support women candidates who are often challenged in primaries.

In a letter to new women voters in 1920, suffragist leader Carrie Chapman Catt tells why voting is important.

> The vote is the emblem of your equality, women of America, the guaranty of your liberty. That vote of yours has cost millions of dollars and the lives of thousands of women. Money to carry on this work has been given usually as a sacrifice, and thousands of women have gone without things they wanted and could have had in order that they might help get the vote for you. Women have suffered agony of soul which you never can comprehend, that you and your daughters might inherit political freedom. That vote has been costly. Prize it!
>
> The vote is a power, a weapon of offense and defense, a prayer. Understand what it means and what it can do for your country. Use it intelligently, conscientiously, prayerfully. No soldier in the great suffrage army has labored and suffered to get a "place" for you. Their motive has been the hope that women would aim higher than their own selfish ambitions, that they would serve the common good.
>
> The vote is won. Seventy-two years the battle for this privilege has been waged, but human affairs with their eternal change move on without pause. Progress is calling to you to make no pause. (Peck, 1924, p 3)

State Laws Regulating the Voting Process

We do not have a national system for registering voters. Voter registration is regulated by state laws. For a summary of the voter registration law in your state, refer to "Voter Registration Drives" in Appendix A. For more information, call or write the office of your secretary of state. An excellent source is your local League of Women Voters. Early in an election year, the League (1983–84) produces its poster, *Easy Does It: Registration and Absentee Voting Procedures by State*.

Voter Registration Drives

One of the best ways to get political experience is to begin with involvement in a voter registration drive. This is an organized plan to register a specific number or targeted group of citizens, for example, nurses in a congressional district or nursing students in a university. A voter registration drive includes registering voters, educating voters on the issues, and getting-out-the-vote (known as GOTV) on election day.

Since voter registration drives are nonpartisan, one can often obtain start-up funds from organizations that would hesitate to be involved in specific party candidate elections. It is an excellent project for a local nursing district for a number of reasons. Voter registration drives are noncontroversial. One can form a coalition with other women's organizations and health care groups around the project. It is an excellent way to recruit new volunteers who would like to be more political but don't know how to begin. But perhaps most important, the organization and planning of the drive involve the same steps as any other successful campaign, political or otherwise. Before initiating a drive, you will need to identify the goal, objectives, tasks, resources, budget, timetable, publicity, and evaluation process. (See Appendix A, "Voter Registration Drives.")

Comparing Lists

To know whether you have been successful in registering, say, all the nurses in a congressional district, you have to obtain the list of all the nurses in the congressional district. This would be a subplan in the organizing process that has just been discussed. The cost of obtaining such lists varies from state to state.

Next, you will need the list of registered voters so you can determine from your list of nurses which are registered to vote. Once you have obtained that second list from your county clerk's office or registrar's office, you compare it to get your targeted list of nurses to register. After you register these nurses, either poll watchers at the voting places or election lists will be needed to check whether your targeted new voters voted. With computers, some firms can compare (for a charge) your list to the registered voter list or actual voters list in that election.

Once you develop your list, card files, or computer discs, keep the original so you can update it in the future. Your list of registered nurse voters who voted is a political tool. Use it wisely.

Voting Power

The success of a voter registration drive is easily measured. You either reached your goal of registering 2,000 new voters by your state's deadline, or you did not. Either 65% of those new voters actually voted on election day, or they didn't. If you were successful, you have just played an important role in empowering others to take charge of their own lives. Even if you didn't meet your goal, you have learned how to organize a campaign, explain your issues, and meet new political friends. You have influenced volunteers, and understand your state's voting and election procedures.

The ANA is encouraging nurses to participate in voter registration drives sponsored by a variety of coalitions such as Project Vote and the National Coalition on Black Voter Participation. The ANA itself is part of a coalition of women's groups doing voter registration. For more information on this or other voter registration coalitions contact: Women's Vote Project c/o American Nurses' Association, 1101 14th St., NW Washington, DC 20005, Executive Director: Joanne Howes.

CAMPAIGN: STRATEGIES AND TECHNIQUES

You have decided upon a candidate. You know what you want from working on this campaign. You are aware of the importance of campaign planning.

Now you have been asked to become part of the yet undeclared candidate's exploratory committee. Another volunteer mentions the importance of individual voter contact.

Exploratory Committees

These committees may range from being formal with a long list of prominent names on a raised letterhead to a small group of the candidate's closest associates. The significance of these committees increases with the level of office sought. The legalities surrounding forming exploratory committees for fund-raising purposes is regulated by the Federal Election Commission or by state election commissions.

This is the candidate's opportunity to test the water. Before the campaign begins, a candidate must determine which of the people encouraging him or her to run for office are ready to commit time and money.

Seats on these committees are prestigious. Membership is a sign of your having arrived as a valued political participant.

Campaign Managers

How do candidates find campaign managers? The political network of former candidates and current activists will supply a candidate with suggestions for managers. Politics involves getting to know who knows what and keeping in touch.

It is important from the beginning that the candidate and the manager understand each other's roles. A campaign can begin to fall apart when the candidate is managing the campaign instead of the person hired to do so. A trusting relationship is essential. How much experience should a manager have? Experience is useful especially if it has been successful. In campaigns for higher public office, it is often required. I have seen, however, enthusiastic and energetic organizers successfully manage their first campaigns. In most cases, the campaign manager for national campaigns becomes the chief staff person for the newly elected member of the House or Senate.

In 1984, we had a nurse (Andrea Christenson) managing the campaign of a woman candidate (Joan Growe) for the U.S. Senate for the first time.

Campaign Calendar

A campaign calendar is a critical part of campaign planning. It is a tool to divide the numerous campaign activities into manageable pieces. The calendar forces one to look at the mechanics of a campaign. Joanne Symons, Director of the Political Education Department for the American Nurses' Association, recalls her first campaign when she covered the kitchen cabinets with white paper outlining what needed to be done. She used colored markers to highlight activities and pinpoint when action was needed.

The calendar gives you a time schedule to avoid crises. For example, in planning the three weeks for GOTV phone banking prior to election day, you would have discovered that the telephone company needed three weeks' notice to add additional phones. If this had not been built into the plan, the campaign would have no phones, angry volunteers, and additional expense to the campaign. The calendar helps staff to focus on details.

Recruitment and Training of Volunteers

Volunteers are the heart of a political campaign. In a low budget campaign at the local level, volunteers *are* the campaign.

They should be treated with respect; their time should be well used, accounted for, much appreciated, and recognized. Unfortunately, that is not always the case. If you manage a team of volunteers for a campaign, make sure they feel an integral part of that effort.

How do you match volunteer skills with campaign needs? There are numerous assessment tools available in political circles to assist the campaign staff. Figure 30-1 is the assessment tool I have used in helping the nurse Congressional District Coordinators, ANA's grass roots political network, to determine their potential role in a campaign.

These are suggestions from ANA's organizing manual (Nurses Coalition, 1981) for nurse political activists on recruiting volunteers:

> No candidate, campaign or nurse political project will function without the help of volunteers. Look for active, enthusiastic nurses drawn from all health-related areas—hospitals, clinics, doctors' offices, temporary agencies, community health nurses and more. Try to recruit enough volunteers to avoid overburdening anyone.
>
> An ideal way to recruit volunteers is to schedule an event involving candidates. This can be a coffee in someone's home or at a public meeting place. Candidates should each make opening remarks, respond to questions and ask for the support of nurses. Here are steps to take in putting together such a candidate night and to taking full advantage of it to recruit volunteers.

1. Contact area candidates' schedules and select a date when the candidates are available. Bill the event as a special reception for nurses.

2. Once you have a go-ahead from the candidate, think through every detail. Things to be done include: flyers to area nurses; other publicity; arranging for a hall; refreshments, introduction of the candidates, and determining the format including how long each speaks, whether there is question/answer period. Make sure that working back from the event date you plan every detail—then delegate tasks to others to get the job done.

3. At the event itself, have an attendance sheet at the entrance, requesting name, address and phone number. If feasible, spend time with each person attending and ask if they are interested in volunteering for upcoming political activities. Make note of their name, address and telephone number and follow up with a phone call. For larger crowds, have volunteer cards and make a strong pitch for volunteers.

There are other ways to recruit volunteers. A few ideas include:

1. Host a social event with a political theme for area nurses. Make it festive and fun. Have several local political personalities in attendance.

2. Perhaps in conjunction with your local political parties, hold an all day political skills seminar. At the conclusion, sign people up for jobs that appeal to them.

3. Hold a meeting to discuss upcoming political projects. Encourage members of the core group to each bring two friends. Then, involve guests in the conversation, planning and strategy. By evening's end, they will be ready to help.

	"A" MOTIVATION					"B" PERSONALITY					"C" RESOURCES					"D" SKILLS					Total	Rank
Place check marks here →	Feel I should get involved	Want public recognition	Believe strongly in issues	Want to advance my career	Want to run for office	Like leadership role	Detail-oriented	Persuasive/articulate	Self-starter	Find routine work relaxing	Want to work part-time	Can work full-time or more	Can work Election Day	Want to work at home	Have access to car	Bookkeeping/typing/clerical	Planning/organizing programs	Hiring/supervising personnel	Writing/public relations	Telephone/personal sales	Total	Rank
Campaign Manager		O		O	O	O		O	O			O	O				O	O				
Headquarters coordinator	O		O		O		O	O			O	O				O	O	O				
Finance chairman		O	O	O		O		O	O		O	O					O			O		
Treasurer or assistant	O		O			O		O	O	O	O	O				O	O	O				
Fund raiser		O	O	O				O	O		O			O	O				O	O		
Clerical support	O	O				O				O	O	O	O	O		O				O		
Scheduler		O				O	O	O		O		O			O	O			O	O		
Advancer or candidate aide		O		O		O	O				O	O			O	O			O	O		
Press secretary		O	O	O				O	O		O	O				O			O	O		
Speechwriter/copywriter	O		O	O		O	O	O	O		O			O		O			O			
Researcher	O		O	O			O				O	O		O		O			O			
Volunteer coordinator		O		O	O		O		O	O		O	O				O	O		O		
Door-to-door canvasser	O		O				O	O		O	O	O		O		O				O		
Candidate	O	O	O	O	O	O			O	O		O	O				O					
Host/hostess	O	O	O		O			O	O		O			O			O			O		
Phone bank supervisor	O					O	O		O			O	O	O			O	O		O		
Phoner	O		O				O	O		O	O	O		O		O				O		
Election Day driver	O		O				O			O	O		O		O	O	O	O		O		
Event organizer		O		O	O	O			O		O			O			O	O				
Poll watcher/checker	O	O	O	O			O			O	O		O		O	O	O					

MATCH WHAT YOU HAVE TO OFFER WITH WHAT'S NEEDED IN CAMPAIGN JOBS

Examine the descriptive phrases within the four vertical columns, A through D, at the top of the page. Select the 10 phrases which best apply to you, with a minimum of two phrases chosen from each column.

Place a check mark in the empty box below each phrase you select. Then, moving down the page, darken each circle below your 10 check marks.

ADD UP YOUR SCORE!

Counting from left to right, add up the number of darkened circles for each campaign job. Put the sum in the box marked "Total". Then rank the jobs from 1 to 20, beginning with the job with the highest total points. This ranking will give you a good idea of where you fit in a political campaign.

Figure 30-1 Campaign Skills Assessment Tool

4. Have informal get-togethers, such as brown bag lunches, at or near nurse workplaces. Invite a local campaign manager or politically active nurse to speak, then sign up volunteers.

In all dealings with volunteers, keep in mind that few things are more precious. Volunteers must be carefully cultivated, cared for, trained, appreciated and thanked. Here are some tips:

1. Volunteers are just that—they do not get paid. So, you can't threaten to fire them. They must feel needed and appreciated, or they will play tennis or watch television, instead.

2. Nothing is more frustrating than to volunteer and not be called on. If someone offers to tackle a job, don't delay. Put her or him to work immediately.

3. Don't leave anything to chance. Volunteers benefit from clear, detailed instructions. So do you.

4. Don't think you can overdo the thank-you's. Volunteers need to feel appreciated.

5. Don't try to pull the wool over a volunteer's eyes. If you convince someone to do a two hour job that grows into 20 hours, she or he has every right to quit in the middle.

6. Everyone has strengths and weaknesses. Most people will be honest in assessing whether their talents lie in answering the phone or writing a speech. Enlist the volunteers' help in making good assignments from the outset. Underutilized and overwhelmed volunteers are frustrated; they quit.

7. Keep records of jobs the volunteers have done, so you or someone else may call on them again. (pp 9–11)

For additional information on volunteer recruitment, start by checking with issue groups in your local community. Handbooks are developed on a regular basis by a broad range of organizations. Some suggestions include local chapters of the National Organization for Women, the American Association of University Women, the National Council of Senior Citizens, the National Education Association, and the National Association of Social Workers.

Fund-raising

You have to raise money to get money. Major contributors who give $1,000 to a national campaign want to know how much money a candidate has raised before they will contribute. It is also the first question asked by political action committee directors. The candidates' ability to raise money demonstrates the seriousness of their candidacy in the political arena. How one will raise a campaign budget is critical to any effort no matter the level. A volunteer who becomes a successful fund-raiser will definitely be appreciated.

Women have a history of volunteerism. Now, with more women moving into the workforce, serious attention is being given to raising money to support our concerns (Crone & Stegal, 1981).

Fund-raising is both an art and a skill. Most organizations see the value of contracting with professional fund-raisers. It is worth the initial outlay. The manner in which a fund-raising appeal is conducted can make all the difference in the world. An error-free, attractive, and creative appeal for donations is worth the effort. An expert fundraiser can tell you how to do it and probably know how to get you the best price.

As a candidate or volunteer fund-raiser, you again start with family, friends, and colleagues. If money permits, you want to target your messages to specific groups to get the most from the appeal.

Much can and should be explored about fund-raising. The "Fund-raising Tips" in Chapter 34 will help you with initial, small-scale fund-raising activities.

One final message about giving money: Women have not been quick to open their checkbooks and write a check for their candidate. It is time to give. You must ask yourself if you do not give to candidates who support your concerns, who will? Women workers earn a little more than half what men do. You have to spend money to change that.

Individual Voter Contact

You are in a campaign to win. You or your candidate have to convince more voters to support you rather than the opponent. To do this you need a plan based on your knowledge of the district. The plan should identify the following:

1. voters who will support the candidate
2. voters who will not support the candidate
3. undecided voters

Once voters have been identified, the task becomes how to contact them personally. One important fact that may surprise the new politician: you don't want to contact all voters—just those who will or might vote for your candidate.

There are many ways to contact the individual voter. The three most commonly used are telephone banks, canvassing, and direct mail. Voters are bombarded by information daily. You must get the voter to notice your candidate. Think about that commercial you laugh about. Why do you notice it? Because the message is presented clearly and creatively and repeated over and over. Repetitive contact and follow-up are essential in persuading voters to vote for your candidate.

Phone banks and door-to-door canvassing are labor intensive. A large number of volunteers must be recruited. They will be needed not only for the calling and canvassing but for the follow-up as well. Phone banks, if well organized, can reach more voters in a shorter amount of time than canvassing. For phone banks, a well-prepared script for volunteers is necessary (see Appendix B). For canvassing, you need a campaign kit. The numerous details involved in these efforts necessitate good planning. For example, two or three hours of telephoning a night is all a volunteer can usually do. You have to take this into account in figuring out the number of volunteers × telephones × days needed. Phone numbers will have to be looked up before the actual telephoning. One has to be aware of important events when other activities would be at a loss, like canvassing during the World Series.

Direct mail should be attractive and personalized. If possible, the message should be targeted to the concerns of that voter as a nurse, a senior citizen, parent, or teacher. That is when it can be most effective. Professional help again is worth the expense.

Media

The media plan should complement efforts to contact the individual. Next to personal contact, television and radio are the most persuasive. Local papers are often useful in local races, especially when money is tight. Television time is expensive. If you can get free coverage as a result of innovative campaign techniques, do it.

For further information on how to develop a relationship with and work the media, see *The American Nurses' Association's Handbook for Political Media* in Appendix C.

Getting-Out-the-Vote (GOTV) on Election Day

The final strategy is getting out the vote on election day. Volunteers will be needed to phone voters reminding them to vote. Voters may need rides to the polls or babysitters. You want to assist voters any way you can. Besides poll watchers, you will need volunteers to canvass outside the voting place to persuade undecided voters.

Thank-you's

Not enough can be said about thank-you's. Whether the campaign is successful or not, those people who gave their precious time to the campaign should be recognized and appropriately thanked.

CHOOSING A CANDIDATE: GETTING INVOLVED IN A POLITICAL CAMPAIGN

Before getting involved in a political campaign, you need to ask yourself what you want to get out of it. Are you doing this as a nurse volunteer where the end result is to get your candidate elected? Or do you regard your involvement in this campaign as a step in your own political career? Do you want a staff position with a campaign? Or are you interested in organizing local nurses into a political power group? Politics is infectious; how will it affect your personal life?

Getting Credit for Volunteerism

As a volunteer you will have to take the initiative to make sure your worth is recognized. Once you figure out who the leaders of the campaign are, tell them who you are, how much your time is worth, and what you are doing or what you would like to do in this campaign. Make a place for yourself in the campaign in an area of responsibility such as scheduling or volunteer coordinator, making your contribution valuable to the campaign. To earn political credit, you need high visibility in the campaign. To get what you want, you will have to learn the art of negotiation (*Tip Sheet*, 1982).

Candidate Selection

You will choose a candidate whose values and beliefs are closely aligned to yours. Being a nurse, you bring with you to the campaign a positive public image, use it carefully.

One of the benefits from working in a campaign of an N-CAP-endorsed candidate is the camaraderie of nurses working side-by-side for organized nursing.

The American Nurses' Association (ANA), in consultation with its state constituents, has adopted a national nursing agenda. This statement outlines the issues that ANA wants addressed through legislation and national policy. Local nursing districts and state nurses' associations have issue committees that have also adopted legislative agendas for issues at the state level. These legislative agendas provide members and the PACs (political action committees) of the state nurses' associations with information about issues on which to judge the voting records and leadership of incumbents.

When you encourage nurses to commit their time to candidates who are clearly friends of nursing, you add to nursing's political power. Whether you join with organized nursing efforts, a group of nurse friends, or work on your own, make sure the campaign knows you are a nurse. It is your professional and political identity.

Some Ways to Tell Whether a Candidate Is Serious

You do not want to waste your time and energy. One would think that candidates would have done their homework before running for an office. This is not always the case.

What do you look for in a candidate and his or her campaign? Do polls show a high positive or negative rating for the incumbent? What percentage of the voting public recognizes the challenger's name? What kind of experience will the candidate bring to the office? Does the candidate have his or her party's backing? If not, why not? Often this is the case for women candidates who enter politics as a result of their concern over local issues. How do they get party backing? Has he or she built up his or her own political credit with peers? Is the candidate comfortable with public speaking? Does he or she appear to enjoy campaigning? How much does the candidate want to win? You bring your personal interaction skills from nursing to the campaign. Use these skills to evaluate the candidate.

On the campaign side, has the staff researched the political unit where the candidate is running? Is this an open seat due to the incumbent's retirement or is it a new seat created as a result of an increase in population? (The latter is known as redistricting.) Is this candidate challenging an incumbent? What is the political makeup of the district? Is it heavily Democratic or Republican? Is there a large independent vote? In the last election what percentage of registered voters voted? In the primary? In the general election? Is this a presidential election year where one can expect a higher voter turnout?

What was the incumbent's margin of victory in the last election? If the incumbent is popular with the voters and received 78 percent of the vote in the last election, the challenger's chances are slim.

Who lives in this political unit? Where does the populace work? What are the major media sources? Wanting to win is not enough. If this campaign does not have an up-to-date profile of the district, how will it develop the campaign plan critical to success?

Campaigns should have an overall plan and component sub-plans. Using your own professional skills in planning and organizing, ask yourself if these plans seem realistic. For example, the campaign has a projected budget but has no subplan of how it intends to raise funds. A hard lesson in politics is that you have to have money to raise money. The campaign must have a good plan to do so.

Is the campaign managed in a professional manner? Are schedules adhered to and tasks completed on time? Do the candidate and campaign manager work well together? Does the campaign recognize that in areas such as polling, public relations, and fund-raising, hiring political professionals may be well worth the cost? There are creative ways to combine professional and volunteer help on a limited budget.

Recruiting Candidates

New nurse politicians often find recruiting candidates a novel idea. But it is done all the time by political parties, activists, and interest groups.

Incumbents leaving political life often endorse a successor. This makes it tough for those not in the old boys network, namely, women and minorities.

Nurses active in politics are beginning to recruit candidates who support our issues. If you recruit a candidate and he or she wins, not only do you have influence with this new member of that particular political body, but you also may have accomplished another goal. If in the process you helped to defeat one of nursings' opponents in the state assembly, you have sent a clear message to the opposition. If you can affect one election, you have political power. Remember, for politicians, getting elected and re-elected is the bottom line.

There are responsibilities to recruiting candidates. Campaigns need time, money, and volunteers. You will have to deliver some of each.

Nurses as Candidates

Nurses make great candidates. The public's view of nursing is positive. We are seen as leaders in our communities by the nature of our professional identity. I call this the "Aunt Lucy" theory. Once you publicly identify yourself as a nurse, the voter then mentions a relative who is also a nurse. Usually this relative is regarded with a sense of pride. You can use this to your best advantage as a candidate. Nurses also have natural constituencies; for instance, the senior citizens and other consumers, women working in or out of the home, and other "helping professionals."

In 1984, there were 35 nurse state legislators. I have met a number of them. They are articulate, elected officials respected by their colleagues.

There are no nurses in the U.S. Congress. We need representation there. Nurses need to bring their skills, their caring and compassion, and their expertise to the national political arena.

Organizational Endorsements

Organizational endorsements are important. They provide a way to reach a larger audience that, due to limited resources, may never have been tapped. N-CAP endorsements mean a great deal to candidates. They are sought because of the positive image of nursing. When the N-CAP board of directors has given early endorsements in tight races, other incumbents have called to find out what happened to their endorsements. An endorsement can mean resources such as money, volunteers, and votes. To other politicians it shows nurses are willing to risk and that legitimatizes us in the political community.

Membership organizations should have written guidelines for endorsement (see Chapter 34 for sample guidelines). These should be available to members upon request. While there will always be members who will think their candidate should have been endorsed, the organization needs to be comfortable with its decision. It makes no political sense for an organization to endorse both candidates for the same office.

As an individual nurse, you have a right to vote and work for the candidate of your choice. Either way, get involved in the process. And remember that PACs need your monetary support. Your political contribution to N-CAP qualifies for the 50% federal tax credit for political contributions.

Going Public

Once you have made an endorsement and taken that political risk with say, "Nurses for Smith" or as the PAC of your SNA, publicize it. You want to reach the widest audience possible. It is crucial to develop a way to reach every member or nurse voter to let them know why this candidate has been endorsed and how they can get involved. In Wisconsin, the state nurses' association's PAC places ads in local newspapers to publish their endorsements. Other states use newsletters. Phone banks and direct mail are other ways to reach the individual nurse.

CONGRESSIONAL DISTRICT COORDINATORS NETWORK

Suppose that when you decided to engage in campaign activity, there already was a large pool of identified nurse volunteers. Wouldn't that have been easier? Now you know the point behind developing a grass roots political network for nursing. In modern campaigns, only organized groups visible to candidates get noticed. While individual nurses have been involved in campaigns for years, the Congressional District Coordinators (CDC) Network is becoming the means for identifying and organizing these nurses. The difference is that it is the nurses' own political network.

The goal of the network is to devise a system within ANA and its fifty-three state nurses' associations (50 states, the District of Columbia, Puerto Rico, and the Virgin Islands) by which nurses can influence legislation at the federal level through collective action at the local level. This goal is achieved by the following:

1. the election of pro-nursing candidates
2. the candidate's realization that he or she is indebted to nursing
3. the perception in the political community (including the media) that nurses are important to have on your side in an election

The objectives of this CDC network for political and legislative action are to:

• Recruit and prepare nurses to work on the campaigns of federal candidates who are friends of nursing and have been endorsed by N-CAP.

- Reach every nurse voter in the congressional district with a unified message of support of the N-CAP-endorsed candidate or federal level nursing issue.
- Establish a system of communication between the local nurses and each U.S. representative on issues of importance to ANA at the federal level.
- Provide a means to inform nurses about the policies and positions of the American Nurses' Association concerning legislative and regulatory issues at the federal level.
- Provide a means of monitoring the potential impact of legislation or regulation before any action takes place.
- Limit the number of requests from the ANA Washington office for legislative or regulatory action by targeting congressional district activity.
- Identify and recruit potential nurse candidates for public office.

History and Development

It became evident to the board members of N-CAP that there was a need for a concerted effort by nurses in the political arena. They recognized that campaigns certainly needed money, but they also needed volunteers and organization. The N-CAP Board of Directors became the catalyst for creation of ANA's Department of Political Education in 1982 and subsequently the development of the CDC network.

As of 1985, over 362 nurses have volunteered as lead political organizers in their congressional districts. With a total of 435 congressional districts, we are over one-half the way there. The congressional district is used as the geographic unit since it is the only way to organize for congressional campaigns. In states like North Dakota, the entire state is a congressional district while there are forty-five congressional districts in California. Each CDC volunteer is nominated, recruited, and approved through his or her state nurses' association.

In 1982, through the CDC network, nurses helped elect over sixty new members to Congress. Over 2,000 nurses emerged through this network to work on campaigns of N-CAP-endorsed candidates for Congress and the Senate. This has made a difference on Capitol Hill. Representatives are now asking what they can do for us.

Potential Nurse Power

Political nurses have been welcomed with open arms into the Washington political community and in their states. We have been successful partly because of our positive image and because of the conspicuous political activity of nurses at the local level.

ANA has been hosting a series of breakfast forums with the leadership of national women's health, labor, and business organizations, the Senate and Congress, executive branch, and other government agencies. The potential for building a strong political grass-roots organization that will give SNA members a sense of control over their future and make nursing an important political force has turned into a budding reality. Public opinion leaders are seeking nursing's input. I have been asked directly for the names of the nurse CDC's by members of Congress. Nurses are writing candidates' health issue papers. They are also being asked by elected Congresspersons to prepare background papers on relevant issues from a nursing perspective. Subsequently, this information is distributed to the representative's constituency as a service to the public. The aim of ANA's Congressional District Coordinators' Network is to create a public awareness of the political clout of nurses.

In the past, nursing's input into the development of major health care legislation has not been sought by high ranking government officials. Nursing has reacted to such legislation after the fact. State government officials, medical societies, and hospital groups have tried to control the practice of nursing by attempting to place restrictions on state nurse practice acts. These attacks on nursing in the past have been due, in part, to the lack of a strong political perception of nursing as a unified and effective political force. This perception is changing rapidly with nursing's growing political clout in the election of pro-nursing candidates, in the legislative effectiveness at the national and state levels, and in nursing's own self-image.

References

Barone M, Ujifusa G: *The Almanac of American Politics*. The National Journal, 1984.

Crone B, Stegal L: *Fundraising Events: Making Womenpower Profitable*. National Women's Political Caucus, 1981.

League of Women Voters Catalogue. League of Women Voters, 1984.

Livingston D: *Power at the Polls*. National Association of Social Workers, 1983.

Nurses Coalition for Action in Politics: *TIME: for Nurses to make a Difference Through Politics*. American Nurses' Association, 1981.

Peck MG: Carrie Chapman Catt. Page 3 in: *The Women's Vote: Beyond the Nineteenth Amendment*. Stone M, Cohn M, Freeman M. The League of Women Voters, 1924.

Stone M, Cohn M, Freeman M: *The Women's Vote: Beyond the Nineteenth Amendment*. League of Women Voters, 1983.

Tip Sheet for Women Campaign Executives. National Women's Education Fund, 1982.

Vignette: **The Nurse Politician**
Shirley A. Girouard, RN, MSN

Nurses are becoming increasingly active in politics. Their involvement takes many forms: participating in campaigns, networking, contributing money to candidates, and acting as consultants to candidates on health care issues. They are even running for office and getting elected. The September 1984 *American Journal of Nursing* reported that 37 nurses were serving as state senators, state officials, or members of their houses of representatives or state assemblies.

Why do nurses run for office? How do they succeed? What do they do once they are elected? Who benefits when the nurse applies her knowledge and skill to the role of elected official? I would like to share my story—how a nurse became a state legislator.

Before 1982, I was, like many other nurses, an average participant in politics. I occasionally wrote letters to my elected representatives, I did a little work on two presidential campaigns, I voted regularly, and I followed issues of particular interest to me or my profession. In 1981, the state law that authorized our nursing board expired. Nurses across New Hampshire including myself learned about and became involved in the legislative process. We were successful in renewing the law and were excited at our ability to influence the political process.

Soon after this, a group of enthusiastic and politically aware nurse friends convinced me that I would make a great representative. They argued that having a practicing nurse in the State House would prevent similar things from happening. Although there were other nurses in the legislature, my colleagues convinced me that my active involvement with the profession and my clinical background would enhance the profession's ability to influence legislation. I ran and won!

My victory may not sound particularly dramatic except for the following facts: (1) no Democrat had been elected from my community for eight years; (2) I was a relative newcomer; and (3) I was virtually unknown. How did I win? The editor of the local newspaper is still asking that question. The secret to my success was nurse power. My campaign manager, Laurie Harding, was a nurse. Most of my campaign funds were contributed by nurses or were raised at fund-raisers organized by nurses. The people who knocked on doors, distributed leaflets, and made phone calls were nurses. My ability to campaign, and my desire to win the election were only possible because of the tremendous support I received from other nurses. I felt I had an obligation to my colleagues to win.

During the campaign we discovered two important things. First, we had the knowledge and skills to deal with issues, organize people, and manage a campaign. Secondly, the members of our community were receptive to nurses on the campaign trail. As we received positive feedback, our self-confidence grew, and we became more assertive and active.

Still elated at victory, I went anxiously off to the State House to become a legislator. I was amazed to discover that after a little tutoring and some study, I was quickly able to integrate myself into this new arena. My nursing background was relevant to the legislative process because much of the legislation we considered had to do with people. Issues relating to the environment, housing, income, health, and social services were familiar because of my nursing education and practice. Also, the process of lawmaking was similar to that of policy-making in settings I had practiced in—negotiating, articulating, persuading, and convincing were all skills I had learned as a nurse. My legislative colleagues generally had good feelings about nurses, and because of this I often acted as their personal consultant for health care problems. Thus, I was able to establish important relationships early in my tenure.

Nurses discovered there were many benefits associated with having a nurse in the State House. Nursing's image was enhanced, legislators who were inactive nurses became more aware of nursing concerns, and other nurses became more interested in the political process. I was able to channel information to the nursing community in a timely fashion, provide contacts when there were issues that needed to be discussed, help other nurses find their way in the legislative process, and mobilize the nursing community to respond when there were issues of concern to us. By the time the presidential primaries began in 1983, New Hampshire nurses were in a prime position to get involved. We held meetings with most of the Democratic candidates and thus further enhanced our image as an involved and concerned constituency.

My experiences have convinced me and other nurses that we *can* run for office, we *can* win, and we *can* be effective legislators. Moreover, our nursing knowledge provides an important perspective in the political arena. I encourage all nurses to work together to elect colleagues to city halls, state houses, the U.S. Congress, and perhaps, someday soon, to the White House. What we have to offer is unique and important to society.

How to Elect a Nurse

Identify an interested, motivated, and politically active nurse.

Organize a group of supporters and assign tasks: a coordinator and individuals to be responsible for fund-raising, canvassing, volunteer recruitment, media, telephone banks, etc.

Raise money.

Hit the streets: knock on every door, leaflet every household, call every resident.

Register voters.

Make a special appeal to nurses in the community.

Make the candidate visible: send letters to the editor of local papers, send press releases, attend public functions and meetings with the candidates, advertise.

Vignette: **Nurses in the Running: A Campaign Story**
Nancy West, RN, MSN

In 1983 three nurses, Theresa Smith, Karen Podmore, and I each ran for a different public office in our local communities. The three of us, a critical care nurse, a head nurse on a surgical unit, and a nurse practitioner/faculty member, were no different from other nurses in our communities and that is why our running for office is important. Since none of us had run for office before, we formed an informal support group, sharing what we learned, our experiences, and feelings.

Most people, like us, become involved in politics as volunteers on a campaign. This gives them an opportunity to meet the leadership of the political party and to learn about effective campaigning. Individual campaign workers who are bright, capable, hardworking, and good with people (attributes most nurses possess), stand out in a campaign. In addition, campaign volunteers who understand and can communicate the issues of a campaign, who speak well, and present themselves well in public are often noticed by political party leadership. Often party leaders ask these individuals to seek nomination for elected office and run as candidates.

Being a candidate is exhilarating, challenging, fun, and sometimes intimidating. Suddenly you are a public person. During the campaign you are scrutinized as a candidate by individual voters, the media, and community groups. People notice how you dress, how well you are groomed, how you shake hands, whether you're relaxed and cordial, how you speak, whether you listen, what your ethnic heritage is, what your religious affiliation is, and in what community groups you participate. We were advised to remember that a candidate is on review at all times. As your name and face become more widely recognized, trips to the supermarket in sweatpants are impossible and a night on the town with friends drinking and dancing seems less appropriate. We all handled the stress of being public persons well, but each of us felt intimidated about being a knowledgeable spokesperson on community problems.

As a candidate, you are expected to speak out publicly on issues and have not only an opinion about problems in the community, but also solutions. While we all read the papers and were aware of issues in the community, it was more difficult to stand before strangers and publicly explain the problem, express our views, and offer solutions. We were fortunate to have attended a Candidate's School sponsored by our political party. This was a crash course on all the issues: pollution of the underground water supply, solid-waste disposal and land-fills, the abuses of one-party government and budgetary control, and excessively high utility rates. (At times we felt like Florence Nightingale as she wrote in *Notes on Nursing* about clean water, waste disposal, and focusing the energy of a bureaucracy to meet the needs of the people.)

Occasionally people asked if we were running for office to get out of nursing—a question we welcomed since it gave us the opportunity to talk about nurses' involvement in politics and public policy. Our experience as candidates did give us an opportunity to speak with thousands of people and a chance to talk about nursing's role in health care.

Being a candidate is hard work. Campaigning is exhausting, and there is never a day off. A typical weekday schedule follows:

5:30 am	Get up and get groomed for campaigning.
6:30 am	Campaign at a commuter railroad station—shaking hands and greeting sleepy voters—all the while smiling and exuding good cheer.
8:30 am	Rush off to work, or if day off, then hit the "Bs": Bowling alleys to meet people in the day leagues, Beauty shops, Bakeries, and Bagel shops (especially good for crowds on weekends).
Noon	Attend luncheons and afternoon meetings of community groups to greet members and sometimes speak.
3 pm	If time (and energy) allows, go to supermarkets and greet voters at the entrances.
5 pm	Check up on campaign progress with campaign manager: check on printing of literature, volunteers scheduled for evening work, go over details of planned fund-raisers.
7 pm	Attend evening functions—usually four or more (one night we did 8 appearances)—at each one make a short speech and shake everyone's hand.
9:30 pm	Stop by headquarters and thank volunteers who made phone calls.
10 pm	Go over next day's agenda and find locations of events on county street map; talk with campaign coordinator.

All of us were working full-time as well as campaigning; so our days were very busy. The real challenge was to find time to see friends and family, to do mundane things such as laundry, and to relax. One candidate found time to manicure her nails while waiting for traffic lights as she was driving between campaign appearances. We learned that taking care of one's self—physically and emotionally—is an important part of maintaining the stamina necessary to campaign again the next day.

We learned many things about campaigning:

• Summer campaigning leads to sunburn, prickly heat, and tired feet; but we learned to look cool, crisp, and confident.

- Rainy days make people disgruntled, and candidates look droopy.
- Chilly autumn morning campaigning at 6:30 am makes separating literature and handshaking uncomfortable (as a bare hand is the best handshake).
- Shaking hands, smiling, and introducing oneself as a candidate becomes instinctive. Meeting hundreds of people in this brief way becomes a daily event. Eventually, speaking before groups of 100 people on issues becomes comfortable.

Nurses who think they might like to run for office can begin to prepare themselves by doing the following:

1. Decide on a political party affiliation and become active in the political organization.
2. Begin to read all local and regional papers and keep a file of clippings.
3. Brush up on grooming and plan well-tailored and professional-looking additions to your wardrobe.
4. Take a course in public speaking.
5. Join a wide range of community organizations (not just nursing organizations) and participate in their work. Groups focusing on community and civic issues, religious, environmental, tax reform, and women's issues are excellent places to learn about issues and to develop a support base.
6. Attend political functions and meet political party activists.
7. Work on a campaign of someone who is known to be a good campaigner, who will let you see the campaign operation and show you how to do campaign appearances.
8. Expand your world of interests beyond nursing and health care. Learn about issues in your community that are unfamiliar to you, such as municipal budgets, transportation, housing, highways, business development, police, and utilities.

Running for public office is a challenging act of self-definition. You must decide on the image of yourself and the nursing profession you wish to project. You must be knowledgeable and able to communicate your views persuasively. You must stand up, speak out, and go on record with your views. You must appear self-assured and confident. You must be worthy of the public trust. These are all attributes of a professional nurse. As we found in 1983, nurses make superior candidates.

Chapter 31

Educating Nurses for Political Action

Teaching Policy and Political Process

Barbara E. Hanley, RN, PhD

Maturity in the political and policy-making sphere will occur when the nursing profession incorporates these subjects into educational and organizational structures. Movement toward this goal is evident as increasing numbers of generic, graduate, and doctoral programs offer courses in health policy and politics. Additionally, state nurses' associations and specialty organizations are offering legislative workshops and continuing education programs on health policy and political participation.

NURSE POLICYMAKERS

The political imperative confronting nursing is the incorporation of both policy and political theory to vitalize nursing's practice, administration, and research. Nurses must see themselves as participants in all phases of policy and political cycles.

The purpose of this chapter is to discuss nurses' roles and to suggest strategies for teaching health policy and political participation, including course content and learning strategies. It is geared toward faculty and nursing leaders to encourage their developing specific courses, as well as to students (generic, graduate, or continuing) to encourage them to seek independent or formalized political learning experiences.

POLITICAL SOCIALIZATION

Nursing leaders set the political tenor in nursing organizations and educational or health care institutions. Faculty who lack experience in political and health policy arenas may stifle nurses' and students' growth because their noninvolvement reinforces the perception that political activities are not part of the professional role. While nurses may be recognizing the importance of policy and political participation as a result of the political consciousness-raising, they frequently lack knowledge or skills in these areas and are less likely to participate.

Role modeling of political behavior by nurse educators or administrators, an essential component of professional socialization, may increase the likelihood that nurses will adopt similar behaviors. A recent study of female nurse political behavior (Hanley, 1983) determined that having a mother at least as politically active as one's father was a significant predictor of political participation.

EDUCATIONAL SOCIALIZATION

The importance of professional education in shaping nurses' political interest and participation is supported by a study of 267 women members in a district of the Michigan Nurses' Association (Hanley, 1983). As seen in Table 31-1, 69 percent of nurses with diplomas or associate degrees found their education "not at all" or "low" as a politicizing force in contrast to 39 percent of BS graduates and 19 percent of nurses with higher degrees. Further, while approximately 44 percent of BS and higher degree prepared nurses found their education moderately politicizing, 36 percent found their graduate preparation "a great deal" so.

The perceived level of educational politicization translated into higher levels of overall political activity ($p < .05$). On a scale of one (never) to four (always), nurses who perceived a high level of educational socialization had significantly higher overall participation and communal activity (a combination of community activity and communication with policymakers), and protest scores.

TEACHING POLITICAL PROCESSES

Since the midseventies nursing leaders have been urging the profession to politicize both nurses and students (Kalisch & Kalisch, 1976; Leininger, 1978; Fagin, 1981). An exploratory study of nurse administrators measured both their level of participation and their recommendations for content in political education courses (Archer & Goehner, 1981). The area most frequently cited (43 percent) was "legislative processes at all levels of government" as course content in curricula which encourage nurse political activism (Archer & Goehner, 1981). Consistent with this recommendation, several nurse authors have reported on model elective courses for teaching nursing students the legislative process (Cowart, 1977; Jones, 1980; McMahon & Westfall, 1984). The key learning strategy in these courses is direct involvement, whether in formal courses or independent study. Provision of information alone is not adequate; direct participation or interaction with legislative and regulatory officials and staff throughout the policy or political process is essential.

Archer and Goehner (1981) emphasize the use of nurse faculty and guest speakers to enhance the role model effect. State nurses' association staff, political action and legis-

Table 31-1 Female Nurses' Perception of Political Socialization in Professional Education

	None to Low	Moderate	High
Diploma/ Associate degree	69%	32%	5%
Baccalaureate	39	43	18
Graduate	19	45	36

lative committee members, and ANA congressional district coordinators are potential resources.

The course focus, whether on legislation, political action, or forces shaping health care delivery, will determine specific objectives. In schools with no formal policy-related course, independent studies can be devised around a student's particular interest or a current legislative issue.

INDEPENDENT STUDY

Faculty interested in offering policy and political behavior courses may find development of independent studies a feasible starting point. A course can be designed around a series of field experiences in numerous policy-making offices. Field experience can include visits to state or local health department officials, such as the state health planning director; and attendance at health meetings of policy-making bodies such as the city council, the health committee of the state legislature, or floor debate on a health bill. Preparatory or debriefing sessions with office or committee staff may enhance the learning value of the experience. Students particularly value discussions with nurses who hold elected or appointed public office.

For example, a student may have particular interest in third party reimbursement for nurses and wish to help develop enabling legislation. An independent study could be developed around a student's unpaid internship in a supportive legislator's office or with a nursing association's government relations staff. Later in this chapter, a nurse describes the independent study she arranged with the help of the staff in ANA's Washington office.

Working in a legislator's office or with a professional nursing association, students will gain indepth knowledge of the political process as they explore the pro's and con's of issues. While learning the legislative process and negotiation, students educate legislators and their staff about nursing roles and provide a nursing perspective on health care problems. Further, they can convey legislators' concerns to nursing constituents and suggest strategies for improving their lobbying.

Weekly logs or journals can be organized to analyze issues under study, their movement through the process, and students' interactions with legislators, staff, and lobbyists. Seminar or class sessions focus on policy and political science background specific to the internship, as well as related policy trends.

HEALTH POLICY COURSES

A general course introducing students to health policy is recommended for all graduate programs. Ideally, however, the process should begin at the undergraduate level. An option is to open the graduate introductory health policy course to senior students as an elective.

In a two-credit graduate core course offered by the University of Maryland School of Nursing, entitled "Influential Forces, Health Care and Health Care Systems," the faculty strives to expand nurses' horizons and encourage them to explore health policy.

Students write a health issue paper and a report of an issue-based field experience. The student determines the issue and traces its evolution; identifies the major policymakers including legislators, regulators, interest groups, and their positions on the issue; cites nursing's involvement or describes how the issue affects nursing; and identifies options for resolving the issue. Finally, the student states her preferred solution and provides a rationale to defend the position.

Students may write an action plan instead of a field experience report. An action report is a description of the process involved in supporting a particular piece of health legislation.

Requirements for an action plan include:

- selection of an appropriate bill, including one's supportive rationale
- contacting involved health care organizations to learn their position on the bill and their rationale
- identification of a supportive coalition for the bill
- development of a lobbying strategy including rationale for each phase and copies of materials used, such as letters to policymakers, summaries of verbal communication, minutes from organizing meetings
- development of an action timetable
- implementation of the plan
- evaluation of the plan

An integral part of the course is a weekly "issue update." Students are encouraged to scan the various media for news and portrayals of health or professional issues, upcoming meetings of policy interest, and political activities. Class format is lecture with guided discussion. Guest lecturers provide expertise on selected topics and nurses who can act as role models are also invited.

The first phase of the course focuses on providing students with the social science tools necessary for policy analysis:

Legislative and Policy Processes. Initial course readings and discussions reinforce fundamentals of American government such as the Constitution and the structure and function of the executive, legislative, and judicial branches. The legislative process is illustrated by tracing nursing or health legislation from idea to enactment. The policy process becomes meaningful when a health program is traced from problem area to program evaluation.

Health Economics.   Principles and concepts of health economics are essential to understanding how health policy is developed, financing of health care, reimbursement practices, and subsidization and distribution of health manpower.

Ethics.   With technological advances blurring the distinction between life and death, ethical concepts provide analytical tools for decisions associated with allocation and rationing of scarce resources.

The next phase includes the structure and roles of government systems in shaping health care and professional practice:

State Health Planning.   Although federal initiatives of the seventies, based on the State Health Planning and Resource Development Act of 1974, have been dramatically reduced, the new federalism of the Reagan administration is increasing state health policymaking influence.

Federal Regulation of Health Care.   As federal dollars now pay for 40 percent of health care, an understanding of the structure, function, and priorities of governmental health institutions is necessary for appropriate interaction with them in policy development.

State Regulation of Nursing Practice.   Legislation and regulation of nursing practice are state responsibilities. The state is the policy arena in which unresolved professional issues will be debated. Included among these are educational requirements for entry into nursing practice and issues related to the scope of practice. Equally important is the role of the state board for nursing in monitoring licensure and standards of practice.

A particularly useful segment of the course focuses on legislative and policy initiatives of the state and national professional nurses' associations. Presentations by nurse lobbyists or policy advocates, both state and national, reinforce the positive image of political nurses while increasing students' understanding of the process. They clarify the complex political roles of the American Nurses' Association's government relations office, in collaboration with the National League for Nursing and the American Association of Colleges of Nursing (the Tri-Council) and other specialty organizations in providing a united nursing lobby in Washington.

The last phase of the course focuses on major health policy issues. Selected readings provide the background for class discussions and analyses. Topics include long-term care, technology assessment, access to care, cost containment approaches, and prospective payment and capitation systems. Presentation of student issue papers is a useful learning strategy. The wide variety of topics, the tracing of political dynamics, and the creative suggestions for solutions stimulate class participation.

Course evaluations reflect the students' excitement as their horizons are expanded through increased understanding of the policy-making process. The possibility for influencing change is exemplified by one student's report of the payoff from her field experience after the first month of the course. An associate director of nursing in a leading private urban hospital, the student reported to her director on the hearing and the state legislative conference she had attended. The conference had addressed the policy options for rehabilitation, while the hearing focused on developing criteria for extending Medicaid funding to cover heart transplantation. The administrators asked the associate director to represent the hospital at three community health policy forums and to present a seminar for the nursing staff.

NURSING–HEALTH POLICY PROGRAM

Recognizing the need for nurses to serve in health policy-making positions and capitalizing on its proximity to both the national and state capitals, the University of Maryland School of Nursing offers a nursing-health policy major and a clinical minor in its graduate program. Students are prepared for health policy positions such as legislative or regulatory agency staff doing policy analysis or program planning, government relations for institutions or organizations, and health-related corporate policy planning.

Students learn policy analysis skills in a series of three courses offered by the policy science department. The interdisciplinary atmosphere facilitates their understanding of diverse orientations of those in policymaking roles. The courses include: political and social context of the policy process, public policy-making in the United States, and planning theory and policy formulation.

For electives, students are encouraged to take health economics, the politics of health, or other relevant courses. Nursing-health policy students are also eligible to receive policy science certificates upon completion of fifteen credits in the department. Students integrate their clinical interests into their policy course assignments. Particularly appropriate in this phase are clinical course assignments and practicums directly related to policy components of their areas of clinical expertise. For example, students with medical-surgical clinical backgrounds coupled with health policy interests could benefit from a practicum in a clinically related experience such as the quality assurance or DRG coordination department.

A nursing-health policy theory seminar provides indepth study of major national health policies, including analysis of historical background, development, implementation, and evaluation. Students make at least six field trips to health policy-related bodies. Selections are based on meetings scheduled by private, state, or federal agencies with particular relevance to current health policy trends and student interest. Assignments include two short issue analysis papers based on the field experiences and one indepth policy analysis paper.

The final semester includes a practicum in a policy setting based on the student's interest. Students negotiate with their preceptors for an assignment to augment their learning while providing assistance to the agency. Although twelve to sixteen hours a week are required, some students increase their time commitment. Field experience, carefully selected, may provide a student with an opportunity for future employment.

Nursing-health policy graduates are involved in a variety of endeavors. Two are seeking higher degrees, one in law, the other a nursing PhD with specialization in health policy. One is director of government relations for a major hospital corporation, and another is a director of quality assurance and DRGs in a veteran's administration hospital. A prospective graduate is planning to work as a congressional staff member.

The program is young and the promise is great. Nurses are actively seeking policy-making roles. The ripple effect of their advance into this area creates an awareness among policymakers of nurses' competence to contribute to the policy-making process. Nurses who have expertise in health policy development will help colleagues articulate their unique perceptions on health care needs, prevention, health promotion, and quality of life so that nurses will expand their influence on the design of a coordinated health policy at all levels of government.

References

Archer SE, Goehner PA: *Nurses: A Political Force*. Wadsworth, 1982.

Archer SE, Goehner PA: *Speaking Out: The Views of Nurse Leaders*. National League for Nurses, 1981.

Baker N, Hart CA: Nurses in action . . . developing a grass roots action committee. *Nurs Health Care* 1981; 2:130–32.

Cowart ME: Teaching the Legislative Process. *Nurs Outlook* 1977; 25:777–80.

Fagin CM: Health policy in the nursing curriculum—why do we need it? *J Adv Nurs* 1981; 6:72–73.

Hanley BE: Legislative and political domain: challenge to community health nurses. In JA Sullivan (Ed.) *Directions in Community Health Nursing*. Blackwell, 1984.

Hanley BE: Nurse political participation: an indepth view and comparison with women teachers and engineers. (Dissertation.) University of Michigan, 1983.

Hunter PR, Berger KJ: Nurses and the political arena: Lobbying for professional impact. *Nurs Adm Q* 1984; 8:66–79.

Inouye DK: A message from Capitol Hill. *Nurs Health Care* 1984; 283.

Jones L: Students participation in legislative process. *Nurs Outlook* 1980; 28:438–40.

Kalisch B, Kalisch P: A discourse on the politics of nursing. *J Nurs Adm* (Mar–Apr) 1976; 6:29–34.

Kijek JC: Nurses need political experience. *Image* 1984; 29–30.

Leininger M: Political nursing: Essential for health service and educational systems of tomorrow. *Nurs Adm Q* 1978; 2:1–16.

McMahon MA, Westfall J: A legislative journey: One way to teach political awareness. *Nurs Health Care* (June) 1984; 5:341–42.

Legislative and Political Internships and Fellowships

Barbara DiCicco-Bloom, RN, MA

with
Patricia A. Payne, RN, PhD
Sandra A. Haff, RN, MPA
Diane Welch Vines, RN
Janet Braunstein, RN, MPH, CPNP

Exposure to the political process through formal and informal legislative internships and fellowships gives nurses an opportunity to participate in the formulation of health care policy.

Besides the obvious educational benefits, a political internship or fellowship can result in: (1) broadening your views of issues; (2) fulfilling college credits in an exciting way; (3) establishing contacts with influential people; (4) educating legislators and government officials about nursing; and (5) introducing those for whom you work to your skills and knowledge for possible future employment.

MAKING A CHOICE

When deciding on a specific experience, you should follow several guidelines. First, your goals should be clear. You may be interested in familiarizing yourself with specific legislative issues. For example, you may wish to learn about women's rights legislation. There are a variety of organizations that lobby to further rights for women. As a volunteer, you can join one of these organizations' health committees that work to educate the public about issues affecting women's health. You can accompany the organization's lobbyists. In the process, you will learn about issues of interest to you, and you will become familiar with the legislative process. This type of experience can be found on the local, state, and federal level in many agencies and organizations.

Perhaps you prefer to learn firsthand about the role of a legislator, such as your congressperson. There are many educational experiences available in your congressperson's local and national offices. In this experience, you would learn about the legislative process and the contributing roles of an elected representative and his or her staff.

Second, you need to consider the practicalities you are faced with to help you make a realistic selection of experiences. If you are a full-time college student with one free half day per week, involvement in politics will be on a local level unless your college or university is in a state capital or Washington, DC. If you are not in the same city as the experience you are interested in, then the amount of time you can spend away from home will affect your choice.

Third, unless you are living at home, living accommodations and costs must be considered. Sometimes the sponsoring agency or office can make helpful suggestions. More often, you will be on your own and have to rely on family, friends, or your own ingenuity. In the case of a nonsalaried internship or volunteer situation, the experience can be costly. If you are working and want to be away from home, a leave of absence without pay may be necessary.

All these variables will have to be considered before selecting the appropriate program. The experiences reviewed in this chapter represent only a fraction of the possibilities. Many other opportunities exist or can be negotiated. If you have other ideas for an internship, investigate them. City, state, and federal officials are responsive to volunteers. If you want to work with a specific individual or agency, present a plan and offer your time. Your chances for success are good.

LOCAL PROGRAMS

In local politics, involvement can lead to easily maintained contacts. Because of budgetary limitations, local government officials are often eager to arrange legislative or political internships to augment the work of paid staff.

There are several entry routes. The local professional nursing organization will usually have a variety of committees. Membership on the legislative committee offers an excellent opportunity to learn about legislative issues affecting health care in your area and enables you to meet nurses actively involved in politics. It may also provide contacts that could result in further educational experiences.

Another possibility is your mayor's volunteer office. Positions can vary from clerical help to research assistants. There may be an opportunity to study a health care issue in your city or town.

Patricia Payne, a nurse from Austin, Texas, relates her frustrations as a practicing nurse, and her efforts to make changes by involvement in local politics through a variety of nursing and other organizations:

Working three or four nights a week in the infirmary at the state school for the mentally retarded opened my eyes to the impact of state and local politics on health care. We had beautiful buildings; the construction lobbyists had been persuasive. Unfortunately for the children, no one had lobbied as effectively for quality child care. Evening and night child-staff ratios made even custodial services difficult to provide. One day's leftover food, when ground, became the next day's tube feedings. Too busy, too tired, and too alone, I did not believe I could protest, much less affect the reallocation of resources.

I thought I could escape. My husband's career change allowed us to move to another city and me to stop practicing nursing. I continued to complain, however, and my sister challenged me to change the system. I confessed I did not know how to begin such a task. She assured me it was as easy as picking up the phone, calling one of the local League of Women Voters (LWV) groups, and going to the next meeting.

I persuaded my best friend to go with me to the next meeting, which happened to be "Meet the Candidates Night." The LWV members were eager to have a new member and went out of their way to discuss issues and candidates with us. They encouraged us to ask the candidates about health care issues. I was hooked. My ideas and input were valued and sought.

Since that first meeting, I have become involved in a variety of politically active organizations including the League of Women Voters, Women's Political Caucus, Common Cause, and the Nurses Political Action Coalition. With each involvement, new opportunities for learning have presented themselves.

On the program committee of the League of Women Voters, I learned to research an issue and present the pros and cons to a group so it can arrive at a consensus on action to be taken. Indeed, all issues have two or more sides. One has to address all aspects of an issue to propose a meaningful and workable resolution the group can support. I learned to broaden my perspective and deal in the art of meaningful compromise.

The Texas Women's Political Caucus (TWPC) taught me the importance of an organization's legislative platform. I was again working with children—this time in day care. Several issues affecting children, including minimum standards for child care, were on the agenda for the next legislative session. I wanted to have as many voices as possible to speak and work on my side. The issue was a question of focusing on making money from child care by reducing the quality of services required or focusing on the welfare of children by requiring services adequate to foster their healthy development. I turned to LWV, TWPC, and the Texas Nurses' Association (TNA) for support.

I made an appointment with the TWPC chairperson. She said she would be happy to support the legislation, but TWPC had no plank in its platform regarding child care. After meeting with TNA personnel, I realized TNA was in a similar position. I asked the TWPC chair what had to be done to get child care on the platform. She said I would have to write a resolution showing the relationship and the importance of the issue to the purposes of the organization and submit the resolution for consideration. It would be voted on at the annual meeting, and I would have to get it approved and funded. The same process was necessary for TNA and most organizations: they cannot go beyond their legislative platforms.

I used my writing and public speaking skills and learned how to garner the votes necessary to pass my resolution. I learned to cut a deal. In this case, I spoke in favor of the Lesbian/Gay Rights resolution, and the Lesbian Caucus voted for the child care resolution. In each organization, the child care resolution passed. The lobbying support was in place.

Twelve years have passed since I entered the world of politics and learned how to change the system. I have learned how to call upon others so that together we can affect the allocation of resources. In the process, I have had some of the most exciting experiences of my life.

STATE PROGRAMS

State politics offers many opportunities for educational experiences in the legislative process. Your state nurses' association may have a legislative program director who is responsible for making nursing interests known to state legislators. It is often possible to accompany the director or her assistant to learn about their roles, as well as state legislative issues that affect health care and nursing. Files are accessible to students for indepth study of issues. The time frame for this experience is flexible. College students who live within commuting distance of the capital may prefer to work once a week. If you prefer to work directly with an elected official or have other ideas, your state nurses' association will have suggestions about whom you should contact.

There are usually structured programs associated with the state legislative body. For example, New York State has legislative internship programs available to undergraduate students from a variety of academic backgrounds. The Assembly Interns Program provides an opportunity to learn about the legislative process through assignment to an assemblyperson. Interns participate in the daily activities of an assembly member's office by attending public hearings, committee meetings, and researching proposed ·legislation.

The New York State Senate has two similar programs: the Sessions Assistant Program for full-time undergraduate students, and the Legislative Fellows Program for graduate students.

The following summary of a legislative fellowship experience was contributed by Sandra Haff, RN:

> After twelve years of working in an emergency department, I had become concerned about issues affecting crime victims, abused children, rape victims, drunk drivers, improper collection of evidence, and the impact of decreased health care funding. My concern led me to seek an educational experience in government on the state level.
>
> My initial involvement as a student of public administration was through my state nurses' association. I found out about their legislative program, and I was accepted for an independent study. I live within commuting distance of Albany, the capital of New York

State, so housing was no problem. While involved in this experience I learned about the Senate Legislative Fellowship Program. No nurses had ever been accepted into it.

Applying for the Senate Legislative Fellowship Program involved writing a statement of purpose and a paper concerning a legislative issue as if addressing a group of legislators. A paper of support or rebuttal of the issue must then be submitted. I chose a legislative issue involving rape: repeal of the earnest resistance clause.

A selection committee decided who would be accepted into the program and included the program director, senior legislative staff, and three educators, a total of ten individuals. They selected me as one of that year's ten recipients of the fellowship.

During the year of my fellowship, I was placed in the office of the Senate Deputy Minority Leader Emanuel R. Gold, as a full-time staff member. Fellows are encouraged to participate in all activities associated with the office routine. This involves dealing with constituents, meeting with lobbyists, attending committee meetings, public hearings, and receptions, and drafting and assisting with legislation.

While gaining firsthand knowledge of the workings of the senate, a fellow has the opportunity to bring new insight to bear on the senate proceedings. Since about one-third of the budget is devoted to health care, it seems appropriate that nurses influence the allocation of funds.

One issue I have focused my energy on this year has been the proper collection and maintenance of rape evidence, especially when the victim chooses not to report the crime to the police. As a result of my position I was able to draft legislation that, if passed, would correct the deficiencies that now exist in the evidence collection process. Uniform procedures would exist throughout the state.

It was interesting to research this bill with the state police crime lab and work with the various groups to make it suitable for passage. The bill had one senate sponsor (Senator Gold) and seventeen assembly sponsors. I look forward to seeing this bill reported out of the health committees of both houses to go on to full debate, passage, and the governor's signature. To see the passage of a bill I had drafted would be rewarding.

To find out if your state has legislative programs similar to the ones described, call your state nurses' association or the office of your state legislator.

New York State also has the Legislative Fellowship Program on Women and Public Policy, sponsored by the Graduate School at the State University in Albany. Matriculated students from accredited graduate programs in New York State are eligible. The program is designed to develop specialists in policy issues of concern to women and improve the legislature's ability to address such issues. Similar opportunities for women exist throughout the country.

NATIONAL PROGRAMS

The numerous internships and fellowships on the federal level are open to individuals of various educational and occupational backgrounds. The following programs are a sample of structured experiences presently available (see Buckalew, Francis, Johnson & Ragone, 1984, for a list of additional programs).

The American Nurses' Association

The American Nurses' Association (ANA) Division of Government Affairs in Washington, DC, offers an informal, noncompetitive internship. No stipend is available, and the length of time is flexible depending on the interests and needs of the intern.

The following summary of an internship with the ANA was contributed by Barbara DiCicco-Bloom, RN, MA:

> As the long-term home health care program for which I worked gained recognition, state and national legislators made frequent visits. They communicated with the physicians and administrators, but were seldom exposed to the expertise of other health care professionals. The frustration I experienced from not being included in these visits or in the policy decisions affecting patient care caused me to seek another outlet for my professional expertise. I needed a way to share my knowledge with people who influence policy development in the health care system.
>
> I had been a member of the Legislative Committee of the New York Counties Registered Nurses' Association since 1978. Committee members who had connections in both state and national government suggested I discuss my thoughts with the staff of the New York State Nurses' Association and the ANA.
>
> Before calling, I decided I wanted to be involved in the legislative process. I established the following goals: (1) to familiarize myself with employment opportunities for nurses in the legislative branch; (2) to investigate the educational and occupational background of nurses already employed; (3) to learn about legislative issues affecting the elderly and nursing; and (4) to share my experiences and concerns for the elderly with elected representatives. Meeting these goals would help me determine whether the day-to-day experience of nurses working in the legislature interested me. Also, I believed that the knowledge and insight I would gain would enhance my nursing skills.
>
> In January, 1982, I contacted the state and national nursing organizations. In both cases, my proposal to work with them was met with enthusiasm. Most nurses requesting similar experiences were college students who would receive credit towards their degree. However, my experience would have to be short-term because my husband would remain at home in New York City, and I would have to arrange coverage at work during my unpaid leave. Housing was a problem until a close friend moved to Washington in April and offered to share her home with me. Once I had a place to live, I called the ANA to make a formal plan for my internship. They recommended a four- or five-week full-time experience so that I could accomplish my goals. We agreed that I would spend September at the ANA because Congress would be in session, and I would have time to make arrangements to be away from my job.
>
> I spent my first few days of my internship reading about the structure of the ANA and its relationship with the state nurses' associations. I was given materials on a range of legislative issues relating to nursing and health care. Congress would be voting on many of them, and the association would be lobbying for nursing's and consumers' interests. Once my orientation was complete, I chose several assignments. I planned to work on these independently when I was not visiting representatives, congressional staff, or special hearings. I was encouraged to observe office activities and to accompany staff when their assignments interested me.
>
> After several days, I decided to take on the following challenges: (1) to trace every bill affecting the elderly that was introduced into Congress in 1982; (2) to learn the workings

of the legislative branch of government; (3) to organize the welcoming party for Eunice Cole, the new ANA president; and (4) to contact all nurses and nursing students involved in political internships and learn about their experiences and aspirations.

The most memorable and educational experiences during my stay in Washington involved meeting with various government officials who wanted to improve health care for the elderly. On one of these occasions, I met with a staff person from the Special Senate Committee on Aging. We discussed the fact that nurses could be primary health care providers in a number of health care settings. We discussed the concept of the community nursing center being promoted by the ANA. She asked questions about the independent function of nurses and was interested in my role as a nurse caring for homebound elderly. I emphasized the fact that care administered by health care professionals other than physicians was often more effective and less expensive.

On another occasion, I was introduced to the Director of the Office of Administration of Health Care Financing Administration. He was familiar with the program in which I worked in New York City and sought my opinion about additional supports for the elderly homebound. I expressed concern over the fact that families caring for their elderly receive little rest from the limitations and constancy of their commitments. I suggested that formal respite care be incorporated into long-term home health care programs. Having the opportunity to discuss my concerns was both exciting and constructive. The director shared some insights he had into the political climate with respect to such programs, such as his concern about cutting programs for care of the needy.

I had several opportunities to talk with nurse leaders in Washington, including a health aide to Senator Orrin Hatch. Because the senator had sponsored bills to allocate funds for a nationwide system of long-term home health care, I made it a point to meet with his aide and share some of my ideas about the way long-term home health care should be organized.

Looking back, I am aware of subtle changes resulting from my internship experience. I am more confident about lobbying, and I have a clearer sense of its importance. My ability to analyze legislation has become more sophisticated. I am more committed to the notion that to improve health care, nurses must become politically active.

The nurses I met in Washington have given me a sense of the direction nursing must take if we are to have the power to improve health care.

For further information, write or call the American Nurses' Association, 1101 14th St., NW, Suite 200, Washington, DC 20005: (202) 789-1800.

The White House Fellowships

A highly competitive program, the White House Fellowships provide qualified and motivated individuals with firsthand experience in government for one year with pay. Diane Vines, White House fellow 1982–83, describes her experience:

> The national political leaders of the past were ordinary citizens who dedicated some years of their career to serve in federal government. In 1964, President Lyndon Johnson observed that young professional and community leaders were no longer motivated to serve their country. Since he felt this reflected a lack of understanding and firsthand experience with the running of the federal government, he instituted the White House Fellows' Program.

There had never been a nurse White House fellow when I read a short note about the program in a professional journal. I clipped the article and entered the competition despite the fact I felt that my nursing background had not prepared me for the rigorous competition for the program since only 12 to 20 persons are selected from several thousand applicants. To my surprise, I was a regional finalist and was scheduled for a full day of interviews by a panel of judges. Surviving that cut and a top security clearance, I moved to the national finals.

The national selection process involved three days at a resort hotel with 33 commissioners/judges. All activities, including interviews with panels of commissioners and meals, were considered part of the selection process. Candidates were informed that the commissioners were judging character, competence, and achievement.

Once President Reagan officially appointed me a White House fellow, I journeyed to Washington to interview for my job placement for the year's fellowship. I chose to serve as a special assistant and policy advisor to Secretary of Education T. H. Bell.

In my work capacity, I advised the secretary on issues relating to disabilities, rural education, child and adolescent health promotion and education, school nutrition, and the health and education interface. I represented the secretary on the federal emergency mobilization health working group, the alcohol and drug abuse task force, and the private sector initiative task force. I conducted, with the Department of Health and Human Services, an interdepartmental conference on health promotion through the schools. I also wrote speeches for the under secretary.

During my year with Secretary Bell, I developed a policy statement that resulted in a national adult literacy initiative. I agreed to remain after my fellowship year to direct the initiative, which was announced by President Reagan at a White House event that I planned.

In addition to the job experience, a White House fellowship has an educational component that includes several seminars a week with the president, vice-president, cabinet members, members of Congress, members of the judiciary, White House senior staff, public figures in the political and entertainment fields, and leaders in business and industry. In addition, the fellows travel nationally to meet with political and business leaders and other persons who influence public policy at all levels of government. Also, as White House representatives, the fellows visited several Southeast Asian countries and met with their national leaders.

In addition to the fellowship contacts, I sought contact with nurses in the Washington area. I joined the Nurses in Washington Roundtable, which is composed of the nurses in Washington-based leadership positions. I sought opportunities to discuss issues with the health care policymakers in the White House and the Department of Health and Human Services.

We live in an era of shrinking resources and huge federal budget deficits. The intergroup fights over those resources are likely to intensify until Congress decides to exercise reasonable control over the influence of special groups. In my opinion, nursing, as one of those special interest groups, will need to function more effectively as a lobbying group until Congress exercises such control. I encourage qualified nursing leaders to apply for Washington-based fellowships. The experience is an opportunity for contact with the "movers and shakers" of the political world and a personally enriching experience.

For further information on the White House Fellowships write or call 712 Jackson Pl., NW, Washington, DC 20006: (202) 395-4522.

The Institute of Medicine of the National Academy of Sciences

The Institute of Medicine administers the health policy program funded by the Robert Wood Johnson Foundation. This program provides midcareer professionals working in academia a chance to study major health care policy issues. Six fellows participate for one year of full-time work. Stipends up to $40,000 are based on salary before entering the program.

The Institute of Medicine is located on 2101 Constitution Ave., NW, Washington, DC 20037: (202) 334-2330.

The American Association for the Advancement of Retired Persons

This association offers six to seven internships for graduate students with demonstrated interest in issues affecting the aging population. A stipend is available, and the experience is for six months. For further information call Monica Brown at (202) 872-4700, or write to 1909 K St., NW, Washington, DC 20006.

The Department of Health and Human Services

The Department offers summer internships for students in baccalaureate, master's, and doctoral programs. The experiences are in health-related fields. Brochures are available upon request. The Department is located in the Parklawn Building, Room 4-35, 5600 Fishers Lane, Rockville, MD 20857.

The Health Care Finance Administration

The Health Care Finance Administration has internships to acquaint nurses with the function of major government agencies and the process of health care financing. Nurses with a graduate degree, demonstrated interest in public policy, and management or leadership experience are eligible. The experience is for one month, full-time without pay. For further information, contact Maureen Rothermich at the HHH Building, Room 310 G, 200 Independence Ave., SE, Washington, DC 20003: (202) 245-8502.

The National Hospice Organization

This organization has internships available that require a letter from the candidate stating interests and availability. They are usually unpaid. For further information write to Louise Bracknell, National Hospice Organization, 1901 N Fort Meyer Dr., Suite 402, Arlington, VA 22211.

The Congressional Placement Office

Internships are available through members of Congress. Assignments are usually made in March or April. For further information call (202) 224-3121. Applications can be obtained at the Canon Building, B26, at the Capitol from 10 am to 4 pm weekdays.

The following internship is an example of a nursing student, Janet Braunstein, interested in expanding her knowledge of policy development in health care, who arranged her own experience with her congressman.

A requirement for completion of the master's of public health (MPH) degree involves a practical experience that combines the knowledge and theory of public health nursing. I received a mailing stating that my congressman, Gerry Sikorski (D-Minn) had been appointed to the newly formed select committee on children, youth, and families. I decided to investigate the possibility of participating in an internship with his office for credit towards completion of my MPH degree.

I spoke with the legislative aide responsible for health issues and discussed my interests and knowledge of child health, public health, and public health nursing. We agreed that an internship would be mutually beneficial since my expertise would complement and broaden their knowledge of health issues, and I would learn about the political process. I was accepted as one of eight nonsalaried interns in the Washington office. I would work for five weeks and be primarily responsible for following health issues and the select committee's hearings. My goals for the internship were learning how: (1) a congressional office operates; (2) one can affect the political system; and (3) policymakers make decisions.

My responsibilities included a fair share of office work, which is essential for the operation of a busy congressional office. It was important that a staff member attend testimonies or hearings to brief the congressman on changes that were occurring. I was assigned to meetings on issues such as Central America, nuclear waste, and acid rain. I would then provide a written brief on what had transpired. I worked on "Dear Colleague" letters that involved calling or writing another congressional office sponsoring a bill and discussing the pros, cons, and previous legislation related to the bill. I was usually responsible for health issues from Medicare and Social Security to the proclamation of "National XXX Week."

I took the opportunity to set up appointments with children's and nurses' organizations such as the Children's Foundation and the ANA. I shared my thoughts about practice priorities for children and public health nursing, and I was introduced to the complexities of the political process for these organizations.

The internship offered the opportunity to broaden my fellow staff members' view of the professional nurse. It was extremely satisfying to educate my colleagues about the fact that nurses are active in the promotion of health and the prevention of illness.

I also had several educational opportunities. There is a lecture series each noon for interns on Capitol Hill. I attended several, one by Casper Weinberger, and others by senators and house leaders. The Library of Congress offers classes on the political and legislative process and makes briefs available on hundreds of topics.

The brief time I spent in Washington was one of the most exciting and educational experiences of my life. Most importantly, the experience taught me that a politically active nurse can change the health care system to meet the needs of its consumers.

The internships and fellowships reviewed in this chapter are by no means a complete list. Nurses are encouraged to investigate other possibilities.

Involvement in an internship requires commitment and work. It is one of the steps nurses can take towards moving into their rightful positions among the leaders and directors of the health care system.

References

Buckalew J, Francis Y, Johnson J, Ragone M: Policy internships for nurses. *Nurs Outlook* 1984; 32:128.

Donley R: An Inside View of the Washington Health Care Scene. *Am J Nurs* 1979; 79:1946–47.

How Can I Get a Job on Capitol Hill? *Am J Nurs* 1981; 81:112–16.

Case Study
Putting It All Together

Julie A. Sochalski, RN, MS
Deborah Oakley, PhD

It's an election year, and nurses in a midwestern congressional district are actively involved in the reelection effort of a nursing supporter in the U.S. Congress. Nurses are sending out brochures to registered nurses, handing out leaflets at university football games throughout the district, and running get-out-the-vote and phone campaigns. Between election years, these same nurses maintain a presence in the political process, staying informed on issues and contacting legislators as issues of importance arise. And each year, the number of politically involved nurses in the second congressional district in Michigan grows.

The Beginning

In February, 1979, first-year graduate students in nursing at the University of Michigan were discussing in their research seminar the impending rescission, or canceling, of appropriations for the 1979 Nurse Training Act (NTA) proposed by President Carter. There was a sense of futility in the room as the implications of the rescission were reviewed, and possible strategies to deter such action were explored. As frustration mounted, a half-serious suggestion was offered: "Let's just go to Washington, DC, and tell these legislators exactly how we feel." This single remark resulted in a legislative triumph for nurses in Michigan and marked the beginning of our efforts to organize nurses for effective political action.

The story of the lobbying trip made by nurses in the second congressional district of Michigan and others is well known. What would be of benefit to illustrate here are some of the organizational issues that arose during our involvement in the successful reversal of the rescission.

USE OF LOCAL EXPERTISE:
Most of those traveling to Washington, many of whom were students, had no formal experience in lobbying. In less than one week, this group was outfitted and prepared for what turned out to be two intense days of lobbying. Nursing faculty and other local leaders with expertise in this area served as a resource, offering their experience, guidance, and organizational skills to ensure a successful endeavor.

DEVELOPMENT OF THE GROUP:
The group was united by the issue at hand and was not organized under the auspices of any formally established professional group, committee, or organization. Rather, many of the people were strangers prior to the trip and chose to go to Washington because of information shared informally, (ie, by word of mouth) and formally (ie, through memos and meetings). This group formed a loose coalition with a new identity.

LEADERSHIP:
Strong leadership was essential to the success of this trip to draw together a diverse group of persons and activities and develop a well-coordinated movement. This lead-

ership was provided by a core of legislative activists at the University of Michigan and augmented by nursing leadership in professional organizations.

An Organization Is Born

As the excitement and celebration about the trip settled, several issues required concerted attention. Nurses in our district had identified a local congressman who supported nursing issues in Washington, Carl Pursell. It followed that it was critical to nurture his support, especially in light of his important seat on the House Appropriations Committee. This conclusion led to the development of the Nurses Political Action Committee for the Second Congressional District of Michigan.

A core group of nurse activists involved in NTA lobbying gathered to brainstorm future directions for nurses' political action. Two major goals for the district were identified: (1) to enhance Congressman Pursell's understanding of nursing's concerns, and (2) to assist his return to Congress in subsequent elections, thus improving opportunities to influence nursing's legislative concerns.

Looking at these goals collectively, it was felt that the first goal could be accomplished most effectively by encouraging nurses in the district to meet and discuss their concerns with the congressman. This, in turn, would engender support among nurses for his reelection, accomplishing the second goal. Discussion focused on planning an event that would provide an opportunity for nurses to talk with Congressman Pursell.

First, we decided to expand the core group planning the event to include nursing representatives from major nursing organizations and institutions employing nurses (eg, hospitals, schools of nursing, state associations). It was hoped this would help nurses throughout the district recognize the group and its activities as legitimate and to become involved.

A meeting was held at the home of a well-known local nursing leader who was also a core activist. Members of our core group and nurses from a wide variety of agencies, organizations, and academic institutions in the district were invited. At the meeting, the goals of the core activist group were discussed as a potential direction for nurses in the district and were agreed upon. With this decided, the group turned its attention to arrange for Congressman Pursell to meet with nurses in his constituency.

Meeting With the Congressman

It was decided to schedule two meetings in the district. This required close work with the congressman's office to identify dates, generally weekends, when he would be in his district. Then the group compared these dates with the calendars of events of all major nursing groups in the area to allow optimal attendance. A Saturday afternoon in November was selected for the first two-hour meeting. The director of the nursing program at the community college offered to provide a large meeting room and refreshments. The agenda included brief remarks regarding nursing concerns by several key nursing leaders in the district. The congressman would then present an update on federal funding for nurse training. Time for questions and answers would follow the congressman's remarks.

Several committees were formed to handle specific planning tasks. An invitations committee designed and mailed the invitations. To ensure good attendance, invitations were sent out to about 200 nurses suggested by the planning group. A personal invitation to a select group, rather than a flyer or mass mailing, was less costly and would encourage a better response. Everyone who received an invitation was encouraged to bring a friend. A return postcard was included.

Another committee prepared information packets for the attendants, which included the agenda, an outline describing Congressman Pursell's background and activities related to nursing, and an update on current federal legislation regarding nurse training appropriations.

A publicity committee advertised the meeting in local professional bulletins and constructed signs to direct attendees to the meeting area. A registration/welcoming group handed out name tags and the information packets and made sure that all walk-in attendees, or those who had not responded prior to the event, signed an attendance list. And finally, several nursing activists met the congressman when he arrived for a short briefing on nursing concerns in his district.

The first event met with great success, with 75 to 80 persons attending. The congressman had an excellent opportunity to converse individually and collectively with nurses in his district, and they in turn became more familiar with him and his stand on nursing issues.

Building on this initial success, the planning group organized the second meeting. This was scheduled for a Saturday morning in the early spring of the following year. The same location was used. The agenda focused on the congressman and remarks from nursing leaders were reduced. This was done to maximize time for attendees to discuss their concerns with the congressman. This event was successful, with nursing supporters for the congressman in the district expanding well beyond the initial group.

At the end of the meeting, nurses indicated their willingness to assist the congressman in his reelection efforts later that year and asked how they could become involved. The first step in the reelection process is to get the candidate's name on the ballot, so the congressman's staff circulated petitions to nurses who offered to obtain signatures. This action set the stage for our first collective attempt to influence the electoral process, working on the campaign of a candidate strongly supportive of nursing. "Nurses for Pursell" was born.

Lessons Learned: Part I

Some of the lessons learned from these events were:

Initiating a new group and set of activities takes a lot of "start-up" energy and time. With perseverance, the payoffs will come your way; it is important to be aware of the costs of personal commitment and the need to be patient.

When bringing a diverse group together, keep the focus on common interests. Differences should be expected; they can be overcome through identification of the group's goal and allowing all involved to grow as a result of the group's efforts.

Locating resources (eg, financial) to host events can be a challenge and should be handled creatively. We found that expanding the planning group helped us to identify other nursing groups and individuals willing to donate money.

Record any events with your legislators through written notes on what went into the planning, a summary of the meeting itself, and photographs.

Campaigning

The next step in our campaigning efforts was to use the expertise of the politically active and experienced nursing leaders in the district and the congressman's campaign staff to develop a plan to involve nurses in his reelection activities. A core group from "Nurses for Pursell" met with the campaign coordinators, and after considerable discussion, three major areas of activity were identified: (1) mailings to nurses in the district; (2) a get-out-the-vote telephone campaign; and (3) distribution of campaign literature. Members from the core group distributed the responsibility for each activity among themselves. To monitor the progress of these activities, the core group maintained close contact with one another and the congressman's campaign headquarters.

A special brochure to mail to nurses in the district was developed jointly by the leadership of "Nurses for Pursell" and the campaign staff. This one-page brochure detailed the many actions Congressman Pursell had taken in support of nursing and explained the significance of his reelection. The mailing list for the brochure came from the state board of nursing computerized list of all registered nurses in the district. A local nursing leader offered her home for a mailing party, and nurses who had attended the meetings with the congressman were contacted for help. A large turnout of nurses and friends made the evening of stuffing, stamping, and labeling envelopes enjoyable. After two mailing parties, we had prepared a mailing for the almost 4,000 registered nurses in the district.

Using the same list of registered nurses, a comprehensive telephone campaign was undertaken. Volunteers spent hours looking up phone numbers of everyone on the list. Once completed, these lists were photocopied and distributed to other volunteers, who were responsible for contacting as many nurses as possible and encouraging them to support Congressman Pursell. The volunteers were given a sample script to guide their conversations and instructions on how to record their efforts and the responses. From this activity, it was learned that many nurses were aware of Congressman Pursell's record on nursing issues, perhaps from the mailing done some months before, and he appeared to have a broad base of support.

The final major activity was distribution of campaign literature at football games of two universities in the district. The campaign staff organized the effort, with the assistance of nursing students and faculty each weekend throughout the season. Nursing's commitment to the reelection effort was underscored when the "show-rate" among nurse volunteers was nearly 100% each weekend, while other volunteers had a rate around 50%.

Nurses were also encouraged to volunteer at the campaign headquarters for any number of tasks, from helping with mailings and telephoning to typing and running errands. The continued exposure of nurses to key campaign staff reiterated nursing's interest in the congressman's reelection.

These successes in nurses' first involvement in an active and close campaign were topped only by Congressman Pursell's victory at the polls. He returned to Washington to continue, among other things, his work on the powerful House Appropriations Committee, and in particular, its HHS Labor Subcommittee.

Lessons Learned: Part II

With each step taken towards greater involvement of nurses in the political process, we gained increasing awareness of the costs and benefits of active participation. While organizing a volunteer group, we learned that it is important not to ask too much of each person. Start by asking the leadership group and those you hope to attract to the larger group to do only limited, specific tasks that they know about and enjoy; reinforce any success; and then ask them to become more involved. Show appreciation when a person is willing to take on one commitment. If you are asking people to do something new, be sure they have adequate orientation and support. Briefing sheets and a buddy system can reduce anxiety. Telephoning in advance of an activity can encourage participation and detect any need for substitutes or additional help. Our experience showed that nurses appreciated the respect shown by only asking them to do something manageable and often would offer to take on more.

We also learned the importance of process and outcome indicators of success. Examples of process indicators are: mailing a certain number of letters, making a specified number of phone calls, distributing literature for a certain number of hours, or recruiting a specified number of volunteers for these or other activities. Counting and totaling these figures will impress the nurse volunteers and the candidate as well.

Between the Elections: Organizational Action

After the successful reelection came a year of respite from the intensity of organizing campaign activities. But during these two years, nurses in the district faced new challenges on the federal scene as well as locally. On the federal scene, a new administration came to Washington with strong ideas regarding spending priorities. Federal support for nurse training and research were falling under the administration's budget-cutting axe, requiring close monitoring of the legislative process and communication with the congressman's Washington office. Thanks in part to that effort, drastic cuts were averted.

Locally, nurses were indirectly faced with another crisis. The president of a state university in a neighboring district proposed closure of the college of nursing for fiscal reasons. Nurses and others questioned the process by which this decision had been made and supported its reversal. Nurse activists in the second district were informally contacted and asked to register their complaints with the university's board of trustees and state legislators. Nurses responded with letters and phone calls. They also served as an information source for other nurses in the district. With that effort and those put forth by nurses across the state, the status of the college of nursing was preserved.

In another local challenge, nurses working at a hospital in the district became involved in a nursing strike. After the strike had been in place for some time, a gathering of striking nurses and sympathizers was planned for a Sunday afternoon in a nearby park. Congressman Pursell was home in the district that weekend for an unrelated event when he learned of the nurses' gathering. He came to the park and met with the nurses to obtain a better understanding of the key issues of the strike. He subsequently submitted a letter to the editor of the local newspaper, expressing his concerns regarding the strike and encouraging a quick resolution.

A Rebirth

In the next election year, 1982, a meeting of many former nurse activists was held to reactivate nurses to political action. The group discussed its role and began to plan the year's activities. The new American Nurses' Association's (ANA) project to organize nurses for political action was also discussed. Through the ANA's Department of Political Education, grass roots organizing of nurses for political action in each congressional district had been targeted. An identified leader, the congressional district coordinator (CDC), was to direct this effort (see Chapter 30). Because political action had been the direction the district had taken for the past few years, it seemed natural for "Nurses for Pursell" to become part of the congressional district organizing network. The group adopted a new name, "Nurses for Political Action Committee (N-PAC) Second District," and developed its own logo.

Based on our experience establishing "Nurses for Pursell," an executive committee was chosen to oversee the group's development and activities. This committee was made up of both former activists and new nurse leaders who represented the diversity of the district and profession. The recruitment of new members interested in political action was our primary goal. Recruitment was critical because in the spring a redistricting plan for Michigan was approved that changed the geographical complexion of the district notably. A two-step plan for member recruitment was put together: (1) hosting house parties, and (2) developing brochures with applications for membership.

Several nurses who attended the reactivating meeting offered to host similar house parties. A small group from the executive committee coordinated the parties and assisted the hosts in party activities. About three to four weeks before each house party, the host and the party coordinator met to discuss the arrangements for the event. At the party, the coordinator was responsible for reviewing the goals of political action in the district, the history of activities in the area, and asking nurses to sign up to become more politically involved. The host was primarily responsible for providing the location for the party, generating a guest list, sending out invitations, and providing refreshments. A sample invitation and suggestions regarding who and how many persons to invite were offered to each host.

As the second part of the membership plan, a newsletter committee was formed to send out a quarterly newsletter to past and potential nurse activists in the district. These newsletters contained political/legislative updates along with an N-PAC Second District membership form and an explanation of its goals and objectives. A separate membership application brochure was developed. Executive committee members took these brochures to meetings, classes, and informal gatherings of nurses.

Political Action: Expanding Our Efforts

At election time, nurses in the district again campaigned for Pursell. By this time Pursell had significant name recognition among nurses, therefore, an intense informational campaign for nurses was not considered necessary. A new brochure describing the congressman's commitment and actions on behalf of nursing was mailed to all registered nurses in the district. This was done through another mailing party, which had by this time achieved the reputation of an event not to be missed. A telephone campaign on a smaller scale targeted only the areas added by redistricting. Nurses again handed out literature at football games. This time there was a single Saturday dubbed "Nurses Day," and many student nurse volunteers distributed leaflets.

N-PAC Second District also decided to become active in a state office campaign. The local state senate seat had been vacated by its incumbent. One of the five candidates, the only woman, had learned that nurses in the district were organized and politically active. After she won the primary election, her campaign staff contacted N-PAC to set up a meeting with key members. Her purpose was to learn more about nurses' concerns and to seek an endorsement from area nurses.

The candidate left the meeting with a greater understanding of nurses' priorities as well as their endorsement, and nurses left with the incentive to work for her election. While working with the candidate's campaign staff, nurses learned there was a need for volunteers to help in the office and staff fund-raising events. Nurses responded by working in the office on mailings, telephoning, and cohosting and staffing fund-raising parties held across the district. Some "nursing specific" activities were also undertaken. Nurses sent a letter to all nurse activists in the state senate district, identifying the candidate and the reasons to support her. A list of 12 to 20 nurses was included, with a request to contact the persons on the list and encourage them to vote for the candidate. An advertisement stating nurses' support for the candidate was placed in the local newspaper. For a $2 fee, interested nurses had their names listed in the advertisement. Almost 100 signatures were collected, generating enough money to pay for a large ad.

After consultation with the candidate's press relations staff, the ad was put in the paper on its best circulation day. Once again we met with success. The candidate became state senator.

The Payoff

After the postelection euphoria had settled, the opportunity arose for nurses to have an increase in funding for the NTA, based on the recommendations of an Institute of Medicine study. N-PAC Second District was asked by the ANA government affairs office to help involve Congressman Pursell in introducing an amendment to the NTA appropriations for an additional $3 million for nursing research.

Representatives from N-PAC met over breakfast with Congressman Pursell on one of his trips to the district. They discussed the issue, outlined supporting arguments, and explored strategies. The congressman agreed to introduce the amendment and asked that a panel of leading nurses with expertise in research testify before his subcommittee to the need for additional research funding. This testimony was coordinated by ANA and included a local nursing leader in the presentation. Thanks to these efforts, the amendment passed in the subcommittee and the full House. Subsequently, funding was increased an additional $1 million by a House-Senate Conference Committee.

The impact of the political activities of nurses was being felt locally. A local hospital organized a "Meet Your Legislator" day for the staff and others. Congressman Pursell was featured. During his address, he made clear his support for the nursing profession and the importance nurses had had to his reelection success. The congressman was also a guest at the opening of a hospital in a newly acquired area of his district. Prior to the event, his office contacted one of N-PAC's executive committee members in that area to arrange for a special reception with the nurses. The hospital's public relations office was amazed that the congressman's office had contacted the nurses and was specifically interested in meeting with them. On his tour of the hospital, Congressman Pursell was asked by an incredulous hospital administrator why he was so interested in nursing. The congressman lauded nurses' importance to health care in this country and their involvement in his reelection. His praise of nursing to other health care professionals and in the community validated nurses as a credible, influential political force, with potential for broader legislative involvement.

The effects of political participation are also reflected in the recent attempts to introduce state legislation for third-party reimbursement for nurses. Several legislators, including the local state senator in whose campaign we have been involved, indicated an interest in working with nurses and offered their support. This has facilitated development of a bill and an effective strategy for its passage.

Continued Organizational Growth

During this off-election year, the executive committee, with several new members, reconvened to assess our current status and future plans. The group identified the need to redefine our goals and objectives as a group as well as to clarify our relationship with other nursing groups in the community, particularly those that were involved in legislative/political activities. Consensus was that clear lines of communication and definition of group roles were needed, especially if we were interested in expanding. We decided that this could be accomplished in several ways: (1) the CDC should be a liaison member on the state nurses' association's (SNA) district legislative committee, to promote communication between the SNA and the local PAC; (2) a member of the SNA district legislative committee should be on the executive committee of the PAC for the same reasons; and (3) an organization/communication chart that would clearly define roles, responsibilities, and interrelationships between these groups should be developed and shared with the PAC and district association members.

Liaison membership strengthened our position, allowing us to broaden our activities and network within the district. An organizational/communication chart was developed by the CDC, approved by the executive committee, and published in the district SNA newsletter. Through this process, several subcommittees of N-PAC were formed, each chaired by members of the executive committee. These committees included: (1) membership; (2) newsletter; (3) campaign activities; (4) research and data collection on our activities as a group; and (5) programs and special projects. We plan to expand the activities of each committee during the coming year.

Our prime thrust continues to be recruitment, with each committee tailoring its activities to that goal. The newsletter informs members of current issues, serving as a recruiting method and a membership benefit.

Lessons Learned: Part III

The growth of N-PAC Second District over the past five years is rooted in the same organizing themes present in our first trip to Washington: use of local expertise, development of the group, and appropriate leadership. These themes have significant implications for successful group building.

Effective groups have active participants and identified leaders. Groups can differ in size and in how active their members are; leadership can be centralized or shared. But to be effective, the leadership must provide a sense of direction, and the participants must provide considerable energy. In our experience, effective leaders have had prior political experience. Perhaps their families were active in politics, they grew up in politicized neighborhoods, or they had done political work or run for elective office themselves. Nurses who took college or graduate courses in the politics and/or history of nursing may also be potential leaders. The leaders of local nursing groups are often already overextended, but can help identify other nurses who could serve as leaders.

Once a PAC leader or a CDC has been appointed, action can begin. In a voluntary group, leaders may have little power. They have influence, but even that may be restricted. We have found that the development of a core group of activists may be helpful. This group would be designated as an executive or steering committee and at first would be self-appointed and eventually elected. In addition to activists eager to work in campaigning, this committee should include key local leaders or people with access to those leaders. The ANA can assist the group by writing a personal letter to the local district nurses' association president and legislative committee chairperson, conveying the legitimacy of the local CDC position and requesting cooperation.

Leadership styles are also important. PACs are a good arena in which to practice participatory leadership. Voluntary groups require lots of energy and time from their members and have no formal job-related or role sanctions. Participatory leadership is one of the best ways to recruit and retain members. In our groups, we have also found that leaders must nurture active participation. When we want to organize people to distribute literature to crowds at the football stadium, we sometimes provide tickets for the game as an enticement. When we want people to attend meetings, we sometimes offer transportation. When we want tasks done, we often have to spend almost as much time monitoring and following up as if we had done it all ourselves.

PAC leaders must remember that people participate because the group meets their needs. Each member has a need for recognition, a sense of affiliation, some realization of his or her role as a professional. Groups that stay together help one another to meet those needs. The wise leader will monitor each person's progress. When people miss meetings, exhibit ambivalence or hostility, or forget commitments, a group leader must consider whether he or she needs to provide more or better opportunities for that individual.

PAC groups can offer many rewards. For instance, many of us in the district group are expert in getting out mass mailings, a skill few of us had in advance of our political activities. Some members have developed closer contact with the offices of elected officials. A few have achieved local or national recognition. One member used PAC activities as the springboard for a doctoral dissertation. Three members have been granted National League for Nursing (NLN) summer fellowships to study legislative processes in Washington. A sophomore nursing student, active in N-PAC since her freshman year, is now the president of her school student nurse association chapter.

PAC participants must have realistic expectations of a candidate they have helped to elect. Our campaign help only gives us the opportunity to work harder to exercise influence. If a candidate made campaign statements favorable to nursing and was elected with our help, then we can expect to gain a hearing for our point of view on particular legislation. We can ask the politician to sponsor or introduce a bill, deliver a speech, help us make high level contacts, or do some other specific activity. But his or her response will depend on a spectrum of concerns, priorities, and the political capital required by our request.

Since one of our primary goals is to maintain our organization, we are always planning new activities. One technique our group is considering is the production of a nurses' political action calendar. Our area is rich in nursing history and photographic records of nurses in politics. A calendar could capitalize on these resources and attract members. A calendar, put on sale at local nursing meetings, state conventions, and elsewhere, could raise some money for the group.

To be effective, local and national political action groups have to work in tandem with others, building coalitions on subjects of mutual interest. Local political groups have taken the first steps by working together with local political parties, sometimes with more than one party. Political coalitions are not just tradeoffs of "you work for me and I'll work for you," but working together on issues and activities of mutual interest. The organization that most strongly identifies with the topic will take the lead.

For local PACs to promote specific issues, they must generate other groups' support. Existing nursing groups cannot be taken for granted, but must be cultivated. The local district nursing association, specialty groups, bargaining units, black, Hispanic, workplace, and other networking groups should be recruited for coalition work. They should be asked to cosponsor political action gatherings. The PACs may even be catalysts to build more cooperative relationships among these nursing groups. Eventually, the coalition must expand beyond nursing, eg, to hospital groups, other professions, and the local political parties. And, it has become increasingly clear to us that no matter what strength we build locally, our work will be maximally effective if we collaborate with the national and state nursing communities.

Finally, a central feature must be leadership renewal, because leadership in the group should be a springboard to opportunities elsewhere. Groups must provide a written history, how-to-work records, and leadership development opportunities that will keep the group active and effective.

To summarize, our experience has shown that the four spheres of political influence discussed in this book are both the beginning and the endpoints of local political activity. Active membership in our group was drawn from all sectors, including government agencies and private or public hospitals or agencies. We built strong ties via our membership and communications systems with other nursing organizations, such as bargaining units, the district and state nursing associations, and other specialty nursing groups. Our work would have been unsuccessful without local community resources such as local political parties. Even before we helped to elect public officials at both the congressional and the state senatorial level, leaders in our group began to work with government agencies, community groups, and professional nursing organizations to enhance professional opportunities for nursing. The four spheres of influence are both the source of resources to begin political activity and the areas in which nurses must use their political clout.

POLITICAL ACTION AND THE PROFESSIONAL ORGANIZATION

The professional organization is one of the primary mechanisms for nurses to exert their collective influence on the workplace, government, and community spheres. Chapter 32 discusses how the nurse can influence the organization. The first part of the chapter examines the structure and functions of organizations—a necessary beginning for any novice to this arena. The second part provides specific strategies to assist nurses in influencing the organization by participating in its functioning. One vignette describes how the Colorado Nurses' Association encouraged nurses in the state to be risk takers. The second vignette is a personal account that demonstrates the importance of mentoring to involve nurses in the professional organization.

The role of the professional organization in collective action in the government sphere must be understood. Chapter 33 presents a discussion of the legal restrictions on political activity by tax-exempt professional organizations. The second part of this chapter, "Don't Bite the Hand that Feeds You!" examines this issue from the perspective of a tax-exempt professional organization receiving federal funds. The chapter ends with a vignette on how nurses from Washington, DC, used their professional organization to influence the issue of practice privileges.

Political action committees (PAC) provide nurses with a means for pooling their resources for influencing government. Chapter 34 begins with an overview by a member of the first board of N-CAP. The history of nursing PACs demonstrates what can happen when nurses refuse to remain powerless. The chapter concludes with strategies for organizing a PAC or a regional unit of a state PAC. Since monetary campaign contributions are an important tool for PACs, some fund-raising tips are included in the chapter.

Unit VI concludes with the case study of a controversial action by the Board of Directors of the American Nurses' Association in 1984 to endorse a presidential candidate. The author, a supporter of the endorsement, presents her own account of how the decision came about and what it means to nursing.

Chapter 32

You and Your Professional Association

Structure and Function

Betty J. Skaggs, RN, PhD

Individuals organize into groups to meet basic human needs. Families, churches, and social clubs provide contacts through which physical needs for food and shelter are met, and make communication, sharing, and closeness possible. Similarly, trade or professional associations are formed to meet basic human needs. Medieval guilds were formed to provide mutual protection and economic advancement for individuals in similar job classifications (ASAE, 1975). As society's needs have changed, trade associations have expanded their purpose from protection of individual members to initiating changes in their professional role. Increasingly, emphasis is placed on keeping members abreast of technological advances and lobbying for change in state or federal statutes to facilitate delivery of services.

"Very early in nursing's history leaders recognized the need to create a nursing organization to serve as a vehicle through which nurses could collectively influence the internal and external factors affecting the delivery of nursing care" (Zimmerman, 1978). Organizational membership has been identified as an important part of one's personal and professional life.

Typically, the active professional nurse holds membership in numerous organizations, taking an active leadership role in some and being a follower in others. The individual locates organizations with concerns and goals that parallel her own and participates at a level dictated by personal commitment and time constraints. For example, an individual concerned about the environment might join the Sierra Club. Although work in her professional association might prevent active involvement, she could participate in legislative alerts and similar activities. Nurses often join numerous organizations, which focus on women's rights, child health, family violence, and other social or health related concerns. Instead of having many concerns, as does the American Nurses' Association (ANA), a multipurpose organization, the "specialized" organization deals with a single issue.

Nurses may express commitment and concern about the nursing profession through involvement in the ANA and a specialty organization. But how does one get involved and make the organization work?

This chapter addresses the following questions. How do organizations work? How does one learn the purpose and functions of an organization? How might one influence the activities of an organization to make it more effective or go in a different direction? How might one use an organization to reach personal and professional goals?

PURPOSES AND FUNCTIONS OF THE ASSOCIATION

According to Merton (1958), associations should serve the needs of society, the profession, and the individual member. In a 1975 American Society of Association Executives survey, associations were found to have many common activities. These were: government relations, membership, communications and publicity, educational programs, certification of products or services, professionalism activities, and advocacy programs. The articles of incorporation and the bylaws of an association outline its purposes.

The articles of incorporation is a legal document that defines the scope of an association and establishes it as an entity. Although it is not required, most large, active associations incorporate to secure tax-exempt status, to define limits of liability for its leaders, and to permit entry into contracts. For example, in 1917, leaders of the newly formed ANA filed articles of incorporation in New York State that stated:

> The purposes of this corporation are and shall be to promote the professional and educational advancement of nurses in every proper way; to elevate the standards of nursing education; to establish and maintain a code of ethics among nurses; to distribute relief among such nurses as may become ill, disabled, or destitute; to disseminate information on the subject of nursing by publications in official periodicals or otherwise; to bring into communication with each other various nurses and associations and federations of nurses throughout the United States of America; and to succeed to all rights and property held by the American Nurses' Association as a corporation duly incorporated under and by virtue of the laws of the State of New York (ANA Certificate of Incorporation, 1917).

Whereas the articles of incorporation (usually found as a preamble to bylaws) are general statements of purpose, bylaws are more specific. For example, the bylaws of the ANA state:

The purposes of ANA shall be to
- work for the improvement of health standards and the availability of health care services for all people, and
- foster high standards of nursing, and

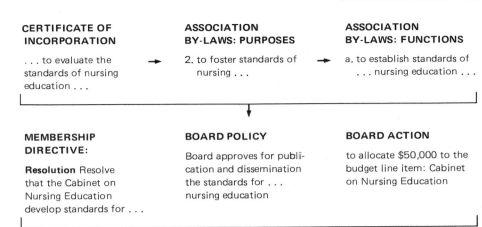

Figure 32-1   Structure and Function of the Professional Association

- stimulate and promote the professional development of nurses and advance their economic and general welfare.

Functions are explicit methods used to achieve the purposes of the organization. Among the functions of the ANA are to:

- establish standards of nursing practice, nursing education, and nursing services
- establish a code of ethical conduct for nurses
- ensure a system of credentialing in nursing
- support systematic study, evaluation, and research in nursing

The functions of the association are most clearly delineated in its policies and procedures (see Figure 32-1).

POLICY AND PROCEDURES

In voluntary associations, in which communication between volunteer and paid staff is critical, it is important to differentiate policies and procedures. Policies are broad guidelines reflecting the values of those individuals making the statement. Policies are established by the voting body, the house of delegates, or by elected officials in collaboration with the chief executive officer. Policy statements established by the voting body take the form of resolutions, main motions, statements of goals and priorities, legislative platforms, and similar documents. In addition, the board of directors adopts operational policies to direct the activities of the organization.

Procedures represent methods that implement the policy, resolution, or legislative platform. Procedures are designed by committees and staff as they implement the policies and directives of the membership and the board. For example, a plank from a legislative platform (a policy statement) might read:

Assure access to comprehensive, quality health care services

State nurses' association will:
> support legislation providing for full utilization of nursing expertise in the delivery of health care, including third party reimbursement for services provided by registered nurses.

Procedures designed by staff, the governmental affairs committee, and the board of directors might look like this:

1. Form coalitions with occupational therapists, physical therapists, and speech therapists to begin developing strategies to pass bill.
2. Begin drafting legislation to introduce next session.
3. Charge the practice committee with the task of reviewing the literature to compile supporting data to use in hearings.

Policy statements provide general guidelines and procedures and direct the day-to-day operation of the association, the staff, and the structural units of the organization.

To change the function of an association, one must decide whether a bylaw, policy, or procedure change must be initiated. For example, using the third party reimbursement issue, if you were opposed to the concept of third party reimbursement, then you would need to bring about a change in the legislative platform—a policy change. Typically, this platform would be adopted at the annual or biennial convention. You would need to mount a campaign to amend that plank of the platform.

Or, using this same example, if you did not think the association should be introducing such a bill at this time, you would have to seek a change in the legislative platform or the procedure by which the platform is being implemented. Obviously, this doesn't necessitate a bylaw amendment, because the bylaws simply enable a legislative program.

Similarly, if you were opposed to the means by which the association was trying to pass this legislation, then you might lobby the elected officer(s) to change the procedures. Another effective mechanism might be to help get an individual whose views you support elected to a powerful position (such as president). Of course you should inform the candidate of your views, expertise, and interest in this area, letting her know that you would be willing to help her get elected and would want to serve on the governmental affairs committee.

In summary, individuals with ideas, causes, or feelings about how the organization should operate should introduce their idea by lobbying appropriate elected or appointed officers, by proposing a position statement to an appropriate committee or the board, and/or by introducing a resolution, main motion, or bylaw revision at convention. This process, then, controls and directs the activities of an association. The process provides numerous points at which one might intervene to influence or change a stand of an association. More strategies to bring about change will be discussed later in this chapter.

THE STRUCTURE OF YOUR ORGANIZATION

The structure of a professional organization must be designed so that authority and responsibility are assigned to the various components. Structure is dictated by the bylaws of the organization. Bylaws define the member, the voting body, and structural units that will perform essential functions of the organization. The ANA bylaws, for example, specify that the association is composed of member state nurses' associations (ANA Bylaws, 1982, article III, section 1).
The bylaws also specify:

- a house of delegates as the governing and official voting body (article IV, section 1),
- a board of directors, consisting of five officers and ten directors with specific responsibilities and duties, as the corporate body elected by and responsible to the house of delegates (article V, section 4), and
- eight different structural units with various areas of responsibility: standing committees, cabinets, councils, a constituent forum, a Nursing Organization Liaison Forum, *The American Nurse*, the *American Journal of Nursing*, and the American Academy of Nursing.

The ANA bylaws create the above entities and clearly define their scope of responsibility and accountability. The document (the bylaws) can be translated into an organizational chart that, through the selection of leaders, development of policies, and the coordination of activities among the various components, defines the scalar process that "organizes" the organization into an efficient, effective group. Ideally, the structure is designed to carry out functions of the organization and is amended by the membership as the functions change or as more effective methods of organizing are identified.

A factor, unique to voluntary organizations, makes the work of professional associations more complex. We have an organizational chart of the members, the voluntary workers, and a cadre of staff members, a chief executive officer hired by the board of directors and staff members to implement the programs of the association (see Figure 32-2).

Williford (1977) describes the two different chains of command: "One line of authority and responsibility in an association runs from the board of directors to the chief elected officer and on down through the committees and task forces. The other line of authority runs from the board of directors to the chief paid executive and on down through the members of the staff" (p 55).

As staff and committees work together, neither has authority over the other when

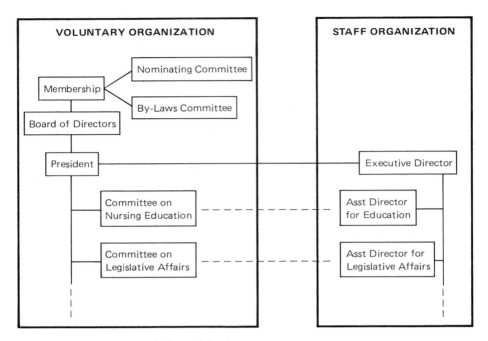

Figure 32-2 Organizational Chart of the Association

decisions are made. Instead, the relationship must be kept at an informal level, a staff versus line relationship. Williford warns us that "the two lines of formal authority and responsibility must be kept separate if administrative chaos is to be averted."

The staff person is hired, managed, and accountable to the executive director. The committee chair and members are appointed (or elected) and accountable to the board of directors (or electorate: the membership or house of delegates). The staff has the final accountability for implementation of procedures stemming from policy. The volunteer component (board, committee, or other structural unit) has the final accountability for policy decisions. For example, the board or committee may decide that a continuing education program on lobbying will be held. It would be appropriate for the committee to outline the program, to write the objectives, and to suggest speakers, establishing policies within which the program will be implemented. However, it would be inappropriate for the committee to select the date, to contract for space, or to commit to speakers on behalf of the association. Clearly, such acts are the responsibility of the staff, and final details of implementation must be handled by staff.

The structure of most professional associations is tiered or subdivided into various regional or state components. The latter may be further divided into districts. Membership in good standing requires conformity to certain requirements (dictated by the bylaws) and communication and articulation with the higher level. Such a structure provides excellent opportunities for its members to learn the ropes at a lower level and to move up as skills develop. Furthermore, a multilevel organization provides instant contact with nurses across the state and nation involved in issues of interest to individual nurses, for example, the hospice movement.

The professional organization, with its meetings, conventions, and continuing education program, is a perfect place to build one's network. Networks are vital to our success personally and professionally. Networks enable us to expand our sources of support and information, to develop collegial relationships, and maybe even establish a mentor relationship. Few nurses are successful through solitary efforts; instead we find a kindred soul who believes as we do and begin to mount a campaign—such as initiating change in the association.

LEADERSHIP: APPOINTED AND ELECTED

Leadership roles within the organization will determine the direction, the effectiveness, and the efficiency, that is, the success, of the organization. The officers and board of directors, specifically the president, provide leadership within the association.

The effective president will, with concurrence of the board, carry out the following functions:

- Planning: forecasting, trend analysis, and providing for the future of the profession and the organization

- Recruiting: providing a well-qualified administrator for the association and soliciting required skills for appointment to committees and task forces

- Coordinating: assuring that all individuals in the association have the information, suppport, contacts, and encouragement needed to perform the assigned task

- Motivating: creating an environment in which the board, committees, and staff are able to advance the goals of the organization

- Evaluating: measuring and assuring the quality of services and products

Elected officers carry the responsibility of implementing mandates from the electorate and the bylaws of the association. Changing or going beyond a directive from the voting body, or violating the ANA Code for Nurses or the bylaws of the organization, would be considered misconduct and subject to disciplinary action. Disciplinary action, which includes due process for the accused, should be explicitly detailed in the bylaws.

Committee chairs share the leadership of the association, albeit within a smaller sphere. They should essentially perform the same functions as the president and board within their area of responsibility. Additionally and more importantly, they advise, counsel, and report to the board.

Committee members monitor areas of practice, advise the board of trends and problems, and suggest actions. Committees are the vital link the organization maintains with the individual—the nurse member.

Finally, the executive director, the chief appointed officer, exerts a specialized type of leadership within the profession. In brief, it is his or her job to "bring about the maximum volunteer responsibility, volunteer involvement, volunteer impact and volunteer satisfaction" (O'Connell, 1976, p 29). The executive director and staff provide continuity and stability to an ever changing and growing cadre of volunteers.

All agree that good leadership is important. Equally important and often overlooked is the importance of good "followership." In some situations, an individual may have the knowledge and skills to assume leadership. In other situations, this same individual may be better suited to the role of follower. Successful group action is contingent upon members' ability to be leaders and followers. "The ability to switch from leadership to followership roles, appropriately and effectively, calls for a great deal of maturity" (Brown, 1980). The follower, knowing and accepting the goals and plan of the effort, allows the leader to coordinate and facilitate activities and provide direction for all members.

INFLUENCING YOUR ASSOCIATION

An association is a tool one might use to improve patient care, to increase the profession's contribution to the health care system, and to enhance individual professional advancement. Sister Thomas Bertel (1975), in a Texas Nurses' Association key note address, "Association man: A study of rigor mortis," compared an association to a vacuum sweeper. The sweeper has much potential to help you, but it will not perform unless it is plugged in and pushed through the house. Likewise, an association will not work for you unless you make it work.

Two vignettes may suggest how an association can benefit the member. The first illustrates how an experienced nurse used the association to change a situation in her practice setting. The second describes how a new graduate worked her way into the association.

The Experienced Nurse

Diane, a nurse with eight years of experience in pediatric and school health nursing, was concerned about children of welfare families. She believed that children's health problems were not being adequately followed up. After consulting with her director of nursing and the school system's medical director, she learned that the best way to remedy the situation involved changing the state welfare rules and regulations governing the program.

She knew that the state nurses' association monitored and provided input to the development of rules and regulations of the numerous state agencies. Therefore, she wrote a letter describing the situation to the council on practice of the state nurses' association. The state practice committee and association staff investigated the situation and suggested alternatives Diane might attempt to see that the children's health problems were addressed. In addition, the association staff, with advice from the state's council on nursing practice, petitioned for rule changes, which were ultimately implemented.

Because of this incident, the association president recognized Diane's talent and commitment. The president contacted Diane, encouraging her to join the district nursing practice committee. The state president also notified the district president of Diane's interests and suggested the district organization invite Diane to work with their nursing practice committee.

Diane agreed to serve on the district practice committee. While working with the district nurses' association and the practice committee, she became more knowledgeable about other practice issues, the state's health delivery system, and the state nurses' association. She also built a network of individuals who felt as she did on practice issues—individuals she could work with to bring about changes.

After two years of dedicated work on the committee, Diane was appointed chair of the district practice committee. Soon she was known as "the contact" for reliable information on child health issues within the association. Based on this track record, at the convention the next year she was elected chair of the state maternal-child health conference group.

In her state nurses' association, the chairs of the conference groups comprise the state council on practice. Diane was now in a position to collaborate on all practice positions issued by the association, to receive timely association communications, and to become a part of the formal and informal lines of authority in the organization.

As an elected official of a state structural unit, she influenced the long-term planning process, presented testimony on behalf of nursing, and was an initiator in the legislative alert system for the state. Through state-level involvement, she broadened her network to nurses across the state and to governmental workers in child health. During this time, she was building a reputation and platform for campaigns for more powerful positions.

Like Diane, any individual who wants to bring about change must go through a problem-solving process. She must identify her dissatisfaction, outline alternative solutions, articulate the solutions and rationale, garner support for her stand, lobby for the requested change, and orchestrate the necessary maneuvers to see the change accepted and implemented.

The New Graduate

Stephanie was a good student and exceptional at managing the student role with her other roles as a wife and mother of three youngsters. She was especially good at using her limited time effectively. Also, Stephanie began practicing some of the skills taught at her school. That is, she began networking, identifying a mentor, and attending district nurses' association meetings, even as a student.

Stephanie's mentor was active in the district and state nurses' associations. Stephanie let her mentor know that she would like to attend an association meeting. The mentor was pleased to see the interest and invited her to attend numerous meetings. Through her mentor, Stephanie learned about aspects of the association that students usually do not see, such as how the organization worked and who the leaders were.

Stephanie felt free to call her mentor to consult about work problems and strategies or to try out solutions or reactions on her. Subsequently, Stephanie settled into her first job and began to examine how she could contribute to the district nurses' association. She volunteered to work on the district governmental affairs committee because she had worked with a similar committee in the state nursing student's association, had taken a nursing jurisprudence elective, and wanted to learn more about this aspect of nursing.

During the next year, Stephanie was building confidence in her professional knowledge and skills and beginning to feel that she was contributing to the organization and the profession. In turn, she found she could apply what she had learned in college and from her mentor to use the professional organization to advance her professional career. In her mind, this was a win-win situation. Soon, feeling like an oldtimer, she was helping other new graduates work their way into the organization.

SUMMARY

Whether as leaders or followers, professional organizations are tools that further professional goals. If we know where we are going and how to use organizations effectively, professional associations will assist us to meet our professional and organizational goals.

References

American Nurses' Association, Certificate of Incorporation. ANA, 1917.

American Nurses' Association, Bylaws, 1982.

American Society of Association Executives and Chamber of Commerce of the United States: *Principles of Association Management.* ASAE and Chamber of Commerce, 1975.

Brown B: Follow the leader. *Nurs Outlook* 1980; 28:357–59.

Merton RK: The function of the professional association. *Am J Nurs* 1958; 58:50–54.

O'Connell B: *Effective Leadership in Voluntary Organizations.* Follett, 1976.

Williford FL: Maintaining lines of authority in board-staff relationships. *Assoc Manage* (August) 1977; 54–56.

Zimmerman A: Toward a unified voice: Individual and collective responsibility of nurses. *J Adv Nurs* 1978; 3:475–83.

Influencing Your Association

Susan W. Talbott, RN, MA, MBA

Thousands of nurses belong to professional nursing associations, each of which has goals and objectives. If nurses choose to join one of over several hundred nursing-related organizations (see Appendix E for a listing of major associations), it is assumed they want something from the association. In some cases, nurses find the organization is meeting their expectations. In other instances, they have ideas about how the association could do more or different things to benefit members or the profession. This chapter outlines ways in which nurses can participate in and influence a professional nursing association on the local, state, or national level.

PARTICIPATION IN YOUR ASSOCIATION

Maintain Membership

The basic way to make an association work is through membership. Simple support through payment of dues provides a necessary financial base to run the day-to-day operations—pay the rent, publish the newsletter, and pay the staff.

Often nurses who leave active nursing practice to raise a family or return to school don't think that they need to maintain membership in their professional associations. Their support, however, both financial and moral, is needed to sustain the profession and the association even while they are not in active practice. Many associations try to accommodate these nurses by offering reduced dues options for inactive or retired nurses.

One reason for nurses to maintain association membership when they are not practicing is to make reentry into practice easier. All members receive the association's publications so inactive nurses can keep up with professional news. Attendance at meetings or other programs help inactive nurses keep in touch with colleagues, issues, and the job market.

Avenues for Involvement

The National Student Nurses' Association (NSNA).   Many RN's have had their first experiences with organized nursing through participation in school chapters of NSNA. Two contributors to this book, Helen Archer-Dusté and Mary Foley, were NSNA presidents and another, Sheila Burke, was president of the California SNA. They are proof that NSNA is a good training ground for future nursing leaders.

Committee Membership.   Many nurses derive satisfaction from working on committees of their professional associations. Most associations have standing committees that deal with issues such as legislation, education, practice, and speciality practice areas (psychiatric mental health and gerontology). New graduates often find committee work rewarding, affording an opportunity to expand nursing networks as well as learn more about particular issues or topics. Membership on a committee is also a good way for the experienced nurse to enter into the activities of the association.

One district association recruits new members by inviting local nursing faculty who are members to help undergraduate and graduate students develop "action projects," for class credit in conjunction with district committees (Vance, 1985). These projects are beneficial to both students and the association:

- Students gain an entre to the association because the executive director or a committee member takes them "under their wing." They get recognition for making a contribution to the association and course credit for their work. Frequently students seek out committee members for advice on career planning.
- The association and committees benefit from student's help with projects or programs and students often join the association and committee as full-fledged working members.

Getting appointed to committees may be as simple as volunteering. Where there is more competition for desirable spots on a committee or task force, you need to plan a strategy. The following suggestions may help:

1. Make yourself known to members of the association board or the committee on which you want to serve. Introduce yourself to the association leaders at an open meeting or get a colleague or teacher who knows one of the leaders to introduce you.

2. Volunteer to work on an association project of interest to you. Your good work will be noticed and increase the likelihood that you will be invited to join a committee.

3. Submit an article to the newsletter or letter to the editor. Publication of your ideas and expertise will cause others to notice you and your ability to help the association.

4. Ask a professor to help you design an action project that you can carry out in connection with an association.

5. Develop an understanding for association politics. Identify formal and informal networks and individuals who have power. Look for opportunities to join others forming a coalition or special task force.

Exerting Influence

After nurses become involved with their professional association, they may want to influence it in some way. There are degrees of influence, ranging from simple projects, such as convincing the board to approve the use of the association's name as a sponsor of an ERA parade to a long-range plan to improve the management of the association.

An effort to influence an association will not always succeed the first time; members may have to be persistent. Sometimes requested change does not occur because other, more important matters demand attention for the moment. Also, matters rarely move fast in volunteer organizations where democratic principles guide the actions of the board and committees.

Nurses use a variety of techniques to influence professional associations. A few ideas and examples are offered to stimulate the reader's own creative thinking.

Propose an Idea.   If you have a good idea or plan that you think the association should adopt or promote, you can present it in a variety of ways. For example, a nurse who had been involved with issues related to safety in the workplace wanted her colleagues in the state association to become informed and to join with her to do something. She wrote an article about her success in setting up a multidisciplinary safety committee in her hospital and described some of the issues with which they had dealt. She included her name and address so interested nurses were able to contact her. The following year at the annual convention, a group of nurses asked the board to form a task force to develop recommended guidelines for hospitals to adopt regarding the mixing of chemotherapeutic medications.

In another instance, a nurse wanted her association to take a stand on the issue of equal pay for comparable worth. Her strategy was to offer to write and present testimony to the city council on behalf of the association.

A group of nurses decided to work together to increase the political savvy and skills of their fellow members. Working through their legislative committee, they planned a series of workshops on legislative and political action and followed up with a day-long trip to the state capital to lobby.

Write a Position Statement   To encourage your association to take a public stand on issues, write a position statement for submission to an association board. A less complicated approach involves writing a letter on a topic of concern and asking that the board or committee send it out over the signature of the president or chair on behalf of the association or a committee. Presentation of your idea via a large professional association will enhance its effectiveness.

Write a Resolution.   Each year at the American Nurses' Association (ANA) house of delegates, at state nurses' conventions, and at meetings of speciality nursing organizations, dozens of resolutions are presented. Many have been written by individual nurses who want to effect change in the organization or obtain formal organizational support for an idea or action. If you have an idea you think should be presented via a resolution, check with the association's parliamentarian or a colleague conversant with the topic of parliamentary procedure.

Raise Professional Issues.   The association is the logical place for nurses to take concerns regarding critical issues. For example, a psychiatric nurse, who teaches in an associate degree program, became concerned about the quality of care she observed at a state hospital where students from the college affiliate. She described the situation to a colleague who is chair of the legislative committee in her district association. The chair asked the nurse to attend the next committee meeting to share her concerns. The committee recommended that the nurse advise the psychiatric mental health and practice committees of the situation. The association president supported the nurse's efforts to share her concern with colleagues and encouraged the psychiatric mental health committee to recommend appropriate action to the association's board. The committee asked the board to send a letter to the director of the hospital. It expressed the association's concern about the safety of patients and staff and offered the association's assistance in finding solutions. A prompt response from the hospital's nursing director indicated that the association's concerns had been acknowledged.

Propose Formation of a Task Force.   An association board or committee might be convinced to appoint a task force to investigate a particular issue or carry out a project. A task force usually has a defined task and time frame in which to complete its work. An association faced with a large increase in rent could ask a task force to study the matter and recommend to the board whether the association should continue to rent or to buy property. The psychiatric nurse referred to earlier, could have proposed that the board appoint a task force, on which she would serve, to study patient care issues. Presenting ideas and offering to work on solutions to problems are good ways for nurses to influence organizations.

Join a Committee.   Committees include individuals who bring a range of knowledge or expertise to bear on a problem. Committees represent the locus of power. They "represent the place where the formal power structure and the informal power structure get together" (Tropman, 1983, p 18). A nurse who has interest or expertise in an area of concern to the committee on which she serves can often sway a committee to support her idea or point of view.

The chair of a committee exerts influence through writing the agenda and conducting the meeting. The committee secretary influences the committee by recording its actions. Minutes should accurately reflect decisions made by the committee, but sometimes items are omitted, inaccurate, or distorted. Minutes should always be closely reviewed by all who participated in the meeting.

A good strategy is to get on a nominating committee so the nurse can influence the ballot and the leadership and direction of the association. Nurses interested in effecting change in organizational structure and function might join the bylaws committee.

Run for Office.   Nurses committed to their professional association sometimes seek elective rather than appointive office. Nurses who want to run for office should have prior experience serving on association committees, including a chair position.

Nurses who want to run for office must consider a number of questions:

- What are the rules relating to nomination and election spelled out in the bylaws of the organization?
- What offices are open, and what are my qualifications for each?
- Why do I want to run? What are my motives? What are my goals for the association and myself? If I am elected, how will the position fit into my professional and personal life? Do I have the time and energy to devote to the position and the association?
- Who will support my candidacy? Do I need to campaign? If so, who will help me? Do I need a formal campaign committee? How much money will it cost? How will I market myself? What are my strengths and weaknesses?

A group of nurses who want to make major changes in their professional association may band together. Strategies might include "stacking" committees and the board by having like-minded members volunteer for committee assignments or run for elective positions. This approach takes years, but it has been done.

Use Outside Experts.   In many situations nurses seem to think that they can do just about anything. Sometimes, however, outside experts are needed. A case in point is the management of association funds. One nursing association board deposited the reserve fund, over $100,000, in a savings bank at 5% interest. When the new treasurer was elected, the board did not heed her advice to invest the funds in a high-yield, fully insured money fund. The treasurer and the finance committee decided to consult the association accountant. Because he was perceived to be an expert, his advice was taken and the board transferred the fund to the high-yield account.

In another instance, a few members of an association board realized that the efforts of their subcommittee on association management were not going to be able to effect the major changes that were needed. One member of this committee consulted a colleague who suggested that the association board do a self-study using an outside consultant. Initially, the board objected to this idea, saying that it could ask members with expertise in administration to take a look at the association. The board ultimately decided to hire the outside consulting team, but it took over two years between the time the board began to seriously consider the idea and the completion of the study. The use of impartial, outside experts accustomed to doing association evaluations, helped the volunteer board members take an honest look at their association. This experience helped them to see the need to design a formal, long-range planning program, including an annual board retreat and periodic association evaluations.

Nurses are well advised to begin their professional association activity at the local level. This permits them to establish a "track record," to demonstrate their knowledge and skills so that they will have a basis from which to seek elective or appointive positions at the state and national levels.

CONCLUSION

Our professional associations have the potential to influence the nursing profession, health policy, and patient care. Too often, they have not achieved that potential because too few of us participate in them. The associations need the energy, expertise, and vision of all nurses—from the student to the renowned nurse leader.

References

Tropman J: *Effective Meetings.* Sage, 1983.
Vance C: On becoming a professional. *J Nurs Educ* (May–June) 1985; 10:20–25.

Vignette: **Risk Takers/Decision Makers Workshops: Empowering Nurses in the Early 1970s**

Karren Mundell Kowalski, RN, PhD, FAAN

While it is incumbent upon individual nurses to join and participate in their professional associations, nurses who already hold elective or appointive positions within associations must work to empower members and encourage their active participation. In the early 1970s, the Colorado Nurses' Association (CNA) did just that through a series of workshops that resulted in significant member participation and an increase in nurses' influence throughout the state.

In November 1971, I was brash, a new master's graduate, a new head nurse, and the newly elected chairperson of the nearly defunct Maternal Child Nursing Conference group. Yet, here I was at a workshop for the nursing education, nursing service, and state association leaders of Colorado. It was unclear to me exactly why I was there, but I came full of enthusiasm and determined to participate. We numbered 74 participants in all and found ourselves in a distant city with nurses whom many had known only by name or position prior to this meeting.

The workshop began with an enthusiastic, challenging, and powerful presentation by Ingeborg Mauksch based on the assigned reading for the workshop, *Future Shock* by Alvin Toffler. Following Mauksch's presentation, a charge was given to the group. Our assigned task for the three days was to leave the workshop with a personal goal, a small-group goal, and a large-group goal—something which could be accomplished before we reconvened in February for phase two of the workshop.

We were randomly assigned to eight small groups and went to work. The first rule was that no one could say what their position was in the introductions. They had to say their first name and some personal things about themselves, such as what they liked or what their hobbies were. This later became known in Colorado nursing circles as the risk-takers introduction because persons were to reveal a more personal, intimate, and human side of themselves rather than the authority and power of their professional positions.

After each block of time in the small groups, participants came together in the large group for sharing. A "recorder" from each group was responsible for informing the other participants about what had been discussed, and where the small group was in relation to the charge. After each group had reported, there was a general discussion of any pressing issues, particularly if they were of concern to more than one group.

During the three days, one key issue for the entire group did emerge. The Colorado Hospital Association was attempting to influence the governor to place the Colorado Nurse Practice Act on his 1972 legislative call list so that the act could be amended to lower the prerequisites for writing the licensure examination. This would allow lesser prepared nurses to be brought in to staff rural hospitals. The state association and state board of nursing were not prepared to have the practice act opened. Thus, the large group made the commitment to contact the governor individually, expressing their concerns over the precipitous opening of the act. On Monday morning following the workshop, there were more than 50 telegrams on the governor's desk requesting that the practice act not be on his call list. And it wasn't.

What Happened

Frankly, I cannot remember either my personal goal or the small group goal from the November workshop. However, nothing succeeds like success, and I was smitten with the small taste of power and influence from having achieved our November goal. Consequently, when the February keynote speaker happened to be Representative Shirley Chisholm and the theme of the workshop was "Utilizing Political Strategies for Change," my small group made the commitment to organize a political action committee that would serve as the political action arm of the state nurses' association. I was elected chairperson of our small organizing committee, and we went to the house of delegates at the state convention, asked for, and received official sanction. Thus, the group became separately incorporated as Involved Nurses' Political Action in Colorado (INPAC). This group became a viable political force and helped the state association pass the revised nurse practice act through the state legislature in 1973.

Other small groups from the follow-up meeting in fall 1972 were empowered to produce new ideas. One group formed Creative Health Services, Inc., the first private group practice for nursing in the state. Another small group developed peer review projects under the auspices of the Colorado/Wyoming Regional Medical Program. I was a member of this group, and we used my hospital unit as one of the project sites in which we developed peer review by staff nurses as a significant portion of the evaluation process rather than relying totally on the superior/subordinate review.

Why Did the Risk Takers/Decision Makers Format Work?

From my perspective, the key element to the success of the risk takers/decision makers format is that the participants felt empowered. As I reflect on the early 1970s, I do not

Table 32-1   The Risk Takers/Decision Makers Format

A Theme: Current and provocative.

Inspirational keynote address: A good speaker is essential.

The Charge: Participants will leave the workshop having accomplished the following:

1. a personal goal or commitment
2. a small-group goal or commitment
3. a large-group goal or commitment.

Staff: who are enthusiastic, good small group facilitators, empowering rather than controlling, and committed to the concepts.

Techniques and Tools:

1. a tool for establishing priorities (such as the Delbeque) to be used in small groups and later in the large group as needed
2. fun exercises such as modeling games (ie, Star Power) or a topical, partially extemporaneous skit.

Flexibility: The schedule can be changed as needed by small groups, the large group, or as requested by group leaders.

Timing: There should be at least one large group meeting each day and more likely two.

---

believe many nursing leaders felt empowered. They felt controlled and at the mercy of physicians, hospital administrators, politics, and other nurses but rarely had they felt empowered. Special leaders and staff are necessary to develop a sense of mastery and control in a group of participants unaccustomed to such feelings. They empower participants rather than control them. The staff must have a high level of commitment because at meals and at the end of the day, staff do not relax—they have a meeting to troubleshoot any problems or difficulties with the workshop or the participants.

Another important aspect is the environment for the workshop. It needs to be specifically designed so that participants come together in a pleasant residential setting and in a group that is small enough to provide informal and intimate one-to-one interaction. There also needs to be a balance of fun, energy, and creative problem solving. The small groups were designed to promote the development of support networks extending past the workshop and serving to counteract prior perceptions of isolation. Many long lasting friendships can develop.

Risk taker/decision maker workshops were done all over Colorado as well as in neighboring states such as Wyoming, New Mexico, Oregon, and Arizona. The state association also sponsored one at their summer Chautauqua conference for several years. When we started taking the workshop to other states, I moved from the participant role to the provider role, always striving to maintain the empowering atmosphere. This is one model of action-oriented concepts that worked for nursing. The format for the workshop appears in Table 32-1. Other nurses can take these concepts, adapt them and create workshops that empower the nurses in their area.

Vignette: **Getting Started**

Ann M. Newman, RN, MSN

My low key entry into involvement in nursing politics should cause the reader to think, "If she can do it, so can I." Until 1980 my involvement consisted of being a registered voter, keeping an occasional eye on local issues, and voting. You don't have to have prior experience in politics to get involved. You just have to "get started." In this vignette I have included specific, concrete suggestions for getting started.

I returned to school to get a BSN. In an elective class, Women and Politics, the professor said, "You either act, or you are acted upon. This is what politics is all about." She also made the point that every profession is affected by politics. It was an interesting thought, but I was much too busy studying, raising kids, maintaining a household, and working PRN, to dwell upon it; however, I did reactivate my membership in the American Nurses' Association (ANA), and sporadically attended local district meetings. At one of the meetings, I began to hear about a new nurse practice act for North Carolina and how members would need to write letters and call legislators to encourage passage of the bill.

The practice act was passed, and my involvement consisted of writing a few letters. But it had sparked my interest. So, when our district president asked for volunteers for North Carolina Nurses' Association (NCNA) committees for the 1981–1983 biennium, I agreed to have my name submitted for the legislative committee. I knew nothing about this committee, but I agreed to go to Raleigh with other local nurses who were selected for committees for an orientation day.

This day was memorable in several ways. I became aware of the structure of my professional organization, how the committees interrelated, and most important, I got to know two mentors, Mary Ann Felts and Cathy Hughes, who nurtured my interest in the political aspects of nursing. This one-on-one nurturing by these nurses was the single most important stimulus to getting me started in politics.

Through serving on the legislative committee, I became involved in a political action committee (PAC). Cathy Hughes, chairperson of the North Carolina PAC (NC-PAC), asked Mary Ann Felts and me to serve on the PAC and to act as liaisons to the nursing association's legislative committee. I learned to be comfortable with calling my legislators on the telephone (the first few times using a "script"). I made numerous trips to Raleigh to speak with legislators in person. I introduced the candidates at our District #5 "Meet the Candidates Night."

My involvement in politics is minute compared to others. But involvement in the political process can be a major focus of your career or a minor focus, as it is with mine. It is important, however, that all nurses realize that political education and involvement are a necessary part of our nursing practice. The key to getting started is through your local nurses' association.

I spoke to my nursing alumni group last year and issued a challenge to them to do one of the following things this year to demonstrate their willingness to begin the process.

1. Become an active member of your district.
2. Volunteer to be on one district or NCNA committee or commission.
3. Contribute to your state PAC and N-CAP (Nurses Coalition for Action in Politics, the national PAC for nursing).
4. Volunteer or ask to be appointed to an advisory board in your city, county, or state.
5. Choose a political candidate you want to support and call his or her headquarters and volunteer to help.
6. Become familiar with how to contact your legislators.
7. Call a legislator to thank her or him for supporting a nursing/health care bill.

My goal for this year is to attend my precinct meeting and find out how to get elected as a delegate to a political party convention . . . not to *get* elected but to find out *how*. "Getting started" is a continuous process.

Chapter 33

The Influence of the Tax-Exempt Professional Organization

Who Can Do What?

Diana J. Mason, RN, MSN*

Nurses want their professional organizations to be more visible in the legislative and electoral processes. The novice member and even the experienced member, however, may be unfamiliar with the legal restrictions on such activity.

While each association should consult its attorney about specific activities, members should be familiar with the law so that they can clarify their expectations of the association. With local organizations, the officers and executive director may be unclear about the limits of the law and may impose unnecessary limits on legislative and political activity.

TAX-EXEMPT ORGANIZATIONS

Not-for-profit organizations (NPO) enjoy certain tax exemptions depending upon the nature of the organization. The Internal Revenue Code categorizes various kinds of tax-exempt organizations; the ones of concern here are the 501(c)(3) and the 501(c)(6).

The 501(c)(3) tax status is conferred upon organizations that engage in charitable, educational, and/or scientific endeavors. Examples of nursing organizations with this tax status include Sigma Theta Tau, the American Association for the History of Nursing, Nurses' House, and the American Nurses' Foundation. This tax status enables

* The author wishes to acknowledge the expert legal counsel provided by Louis Frost, JD, a partner in the firm of Davidson, Dawson and Clark, New York City.

these organizations to receive tax deductible donations, such as grants for research, funds from philanthropic foundations, and gifts from individuals. Organizations with this tax status do not pay income taxes (other than on unrelated business income).

Why don't all nursing organizations seek this tax classification? Along with these benefits come certain restrictions on the organization's activities. In general, the 501(c)(3) organization cannot engage in substantial lobbying or any partisan political activity. The missions of state nurses' associations (SNA) and many specialty organizations include promoting legislation of importance to nursing and quality health care. As such, the SNAs cannot be classified as 501(c)(3) because they need greater freedom to lobby than is permissible under that classification. Most of these organizations have the 501(c)(6) tax status, but many have formed separately incorporated 501(c)(3) organizations to carry out the educational activities permitted with that tax status.

For example, the American Nurses' Foundation is a 501(c)(3) arm of the American Nurses' Association (ANA), which has the 501(c)(6) status because of its lobbying activities. The foundation awards monies for research and receives tax deductible contributions for this purpose. It does not engage in lobbying or political activities. Similarly, the New York Counties Registered Nurses' Association in New York City is a 501(c)(6) organization because it engages in legislative activities. It recently formed a separately incorporated educational foundation that enjoys the 501(c)(3) status. This foundation cannot devote a "substantial part" of its budget to lobbying activities and cannot engage in partisan political activities.

PARTISAN VS. NONPARTISAN ACTIVITIES

Partisan political activities include endorsing a candidate for elective office, making a monetary contribution to a candidate's campaign, and listing the association's name on campaign literature. Individual members of any 501(c)(3) organization cannot engage in these activities as representatives of the association. So, while the members can and should participate in individual candidates' campaigns, they must do so as citizens, nurses, or members of some other organization that does not enjoy a 501(c)(3) tax exemption.

Even if nurses are told their affiliation with a 501(c)(3) association will be listed on campaign literature "for identification purposes only," such a listing could jeopardize the tax status of their association. The nurse who participates in a campaign as a member of a 501(c)(6) organization should do so only with the consent of the organization, since endorsing a particular candidate may not be in the best interest of the organization for other than legal reasons.

If nurses want to participate fully in political activities as an organized body, they can form a political action committee (PAC). Indeed, a growing number of local and state nurses' associations are forming PAC arms to enable nurses to exert greater influence on the electoral process in their communities. The 501(c)(6) association can provide monies to support the administration of the PAC, but none of the association's funds can be used for political contributions. The PAC must solicit individual members of the association for monies to use for campaign contributions.

While 501(c)(6) organizations can endorse and campaign for candidates, most prefer to engage in nonpartisan political activities. Such activities include voter registration drives, candidates' "nights" or forums (to which all candidates running for a particular position are invited to present their views), and publication of the views of all candidates or the platforms of all political parties. While the 501(c)(3) organization can also engage in such nonpartisan activities, most do not.

Although some 501(c)(6) nursing organizations are not taking advantage of the political activities in which they are permitted to engage, others are moving ahead in bold and effective ways, as the following example demonstrates.

CANDIDATES' NIGHT

Members of the local nurses' association in Syracuse, New York, were concerned about the reelection of a major state senator from their city who had been particularly unsupportive of nursing. This election year, he was being opposed by a woman with strong, supportive positions on nursing and health care issues. Nurses across the state were excited by this campaign because the senator had been a thorn in the side of nursing for some time. On several occasions, the insurance committee, which he chaired, had refused to pass the nursing association's third party reimbursement bill for nurses out of committee. He had been in office for a number of years and was powerful within his party, the majority party in the city. The senator was deemed to be a shoe-in.

Members of the local nurses' association, however, believed that a candidates' night would give nurses the opportunity to see the differences between the two candidates. The association decided to sponsor this nonpartisan event and expanded it to include candidates for other elective positions in their city.

Candidates were invited and told they would be given five minutes to make a statement, followed by questions from the audience. Candidates would speak on a first-come-first-serve basis—the first to arrive would be the first to speak.

The candidates' night, held after a regular dinner meeting of the nurses' association, was publicized in the association's newsletter and fliers. Attendance at the dinner was larger than at other dinner meetings; by the time the candidates began to speak, nurses were literally lining the walls.

The candidates' night had also been publicized by the local media. Press releases were sent to the local newspapers, radio, and television stations. In addition, the nurses wisely selected a well-known Syracuse news reporter to moderate the candidates' presentations. Of course, the reporter told his colleagues of this event. As a result, the room was filled with television cameras, microphones, and reporters to record the event. One local television news program reported the event on the nightly news, with video replays and a printed listing of the major bills of concern to the association.

The candidates took turns presenting their statements and answering questions. A few of the invited candidates did not come and several sent staff members in their place. Both the incumbent and challenger in the race for the state senate addressed the nurses.

The challenger made her case well—after the candidates' night the number of nurses participating in her campaign, and making monetary and other contributions, increased dramatically.

The chair of the association's legislation committee played an active role in the challenger's campaign, although he did so as an individual nurse. (From a legal standpoint, he could have done so as a member of the association. The association, however, had decided not to engage in partisan politics.) He traveled widely with the candidate, enlisting support for her campaign. The president of the nurses' association also invested time and energy in behalf of the challenger's campaign as an individual citizen, not as president of the association. She used her nursing contacts throughout the state to enlist support of nurses outside of the city interested in seeing the incumbent defeated.

These two nurses led the entire nursing community, in appropriate ways, to work for what became the biggest upset in the state—the challenger defeated the state senator by fewer than 200 votes. Nurses had made a difference, and the entire community knew it.

The candidates' night enabled the local nurses' association to participate in the electoral process in a meaningful and appropriate way. Doing so brought benefits to nurses and the nursing profession and the community at large. Besides having a good friend in the state senate, the association was in the news. In addition to the news coverage of the candidates' night, one reporter has written several favorable news articles on nursing.

Many state and local nurses' associations limit their legislative and political activity for fear of running afoul of the law. Many organizations have found ways to expand legislative and political activities while complying with regulations by consulting legal counsel when questions about rules and regulations arise.

Nursing association board members and staff may find regulations relating to tax status complex and vague. The next section of this chapter describes some of the questions and difficulties that a 501(c)(3) nursing organization faces when it accepts federal funds.

This will be followed by a paper on ANA's historic 1984 presidential endorsement. It represented a bold effort by this tax-exempt organization to influence the political arena. Keep in mind that, although the ANA is a 501(c)(6) organization, endorsements are permitted; and second, the author of this paper is presenting her own views on the issue, and is not speaking for the ANA or its board of directors.

Don't Bite the Hand that Feeds You!

Jacqueline Rose Hott, RN, PhD, FAAN
Pearl Skeete Bailey, RN, EdD

What are the legislative and political action problems that administrators of a federal grant-supported, tax-exempt 501(c)(3) professional organization may encounter when the caveat is "Don't bite the hand that feeds you"? This question is faced by many organizations, including MARNA (Mid-Atlantic Regional Nurses' Association).

MARNA is funded by the Division of Nursing, the Department of Health and Human Services, through a special project grant. It was officially established in July, 1981 as a non-profit regional nursing association in the mid-Atlantic area. Five states comprise MARNA's jurisdiction: Delaware, New Jersey, New York, Pennsylvania, and Washington, DC.

The authors, MARNA's executive director and former associate director respectively, have frequently found themselves in predicaments trying to carry out activities related to the purpose and objectives of the association while, at the same time, abiding by the restrictions related to legislative and political action imposed on organizations receiving federal grant funds. The following anecdotes illustrate the problems faced by many government-supported organizations.

1. The regional newsletter is being compiled. It includes a legislative update. Can we identify potential or actual political issues before they have been formally presented to a legislative body? Can we indicate support for pending state or federal legislation? Can we ask our readers to react to such legislation? Can we participate in lobbying activities?

2. The regional maternal-infant project investigators are meeting. They are discussing replication of a nurse researcher's proposal to study the impact of federal budget cuts on maternal-infant health care. Will undertaking this study imply criticism of the federal government? Will this study be embarrassing to the current administration? Does conducting this study demonstrate a political bias against the government's socio-economic policies?

3. The regional program committee has planned a meeting on nursing and cost containment. DRGs and other prospective payment schemes are to be discussed. The committee suggests a panel of legislative experts, representative of each of the five jurisdictions in the MARNA area, to address these issues. Who should be invited? Who should do the inviting—the local members, state organizations, or the regional MARNA office? Does the panel have to be bipartisan? Should federal or state legislators be invited? Which ones should be particularly sought after? Does inviting legislators to a wine and cheese party after the program constitute lobbying?

4. A solicitation letter, addressed to MARNA, requests an organizational contribution to the New York State Nurses for Political Action (NYS-NPA). Should the regional association contribute? Should members of the MARNA staff refrain from making personal political contributions to NYS-NPA, other political action committees, or individual candidates?

5. The bill authorizing third party reimbursement for registered nurses awaits the governor's signature after passing both houses of the state legislature overwhelmingly. The state nurses' association asks its members to contact the governor and ask him to sign the bill. What are the MARNA staff's private, personal, and public actions and responsibilities in response to this request?

With these examples in mind, the authors decided to try to develop generic guidelines for the 501(c)(3) professional organization that will:

• preserve the delicate balance between personal and organizational accountability

- ensure that a nonprofit, tax-exempt organization uses federal funds legitimately
- advance the purposes and objectives of an association.

As a first step, the authors interviewed leaders of comparable federal and state organizations. In general, they were asked how they handle federal and state policies that affect their personal and organizational involvement in influencing legislative and political activities. Two specific questions were asked:

1. How does a nonprofit foundation that receives private or federal funds maintain its tax-exempt status while pursuing its social advocacy role?
2. Under what conditions can a nonprofit organization that receives federal funds engage in legislative or political activities?

In response to question one, the legal contract officer of a large private foundation, noted for its support of social policy change, said "You ask a question that has many answers." Discussions with other large grant-funding agencies disclosed similar difficulties in giving direct answers. "The answers are inferred and between the lines with few things written down," said one major grants officer. Another said, "Each has his own approach. You are covertly and overtly encouraged to obey the rules. You do not publicly violate these rules. Many times, restrictions appear to be in direct conflict with the purpose of an organization, eg, to effect social change."

Queries about the political and legislative activities of nonprofit organizations produced more questions than answers, but the consensus was the less said, the better. For example, a grants officer at a private foundation said: "It's a very narrow line to walk and we tend to be conservative about what is, and is not said." Another stated, "Rules for private nonprofit foundations are promulgated in the Internal Revenue Code, which is one dimensional. The private foundation is not one dimensional. The whole thing gets tacky."

A review of government efforts to clarify the responsibilities of tax-exempt organizations receiving federal funds revealed the following information.

In April, 1984, the federal Office of Management and Budget (OMB) issued a revised circular (A-122) outlining the lobbying and other advocacy activities that organizations receiving federal funds are permitted to undertake. This revision was adopted to ensure that appropriated funds are not used in subsidizing lobbying by federal grantees or contractors. The revision protects the First Amendment rights of federal grantees and contractors and, in some respects, strongly advances their interests. By giving nonprofit entities clear guidelines and limiting the bookkeeping work that can be required (for example, to refute an auditor's claim of unallowable costs), the revision removes a potentially severe burden from those receiving federal grants or contracts, especially the smaller and less well-financed groups. Although the revision cannot resolve, in advance, every problem which may arise, a mechanism has been developed to assist nonprofits to find out in advance if certain costs are allowable. This means that MARNA and similar groups can apply for a ruling before going ahead with plans for an activity such as the wine and cheese reception for legislators.

A FURTHER LOOK AT LOBBYING

An organization is considered to be lobbying when:

- A substantial part of its activities and resources are directed towards attempting to influence passage of legislation.
- It contacts, or urges the public to contact, members of a legislative body to propose, support, or oppose legislation.
- It advocates the adoption or rejection of legislation.
- Its members, on behalf of the organization (including identifying oneself as a member of the organization), participate, directly or indirectly, in a political campaign on behalf of or in opposition to any candidate for public office. (However, members may participate in campaigns as individual citizens, a nurse, or other sanctioned capacity.)

What legislative or political activities are or are not permitted to be undertaken by the 501(c)(3) organization? The following guidelines are related to the situations described earlier.

1. The 501(c)(3) organization can inform its members, but not the general public, about legislative activities critical to the purposes and objectives of the organization. For example, MARNA includes a legislative update in its publication, *Marnagram*. The status of pending legislation that may affect nursing and health care, such as third party reimbursement for nurses, is reported. When the National Institute for Nursing bill was introduced into the House of Representatives in 1984, the MARNA editors printed the position statements of major nursing organizations. The editors did not urge members to support or oppose the bill or report their personal opinions, because exhorting others to influence Congress on a pending bill is not permitted. In another instance, however, when the MARNA task force on regional planning for nursing completes its study projecting supply, demand, and distribution of nursing personnel and resources, the report, including the recommendations, can be given to the membership. The report will also be available to legislators, but only if they make a written request for a copy. Distribution of such reports to legislators must be done this way to guard against an accusation that the organization is trying to influence legislation by sending out reports that may affect legislators' opinions.

2. An organization such as MARNA can engage in nonpartisan analysis, study, or research on issues as long as the work is not being done in preparation for a lobbying effort or the results are not ultimately used to influence the legislative process. MARNA's original plan to replicate an Oregon study on the impact of federal budget cuts on maternal/infant care has been revised to avoid possible criticism that the work was planned to influence legislation. The current design will provide important information, but the analysis of the issues will be nonpartisan and will be used to educate the membership. In keeping with the law, legislators will be advised that they may make a written request for the report.

3. Legislators and their staff aides may be invited to a program by an NPO (not-for-profit organization) that receives federal funds when they wish to:

- gain factual or technical information relating to a particular issue
- contribute information on a particular topic
- advise the membership about how legislation may affect an issue of concern to the group.

For example, when MARNA was planning its program, "The Dollars and Sense of Cost Containment in Nursing within the Mid-Atlantic Region," a bipartisan panel of state and congressional representatives was invited to provide information. None received an honorarium and each paid his travel-related expenses. After the conference, a reception for the legislators and their aides was held in the Senate Office Building. The purpose of the party was to provide an opportunity for MARNA members to meet their representatives informally and to discuss nursing and health care issues related to each of the MARNA jurisdictions. MARNA defrayed the cost of the reception by using the proceeds of the conference. This ensured that no federal funds were expended for an activity that could have been perceived as lobbying.

4. MARNA may not contribute to political action committees, (PACs) such as NYS-NPA. The purposes of PACs includes active support of candidates for political office, an activity that NPOs are forbidden to undertake. However, staff and individual members of MARNA, or any NPO, may work on their own time, as private citizens, on any campaign, or for any PAC. Public endorsement of a candidate is permissible, as long as the nurse does not imply that the endorsement has been made by MARNA. Current law permits individuals who work for NPOs to put political signs, such as bumper stickers, on their cars. Writing this paper, however, has been done on the authors' days off, using a word processor purchased with nonfederal (membership) funds. In addition, after the presidential endorsement by ANA in the fall of 1984, MARNA was advised by the federal government, through the Division of Nursing, that staff could not do ANA work on MARNA's time.

Other activities of NPO's receiving federal funds are specifically prohibited by the guidelines referred to earlier (Circular A-122). They include:

1. lobbying the executive branch in connection with decisions to sign or veto legislation
2. efforts to use state or local officials to lobby Congress or state legislatures
3. grass roots lobbying concerning federal, state, or local legislation, through attempts to affect the opinions of the general public, or any sector thereof
4. lobbying with resources that are considered a match for federal funds.

Federal funds may be used for:

1. Any lobbying to influence state legislation to directly reduce the cost or to avoid material impairment of the organization's authority to perform the grant, contract, or other agreement.
2. Use of NPO funds for travel-related expenses for a legitimate meeting or program and lobbying legislators in the same location on one's own time.

There are guidelines for NPOs to follow. Failure to follow them, especially the ones described above, may result in the organization being penalized. A usual penalty is repayment of misspent funds. In cases of serious abuse, the grant or contract may be suspended or terminated, or the recipient may be prohibited from receiving grants or contracts for a certain period.

If you are uncertain about how to proceed, consult representatives of the federal agency from which your contract derives. In our experiences, we have found the Division of Nursing in the Department of Health and Human Services has provided MARNA with helpful information and guidance. We have also consulted the grants officer of the university in which our offices are housed as well as lawyers associated with other NPOs.

In any case, when determining what legislation or political activities are permissible, it may be wise to consider the question, "How do porcupines make love?" The answer: "Very carefully."

Vignette: The Organization in Action: Washington (DC) Nurses Work for Practice Privileges

Elizabeth Calderon, RN

On October 7, 1983, the City Council of the District of Columbia (DC) passed an unprecedented bill that prohibits hospitals from discriminating against nonphysician providers seeking practice privileges. The efforts of the District of Columbia Nurses' Association (DCNA) in securing passage of the bill illustrate how the professional organization can successfully exert its influence in the legislative arena.

The Health Care Facility and Agency Licensure Act of 1983 was considered in a hearing by the District of Columbia (DC) Committee on Human Services in May 1983. This Licensure Act was routine except for a section dealing with anticompetitive practices and discrimination against nonphysician health professionals, namely: podiatrists, psychologists, nurse-midwives, nurse anesthetists, and nurse practitioners. Under this bill, institutions could not prohibit podiatrists, psychologists, nurse-midwives, nurse anesthetists, or nurse practitioners as a class from being accorded clinical privileges and appointed to active staff membership with full voting rights.

Political lines were clearly drawn. During the hearing, the DC (District of Columbia) Medical Society allied with the hospital administrators for a united front. The medical society wanted this section removed from the licensure bill. It made statements such as "boy scouts with rusty knives" to describe what would happen to the public if nurses were allowed staff privileges. It called us "subprofessionals." It placed flyers in their offices with a cut-out section for the patient to mail to the council member, stating, "I vigorously oppose the passage of bill 5-166 and the lowering of patient care standards in the hospital." It called the media and stated it would cause chaos for the community if this bill is passed. The medical society had a great deal of support.

The DCNA called a meeting with representatives of all the health professions named in the bill to discuss ideas and decide strategy. The psychologists and the nurse anesthetists hired attorneys. An attorney came forth to work pro bono for the nurse practitioners. DCNA encouraged communication and the District of Columbia Nurses' Association Political Action Committee (DCNA-PAC) offered its political organizing tools and skills. The podiatrists decided not to join us but to bargain separately with the medical society. The Health Coalition was formed, and labor and consumer groups were invited to join us. Our strategy was forming.

This bill had been researched, written, and introduced by the chair of the Human Services Committee. This was to our advantage; however, not all members of the committee shared the same view. The bill was due to be voted upon by the committee on July 7, 1983, which did not provide much time to organize, educate, and lobby. The DCNA nurses met weekly to make telephone calls and write letters. We generated thousands of letters and flooded the committee members' offices. They had never seen nurses respond to an issue like this before. We made lobbying visits. The Health Coalition called a press conference to give our side of the issue. We were invited to local talk shows on radio and TV. We presented ourselves to the media as concerned about costs and better utilization of health care professionals. We got consumers to speak for us too. Women who had babies delivered by nurse-midwives were excellent spokespersons. The issue was in the newspapers almost daily. The DC Medical Society gave dire warnings of a "two-tier medical system," in which the rich would still go to a physician, and the poor would be forced to use a lesser-educated health professional. The committee voted a unanimous "yes" on July 8, 1983, and the bill went to the full council.

The fight remained in the media from July 8 until October 7, 1983. During the summer, we met every Wednesday to make calls and write letters. We generated hundreds of letters for each of the twelve council members. Nurses lobbied the council members and their staff and tried to dispel misconceptions about nurses. Receptions were held in key wards to bring together the nurse constituents and the council members. Press conferences were held, and the media kept the issue before the public. On October 7, 1983, the City Council voted a unanimous "yes" to a full chamber of health care professionals. After the vote, many of the council members commended the nurses' educational and lobbying efforts and their involvement in this political issue.

Once you get involved in politics you learn that nothing is clear-cut. The DC Medical Society does have many friends on the City Council. The pressure of the unions, consumers, psychologists, and nurses was too strong, however, and they voted against the Medical Society. The Medical Society pulled out some old legislation—the Nurse Practice Act—and rewrote some parts of it to reduce our autonomy. They had always been our key opposition on the Nurse Practice Act, but suddenly they wanted it reintroduced with their changes. They also had three new bills introduced to require specialty licensure for nurse-midwives, nurse anesthetists, and nurse practitioners. The bills would also place these nurse specialists under the physician's supervision with specialty boards. While hearings on these bills were held in 1984, they have yet to be enacted.

Furthermore, the physicians are continuing to try to undermine the practice privilege law by influencing how the regulations for the law are drafted and enforced. The American Medical Association, at its 1984 House of Delegates meeting, pledged financial resources to fight expanded practice privileges for nonphysician providers and continues to monitor the DC law.

The DCNA-PAC continues to meet every Wednesday evening for work sessions. We are holding training seminars to teach our members how to lobby. We are also considering the possibility of hiring a part-time lobbyist. We realize that the fight is far from over, but we have gained recognition and some respect with politicians. It is now important that we keep up our momentum and involve more nurses in this kind of political action.

Chapter 34

Political Action Committees

Overview

Barbara Thoman Curtis, RN*

The formation of political action committees—PACs—is the current political style—the means by which groups gain access to elected officials. In 1984, the PACs numbered over 4,243, up from 2,551 in 1980 and 113 in 1972. There are approximately 614 association PACs. AMPAC, the political action committee of the American Medical Association and one of the oldest political action groups in the health field, was formed in the early sixties. In 1982, AMPAC contributed in excess of $2.4 million to congressional campaigns. In 1984, AMPAC ranked sixth among the 25 largest PACs, but was the largest among the association PACs, having raised $3.7 million.

The Constitution of the United States gives its citizens the right to petition the government. That's exactly what lobbyists do, assisted today by the political action committees. Political action groups reflect a wide spectrum of interests: labor, business, environment, association, women, independents' (primarily conservative groups), and education. Because so many elections are decided by just a few votes, active interest groups can rightfully claim that their support made the difference in countless races for Congress and the state legislatures. There's clout in numbers. Candidates know it, they respect it, and they respond to it.

Back in 1907, it was illegal for a corporation to make contributions to a political campaign. Through the years, the law has evolved, with significant amendments added in 1971 and 1974. These recent statutes carry strict reporting and disclosure

* With special thanks to Joanne Symons, Director of Political Education, and Pat Ford-Roegner, Political Field Director, American Nurses' Association, Washington, DC. Information on N-CAP program and activities was obtained from N-CAP policies and materials. As of January 1986, N-CAP's name will be ANA-PAC.

requirements. But the law explicitly recognizes that a trade association or corporation, such as the American Nurses' Association (ANA), may pay the costs of "establishment, administration, and solicitation of contributions to a separate, segregated fund to be utilized for political purposes by a corporation or labor organization." In such a political action committee, the law requires that the monies collected from voluntary contributions be kept in a separate, segregated fund and that no corporation/association money may be used for candidate support. (See Chapter 33 on the Tax-Exempt Organization.)

N-CAP, the Nurses' Coalition for Action in Politics, was established in 1974 as the political action arm of the ANA. Because of the changes in the law, the impetus of an existing group (NPA—Nurses for Political Action), and the establishment of several state nurses' association PACs around the country, the ANA board of directors decided to establish a national PAC and allocated an initial grant of $50,000 that first year. (N-CAP's administration continues to be subsidized by ANA.) A director for N-CAP was hired, and the office located in the ANA Washington facility. This arrangement enabled N-CAP to solicit contributions to a "separate, segregated fund to be utilized for political purposes . . ."; more specifically, to be used to provide financial support for officeholders and candidates. At no time have members' dues been used for candidate contributions.

The purpose of N-CAP is to establish political power through endorsements and contributions. This activity gives nurses visibility, credibility, and influence. N-CAP endorses candidates who are friends of nursing and who will increase nursing's impact on issues that affect health care consumers and nurses. N-CAP exists solely for the purpose of creating power and influence for nursing.

The N-CAP board of trustees includes five members appointed by the ANA board from its membership, and four members appointed by N-CAP from the state nurses' associations' (SNA) membership-at-large. The board is bipartisan. It meets three times during the election year and reviews every House and Senate race in the country—435 House races and 33 Senate races.

All money donated to N-CAP must come from voluntary contributions by SNA members. Federal law prohibits solicitation of funds from other than SNA members, nor can money collected from association membership dues be used to support candidates.

In 1984, the average United States Senate race cost $1.5 million, with some races costing in excess of $20 million. (The National Conservative PAC spent over $5 million on the North Carolina Senate race; it raised a total of over $16 million.) A candidate for a contested seat in the House may spend as much as $400,000. Money is the major factor in elections. A large contribution from N-CAP in the name of nursing gives nurses more political clout than smaller individual campaign contributions. N-CAP enables nurses to pool resources and maximize the benefits. In federal elections, a contribution to a candidate in Massachusetts will affect nurses in California and Texas because, once selected, that officeholder will vote on issues affecting nurses all over the country.

Political action committees were born out of a need for individual and collective action. The ANA and state nurses' associations hire lobbyists to persuade public officials to work for legislation nurses consider important. They primarily work to convince those already serving in public office. But political action committees aim at influencing the elections' outcome. By endorsing candidates and contributing time and money, nurses can help elect to office and keep in place public officials who support their point of view.

Political action and lobbying are both necessary if nursing is to have a strong voice in health care decision making. It must be recognized, however, that political action committees such as N-CAP do not set priorities or establish general policy for the profession. That is the responsibility of the parent organization. The PAC is an "arm" of the association. It operates on behalf of the association, and reflects its philosophy, goals, and objectives. The goal of the PAC is singular and should not conflict or compete with the parent organization.

The functions of N-CAP are distinctively different from those of the ANA Congressional Relations Department and the Department of Political Education. N-CAP does not lobby. The only criteria for N-CAP involvement are a monetary contribution and interest in participating in politics, particularly at the grass roots level. N-CAP is primarily made up of nurses, but contributions are welcome from families and friends as well.

PAC FUNCTIONS

A political action committee such as N-CAP has several functions. The primary task is to endorse and support candidates and officeholders who support goals important for nursing and health care in this country. In addition, the PAC can educate others about the democratic process. PACs can also inform nurses and others about the records of officeholders and candidates on key political issues, primarily health related issues.

Within the ANA, the Department of Political Education works with N-CAP to ensure that nurses are a political force. This department, established in 1980, helps nurses use effective political skills. Staff work with the SNAs to help nurses become more effective campaigners and lobbyists.

Fund-raisers are a major political activity in Washington, not merely a social event. Since N-CAP has been in existence, representatives of the PAC have attended fundraisers sponsored by individual candidates, political parties, and other groups that share interests with nursing. This has provided many opportunities for the official lobbyists and strategists of ANA and recognized nursing experts to be recognized and heard. Fund-raisers are a major means of access to those who make and implement laws and policy at the federal level.

CONGRESSIONAL DISTRICT COORDINATOR NETWORK

A qualified staff in Washington, DC, cannot be effective without grass roots support and the constant display of broad-based strength. A source of national nursing strength is the Congressional District Coordinator (CDC) Network, an activity of the ANA

Department of Political Education. By mid-1985, there were 362 CDCs throughout the country, out of a total of 435 congressional districts. The main goal of the CDC is "to organize nurses to help elect N-CAP endorsed candidates." CDCs monitor the political scene, and through the SNAs and the Department of Political Education, they provide N-CAP with essential advice and information for the endorsement process.

The ultimate identity of the PAC comes through the involvement of its contributors in the political process in the home districts. When the call goes out from ANA's Washington office for a particular nurse or CDC to contact a specific congressperson on a key committee, that nurse will have an already established direct line of communication with the elected official. That nurse will have been active in the congressperson's campaign, served as a resource person for position statements on health related issues, or shared her knowledge and experience in other ways. For example, a legislator called upon a nurse constituent for information about the plight of the homeless and chronic mentally ill. Another representative consulted a nurse about the incidence of domestic violence and asked her opinion about what legislation should be initiated.

ENDORSEMENT PROCEDURES

The process of interviewing candidates and making endorsements is a basic activity of any political action committee. Endorsement policies should be developed and should identify who the endorsing body should be. The endorsement committee may consist of representatives of the PAC board or include the board as a whole. Policy should also establish how recommendations for endorsements should be received and from whom, as well as what the priorities are for endorsement. (Contact your SNA or PAC to obtain a copy of the state PAC's endorsement guidelines.)

There are numerous factors to be considered when planning endorsements. Key races that will draw significant public attention and where nursing's input would be valued might receive priority. Many candidates will receive nursing support if they meet PAC endorsement criteria, such as:

- consistent supporters of the SNA who face a tough contest
- pronursing incumbents (those currently holding office) who face little or no serious opposition
- candidates with positive voting records on major health related issues
- candidates supportive of nursing or responsive to nursing input who are challenging known adversaries of nursing
- candidates in swing races (no incumbent running) who are clearly more in agreement with nursing goals and SNA positions.

In deciding what the priority for endorsement should be, factors to be considered include the leadership position of the candidate, committee chairmanship or membership, sponsorship of key bills, and political potential and position in the political party.

Categories of endorsement include:

- major endorsement, including significant financial assistance and commitment to work in the campaign
- general endorsement for candidates who demonstrate need for some "in-kind" contributions (staff services, such as consultation, campaign organizing, or office assistance) or financial support
- name-only endorsement for candidates who have little need for assistance other than "in-kind" services and announcement of the endorsement
- no endorsement when the PAC decides to stay out of a race or that a candidate has not met the criteria.

Included in the criteria for endorsement are:

- the candidates' expressed willingness to support, or past demonstration of support, for SNA programs
- "winability" of the race, including the capacity to mount an effective campaign
- willingness to accept PAC contributions.

One of the most significant steps of the endorsement procedure is delivering a written endorsement or a check to the candidate. The timing of this activity is crucial and should be coordinated by the campaign staff to provide the best visibility for the candidate and for the nursing PAC. Another consideration is timing of the endorsement. There may be occasions when an early endorsement could be critical, so the procedure should be easily called into action.

Notification of the nursing community about the endorsements is a crucial step in the process. After the decision is made, the SNA board of directors and the membership, along with the student organization, should be notified as to who the endorsed candidates are. Suggestions as to how to get involved in the individual campaigns should accompany the endorsement information.

N-CAP Endorsements

According to N-CAP's endorsement policy:

Each board member reviews a confidential report on each candidate using a variety of measures including input of the SNA and the candidate's voting record and issue positions. Once the board members have reviewed candidates in each race in question, the board votes on whether to endorse a candidate. If the board votes to endorse, it must then determine whether to endorse and contribute money, and if so, how much money to contribute. N-CAP has a limited amount of money to dispense, so it is important that the money go to those races where it will count the most. Some candidates receive an endorsement but no money, since their races may not be close enough or crucial enough to warrant a financial contribution. For those candidates who do receive a donation, the amount of money contributed varies from candidate to candidate.

Since money is a scarce commodity, special attention should be paid to certain kinds of candidates for contributions. Since 97 percent of the nursing profession are women,

N-CAP carefully reviews all women candidates. Women traditionally have a more difficult time raising money than do men, so the impact of a monetary contribution to them is greater. N-CAP may invest in a well-qualified woman even though her chances of winning are considered a long shot. In such cases, the PAC contribution may be that little extra that will make the difference. In November, 1984, the hard work of nurses in Syracuse, NY, coupled with contributions from NYS-NPA (the PAC for New York State nurses), helped a woman candidate for the New York State Senate defeat the incumbent by fewer than 200 votes.

Endorsements are strengthened when volunteers are part of the deal. This type of a contribution—endorsement, money, and nurse power—will be long remembered by the officeholder.

The Interview

The interview process is an important component of the endorsement procedure. Preparation of a list of questions to ask each candidate will facilitate the interviews.

The interview team should consist of two to five persons. They decide in advance who will be the leader or chair for the meeting. The leader should introduce each member of the team at the beginning of the interview. Name tags are helpful.

Interviews and time limits should be scheduled in advance, including time after the interview for people to review and record comments. If possible, candidates for the same race should be interviewed at the same time by the same team of interviewers.

The interview should increase the candidate's respect for nurses and their political action program. The setting should be appropriate, and every effort should be made to make the candidate comfortable.

Following introductions, the candidate may deliver a brief opening statement. The interview is an opportunity to educate candidates or officeholders about nursing's position on the issues, but the interviewer should not do all the talking. On the other hand, the candidate should not be allowed to take over the interview. The team should be careful not to argue and not to comment on the candidate's answers. This should be reserved for the postinterview session. Vague or incomplete answers, however, should be followed up.

At the close of the interview, the team should tell the candidate when he can expect a decision. The meeting should be followed up with a thank-you letter and, if the decision is to endorse, the candidate should be informed of this decision in writing.

When an endorsement is to be made, a number of things must be decided:

- who will announce the endorsement
- when the announcement will be made
- who will present the check.

It is preferable to allow the candidate some control over these activities so he can get the most mileage out of the endorsement. For example, the candidate's public relations staff may develop a "media event" to publicize the nursing PAC's endorsement. If possible, involve nurse volunteers who plan to work in the candidate's campaign. This often means as much as the money or the endorsement itself.

FUND-RAISING ACTIVITIES

Raising money is a key function of political action committees. N-CAP has run the gamut from gala affairs—a luau in Honolulu and a rodeo in Houston—to a celebrity auction in Washington, DC. Although successful, none was more successful or easier to plan than the "challenge" held at the 1985 ANA meeting in Kansas City. Nurses were reminded that it costs money to demonstrate strength. In a little over fifteen minutes, $33,000 was raised in contributions from approximately 675 nurses in the ANA House of Delegates. A state nurses PAC held a similar challenge during its annual meeting and raised over $4,000. The best approach might well be a straight-forward request for funds.

There are a few basic factors to remember when a group wants to raise money for a PAC:

- Only association members can be solicited (unless your state law permits non-member solicitation).
- All PAC contributions must be voluntary—they cannot automatically be attached to association dues.
- Funds for a PAC may be solicited at the same time dues notices for the nursing association are sent.
- Fund-raising literature should carry a sentence explaining what is to be done with the money. N-CAP states on its literature, "Your voluntary contributions to N-CAP will be used to help elect to federal public office, through partisan effort, those who have proved or are deemed to be friends of nursing."
- Most fund-raising activities require the expenditure of considerable time and energy; analyze the costs to PAC members versus the benefits to the PAC.

People are always trying to come up with new ways to raise money. In a tight economy, many groups compete for the same dollar. Creative ways to raise funds are really variations of the same four themes: direct mail, sale of merchandise, special events, and personal solicitation. (For additional tips on fund-raising, see box.)

Direct Mail

If a direct mail campaign is planned far enough in advance, it can be a smooth and efficient way to raise money. Using a known list, such as the state nurses' association membership, the cost can be calculated fairly accurately.

When planning a direct mail campaign, it is important to provide sufficient time for the following: obtaining labels; writing the solicitation letter and preparing other materials to be included; printing the letter, literature, envelopes, and return envelopes; stuffing and sealing the envelopes; and sorting the envelopes for bulk mailing. There should be a coordinator, possibly a staff person. Direct mail companies perform all these tasks, but this can be quite expensive. Volunteers should be considered, particularly for the time consuming tasks of stuffing envelopes and zip code sorting.

It is also important to devise a record-keeping system before the mailing is done. As

---

Fund-Raising Tips

Nancy West, RN, MSN

Have a goal of the amount you want to raise and state it publicly. Always ask individual donors for more than you expect them to contribute (people will never give more than what you ask them to give).

The most effective method of fund-raising is one-to-one, direct, personal contact with a potential donor. (It is much harder for people to say "no" face-to-face.)

Mailings to solicit money are expensive and the response is usually less than 1 percent. Don't choose this method of fund-raising for your first endeavor.

When doing a fund-raising event, expenses should be no more than one-third of the price of the ticket, or you will not make enough money to justify the effort required to put together a good event.

People like raffles and 50/50 drawings. These small individual contributions can add up. Always do one at any fund-raising event. You will take in more incidental money from those in attendance. These can also be done at meetings and other types of gatherings.

Keep asking. You can vary the techniques of fund-raising (mail solicitation, phone calls, personal contact) but be sure to ask repeatedly.

Be sure to keep records of those who contribute and be sure to ask them to give again.

Never give your list of donors away. Lists are power. (If some other group asks them for money, the persons on your list may give to them and not to you next time.)

Be sure to thank people—in person, if possible, and in writing.

People expect to be asked to give money and most people don't give unless you ask. Don't be shy. If you believe in your cause/your organization, then you should be asking for support and contributions of money.

---

responses are received, the name and address of each donor should be recorded in a file so each can be contacted again the following year.

It is often helpful to include suggested donations on your return enclosure. Analyze the state's economy to determine a sum. The PAC should be bold. The donations will eventually result in better health care for all as well as a better life for nurses.

Sale of Merchandise

A logo design or slogan can be printed on almost anything, from T-shirts to tote bags. It is possible to buy at a bulk rate and sell at a higher price. The profit represents a donation to the PAC. This can be a high-risk business. A realistic assessment must be made of how many items can be sold, and how they will be sold. An advertisement offering an item for sale could be placed in the state association's newsletter, or the item can be given as a premium to nurses who make a large donation to the direct mail campaign. The items may be sold at SNA meetings and conventions. Before getting into merchandising, all the ramifications should be considered. It's important to consider the initial cost of the merchandise, the advertising expenses, cost of shipping, storage, and distribution.

Special Events

Special events are fun and can provide visibility and supplementary funds for the PAC. Again, long-term planning is essential to ensure a smoothly run event.

Events may be built around a special appearance by a person who will attract a crowd, a benefit performance where an amount is added to the cost of the ticket for the donation, or a group activity. The latter can include auctions, house tours, garage sales, walks, or marathons. It must be remembered that money can only be solicited from association members, not the public-at-large.

As with merchandising, the PAC can run financial risk by guaranteeing a certain number of participants for an event (the group must pay whether the people show up or not).

Personal Solicitation

The most effective way to raise money is to ask for it. It costs little and has a high return. The most important factor in personal solicitation is a group of trained volunteers who believe in what they are doing.

Many people will say that they will do anything but ask someone for money. It is difficult for some people to do. They key is to make sure solicitors have a full understanding of what they are doing and why. A training session is essential.

Personal solicitation can be done in several different ways. The SNA membership list can be broken down into local calling areas and solicitors can spend a specific number of hours on the phone. It is always important that volunteers know in advance what is expected of them and how many hours their task will take. Personal solicitation is often used to follow up on a direct mail campaign. If that is the case, make sure that the names of nurses who have responded by mail are removed from the solicitor's telephone list.

Another follow-up to direct mail is solicitation of nurses at a specific location. Since many nurses are employed in central locations, such as hospitals or clinics, solicitors can be located in each workplace to approach fellow nurses. Care should be taken that solicitation is done methodically rather than randomly. Lists of nurses should be provided so donors' names can be checked off.

A special approach may be taken with nurses in a position to give more than an average contribution. Once such nurses have been identified, the solicitor should visit that nurse at home or over lunch or dinner. The solicitor should describe the PAC's program, how the money is spent, and results to date. A specific amount should be asked for.

A board and/or staff person should be responsible for planning the total fund-raising program each year. In fund-raising, the more methodical the planning, the more satisfactory the results. The real source of income should be direct mail and personal solicitation. Merchandise money is that extra bit, as are dollars gained from special events.

PAC POWER

In June, 1984, the ANA House of Delegates voted to promote the selection of a woman vice-presidential nominee who would endorse ANA's National Nursing Agenda. Later that summer, after Geraldine Ferraro was nominated by the Democrats, the ANA Board voted to endorse the Mondale-Ferraro ticket. While this proved to be a controversial decision (see the Case Study on p 501 for an account of the ANA Board endorsement), the 1985 House of Delegates authorized the association to make future presidential endorsements via N-CAP. The endorsement procedure will undoubtedly involve the organization of extensive grass roots campaign activities for nurses.

Political clout, translated into increased activity through N-CAP and the 41 state political action committees, is being acknowledged by nurses and politicians. Nurses are demonstrating their willingness to accept responsibility as well as accountability for making health care more accessible. Nurses are monitoring the scene, seeking, and winning appointive and elective positions by targeting offices and promoting nurse candidates to fill them. Nurses are joining the political network, working with coalitions, recognizing the importance of partisan involvement, and paying their dues to work their way up—precinct committeeperson, county organization, convention delegate, officeholder.

All of this translates into nurses taking positions as change agents, as political activists, and political strategists. More than ever before, nurses influence the reordering of health priorities, the establishment of political platform planks, and the allocation of government monies. Nurses provide a dynamic voice in decision making at all levels, local, state, and national, using skills learned through their involvement in political action. It takes informed, skillful, articulate nurses to participate in the formulation of policies and laws that have traditionally been developed by lawyers, sociologists, economists, educators, and politicians. Nurses no longer hold back and keep their "proper place." Today nurses are finding new places and new opportunities to demonstrate their knowledge and the strength of their numbers. Nurses are accepting that politics is not a spectator sport. As this book demonstrates, nurses everywhere have made a conscious decision to get politically active, and they are making a difference.

THE FUTURE OF PACS

The proliferation of PACs continues, and one Washington politician has said that no bill to limit PACs will pass the Congress in the forseeable future. While many individuals and some organizations, like Common Cause, believe that there should be a limit to the amount of money a PAC can raise, the Supreme Court has upheld the right of PACs to raise unlimited funds.

Consider the following figures as of September 1984:

• Funds raised by 4,243 PACs: $195.3 million

- Funds contributed to candidates: $50.7 million. (The remaining $144.6 million is the cost of raising the money given to candidates.)
- The top fund-raising PAC in 1984, the National Conservative PAC, raised $16 million
- N-CAP raised and gave candidates $297,000; ANA is permitted by law to pay for administrative costs.

It is clear that if nursing's influence is to grow, its use of political action committees at the local, state, and national levels must be expanded. If every nurse in this country gave $1 to N-CAP, what a difference it would make in nursing's ability to support worthy candidates for Congress.

Running for office is expensive, and those who are not wealthy have a difficult time raising funds. Many refer to the Senate as the "House of Lords," because most senators are men and a majority use their personal wealth and access to sources of funds, PACs primarily, to get elected.

Women and minorities continue to be underrepresented in all legislative bodies. The fact that only 22 of 468 representatives in Congress are women is a disgrace. This circumstance will not be changed by individuals working alone; it will most likely occur as a result of group initiatives. A belief in the value of collective action, through PACs, may motivate more individuals to work together to alter the representation in the legislatures of our country. Nurses can and should be in the vanguard of such a movement. The means to take action, political action committees for nurses, are in place. Have you contributed to N-CAP and your state nurses' PAC recently? If not, why not?

An Idea Is Born: The Beginning of Nursing PACs

Nancy West, RN, MSN

In the early 1970s, things were not going well for nursing on the federal or state level. The veto of the Nurse Practice Act (NPA) in New York State and difficulties in getting the federal Nurse Training Act passed had caused frustration among nursing professionals. Many nursing leaders had been lobbying, but passage of legislation to promote the profession of nursing seemed at a standstill.

Many nurses wondered why their professional organizations (American Nurses' Association [ANA], National League for Nursing [NLN], American Association of Colleges of Nursing [AACN]) could not seem to get things moving legislatively; why a million nurses in a democratic country had no say, no power in the health care system, the workplace, the state and federal governments.

Two nurses, Rachel Rotkovitch, then Director of Nursing at Long Island Jewish

Hospital, and June Rothberg, Dean of Adelphi University School of Nursing, began to discuss what they could do, who could help, who the local active and savvy RNs were, and where they could go to develop new approaches for nursing's problems. If lobbying wasn't working, how else could nursing gain clout to influence executive and legislative decision making?

They both agreed to get a group of people together to think of new solutions to nursing's lack of power. From their first conversation came the idea for a meeting of a select group of nurses representing nursing education and nursing service. Only later would Rotkovitch and Rothberg realize how important that first phone conversation would become to the future of the profession of nursing.

Many readers will identify with the frustration these two leaders felt. An important and recurring theme in the history of political action in nursing at this time is that the frustration experienced by nursing leaders led to action.

THE FIRST MEETING

On July 10–11, 1971, a small group of nurses, primarily from the Long Island area of New York, met at the Tappan Zee Inn in Nyack, New York. The first meeting was held away from home to allow the group freedom from the interruptions of phone, work, and family responsibilities. During that weekend, the nurses concentrated on the question of why, in spite of nursing's huge number of professionals, the profession continued to have little power or influence.

They discussed the notion of acquiring clout by establishing the political power of a professional group. This avenue was being explored by physicians and other health care professionals. In fact, other professional organizations were forming political action committees (PACs) that year. Lobbying by special interest groups had also seen a tremendous increase. The strong, positive influence of the women's movement was present as the group began to recognize that to get power, nursing had to move into the political arena and organize the clout inherent in its numbers.

The group agreed to continue meeting. They spoke of influencing the upcoming 1972 elections, of mobilizing the nursing community, and of educating nurses for action in the political arena. Several months later, the group crystallized these ideas into the formation of a political action committee for nursing. There was, as yet, no organized political action within nursing.

EARLY COLLABORATION WITH ORGANIZED NURSING

At the second meeting in October 1971, at Adelphi University, New York, the group invited Veronica Driscoll and Cathryne Welch of the New York State Nurse's Association (NYSNA) to attend. The group recognized the importance of working with the professional organization for nursing and used this meeting to brief the guests on their purpose: To make nursing a viable force in changing the health care delivery system. The group decided to organize formally and incorporate as a separate organization from the ANA and the state nursing association (SNA). The new organization based on their ideas would be called "Nurses for Political Action (NPA)." The group hoped that the new organization would be viewed as the political action arm of professional nursing organizations.

Also from this meeting came some concrete ideas for early action:

- to campaign against legislators seeking reelection who didn't support the state Nurse Practice Act to demonstrate political power
- to do a statewide (or nationwide) mailing to RNs to gain interest and financial support for NPA
- to contact Senator Edward Kennedy (D-Mass) to offer nursing's support for national health insurance
- to consider supporting the campaign of a woman running for lieutenant governor in the state of New York
- to solicit support of NYSNA members at the fall convention
- to contact nursing publications to get publicity for NPA
- to contact student nursing organizations.

SPONSORSHIP OF NPA: A SYMBOL OF COMMITMENT

Organizational minutes reflect that in November, 1971, the new organization received its first contribution of $10 from R. DeVaney of Long Island City, New York. While interest in NPA and small contributions continued, the group recognized the need to put together seed money to hire a public relations firm to do nationwide promotion for the organization.

The most outstanding symbol of the commitment of the members of the new NPA was their willingness to become early sponsors of the organization. The minutes of the January 4, 1972 meeting read: "The group was polled as to their willingness to each loan NPA $1,000 apiece; money to be repaid when and if contributions exceeded first year's operating expenses; to be repaid without interest." Something magical happened at that meeting. These committed, professional nurses stated, one by one, that they were willing to contribute $1,000. Not only were they each contributing their name, their time, and tremendous energy to creating NPA, but they were also willing to loan the money without any guarantee that this loan would ever be repaid.

In February, 1972, the bank account of NPA had had $400; in less than two months, the account had a balance of $5,902.50. Contributions from nonnurse professional colleagues came in the form of money and in-kind work, such as legal services and consulting. At the same meeting, each member pledged to solicit funds from other nurses, nursing organizations, and interested lay people.

THE KICK-OFF

The money raised or donated by the early sponsors was used to do a 10,000-piece nationwide mailing. This mailing was an attempt to reach out to the grass roots level of nurses—staff nurses and head nurses. NPA board members felt that this effort was essential to build a strong organization composed of more than the already identified nursing leaders. In fact, the early letterhead of the organization included few nationally known nursing leaders, and the minutes express concern that the "rank and file nurse would not necessarily be interested in membership in an organization that was sponsored by well-known national names in the field of nursing."

Unfortunately, the response to the first mailing was a disaster. NPA received a return of less than one-half of one percent on the 10,000 pieces mailed out.

Meanwhile, by September, 1972, NPA membership had grown to 136. Also, an additional 15,000 pieces of literature about NPA had been distributed by NPA members.

THE POLITICAL ACTION PROCESS BEGINS

In July, 1972, just one year after the idea of political action for nursing had been born, the NPA subcommittee for political planning had their first meeting. Members discussed and recommended to the NPA board ways to implement goals and objectives of NPA through political action. Most importantly, the subcommittee noted the importance of bipartisan support of candidates. Support should be based on favorable positions on issues of importance to nursing and health care consumers. The endorsement of candidates (letters of support and/or contributions to campaigns) began in 1972.

NPA IN THE NEWS

The first press release about NPA appeared about the same time, informing politicians of the existence of NPA. The July, 1972 press release was sent to newspapers and magazines, all U.S. senators and congresspersons, President Nixon, all governors, and state nurses' associations and their local districts.

As a result of the press release, news items about NPA began to appear:

* *RN* magazine had a paragraph on the formation of NPA in its June, 1972 issue.
* *MS* magazine had a news item in the August, 1972 issue, and NPA received 50 letters in response.
* In August, the *Amarillo* (Texas) *Globe-Times* did a feature article about Martha Ann Bobbitt (one of the 14 nationwide advisors/sponsors to NPA). It was entitled: "City Woman Thinks Nurses Deserve Greater Policy Role."
* Also in August, the *American Medical News*, published by the American Medical Association, had a news item, "Nurses Form Political Action Group."
* The September *Nursing Outlook* mentioned the formation of NPA in its news section.

- Editor Dorothy Kelly wrote an editorial about NPA in the September, 1972 *Supervisor Nurse.*

NPA AND ANA COLLABORATION BEGINS

As early as January, 1972, the NPA minutes reflected the importance of NPA working as the political action "arm" of the professional nursing organization. In September, 1972, a formal motion was made that NPA "establish a formal liaison with ANA. We wish to be put on record that we want to complement and supplement ANA's legislative activities," the minutes stated. The motion was carried unanimously.

While pressure for this close affiliation came from across the nation, the October minutes of NPA reported that "a letter from ANA was sent to the state associations indicating that they were not to support NPA until ANA finds out what they are about. It appears that ANA feels we are stepping on their toes in the matter of health legislation and other political issues such as institutional licensures, etc." The board of NPA decided that two representatives, June Rothberg and Marjorie Stanton, should "go to Kansas City and attempt to establish a working relationship between ANA and NPA." In November, 1972, two letters arrived from ANA: one from Rosamond Gabrielson, ANA president, and one from Eileen Jacobi, ANA executive director. A meeting was finally agreed upon.

The meeting was held on January 17, 1973, in New York City. Gabrielson, Jacobi, and Constance Holloran, head of the ANA Washington Office, represented ANA, and Stanton, Rothberg, Rotkovitch, Fahy, and Doyle represented NPA. The minutes reflect ANA's concern that there be a clear division of ANA and NPA legislative activities. ANA agreed, however, to recognize NPA as "an organization which could enhance positions taken by ANA which affect health care delivery and nursing"; and that "a viable and visible political arm for the ANA was highly desirable." A group of two representatives from each organization was formed to "pursue strategies for mutually agreeable organizing effort." That group met the following month at ANA Washington Office in hopes that a "political arm" for ANA could be presented to the House of Delegates at the ANA Convention in 1974.

On September 6, 1973, the ad hoc committee of the ANA Board of Directors met at the Kansas City headquarters. Representatives from the Washington, Colorado, and California state nurses' associations and from states with political action arms served as resources. This group, chaired by Board member Rebecca Culpepper, reported to the ANA Board of Directors at their September 29th meeting, and the following recommendations were accepted:

Recommendation 1:

That ANA establish a carefully structured nonpartisan political action unit. It will be a voluntary, unincorporated nonprofit organization of nurses and others. The policies, positions, and platform of the ANA will guide the actions of the PAC. It will function in areas of political activity not open to ANA. The national unit will be independent but work in a close cooperative relationship with state and local nursing political action units.

The purposes of the PAC will be:

- To educate nurses and others on the relevant political issues
- To assist nurses and others in organizing for effective action in the political arena and in carrying out their civic responsibilities
- To raise funds and make contributions to candidates for public office who have demonstrated or indicated supportive positions on the issues of importance to nurses and health care

Recommendation 2:

That bylaws for the Political Action Unit provide for up to fifty percent of its board of trustees to be named by the ANA Board of Directors. There should be provision for limitation of terms of office, of officers and trustees. A method(s) for selecting trustees not appointed by ANA must be designated.

Recommendation 3:

That ANA provide budget support for the Political Action Unit. It is anticipated that minimal costs for the initial year of operation would be $50,000. A projected five-year minimal cost is $350,000. This budget assumes utilizing the Washington Office of ANA to the extent possible under federation law. It is recommended that the staff for the PAC work closely with ANA in the development of its activities.

The closing statement of the ad hoc committee report was as follows:

In publicizing any action taken to establish a political action unit, recognition should be given to Nurses for Political Action and existing state political action groups. NPA was instrumental in focusing ANA's attention on the need for a national political action program. State nursing groups have proven the feasibility of state and local units. All organized political action groups of nurses should be encouraged to cooperate with the (political action committee).

The first meeting of the newly constituted political action committee was held on May 4, 1974, in Chicago. The following persons were appointed to the Board of Trustees representing both organizations. Appointed by NPA were Marjorie Stanton, June Rothberg, and Martha Bobbitt Schrock. Appointed by the ANA and representing the Board of Directors were Rebecca Culpepper, Dolores Little, and Ethelrine Shaw. ANA then named three at-large members, JoAnn Ashley, Roy Campbell, and Barbara Curtis. The National Federation of Licensed Practical Nurses named Mary Runnels, and the National Student Nurses' Association named Kenneth Dellefield. Bylaws, a logo, and a name were decided. Valerie Fleischhakker was named the first executive director. The formation of N-CAP was announced at the June 1974 ANA Convention. The 1985 ANA House of Delegates voted to change the name of N-CAP to ANA-PAC by 1986.

NPA CELEBRATES AND PLANS TO DISBAND

NPA celebrated its third birthday with a dinner party given by the Board. Conversation centered around the organization's success and the development of a phase-out for NPA, which was to disband as the national PAC for nursing.

The final NPA Board of Directors meeting was held January 26, 1976, in Plainview, New York. The Board decided to place all minutes and data of historical importance from the development of the idea of and the organization for political action for nursing in the Nursing Archives of Boston University. At this time, NPA had 861 members (with all states represented) and twenty-three functioning regional units in eleven states.

From this review of the early history of political action in nursing, some outstanding strengths of the profession of nursing emerge. First, frustration led to action rather than acceptance of the status quo. Nurses looked for new solutions to old problems. The creativity and determination of the founding nurses of the NPA were backed up by commitments of time, energy, and money. The nurses who sponsored the idea and the organization were risk-takers, stepping out of the mainstream of nursing at a time when nursing organizations were facing an identity struggle. They remained determined in spite of the disappointment of their first mailing and the frustration of over a year's worth of meetings before the beginning of collaboration with the ANA. Fewer than fifteen years have passed since the first meeting of NPA. Although the first chapter in the history of political action has been written, its future will be written by the readers of this book—by those willing to make the same commitment to the profession of nursing made by the nurses who founded NPA and N-CAP.

Organizing a Nursing PAC

Patricia A. Eberle, RN, PhD

Nursing political action committees (PACs) have been formed in forty-one states. Considerable time and effort are required to organize a PAC, and the work is usually accomplished by a small group of dedicated nurse political advocates. It is often easier for organizers to gather volunteers, support, and interest in a PAC if a powerful nursing-related issue is the focus. People are more likely to rally around an identifiable cause, and there are many political issues that will arouse nurses' interest and support. First, the PAC organizers must establish the PAC and its goals, preferably in conjunction with the existing state nurses' association (SNA).

A PAC must have a strong organizational base to administer its goals and purposes. This section provides some guidelines, examples, and resources that should be helpful to nurses who wish to start a state PAC or strengthen an existing PAC.

Nurses who wish to endorse and support local candidates (mayor, town council, etc.) are encouraged to organize a "nurses for _____" group. This should be separate from the state PAC, which regularly endorses candidates in state elections. Those who wish to support local candidates are urged to use the guidelines outlined for PACs and to consult their local election board about requirements for reporting on fundraising and other political activities on the local level.

ORGANIZING A NURSING PAC

1. Form a Steering Committee
   - Investigate state laws governing PACs
   - Contact state nurses' associations with rationale for state PAC formation
   - Make policy decisions as to monetary support for state and local candidates
   - Plan membership/contribution recruitment strategies prior to first meeting

2. Complete the Organizational Structure
   - Selection of officers
   - Approval of bylaws or memorandum of understanding
   - Identification of possible committees

3. Form PAC Committees
   - Membership/contributors committee
   - Fundraising committee
   - Candidate screening committee
   - Strategy planning committee
   - Political education committee
   - Talent bank

FORM A STEERING COMMITTEE

There are basically two approaches nurses can take to establish a nursing PAC within their state. Under the auspices of the state nurses' association board of directors or the committee/commission on legislation, a group of interested nurses can draw up the rationale for creating a PAC. If no one from the SNA takes the initiative, an independent group of nurses can create a steering committee to promote the establishment of a state PAC. One of the committee's basic goals will be to get the SNA to embrace the concept of a PAC. There are several preliminary organizational tasks.

Investigate state laws governing PACs. These laws vary from state to state and must be understood before the group goes any further. The secretary of state's office or the election commission has this information.

Determine feasibility of the PAC being associated with the SNA. The PAC should have an open relationship with the SNA, with access to monetary support and membership and administrative services. A report should be made to the SNA board of directors that includes a preliminary budget reflecting start-up costs such as secretarial services, letterhead stationery, a brochure or leaflet, postage, and printing; and a statement of rationale with a resolution that can be acted upon by the board of directors or forwarded to the SNA house of delegates for action. If the SNA decides not to accept the PAC as the official political action committee, the group may opt to have a freestanding PAC. Although this is not recommended, there are several such PACs in existence.

Make decisions regarding monetary support for state and federal candidates.
N-CAP, the Nurses Coalition for Action in Politics, focuses its support on the U.S. Senate and House races, with input from the SNAs and the PACs. For a variety of reasons, state PACs should anticipate focusing their scarce resources on state and local races, leaving the federal election support to N-CAP.

Plan public relations campaigns to promote PAC acceptance.   The steering committee should be responsible for the initial recruitment of members/contributors. A good technique is to hold the kick-off meeting in conjunction with an SNA convention or program, distributing membership/contribution forms and other appropriate information. Invite a well-known public figure to speak about a popular nursing issue, and follow up with an informal meeting to recruit additional persons for the basic organizational structure. Encourage interested persons to submit their names for appointment to committees. Inform the attendees when they can next expect to hear from you. It is important to explain that a PAC differs from most organizations in that a primary goal is fund-raising. Another goal, the development of a cadre of volunteers who can meet a variety of campaign needs, needs to be discussed.

COMPLETE THE PAC ORGANIZATIONAL STRUCTURE

The first item of business at the organizational meeting should be the selection of a chairman and a secretary/treasurer. These positions are required by law, and the PAC is not permitted to receive contributions or make expenditures when there is a vacancy in either office. In addition, bylaws or a memorandum of organization should be approved and submitted to the SNA board of directors for review.

FORM PAC COMMITTEES

The PAC will decide on the committees needed and how to organize them. The following are suggestions for committees and guidelines for their structure and purpose.

Membership/Contributors Committee

Recruitment of Members/Contributors.   One of the most important reasons for nurses' political clout is the large number who vote. N-CAP states that if just ten percent of all nurses could be mobilized into a political organization, they would be one of the strongest political forces in the nation. A minimal political contribution and a commitment to volunteer time to a political cause are appropriate actions for money-conscious nurses.

Soliciting Contributions.   Contributions should be solicited, if state law permits, from various nursing organizations and nursing education groups.

Development of a Contributor File.   Records must be kept of all those who contribute over the amount established by law. Included in this file should be information from the initial application: name, address, phone number, place of employment, position, political party affiliation, and election district in which the nurse resides. A creative way to handle this data would be to recruit someone to code the application for computer analysis. Software programs are available.

Fund-raising Committee

This committee will decide what method will bring in the highest level of contributions with the smallest expenditure. Talk with persons in the community who have run successful fund-raising campaigns. Phone banks are successful in raising money quickly for candidates but take considerable organization. The fund-raising committee should decide what method will work best given their people and resources. (For additional fund-raising tips, see Curtis and West in this chapter.)

Candidate Screening Committee

Establish criteria for endorsing candidates prior to interviewing any candidate. N-CAP can provide guidelines. The best screening technique is a personal interview. Candidates receive many questionnaires in the mail and may not respond to a mail survey. A face-to-face interview gives PAC members the opportunity to introduce the SNA and PAC organizations to the candidate and to obtain more complete responses. The interview is also a forum to educate candidates about nursing issues. Phone interviews are less time-consuming, but are not as effective.

Maintain a file of all legislators and political officeholders of interest to the PAC. Include as much information as possible on each elected official, such as a summary of interviews with PAC members, voting records, newspaper clippings, and comments. Other PACs, such as the National Organization of Women, the Women's Political Caucus, labor groups, and teachers are all resources to supplement your data.

Create a list of officials to target. These are people known for their lack of support for nursing issues. If efforts to make them a friend of nursing are unsuccessful, the PAC may decide to support their opponent at election time.

Strategy Planning Committee

Plan strategies to make nurses visible in a campaign. Although donations of money are effective, many nursing PACs cannot compete with the contributions of larger and better financed PACs. The usual volunteer campaign work includes telephone calling, envelope stuffing, literature distribution, and door-to-door canvassing. Nurses have creative skills to offer the politician. The following activities might be considered:

Blood Pressure Screening Clinics.   Nurses can sponsor blood pressure clinics on behalf of the PAC-endorsed candidates at political functions, neighborhood events, county assemblies, and state conventions.

Health Fairs.   Plan a fair for a shopping center, large apartment complex, or any central location that will attract a large number of people. Staff it with nurse clinicians, nurse practitioners, and specialists. Have the candidate attend, and use a preprinted form with the candidate's information to record the blood pressure reading or other screening data.

Political Education Committee

Educate nurses about the political process. This important committee can sponsor workshops, speak to nursing groups, hand out information sheets on the political process, register nurses and others to vote, and work on "get out the vote" campaigns. Any number of activities can be planned to help nurses become more knowledgeable about the political process.

Talent Bank

Work to get nurses appointed to boards and commissions. Many of these positions are unpaid, but they can give nurses a visible and powerful means to effect public policy and regulation. A talent bank can find out about future vacancies and the requirements for candidates to be appointed or elected. They can publicize these vacancies and nominate nurses to be considered for appointment.

Organizing a Regional Unit

Karen Duffy-Durnin, RNC, MS

In October, 1981, the annual New York State Nurses' Association convention was held in Rochester, New York. At the convention, the New York State Nurses for Political Action (NYS-NPA) presented a program on political action, with Pamela Maraldo, then Director of Public Policy, National League for Nursing, as the keynote speaker. As I listened to the speaker call for political participation by all nurses to assure a voice in the health policy arena, I observed an instant change in the atmosphere. Nurses were interested in political action; the excitement was apparent. A successful fund-raising effort and a dramatic display of enthusiasm followed.

WHY ORGANIZE?

At this meeting I became involved with the NYS-NPA. I discussed with the board the possibility of identifying Rochester as a regional unit. The NYS-NPA board wanted to increase participation and representation across the state through the establishment of regional units.

Establishment of Regional Units—Why?

The establishment of regional units promotes dialogue between nurses in diverse settings and circumstances. Sharing common and unique concerns provides the nurses with a profile of the condition of nursing in their state. Regional units facilitate participation statewide and promote geographic representation.

Nurses need a vehicle whereby they may affect political outcomes regionally and statewide. Joining the political action committee's regional unit provides nurses with the opportunity to collectively share political skills and strategies at their home base. Politically active nurses joining the unit enhance the influence of nursing in state politics.

To establish a regional unit, we needed a regional coordinator. I spoke with colleagues in the Rochester area about establishing a regional unit, and the idea was favorably received. I assumed the position of regional coordinator, supported by colleagues who were ready to help organize.

Existing Nursing Networks—Resources to Mobilize

We had carefully analyzed our region's need for political action before deciding to establish a regional unit. A variety of nursing groups, such as the district nurses' association legislative committee and a university-based legislation committee, were involved in legislative affairs in the region. However, no group was organizing nurses to participate in political campaigns. I believed a regional unit of NYS-NPA would increase political participation by nurses in a region rich in nursing resources.

I was involved with these other groups, as were many of my nursing colleagues. These colleagues helped me establish contacts with interested nurses. The nursing groups spread the word about the regional unit and provided information about possible members.

Active Nurse Involvement—Impact on the Future

Nurses from a variety of settings participated in the first organizational meetings. The names of nurses interested in political action had been obtained at the annual state nurses' association convention and through informal referrals. Meeting announcements had been sent out for the first meeting. In addition, nurses I worked with or had attended graduate school with who expressed interest in political action received mailings.

The agenda of the first meeting focused on the following: (1) a general overview of the history and purpose of NYS-NPA; (2) discussion of ways the organization could establish coalitions with other local women's groups; (3) the need for fundraising; and (4) the importance of educating members about political action so they could educate others. The second meeting featured two board members of NYS-NPA, and the agenda was as follows: (1) background information; (2) future goals; (3) long-range plans; (4) ad hoc groups; (5) program planning; and (6) general discussion.

Throughout the initial months of organizing, the momentum increased. As we met and exchanged ideas for an agenda for action, we knew we had the numbers, if mobilized, to make significant strides in the upcoming elections. This challenged us and gave us the incentive to continue working.

HOW TO ORGANIZE

Recognition of Obstacles to Organizing

The numerous obstacles one encounters when organizing a regional unit may not be immediately apparent. During the initial stages, three common obstacles from nurses themselves may be encountered: a lack of knowledge about politics; apathy; and time constraints. To overcome the obstacles nurses express, the regional coordinator should clearly outline all roles and responsibilities.

Other possible obstacles are: disapproval of political action by small or sometimes large groups of nurses; existing groups' fear that the political action committee will erode their power base as "the" nursing organization; and pressure from individuals' employers not to belong to political action groups. One way to alleviate these fears is to provide potential members with a clear understanding of the history and goals of the political action committee.

Membership

Securing members is a critical element of organizing a regional unit. Previously, I discussed networking. Contacting existing groups will put the regional coordinator in touch with increased numbers of nurses. One strategy I employed was to print an update on the regional unit's progress in the SNA district newsletter. In the update, I encouraged anyone interested to contact me. The one-to-one recruiting approach is also effective. It may be possible to get membership lists from state political action committees and other nursing organizations.

Meetings

The frequency of meetings should be established from the beginning. Initially, we held many meetings to organize the group, get to know one another, and clarify our goals. Without a regularly established meeting date we met less frequently, until right around election time when we focused on endorsements. (Recommendations for endorsement of candidates for state office from our region were sent to the NYS-NPA endorsement chair.) Following the elections, many months passed without a meeting. This had a devastating effect on the group and resulted in the loss of a few members and the need to reorganize and recruit. A year-long schedule could have kept the group focused and involved.

During the months or years when no election preparation is required, there are a number of ways the regional unit can remain active. Linking up with the legislative committee of the region's district nursing association is valuable. The link or exchange of information between the two committees can be ongoing. Frequently, the same nurses serve on both the district legislative committee and the regional or state PAC boards or committees.

We found that we did not need large numbers of people to get the work done. However, the unit needs an extensive network of area nurses to mobilize during campaigns.

Publicity—Effective Use of Media

We primarily sought publicity for our regional unit through local newspapers. We announced meetings in the local papers. During election time, the NYS-NPA endorsement of a local candidate for state office was publicized only once, even though we sought publicity from radio, television, and the newspapers. The media decides what to publish, but this fact should not dissuade you from seeking publicity. Developing contacts with the media is an important, ongoing effort. (See Appendix C.)

Relationship of Regional Unit with NYS-NPA Board

The regional unit stays in constant contact with the board of NYS-NPA. This assures that the board is kept up-to-date regarding the region's progress. Selection of candidates for endorsements is one of the primary goals of NYS-NPA. Therefore, the regional units must frequently apprise the board about candidates for state office in their regions.

The regional coordinator collaborates with the board to develop policies for the regional unit's approach to fundraising, endorsements, and overall organization. Support from the NYS-NPA chair is always available to the regional coordinator. This is one of the most positive features of the organization.

POLITICAL OUTCOMES—IMPACT OF THE REGIONAL UNIT

Mobilizing for a Special Election

The Rochester Regional Unit had an exciting opportunity to participate in a campaign less than one year after the group was organized. In April, 1982, a special election was held to fill a vacancy in a state senate seat. The senate race was between two candidates, William Steinfeldt and Andrew Virgilio. As a past member of the New York State Legislature, Virgilio had a long history of support for nursing. This was a prime opportunity for our regional unit to participate in an election.

Members of the regional unit reviewed Virgilio's record and agreed that he deserved NYS-NPA endorsement. Then two representatives of the group met with his opponent. Following the meeting with Mr. Steinfeldt, the group decided to recommend Mr. Virgilio's endorsement to NYS-NPA.

We gave the NYS-NPA board information on both candidates, with our recommendation for endorsement of Virgilio. The board approved the endorsement and allocated a financial contribution.

This was our first endorsement, and we looked forward to presenting Virgilio with the check. Several members of the regional unit were sent to do this. We had informed the media of the endorsement and expected them to attend and cover the story. Al-

Guidelines for Organizing a Regional Unit

1. Organize the regional unit in response to an identified need and in cooperation with the board of your state PAC.
2. Assess political climate of the region by reviewing voting patterns and profiles of current office holders.
3. Determine the total number of nurses in the community by obtaining information from state and local agencies and nursing organizations.
4. Make lists of existing nursing groups and "contact" people. Ask to speak at their meetings; use their mailing lists or network trees; publicize meetings in their newsletters; cosponsor programs on political action for nurses and help them with voter registration drives.
5. Identify nonnursing organizations within the region that influence the political climate, exchange information, and sponsor programs jointly.
6. Develop a network file of interested nurses who can be contacted when assistance is needed.
7. Establish committees for publicity, fundraising, membership, media contacts, and letter writing.
8. Develop a plan for meetings and activities for the year.
9. Hold monthly or bimonthly meetings.
10. Maintain records of candidates seeking reelection to state assembly and senate.

though the cameras didn't show up, the local paper wrote a paragraph on our endorsement. Virgilio lost the election in April by fewer than 600 votes, out of 36,000 cast.

Nurses who wish to endorse and support local candidates are encouraged to organize a "nurses for _____" group. This should be separate from the state PAC, which regularly endorses candidates in state elections. Those who wish to support local candidates are urged to use the guidelines outlined for regional units and to consult their local election board about requirements for reporting on fund-raising and other political activities.

Lessons Learned—Evaluation of Outcomes

The special election in April of 1982 taught our regional unit a few important lessons. We had to support a candidate early enough in the race to make a difference. Many more nurses could have worked on the campaign if we had become involved sooner. When an endorsement is made, it should be far enough in advance to not be overlooked by the media during hectic, last-minute campaign coverage. Nurses might have made a difference in the outcome had we been available earlier to hand out information, go door-to-door, get nurses registered, and contact nurses by phone.

Role of the Regional Unit in a General Election

Having learned these lessons, in November, 1982, the regional unit got involved in the campaigns of two women running for the state legislature. This time, we made our plans well in advance of the elections. We sought an endorsement from the NYS-NPA board for incumbent Pinny Cooke of the 132nd Assembly District and for challenger Louise Slaughter of the 130th. Both endorsements were approved, and we began to mobilize our strength.

Pinny Cooke had been known by nurses in the region for quite some time. The regional unit had received a request from her staff for nurses to distribute literature at local shopping centers. The regional unit contacted many nurses and asked for help.

In the 130th Assembly District, the incumbent had met several regional nurses on a variety of occasions, when they attempted, to little avail, to get his support for legislation affecting nursing. Following the endorsement of his opponent, Slaughter, members of the regional unit who lived within her district were asked to call friends, co-workers, and relatives to seek support.

Both Cooke and Slaughter were victorious. Unlike the previous election, nurses got to work early to secure additional support and votes for the candidates. Slaughter's win was particularly sweet for our regional unit, because she had not been the frontrunner. The campaign work organized by the regional unit of NYS-NPA paid off.

INDIVIDUAL AND COLLECTIVE RESPONSIBILITIES

To understand the need for strategic planning in organizing for political purposes, we must involve ourselves in the existing political groups or committees in our regions. Nonnursing networks of support are essential to strengthen nursing's image and influence in the political arena.

Reaching Out

The regional coordinator can help other regions to organize. When someone requests assistance in organizing an area, the regional coordinator should make plans to meet with that region on a number of occasions.

For example, such a request was made by a group of nurses in Ithaca, New York. The nurses were aware of the Rochester Regional Unit and asked the coordinator to join them for a meeting and share some ways to strengthen their group. During the meeting, organizational strategies were described and the nurses discussed whether they wanted to become a regional unit of NYS-NPA. As a result of this meeting, the regional coordinator for Rochester organized a follow-up meeting in Ithaca. Another board member of NYS-NPA joined Rochester's regional unit coordinator at that meeting and presented a morning workshop on political action.

The follow-up meeting was a success. Since that time, the nurses in Ithaca have agreed to join the NYS-NPA as a regional unit. As regional units form, more and more opportunities such as this one will evolve.

In another instance, a group of nurses from the state contacted the Rochester regional coordinator to discuss the possibility of sponsoring a meeting with interested nurses. After assessing the situation, it was found that the nurses were not seeking consultation on political action. The regional coordinator discussed the circumstances with the contact person and suggested that she contact the coordinator at another time, when the group was indeed interested. Often, nurses are seeking immediate solutions to institution-based problems and misinterpret the goals of NYS-NPA. The regional coordinator must clarify the purpose of NYS-NPA and make referrals to others for consultation.

Case Study
ANA Presidential Endorsement

Susan Harris, RN, BSN*

On September 18, 1984, the American Nurses' Association (ANA) held a press conference in Washington, DC, to announce that for the first time in its 88-year-history, the association was endorsing a presidential candidate. This decision was a historic one for the profession in a year that will be noted as the first time a woman was selected to be the vice-presidential candidate for a major political party. The decision to endorse a presidential candidate, however, was marked with anticipated controversy among nurses.

While some nurses viewed the endorsement as that next step in ANA's long history of political and legislative involvement, others took the view that this action was ill advised and carried too great a risk for the profession. Some questioned why the ANA Board of Directors made the endorsement when it appeared that there was much to risk and little to gain when the ticket it was endorsing—Walter Mondale and Geraldine Ferraro—was so far behind in the polls. Others believed that 1984 was too soon for ANA's involvement in executive-level politics, and that the association should have waited until 1988.

But, as the political campaigns took shape, it became apparent that 1988 would be too late to address health and social issues ignored in the 1984 campaign, such as nutrition programs for mothers and children, health and social programs for the elderly, unemployment, and poverty. One of the major concerns of the ANA is the health of the American people. As such, the association has a responsibility for leading efforts in any arena to address issues that affect health. While the political involvement of nurses has been evolving, the ANA presidential endorsement marked the profession's coming of age in the political arena by daring to take a stand for the nation's health.

Nurses: Visible in Politics

The issue of the presidential endorsement had been discussed several times throughout the 1982–1984 biennium. Early in 1983, the ANA political action committee, Nurses' Coalition for Action in Politics (N-CAP), brought forth proposals to the ANA board for presidential endorsement and a request for funds to implement an association-wide political campaign aimed at strengthening ANA's grass roots involvement. The N-CAP board believed that the political involvement of nurses in congressional campaigns was increasing and making a significant impact, and that this involvement must move on to the executive branch of government. N-CAP had also heard from many state nurses' associations that, since nurses' interest in politics was increasing, the associations needed ANA to assist them in bringing political action within the framework of the association. A majority of the state nurses' associations already had PACs with varying levels of activity. The N-CAP Board believed that the "Nurses: Visible in Politics" (N:VIP) proposal was a start in that direction.

*This paper is the author's interpretation of the ANA endorsement. It in no way represents the ANA Board of Directors or an official position of the ANA.

The N:VIP was a program to encourage ANA and state nurses' association members to contribute to N-CAP, to support candidates who were supportive of ANA's legislative priorities, and to educate nurses about political action through weekend workshops held across the country. The original proposal also included a call for the ANA board to endorse a presidential candidate. It also proposed a request for funding several positions for regional field organizers who would coordinate the ANA's grass roots support of the endorsed ticket.

The proposal initially ran into trouble when it was submitted to the financial committee. The ANA annual budget had already been adopted by the board. Since the N:VIP proposal called for a $100,000 budget, the finance committee was concerned about the fiscal implications of approving a project of this size that would fall outside of the approved association budget. The Committee sent the proposal to the board with the recommendation that the board disapprove it for procedural reasons.

At this time, members of the ANA board held mixed viewpoints on the subject of a presidential endorsement. While the process used by the N-CAP Board to bring this proposal forward seemed to be the first concern, discussion then moved to a debate over how the ANA was to be involved in grass roots political education and action as well as a presidential endorsement. The structure of the ANA had recently been changed to a modified federation model under which the states, rather than individual nurses, were the association's members. Thus, one concern voiced by members of the board was that the ANA's role in political action might also change. However, debate centered around the role of the association in presidential campaigns. Advocates for the N:VIP talked about political influence and the need for ANA to support candidates who share its concern for nursing and the nation's health. To not work to influence our country's highest leadership could keep the association from attaining its goals. While most board members agreed that the association's activity on the congressional level had been successful, the risks of endorsing a presidential candidate appeared to outweigh the benefits. The ANA board supported a revised N:VIP proposal that excluded the presidential endorsement and activities to support it.

The National Nursing Agenda

The discussion did point out the need for a working committee to assist the ANA board in managing the legislative direction of the association. Eunice Cole, president of the ANA, appointed a legislative committee composed of board members and cabinet chairs. The design of the committee would be kept fluid so the composition could be changed as the issues changed. The work of this committee was very detailed. It used existing goals and priorities of the association, resolutions passed by the house of delegates, and adopted policies. In addition, the chairs of the respective cabinets brought forth issues of concern to their constituents and identified trends for the committee's consideration as it formulated the legislative statement for the ANA. The committee's efforts culminated in the National Nursing Agenda, approved by both the ANA board of directors and the house of delegates.

With the approval of the agenda came the recognition of the need for the association to publicize it while promoting grass roots political activity. The ANA board authorized funding for circulation and promotion of the agenda, particularly in congressional campaigns where nurses were involved. It was also recommended that both the ANA president and the N-CAP chairperson be visible in these promotional activities and present the agenda to both political party conventions.

1984 ANA Convention

At the 1984 house of delegates in New Orleans, the association dealt with several reso- lutions that addressed a presidential endorsement, political action, and education. The resolutions were discussed at length at reference committee hearings. This committee reported out positions of support for the intent of these resolutions, but expressed con- fusion about the process by which they would be implemented. Strong support was ex- pressed for the resolution that called for the ANA to urge the major political parties to nominate a woman for vice-president. Subsequent motions were passed in the house that directed the ANA board to develop a process for endorsement by 1988, present the association's position on issues that were crucial to the nation's health to the major politi- cal parties, and support the nomination of a woman for vice-president.

California Nurses' Association's Proposal

After the ANA convention, the California Nurses' Association developed and submitted to the ANA board a proposal that brought a new dimension to the arguments in favor of the ANA making a presidential endorsement. The proposal outlined a comparison of the two major parties' platforms on health and the positions of the candidates on issues related to the National Nursing Agenda. While the ANA board expressed mixed inter- pretations on the intent of the house on whether a presidential endorsement could be made in 1984, a majority now supported endorsing a presidential candidate. The issue of propriety was again brought up, as was the fear of jeopardizing ANA's nonpartisan political stance. However, a factor crucial to the board's support of the endorsement was the overwhelming split on the issue between nurses of both political parties. One member polled her Republican nurse colleagues and found that most of them sup- ported the idea of the ANA endorsing a presidential candidate. Many board members argued that to continue to claim and legitimize the Association's role as a leader in health care, it must be willing to support, with action, those things that the association says it believes in. The timing was crucial. This time the risks outweighed the benefits if we failed to act.

The Fallout

Early returns indicate that while the endorsement has bolstered the position of the ANA in the external political world, the responses from within the profession have been mixed with surprise, excitement, and anger.

Those nurses already involved in congressional and the presidential campaigns were excited about the endorsement. It permitted them to identify themselves officially as part of the ANA. And, some state nurses' associations supported the endorsement, cit- ing their understanding of political realities and the importance of being visible during the elections.

Immediately following the endorsement, nurses across the country were invited to participate in local, state, and national political activities in an unprecedented fashion. Nurses were invited to briefing meetings with Mondale and Ferraro, their staff, and state party leaders. These nurses have continued to work with the state party leaders and undoubtedly will have greater access to and influence with the state leadership in the years ahead. In North Carolina, Michigan, Illinois, Pennsylvania, and other states, nurs- ing leaders participated in invitational meetings of small, select groups of women lead- ers in the state to discuss issues and devise strategies for the presidential and other important state and national campaigns. Press conferences held by nurses saw the presence of governors and other state leaders in an unprecedented fashion, as these leaders recognized that nurses were part of the political leadership of their states. In Texas, the state nurses' association was invited to give statements at a press conference called by the governor's wife and the state's political leaders. The president of another state nurses' association was invited to tea by Rosalyn Carter, the wife of former President Jimmy Carter and a political leader in her own right.

The endorsement also brought more visibility to the ANA through media coverage. The endorsement was publicized in the nation's leading newspapers. Further recognition was accorded the ANA when the paper on health it drafted, at the request of the Mondale-Ferraro campaign staff, became the official statement on health for the ticket.

Despite these favorable outcomes, some nurses and some state nurses' associations condemned the endorsement. The prime concern of those who opposed the ANA endorsement relates to the way in which the endorsement was made and the belief that the board violated the intent of the house of delegates. Some of those who attended the convention believe that the house told the board not to endorse before 1988, while others disagree with this interpretation. In addition, some are ignoring the fact that circumstances changed after the house of delegate's actions at the convention and that the board believed it was acting in the best interests of the association.

Furthermore, few speak to the real reason the board chose to make the endorsement; eg, nursing has largely been ignored by the Reagan administration, despite efforts by the association to work with the administration. It is the Reagan administration's negative impact on health care, the targeting of selected populations (such as the poor, single mothers, and the elderly) for cutbacks, the replacement of individuals on the National Labor Relations Board with antilabor members, and the failure to support and promote women's issues (such as equal pay for comparable worth) that caused the board to endorse the Mondale-Ferraro ticket.

Some nurses were also concerned that the endorsement would jeopardize the tax status of the ANA because they were unaware of the federal election laws. Federal law permits tax-exempt organizations to endorse federal candidates, although organizations may not make monetary campaign contributions.

A number of nurses believed that President Reagan's subsequent vetoes of the National Institute of Health Reorganization bill, which included a National Institute of Nursing, and the Health Professions Act, which included funding for nursing education, were due to the ANA's endorsement; however, it was known prior to the endorsement that he opposed both bills (which also included appropriations desired by other groups such as organized medicine) and was likely to veto them. Certainly, nurses who were appointed to governmental positions by the Reagan administration were distressed by the endorsement.

Of particular distress to some nurses who supported the endorsement were public disclaimers issued by other nursing organizations. These pronouncements only served to send a message to the public that the nursing community is still not cohesive and that nurses continue to air their disagreements in public.

The earliest recollections in ANA's history pointed out the need for nurses to be involved in political and legislative action. In 1908, Lavinia Dock wrote regarding support of women's suffrage: "To give moral support and endorsement takes no time; to feel intelligent sympathy costs no money." The professionalism of nursing is not restricted to those matters that enhance our territorial boundary but includes the association's responsibility to address external, as well as internal, matters. It is disturbing to read those letters in response to the endorsement that label the ANA's endorsement as unprofessional. It is regrettable that our own politicalization has not kept pace with the times. To be a self-directed profession, we must contribute to that process that will ultimately make the decision for us, our health care colleagues, and our fellow citizens.

Since the endorsement, the ANA has received more positive public attention and had its positions promoted by a larger segment of the media than ever before. Members have been asked to participate in a variety of local, state, and national political activities. Although many nurses were concerned about the effects of the endorsement on the association's effectiveness in Washington in the next four years, those who are experienced in the political arena and understand endorsements know that the day after an election, fences are mended and a new dialogue started.

What the endorsement has done for ANA is to generate a new level of public respect. Society recognizes that the ANA will stand up for its beliefs, will take risks to make these beliefs known, and has the courage to act as an advocate for the nation's health. This is a vision that most nurses hold for the association's future. The ANA Board of Directors' historic presidential endorsement represented a major step towards making that vision a reality.

POLITICAL ACTION IN THE COMMUNITY

The three previously discussed spheres of influence are encompassed by the community, be it local, regional, or international. Developing one's influence in this sphere enhances one's ability to influence the others and vice versa.

Unit VII examines how to influence the community from three points of view. The local community, the first focus, is discussed in Chapter 35. Rather than using the traditional approach to community action, the author uses a marketing model for analyzing and influencing one's community. The vignette that follows describes one nurse's efforts to mobilize her community to take action on a nearby international airport's violation of noise and safety standards. The focus then shifts to the international community in Chapter 36 with a discussion of the relevance of this community to nurses in the United States, and follows with two vignettes. One describes a nurse's experience with the politics of practicing in another country. A second vignette describes a nurse's appointment to a commission studying public health in El Salvador. Excerpts from the commission's official report illustrate the politics of practicing nursing in a country torn by civil war.

The corporate world is an increasingly controversial and influential part of the health care system and the community. Chapter 37 describes corporate structures, how the nurse can operate effectively within them, and how nurses can apply for corporate funding for projects, programs, and research. Some of the ethical dilemmas that may confront the nurse who works in a corporation are also included.

The case study for Unit VII describes the efforts of two nurses—one a citizen of Canada, the other of the United States—to introduce maternity care options into the Canadian health care system.

Chapter 35

Working Together: Local Community Action

Anne DuVal Frost, RN, MA

Nurses commonly separate their professional role from their role as community resident. The development and use of political influence in the local community, however, can create an important base of support for the accomplishment of nursing goals on a local, as well as state, and national levels. Many of the current issues in nursing and health care require legislative and philanthropic support. Enlisting such support requires that nurses move beyond tapping resources in the profession to seeking the assistance of nonnursing advocates. We need the advantages provided by large numbers of advocates as well as the political networks and corporate resources they can make available.

Political influence often begins with a commitment to the health and welfare of the community. This is in keeping with a nurse's professional perspective and expertise. Too often, nurses do not recognize and use this expertise for the benefit of their own communities.

At the same time, community involvement provides the advantage of the informality of social relationships to develop non-nurse advocates. While these relationships may differ in their degree of intensity, they are founded on a "common ground" of compatible attitudes, values, and beliefs. This fosters a receptivity for one's messages and avoids the disadvantage of anonymity. Identity as just another member of a special interest group is far less powerful than identity as someone who has established credibility through personal involvement in the community. The form letter that solicits legislative or philanthropic support is less effective than a telephone call to someone who knows you as a member of his or her organization or who has recently enjoyed dinner in your home.

This chapter examines some of the common barriers to nurses using their political influence in the community and presents a marketing model for nurses to use in developing this power base. It will also explain how my involvement in community service created opportunities to foster nonnursing advocates while improving the health and welfare of the community. In this latter part, I will describe how I used my nonprofessional role as a friend, neighbor, and concerned citizen to contribute to the well-being of the community and introduce my professional role as clinical specialist and nurse educator. I will also describe how I capitalized on my professional identity to establish the community as a unique clinical laboratory for masters-level students. By using the community as a clinical site, the intensity of political influence was increased through the greater visibility and involvement of a larger number of nurses.

BARRIERS TO DEVELOPING POLITICAL INFLUENCE

Separation of Personal and Professional Roles.   There are a number of reasons why nurses have often separated personal and professional roles. First, doing so creates an air of objectivity to foster the client's comfort in expressing attitudes, values, and beliefs. While this may be appropriate in many clinical settings, it is a barrier to the use of nursing expertise for promotion of both the community's health and the profession. Ideally one can combine the power of professional expertise and personal credibility. As Epstein (1982) suggests:

> The community leader who is not only articulate and skillful in effecting change but also a resident of the community acquires a unique legitimacy. She can affirm, "not only do I know this as a nurse and a scientist, but I know it as a resident of this community." Such a leader is difficult to co-opt. (p 199)

A second reason why nurses often separate their professional and personal roles involves the antipolitical socialization of women. To use self-promotion and political activism to support one's beliefs may have been inculcated as unfeminine (Kalisch & Kalisch, 1982). To weaken sex-linked roles, we first need to acknowledge them. Then we should ask who, if not us, can be expected to introduce perspectives and suggest policies derived from educational and professional experiences specific to nursing.

A third reason is the fear that self-promotion might be viewed as sexually provocative. The connotation of using self to "gain favor" or influence is reminiscent of sexuality as power. This has long been associated with the nurse-physician relationship (Archer, 1982). However, it is a waste of valuable time to legitimize inapplicable stereotypes. Instead, nurses should use the combined strengths of personal and professional roles for the reciprocal benefits of promoting community health, as well as the power and authority of nursing.

Class Differences.   Although Florence Nightingale was from an upper-middle class family, the majority of contemporary nurses are from lower and middle socioeconomic classes. In addition, nursing education usually provides clinical experiences with clients from lower and middle socioeconomic classes. This creates a natural barrier, or even alienation, to potential advocates, who are usually well-connected politically and philanthropically.

There is little in the nursing literature that addresses class differences between nurses and patients. In "The Hospitalized Rich and Famous," Henry and Digiacomo-Geffers (1980) identify envy and anger as two common responses of nurses to upper-middle class and upper class patients. They explain this as a lack of familiarity with the problems of the wealthy, as well as a professional ideology that supports service to the needs of the less privileged. They suggest, however, that the demonstration of professionalism and excellence by nurses can influence not only the philanthropic patterns of the wealthy, but also the use of their power to promote a positive image of nursing with the media. This, they explain, was particularly true of their Hollywood-based patients because of associations with the motion picture industry.

Epstein (1982) also identifies envy and antagonism as possible reactions of nurses who are assessing higher income communities. She also points out that those who choose to work in affluent areas may feel guilty that they are not caring for the poor. She counters:

> Nurses can resolve this conflict by considering their objectives within the context of our total national and world systems. It is true that, whatever problems the affluent suffer, the poor also suffer, but always with the added problems generated by poverty. So we can safely generalize that the poor need us more than the rich. However, the more affluent who have not been helped to become self-actualizing can seriously hamper local, national, and world efforts to improve the quality of life. (p 236)

Thus, developing influence within the ranks of the wealthy can further nursing's commendable tradition of serving the poor. Lillian Wald, an exemplary figure in nursing's history, knew of the importance of cultivating the philanthropic reserves of the wealthy. Indeed, the famous Henry Street Settlement House, which she started on the Manhattan Lower East Side in the early 1900s, thrived as a health and social service center for the community's poor because Wald got wealthy patrons to underwrite it (Siegel, 1983).

If nursing is to become politically astute and continue in the tradition of Lillian Wald in serving the country's communities, we must seek the support of health care consumers from all socioeconomic classes. However, as indicated, we need to examine our values for barriers that might preclude us from tapping resources of the upper socioeconomic class, with which we are least familiar and which is probably the least informed about the range and efficacy of nursing. To this purpose, the community selected for discussion later in this chapter is characterized by an upper-middle and upper socioeconomic population.

Nursing's Image.   To build a base of support of nonnursing advocates, nursing must be viewed as relevant and valuable to the wide range of needs of the community's health care consumers. Potential advocates should learn that nursing is an accessible, cost-effective source of expert guidance, support, and management in prevention, restoration, and maintenance of health. This must begin with discrediting the existing inaccuracies of nursing's image, which can be done in large part through community involvement if nurses consider themselves representatives and "image-makers."

Participation in local community groups and organizations provides an excellent opportunity to demonstrate intelligence, creativity, leadership, and social responsibility. While the public's image of nursing may easily incorporate social responsibility, it usually excludes the preceding "executive" characteristics. These are incompatible with the dependent and subordinate behaviors often attributed to nurses as auxiliary health personnel and physician extenders. Community involvement, especially if leadership positions are assumed, may be the most efficient and effective way to change this negative image of nursing. In addition, the knowledge and skills that nurses use to address local issues should be publicly credited, at least in part to professional education, insight, and expertise.

Nurses should also be promoting nursing as a professional discipline that fosters careers, not jobs. Many potential advocates have viewed nursing as a hobby that gives women a "break" from housework and children or which is used to provide a financial supplement for household projects such as new curtains, carpeting, or a refrigerator (the nurse who works with this motivation has been referred to as the "refrigerator nurse"). The public has often considered career nurses to be women who did not marry and who worked out of financial necessity or lack of choice.

To correct this stereotype, nursing must be identified as a profession based upon theory and scientific inquiry and stabilized by women and men who share common professional goals, as well as a desire for personal growth and self-actualization. An important part of the image nurses should be conveying is that nursing is a stable profession with a long track record. This notion of stability is particularly important for potential business allies, especially those in upper management positions. If we want to gain support for practice and legislative trends, we need to explain the basis for current practice; but like any "good business" demonstrate a "critical eye" for appropriate growth and expansion.

The image of nursing, then, should reflect a social consciousness supported by professional commitment and expertise and implemented with effective executive skills. The nurse whose contributions are credited with adding to the well-being of the community has added to the strength and authority of nursing as an appropriate voice for health practices and policies in any community, whether local, state, or national.

Lack of Promotional Skills. Political influence is a change process in which conscious effort is devoted to a modification of the targeted person's or group's attitudes, values, beliefs, and behavior. While there are numerous models for change such as those developed by Lewin (1951), Pitcher (1967), and Seifert and Clinebell (1969), their emphasis is on the process and its guiding steps. There is less specificity given to strategies.

Since these theories are the ones most often used for teaching nursing students about change, we have generations of nurses skilled at analyzing the factors that need and can be changed, but less skilled at promoting the change. Indeed, imparting information is the strategy most nurses would identify as their primary tool for change. However, developing an effective change strategy entails designing a message with culturally relevant values, themes, and symbols.

This approach to change is part of a marketing framework compatible with process models, but emphasizes the design of the message or interaction used for influence or

```
┌─────────────────────────────────────────────────────────────────────┐
│  Market Assessment               New Product (Message,               │
│  • Consumer Profile              Interaction, Service)                │
│  • System Profile                • Cost                              │
│  • Nurse Profile                 • Availability                      │
│                                  • Potential Supplier               │
│  Targeted Population             • Trend Compatibility              │
│                                  • Market Readiness                 │
│  Competitive Product (Message,                                       │
│  Interaction, Service)           Promotional Strategies             │
│  • Cost                          • Benefit Exchange                 │
│  • Availability                  • Coalitions                       │
│  • Current Supplier              • Advertising                      │
│  • Performance Record                                               │
│  • Trend Compatibility           Pilot Testing                     │
└─────────────────────────────────────────────────────────────────────┘
```

Figure 35-1   A Marketing Model for Change

change. This model was developed from synthesis of collaborative meetings with marketing professionals and my own consultative experiences with consumer groups.

A MARKETING MODEL FOR COMMUNITY ACTION

In essence, the marketing model views a message, interaction, or service as a product (see Figure 35-1). The determination of the need for a product is based on an assessment of the involved individuals or groups, as well as the characteristics of the nurse who would be the "provider." In addition, development of the new product would be based, certainly in part, on the existing "product," its deficits, as well as its strengths. Introduction of the new "product" would be facilitated by promotional strategies that include the selection of pertinent themes and symbols based upon relevant sociocultural values (Frost, 1984). This chapter emphasizes assessment criteria and their use in the development of three promotional strategies: benefit exchange, coalitions, and advertising.

BENEFIT EXCHANGE

Many nurses are uncomfortable with benefit exchange as a promotional strategy because of its self-promoting aspects. Benefit exchange is analogous to the cliche, "One hand washes the other." In other words, when attempting to influence, one should consider the reciprocal nature of the process. This means that benefits are often given to receive benefits. Benefits may be concrete, behavioral, or affective. Concrete benefits may be tangible property such as gifts or financial contributions. They may also include a service such as training programs or "hands-on" care. Behavioral benefits may be networking arrangements in which introductions are made to key contacts, or support is given through the persuasive presentation of pertinent issues or information. Affective benefits may be a state of receptivity, agreement, loyalty, or obligations that lead to future behavioral or concrete benefits.

In all nursing transactions, the two-way flow should be a conscious part of the nurse's planning for the successful development and use of influence. This does not mean, however, that the person or group with whom one is engaged in an exchange must be aware of the benefit to the nurse. Some nurses have initial difficulty with what they view as the manipulative quality of this concept. Their discomfort may be a result of our historical orientation to nursing as a "duty" and a "service" along with the idea that anything that provided personal benefit was thought to erode professional integrity. The behavioral sciences, however, have taught us that human attitudes, values, and beliefs are multifaceted and self-protective. It is naive to expect that the value of what we say and do will be accepted without first establishing a relationship based on the production of benefits. Having "good" ideas and clinical expertise is not enough. Promoting opportunities in which they will be demonstrated as important and essential should be a primary goal.

MARKETING ASSESSMENT

To develop promotional opportunities and strategies and implement benefit exchange, a profile of significant personnel and systems should be prepared as a guide. With the use of the marketing model in a community setting, powerful individuals within organizations and groups are given key roles. This is not to negate the power of the group as a system, but simply recognizes that the group "culture" is not determined by an even distribution of individual influences. Rather, this culture is more often determined by a small number of leading "players."

The following format is helpful in the market assessment process:

- System profile (organization, institution, family)
    sociocultural values
    community role
    role needs
    communication structure
    health-related needs/goals
- Consumer profile (friend, neighbor, concerned citizen, community official, agency member, patient)
    sociocultural values
    community/agency role
    role/personality needs
    communication patterns
    health-related needs/goals

- Nurse profile

    compatibility of sociocultural values with targeted personnel and systems

    strengths/weaknesses of community role

    personality style and impact

    communication/promotional skills

    professional expertise

The nurse profile reflects the necessity for establishing a facilitative match between the nurse and the community member or system. There is nothing wrong in concluding that one nurse is a more effective choice than another for instituting a particular benefit exchange. However, choosing from a small number of available nurses may prevent an ideal match. In either case, the nurse can enhance the chances of success by designing a presentation and message that will gain the attention and receptivity of the targeted person. Again, this is part of the shedding of the idea that if we have something "good" to say, people will listen. Instead, we should adopt the philosophy that, "If the presentation and message are appropriate, people will listen."

SOCIOCULTURAL VALUES

The design of a promotional strategy depends on using the relevant sociocultural values of a targeted community and individuals. There should be caution, however, to avoid overgeneralization of particular segments of the population: For example, sweeping judgments are often made regarding community location; socioeconomic status; or individual gender, age, ethnicity, and occupation. We are all familiar with generalizations such as "cities are dangerous, suburbs are rich" or sentences that begin with "women believe," "adolescents are," "all Irish," and "doctors never." However, a focus on communities, the individuals within them, and their unique value systems must follow assessment of more general categories. A few of the typical categories are:

1. Community status

    urban vs suburban

    socioeconomic level of residents

    ethnicity of residents

    quality of dwellings

    quality of schools

    quality of government services

2. Individual role prescription

    - Family

        gender

        birth order

marital status

parental status

financial contributions

- Occupation

educational preparation

financial capability

humanitarian worth

esthetic worth

- Community

number of agency/organizational memberships

length of residency

status of dwelling

3. Individual physical appearance

height

weight

hair

clothes

4. Individual health practices

diet

exercise

preferred health professionals

To demonstrate the use of these categories, I will give a brief overview of my community. It is a small suburban community of New York City. Most of the residents are in an upper socioeconomic bracket. Most young adults are married for the first time. A growing number of middle-aged adults are married for the second time or recently divorced. Most older adults have lost one spouse, usually the husband. Most of the employed adults commute to the city. The predominant sociocultural values include academic achievement, professional careers, spontaneous but not unbridled behavior, casual but good quality clothes, a high level of personal grooming and property maintenance. In addition, community involvement is applauded, with churches, synagogues, and service agencies as prime recipients. Children are supported through sports, scouts, and music and dance lessons. Men are considered the primary breadwinners, but women with executive earnings are admired. Older residents are respected but expected to relinquish power and move from their large homes to community apartments when they retire. Long-term residents, especially those who grew up in the town and continue to reside there as adults, are both revered and viewed with suspicion for being "stuck in a rut." "Old" money is better than "new" money, but new money is respected if the recipient has at least one college degree and is an entrepreneur. Highly suspect are large amounts of money carried in shoe boxes. Teeth are checked every six months, with physical exams undertaken annually. Jogging and aerobics are in, but yogurt will never replace red meat.

FOUR AMERICAN VALUES

After completing a general sociocultural assessment for a community, four additional values should be integrated. I believe these four values are indigenous to the American culture regardless of regional or ethnic influences. This modifies Kluckholm's (Kluckholm & Strodtbeck, 1961; Brink, 1984) view of the American core culture as being only future oriented. While I agree that future orientation is greatly valued, the relative newness of our culture and our respect for success borne out of our past fosters the continued use of traditional or indigenous values. These indigenous values are as follows:

- authority
- majority
- validity
- stability

First, the substance of a message must be credited to some *authority*. Most Americans have an image of their ancestors as good, hard-working people, but nevertheless of peasant stock. We compensate for our lack of inherited rank by checking the source of information and giving greater value to that which comes from those above us, those with authority. This of course hits at the heart of one of nursing's greatest difficulties in the attempt to use political influences. Nurses are generally not seen as authorities. This is why at present our use of political influence has the simultaneous purpose of developing authority while learning to implement it.

Second, the message must appear to represent the *majority* of persons to be affected by any change. Naturally, the actual number of people in a particular majority can refer to as few as the residents on one block or all the senior citizens in the town. The point is that the basic value is majority rule. It is a throw-back to the founding of our country, and the fear of rule or preference by and for a select few. For example, support for an increased town budget to expand a youth soccer program was initially questioned. When I and others joined town officials in explaining that such a program would benefit all children and therefore affect the majority of families, the budget was passed.

Third is the issue of *validity*. Whatever is suggested must appear to be "tried and true." While Americans may applaud innovation, it is best accepted if it appears to be based not only on sound thinking but on experience. Our heritage bespeaks a certain skepticism on decisions based only on "book learning." On this point nurses can take advantage of associations made with our "hands-on" skills and "firsthand" experience to qualify certain opinions. For example, at a recent community school board meeting I spoke against a plan to organize the town's four elementary schools with two grade levels per school. I stated that from my experience as a nurse-counselor (I did not say therapist because it is a term that arouses defenses) with children, having them change schools four times during grades K through six disrupts the continuity of identity that benefits the development of school-age children. The plan was defeated.

Fourth, the change should add *stability*. Again one of the premises upon which our country was founded was the desire for the security of being able to count on a stable framework of rules, regulations, and responsible leadership. Our system of checks and balances permeates the need to stabilize, maintain, and defend what we consider in the broadest sense, our "way of life." While some communities better represent a more positive image of that concept than others, stabilization of whatever is representative will be defended.

A controversial issue relating to stability, and which included the first three values, arose in my community regarding the initiation of a school lunch program for elementary school children. The largest contingency of citizens opposed to the plan were those whose children were adolescents and young adults and who had "been there" when their children came home for lunch. They argued that a school lunch program would interfere with the *stability* of the family unit by limiting the mother-child contact during the day. They further substantiated their views by testimony that their experience of raising children who had "turned out OK," *validating* their *authority* to protect the *majority* of young children whose parents were willing to institute a new and potentially dangerous practice.

Again, during a school board meeting, I countered this argument with a rationale that also emphasized *stability*. My intent was that my view of what supported *stability* was more accurate. I began with a value shared by everyone present, the "high quality of life" in our town. I emphasized that the beauty of the town, the safety of the town, and the excellent quality of the schools were valued by each of us. I then pointed out that they existed in part because of the high rate of local taxes. I specified that these taxes pay for regular street and sidewalk repair, maintenance of town property, as well as frequent sanitation services. I continued the emphasis by reminding everyone that these high taxes also provided the highest per capita fire and police services in the state as well as support for a nationally ranked school. However, I continued, "the high taxes require that even in two-parent families (more highly valued as *stable* than single-parent families) of well-educated professionals (highly valued) both often chose to work to maintain and *stabilize* their accustomed life style." Next I added that, based on my professional experience (*authority*), children felt the greatest security when their parents believed that they were doing a good job of parenting by providing a good community in which to "grow up." I later pointed out that a lunch time recreational program could be designed that would enable healthy exercise and peer play (*validity*). This, I pointed, out would serve the *majority* of children well by replacing travel time with recreation and relaxation (*values*). Refocusing on my professional expertise, I concluded by saying that reducing the need for travel in inclement weather might reduce the risk of illness. The lunch program won a majority vote during the school board elections.

It seems obvious that the sociocultural value system is a major determinant in the process of political influence. The benefit to the majority of the voters was the belief that they were participating in securing the stability of a quality of life they enjoyed. The benefit to me included the same assurance, but there was the additional advantage of an opportunity to establish my professional identity and participate as an "image-maker." By providing a rationale based upon nursing education and expertise, I was demonstrating and strengthening the value of nursing in the development of policies related to the health and well-being of the community.

POWER OF COALITIONS

Coalitions can be considered a promotional strategy because they are a "contrived" grouping created to influence the marketing of a message, interaction, or service.

One of the most dramatic opportunities for the use of coalitions for image-making occurred shortly after my husband and I moved from New York City to this small suburban community. One of the expectations of the move was the reduction in environmental noise from the city to the country, even though our new home was located on one of the main streets of the town. Soon after moving, we were startled by the realization that the intensity of the street noise was far greater than anything we had experienced when "tucked away" in a brick and cement high-rise apartment house in Manhattan. An initial investigation revealed that road repairs in the industrial section of a nearby community were resulting in the rerouting of a steady flow of trucks down our street. The noise and constant vibrations were extremely annoying. A call to the village government revealed that there were no zoning regulations to prevent the rerouting. The response of the administrator was matter-of-fact and apathetic. I concluded that the power of a coalition was needed to influence the village government.

I began by interviewing all of the neighbors on the street and proposing a plan to organize. I discovered that while they were annoyed, many felt that "our hands are tied" and that change would be impossible. Nevertheless, the first meeting of the coalition was well attended. First we discussed the values that would be used and then selected the primary benefit exchange. It was concluded that an official organization would receive more attention from the board of trustees of the village than would a "group of neighbors." The coalition became "The Manor Community Organization." We ordered stationery printed with the name, which we decided would be used in all correspondence with the Mayor and village officials. I was offered the position of president of the organization. I suggested that I assume the informal leadership role and that the president be someone who was well established with formal power. The selection was a man who headed the government party that represented the opposition to the members of the board. While his opposition status was initially considered a potential problem by some members of the coalition, it was negated on the basis of the "working relationship" that he had formerly established with the board. His gender was also considered favorable because of the traditional values of the all-male board.

We believed that the board, who were all members of upper management, would respond to a constructive alternative to the situation. Consequently, we investigated the delivery needs of the companies represented by the trucks and found a new route with a limited number of private homes. Secondly, my husband, a lawyer, prepared an extensive legal brief demonstrating the precedents and need for a change in the existing zoning law. We also used the talents of one of the neighbors who was a commercial artist to draw a series of professional graphs and maps. We were business-like in our formal request for a hearing at a board meeting.

At the appointed time, all residents on the street (*majority*) attended. Both men and women wore business clothes to add to the business-like effect of our presentation. The president of the organization gave an opening address relating to the need for *stability* in the "quality of life" in the community. He used his many years of residency and involvement in the community to emphasize both *authority* and *validity*. I then addressed the board using my *authority* as a nurse to *validate* the health hazards of noise pollution. My husband then presented the legal issues using professional visual aids to show the dramatic increase in both the number and size of the trucks. The implied benefit to the board was the *stability* of the "quality of life" as well as preventing the costly damage to the heavily trafficked streets. Nevertheless, we were given polite attention, and promptly dismissed. However, while slightly outraged, we decided that the stage had been set and that we would increase our strength if we demonstrated that we expected results.

We arranged a second hearing with the board, and this time increased the components of the benefit exchange to include the prevention of legal action. After reiterating the health hazards, the reasonable alternatives to the traffic problem, and the legal justifications, it was stated that there seemed to be no logical reason to refuse the organization's request for a change in the zoning law. It was further stated that if we could not count on their assistance, the organization would have to seek legal recourse. Shortly after this meeting, our requests were granted.

There were also additional benefits. I was asked to run for mayor of the party that the president of the Manor Community Organization represented. In addition, my husband was asked by the village board of trustees to become the village attorney. Implied in this position was the opportunity to become trustee and, eventually, the mayor. Because we did not have strong ties with either one of the national parties, we did not feel compromised in considering both offers. I decided that I would decline the offer to run for mayor because of a limited chance of being elected. The minority party that I would represent had never had a candidate elected. My husband accepted the position as village attorney and, by doing so, became affiliated with the party of power. We knew that his position would provide more *authority* to facilitate common goals. Among the goals realized was the precedent of a female member elected to the board of trustees as well as the introduction of health-related issues into many of the community policies enacted by the board. On such issues I was cited as the "consultant" along with other nursing colleagues in the community.

CLINICAL SITE: A COALITION OF AGENCIES

When my husband became a trustee of the village, I decided to take advantage of the fact that my surname was firmly associated with responsibility and productivity. To further increase my personal credibility and professional identity, I submitted articles to the local newspaper about my presentations at national nursing conferences. In addition, I volunteered to run a series of parent training seminars at one of the local elementary schools. One reason for increasing my professional visibility was to facilitate the development of a clinical learning site in the community.

As a teacher of masters-level students, I find that there are fundamental frustrations in the workplace that prompt nurses to pursue graduate work. Prospective students cite an inability to influence the health beliefs and practices of patients as well as the professional philosophy and conduct of peers and coworkers. They hope that graduate education will increase their effectiveness in these arenas. Both patients and coworker groups are targeted in my graduate curriculum along with a third group called community members. This latter group includes all those who could become nursing advocates. To meet both the curriculum objectives and student needs, a clinical site was needed to support the practice of political influence.

I felt it was imperative to find opportunities for autonomy above and beyond that afforded by role prescriptions based on the medical model. I also wanted the students to have access to all three target groups: patients, coworkers, and constituents. I have found, however, that nurses who don't have experience with upper-middle and upper class patients, particularly outside of the hospital, often possess negative stereotypic expectations of these patients. Again, because this group often has an advantage for legislative and philanthropic contacts, it is important for students, as part of their professional socialization, to test their expectations for confirmation or reevaluation.

Finally, the clinical site had to have a population of preschool, latency, and adolescent patients to represent the developmental life cycle that was the specialty focus. The clinical site that most closely approximated all requirements was not an agency but the entire community. The health-related agencies included four elementary schools, one junior high school, one senior high school, a day care center, a family counseling service, and several nursery schools. I will share a series of case studies that demonstrates how the graduate students were able to learn and use political influence to build a coalition of these agencies. The use of benefit exchange will be related to personal and system profiles as well as general sociocultural values.

CASE STUDIES

The first program the students elected to do was one of play therapy for latency-aged children. Of the four elementary schools that provided this age group, school A was chosen. Initial benefit determination concluded that the program was potentially controversial. After compiling a personal profile of the principals of the four schools, it was decided that the principal in school A was the best choice. She was reported to be efficient, conscientious, ran a tight ship but was open to innovative interventions that would add to her image of being a forward thinker. In addition, her daughter held a PhD in child psychology and would probably be used by the principal as an informal sounding board regarding our philosophy and methodology. Not incidentally, this was also the school where I had presented the parent-training programs.

In the first planning session with the principal, the students and I described the potential benefits of the program for the participating children's psychosocial as well as academic achievements. For example, often grades improve when anxiety decreases. This benefit would add to the school's academic profile, which in turn would reflect on the effectiveness of the principal. All of these, as well as a genuine interest in the well-being of her pupils, gained the principal's receptivity, acceptance, and involvement in the implementation of the program. Even though a profile of the agency system revealed a particularly conservative attitude toward mental health interventions, the students and I concluded that the power of the principal would encourage the teachers' cooperation with the participating children. The status of principal A as the most powerful and influential of the four elementary school principals was the final consideration that led to the selection of school A. If the program proved successful, she could facilitate important connections with the other schools.

Next, we developed a collegial relationship with the psychologist in school A. Her educational background most closely approximated that of the nurses and also represented the specialty that was a major theoretical thread for their interventions. She was also respected by principal A and had important ties to the small group of psychologists and counselors who wielded power regarding "entry" into some of the other schools. Conversely, if we didn't include her, we would risk territorial problems. The benefits we offered were acknowledgment of her expertise, respect for her position, and assistance in caring for the children, which she needed because of time constraints. She accepted our plans, and her help was elicited in the development of recommendations and selection of participants.

The next step was to introduce the program to the parents of potential participants. We were aware of the sensitivity of this process. Both the name of the program, "Creative Play," and the description were designed to neutralize associations with sickness or unreconcilable problems. We offered the benefit of regular meetings with the parents for progress reports and reassurance that if the program seemed inappropriate for their child or if the child proved resistant, it would be terminated. At the same time, the parents were helped to consider their permission as providing a special growth opportunity for their children. We concluded that this had the benefit of decreasing their guilt and increasing their esteem as responsible parents.

The program proved to be highly successful. The children, their parents, the teachers, the psychologist, and the principal were all pleased with the observed benefits. The nurses had benefitted from a successful lesson in the process of influence and felt that they had made a definitive impact on the image of contemporary nursing. One of the informal promotional opportunities that arose with the teachers and parents was the discussion of the benefits of obtaining a master's degree in nursing, both from the viewpoint of the nurse and the health care consumer. To promote this image for the community at large, I submitted to the local newspaper a picture of the students and an article explaining the program.

The next semester, I visited two of the other elementary schools that have special-education classes and could provide a group of children who could use the "Creative Play" program. I cited the successful experience at school A as a reference, along with written verification from principal A and the school psychologist. There was no difficulty securing the placement. Similar benefit exchanges were demonstrated in these schools. The proof of our skill in influencing was reflected in the ease with which we were able to enter and align with these two new subsystems of the community.

The day care center was the next agency selected because of the nursing students' need to work with a preschool population. It also offered the potential opportunity for fulfilling consumer education requirements through participation in agency-sponsored parenting programs. The director of the program was a master's-prepared teacher in her sixties. A personality profile indicated that she was conservative in her view of nursing roles. It also became apparent that her short stature (4'11") was inversely related to her need to control the staff, children, and program. Her grey hair, recurrent bouts of asthma, and cherubic-like smile were manipulative tools to maintain things "her way." I approached the use of this agency with caution because of the need to secure sites that would support professional innovation. From the system's profile, it was ascertained that the teacher-pupil classroom ratio was often too large with resulting stress for the teacher and director. Secondly, the "showcase" parenting program called "Coffee, Chat, and Children" was short of adults to participate in the concomitant babysitting service. I decided to offer benefits that would serve both agencies' needs. First, I suggested to the director that the nurses participate in the classroom by assisting a designated group of children or one or two who presented behavioral difficulties. In addition to this being an ideal benefit for the students, I also offered a program of physical and developmental screening. I felt that the idea of physical or "hands-on" care would decrease her fear of the nurses departing from what she viewed as a typical nursing role and encroaching on the teachers' "territory" of curriculum integration. I also pointed out that the students could make home visits and would be available to consult with any of the parents regarding their findings. This would also allow the students yet another opportunity to work with community members to demonstrate nursing expertise. I pointed out to the director the value of this benefit as one of good public relations for the agency.

Next I offered the benefit of the nurses' assistance in the babysitting program. This was received enthusiastically. I suggested that the students could design developmentally stimulating programs which they would implement and also explain in a parent's handbook along with recommendations for implementation at home. Again I pointed out the public relations value of enhancing the agency's image as a resource for educational experiences and materials. The director agreed and accepted these student roles along with the introduction of several students into the consumer education role as presenters in "Coffee, Chat, and Children."

The selection of the students for the various roles was based on personality profiles they performed for each other in a seminar discussion. We used ethnic, sociocultural, and even physical determinants to match the nurse and staff member. Several news releases were given to the local paper emphasizing the role of the nurses. The director approved the release and was pleased that the center was receiving publicity. The programs were successful although it was apparent that, with some contacts, more time and demonstration would be necessary to convince them of nursing's expertise and rightful autonomy. The group accepted this as a positive challenge and concluded that through successive student placements, the new image of nursing would strengthen.

CONCLUSION

In summary, barriers that could have undermined the development and use of political influence were reframed and used as assets. Personal and professional roles were combined to maximize credibility. The stringent lines of class differences were softened by recognizing mutual goals and dovetailing resources. A marketing framework provided promotional strategies to add specificity to the design and inauguration of new liaisons. The image of nurses as socially aware professionals was greatly expanded through political assertiveness and demonstration of executive skills. The new advocacy and clinical roles filled by the graduate students and myself added clout to nursing's authority as a policy maker in this community.

Residents are now willing to make phone calls to the state capital or Washington to support nursing legislation. Corporate businessmen have indicated their willingness to lend financial and professional support to nursing projects. This local community became a much needed base of support for nursing, while benefiting from the expert contributions of nurses.

References

Altman I: *The Environment and Social Behavior.* Brooks/Cole, 1975.

Archer SE: Selected concepts fundamental to nurses' political activism. Pages 71–80 in: *Nurses: a Political Force.* Archer SE, Goehner PA (editors). Wadsworth Health Sciences, 1982.

Archer SE, Kelly CD, Bisch SA: *Implementing Change in Communities: A Collaborative Process.* Mosby, 1984.

Bernal H: Power and interorganizational health care projects. *Nurs Outlook* 1976; 24:419–21.

Blattner B: *Holistic Nursing.* Prentice-Hall, 1981.

Brink PJ: Value orientation as an assessment tool in cultural diversity. *Nurs Research* 1984; 33:198–203.

Chin R: The utility of systems models and development models for practitioners. Pagers 90–102 in: *The Planning of Change.* Bennis WG, Benne KD, Chin R, Corey KE (editors). Holt, Rinehart & Winston, 1976.

Craig JH, Craig M: *Synergic Power: Beyond Domination and Permissiveness.* Pro Active Press, 1974.

Dornbusch SM, Scott WR: *Evaluation and the Exercise of Authority.* Jossey-Bass, 1975.

Epstein C: *The Nurse Leader: Philosophy and Practice.* Reston, 1982.

Frost A: The use of SMURFS for increased body control and self-accountability. *Holistic Nurs* 1984; 2:38–42.

Goodstein LD: *Consulting with Human Service Systems.* Addison-Wesley, 1978.

Henry BM, Digiacomo-Geffers E: The hospitalized rich and famous. *Am J Nurs* 1980; 80:1426–29.

Kalisch BJ, Kalisch PA: *Politics of Nursing.* Lippincott, 1982.

Kipnis D, Vanderveer B: Ingratiation and the use of power. *Personality and Social Psychology* 1971; 17:280–86.

Kluckholm FR, Strodtbeck FL: *Variations in Value Orientations.* Row Peterson, 1961.

Lewin K: *Field Theory in Social Science.* Harper & Row, 1951.

Lippitt G, Lippitt R: *The Consulting Process in Action.* University Associates, 1978.

Maslow AH: *Motivation and Personality.* Harper & Row, 1970.

Pitcher A: Two cities—Two churches. *Chicago Theological Seminary Register*, (May) 1967; 4–5.

Reinkemeyer AM: Nursing's need commitment to an ideology of change. *Nurs Forum* 1970; 9:340–55.

Riccordi BR, Dayani EC: *The Nurse Entrepreneur.* Reston, 1982.

Ringer RJ: *Winning Through Intimidation.* Los Angeles Book, 1974.

Rodgers J: The clinical specialist as a change agent. *J Psychiatric Nurs* (Nov–Dec) 1974; 12:5–9.

Rodgers J: Theoretical considerations involved in the process of change. *Nurs Forum* 1973; 13:160–74.

Seifert HH, Clinebell H: *Personal Growth and Social Change.* Westminster Press, 1969.

Siegel B: *Lillian Wald of Henry Street.* Macmillan, 1983.

von Bertalanffy LV: *Perspectives on General Systems Theory.* George Braziller, 1975.

Vignette: Keeping a Community Healthy

Margaret A. Kessenich Meagher, RN, MS, CS

In 1973, my small son and I watched two small planes crash in midair, seemingly directly over our urban neighborhood. When I called Denver's Stapleton International Airport to see what had happened, I was told it was none of my business. Somehow, the prospect of plane wreckage in my backyard seemed very much my business.

In 1979, when I called to ask why a jumbo jet had just passed what seemed like inches over our home, I was again refused any information. According to airport authorities, ordinary citizens were not due any explanations, even for such blatant disregard of city noise and safety statutes.

Today, the situation is different. News coverage on all three of the city's TV network affiliates made the city and the community aware of our unpreparedness for an air disaster over an urban neighborhood. And the airport mans a 24-hour hotline to answer questions and to file complaints about airport noise.

Those changes came about primarily through my efforts, at least initially. They were well worth the hundreds of hours of my time, not only in terms of improving the quality of life in our city, but by teaching me that a single individual can change city government policy.

My family and I live in a sprawling Denver neighborhood called Park Hill. About two miles from downtown and a mile from the airport, it is the city's most completely integrated community and is filled with comfortable brick homes that date back to the 1920s and 1930s. Most of my neighbors understand that a nearby airport is going to generate some noise and some inevitable safety hazards. But what stimulated my involvement was the realization that neither issue was being adequately addressed by the city. Nor were the citizens being asked for input on future airport planning.

After I was refused information about the midair plane crash, I began to wonder what would happen if a plane did crash in one of the neighborhoods surrounding the airport. As a nurse, I had seen how important emergency planning was in handling a disaster situation. Did the city have a plan for an air disaster? I began a campaign of phone calls and letters to find out.

"Of course," said the Office of Emergency Preparedness (OEP). "We hold a mock disaster at the airport every year"—at the airport, not in the community. In fact, the mock disaster at the airport in 1980 went so poorly that the "injured" had to be downgraded from critical to serious because there weren't enough ambulances available.

I was told that there was a plan for an air crash over an urban area, but when I requested a mock disaster to help the community understand the plan of action, I was told, "It would be too frightening for the public." Further conversation with the Fire Department shed a new light on the situation: the necessary rescue equipment was too big to get through the residential streets.

Since I was getting little cooperation from the OEP, I decided that what was needed was a graphic demonstration of what could happen. Through a neighborhood newspaper, I solicited volunteers to participate in a mock disaster on the same day that the OEP did its mock disaster on the runway. We called ourselves "The Ground Crew," and on a Saturday morning in June, 1980, we enacted the results of a plane crash. Kids with ketchup and bandages all over them were everywhere and so was the press. We became headline news on all three television stations and so did the fact that Denver's planning for such a disastrous event was inadequate.

As a result, my cohorts and I were invited to a meeting at the OEP. We were greeted not only by OEP personnel but by big guns from the Police Department, the Fire Department, and the mayor's office. They didn't promise a real live enactment, but they did arrange an on-paper walk-through of the plan, and they underwent some serious consciousness-raising about air disaster issues.

My second area of concern involved air traffic noise. Noise is an insidious problem for city dwellers. Studies show that excessive noise contributes to alcoholism, hearing loss, high blood pressure, family violence, and loss of the ability to problem solve.

Complainers are frequently asked why they moved near an airport if they can't live with the noise. But I wasn't suggesting that the airport be moved: merely that laws involving air traffic and the related noise factors be observed, and that citizens be given adult information about situations affecting air traffic noise.

This time, I went straight to the top. After being refused information by the airport authorities, I requested—and received—an interview with Mayor William McNichols. I took my seven-year-old son with me, and the Mayor agreed to establish a temporary line— open 24 hours a day—to the office of the airport operations manager. For a time, the city administration operated the hot line as agreed. But when the airport stopped answering it, I collected over 450 signatures to reinforce the need for the line and sent it to the mayor and our congresspeople and senators. It worked: the mayor agreed to establish a permanent 24-hour line where we would not only get information, but file complaints about noise. The following year, the line logged over 1,000 calls.

In the process, we discovered that there are things that can be done about air traffic noise—such as trees, runway layout, landing direction, engine fanning, etc—and that we need not helplessly accept more air traffic noise. I also learned to ignore authorities who fought back by treating me like a public nuisance. I had discovered that I did have something to offer, that my opinion and that of my neighbors counted and could be used to effect change for the better.

As a result of my work around airport issues, I was asked to become a board member of Greater Park Hill Community Inc, a powerful civic group. I became a plaintiff in the organization's lawsuit against the city that stated that the airport was in violation of state statutes on noise. That lawsuit resulted in the current noise mitigation study partially funded by the city.

Although noise levels are still in violation of state statutes, the City and County of Denver are now using more noise abatement procedures. We are already experiencing a decrease in noise.

The lawsuit also taught me more about basic political action and how it works. Learning that I could be a part of the political process took many years. I grew up in an economically poor area of Milwaukee, where my mother and father—neither of whom finished high school—worked in a bar. It would never have occurred to them that they could negotiate with people in power to effect change. At first, I was scared to even try. But each step in community activism, from my days as a Student Nurse of the Year in Wisconsin in 1965 to the present, proved to me that an individual can make a difference.

Our elected officials—including the mayor, Gary Hart, and Rep Pat Schroeder, whom I contacted as a part of my airport involvement—are people who seek good information.

In addition to accomplishing specific goals, the most surprising dividend of activism has been intangible. It has helped me to recapture the feeling of community that I knew as a young girl in our close-knit German-Catholic neighborhood. My involvement has made me part of my new community, developing the kind of roots and belonging that I had missed for many of my adult years.

Political action is a two-way street. I give and my city and my community give to me, making me a more effective practitioner in every aspect of my life.

Chapter 36

Nursing and the International Community

Veneta Masson, RN, MA

The international community? It's us. All 4.5 billion of us who inhabit this planet. From many perspectives, it seems as if we have little in common and that the word community gives a false impression of harmony and homogeneity. We are separated by geographical, national, cultural, and language barriers. We are divided into sexes, races, age groups, social and economic classes, religions, occupations, political parties, and neighborhoods. Some of us have more food than we can eat, more clothes than we can wear, and more space than we can fill; others can claim little more than their bodies as their own. Some of us expect our children to thrive; others wait and wonder whether theirs will survive the first years of life. Some of us decide what we will do on a given day; for others, what they do will be decided solely by tradition or necessity. Some of us live in peace; others, at war. A few of us monopolize the resources of the world and determine the fate of all the others. But despite all that separates us, we are bound together once and for all by our common humanity, our mutual dependence, and the fact that this world provides us with all that we know of life.

The international nursing community? It's us. All 4 million of us whose occupation bears the rough equivalent of the English titles nurse or midwife. We have different occupational roles, expectations, and aspirations. We work in cities or in the countryside; in institutions or homes; with individuals or whole populations; alone or as part of a team; as directors or supervised by others; as employees of the state, private organizations, or ourselves; with sophisticated equipment or none at all. What we have in common is responsibility for people and their health and our practice that is rooted in traditions extending back to the earliest times.

The international community? It's Maria, the director of nursing, and Mary Ann, her North American counterpart, making administrative rounds in the new regional hospital just outside the capital of this South American country and trying to find a way to staff it with one qualified nurse, a few auxiliaries, and a complement of untrained assistants. It's Moustafa and Eleanor and their North African colleagues, seated around a table, searching for a common language as they review plans for a training program to prepare traditional healers to provide primary health care in their own villages. It's nurses from twelve countries arriving in the Netherlands to present papers at the Conference of European Nurse Researchers. It's thousands of nurses from over 90 countries making their way to Israel to attend the 18th Quadrennial Congress of the International Council of Nurses (ICN).

This chapter presents a series of questions and answers about nursing and the international community. They are questions American nurses would ask if they knew how important the answers were.

WHY SHOULD I CONCERN MYSELF WITH INTERNATIONAL HEALTH?

The answer is simple. Because international health concerns itself with you. While the population of the United States accounts for about five percent of the population of the world, approximately twenty-five percent of the world's nurses are in the United States. Because of our numbers, our relatively high status within our society, our organization into strong associations, and our indispensability to the health sector of this nation, we are among the most visible of national nursing groups. We are recognized as pacesetters by our international colleagues and, at minimum, as highly valued commodities for import by technologically minded countries. Our textbooks are translated and distributed worldwide, and our theories are discussed and often adopted in foreign schools of nursing. U.S. nurses have organized hospitals, schools, and public health programs around the world. They have advised health officials at the highest levels of government.

We have often assumed, however, that what works for us will work for colleagues in other countries, and that what is important to us is equally important to them. We have acted without a full understanding of their values, needs, or resources. For these reasons, we have sometimes failed to communicate or to contribute.

Our mutual dependence as people and as nurses demands that we take a world view. The object of nursing is health. Health is associated with prosperity, prosperity with peace, and peace with integrity and creativity. A strong nursing profession worldwide can make an important contribution to all these. We can start by finding out about nursing in other countries and cultures. We can begin to concern ourselves with the social and economic welfare of our international colleagues. We can benefit from the wisdom and experience of individuals and institutions in other nations.

WHAT DOES HEALTH MEAN?

How do you define and measure health? For many people of the world, particularly in underdeveloped countries, health is a vague notion. It is seen as a gift or a fact of life rather than something one works to attain. It is the ability to do what one has to do rather than a sense of optimal mental and physical well-being. Rarely in history has it been conceived as a right.

Morbidity and mortality, which can give a distorted picture of health status, constitute the main tools used to assess it. It is generally agreed that health conditions in poor regions are inferior to those in affluent regions. Life expectancy is substantially less, and disability, debility, and temporary incapacity are serious problems. According to a World Bank report (1980) one-tenth of the life of the average person in a developing country is seriously disrupted by ill-health.

Until recently, health care was considered the answer to health problems. Health care meant highly trained health professionals, principally physicians, and well-equipped, modern hospitals, where technology could be applied to the treatment of acute or complex medical problems. Nevertheless in both poor and rich countries, large expenditures for health have had only a modest impact on health statistics. By any standard, the health of hundreds of millions of people in the world today is unacceptable, particularly in developing countries. In too many places, an infant remains an unnamed "child of God" until his first birthday, and death during that year is accepted with resignation. In too many places, major diseases, such as respiratory and gastrointestinal infections, could have been prevented or treated by technically simple, inexpensive means.

WHO ARE THE HEALERS?

Studies of healers often group them into two major categories: traditional and modern. The traditional birth attendant is compared with the trained midwife or obstetrician, the bone-setter with the orthopedic surgeon, the medicine man or curandero with the physician, and the nurse with, well, the nurse. In many parts of the world, people avail themselves of the services of healers from both traditional and modern systems.

Healers can also be classified according to the two prototypes—physician and nurse. The physician applies technology (medicinal substances, manipulations, incantations, or surgical procedures) to the systematic solution of problems affecting bodily functioning. Doctoring is associated with the use of tools, a focus on the diseased body part, and prescription of a course of treatment.

The nurse prototype (usually female) uses herself as her principal tool and time as her medium. She views a person and his problem in the context of his internal and external environments. She mediates rather than prescribes, putting patients in touch with their own strength and potential for healing, while at the same time letting them draw temporarily on those of the nurse. Like most classifications, this one has limited usefulness, because the roles of physician and nurse overlap and defy attempts to define them in mutually exclusive terms.

Nursing exists in every part of the world on at least three levels. It is, first of all, one of the oldest and most universal of human activities—caring by families or communities for their own members. Second, it is an occupation, carried out by registered or, to use a more common term, qualified nurses and the trained or untrained personnel who assist them. The ICN (1983) defines this first-level nurse, who has completed a program of basic nursing education and is qualified to practice nursing, as responsible for planning, providing, and evaluating nursing care in all settings for the promotion of health, prevention of illness, care of the sick and rehabilitation. In countries with more than one level of nursing personnel, the second-level program prepares nurses to give nursing care in cooperation with and under the supervision of a first level nurse.

Finally, there is the group of nurses for whom nursing is not simply an occupation. Their practice is characterized by academic rigor, the exercise of independent judgment, personal accountability, and, because it is in the nature of nursing, feminism. They form the profession of nursing. Out of this group comes an even smaller subgroup of nursing leaders whom I call the international elite, because they travel and collaborate as representatives of their countries and their profession.

Given the broad range of practitioners called nurses, it is no surprise that there is continuing confusion in the collection and interpretation of nursing statistics. In the category of nurse, one finds variable groupings of nursing auxiliaries, qualified nurses, and trained midwives who may or may not be qualified nurses or auxiliaries. There is no international standard such as graduation from high school for entry into a school of nursing, no standard content or length of training, no uniform nursing role. Nursing, while fundamental to any concept of healing, is culturally determined.

WHO MAKES DECISIONS ABOUT NURSING AND HEALTH CARE?

Health and the practices, practitioners, and institutions required to attain it are determined by society. Society decides who is sick and who is well, values some modes of healing over others, and dictates the structures through which health services will be provided.

In this, government is the principal instrument of society. Even in the United States, government is the major bill payer for health. Through the allotment of monies for programs, institutions, and services, it assigns health a practical priority in relation to defense, education, housing, social welfare, public safety, transportation, and other societal concerns. Its legal code regulates who gives health care, what services each type of health worker may provide, where they will provide them, how they will be paid, and what legal remedies are available to an aggrieved recipient of care. Professions, said to govern themselves, may do so only within the limits set by law and custom.

In many countries, government is also the major employer of nurses and other health workers. Through a ministry of health at the national level, government builds, staffs, and runs hospitals and other institutions. A ministry of education may publish standard curricula for the training of nurses and other professionals and confer automatic licensure on graduates of its schools. Developing countries are often influenced by the ideologies of allied governments or international organizations that grant funding and material or human resources. Invariably there are strings attached that may result in the creation of new types of health workers, the reorganization of health systems, or emphasis on certain health problems over others.

In most countries, physicians are the main spokesmen for health and the most likely to hold positions of power. With the gradual shifting of health priorities in many countries, however, health service administrators and sometimes nurses are assuming high-level positions of authority and influence.

HOW DO NURSES INFLUENCE THE POLITICAL PROCESS?

Nurses could be called the invisible healers. We have been an essential but amorphous part of the health infrastructure, visible to patients in the act of giving nursing care, but not to the public when issues are being debated and decisions about health care and the allocation of resources are being made. There have always been individual nurses who have advanced nursing as a profession and contributed directly to the improvement of the health of nations, but their influence has been as much a result of their personal qualities, social status, and political connections as the fact that they have been nurses. In many countries, a nurse relative of the head of state or member of the ruling party has exercised great power that would not have come to her except by accident of birth.

The strength of nursing as a profession is linked directly to the status of women in a country or region. If women are strong, active, and independent, so is nursing. If women are anonymous and silent, so is nursing. Is it different where nursing is a predominantly male profession? Curiously, it is not. Where men have been dominant, in some of the French-speaking countries, for example, nurses have aligned themselves with medicine and have been less likely to seek an independent voice or role.

British nurses may be the most politically astute of national groups. Since the Nightingale era, they have been recognized and respected. With the institution of socialized medicine in 1948, nurses became civil servants, directly dependent on the state for their education, employment, advancement, conditions of work, and the governance of their institutions. As a result, all British nurses share common concerns. They have come to the "vital realization that health care without politics is simply not possible" (Schrock, 1977). The Royal College of Nursing, the professional association and union, closely monitors government actions and policy changes and speaks forcefully for the profession. Two major nursing magazines, published weekly, give regular and extensive reports on political developments. The many letters to the editor published in each issue reflect intense interest on the part of large numbers of nurses in everything from salary negotiations (Howie, 1983) to the presence of a chief nursing officer on the supervisory board of the National Health Service (New-look, 1983). Nurses are included in management teams at every level within the NHS—local, regional, and area—and will continue to be influential in policy-making and administration, even though a recent experiment in consensus management (giving each nursing member veto power over any decision taken by the management team) has been terminated as unwieldy ("Griffiths Report," 1983).

By and large, however, nurses are notable for their diversity rather than their conformity, for a concern for individuals and their immediate health care needs rather than broad health goals subject to political wrangling. As a result, their impact on the political process has been subtle and indirect.

WHAT IS THE INTERNATIONAL COUNCIL OF NURSES?

The American Nurses' Association is a member of ICN, represented on its Council of National Representatives by the ANA president. The oldest international professional organization, ICN was formed largely on the initiative of British nurses at the 1899 meeting of the International Council of Women and has had a decidedly feminist orientation ever since.

ICN's official purpose is "to provide a medium through which national nurses' associations share their common interests working together to develop the contribution of nursing to the promotion of the health of people and the care of the sick" (1983). Today, it remains an independent, nongovernmental federation of ninety-five national nurses' associations (only one from a country may belong), headquartered in Geneva. Many nurses attend the Quadrennial Congress, held every four years in a different host country. Between congresses, the work of the organization is carried out by its staff, committees, and the Council of National Representatives, which meets every two years.

ICN aims to serve as the authoritative, international voice for nurses and nursing. This takes the form of policy statements, participation in international meetings of health organizations, and publications such as its official journal, *International Nursing Review*. It also assists in building strong nurses' associations, particularly in the developing world, and helps these groups to improve standards of nursing care and the professional, social, and economic position of nurses. It does this through sponsorship of consultations by ICN staff, international meetings and workshops, and cooperative relationships between associations in developed and developing countries.

The ICN is the profession's United Nations and, like the UN, its meetings often generate more rhetoric than action. Nonetheless, it is the only forum of its kind for international exchange among the world's nurses and merits our attention and support.

WHAT OTHER FORCES SHAPE NURSING WORLDWIDE?

How does an idea or a way of doing something find its way from one place to another? Three major forces have been responsible for the dissemination of nursing innovations around the world: religion, war (or natural disaster), and technology.

Let's use China as an illustration. Nightingale nursing was first brought to China in the late nineteenth century by American missionaries, whose intent was to propagate the Christian faith by preaching, teaching, and healing (Abu-Saad, 1979). Then came the Russo-Japanese War of 1904, and with it the formation of the Chinese Red Cross Society and the establishment of new hospitals and schools of nursing. During World War II, hospitals again proliferated, influenced by the International Red Cross and the United Nations agencies. With the Communist victory in 1949 and the subsequent cultural revolution, schools of nursing and many hospitals were closed, and missionaries and other foreigners were expelled from the country. Ideological shifts, beginning in 1976, awakened interest in exchange with the Western world and the import of technology and consultants in many fields, including health and nursing (Liu, 1983). Meanwhile, innovations from China—acupuncture, the barefoot doctor, and herbal medicines—have been finding their way to the West.

These seemingly anonymous forces of change assume many forms. In addition to medical missionary societies, there are foundations and agencies whose philosophies are humanistic, if not specifically religious. The Kellogg and Rockefeller Foundations, Project HOPE, CARE, and many more transmit knowledge and resources across national and cultural boundaries. The World Bank, officially known as the International Bank for Reconstruction and Development, established to assist in the reconstruction of countries devastated by World War II, lends money for economic and social development to its member countries. The Agency for International Development of the United States Department of State, exports American goods and services in the name of development. The World Health Organization, an agency of the United Nations, serves as an international forum for the exchange of ideas and sponsors health projects worldwide. Multinational corporations buy and sell technology to anyone or any country with an acceptable credit rating.

The place of nursing in these organizations is generally a function of patient demand. Sometimes a health project is planned and executed with no nursing consultation. The planner, perhaps an economist, may say, "Oh yes, I put some money into this rural development program for two regional hospitals, six health posts, equipment, supplies, and staff." In other projects, particularly when health professions' education and the design of health systems are the focus, nurses are an integral part of the planning, implementation, and evaluation. Private organizations that focus specifically on health are most likely to have nurses in key positions. Large, politically oriented bureaucracies are least likely to recognize what nurses can offer.

"HEALTH FOR ALL BY THE YEAR 2000"— WHAT DOES IT MEAN?

> Nursing, like medicine, has for far too many years been predominantly oriented to meeting the needs of the privileged few. . . . To those who ask whether the "world needs nurses," my answer is that billions of people need health services and care, no matter what we may call the respective collectivities needed to promote such care. If those who are now called nurses, or will be so called in the future, are willing to confront the formidable challenges implicit in primary health care, and to acknowledge primary health care as the medium for achieving an acceptable level of health for all people in the foreseeable future, then the world does, indeed, need nurses (p 3).

Thus wrote Halfdan Mahler, director-general of the World Health Organization, in 1978. This was also the year of the Declaration of Alma-Ata. There, in the capital of the Kazakh Republic of the USSR at the International Conference on Primary Health Care, the goal of "health for all" was first etched into the thinking and planning of health officials and governments. Primary health care, which seems at first to be an unattainable political ideal, was further defined as:

essential health care based on practical, scientifically sound and socially acceptable methods and technology made universally accessible to individuals and families in the community through their full participation and at a cost that the community and country can afford to maintain at every stage of their development in the spirit of self-reliance and self-determination (WHO, 1978, p 3).

With this new philosophy has come a distinct change in the way nursing is viewed within WHO and its American regional office, the Pan-American Health Organization. Before Alma-Ata, priority had been given to producing sufficient nursing personnel to provide institutionalized patients with safe levels of nursing care. Programs were frequently directed toward the creation and strengthening of nursing education programs, often along the lines of U.S. models.

In recent official resolutions, member governments are urged to "redirect educational programs in order to strengthen the contribution of nursing to the enterprise of extending care services to the entire population," and to "strengthen the preparation of teaching staff in aspects of community health" (PAHO, 1983).

Only fifteen percent of the world's qualified nurses are in developing countries, where sixty-six percent of the world's population lives (Mahler, 1978). That is one reason new types of middle-level and village health workers are emerging. It is also thought that health professionals like physicians and nurses are less suited to meeting basic health needs through the application of "appropriate technologies" in community settings and on the community's terms. Yet these appropriate technologies can save millions of lives. James Grant, executive director of UNICEF, observed that:

oral rehydration therapy, universal child immunization, the promotion of breastfeeding, and the mass use of child growth charts are all low-cost, low-risk, low-resistance, peoples' health actions which do not depend on the economic and political changes which are necessary in the longer term if poverty itself is to be eradicated. They are therefore available *now* (1983, p 22).

Some countries espousing primary health care still spend disproportionate amounts of money on tertiary care. Even affluent countries like the United States, where the slogan of "health for all" is heard less often, are recognizing that the health dollar does not buy as much as it used to, and what it has bought has not been sufficient to significantly reduce mortality and morbidity from most of the ills that plague us. Nurses in all countries would do well to examine their orientation to health care and nursing practice in light of the primary health care movement and the coming reallocations of health resources.

HOW CAN I CONTRIBUTE TO THE WORLD'S HEALTH?

There are countless ways to become involved in international nursing and health, directly or indirectly. Direct participation most often takes place in an international development project, disaster relief effort, or a program of professional exchange. Any of these may necessitate a short- or long-term overseas commitment. These may be sponsored by private, governmental, or multinational organizations. They may involve direct patient care, but more frequently they mean teaching (and, always, learning), planning, managing, or evaluating, with or without host-country counterparts. The work setting may be a rural health post, a university hospital, a school of nursing, or a government office. Some U.S. nurses work abroad in extensions of the American health care system—in the military, for example, or on the staff of U.S. companies with overseas branches.

Participation in international health is also possible by attending international meetings, undertaking courses of study, or joining international organizations. There are, at any given time, thousands of foreign-trained nurses working or studying in the U.S. who can serve as valuable sources of information about health in their countries. You can study a foreign language and, in doing so, gain entry to a previously unknown culture in a way that will enhance your understanding of people, their beliefs about health and illness, and their use of words to express values, feelings, and needs.

Many nurses lend their support to international causes. Certainly one of the most well-known causes was the Nestlé boycott, which ended in 1984 when the Swiss-based company that controls almost half the world market in baby formula agreed to comply with the WHO infant formula sales code (Hilts, 1984). For six and one-half years, consumers in many countries refused to buy any Nestlé product because its marketing methods persuaded millions of mothers to switch from breast-feeding to bottle-feeding, a practice that can threaten the health of the infant when the formula is misused and strain the finances of a family probably already desperately poor.

A note of caution. Cultural sensitivity is crucial in any international endeavor, and even a seemingly just cause can generate conflict. Female circumcision, for example, has been debated repeatedly in international meetings, including the 1981 ICN Congress. Far from welcoming support from Westerners who abhor the custom and would see it abolished, many women in countries where it is practiced resent the intrusion of Western values and maintain that they not only condone circumcision but plan to have their daughters circumcised. Another fiercely argued issue is the use of the hormone diethylstilbestrol (DES) for long-term contraception in many other countries, sometimes with the advice and support of U.S. agencies, despite the fact that the U.S. Food and Drug Administration has not approved it for use in this country. While some Americans are appalled by the promotion of the contraceptive, many in the countries in question maintain that it has solved more problems than it has caused.

Any American nurse, regardless of the degree to which she is attracted to international nursing, is responsible for two things: keeping abreast of world events, especially as they affect health, and supporting the work of the International Council of Nurses. Nursing can provide a framework from which to look at the world. It can become your world within the world. When someone talks about nursing, whether in Chile or China, they are talking about your profession. And the nurses of the world, whatever their language, culture, training, or patterns of practice, are your colleagues. Nurses have natural counterparts in every country and skills that are in demand.

References

Abu-Saad H: *Nursing—A World View*. Mosby, 1979.

Grant JP: Four Ways to Save Lives. *J Society International Development* 1983; 1:22–24.

"Griffiths Report—have we been this way before?" *Nurs Times* (Nov 23) 1983; 79:9–10.

Hilts PJ: 6½-year boycott of Nestlé is ended as firm adopts baby-formula code. *The Washington Post* (Jan 27) 1984; A1, A23.

Howie C: The concensus begins to dissolve. *Nurs Times* (Mar 30) 1983; 79:10–11.

International Council of Nurses: *Constitution*. ICN, 1983.

Liu Y: China: Health care in transition. *Nurs Outlook* 1983; 31:94–99.

Mahler H: Action for change in nursing. *World Health* (Dec) 1978; 2-3.

New-look NHS threatens nursing voice. *Nurs Mirror* (Nov 2) 1983; 157:5.

Pan-American Health Organization: *Final Report of the XXIX Meeting of the PAHO Directing Council and the XXXV Meeting of the WHO Regional Committee*. PAHO, 1983.

Schrock RA: On political consciousness in nurses. *J Adv Nurs* 1977; 2:41–50.

World Bank: *Health Sector Policy Paper* (2nd ed). World Bank, 1980.

World Health Organization: *Primary Health Care—Report of the Internationl Conference on Primary Health Care, Alma-Ata, USSR*. WHO, 1978.

Vignette: The Politics of Practicing in Another Country

Martha Fortune, RN, MS

The challenges I faced as a nurse educator, working for Project Hope in Tunisia at that government's request from late 1974 to 1976, were dynamic and sometimes elusive. Differences in language, customs, values, material resources, and other variables, including my own inexperience in international work, set the tone for what could have been another story of the "ugly American." Fortunately, my political skills enabled me to turn a potential failure into a success, small though it may have been, for myself and my Tunisian colleagues.

A Portrait of Tunisia

A small, poor, yet picturesque North African country on the Mediterranean Sea, Tunisia has been invaded and controlled by Phoenicians, Romans, Turks, and the French. Although Tunisia's current culture reflects these influences, its history has made Tunisians suspicious of outsiders. The predominant religion is Islam. The government is a democratic republic, with a president elected for life. Education is free and mandatory for all children through primary school. Baccalaureate and professional education is also free.

Tunisians have a fatalistic view of life and health problems. Due to a lack or transitory supply of material goods, Tunisian leaders in many fields struggle with problems that have become obsolete for most Westerners. The use of technology for early diagnosis, treatment, and prevention of health problems was almost nonexistent during my stay. The availability of basic health care was of primary concern to the country. There was at least a two-year waiting list for corrective surgery at the orthopedic hospital in Tunis, where all the major specialty hospitals are located. Persons living in smaller cities, towns, and in the large rural areas had limited access to a physician, hospital, or pharmacy. Nurses assigned to local communities were available to administer injections, dressings, and other nursing care. Clinics were established in some of the towns, primarily for maternal and infant care.

Factors that contributed to the poor health of the country included malnutrition, contaminated water supplies, and lack of solid waste disposal. These factors facilitated the spread of communicable diseases. Although health promotion and disease prevention efforts were widespread, often with assistance from a number of other nations, those persons most at risk were not greatly affected—infant mortality occurred at a rate of about one in three births, and the major cause of death after infancy was attributed to communicable disease.

Freedom of speech was not guaranteed the same protection as it is in the United States. Public meetings to discuss the difficult socioeconomic conditions, even if held in private homes, were discouraged. Rumors were sometimes heard about people missing for several months—people who had spoken against the president or government's positions. Fear of punishment prevented interpersonal and public display of discontent.

Those of us who had been invited by the government to give assistance remained as neutral and uninvolved in the country's internal politics as possible. Nonetheless, the inadequacies inherent in the health care system presented diplomatic dilemmas. Apart from the stress caused by a lack of supplies and insufficient knowledge, there was an overriding atmosphere of denial of problems. This attitude of denial, among citizens and officials alike, proved to be a major stumbling block in my efforts to help bring about needed changes in the delivery of nursing care.

Building Relationships

I was part of a health care team invited by the Tunisian government, specifically the Ministry of Public Health. As one of six nurses on a team of twenty professionals, I helped to identify ways that hospital-trained Tunisian nurses could improve health care. My first assignment was to work with four nurses on a twelve-bed intensive care unit of the endocrine and urology service, which in turn was a part of the 1,000-bed hospital in Tunis. I spent my mornings learning French and my afternoons observing how the unit functioned.

My first challenge quickly arose. On this busy unit, the nurses tended to speak to each other in their native tongue, Arabic. Moreover, many of the patients spoke various rural dialects, which were sometimes difficult for even the Tunisian nurses to understand. This communication problem limited my ability to share my ideas and to understand nurses and patients.

I had to earn the nurses' respect and establish my credibility before they would agree to either translate their discussions into French upon my request, or to speak French in my presence. Some of the nurses felt degraded because I had been asked by their government to work with them. I had to convince them of my willingness to work with them toward their goals. By using the French I was learning, as well as some key Arabic terms, I demonstrated that I was willing to work with them on their terms.

My second challenge was the medical system itself. Since Tunisia had been a French protectorate, the framework for much of the government's agencies and, therefore, the health care delivery system, was the French political system. In the hospital, this meant that physicians gave orders, and nurses carried them out without discussion or question. Nursing care procedures and routines were often based upon tradition and hearsay rather than on documented scientific principles or research. While the nurses had worked out a system for obtaining blood, urine, and other laboratory samples, there was no documentation because of a lack of emphasis on recording procedures. Intake and output were not measured routinely, even for patients on peritoneal dialysis. Drugs and vital signs were not recorded.

Another major problem was the administration of medications. Intramuscular drugs were often drawn up into one syringe to decrease the patient's discomfort by reducing the number of injections a day. Indeed, each nurse was issued a limited amount of supplies, including glass syringes and needles, and any breakage had to be accounted for. Thus, the fewer syringes used, the less chance of damage. Because there was no list of contraindications in the drug index, I had no objective way of proving that combining up to six or seven drugs in a syringe could be dangerous. In addition, the nurses interchanged insulin and tuberculin syringes to administer insulin and PPD, because both were marked in units and there was no literature available to define the difference in these units.

Medical, nursing, and pharmacologic texts were lacking, and advanced education was in the form of lectures. Students were responsible for taking detailed notes. Foreign (French and German) medical texts were taxed 100 to 150 percent over their retail cost and were therefore unavailable to the students. I would often bring my American nursing texts to demonstrate a procedure or try to prove why a procedure, such as sterile technique or the basics of patient positioning, should be done in a certain way. Use of American texts was often unproductive, however, because of the language barrier and the different equipment and supplies.

Some of these obstacles were overcome during the course of my twenty-month stay. My daily encounters with Tunisians, both personally and professionally, helped me to integrate their approach to problem solving, which I saw as essential in the face of limited supplies and expectations—expediency and fatalism. I also learned to appreciate their coping with frequent equipment malfunctions, limited sanitation and a general lack of successful treatments for the acutely ill. I gradually shared my knowledge and ideas with them by working with staff nurses on an individual basis.

Learning a Lesson

My greatest challenge, however, came when I began working with nursing students. During my six-month observation and orientation period, it became apparent that beginning students were assigned to a unit without adequate supervision by their instructor. The staff nurses assigned patients and tasks and instructed the students about procedures. I watched a nurse hold up a syringe full of different drugs and ask, "Who needs to give an intramuscular injection?" It appeared that students who volunteered to administer the injections made no attempt to find out who the patient was; his diagnosis; what the drugs were; or the normal dose, route, and time of administration.

Students were responsible for correctly performing a list of tasks on each service. The nursing instructor met with the staff nurses to verify the list. There were simply not enough nursing instructors, and the system of clinical education bore no resemblance to the problem-solving approach we use in the Western world.

My American nursing colleagues had identified similar problems with other services in the Tunis hospital. Together with our nursing supervisor, we documented the problems and recommended that we meet with the director of the school of nursing to offer our services in the following academic year.

We held several meetings to gather data from our project's team director and from the Tunisian instructors, who were our professional counterparts. It was agreed that we would be allowed to supervise the students in their clinical rotations on the units where we were assigned. We were also expected to participate in classroom teaching and laboratory demonstrations. Naturally, we welcomed this opportunity to introduce scientific, systematic, and safe nursing care to beginning students and to work side-by-side with our Tunisian colleagues.

We spent three summer months building a nursing curriculum and teaching plans from scratch, using Maslow's hierarchy of needs as a framework. It was a major feat just to agree on a common foundation on which to constitute a generic nursing program. Although the Tunisian and French educators had been asked to participate, they were unwilling to relinquish their vacation to do so.

Before the beginning of the school year, we met again with the school's director and the instructors to clarify our roles and the teaching schedule. We began teaching Foundations of Nursing in the classroom and in the lab. However, problems arose when we observed the lectures given by one French and two Tunisian nurses. The material they presented was sometimes too narrow in focus or even incorrect: for example, they taught that the normal pulse was 70 to 72. When we asked the students to take each other's pulses, they reported a range from 48 (a long-distance runner) to 92.

Although we tried to be polite when offering our viewpoints and conflicting data, we embarrassed our Tunisian colleagues. Because saving face is more important than adherence to a principle in their culture, the situation offered a valuable lesson in diplomatic relations. Professional integrity was also a factor, and eventually the working atmosphere between the American nurse educators and our Tunisian and French counterparts became uncomfortable. Despite daily attempts to socialize, share common concerns, and plan classroom and lab instruction, communication rapidly deteriorated. By the end of the first quarter, we were asked by the director of the nursing school to discontinue the didactic portion of our commitment and to confine our teaching to clinical work with students. Although the director was sympathetic to our cause, she had to support her own staff, with whom she would be working long after our departure.

Enduring Changes

When I returned to my original unit, I felt angry and discouraged. Therefore, I was happily surprised to find that the staff nurses were still using the procedures I had taught them when I first came to work at the hospital. Clearly, they had learned and accepted the rationale I had explained months before. I found that the Kardex I had helped them create, at their request, was being successfully used to record both physician and nurse-generated orders. Some intramuscular drugs were actually being injected separately. Disposable syringes had been introduced at our urging, following an increased incidence of hepatitis. The nurses were operating from their own sense of autonomy and problem-solving abilities. The changes that I had wanted to make on this unit had become routine during my six-month absence.

Another incident occurred that strengthened my relationship with the staff nurses. The nurses in the hospital were striking for better wages. The intensive care nurses discussed the strike with me. While I refrained from offering a personal opinion, I did offer to "cover" the unit, together with my students, during a demonstration in which the nurses wanted to participate. This earned me enormous credibility with the staff nurses and students.

During this international experience, my own challenge was to maintain a balance between my yearning for a more advanced level of nursing and health care and the facts before me everyday. I maintained this balance by increasing my appreciation of the culture, the long and varied history, the language, the subgroups in the population, and especially the political climate. The interpersonal and small group approach to change had succeeded, instead of a new curriculum, primarily because of interpersonal grass roots politics. I learned from my gracious hosts that the daily struggle for small changes was worthwhile and would eventually yield better health care for Tunisians.

Vignette: A Report on the Second Public Health Commission to El Salvador

Anne G. Montgomery Hargreaves, RN, MS, FAAN

> . . . the traditional protection conferred on doctors and other health workers has been increasingly ignored as military and paramilitary gangs have assassinated, tortured, and threatened doctors, nurses, and medical students; military and paramilitary personnel have flagrantly entered hospitals and shot down patients in cold blood. . . . (Public Health Commission to El Salvador, 1981)

This report was written by the first Public Health Commission to El Salvador after its 1980 investigation, which documented government-sanctioned repression in the health care sector. At that time, El Salvador was a country torn apart by a bloodless civilian and military coup. The coup had overturned a decades-old military dictatorship and replaced it with a military-dominated junta. Political control quickly returned to the country's traditional power groups—the military and paramilitary and the two percent of the population that owned sixty percent of the land. Reforms in housing, land distribution, and community development that the civilian members of the coup had wanted were resisted. To quiet these calls for reform, the ruling junta resorted to repressive tactics, such as threats, harrassment, and assassination. Because of threats to and killings of both patients and health care workers, including nurses, and because of the military's closing of the country's only medical school, the Committee for Health Rights in El Salvador organized the first commission to investigate conditions there.

In spite of the commission's appeal for ending the repression, abuses of human rights in the health care sector continued. For example, "Eight of 11 physicians who founded the National Commission for the Defense of Patients, Workers and Health Institutions had been killed, 'disappeared' or forced into exile by 1982" (*Health and Human Rights in El Salvador*, 1983, p 7). A second commission was organized to investigate continued charges of repression and the resultant deterioration in health care services and the health of the people of El Salvador.

Early in December, 1982, I received a call at home from a long-time colleague in nursing who was active on The Committee for Health Rights in El Salvador. I had known of her interest for some time, but was not especially concerned about the plight of these people. She asked if I would be willing to be considered as a candidate for a commission being formed to visit El Salvador in January to assess the situation since the visit of a similar group in 1980. A nurse had not been in that delegation, and they wanted one to go with this commission. She was asking me because my attitude was neutral, but I had political experience in nursing. Besides on-the-scene observation, there would be the back-home work of interpreting the findings. I expressed interest and submitted a copy of my credentials for review by the selection committee. I received a telephone call from members of the committee who sounded out my commitment. A week or so later, I was notified of my selection. Because of the political implications of the trip, I requested vacation time from work.

The Delegation

The delegation included myself, five physicians, and a health educator. Sponsors and endorsers of the group included the American Medical Student Association; the American Orthopsychiatric Association; the American Public Health Association (APHA); the Committee of Interns and Residents; the District Council 37 of the American Federation of State, County and Municipal Employees (AFSCME); the Massachusetts Nurses' Association (MNA); the National Association of Social Workers; and the Physicians Forum. Grants to support the delegation were made by the Libre Fund, the Committee of Interns and Residents, and the District Council 37 of AFSCME, along with numerous private donations. The APHA provided meeting space and support services in Washington, DC, for the commission upon its return.

A series of group meetings were held to orient us to the country and the purpose of our mission and to provide the opportunity for us to become acquainted and begin working as a group. The stated purpose of the visit was to determine the level of repression in the health sectors, the impact of repression on health delivery, and the status of training of health personnel.

Plans called for us to meet in New York City for further orientation, then to fly to Mexico City where we were to meet with El Salvadorans in exile. These included representatives of a Committee of Exiled Physicians, members of El Salvadoran political parties that had been forced underground, and family members of political prisoners and missing persons (desaparecidos) in El Salvador.

From Mexico, we flew to San Salvador, the capital of El Salvador and a modern, bustling city. Because of the political situation, we were advised to stay within the city, together, and off the streets at night. During our stay in El Salvador, we met with religious, government, health care, and American personnel, as well as representatives of international relief organizations. For example, we met with U.S. Ambassador Hinton, the chairperson of the El Salvador Human Rights Commission, the attorney general, the International Committee of the Red Cross, the U.S. Department for International Development, the chief of National Police, the vice-minister of health, the El Salvador Nurses' Association, and the Catholic Relief Agency. In addition, the delegation made field trips to refugee camps, prisons, hospitals, and clinics.

Upon completion of our trip, the delegation flew to Washington, DC, to meet with concerned officials and draft our report.

The Findings

The commission's findings were recorded in the document, *Health and Human Rights in El Salvador: A Report of the Second Public Health Commission to El Salvador* (1983).

The commission found virtually a complete breakdown in the country's health care system. Numerous health care workers, including nurses, had been killed by military or paramilitary forces, imprisoned, or forced to leave El Salvador because of the climate of terror generated by the government. The training of health professionals was at a near standstill, while the practicing workers continued to be abducted, tortured, and killed. The health and sanitary conditions of refugees was appalling. Political prisoners were subjected to physical and psychological torture. They were held indefinitely in prison without formal charges or trial. The leading cause of death had become violence. And the children and youth were suffering a terrible toll from the militarization of their society. The commission's report documents these findings:

> At the Maternity Hospital, we observed about 20 women in various stages of labor. Two or three women occupied each bed. Women in labor sat together on a hard bench until shortly before delivery, when they walked up a steep flight of stairs to the delivery room. If they could not pay the fee for admission to the hospital and for medications, they were sent home immediately after they had delivered. . . . The death rate of infants admitted to the sick newborn nursery approaches a staggering *80 percent.*

> . . . Representatives of the refugee relief service of the Lutheran Synod of El Salvador informed us that in a rural area served by one of their clinics, infant mortality now reaches 60 percent. . . . One-third of their patient population has clinically apparent anemia. . . . Salvadoran government forces, operating with U.S. military advisers, are destroying crops and livestock and displacing or killing the peasants who work the land. The abandonment of farms contributed to the deteriorating nutritional state of the population and the attendant rise in disease rates. . . . Lutheran health workers we met . . . reported increased military harrassment. . . . They expressed the fear that their activities would no longer be tolerated. On April 27, 1983, Dr Angel Ibarra, who was medical director of the refugee relief services of the Resurrection Church of San Salvador, was abducted by the National Police and tortured in their headquarters. . . . As recently as six months before our visit, patients had been abducted from hospitals in rural areas.

> . . . Health workers said that any criticism of the government carries the risk of being labeled an insurgent or a supporter of the opposition. This label in turn can lead to loss of one's job or reprisal by government or paramilitary forces. . . . We were told of health workers who were threatened or killed for treating persons suspected of being "guerillas" or "insurgents." Even engaging in health planning, such as the collection of statistics on the incidence of disease, renders health workers liable to reprisal. . . . While physicians, medical students and their families have been primary targets in the past, nurses have increasingly become subject to abduction, assassination and disappearance. This led the Salvadoran nurses' association . . . to take the unusual step of making a public appeal for an end to the violence. (*Health and Human Rights in El Salvador*, 1983, pp 8–10)

These and other findings guided the commission in its recommendations. These included:

- The United States cease all military aid to the government of El Salvador and instead encourage a political settlement through negotiations between the government and opposition.
- The government of El Salvador and its security forces stop the abductions, executions, and imprisonment of health workers and respect the neutrality of health institutions, professional associations, religious and relief organizations, and grant prisoners of war their appropriate rights under the Geneva Conventions.
- The National University with its medical school be reopened under civilian auspices with guarantees of academic freedom and no reprisals against faculty members who return from exile.
- Health services, medicines, food, and clothing be provided for displaced persons within El Salvador.

The Delegation's Return to the U.S.

Needless to say, my experience on the commission erased my neutrality about what was happening in Central America. Once over my initial depression, I mobilized my resources to share what I had observed with any groups or individuals who would listen.

On returning to Washington, DC, the commission held a press conference. There was extensive coverage by the *New York Times* and *Washington Post*. We visited with representatives of the State Department, staff of the Committee on Foreign Affairs, and congressional representatives from our own states.

When I returned to Boston, there was a flurry of interviews by radio and television, newspapers, and popular magazines regarding the commission's findings. The president was interviewed on television about the upcoming elections in El Salvador, and I was asked to follow with comments on two television stations for the evening news. Community groups, schools, organizations, churches, human rights advocacy groups, and town meetings asked me to speak. Within a few weeks, I was asked to come to Washington to appear before the Congressional Subcommittee on Inter-American Affairs. I was in communication with state and national public officials such as U.S. Sen. Edward Kennedy and House of Representatives Speaker Tip O'Neill, who received reports and expressed their support of our recommendations.

Taking the Report to the Nursing Community

I felt a special urgency to communicate with nurses in this country about what was happening to our colleagues in El Salvador. The colleague who had initiated my going on the trip and I held a meeting to report to the Board of Directors of the MNA, which was one of the sponsors of the delegation. My colleague testified in Washington and briefed the staff in the Washington office of the American Nurses' Association (ANA). Accounts of the commission's findings were published in the *Massachusetts Nurse* (MNA's monthly newspaper), *The American Nurse* (the ANA newspaper), and *Nursing Outlook*.

At the ANA 1984 convention, the MNA introduced a Resolution on Health and Human Rights in El Salvador. With revisions, it was adopted by the House of Delegates and is being followed by the ANA Committee on Human Rights. The resolves state:

> That the 1984 American Nurses' Association House of Delegates direct the ANA Board of Directors to have the ANA Cabinet on Human Rights determine what support the ANA might offer nurses in El Salvador and make recommendations for action to the ANA Board of Directors;
>
> That the ANA forward its plan to the International Council of Nurses; and
>
> That the members of the 1984 House of Delegates express their concern in writing to the President of the United States and their congressional representatives that the direction of aid to El Salvador should be for humanitarian purposes.

Questions were raised at the convention as to why the International Council of Nurses (ICN) did not take action. A nurses' association has to ask for help for the ICN to act. For Salvadoran nurses to ask would have put them at risk of torture, prison, and death. It is difficult in the U.S., where we are free to speak our mind and to take issue with the government, to understand what it means to be so intimidated that you dare not express displeasure with what is happening to you and your people.

Human rights are predicated upon physical and psychological integrity. Integrity cannot be maintained in a society disintegrating under political repression, militarization, and economic adversity. The provision of health care and training of health care personnel are dependent upon social organization. In El Salvador, such social organization had been crushed. As stated in the commission's report, "Health and general social processes are intimately connected. Health rights can unite concerns of a legal, moral and political character with those that are more specifically medical."

References

Public Health Commission to El Salvador: Abuses of medical neutrality. *Inter J Health Services* 1981; 11:329–37.

Health and Human Rights in El Salvador: A Report of the Second Public Health Commission to El Salvador. Committee for Health Rights in El Salvador, 1983.

Chapter 37

Nursing and the Corporate World

M. Elizabeth West, RN, EdD

As large corporations increasingly dominate the American economy, nurses are finding they need to know how they can influence corporate decision making. Nurses may interact with corporations in several ways:

- as an employee of a corporation
- as a consumer of services or products of the corporation
- as a beneficiary of corporate funds through grants or gifts to individual nurses, or to nursing groups or to community projects sponsored by nurses and others

This chapter discusses how nurses can interact with corporations on behalf of nursing and the general public.

TYPES OF CORPORATIONS

A corporation can be defined as "any group of people combined into or acting as one body." A corporation allows a group of individual owners to operate under the law of the state in which it is incorporated. All states require corporations to register their articles of incorporation, which specify the purpose and functions of the organization.

The purpose of a corporation is frequently determined by its type of ownership, ie, private or public. A private corporation is owned by an individual or a group of private individuals. It is termed a private corporation because the rules it makes within the law are final and not reviewable by any public body. In the case of health care corporations, a community may operate a hospital as a private corporation. Private corporations may be "proprietary," ie, operated for-profit, or they may be not-for-profit.

A public corporation differs from a private corporation in that it is held in public trust and is subject to governmental regulation. Under certain conditions, a publicly held corporation may issue and trade stock in accordance with rules and regulations of the Securities and Exchange Commission (SEC). It is expected to return a profit to the owners of the stock. Most individual investor-owned hospitals are operated for profit, but are privately owned, eg, are not public corporations. Many hospital management firms, however, are publicly held corporations that may own and manage a variety of individual hospitals of both types—for-profit and not-for-profit.

CORPORATION POWER STRUCTURE

A public corporation operates under the regulations of the SEC. Under the SEC's strict guidelines, it is authorized to issue or sell stock. The officers of the company, under the direction of the chief executive officer (CEO) or president of the corporation, are responsible for management decisions. The key officers are employees of the corporation and most own stock in the firm.

The CEO is responsible to the board of directors. The board is elected by the stockholders. A chairman of the board is also elected to manage board affairs and determine the direction of the corporation.

Because of the structure of a public corporation, its immediate concerns are focused on corporate growth, profits, and stockholder dividends. Management decisions are made with these three goals in mind. Pursuit of corporate growth often leads companies into mergers, buy outs, and other business transactions designed to increase the value of the business and its stock. This dedication to corporate growth may not be in the best interests of the public. Currently, the concept of corporate social responsibility, that suggests businesses should promote the well-being of the community at large, seems to be at a low ebb. For example, chemical companies have improperly disposed of wastes, resulting in dangerous pollution of community water supplies. Some believe the motivation for such apparently short-sighted and irresponsible actions derives solely from the desire of management to increase corporate profits.

Private corporations also have boards of directors accountable to private stockholders for growth and increased dividends. Because private corporations do not sell stock publicly, they are not regulated by the SEC. Because the source of growth capital derives from reinvestment of profits or loans, the growth of private companies is typically slower than that of public corporations. Most private corporations, therefore, are smaller than public corporations. Private corporations may be either for-profit or not-for-profit.

Nurses are more familiar with the power structure of the not-for-profit corporation because traditionally nursing schools and medical schools have affiliated with not-for-profit hospital corporations. Typically, not-for-profit corporations have operated with a high-degree of autonomy even when owned by religious groups and communities. Without the responsibility of a return on investment or the necessity to pay taxes on surplus funds, the local boards of directors were able to subsidize nursing and medical education and marginally profitable patient services; eg, obstetrical and pediatric services, which have traditionally cost more to operate than they returned to the hospital.

Within the last decade, not-for-profit corporations faced with serious financial pressures are reevaluating their organizational structures. With this restructuring, poly-corporations are emerging that manage a group of not-for-profit hospitals and for-profit health care subsidiary corporations. The voluntary hospital power structure is becoming more complex, and corporate values are changing to include not only a goal to provide community service but also to assure fiscal accountability for each operational entity.

The 1970s has seen the emergence of large multihospital corporations within the health care sector. Starr (1982) states that "of all the forces fragmenting the (medical) profession in the 1980s, none promises to introduce more antagonistic divisions than the growing presence of corporations in medical care" (p 420). If nursing is to survive within this environment, it is important that individual nurses understand how a corporation functions.

NURSES' POWER IN CORPORATE HEALTH CARE ORGANIZATIONS

Nurses' involvement in corporate health care settings is not a new phenomenon. The first incorporated hospital in the United States was the Pennsylvania Hospital. Still in existence today, it received its charter in 1756. In the early 1900s, a substantial number of hospitals were built and owned by individuals or groups of individuals, frequently physicians, and were operated for profit. During this period, governmental, charitable, and religious groups established hospitals. During the depression, when many individually owned hospitals were bankrupt, nonprofit hospitals became increasingly important. Nurses held high-level positions within these settings. Regardless of the hospitals' ownership, the level of authority and responsibility given to nurses who oversaw the operation of these facilities was corporate in nature. Readers familiar with the many Catholic hospitals and charitable hospital systems understand the responsible roles nurses assumed, especially those in religious orders, in the provision of health care and the process of corporate decision making.

The power structure of the voluntary nonprofit hospital corporation has traditionally resided with a board of directors. Board members typically included community leaders, members of the medical staff, (or medical school where applicable) and the hospital's chief executive officer. Traditionally, nursing has been esteemed because of its service orientation and has operated with a high degree of autonomy within the organization. Chief nurses were consulted about changes in policies and services and frequently had responsibility for the school of nursing, which subsidized the labor needs of the facility.

Corporate politics in the voluntary not-for-profit hospital setting was complex due to the integration of many professional disciplines. These organizations often recruited executives and managers who shared goals of community service with nursing and medicine. Therefore, nursing and medicine rarely found themselves in conflict with the corporate mission and goals. A commitment to patient care and community service was shared by hospital boards of directors, physicians, administrators, and nurses.

The role of the nurse in contemporary corporate hospital settings has changed remarkably. In this age of accountability, nurses are increasingly called upon to defend their positions and prove that nursing contributes to the improvement of health care and the corporation. It is not enough to say that nurses have always had an active part in corporate settings and therefore have earned their rightful place.

A major change in the management of health care corporations is related to the increase in the number of professional business managers in key positions. Few of these "MBA types" have had any health care experience and are looked at askance by many health professionals. Because nursing and medicine were not sufficiently prepared to play the bottom-line game with the new breed of administrators, they have experienced a weakening of their professional sovereignty within the health care system. The expansion of the large multihospital system chains further jeopardizes the medical and nursing professions' control of health care organizations and their professional standards. Nursing finds itself in a particularly weakened state due to its lack of professional and workplace-based cohesiveness.

What are nurses doing about this? Individual nurses and groups of nurses are banding together to influence the direction of the corporate health care. This commitment requires nurses to explore new ideas such as:

- the nature of institutional politics
- ways to market clinical skills
- accounting methods for costing out nursing care

The 1970s and 1980s have brought harsher times for many public and nonprofit hospitals and greater opportunities for nurse managers. Cutbacks in reimbursement rates under government programs threaten the survival of large teaching hospitals and public hospitals, which care for large numbers of indigent patients. Hospitals face a more competitive market, and many will not survive. On the other hand, multihospital systems, constantly seeking ways to improve productivity, are expanding rapidly. Also, voluntary hospitals are diversifying. They are reorganizing corporate structures to create holding companies or parent corporations, which own and manage a variety of subsidiaries. The ambitions of hospital and nurse administrators now go considerably beyond the traditional hospital functions.

With the health care segment of society growing and changing rapidly, nurses have opportunities to create new roles and responsibilities. Some of these opportunities are described below.

MULTIHOSPITAL SYSTEMS

Investor-owned hospital corporations emerged in the 1970s to form multiunit, for-profit hospital systems. In 1980, the 10 largest investor-owned corporations owned or leased about 340 hospitals totaling 52,000 beds. Management contracts added another 220 hospitals, totaling 25,000 beds. In 1980, industry forecasted that the number of hospital beds controlled by investor-owned hospital chains would double in the 1980s. By 1983, the ten largest multifacility systems operated 944 hospitals worldwide representing 141,897 beds. One firm, Hospital Corporation of America, operates 390 hospitals with 56,226 beds (Johnson, 1985). This phenomenal growth brings opportunities for nurses.

Even though most investor-owned companies hired nurse consultants to trouble shoot, Hospital Affiliates International was the first (1976) major multifacility company to place a nurse in an executive position within the corporation, ie, vice-president for nursing. Humana created a similar position in 1978. Nurses in these positions focused on productivity, management systems development, monitoring quality of care, recruitment, seminar development, and general trouble shooting. Other hospital management firms hired nurses in a variety of positions including: corporate director of nursing, director of recruitment, director medical information systems, director of quality assurance/risk management, director of education, and other nurse consulting roles.

Nurses hired for corporate positions had varied backgrounds and gained entry in a variety of ways. Some were transferred to the corporate office after having been in a management or education position within a hospital owned or managed by the corporation. Others were hired because of a particular specialty, ie, recruitment, management systems development, seminar development. All had a track record of success in previous jobs and a specific skill needed by the corporation.

Nurses within the corporation are highly valued as specialists. As the multihospital systems have become larger, however, most specialists have not been promoted to line positions, eg, they do not direct the work of numbers of professional or ancillary staff, because they lack managerial experience and graduate business degrees. Those that remain in high level positions in multihospital systems perform a staff function (such as assistant to the president) rather than holding positions with line authority, such as assistant administrator. Even though these nurses are influential and consulted about problems of a specialty nature, most are not in a position of direct line organizational power.

Nurses in high level positions, particularly those who are officers of the corporation, are able to influence the practice of nursing within individual hospitals. They can do this directly by offering their expertise within the hospital or indirectly by stimulating development of nursing care delivery systems, productivity standards, and company-wide seminars. It is interesting to note that the largest multihospital chain, HCA, does not have a nurse in a high level executive position within the company. The centralized corporate nurse position was eliminated in 1982 when decentralized regional offices were created.

VOLUNTARY HOSPITAL SYSTEMS

Many nonprofit hospital corporations as well as other health care corporations are operationally efficient and may produce a substantial financial surplus each year. Because of the nonprofit label, however, this surplus must be invested in new equipment and expansion of facilities.

Through corporate restructuring, individual voluntary not-for-profit hospitals are expanding their bases of operation to include ownership or management of smaller hospitals. The unbundling of costs is also occurring. For example, the cost of direct nursing care is being recorded separately rather than being lumped in with the cost of housekeeping and laundry. Nursing administrators, frequently titled vice-president of nursing or vice-president of patient services, have been assigned responsibility for coordination of nursing and other patient care services for the parent hospital as well as for the management contract hospitals. In this role, the nurse administrator has direct line authority over the nursing organization and other patient care services and may also have either direct line authority over nursing organizations within the management contract hospital or a consulting relationship (functional authority) over nursing in the managed hospital. In either case, because of the nurse administrator's line authority in the parent hospital, and the smaller number of contract hospitals involved, the corporate nurse in this setting may have a power base equal to or greater than the corporate nurse in the major multihospital system. This may also be due, in part, to the fact that the power of the organization is held primarily by hospital professionals, who have a greater understanding of the role of nursing than the many nonhealth care business professionals in the major multi-hospital systems. As smaller voluntary hospital systems expand, the nurse administrators will have an excellent opportunity to expand their authority and influence. The nurse administrator in the progressive voluntary hospital system has a potentially greater opportunity to expand the influence of nursing within the corporate setting.

OTHER HEALTH CARE CORPORATIONS

Another significant trend in the 1980s is the decentralization of the health care system. Until the 1980s, the hospital was the central core of the health care delivery system. With the diversification and decentralization of the health care industry, new opportunities are emerging for nurses, which may include operating subsidiaries of parent hospitals. For example, in Kansas City, Missouri, a 600-bed nonprofit research medical center operates a profit-making subsidiary, Health Services Management, Inc. It sells assertiveness training, stress management, continuing medical education, and group therapy for children. Other new ventures being considered include a chain of health food restaurants and retail pharmacies. Other hospital corporations have entered the hospital management business through purchase or management of smaller hospitals within their geographic area. Nurses employed in these systems as administrators of subsidiary hospital corporations serve as chief operating officers of ambulatory clinics, surgical care centers, and nursing homes.

Opportunities also exist for nurses to operate their own corporations. For example, nurses now own and manage small and large home health companies. This gives them ultimate control over the direction of the organization. One such company, Health Care Partners (HCP), of Nashville, Tennessee, originated because the owners, as employees of another health care corporation, believed that their professional practice of nursing and their personal goals for patient care were compromised. Not able, as employees, to influence the corporation to uphold nursing standards, these nurses founded their own health care corporation. In 1984, it had revenues of $4.2 million and operated in three states. Starting a business is risky, but perhaps it is the most honest stand nurses can take to effect change in the health care system. Indeed, the subject of nurse entrepreneurs is growing increasingly popular as more nurses do establish their own corporations (Millhaven, 1984).

Through their own corporation, the owners of HCP have demonstrated their belief in and commitment to nursing as a profession by:

- submitting a certificate-of-need to construct and operate a midwifery birthing center
- providing an avenue for professional RNs working for the home health care company to function as independent practitioners, rather than employees, and take advantage of professional benefits of self-employment
- providing opportunities for individual nurses, through investor participation and stock options, to take an active part in corporate decision making
- starting a foundation to support and finance special projects that benefit nursing. As individuals, they have also actively participated in a consumer coalition to assist nurse-midwives in pursuing an antitrust case initiated when their practice privileges were denied (see Chapter 16).

The diversification and decentralization of the health care system will expand corporate job opportunities for nurses over the next decade. The corporate nurse will increasingly be faced with the need to make decisions about nursing, health care, and management issues. She will be in a position to advance or compromise nursing within the corporation and the community it serves. An essential part of being an effective corporate nurse leader will involve the ability to judge the significance of issues that affect nursing and develop strategies to deal with them.

INFLUENCING THE HEALTH CARE CORPORATION

Gaining Entry

Health care corporations employ large numbers of college graduates as well as those with advanced degrees. Nurses who seek corporate employment should find out what types of degrees are valued by the corporation. The baccalaureate nursing graduate might pursue a graduate degree in nursing or a master's in business administration (MBA). The larger the corporation, the higher the percentage of upper level managers who hold MBAs from prestigious universities. The nurse who wants to become an officer of a large multihospital system is likely to be faced with the question: "Will I need a graduate business degree to seek a higher position in this corporation?"

While educational credentials are important, nurses who seek entry into large multihospital corporations should not assume that possession of the appropriate degrees will provide entry. Corporations may eliminate nondegreed candidates, but will select employees based upon prior successful experience in a similar position. Corporate nurses have often gained entry because they had the right credentials and skills and were in the right place at the right time. Timing is a critical factor, but the nurse who has marketable skills, clinical experience, and appropriate educational credentials will have the edge.

Employment experts have discovered that only twenty to thirty percent of all jobs are filled through want ads and employment agencies or by sending out resumes with requests for interviews. Of course, it is possible to locate a corporate position using these methods. A majority of jobs are never advertised.

Gaining entry to a corporation can be enhanced by: (1) researching the organization where you think you'd like to be employed; (2) establishing contacts with employees to learn about available openings; and (3) securing an inside spokesperson who will speak in your behalf before your interview. If possible, the candidate should bypass the personnel department and arrange interviews with the individuals who have the power to hire. During the interview, the candidate should be as specific as possible about career goals and skills and the potential contribution he or she can make to the company. It is important to have ideas about the kind of position you want, but be open minded.

If a contact cannot be located within the company, identify the individual to whom the person in the desired position will report and write the individual requesting an interview. A candidate is advised to use corporate contacts to open doors, but the selling of your skills is entirely up to you. You must market yourself to the corporation.

Up the Ladder

The nurse can influence the corporate structure only after learning enough about himself or herself, the job, and the corporation to develop a strategy for climbing the corporate ladder. Another way to consider this idea is to think about how a nurse might market knowledge and skills within the corporation. To climb the corporate ladder, an individual must successfully perform his or her job and demonstrate perseverance and flexibility. He or she must also acquire an understanding of the corporate structure, institutional politics, sources of power, and decision-making styles.

The role of the mentor is important in understanding the corporate power structure and preparing to climb the corporate ladder. A mentor can provide insight into the politics of the organization and provide advice on how to get ahead. Gaining access to a potential mentor is often difficult for new corporate employees, especially women. A mentor usually takes the initiative, based on personal desire to help the protege grow and develop within the organization. A mentor may devote considerable time and energy on behalf of the employee and take great pride in his or her progress. Because of the need to support professional nursing goals, corporate nurse executives have responsibility to seek out proteges and to act as mentors. This type of leadership will promote nursing and enhance the individual nurse's success within the corporation.

Nurses working in corporate settings also need to support each other to project a consistent voice on behalf of nursing. When nurses are divided, it undermines individual nurses' effectiveness and confuses the corporation's view of nursing. Corporate nurses who work together as a team can positively influence the corporation's view of nursing.

Traditionally, corporate nurses have worked independently within the corporation, resisting a centralized authority. Because of this, corporate nurses within a large, multi-facility corporation have not been viewed as a united group. This has reduced their power to exert influence within the corporation. For example, in one major multifacility corporation that employed a vice-president of nursing as well as regional nursing consultants, the nursing consultants could not agree on the role of the licensed practical/vocational nurse (LPN/LVN). In some cases, the LPN/LVN worked in the capacity of a registered nurse. In other instances, the LPN/LVN role was limited to that of a nurse's aide. The corporate nursing consultants continually argued among themselves about the LPN/LVN role and failed to recommend a corporate policy. In this case, the vice-president of nursing had no direct line authority over the regional consultants and could not order them to develop an appropriate policy. The regional consultants resisted development of specific nursing standards to maintain personal autonomy and control of their particular settings. The lack of team work prevented the development of corporatewide nursing standards and gave credence to the belief that nurses do a lot of infighting.

Dealing with corporate politics requires the ability to analyze organizational power structures. This involves identifying the level at which decisions are made. For example, what level of authority is given to the individual health care institution, and what decisions are controlled at the corporate level? It is also important to determine who will be affected by a decision or change in policy before it is implemented. If a decision negatively affects only one powerful person, and that person was not consulted in advance, the decision and the decision maker may both be rejected. A corporate nurse is well-advised to become a serious student of institutional politics (Longest, 1975).

Many nurses hold middle management positions in health corporations such as Upjohn Healthcare Services and health care insurance companies. These nurses often work independently, so that opportunities for work-related collegial relationships are limited. Frequently, these nurses realize that within the corporation, they alone speak for nursing. Because professional isolation of this sort causes nurses to lose touch with nursing and its professional goals, it is important for them to find ways to maintain contact with professional associations. The corporate nurse can rely on the association not only to provide the usual benefits of association membership, but also to develop professional networks that can help reduce isolation from the profession.

SUPPORT FOR PROJECTS THAT BENEFIT NURSING

Obtaining support for major projects requires preparation. The amount of preparation required is directly proportional to the cost impact and the number of persons affected by the project as well as the power base of the individual seeking approval for a project. For example, if the president of the corporation proposes to the board of directors a change of policy that is not costly and will benefit the board as a whole, little more than a verbal request may be required. If, however, a middle manager proposes a policy that is not excessively costly and will benefit middle managers primarily, she may be required to provide more documentation. It is generally true that individuals who have limited authority or power will be expected to provide more documentation as to the need for and benefits of a project. A controversial project that will require considerable funding or will result in major operational changes, must be thoroughly planned to prevent costly errors and avoid confusing employees (see Figure 37-1).

1. Clear definition of the project or issue and its impact on the company

2. Discussion of the potential benefits

3. Acknowledgment of the potential implementation problems

4. Projected cost

5. Proposed implementation time-line

6. Project evaluation methods

Figure 37-1   Project Development: Key Steps

For example, a corporate nursing executive proposed the development of a one-year preceptorship program to prepare nurse administrators. The projected program cost was high, but the nurse executive was able to demonstrate that improved preparation of nurse administrators would reduce turnover rates and recruitment costs among nursing directors. She also projected that a more stable nursing management team would provide improved management in the corporate hospitals. The corporate nursing director followed the steps outlined in Figure 37-1, and her project was approved and funded.

The more complex and controversial the issue, the more need for marketing the project. Managers frequently become so involved in the "pride of authorship" of a project that they fail to identify potential problems. They expect their ideas to be enthusiastically received by others. Politically astute managers consult decision makers and other key players during the development of a project to obtain helpful suggestions and support. Following several revisions of a project proposal, it is always prudent to review the final document with one or more objective reviewers before its submission or presentation.

Resolving Ethical Issues and Conflicts

In working within a corporation, a nurse's professional values may conflict with a corporate policy or direction. The corporate nurse must decide whether to take a stand on the issue. The issue may take the form of a problem, conflict, differing opinion, or a matter of serious controversy. It may be an isolated incident or it could affect professional nursing on a corporatewide basis.

Examples of ethical issues range from individual conflicts with a hospital administrator or physician regarding patient care to changing the legal practice of professional nursing within the corporation. Regardless of the issue, corporate nurses must analyze and judge the issue from two points of view, that of a professional nurse and as a corporate employee. Corporate nurses also need to examine the issue or position from the consumers' point of view.

Before action is initiated, the corporate nurse must weigh the significance of the issue and the price of pursuing the conflict. Probing more deeply into the facts and verifying essential information clarifies the significance of the problem and each participant's role. Once the issue has been clarified and the chronology of events established, the simplest approach should be sought. The more controversial the issue and the more people affected by the problem, the more complex the solution becomes.

An example of choosing the simplest approach to solving a conflict occurred when a nurse consultant at a large investor-owned corporation received a call from a director of nursing in an eighty-bed rural midwestern hospital concerning a physician/nurse conflict. A nurse had refused to administer a penicillin injection to a hospitalized patient who stated he was allergic to penicillin. She called the attending physician, and informed her of the patient's allergy. The physician instructed the nurse to give the injection. When the nurse questioned the action, the physician threatened to have her fired for insubordination. The physician complained to the hospital administrator who, in turn, instructed the director of nursing to fire the nurse. The director of nursing supported the employee's action, based on her understanding of a nurse's responsibility to "protect the patient from harm" and the nurse's liability if a patient injury resulted from her action.

The director of nursing requested that the parent corporation intervene. The corporate nurse analyzed the situation and saw no need to involve the regional or national corporate office unless the parties were resistant to a solution. The corporate nurse spoke jointly with the hospital administrator and director of nursing, explaining the nurse's legal responsibility to protect patients. The corporate nurse recommended that the hospital pharmacist be asked to evaluate potential action of the drug and that the pharmacy and therapeutics committee of the medical staff be convened, if necessary, to evaluate the problem. These steps were taken, and within a few hours it was determined that:

- The nurse had acted judiciously in questioning the administration of penicillin in view of the facts available to her.
- The patient was not allergic to penicillin, but to a drug solvent used to mix penicillin. The physician knew this, but did not communicate this fact to the nurse. The patient could in fact receive the drug ordered.
- The physician had acted inappropriately because she had not provided the nurse with the necessary details and supporting information.

The simplest solution was chosen, thereby avoiding both a personal disaster (termination) for the nurse and the possibility of legal action against the physician and hospital by the nurse.

There are times when a corporate nurse must be willing to take a personal stand and risk losing her job to uphold professional standards. Such a situation arose in a small southeastern hospital when an administrator imposed unsafe staffing levels on the evening and night shifts. Several "near miss" patient incidents occurred because of low staffing levels, and the administrator threatened the nursing managers with reprisal if they complained. The director of nursing called the corporate nurse in confidence. She evaluated the situation and, based upon the immediate potential hazard to the patients and her knowledge of the administrator, she called the regional director in charge of that area.

The regional director recognized a potential hazard but could not respond immediately. He said he would handle the problem within a few weeks. The corporate nurse reiterated her concern and recommendation for immediate action. She requested permission to visit the hospital, which was denied. When she insisted, she was told that it was not her concern. Believing that the hospital's nurses and patients were being subjected to dangerous conditions, the corporate nurse stated she would allow the regional director eight hours to solve the problem, after which she would be on site personally to resolve the issue. The regional director stated he would have the corporate nurse fired if she appeared on site, but she firmly stated she would come to the hospital if the problem was not resolved within eight hours.

The regional director appeared unexpectedly at the hospital within six hours. He uncovered serious problems and fired the administrator on the spot. The situation was resolved, but only after personal risk had been taken by the corporate nurse.

There are times when a corporate nurse must also take a stand on issues that affect patient care in a large number of health-care settings. Projects designed and instituted by corporate nurses that positively affect patient care include: the establishment of corporate-wide standards for nursing, introduction of corporate-wide quality assurance standards, creation of salary scales for nursing managers, institution of grievance procedures, development of nursing care delivery systems, and productivity standards.

Once a nurse or group of nurses request funds and support for projects to enhance nursing and patient care, their individual and collective effectiveness as corporate employees is on the line. If nursing-sponsored projects do not meet projected outcomes, the management of the nursing department or unit is called into question. If nursing projects are successful, then the corporate bosses will be more likely to support further proposals.

Other issues that must be dealt with by nursing leaders and their administrative colleagues in health care corporations include third party reimbursement of nurse practitioners, and practice privileges for nurse-midwives, psychiatric nurse practitioners, and other nurses in expanded roles. Also, because of the purchasing impact of large health care companies, corporate nurses should influence large health supply corporations to improve the safety of patient care products.

Corporate nursing leaders are working together nationwide to influence nursing within the multihospital corporations. In 1981, through the Federation of American Hospitals, a nationwide organization representing multihospital chains, a nursing task force was formed to review nursing issues that affect proprietary hospitals. Although in its infancy, this group promises to support nursing's agendas within these large corporations.

THE NURSE AS A CONSUMER ADVOCATE

The Consumer Movement

A corporation provides a service or product to its customers. The corporation justifies or measures its success on profits, which in turn are affected by the number and degree of satisfied customers. If, for example, a hospital fails to deliver good nursing care, it may run into conflict with the law or be sued by a dissatisfied consumer.

What is good for business is not necessarily good for society. Consumers have been harmed by the sale of unsafe products, such as the Dalkon Shield (an intrauterine device for birth control). Improper and dangerous disposal of pollutants has caused a public outcry against corporate policies that harm the public. In the short run, corporations "won"—they made money. But in the long run, when consumer dangers were documented, these firms paid a heavy price in monetary losses (through lawsuits) and in damaged reputations.

Society has become increasingly aware of corporate practices that endanger consumers' health. In the July, 1962 message to Congress, President Kennedy stated the four rights of consumers:

- *The right to safety*—to be protected against the marketing of goods that are hazardous to health or life.
- *The right to be informed*—to be protected against fraudulent, deceitful, or grossly misleading information, advertising, labeling, or other practices, and to be given the facts he needs to make an informed choice.
- *The right to choose*—to be assured, wherever possible, access to a variety of products and services at competitive prices and, in those industries in which competition is not workable and government regulation is substituted, to be assured satisfactory quality and service at fair prices.
- *The right to be heard*—to be assured that consumer interests will receive full and sympathetic consideration in the formulation of government policy, and fair and expeditious treatment in its administrative tribunals.

He also established the Consumer Advisory Council which identified ten major fields of interest to consumers:

1. consumer grades, standards, and labels
2. two-way flow of information and opinion between government and consumers
3. effective consumer representation in government
4. consumer credit
5. cooperation among federal agencies and between federal and state agencies
6. acceleration of economic growth
7. increased consumption by low-income groups
8. antitrust action and prevention of price fixing
9. adequate housing
10. adequate medical care (Nicholson, 1974, p 126)

In 1964, President Johnson appointed a special assistant for consumer affairs. In the following months, the 92nd Congress passed legislation to strengthen the Office of Consumer Affairs, including the power to obtain court injunctions, to issue cease and desist orders, to prosecute cases, and to levy stiff penalties on violators. Major consumers' rights and positive actions include:

- *Truth in Lending Bill*, 1968, provides full credit disclosure as to the costs and rates to the consumer for credit

- *The Fair Packaging and Labeling Act*, July 1, 1967, provides the customer product information through product labeling
- *Enforcement of Federal Trade Commission Act*, 1914 and the 1938 Wheeler-Lee Amendment, to protect consumers from false advertising

Other areas of government interest have included product safety, branding, and environmental issues.

Nursing's Involvement in the Consumer Movement

Nurses are in an excellent position to alert the public to dangerous consumer products or services and to initiate legislation on behalf of the general public. As consumer advocates, nurses are challenging the actions of large corporations that are in conflict with the public interest. Nurses are recognizing their personal and professional responsibility to take a stand on health care issues. Legislators are also recognizing professional nurses' political clout, for they represent a formidable voting block when they stand together on consumer and health care issues.

Ethical conflicts arise when corporations mislead the public, intentionally or unintentionally, to market a product and make a profit. Some of the unethical practices objected to by nurses and consumers may be completely legal, "fuzzily" legal, illegal with light penalties, or illegal with heavy penalties. Examples include deceptive advertising, pollution violations, and price fixing. Some corporations avoid unethical practices, especially if the gains are small. Some stay just inside the border of legality, and others gamble on not getting caught. At the other end of the spectrum are corporations that have a well-developed social conscience; some even sponsor consumer advocacy legislation.

Nursing has a responsibility to make the public aware of dangerous or unethical corporate actions that negatively affect the health care of the public. For example, deceptive advertising is still largely unregulated. The Federal Trade Commission has cracked down on some dishonest practices, but advertising still promotes deceptive impressions while avoiding specific misstatements of fact. For example, "(brand x) is stronger than any other painkiller on the market" simply means the manufacturer has increased the amount of aspirin in each tablet.

Large corporations employ legal staffs and other personnel to represent their best interests. Many large corporations have unlimited resources at their disposal, and if an issue is important enough to the corporate image or profits, the corporation may outlast the efforts of an organized but less well-financed opposition.

Nurses who decide to oppose a corporation's position or product should prepare carefully. Banding together through coalitions is one way in which nurses are forcing change. In one instance, nurses and others formed a coalition (INFACT) to fight the Nestlé Corporation. At issue was Nestlé's international practice of using employees dressed like nurses to market infant formula to new mothers in poverty-stricken areas of the world, despite the fact that the mothers could ill afford the formula and did not have the skill or a safe water supply to ensure appropriate use. INFACT conducted a seven-year boycott of the Nestlé Corporation. Nurses in Massachusetts, through the nurses' association, passed a resolution to boycott Nestlé, obtained petitions, and distributed leaflets throughout the state. The boycott resulted in passage of legislation in several states, including New York and Massachusetts, to promote breast-feeding.

Professional Organizations and the Consumer Movement

Consumerism was begun by those who saw it as an opportunity for sales or needed reforms. Ralph Nader urges professional and technical societies to take a stand within the consumer movement. Nader called these societies "sleeping giants where the protection of the consumer is concerned" (Nicholson, 1974, p 142). He was shocked that societies such as the American Society of Mechanical Engineers, the American Chemical Society, and the American Society of Safety Engineers had done so little to work out public policies to deal with pollution.

In health care, the professional nursing organizations have testified on behalf of the public, particularly on issues related to protection of the elderly. For example, at a March, 1984 hearing on the Senate Labor and Human Resources Committee, leadership of the Tri-Council for Nursing—the leadership of American Nurses' Association (ANA), National League for Nursing (NLN), American Association of Colleges of Nursing (AACN)—testified that "the federal research enterprise is out of touch with the needs in long-term care" and "that the National Institutes of Health provide next to no support for the sciences that serve the aged and chronically ill (Nursing groups step up, 1984, p 667). The ANA, through its Washington Office, continually monitors issues that affect public health and nursing.

The consumer movement continues to be a feeble force in American power politics. Some people hold that there is a clear case for setting up professional firms to act in the public interest at federal and local levels. Support for such firms could come from foundations, private donations, dues paid by consumers and the professions, or government subsidies. The Neighborhood Legal Services is a precedent-setting example of this concept.

As patient advocates, nurses must take an active part within the community to protect the public's health and safety. This may be accomplished through: (1) the establishment of a consumer arm of local, state, and national professional organizations; (2) the establishment of coalitions to fight specific consumer issues; and (3) individual participation in consumer issues through local political arms, letter writing campaigns, and boycotting of certain products and services.

CORPORATIONS AS SOURCES OF FUNDS

Large corporations are sources of funds for research. Because large corporations recognize a social responsibility to the communities they serve, more are approving corporate guidelines that provide for assisting community agency projects or causes. Shell Oil, for example, in their "Statement of General Business Principles," stated that "The most important contribution that companies can make to the social and material progress of the countries in which they operate is doing their business efficiently" (Wagner, 1982). It urges, however, that the companies take a constructive interest in social matters, educational assistance, or making financial donations.

The federal government is the largest source of funding for health care projects; however, corporate philanthropy for nursing and nursing-related projects exists. In general, public information on corporate funding is scanty, often because corporations or nurses receiving corporate funds are reluctant to reveal this information.

Corporate Funding Approaches

There are many approaches that a corporation uses to provide grants or charitable funds. Some of these include:

- establishing a nonprofit foundation
- matching employee contributions with donations
- approving grant proposals on an individual basis

Corporations may use a variety of methods to sponsor a project financially. Several of these include:

- establish a scholarship fund administered by the corporation or through application to a specific nursing school, college, or university
- provide a grant to finance a project of interest to the company
- donate supplies, funds, or services to partially support a project
- contract with a health care company or agency to provide a service the company does not provide

Corporations that establish foundations frequently appoint a foundation board to administer the funds. Projects are reviewed on an individual basis, and funds are awarded by the board for projects that meet corporate guidelines. The guidelines vary in accordance with the specific corporation's goals and funding capability.

Types of Foundations

There are five general categories of foundations: general purpose, special purpose, corporate, community, and family. Community foundations usually award grants within a specific geographic area. For example, the Cleveland Foundation and the San Francisco Foundation award grants to individuals and groups within their cities.

Family foundations usually award grants only once a year and often make awards to organizations personally known to the family of the benefactor. Special purpose foundations usually support specific fields of interest. The Anne Fuller Fund, for example, specializes in cancer research and treatment.

Sources for Information on Corporate Funding

Although many corporations do not establish separate identifiable foundations, many contribute to public and private foundations. Several publications list information concerning corporate giving. For example, *The Handbook of Corporate Social Responsibility* (1975) includes a brief description of projects funded by more than 200 larger industrial corporations. Along with other helpful information, *The Handbook* lists a contact person and measures of success used for evaluation. Another source of information is the *Bibliography of Corporate Social Philanthropy* (1977), which organizes articles and speeches under headings such as health and health education, as well as corporate reports that identify projects for which corporate funds have been provided.

More than half the grants awarded by foundations are made by general purpose foundations. Examples of these are The Robert Wood Johnson Foundation, The Lilly Endowment, and the Ford Foundation.

Several corporations, including Republic Steel, Kellogg, and Merck have also established foundations. A valuable source of information about both private and corporate foundations can be found in *The Foundation Directory* (Renz, 1985), which can be located in the public library. In her excellent article, Rosemary Campos (1980) discusses other sources of information on 26,000 private foundations and how to determine a good funding source for a particular project.

Before contacting a corporation to solicit funds for a project, research businesses within your geographical area using a local business directory. The public library, local chamber of commerce or state attorney general's office may be helpful. Request annual reports of corporations from the business section of a public library. These reports frequently outline philanthropic programs.

Applying for Funds

Once a list of corporations has been compiled (starting with a list of 10 potential funding sources is suggested), determine the appropriate contact person. If the corporation has a centralized corporate office, contact that office. Ask for information about the corporation's grant programs, together with the name of a local contact. Follow up the telephone contact with a letter confirming your interest and outlining the following questions:

- corporate guidelines for preparation of grant or project proposals
- deadlines or preferred times for the submission of proposals
- person or committee that ultimately approves project funds
- project review process and whether or not a personal interview is possible
- date and method of notification of approval or denial
- average size of the award.

At this point, evaluate the original list of corporations, and select the two to three most likely to fund your proposal. These should be selected, in part, based upon the similarity in guidelines for proposal development. If guidelines are not specified, one may forward the same proposal to all the prospective corporations.

Methods of tapping these sources of funds are as varied as the number of corporations. General recommendations for obtaining corporate funds include:

1. Develop a written proposal that includes a description of the project, project cost, financial resources available, and need for additional financial resources.

2. Identify local, state, and federal sources of funds. This may include discussions with the local chamber of commerce, as well as requests for information from government agencies. The public library is also an excellent resource.

3. Seek the endorsement of an influential group that supports your cause, eg, a professional association, respected businessman, politician, or newsman. Ask for letters of support.

4. Establish friends on the board of directors who are sympathetic to the cause, and develop an action plan to seek funds.

5. Make a list of ten firms or foundations that may be interested in your project and seek a contact person within each organization. Contact the highest level person possible within the organization.

6. Assign responsibility for personal interviews with these individuals.

7. Do not be discouraged if project approval is delayed or refused. Corporate contacts may make reference to another source or make recommendations on how the project may be changed to appeal to others.

Successful identification of funding sources is primarily dependent upon applicant's development of a first-class proposal or application. The appearance of the proposal, the detailed description of the project, the realistic budgetary requirements, the timetable for implementation, and the projected outcome are all important in the potential for success in receiving corporate or foundation funding.

References

Bauer D: The "How to" Grants Manual. Macmillan, 1984.

Bibliography of Corporate Responsibility for Social Problems. Vol 6. Bank of America, 1977.

Campos RG: Acquiring foundation funds. J Nurs Adm (Jun) 1980; 10:16–23.

Coleman J et al: Nursing careers in the emerging systems. Nurs Manag 1984; 15:19–27.

Human Resources Network: The Handbook of Corporate Social Responsibility: Profiles of Involvement, 2nd ed. Chilton, 1975.

Johnson D: Multiunit providers: Survey plots 475 chains' growth. Mod Healthcare (May 15) 1985; 65–84.

Longest B: Institutional politics. J Nurs Adm (Mar–Apr) 1975; 5:38–41.

Mallison MB: A tale of two coalitions. Am J Nurs 1984; 84:7.

Millhaven A: Professional—for-profit—corporations balance the market for nursing service. Nurs Manag (Mar) 1984; 15:48–53.

Nicholson EA: Business Responsibility and Social Issues. Charles E. Merrill, 1974.

Nursing groups step up lobbying for national research institute. Am J Nurs 1984; 84:667.

Renz L (editor): The Foundation Directory, 10th ed. Foundation Center, 1985.

Starr P: The Social Transformation of American Medicine. Basic Books, 1982.

Wagner, GA: Business in the Public Eye. Eerdman's, 1982.

Wallace C: Foundations are sowing seeds for change in health care systems. Mod Healthcare (Aug 1) 1984; 65–84.

Wegmiller D: Corporate restructuring of hospitals and multiinstitutional arrangements. Issues Health Care 1981; 12:12.

Case Study
An Alternative Birth Center Proposal: The Struggle to Introduce Maternity Care Options into the Canadian Health Care System

Ilene Tanz Gordon, RN, DrPH
Elaine McEwan Carty, RN, MSN, CNM

My adventure (Ilene Tanz Gordon) in international nursing began with a visit to Vancouver. Struck by the beauty of the mountains and beaches, I sought to prolong my vacation by plying my trade—teaching nurses. When I settled into that first winter of endless rain, fascination with the scenery paled. It was replaced by a growing awareness that being a nurse in Canada provided an invaluable opportunity for learning.

I could not remain a disinterested observer for long. Pregnant and unable to find a nurse-midwife to assist in the birth of my child, I became involved, with other nurses and consumers, in an attempt to introduce maternity care options into the Canadian health care system.

Maternity Services in Canada

My interest in alternative maternity services stemmed not only from my personal situation, but also from my familiarity with the issue as an American. Because of the cultural similarities between the United States and Canada (especially English-speaking Canada), many of the health care issues facing nurses and consumers are similarly articulated.

As in the United States, consumers in Canada, who read American literature and watch American television, described the problem with maternity services in terms of a physician-monopoly over childbirth. Unlike the situation in the United States, however, Canadian consumers who rejected traditional hospital and physician maternity care had limited options. Birth centers had not been developed in Canada, and there was legislation prohibiting the practice of midwifery by anyone other than a physician. If women chose to give birth at home, their birth attendants were usually practicing illegally.

My Canadian colleagues, most of whom had studied or worked in the United States, were aware of the alternative maternity care models in the United States. They were eager to import American-style options, including in-hospital and out-of-hospital birth centers with care provided by nurse-midwives, into the Canadian health care system.

I joined with a group of Vancouver women (nursing professors at the University of British Columbia and a consumer) to plan a small, out-of-hospital birth center staffed primarily by nurse-midwives. The alternative birth center was to be in a home-like setting, where women would receive prenatal, postnatal, and parenting education, as well as prenatal assessment, care during labor and birth, and care for themselves and infants for a year following birth.

In spite of a similarity of this proposal to existing alternative birth centers in the United States, the process involved in trying to introduce such an option in Canada differed.

564

What began for me as a relatively simple exercise in articulating goals and objectives became a lesson in negotiating change in a different political context.

Working Within the Canadian Health Care System

The lack of choice in maternity care services reflects the nature of the Canadian health care system. When the federal and provincial governments agreed to pay the bills for health services through public insurance plans, they became increasingly involved in planning and regulating services. In an effort to provide universal access to high quality care, the focus has been on setting standards rather than on stimulating diversity. As a consequence of the high degree of regulation in the health care system, making change is difficult.

In Canada, virtually all women have access to a hospital for birth with little out-of-pocket expense. The medical plans pay for both hospital and physicians' services. To suggest a change of setting meant finding a way that the birth center could be financed. A new category of health care worker, the nurse-midwife, meant developing a plan for paying for the services and finding a legal framework in which to practice.

Since the government is deeply involved in health care, relevant features of the system should be understood. Canada is a federal state consisting of ten provinces and two territories. It was formally created in 1867 when the British North America Act (BNA Act) was passed by the British Parliament. This act and subsequent amendments formed the constitutional framework of Canada.

The BNA Act gave the provinces jurisdiction over health services. Each province has both a hospital insurance plan and a medical insurance plan that pays for the services of designated health professionals. Although the details of these plans differ among provinces, most funding comes from general federal and provincial revenues. Hospital insurance, available to virtually all residents, pays for hospital care. Almost all physicians are paid on a fee-for-service basis through the medical plan.

Specific health policies and programs are delineated by the provincial governments. The influential bureaucrats in each provincial ministry of health are often physicians with backgrounds in community health or hospital administration. Although professional organizations, particularly the medical associations, are frequently consulted, there are few mechanisms for consumer input into the decision-making process. Unless a provincial government decides to provide alternative health services, there is virtually no mechanism for introducing change into the provincial health care system.

Although the provision of health services is a provincial responsibility, the federal government has a major impact on health care. As well as the cost-sharing arrangements with the provinces for funding of medical and hospital insurance plans, the federal department of health and welfare finances health care research including demonstration projects in innovative modes of health delivery.

Seeking Federal Funding for the Birth Center Proposal

Because the birth center was an innovative project and because such a project could not be funded under the existing terms of the provincial health insurance plans, funding was sought from Health and Welfare Canada (the federal department of health and welfare). Funding of this type would allow for a study of an alternative maternity service and would obviate the necessity of charging patients for maternity care.

A plan for sound evaluation of demonstration projects is a requirement for funding by Health and Welfare Canada. Thorough research of this project was particularly important because there were currently no prospective studies evaluating alternative birth centers. The research proposal was designed to measure five areas: safety and quality of care, cost effectiveness, parent satisfaction, impact of the program on parent-child interaction, and acceptability of the concept by health care professionals.

A decision was made to develop the project within the structure of the university. First, it was felt that the proposal would have more credibility coming from the university. Second, the university setting offered ready access to experts for consultation on research design and methodology.

From the beginning, it was clear that more than just a high quality grant proposal was needed for such a controversial project to be funded. Funding would be contingent upon:

- an indication from the provincial government that it would continue to fund the project after the demonstration period, if it proved successful
- cooperation from the medical community
- approval by the university

The approval and cooperation of the British Columbia (BC) Ministry of Health, the local medical community, and the university were interdependent; none of these groups wanted to be the first to commit itself. Moreover, each preferred to wait for an indication that the federal government was willing to fund the project. The process of gaining support was like building a house of cards; the strains of adding a new card continually increased. A discussion of some of the specific problems follows.

The British Columbia Government
To obtain a commitment from the provincial government to continue funding of the project after the demonstration period, officials in the provincial Ministry of Health were approached. On the advice of persons familiar with the ministry, key people were identified and strategies for approaching them were worked out.

After much persistence, the birth center proposal was presented at a meeting with the deputy minister of health, the director of health planning, and the director of the bureau of special services. The Ministry of Health responded positively to most aspects of the proposal, particularly the economic and political implications, and expressed an appreciation for the consumers' concerns about existing services. They were willing to continue negotiations but wanted to hear what the physicians had to say before making any commitment of support.

The discussions with provincial government representatives demonstrated how each group weighed the benefits and costs of supporting the birth center proposal. For the provincial government, even though there were both economic and political reasons to approve the concept, it was important to weigh the potential negative consequences of supporting a project that physicians might oppose.

The Medical Community
The birth center proposal was discussed with a number of obstetricians, pediatricians, and general practitioners, including the heads of the Departments of Pediatrics and Obstetrics and Gynecology at the university, and the chief medical officer of the Metropolitan Health Department. Some physicians disapproved of certain aspects of the proposal, and some offered help, both advice about providing patient care and suggestions about strategy. Although there was some encouraging support from physicians in private discussions, a lack of public acknowledgment of even partial support was frustrating. Several physicians refused to support the project publicly but said they would be willing to work in the birth center once it opened.

Because the British Columbia Medical Practice Act prohibits the practice of midwifery by anyone not licensed as a physician, it was necessary that the licensing body for physicians, the College of Physicians and Surgeons of BC, agree to the practice of nurse-midwifery. Accompanied by a lawyer, the birth center proposal group met with the executive council of the college. As a result of this meeting, the college agreed in writing that nurse-midwives could practice nurse-midwifery in the proposed center under the "ordinary calling of nursing" provided they had passed a midwifery program approved by the Registered Nurses' Association of BC, the body responsible for the regulation of nursing practice. This was the first time in the province that there had been any acknowledgment that the practice of nurse-midwifery might not be illegal. In his letter, however, the registrar of the college added that this was not to be construed as support for the birth center project. Double messages from physicians made it difficult to document support from the local medical community.

The University
Because the birth center proposal was submitted by faculty members at the University of British Columbia for funding as a demonstration project, it was necessary to negotiate an agreement with the university for the administration of the funds and to obtain approval of research involving human subjects. As soon as the university research officer was aware of the project and the controversy likely to surround it, he set up an *ad hoc* committee of senior university administrators to determine whether the birth center project was a legitimate university activity. Members of this *ad hoc* committee included the dean of graduate studies, associate dean of medicine, associate dean of applied science and legal advisor to the president. They agreed that the birth center project was an appropriate undertaking for the university, and a mechanism was developed so that the financial administration would be handled by the university. This was the first time such a committee had been set up to consider research being planned at the university, and the establishment of the committee reflects the intensity of the controversy surrounding the proposal.

The second step in negotiating with the university involved seeking approval for research involving human subjects. The Medical Science Research Screening Committee of the university proved a major obstacle to the birth center proposal. Most of the members of the committee were physicians who objected to the provision of out-of-hospital maternity services. Because approval from the current membership of the Medical Science Research Screening Committee was deemed unlikely, the proposal was rerouted to the Behavioural Science Research Screening Committee, which approved the project.

Not only were negotiations with the university, physicians, and the government necessary, the interrelatedness of these groups complicated the whole process. The problems encountered with each of the groups were different, but because the health care system is highly regulated and centralized, the decision makers in each of the above groups are often in contact with one another in the course of their daily business. It was impossible to know what kind of information, rumors, decisions, and attitudes were transmitted through informal communication network.

Present Status of the Birth Center Proposal

The birth center proposal was not funded. Health and Welfare Canada indicated that the proposal was "relevant and significant" to their objectives, but there were problems with research methodology. They encouraged resubmission of the grant once local support could be more clearly documented and the research methodology strengthened.

As a revised grant proposal was being written, political developments intervened.

The allocation of federal funds for research depends upon the philosophical and political priorities of the governing party. These priorities may change in election years. Shortly after the grant was rejected, health and welfare research funds were frozen due to budget cutbacks. In May 1979, the party forming the government of Canada changed. With yet another federal election in February 1980, the future of many government programs, including health and welfare demonstration projects, remained in doubt.

Secondary Gains

Although funding for the demonstration project was not realized, there have been some positive and encouraging outcomes. The most important has been progress on the midwifery issue. Leaders of the medical community, who opposed the project, publicly stated that they objected to the out-of-hospital birth setting and not the practice of nurse-midwifery. When these same men were later asked to support a proposal for an in-hospital nurse-midwifery service, many did. The first nurse-midwifery service in a Canadian province was established in a hospital in Vancouver by a group of American- and British-trained midwives, including two members of the original birth center proposal group.

While the statutes prohibiting the practice of midwifery by nonphysicians remain unchanged, medical societies in several provinces agreed to allow the practice of nurse-midwifery under certain conditions. Nurse-midwifery services are now available in Alberta and Ontario and are planned for several other provinces as well.

An indirect consequence of the project has been an increase in consumers' awareness about birth practices and maternity care. National newspaper and magazine coverage of the proposal stimulated discussion of the issues. Family-centered maternity care changes have been requested of hospitals all across Canada, and they are beginning to respond. Hospital administrators, nurses and physicians are beginning to ask, "What do these consumers want?"

Conclusion

Trying to implement change within the Canadian health care system is both similar to and different from the American health care system. Many of the problems, such as the opposition of powerful physician groups, also confronted groups trying to establish out-of-hospital birth centers in the United States. If the proposal had been funded, the same difficulties such as arranging hospital back-up services, would have been faced. Because an attempt was made to work within a national health insurance system, however, an alternate birth setting and an alternate health care worker had to be justified to the federal government to arrange funding for the project. To obtain federal funding, it was necessary for the provincial government, the health professionals, and the university to approve the project.

The commitment of the federal and provincial governments to provide quality health care for Canadians has led to greater availability and more equitable access to services. Despite the advantages of such a system, where there is virtually universal access to health care, innovative changes are slow and difficult to implement. While the results of this effort came too late for us, as childbearing women, participating in the process of opening up maternity care options in Canada was an exhilarating experience.

End Case Study
One School's Response to Proposed Deletion

Sandra Simmons, RN, MS

The fight waged to retain Michigan State University College of Nursing after it was proposed for deletion by the university president provided many valuable insights and lessons. To help other schools dealing with proposed deletions, or even preventing the proposal from occurring, those who have experienced the event need to share information. While the specific sequence of events will differ among agencies, certain preventive actions and responses are generally applicable.

Warning Signs

There are two levels of warning signs that schools of nursing need to be aware of—societal and institutional. The societal warning signs are clearly present and increasing in number and severity. These include:

- decreased overall university enrollments leading to decreased revenues
- decreased state funding for educational institutions
- decreased federal money available for institutions and students
- national surveys showing no overall shortage of nurses

The institutional warning signs flow from the societal signs and can be viewed from two perspectives: the overall institution and the nursing program. At the institutional level, one should look for a trend of decreasing enrollments at the freshman (and graduate) level and decreased state funding. These two elements combine to mean less revenue to the institution except through increased tuition, which, at some point, also leads to decreased enrollment because the cost is beyond the means of many potential students. Since nursing programs are high in cost, they are likely targets for review. Many nursing programs must limit enrollments because of available faculty and clinical sites and may say there is no enrollment problem because there are more applicants than student spaces. This can be false comfort if the overall proportion of nursing applicants to institutional applicants and grade point averages are not also reviewed. Nursing may have more applicants than space allows, but there may be a decrease in the overall number of applicants. Likewise, the grade point average of applicants may be dropping, which shows a different applicant pool and may require changes in the curriculum and support services.

The warning signs at Michigan State University were long-term decreased state funding coupled with greater program expansion than could readily be supported. The latter came about in subtle ways over the years, mainly as special programs initiated through grants were picked up by the general fund. Primary precipitating factors seemed to be a marked decrease in proposed state funding and a new university administration with a different philosophy of what the university should be and where it should be going. Enrollment, while down some from previous years, was not a significant factor.

Warning signs related specifically to the nursing program are noted in Table VII-1.

Table VII-1. Areas to Assess to Determine Vulnerability

Centrality to mission of institution

Involvement in campuswide activities

Credentials of nursing faculty compared to other faculty (master's vs doctorates)

Productivity of nursing faculty compared to other faculty (publishing and research)

Leadership of program

Cost/student compared to other programs

Student credit hours generated (direct and indirect)

Political involvement and power

Societal need for graduates

Other state producers of graduates

Each nursing program should assess these areas to determine its vulnerability. If possible, representatives from other colleges should assist in the assessment, adding an objectivity not otherwise possible.

To some extent, all the vulnerable areas in Table VII-1 were present in the College of Nursing. Many of the signs had been present for a number of years with no corrective action taken or planned. The quality of the educational program was good, as evidenced by state board scores. The last National League for Nursing (NLN) visit in 1978 gave maximal approval to both the graduate and undergraduate programs. An internal university review of the nursing program early in 1980 led to its elevation to college status. Unfortunately, this false sense of security and the isolation of the college from the university community muted continuing warning signs.

Unattended problem areas included:

- Strategies were not developed to reduce the high cost of the program (cost/ student credit hour).
- Faculty credentials were not upgraded.
- No action was taken to become more visible and involved in the campus activities and power system. Few nursing faculty served on university-wide committees.
- Luncheon or social events where nursing faculty or administrators joined with others on campus were minimal to nonexistent.
- Visibility of nursing faculty and students on campus was limited, because the nursing program was housed in a section apart from the central campus. Faculty members spent the majority of their time teaching and supervising students in clinical settings—thus few publications were produced and less research was done. There were twelve other universities in the state that also had baccalaureate nursing programs, and two others had graduate programs. No monopoly could be claimed in the service provided.

Response to Proposed Deletion

The budget reflection at Michigan State University was based on agreement by the deans of all colleges that programmatic, rather than across-the-board, cuts should be made. The rationale for this was that the maintenance of the quality of programs was paramount and across-the-board cuts would weaken all programs. A Select Advisory Committee was appointed by the president to propose macrolevel cuts on a university-wide basis, while the deans were to propose college-level cuts. These two sets of proposals were then to be combined at the provost's level, and the total package was presented. The administrative budget reduction process began in October, 1980, and was completed at the Board of Trustees meeting April 4, 1981. There was little time available for planning our response once this process was initiated.

Rumors and informal networks indicated the College of Nursing was being discussed for possible elimination. Since there was no formal mechanism for input into the Select Advisory Committee, the informal communication system was the best route to use. Unfortunately, because of the relative isolation and political naiveté of the College, this system was used poorly. There was also a need for calculated risk-taking, an activity the College was not prepared for. In essence, minimal proactive functioning occurred prior to February 25, 1981, when the first report proposing deletion of the College of Nursing was issued by the Select Advisory Committee.

Prior to the first report, the faculty received mixed messages as to the severity and validity of the rumors. There seemed to be an inability to determine a course of action for the college. This period of inertia may have reaffirmed that the College should be eliminated. Other units that feared they might be on the deletion list were doing offensive lobbying with members of the Select Advisory Committee and asking alumni and legislators to intercede on their behalf.

After the proposed deletion of the College of Nursing was made public, a more action-oriented posture was taken by the college. All action from this point on was of necessity defensive. A short alert stating the proposed deletion, events leading up to it, and action the college desired the reader to take was prepared and distributed to all College of Nursing alumni, the directors of nursing of all health care agencies in the state, and all baccalaureate schools of nursing in the United States. This process was accomplished within three days by using the resources (contacts and mailing lists) of the Division of Lifelong Education in the college. The statewide network established by the Division of Lifelong Education helped to quickly inform and activate significant people. Faculty members were asked to contact persons they knew; and a statewide list of people to keep informed was developed.

From the first signs of possible trouble, the Michigan Nurses' Association suggested strategies and acted as an advocate. Its public relations director scheduled press conferences and helped to write and distribute press releases. The legislative director arranged strategic contacts with significant legislators, prepared statements for the college, and spoke at special legislative committee sessions. Information and calls for action were distributed to the president of every district nurses' association in the state, thus increasing the college's contacts and support. Several district nurses' associations organized marches and rallies in their communities.

Another source of support was the Michigan Hospital Association. Since there was a shortage of nurses in Michigan, the deletion of a major provider of nurses would worsen an already acute situation. The hospital association used its communiques and contacts to support the college's efforts, contacted members of the university Board of Trustees, and spoke at public meetings in support of the college.

Assistance and support from the college alumni was a critical factor. The alumni association solicited donations from its members to finance efforts to save the college. This added financing was crucial as university funds could not be used to subsidize these activities. Alumni also helped to spread the message of our plight nationally.

While no statements of support came from either the state medical society or the

Table VII-2 Groups to Contact for Support

Health Related

   Nursing programs in the state/country

   All health service agencies

   Alumni

   Hospital association

   Health systems agency

   Nurses' associations (local/state/national)

Nonhealth Related

   Political caucus groups (both parties)

   Labor unions

   Women's organizations

   Legislators (local, significant committees, state)

   Major university contributors

   Local/state businessmen (company presidents)

   Local/state newspapers

   Local/state radio stations

dean of either College of Medicine on campus (MD, DO), individual physicians across the state and in the medical schools wrote letters of support for our cause to the university administration and Board of Trustees.

Support came from a number of nonhealth groups, increasing the college's power base. The contact with many of these groups came about through the efforts of individual faculty, alumni, and other colleges and departments on campus that were also proposed for deletion and seeking allies to expand their power base. A list of groups to consider contacting when seeking support is in Table VII-2.

The major sources of support were from outside the university. The budget reduction process was universitywide and affected all units to some degree. Each unit focused primarily on its own problems. To suggest that something proposed for deletion be retained implied a reduction to someone else. For this reason, most units were hesitant to suggest sparing others.

Another technique used by the administration to lessen pressure on it was to promote disagreements between faculty and unit administrators by meeting with each group separately and carrying slanted information between groups. This was but one of the administration's ways of dividing and conquering the opposition, and it worked quite well. The entire academic governance system was bypassed. The Board of Trustees' declaration of financial crisis in February, 1981 allowed most rules and procedures to be waived.

Throughout the sequence of events that occurred, it was necessary for affected units to have ongoing communication with key legislators. Communications varied from taking legislators to lunch to meeting with small groups of local representatives or presenting testimony at public hearings. Legislators like to have significant facts and data presented concisely. Equally significant to legislators are the contacts by their voting constituents. All persons you contact should be urged to contact their local legislators. While contacts must be individualized, generalized data should be widely distributed so various persons or groups can use the segments that apply to them.

The information should be concise, in lay terms, and positive. We found "single issue" papers helpful. One topic would be developed (costs of program, affirmative action, etc.) in each paper and distributed as appropriate. This was done on a weekly basis to maintain the visibility of the College of Nursing or as frequently as needed to respond to misinformation. The regular list of persons receiving these papers included members of the Board of Trustees, legislators, and members of the academic governance system on campus (though this system was bypassed in the budget reduction process).

Another effective means of keeping people informed is through the public media: press, television, and radio. Lessons learned in dealing with the media were:

- Always have several spokespersons available at the college who have all the background, are articulate, and can respond extemporaneously and tactfully to leading questions.
- Make responses short and factual.
- Give only information asked or give only the information you wish to give.
- Don't be led into arguments or expressing value judgments.

It is possible to keep an issue before the public almost daily for weeks through planned press conferences, information given to interviewers, letters to the editor, and editorial support from newspapers and television stations. It is especially important to seek editorial support and have letters to the editor appear in the papers in the cities where members of the Board of Trustees live and papers with statewide distribution.

The support from women's organizations was important. Political caucus groups from both parties listened to nursing representatives and provided support. Labor unions representing the major employee groups in the community were contacted and provided supportive statements. Community and state-wide business leaders who were significant donors to the university were contacted, and many provided supportive letters. Staff members to key legislators were kept informed of events.

The defensive posture of units proposed for deletion was reinforced by the university administration, which did not support the proposed deletions with hard data, yet asked units to justify why they should remain. When forced to document proposed deletions, much of the data presented was distorted, inaccurate, and self-serving. A vast number of proposals, counterproposals, and reports were issued from academic units and the administration. Each report from the administration contained slightly different data, keeping units busy preparing replies as well as waging massive efforts to save themselves.

The university administration's position of proposed deletion of the College of Nursing could not be swayed and the normal channels of academic governance were not being used. This meant that all previous contacts with the president and provost were ineffective. Action needed to focus on the Board of Trustees as it would make the final decision. In addition to direct contacts with Board members, all mailings by the college, hospital association, or nursing association directed recipients to write to Board members. Lists of board members' names and addresses were widely distributed. Another approach was to assign one of two faculty members to meet with each Board member—in the trustee's place of business—and then provide ongoing follow-up information to that trustee. This approach provided the trustee with a specific contact person and allowed for continuity. This approach worked quite well.

Students of the College of Nursing were another valuable source of contacts and support. They organized marches and rallies and contacted student organizations at other nursing colleges in the state. Students from other nursing programs joined in marches and rallies and presented statements at open meetings held by the administration. Parents of students contacted the president, indicating their intent to take legal action if the program were closed before their son or daughter was able to graduate.

At crucial Board of Trustees' meetings where comments from affected units were heard, a well-orchestrated, diversified group of persons spoke on behalf of the College of Nursing. Oral presentations were supplemented with handout packets containing the text of each person's speech. Short fact sheets were presented with points the speakers wished to make. These packets were also distributed to members of the media present. The range of presenters included representatives from other BSN programs in the state, the nurses' association, the hospital association, one medical school at Michigan State University, United Auto Workers local union, the Health Systems Agency, employers, community college, and one of the faculty speaking for the College.

Outcome

The Board of Trustees unanimously accepted the College of Nursing counterproposal that retained the college, but called for some internal changes and reorganization. These changes decreased the undergraduate enrollment by 25 students per year, held the graduate program enrollment constant, and retained the lifelong education division. The chairman of the board stated that he voted to retain the College of Nursing not because he felt it should be retained, but because he could not ignore the 7,000 letters he received in support of the college. Another member of the board stated he was voting to retain the College of Nursing because he was sure that as soon as the board voted to delete the program, it would be given a line item in the budget by the legislature. This was taken as an acknowledgment of the effectiveness of the lobbying efforts with the legislature.

Some questions remain. How much and for how long will enrollments at the graduate and undergraduate levels be affected? How much and for how long will the reputation of the college be damaged? How does one work with a university administration that proposed your deletion? Will the career mobility of faculty on staff during the crisis be affected? Will the students who graduated during the crisis recognize discrimination in employment? To what extent and for how long will faculty recruitment be affected?

Application to the Future

To have experienced such an event and not let it affect your future is to ignore reality. The information obtained in the assessment of your program (Table VII-1) should guide your actions in developing long-range plans for your unit. Many of those plans will pressure persons to do things not previously required. This may be expected to bring about expressions of concern from selected members of the faculty. Cries of "overwork," "unrealistic," or "unnecessary" will arise. We can, however, no longer afford to indulge ourselves in the comforts of the past or the security of cliches.

Nursing must enter into the mainstream of the university; faculty must be doctorally prepared; research and publication must increase; alternative teaching strategies must be developed; and political insights and power must be developed. Nursing faculty and administrators must be urged, invited, pushed, or forced to set long-range plans that address these areas.

We must expand our scope of contacts outside of the academic setting. Broad-based advisory committees or planning committees must be formed. The committees would not only help to keep programs more realistic in their orientation but increase visibility with lay and power groups.

Nursing must begin to view itself as a professional community rather than an aggregate of vested interests. We must develop a much stronger professional network, increase our power base, and expand our political involvements. The political process is used here in its broadest sense, not only to refer to communicating with legislators but with significant and power people. This list should include members of the Board of Trustees; community, business, and labor representatives; and policymakers in all nursing and health-related areas. This orientation and philosophy must also be integrated into the basic nursing curriculum.

One other lesson learned from this experience is that a successful fight may be waged against significant opposition if nurses respond as a unit. This problem brought nurses closer together than they had been in some time, and this strength was noted by legislators and other significant groups in the state.

It is now the responsibility of the College of Nursing to take the steps necessary to build on this new foundation and prevent such a proposal from occurring again. The support gained from others now needs to be nurtured, developed, and refined. It also requires, in most cases, future reciprocal actions of some type from the College of Nursing or individual members. This reciprocal action may mean joining a group; financially supporting an organization, cause, or person; campaigning for a legislator; regularly going to group meetings; or supporting other causes. Repayment of favors or support is a fact of life. We can't receive and not give, and we can't give from positions of weakness. Strength requires involvement beyond ourselves.

Voter Registration Drives

Never done a registration drive? Here's how.

LEARN YOUR STATE'S REGISTRATION PROCEDURES

Registration methods vary from state to state. Voter registration can be as easy as dropping a postcard in the mail, or as complex as appearing at a specified voter registration center on a specified day at a specified (and often inconvenient) time.

Information on the method used in your state may be obtained from the office of the secretary of state. Many states allow local officials great discretion in administering state election laws, so be sure to contact a local election official as well for full information on registration in your community.

REVIEW THE FIVE BASIC METHODS

Most states use at least one of the following types of registration. (Some states use a combination of techniques.)

Postcard Registration.   Under this easy system, volunteers may register people on the spot by having them sign a simple form. Forms are then mailed or hand delivered to local elections offices.

Difficulties can arise when volunteers are unable to obtain enough forms to register large numbers of people. If talking this over with a local elections official fails, contact the secretary of state's office.

States using this method are: Alaska, California, Delaware, Iowa, Kansas, Ken-

Reprinted with permission from *The Women's Political Times*, National Women's Political Caucus, 1984.

tucky, Maryland, Michigan, Minnesota, Missouri, Montana, New Jersey, New York, Ohio, Oregon, Pennsylvania, Tennessee, Texas, Utah, Wisconsin, and the District of Columbia.

Deputy Registration. Under this system, volunteers must be deputized to register voters in homes, workplaces, or other designated sites. Some state laws require deputies to work in pairs, one Democrat and one Republican, and limit the jurisdiction and length of deputization.

States using either deputy registration or branch registration (see below) or both are: Arizona, Arkansas, Colorado, Connecticut, Florida, Illinois, Indiana, Maine, Massachusetts, Nevada, New Mexico, South Dakota, Virginia, Washington, and West Virginia.

Branch Registration. Under this system, certain sites are designated by the state as registration centers (eg, banks, shopping centers, fire houses, or schools) and registration can be conducted only on certain days. Procedures for selecting branch sites differ from state to state. Often, citizens are permitted to petition for additional registration sites.

Centralized Registration. Under this more cumbersome system, new voters are required to appear at one location, usually a court house or city hall, to register. Registration times are generally restricted to regular business hours.

States using this system are: Alabama, Georgia, Hawaii, Idaho, Louisiana, Mississippi, Nebraska, New Hampshire, North Carolina, Oklahoma, Rhode Island, South Carolina, Vermont, and Wyoming.

Same Day Registration. Under this system, new voters may register on election day before voting. States using this system are: Minnesota, Oregon, Wisconsin, and Wyoming.

FORM A COALITION

Many other organizations have made voter registration and get-out-the-vote projects a priority this election year. Among them: American Association of University Women, Planned Parenthood, National Educational Association, Citizens Actions Programs, National Federation of Business and Professional Women's Clubs, National Organization for Women, League of Women Voters, National Association of Social Workers, and National Association for the Advancement of Colored People.

The more groups you can hook up with, the more experience, ideas, volunteers, and woman power you'll have to draw upon for your effort. Working coalitions makes smart political sense, too. For instance, a coalition will wield more influence and clout in the event that local authorities—for their own political reasons—attempt to obstruct your voter registration drive.

When building a coalition, aim toward getting solid commitments on what each group will contribute to the campaign, be it volunteers, money, office space, telephones, postage, refreshments, supplies, etc.

SET A GOAL

Decide on how many people you will try to register. This will enable you to monitor your progress and will give volunteers something concrete to work toward. A realistic goal is to register approximately half of those currently unregistered in your precinct. An energetic volunteer can register between five and fifteen people per hour.

DIVVY UP JOBS

Planning an effective voter registration drive is a big job. For efficiency's sake—and to prevent all the work from falling on one person—consider setting up a steering committee of four or five people who will be responsible for major components of the campaign. One possible breakdown of responsibilities:

Researcher. This person will research registration laws and procedures and negotiate with local officials for additional sites, forms, and deputies.

Volunteer Coordinator. The volunteer coordinator is responsible for mobilizing volunteers, training them, and keeping them happy.

Publicity Director. This person has dual responsibilities: to design announcements, flyers, and other educational material that will encourage people to register and to arrange for media coverage of the registration campaign to make it as successful as possible.

Finance Director. While costs involved in a registration campaign are minimal, a few items will invariably arise, eg, postage, long distance calls, photocopying, supplies, refreshments. It is the job of the finance director to estimate these costs and solicit assistance and donations from coalition groups, local businesses, friends, and civic organizations.

Project Director. The project director is responsible for seeing that all the above jobs get done and that the project runs smoothly and according to a scheduled timetable.

TARGET NONVOTERS

A list of registered voters, arranged by street address, can usually be obtained from the county clerk's office, the local elections office, local political parties, or candidates' headquarters. By studying such a list, you will get an idea of where pockets of unregistered voters exist in your precinct. Use this information to target the areas in which you will concentrate your efforts.

TREAT YOUR VOLUNTEERS WELL

The success of any voter registration drive hinges on the quality and quantity of volunteers involved, so take extra care in how you go about recruiting, training, and supporting your volunteer staff. Some tips:

- When recruiting volunteers, the phone is the way to go. Letters, flyers, and announcements in newsletters seldom bring results, although they can be useful in informing your members about the project and preparing them for your call.
- Have your registration campaign well planned before contacting potential volunteers. The more organized you appear, and the easier you make it for someone to "plug in," the more likely your contact is to say yes.
- When calling, give specific information on where and when the volunteer will be needed, exactly what she'll be required to do, and why the project is important.
- Don't ask for more than two to four hours of a volunteer's time on any one day. While you may find people willing and eager to work all day long, chances are they won't return after such an exhausting experience.
- Before sending your volunteers out on the streets, train them. A training session can take place either in advance or on the actual day of registration. Keep it short, but be sure to cover the purpose of the project, the goal for the day, what approach they should use in encouraging people to register, what problems they might encounter and how to handle them, and the answers to questions they'll most likely be asked.
- Provide each volunteer with a kit containing information and supplies she or he will need. Such a kit might contain the following items: a summary of registration laws, requirements, and procedures; a sample of the pitch to be used when talking with potential registrants; a sheet of answers to frequently asked questions; registration forms; neighborhood or precinct maps; volunteer name tag; report form to be turned in at the end of the day.
- At the end of the day, have volunteers report back to someone for debriefing, refreshments, and thanks.

GIVE PEOPLE A REASON TO REGISTER

Cynicism and apathy are common among unregistered voters. Prepare a flyer stating several reasons why registering and voting are important. Obtain permission to pass it out in churches, shopping centers, office buildings, and college campuses. Work in pairs, with one person handing out flyers and talking with people, and the other person signing them up.

Many people feel that their votes don't count. Point out that many elections are won by a small number of votes and give an example of a recent local election where a few votes made the difference. Say, too, that while one vote may not make a difference, if more women voted it would definitely make a difference. Tell the person how many people have already registered during the drive.

If a person shows any interest at all, don't let her/him get away without registering. Have her fill out the required form immediately. The person who says she will "think about it" or "get to it later" probably won't.

KEEP LISTS

Record the name and address of every person you register. As election day approaches, you will need this information to send out notices reminding people to get out and vote.

SEEK MEDIA COVERAGE

Provided all the other pieces are in place, coverage by a local newspaper, radio, or television station is the final boost that will make your registration drive a success. The publicity will bring credibility to your efforts, increase responsiveness among the people you're trying to reach, educate the community about the importance of registering, and give your volunteers a lift.

Your publicity director should identify the editors and reporters—both print and electronic—most likely to cover your registration activities. A news release that succinctly sums up the what, when, where, who, and why of your efforts should go to these people, followed up with a phone call for clarification and further encouragement.

If yours is a coalition effort, be sure to designate your public spokespersons. It's best to have one person, preferably a community leader. But if you must have a few people, be sure they're all thoroughly briefed and conversant in all aspects of the project. If your program is big, consider staging an event or press conference to kick it off.

Sample Telephone Canvass Script

Patricia Ford-Roegner, RN, MSW

"Hello, is this the Carroll household? My name is Mary Smith. I am a registered nurse and member of the Iowa Nurses' Association. And I'm calling for Elizabeth Wilson, who is in a tough race for the U.S. Senate in the November 6th election. Have you heard much about her or her campaign?" (Wait for response)

"You know, unlike her opponent and some other people we've sent to Washington, Elizabeth cares about, fights for, and understands the problems of working people in Iowa. She and her husband have raised their children on an average income, and Elizabeth knows what it's like to balance a family budget. Elizabeth has been the major sponsor of progressive health care legislation supported by the Iowa Nurses' Association. Could I ask you, do you think you might be able to support Elizabeth Wilson on election day?"

(Wait for response)

If yes: "Marvelous! I'll tell Elizabeth. Do you think you or someone in your household could help us in the campaign by making telephone calls for Elizabeth from one of the campaign's phone banks or going door-to-door?"

If yes: Get name and number and thank them profusely.

If no: "I understand. Be sure to vote on Tuesday, November 6th. The polls are open from 6 in the morning until 7 in the evening. Thanks so much for your support. Good-bye."

If undecided: "I understand. It's a difficult decision and a very important one. I'd like to tell you why I think Elizabeth Wilson would be a great United States senator. Elizabeth has a record of concerned public service. As a state senator she sponsored and fought for legislation to protect the elderly in nursing homes, to provide low interest loans for nursing education, and for comparable worth legislation to put the value so deserved on services provided mostly by women such as nursing. Elizabeth strongly opposes cuts in Social Security and in education programs for our children.

"I hope that you will watch the campaign and give Elizabeth the opportunity to earn your support. Elizabeth is a good friend of nursing and all residents of our state. She is a fine person and she really cares. Thanks so much for talking with me. Good-bye."

If no: "I understand. Thanks for talking with me. Good-bye."

The American Nurses' Association Handbook for Political Media

As the American Nurses' Association (ANA) and your state nurses' association (SNA) become more involved in political activities, nurses will increasingly become news. This means that there will be greater opportunities for favorable coverage of SNA/ANA positions and activities.

There are techniques for dealing successfully with the political media. This handbook is designed to aid SNA's get across nursing's point of view, while avoiding some of the pitfalls in dealing with the political media. Depending on local circumstances, media coordinators will be able to do some or all of the activities presented here. This handbook is designed to be flexible—use those sections best suited to your needs locally.

MEDIA COORDINATOR

The media coordinator (MC) (who may be a staff person, but will most likely be a volunteer) must be able to:

1. Do research
2. Be well organized
3. Write effectively
4. Speak, listen, and respond well
5. Keep records

Reprinted with the permission of the American Nurses' Association

6. Assign responsibility

It will be up to the MC to:

1. Develop reference files of media outlets
2. Maintain contact/liaison with the media
3. Write and distribute news releases
4. Keep records of releases circulated; and the amount of coverage they generate
5. Develop media kits
6. Prepare self and others to grant interviews with print and electronic media people
7. Prepare self and others for participation in news conferences
8. Schedule and conduct news conferences
9. Respond to media inquiries as identified spokesperson
10. Coordinate with ANA to assure consistent response to inquiries
11. Inform ANA of local media activities/issues

MEDIA FILES

Media files, including all outlets that can be expected to carry news of nurses' political activity, should be carefully developed.

The following directories of local and national outlets are excellent resources and should be available from local libraries:

1. Editor and Publisher International Yearbook, 853 3rd Avenue, New York, NY 10022 (newspapers, weekly and daily)
2. Bacon's Publicity Checker, 14 E Jackson Boulevard, Chicago, IL 60604 (major magazines and newspapers)
3. Ayer's Directory of Newspapers and Periodicals, West Washington Square, Philadelphia, PA 19106
4. Gebbie Press House Magazine Directory, The Gebbie Press, Box 1000, New Paltz, NY 12561
5. The Broadcasting Yearbook, Broadcasting Publications, Inc., 1735 De Sales, NW, Washington, DC 20036 (radio and TV)

Additionally, a request addressed to "Press Secretary, Office of the Governor, The State House, Your State Capital" may yield a current list of regional and local outlets—including political correspondents for media not based in the capital (an important source for you).

An effective way to organize your media list is to develop a five-color card file system, assigning a different color for newspapers, magazines, radio, TV, and wire services. You may use the following form as a guide.

Publication: _____ Phone: _____

Address: _____

Daily   Weekly   Sunday (circle one) Circulation: _____

Geographic area covered: _____

Best contact: _____ Other contact: _____

Deadline: Copy _____ Photos _____

Photo requirements: _____

Best time to visit or phone: _____

MEDIA LOG

A complete, accurate, and chronological log of all releases sent to the media—whether or not they were run—should be developed.

Prepare a loose-leaf binder for this purpose, using the following form as a guide.

MEDIA LOG						
Release Number	Date Release Mailed	Subject of Release	Distribution	Photos Yes/No	Page/Program Release Ran	Date Release Used

MEDIA INQUIRIES

All media inquiries should go to the MC, who will respond directly and/or arrange to have a person with special expertise available to respond.

1. Be prepared to be quoted by name.
2. "I don't know" is an appropriate answer when it is true. Do add "I'll find out and get back to you, though" if you are able—and respond quickly.
3. When responding to a question that you feel would be unwise to answer, be polite, but don't be pressured into giving more information than you want to.
4. "No comment" is never appropriate, though occasionally "We're not ready to comment at this time" may be used.
5. Do not give "off-the-record" interviews or make "off-the-record" comments. There are none.
6. Return media calls promptly. Reporters are usually working against tight deadlines.
7. Quash baseless rumors with firm, unequivocal responses. Get facts and a very short quotation from an appropriate person to stop rumors at once.
8. Be on guard against leading questions which are occasionally asked in the hopes of bringing forth a particularly newsworthy response.
9. Work with the reporter to get the best story for the nurses. This is no place for an adversarial relationship.
10. When stories that are negative to nurses appear, don't ignore them. Do:
    - Contact ANA to be sure ANA is aware of the unfavorable publicity
    - Determine proper response and call appropriate local media to volunteer information or comments.

A file should be maintained on all media inquiries and contacts. For this purpose, you may want to use the following form developed by the ANA's Office of Public Information and Policy.

AMERICAN NURSES' ASSOCIATION

Inquiry and Response Record

Caller: _____

Represents: _____

Address: _____

Telephone: _____

Date/Time Received: _____

Date/Time Responded: _____

Action: _____

Sources Checked: _____

NEWS RELEASES

News releases are to be sent out when you have real news, such as the announcement of an N-CAP endorsement. The following format should be rigidly adhered to:

1. Use white, standard letter-size paper, 8-1/2 x 11
2. Use one side of paper only
3. Type all releases
4. Carbons are unacceptable—use quality photocopier
5. At top of page one, indicate:
   - Source of the release
   - Address
   - Day and night phone numbers for further information
6. In upper corner of page one, show release date and time
7. 1/3 of the way down the page, the headline should be typed, all in CAPS, to call the editor's attention to the story
8. Use margins of 1-1/2 inch
9. Double space
10. Break no proper names between lines
11. Break no paragraphs between pages
12. Main elements of story should appear in first or "lead" paragraph
13. Lead paragraphs should seldom exceed 6 to 8 lines and should answer, in order of importance:
    - What?
    - Who?
    - Where?
    - When?
    - Why?
    - How?
14. Correct spelling is vital—use a dictionary
15. End each page of a story that is continued with "(more)"
16. Identify second page and any following pages with page number and one or two words indicating content in upper left-hand corner
17. Except in unusual cases, stories should run no more than two pages
18. End final page with "###" in center at bottom
19. Write "with art" in bottom left hand corner under "###" if photo or illustration accompanies story
20. Hand deliver releases to key media; mail to others marked "to the attention of . . . (contact person)." Allow enough time for release to be received before re-

lease date and time and before deadline of media (weekly newspapers often have deadlines of nearly a week in advance of their publication date)

In addition to the above rules, releases prepared for radio or television should:

1. Be extremely concise. The information dealt with in the lead paragraph (#12 and #13 above) may be sufficient
2. Be conversational in style
3. Be triple spaced
4. Be all in capital letters
5. Include phonetic spelling of unusual names, words, or terms (in parentheses after the correct spelling)
6. Possibly be accompanied by the complete release sent to the nonelectronic media to provide fuller information and for background

SAMPLE NEWS RELEASE

(On state association or N-CAP letterhead or plain paper)

August 1, 1983 *
12 noon

Joan Daniels * *
Indiana Nurses' Association
2915 North High School Road
Indianapolis, IN 46224
Phone: 619/123-4567 (office)
　　　　 619/890-1234 (home)

NURSES ENDORSE (CANDIDATE'S LAST NAME) FOR (CONGRESS/SENATE)

The (state) Nurses' Association of the American Nurses' Association today announced the endorsement of (candidate's full name) for (U.S. Senate/Congress in the
_____ district).

"(Candidate's full name) clearly supports the need to maintain quality health care
for all the American people," said Kathleen Montgomery, RN, chairperson of
N-CAP, political action arm of the professional organization for registered nurses.

Speaking for the state association, President (name) said nurses' support for (candidate's last name) is a reflection of (his/her) (record/position) on health services
issues.

"As the largest health care group, nurses have a stake in health issues," Montgomery said. "One in every 44 women voters is a registered nurse. We're glad to be able

to put our strength behind candidates who show genuine concern for solving problems—at a time when health care has never been more important."

On learning of the endorsement, (candidate's last name) noted "(get brief statement for quotation)."

The (state) Nurses' Association represents nurses from throughout the state. ANA is the largest organization in the nursing profession, with 170,000 members nationwide.

---

* Time for release, if necessary
* * Name of contact, person who can answer questions

PHOTOGRAPHS

As someone once observed, "A picture is worth a thousand words." When there is a good visual opportunity, take advantage of it.

1. Use your imagination to make photographs interesting. The best photos are those that show people doing something.
2. A single head and shoulder shot is appropriate only when it accompanies a release in which the person pictured is the news.
3. Daily papers may prefer to use their own photographers and will often send one to cover an event if requested to do so well in advance. Many papers will print a good picture accompanying a release.
4. Newspapers require glossy, black and white photos with sharp, but not extreme, contrast.
5. Captions should note the occasion for the photograph rather than literally explaining the activity in the picture.
6. Captions should identify all people in the photo with full name and initials, in order from left to right.
7. Captions should be typed on white paper, attached to the back of the photo with tape, and folded over the front of the photo.
8. Never write on the back of a photograph.
9. When mailing a release with photograph, protect the photo with cardboard inserts to prevent bending or cracking. Face the image side of the photo toward the back of the envelope, and mark the envelope: "Photographs, Do Not Bend."

DEVELOPING A GOOD RELATIONSHIP WITH THE MEDIA

An important part of the MC's job is to establish a cordial and cooperative relationship with media representatives.

1. The MC should monitor the media in order to be aware of what is reported as it relates to nursing and the health professions.

2. When a reporter does a good job on a story that is of particular interest to nurses.
   - Call the reporter and say so
   - Write a letter to the editor or producer complimenting the paper or station, and the reporter

3. When a reporter does a poor job or makes a glaring error
   - Call it to the reporter's attention in a constructive way (but don't go over the reporter's head to the editor or producer)

4. Rapport is often best established in an informal setting. It is perfectly appropriate to invite a reporter to lunch—offer to pay, but recognize that a trend in journalistic ethics may require that the lunch be dutch treat. Such an occasion is a good opportunity:
   - Just to get acquainted
   - To discuss a recent or pending story or issue
   - To offer information that may be background material for some future story.

5. When you see something that relates to a story the reporter has written, send it along. This need not be a "nursing" issue necessarily—just something you know the reporter would be interested in. Reporters are building their careers just as nurses are and are grateful for such help and attention.

ELECTRONIC MEDIA: TELEVISION AND RADIO

Interviews given to the print media are different from those granted the electronic media. Whereas an interview with a reporter from a newspaper or magazine will result in a report of what you said, an interview with a television or radio reporter might actually present you saying it.

1. A booking to appear on radio or TV is a firm commitment. Only dire circumstances can justify a cancellation.

2. Meet ahead of time with the on-mike interviewer or her representative to establish ground rules and to determine what the content, subject, or thrust of the interview will be. You have a right to say what you will or will not answer questions about and the reporter should respect your wishes. Occasionally reporters like to "spring" questions, hoping for offguard or especially candid responses. Prepare and submit a list of questions you would like to be asked. They may or may not be used, but they could serve to lead the show where you want it to go. And remember—nothing is "off the record."

3. Familiarize yourself with the style and format of the show by watching or listening to several segments.

4. Give the reporter or her representative an accurate and complete introduction suitable to be used on-the-air. At the very least, it may serve as a guide.

5. Be well informed. Your interviewer will not likely be as well informed as you, nor will your audience. Keep your message concise.

6. Mentally rehearse the interview. Run through all the questions you think you may be asked and develop answers to them. Don't rely on written notices which will hinder your spontaneity. Develop short, succinct answers.

7. If the reporter or another guest makes an incorrect statement, correct it at once. There may not be another opportunity.

8. Do not get into a debate with anyone. Just keep reiterating your points.

9. Be assertive. Be ready to involve yourself in the discussion if another guest threatens to monopolize it. Be prepared to make your own opportunity to get your message across.

10. Use commercial breaks to work with the interviewer to guide the show's direction.

11. Be self-confident.

12. Be relaxed, informal, and positive.

13. Write a thank-you note to the producer and host of the show. It may mean a return engagement!

A few additional tips for television interviews:

1. Television is designed for 30 second spots. Structure your answers accordingly.

2. Assume that you are on-camera all the time. Just because you aren't speaking doesn't mean you aren't being seen.

3. Wear simple, uncomplicated clothing you feel comfortable in. Avoid distracting plaids, colors, elaborate jewelry, and clothing that is uncomfortable to sit in.

CLIPPING PROGRAM

Establish a program of clipping from all papers and magazines that carry news of nurses in general, and your releases in particular.

Assign a person to read and clip every media outlet you will be sending releases to. Clippings should be:

1. Cut from newspaper, including any "jump" (continuation to another page)

2. Mounted on 8-1/2 x 11 piece of paper

3. Identified as to page, date, and paper in the upper right hand corner of the mounting paper

4. Sent to the MC who will distribute them to appropriate people

5. Arranged by the MC in chronological order in a loose-leaf binder

To further record those journals that have run releases, underline or circle the appropriate entry on the media log.

MEDIA KITS

Prepare handout media kits for all those attending news conference or any media-covered event. Consider for inclusion:

1. News release
2. If subject of conference/event is to announce endorsement of a candidate, include:
   - Bio of endorsee
   - Photo of endorsee
   - Statement by endorsee responding to endorsement
3. Bios of those giving speeches at conference/event
4. Captioned photos of those speaking at conference/event
5. Copies of any speeches given
6. Copies of any statements made by others, not present (president ANA, mayor, chairman, hospital board of trustees, etc.)
7. Short "perspective" piece—if, for example, the purpose of the conference/event is to announce the endorsement of a candidate who has a strong position on pay equity in health professions, you may want to include a statement on pay equity
8. Technical backup information—charts, diagrams, financial data, statistics, copy of a study or poll referred to or supporting the story
9. Contact person with day and night phone numbers, for further information

The Hatch Act

SOME FEDERAL EMPLOYEES MISUNDERSTAND HATCH ACT; MANY VOLUNTEER ACTIVITIES OUTSIDE WORK ARE ALLOWED

The Hatch Act of 1939 was the federal government's response to the intimidation of federal employees by corrupt politicians and political organizations. At one time in our history, federal employees were sometimes forced to participate in political efforts against their will in order to maintain their jobs. In addition, the act seeks to eliminate the possibility that a government official might compromise his agency's neutrality by such active partisan participation as seeking partisan elective office.

The Hatch Act is not intended to prohibit federal employees from expressing their political opinions or from engaging in many volunteer political activities on their own time. Such prohibition would clearly be in violation of the first amendment to the Constitution. Some federal employees, however, believe they are restricted from all political activities, and administrators sometimes foster that misconception. It is absolutely not true, and nurses who work for the federal government should be particularly active in pursuing their political interests within the confines of the law.

ANA's legislative counsel, attorney Tom Nickels, has formulated the following list of do's and don'ts based on the Hatch Act. All federally employed nurses are urged to familiarize themselves with the list and to inform others of the actuality of the law, rather than the common misperceptions. Any further questions may be addressed to Tom Nickels at the ANA Washington office.

Reprinted with permission from *The Political Nurse*, American Nurses' Association, (Feb) 1982; 2:30.

Under the Hatch Act, each federal employee has the right to:

- register and vote in any election
- express his or her opinion as an individual privately and publicly on political subjects and candidates
- display a political picture, sticker, badge, or button
- participate in the nonpartisan activities of a civic, community, social, labor, or professional organization, or of a similar organization
- be a member of a political party or other political organization and participate in its activities to the extent consistent with law
- attend a political convention, rally, fund-raising function, or other political gathering
- sign a political petition as an individual
- make a financial contribution to a political party or organization (This means that federally employed nurses can give voluntary contributions to N-CAP.)
- take an active part, as an independent candidate or in support of an independent candidate, in a partisan election
- take an active part, as a candidate or in support of a candidate, in a nonpartisan election
- be politically active in connection with a question not specifically identified with a political party, such as a constitutional amendment, referendum, or approval of a municipal ordinance; or with any other question or issue of a similar character
- serve as an election judge or clerk or in a similar position to perform nonpartisan duties as prescribed by state or local law
- otherwise participate fully in public affairs, except as prohibited by law, in a manner that does not materially compromise his or her efficiency or integrity as an employee or the neutrality, efficiency, or integrity of his or her agency

Employees are not authorized to engage in the foregoing activities in violation of law, while on duty, or while in a uniform that identifies them as employees. The head of an agency may prohibit or limit the participation of employees in any of the activities listed above if such participation would interfere with the efficient performance of official duties or create a conflict or apparent conflict of interest.

The regulations also list a number of activities in which federal employees are prohibited from engaging. Such activities include but are not limited to:

- serving as an officer of a political party, as a member of a national, state, or local committee of a political party, or as an officer or member of a committee of a partisan political club; or to being a candidate for any of those positions
- organizing or reorganizing a political party organization or political club
- directly or indirectly soliciting, receiving, collecting, handling, disbursing, or accounting for assessments, contributions, or other funds for a partisan political purpose

- organizing, selling tickets to, promoting, or actively participating in a fund-raising activity of a partisan candidate, political party, or political club
- taking an active part in managing the political campaign of a partisan candidate for public office or political party office
- becoming a partisan candidate for, or campaigning for, an elective public office
- soliciting votes in support of or in opposition to a partisan candidate for public office or political party office
- acting as recorder, watcher, challenger, or similar officer at the polls on behalf of a political party or partisan candidate
- driving voters to the polls on behalf of a political party or partisan candidate
- endorsing or opposing a partisan candidate for public office or political party office in a political advertisement, a broadcast, campaign literature, or similar material
- serving as a delegate, alternate, or proxy to a political party convention
- addressing a convention, caucus, rally, or similar gathering of a political party in support of or in opposition to a partisan candidate for public office or political party office
- initiating or circulating a partisan nominating petition
- otherwise using official authority or influence for the purpose of interfering with or affecting the result of an election

National Nursing Organizations

The following list of national nursing organizations is included in this book to encourage readers to lend their efforts to building the profession's collective power. It should be noted that one organization requested that it not be listed in a book about politics and, therefore, has not been included.

American Academy of Ambulatory Nursing Administration
North Woodbury Road, Box 56
Pitman, NJ 08071
(609) 582–9617

American Academy of Nursing
2420 Pershing Road
Kansas City, MO 64108
(816) 474–5720

American Assembly for Men in Nursing
% College of Nursing
Rush University
600 South Paulina, 474–H
Chicago, IL 60612
(312) 942–7117

American Association of Colleges of Nursing
Suite 530
One Dupont Circle
Washington, DC 20036
(202) 463–6930

American Association of Critical-Care Nurses
One Civic Plaza
Newport Beach,CA 92660
(714) 644–9310

American Association for the History of Nursing
College of Nursing, University of Illinois
845 South Damen Avenue, Room 1042
Chicago, IL 60612
(312) 996–9171

American Association of Nephrology Nurses and Technicians
North Woodbury Road, Box 56
Pitman, NJ 08071
(201) 926–7609

American Association of Neuroscience Nurses
22 South Washington Street, Suite 203
Park Ridge, IL 60068
(312) 823–9850

American Association of Nurse Anesthetists
216 Higgins Road
Park Ridge, IL 60068
(312) 692–7050

American Association of Occupational Health Nurses
3500 Piedmont Road, NE
Atlanta, GA 30305
(404) 262–1162

American College of Nurse-Midwives
1522 K Street, NW Suite 1120
Washington, DC 20005
(202) 347–5445

American Holistic Nurses' Association
Box 116
Telluride, CO 81435
(303) 728–4575

American Indian/Alaska Native Nurses Association
Box 3908
Lawrence, KS 66044
(913) 749–4335

American Nurses' Association
2020 Pershing Road
Kansas City, MO 64108
(816) 474-5720

American Public Health Association
1015 Fifteenth Street, NW
Washington, DC 20005
(202) 789–5600

American Organization of Nurse Executives
840 North Lake Shore Drive
Chicago, IL 60611
(312) 280–6410

American Society of Ophthalmic Registered Nurses
PO Box 3030
San Francisco, CA 94119
(415) 921–4700

American Society of Plastic and Reconstructive Surgical Nurses
North Woodbury Road, Box 56
Pitman, NJ 08071
(609) 589–6247

American Society of Post-Anesthesia Nurses
PO Box 11083
Richmond, VA 23230
(804) 359–3557

American Urological Association Allied
6845 Lake Shore Drive
PO Box 9397
Raytown, MO 64133
(816) 358–3317

Association for Practitioners in Infection Control
505 East Hawley Street
Mundelein, IL 60060
(312) 949–6052

Association of Pediatric Oncology Nurses
PO Box 7999
% Lorraine Bivalee
Pacific Medical Center
San Francisco, CA 94120

Association of Rehabilitation Nurses
2506 Grosse Point Road
Evanston, IL 60201
(312) 475–7300

Dermatology Nurses Association
North Woodbury Road, Box 56
Pitman, NJ 08071
(609) 582–1915

Emergency Nurses Association
666 North Lake Shore Drive, Suite 1131
Chicago, IL 60611
(312) 649–0297

Gay Nurses' Alliance
% Andrew C. Irish
507 Harvard Avenue E, #108
Seattle, WA 98102

Health/PAC (Health Policy Advisory Center)
17 Murray Street
New York, NY 10007
(212) 267–8890

International Association for Enterostomal Therapy
One Newport Place, Suite 970
Newport Beach, CA 92660
(714) 476–0268

Mid-Atlantic Regional Nursing Association (MARNA)
Teachers College, Box 146
Columbia University
525 West 120th Street
New York, NY 10027
(212) 678–3988

National Association for Health Care Recruitment
111 East Wacker Drive, #600
Chicago, IL 60601
(312) 644–6610

National Association for Practical Nurse Education and Service
10801 Pear Tree Lane, Suite 152
St. Louis, MO 63143

National Association of Hispanic Nurses
2014 Johnston Street
Los Angeles, CA 90031

National Association of Orthopaedic Nurses
North Woodbury Road, Box 56
Pitman, NJ 08071
(609) 582–0111

National Association of Pediatric Nurse Associates & Practitioners
1000 Maplewood Drive, Suite 104
Maple Shade, NJ 08052

National Association of School Nurses
7395 South Krameria Street
Englewood, CO 80112
(303) 850–9023

National Black Nurses Association
PO Box 18358
Boston, MA 02118
(617) 266–9703

National Federation of Licensed Practical Nurses
214 South Driver Street
PO Box 11038
Durham, NC 27703
(919) 596-9609

National Federation for Specialty Nursing Organizations
PO Box 23836
L'Enfant Plaza, SW
Washington, DC 20026

National Flight Nurses Association
%Miami Valley Hospital
One Wyoming Street
Dayton, OH 45409

National Intravenous Therapy Association
87 Blanchard Road
Cambridge, MA 02138
(617) 576–1282

National League for Nursing
10 Columbus Circle
New York, NY 10019
(212) 582–1022

National Nurses Society on Addictions
2506 Gross Point Road
Evanston, IL 60201
(312) 475–7300

National Nurses Society on Alcoholism
733 Third Avenue
New York, NY 10017

National Student Nurses' Association
555 West 57th Street
New York, NY 10019
(212) 581–2211

Nurses Alliance for the Prevention of Nuclear War
Box 319
Chestnut Hill, MA 02167

Nurses Association of the American College of Obstetricians and Gynecologists
600 Maryland Avenue, SW, Suite 200 East
Washington, DC 20024
(202) 638–0026

N-CAP (Nurses Coalition for Action in Politics; "ANA-PAC" as of 1986)
1030 15th Street NW, Suite 408
Washington, DC 20005
(202) 789–1800

Nurses' Environmental Health Watch
RCU, PO Box 1277
NY, NY 10185

Nurses Organization of the Veterans Administration
23341 Milwaukee Avenue
Half Day, IL 60069
(312) 634–1412

Oncology Nursing Society
3111 Banksville Road, Suite 200
Pittsburgh, PA 15216
(412) 344–3899

Sigma Theta Tau, National Honor Society of Nursing
1100 Waterway Boulevard
Indianapolis, IN 46202
(317) 634–8171

Society for Nursing History
Nursing Education Department, Box 150
Teachers College
Columbia University
525 West 120th Street
New York, NY 10027
(212) 678–3946

Society for Peripheral Vascular Nursing
436 Great Road
Acton, MA 01720
(617) 263–5144

Transcultural Nursing Society
4111 53rd SW
Seattle, WA 98116

Index